Russian Culture in War and Revolution, 1914–22.
Book 1: Popular Culture, the Arts, and Institutions

Russia's Great War and Revolution

Vol. 1, bk. 1
Murray Frame, Boris Kolonitskii, Steven G. Marks, and Melissa K. Stockdale, eds., *Russian Culture in War and Revolution, 1914–22: Popular Culture, the Arts, and Institutions* (2014)

Vol. 1, bk. 2
Murray Frame, Boris Kolonitskii, Steven G. Marks, and Melissa K. Stockdale, eds., *Russian Culture in War and Revolution, 1914–22: Political Culture, Identities, Mentalities, and Memory* (2014)

Series General Editors: Anthony Heywood, David MacLaren McDonald, and John W. Steinberg

RUSSIAN CULTURE IN WAR AND REVOLUTION, 1914–22

BOOK 1: POPULAR CULTURE, THE ARTS, AND INSTITUTIONS

EDITED BY

MURRAY FRAME
BORIS KOLONITSKII
STEVEN G. MARKS
MELISSA K. STOCKDALE

Bloomington, Indiana, 2014

SLAVICA

Cover: Kazimir Malevich, *Nu i tresk-zhe, nu i grom'-zhe! (What a boom, what a blast!)*, 1915, lithograph, National Gallery of Australia, Canberra, purchased 1986.

Library of Congress Cataloging-in-Publication Data

Russian culture in war and revolution, 1914-22 / edited by Murray Frame, Boris Kolonitskii, Steven G. Marks, Melissa K. Stockdale.
  volumes cm -- (Russia's Great War and Revolution ; volume 1)
  Includes bibliographical references.
  Contents: Book 1. Popular culture, the arts, and institutions -- Book 2. Political culture, identities, mentalities, and memory.
  ISBN 978-0-89357-423-9 (book 1) -- ISBN 978-0-89357-424-6 (book 2)
  1. Popular culture--Russia--History--20th century. 2. Popular culture--Soviet Union--History. 3.   Political culture--Russia--History--20th century. 4.   Political culture--Soviet Union--History. 5.   World War, 1914-1918--Social aspects--Russia. 6. Soviet Union--History--Revolution, 1917-1921. 7.   Russia--Intellectual life--1801-1917. 8.   Soviet Union--Intellectual life--1917-1970. 9.   Russia--Social conditions--1801-1917. 10. Soviet Union--Social conditions--1917-1945. I. Frame, Murray. II. Kolonitskii, B. I. III. Marks, Steven G. (Steven Gary), 1958- IV. Stockdale, Melissa Kirschke.
  DK264.8.R87 2014
  947.084'1--dc23

                    2014014607

Slavica Publishers   [Tel.] 1-812-856-4186
Indiana University   [Toll-free] 1-877-SLAVICA
1430 N. Willis Drive   [Fax] 1-812-856-4187
Bloomington, IN 47404-2146   [Email] slavica@indiana.edu
USA   [www] http://www.slavica.com/

In memory of Richard Stites, generous friend and inspirational scholar

Contents

The Arts

Institutions: Education, the Orthodox Church, and Museums

From the Series Editors

Origins of the Project

Since its inception in 2006 *Russia's Great War and Revolution, 1914–22* has taken shape through the collaboration of an international community of historians interested in the history of World War I's understudied eastern theater. Timed to coincide with the centenary of the Great War—and, by extension, the revolutions it helped unleash—this series responds to several developments in the historiography of the Russian Empire, its Soviet successor, and the Great War as a whole.

During a century of scholarly and popular discussion about the First World War, the "Russian" part of the conflict received little sustained attention until after 1991. In the former USSR, the war stood in the shadow of the revolutions of 1917 and the subsequent Civil War that resulted in the formation of the Soviet Union; most of all, it was eclipsed by the apotheosization after 1945 of the Great War of the Fatherland, the victory over Nazi Germany, as the defining moment in Soviet history. As a result, the First World War appeared as the final folly of an outmoded bourgeois-noble autocracy, doomed to collapse by the laws of history. Non-Soviet scholars, often hampered by restricted access to archival collections, downplayed the Russian war experience for other reasons. Specialists in the history of the late empire or early Soviet order tended to see the war as either the epilogue to the former or the prologue to the latter. Western historians often focused on the war experience of their own states—most often Britain and its imperial possessions, France, or Germany—or on a welter of issues bequeathed by the outbreak of the war in 1914 and the peacemaking in the years following 1918. These issues included most notably the vexed question of Germany's "war guilt," encoded in Article 231 of the Versailles Treaty, which has continued to provoke a lively and contentious discussion in the intervening 100 years.

The disintegration of the Soviet Union by the end of 1991 cast the history of the Soviet state and the late empire in a different light. Long-closed archives—particularly for military and international history—became relatively accessible to post-Soviet and Western scholars. As important, opportunities opened quickly for collaboration and dialogue between historians in Russia and their colleagues abroad, fostering new research and interpretations that would have been impossible or inconceivable before the late 1980s. Likewise, the

Russian Culture in War and Revolution, 1914–22, Book 1: Popular Culture, the Arts, and Institutions. Murray Frame, Boris Kolonitskii, Steven G. Marks, and Melissa K. Stockdale, eds. Bloomington, IN: Slavica Publishers, 2014, xi–xvii.

dramatic changes of the era led scholars inside and outside the former USSR to re-examine long-held assumptions about the Soviet state and its origins, accompanied by renewed debate over the viability of the Russian Empire as it adapted to the challenges of modernity. As part of this general re-evaluation, Russia's Great War became a subject of study in its own right. By the early 21st century, the war years came to be seen as what Peter Holquist termed "a continuum of crisis." Rather than an abrupt rupture between juxtaposed imperial and Soviet orders, the war now appears not just as a powerful force of disruption, but also a period of intense mobilization—as in the other combatant states—that produced the modes and the "gaze" of statecraft, mass culture, and social control often associated with the totalitarian/authoritarian states of the interwar and Cold War years. Such practices include the nationalization of economies, the increasing application of technology to surveillance, reaching farther than before into the "private" sphere, but also such issues as displaced or refugee populations, racialized nationalist ideologies, and the development of such means as mass propaganda in support of building a utopia in our time.

All of these contexts have been brought into sharp focus by the centenary of the Great War. This occasion has engendered a great deal of scholarly and popular interest, attested by the gathering stream of books, exhibits, and memorials that will, over the coming years, mark the milestone anniversaries in the conflict's history: the war's outbreak in the summer of 1914 and key moments enshrined in the historical memories of the combatant states. All of the one-time enemies will honor the millions of dead, wounded, incapacitated, and displaced by the first "war to end all wars." For the first time, Russians will take part in these rites of commemoration. At the end of 2012, the Russian Federation declared 1 August the annual "Day of Remembrance for the Victims of the First World War" (Den' pamiati zhertv Pervoi mirovoi voiny), first observed in 2013. Similarly, having long been consigned to the margins of the dominant narratives on the First World War, Russia's part in and experience of the Great War has become the focus of a substantial body of new scholarship. This series forms part of that new contribution to the international understanding of that conflict.

If the concept behind *Russia's Great War and Revolution* reflects recent trends in the historiography on the war's meaning for Russian history, its form draws on earlier examples of the sort of international collaboration that have become increasingly possible since the late 1980s. Each of the general editors and many members of the editorial collective had participated in similar partnerships, albeit on a smaller scale. Such projects included two volumes on Russian military history that enlisted the best specialists from the international community. Eric Lohr and Marshall Poe edited *The Military and Society in Russia* (Brill, 2002), while *Reforming the Tsar's Army* (2004), edited by Bruce Menning and David Schimmelpenninck van der Oye, appeared with the Woodrow Wilson International Center and Cambridge University Press in 2004. Other participants in this project had taken part in two other similar collections. In 2005, Routledge published *The Russian Revolution of 1905: Centenary Perspectives*, co-edited by Jonathan Smele and Anthony Heywood. That year also saw the publication by Brill of volume 1 of *The Russo-Japanese War in Global Perspective: World War Zero*; volume 2 came out two years later. Both were overseen by Menning, Schimmelpenninck, and John W. Steinberg. Each of these collections provided instructive examples of how to organize and produce the broad collaborative effort that has led to the appearance of *Russia's Great War and Revolution*.

Aims

Recognizing both the growing scholarly interest in Russia's Great War and the occasion presented by the successive centenaries of the First World War and the Russian revolutions, the editors of this collection have sought to assemble the best current international scholarship on the conflict. Ideally, they have oriented this collection toward several audiences. For those in the academy—scholars, undergraduates and graduate students—we offer a series of edited collections, varying in format and approach, that will provide a "snapshot" of the current state of the field. As a reflection of existing scholarly interests and debate, these materials will by default indicate those topics and issues demanding further attention. Editorial teams agreed on the optimal structure, periodization, and approach taken in their respective volumes. As a consequence, depending on the topic covered, some volumes provide a largely narrative treatment of events—for instance, military operations and engagements—or of developing issues, as occurs in the volume on international relations. Others, most often dealing with the "home front" or Russia as an empire, will present chapters that examine specific problems, groups, or regions.

In addition to addressing our academic communities, the editors seek also to engage non-professional readers in the general public, including secondary school students. To this end, as a supplement to the books in this series, the larger editorial collective have created a dedicated website with such supporting materials as maps, illustrations, sound files, and moving images. Further, the editors plan to house on the web-site special sections devoted to summaries of the published findings and instructional guides to aid teachers in developing school and lesson plans. Finally, alongside its appearance in book form, the series will also be available on the internet through the Project MUSE scholarly database. Readers with access to that platform will be able to conduct searches in and download entire books or individual chapters as they require. In addition to benefiting scholars interested in Russia during the Great War and revolutions, the MUSE edition will provide instructors with a ready trove of materials which can provide specific readings, as well as a valuable research resource for their students.

Conceptualization and Organization

The volumes in this collection reflect the current state of scholarship on Russia's experience of the "long" Great War, spanning the First World War, the revolutions, and the Russian Civil War. Editors have sought to cover all the significant aspects of Russia's history during 1914–22, so far as current expertise permits, under a series of thematic rubrics. These cover a wide range of subjects, including the experience of the soldiers involved, as well as of the urban and rural populations on the "home front"; the course of international relations, both formal and non-governmental; the implications of war and revolution for the empire as a polity incorporating a broad variety of national and confessional populations bound to the imperial "center" by distinctive administrative and legal regimes; and the impact of prolonged "total war" on the cultural, religious, and intellectual life of the region. Looking outward beyond the territories of the Russian Empire/USSR themselves, other volumes address the perspectives of the Central Powers during the Great War, the effects of war and civil war in Siberia and the Far East, the lengthening "arc of revolution" through the peripheries of the former empire and beyond to the global south and New World in the years following 1917, and, finally, the repercussions of total wars and revolution on ideas about and performance of gender, sexuality, and the sphere of intimacy in Russian society. Of course, throughout, the use of the term "Russia" and its inflections connotes, unless otherwise stated, the territory and populations housed within the boundaries of the Russian Empire in 1914.

Given the breadth of the subject matter and the renewed interest of historians in Russia's Great War, this collection does not aspire to offer a comprehensive narrative history of the war, nor is it meant to serve as an encyclopaedia of issues, events, and persons associated with the war and revolutions. Rather, it seeks to provide clear representation of current scholarly interests and debates, while indicating areas in need of more research. Thus, readers will find relatively few articles on the economic history of either the war or the Civil War. Likewise, many areas of international relations remain uncovered, not least the formation of policy-making institutions in the successor states to the Russian Empire. Those interested in the revolutionary period will find the "workers' movement" far less prominent in this collection than would have been the case for much of the late 20th century, while the peasantry and Russia's regions have begun to receive comparatively greater attention.

As noted previously, an underlying aim of this series is to encourage further research into areas as yet insufficiently covered in current scholarship. Thus, despite the increasing prevalence of the "imperial turn" in our historiography, the impact of the war, revolutions, and Civil War in Russia's imperial borderlands has only begun recently to command the interest that it warrants. By the same token, like their counterparts for the history of other countries, specialists on 20th-century Russia have yet to delve deeply into the manifold aspects of religion and religiosity in the wartime Russian Empire, from popular or folk religion and religious practice, through the high politics of spiritual institutions, to the effects of war and turmoil on currents in theology and religious philosophy that had begun to run so strong during the "Silver Age."

Finally, throughout the long process that led to the appearance of this series, the editorial teams have sought to avoid the imposition of an explicit interpretive agenda, in the interests of conveying a sense of current areas of debate and consensus in our historical literature. Thus, while the periodization of 1914–22—i.e., the years spanning the Russian Empire's entry into war through two revolutions, civil war, and the formation of the Soviet state— has taken hold with many historians, others continue to maintain that such an approach risks flattening or downplaying the significance of 1917 and its consequences for the area's subsequent history. In the interest of providing as clear as possible a reflection of the current "state of play," these volumes house a variety of interpretations and periodizations, inviting readers to draw their own inferences and conclusions from the evidence and arguments on offer.

Process

From the beginning, editors have viewed *Russia's Great War and Revolution* as a truly global project, incorporating perspectives from historians across Europe, North America, Russia, Asia, and Australia. In addition to the subject matter treated in the volumes' contents, this global approach informed the composition of the editorial teams that oversaw the production of each volume. Each of these groups included members from North America, Russia, and the United Kingdom or continental Europe. Where the contents required it—for instance, in the book dealing with Asia, scholars from elsewhere joined the editorial team. In the interests of reaching the broadest possible international audience, the editors agreed on English as the language for the series, with the intention of publishing a parallel Russian-language edition when feasible. The chapters in these volumes consist both of submissions in response to a widely circulated open call and invited contributions. Papers were selected in a two-stage process involving initial vetting by editorial team-members, then evaluation by the full editorial board. Throughout, editors strove for the greatest possible inclusiveness, with the result that the articles in the series represent a broad variety of scholars, ranging from graduate students through all ranks of the academic *cursus honorum*.

The project and its publication took shape through a series of editorial-board meetings that began at the University of Aberdeen in the summer of 2008. A meeting at the University of Wisconsin-Madison the following summer resulted in agreement on the thematic areas to be addressed by separate volumes, in addition to provisional topical headings for each volume. At Uppsala University in 2010, board-members refined outlines of desired contents for each volume, leading to a public call for papers the following autumn. From that point forward, editors pursued submissions, while project representatives participated in the presentation of project overviews and draft articles at the annual conventions of the Association for Slavic, East European, and Eurasian Studies (ASEEES), the Study Group of the Russian Revolution, the British Association for Slavonic and East European Studies (BASEES), the Southern Conference on Slavic Studies, and the 2010 Stockholm meeting of the International Council for Central and East European Studies (ICCEES).

The chapters contained in the volumes comprising *Russia's Great War and Revolution* have undergone an intensive multi-stage review process, overseen collectively by the 30-odd members of the full editorial board. The publisher also solicited a peer assessment of the project description and design; the resulting review yielded important and helpful suggestions, as did consultation with the project's advisory board. Next, editorial teams for individual volumes jointly assessed contributions. To select papers for inclusion in individual volumes and to prepare the latter for publication, the editorial board adopted a two-tier review exercise. Editorial teams were paired according to areas of overlapping interest or approach. Each of the teams would read and critique the contents for the other's volume, followed by a general discussion involving the entire editorial board. Finally, after the completion of revisions, that volume's editorial team sent it on to the general editors, who solicited anonymous peer reviews for final review. Once the volume editors addressed any critiques or suggestions from these last reviews, the general editors submitted the volume to the publisher for production.

Acknowledgments

In the eight years from its origins to the first appearance of its results, this project benefited immeasurably from the support of many people and institutions. The editorial board owes a special debt of gratitude to Alice D. Mortenson from Minneapolis, Minnesota for her unstinting support of and generosity to this undertaking, not least through the Alice D. Mortenson/Petrovich Chair of Russian History. This resource proved indispensable in making possible several successive editorial meetings. Special thanks are also due to Scott Jacobs of Houston, Texas, who provided significant support to this project for more than five years. His contributions helped ensure the success of the summer editorial meetings at the University of Wisconsin-Madison in 2012. Both donors also made possible many of the translations in the collection.

The editorial board also benefited from the support of several universities and departments. Significant financial support was provided by the University of Aberdeen, Scotland, through the School of Divinity, History and Philosophy, the College of Arts and Social Sciences, and the

Principal's Interdisciplinary Fund to facilitate our inaugural board meeting at Aberdeen in 2008 and our fifth full meeting in 2014. The Department of History at the University of Wisconsin-Madison hosted the 2009 and 2012 editorial-board meetings; Nicole Hauge played a key role in arrangements for the visitors to Madison on both occasions. In addition, we benefited from the support of the university's Anonymous Fund and the office of the Dean of the College of Letters and Science. Our colleagues in the Department of History at Uppsala University in Sweden gave us the use of their facilities and meeting-space in the summer of 2010, providing an excellent and hospitable environment for our discussion. Many of the home institutions of the editorial board also contributed travel costs and meeting-space for the compilation of several volumes in this collection; some helped underwrite some translation costs as well.

Several other groups and institutions played an important role in the gestation of this series. The Kennan Institute of the Woodrow Wilson International Center, particularly Associate Director William Pomeranz, has actively supported the project since its outset. Grants to support our editorial meetings were provided by the British Academy, BASEES, and the Great Britain Sasakawa Foundation. The German Historical Institute in Moscow very kindly sponsored the translation into English of chapters written in German. The Study Group on the Russian Revolution served as an important venue for the development of many of the chapters, particularly from British and European contributors, that appear in these volumes. George Fowler and Vicki Polansky of Slavica Publishers have proven the ideal partners in this lengthy process, offering sage counsel, clear deadlines, exemplary patience, professionalism, and rigor, all of which have made the production process run with an enviable dispatch and smoothness.

Finally, the editorial board expresses its heartfelt thanks to more than 200 contributors, who offered their skills, effort, insight, and scholarship to *Russia's Great War and Revolution*. At the risk of tautology, it must be said that this series could not have come to fruition without them. Their efforts—and patience with an extended production schedule—allowed us to present our readers with strong evidence for the enduring importance and complexity of this eight-year span in the history of Central and Eastern Europe and Asia, the consequences of which continue to shape our world in ways that we are still witnessing.

Anthony Heywood
David MacLaren McDonald
John W. Steinberg
June 2014

Preface

This book is the first of a two-part collection of essays on the cultural history of Russia between 1914 and 1922, both of which form part of a larger series on Russian history during the Great War, Revolution, and Civil War.[1] The two books that comprise the culture "volume" of the series are intended to complement each other, and they are published separately only for reasons of space. The general aim of the umbrella project to which the culture volume belongs is to consider Russia's experience of war and revolution as a "continuum of crisis"—in Peter Holquist's apt phrase[2]—from the outbreak of conflict in 1914 to the formation of the Soviet Union in 1922. The merits of this approach are at least two-fold: it focuses attention on the history of Russia during the First World War—until recently a largely neglected area— and it connects that history to the early years of the Bolshevik regime, thereby transcending the often artificial partition of 1917 in the historiography of modern Russia. Contributors to this volume were therefore asked to address an aspect of Russian cultural history during the 1914–22 period. Some have taken a slightly broader perspective, and a few are focused predominantly on the years prior to 1917, but all of them advance our understanding of Russia's experience of the Great War, its relationship to the early Soviet period, and the complex memory of the "continuum of crisis."

Definitions of culture and cultural history are now so expansive and protean that the subject matter of these two books is potentially enormous. Emmet Kennedy has defined culture as "any symbolic representation of value, particularly of values that are perpetuated in time through the educational process (schools, churches, press, theater),"[3] and Peter Burke has described cultural history as "a concern with the symbolic and its interpretation."[4] These two statements highlight the difficulty of distinguishing too strictly between traditional understandings of culture as the arts and sciences, and more

---

[1] Details of the larger series, "Russia's Great War and Revolution," can be found at http://russiasgreatwar.org/index.php

[2] Peter Holquist, *Making War, Forging Revolution: Russia's Continuum of Crisis, 1914–1921* (Cambridge, MA: Harvard University Press, 2002).

[3] Emmet Kennedy, *A Cultural History of the French Revolution* (New Haven: Yale University Press, 1989), xxii.

[4] Peter Burke, *What is Cultural History?* (Cambridge: Polity Press, 2004), 3.

Russian Culture in War and Revolution, 1914–22, Book 1: Popular Culture, the Arts, and Institutions. Murray Frame, Boris Kolonitskii, Steven G. Marks, and Melissa K. Stockdale, eds. Bloomington, IN: Slavica Publishers, 2014, xix–xxiii.

recent approaches that imply almost anything can have a "cultural history" (since all objects and behaviors may be read for their symbolic content). Accepting that cultural history has few, if any, boundaries—a liberating yet potentially bewildering condition—we have not aimed for encyclopaedic coverage of the subject, for inclusion of every conceivable topic. Instead, the contents of the two books reflect the work of scholars whose current or recent research falls broadly into the category of Russian cultural history during the late imperial and early Soviet periods. The result is a diverse and stimulating array of original essays on subjects that range from the experience of cultural institutions and the arts, to aspects of identity and memory in popular culture. Many of the topics have rarely, if ever, been explored for this period of Russian history.

Through their close focus on diverse aspects of cultural life in Russia, the essays collectively demonstrate that cultural responses to war and revolution were far from uniform, and they defy simple generalizations. Nevertheless four broad observations can be made. The first is that, despite the traumatic upheaval that Russia experienced between 1914 and 1922, cultural life appears to have persisted with undiminished energy, even accelerating in some spheres—witness, for instance, the exponential growth in native film production from 1914 to 1917, or the myriad proletarian culture projects launched during the Civil War. The reasons for this "cultural acceleration" were complex and varied: patriotic mobilization; commercial demand; the thirst to comprehend global conflict and domestic revolution; the impulse to escape from reality; and notably the political conviction that culture had agency, that it was a tool capable of reshaping society. These factors help to explain why cultural activity was barely disrupted, even when basic material resources were in desperately short supply.

Secondly, according to the findings of several contributors, popular culture manifested greater signs of Russian national integration during the First World War than hitherto assumed. It was not simply that patriotic sentiment prompted a ban on German films or fueled attacks on European clothing fashions, for example, important though such developments were, especially during the first year of the conflict. Rather, a much wider spectrum of the empire's population increasingly engaged with a national public culture— especially through newspaper war reportage and efforts of civil society to organize patriotic work—and this may reflect a level of national unity not ordinarily associated with the final few years of tsarism.

The third observation is that—perhaps inevitably—consideration of the 1914–22 period as an integrated continuum reveals as many continuities as it does discontinuities, with the consequence that 1917 appears less prominent as a turning point in Russian cultural history (at least within the confines of this discrete period). The vibrant cultural experimentation of the Civil War years—the subject of many studies—conveys an impression of rapid cultural transformation under the Bolsheviks. Yet when that story is considered in the context of the Great War, the sense of a sharp disjuncture in the cultural sphere is less obvious. To cite a few examples that are elaborated in the volume's chapters: the attitudes of state and intelligentsia towards culture remained fundamentally similar across the revolutionary divide; changes in sexual mores, often associated with the Revolution, were already underway before 1917; and the history of popular holidays and festivals indicates how traditional cultural forms persisted beneath the veneer of new ideological content. This serves as a reminder that whilst some aspects of a culture—signs, symbols, and names, for example—can be replaced quickly, others—like deep-seated assumptions, values, and conditioned behavior—evolve at a different pace from the welter of military and political events. In that sense, the rhythms of cultural history do not correspond neatly to the chronological parameters of this volume. This does not mean that culture was impervious to the pressures of war, revolution, and civil war—on the contrary, they left indelible imprints on Russian culture—but it suggests that cultural change was less rapid or all-encompassing than political, social, and economic transformations, and that it might be more apposite to think of the period as a transitional rather than a revolutionary one for culture.

Finally, the essays suggest that cultural life was not only tightly inter-twined with its social and political contexts, but that the wider history of Russia's Great War and Revolution cannot be fully comprehended without due attention to culture in its broadest sense. Cultural activity was one of the central mechanisms for circulating information, promoting patriotism, exchanging views, attacking hierarchies, exploring alternatives, and escaping reality. Even after the fall of the autocracy, cultural activity was the principal way in which most ordinary people connected with public life: through reading, viewing, listening, and socializing in a variety of cultural settings. More broadly, popular culture—the values and attitudes of ordinary people—set limits to what was adapted, ignored, embraced, or resisted. It was for these reasons that the Bolsheviks, as much as their tsarist predecessors, placed great emphasis on the importance of cultural policy (the short-lived Provisional Government paid less attention to this matter).

The chapters are arranged into sections that reflect certain thematic syn-ergies. They are bracketed by an introduction (in book 1) that discusses the broader context of cultural policy in late imperial and early Soviet Russia, and by two concluding essays (both in book 2) that draw together the volume's themes from both a Russian and a wider European historical perspective. Given the mercurial nature of culture and cultural history, there is an inev-itable element of overlap between some topics and sections, and certain chapters could have appeared in different sections, but ultimately we think it is more helpful to have some subdivision of the chapters than to present them without any attempt at classification. A few topics that readers might expect to find under the heading of "culture" are treated elsewhere in the wider project on Russia's Great War and Revolution: the intelligentsia, for instance, is discussed as a social category in the Home Front volume, although many of its representatives certainly appear throughout this volume. Moreover, the emphasis in these two books is largely Russo-centric, providing a degree of focus for an otherwise diverse range of subjects. Other nationalities of the tsarist and early Soviet polities feature more prominently in other volumes of the project (albeit not necessarily from a cultural perspective).

ଓଃ ଃଚ

Unless otherwise noted, all dates before February 1918 are given in the Old Style (Julian) calendar, which was 13 days behind the New Style (Gregorian) calendar used in the West. The New Style calendar was adopted by the Russian government in February 1918. Russian names and terms have been transliterated according to the Library of Congress system (with exceptions for rulers' names and a few others that are widely known in their anglicized forms). Russian patronymics (full name or initial) have been included for individuals who are not well-known or readily identifiable (except where their patronymics are unknown). Places of publication of books cited in the footnotes have been included, except where unknown.

ଓଃ ଃଚ

We would like to express our gratitude to the many people who have helped make this volume possible: to the contributors, especially for their patience and professionalism; to the General Editors of the volume's umbrella project, Russia's Great War and Revolution 1914-22 (RGWR), Tony Heywood, David McDonald, and John Steinberg, for their unfailing support and encouragement; to the RGWR Editorial Board—too large to name individually—for all kinds of help and advice, but especially for their tremendous collegiality and friendship, both during and after the RGWR editorial conferences in Aberdeen (2008), Uppsala (2010), and Madison (2009 and 2012); to the translators of the chapters that were originally in Russian or French, Joan Bridgwood, Kirsty McCluskey, Diana Statham, Victoria Steinberg, Hannah Zinn, and Josephine Von Zitzewitz; to the generous sponsors of the translations, David Finkelstein and the School of Humanities, University of Dundee, Gerald Sonnenfeld and Clemson University, and David McDonald and the University of Wisconsin-Madison; to Véronique Wechtler for additional translation advice; to the anonymous volume reviewer for helpful suggestions; and to Vicki Polansky for being such an exemplary editor.

One of the greatest pleasures in preparing this volume was the opportunity to "workshop" the chapters at several events, where contributors discussed themes and shared ideas arising from their research. We were fortunate to be able to hold two volume-based conferences whilst work on the chapters progressed, the first at the European University at St. Petersburg in summer 2011, and the second at Clemson University in fall 2011, for which we would like to acknowledge the support of Tom Kuehn and Gerald Sonnenfeld at Clemson University, and David McDonald. We would also like to thank Joye and Hubert Shuler and Louise and John Allen of Charleston, South Carolina, for their unforgettable hospitality. Volume-based panels were also held at the ICCEES World Congress, Stockholm (2010) and the ASEEES annual convention, Boston (2013). We thank all the contributors to—and organizers of—these events for helping to enhance the volume in such an amicable and stimulating manner.

Murray Frame
Boris Kolonitskii
Steven G. Marks
Melissa K. Stockdale
December 2013

Revolution, Culture, and Cultural Policy from Late Tsarism to the Early Soviet Years

Christopher Read

Speaking at the International Cultural Summit held during the Edinburgh Festival in August 2012, Haris Pasovic, artistic director of the Sarajevo East West Center made a large claim. "Culture," he said, "is a primary need as much as food and sex."[1] Even though almost all children like to draw and most people like to tell a story, the claim was met with much scepticism. It was perhaps appropriate that the claimant was from an East West Center because, in many ways, he had pointed to an issue which divides Europe and beyond. In the artistic sense, as opposed to the anthropological one, culture in Western "bourgeois" society is often considered to be a pleasant but unnecessary embellishment of life. It is often worn as a bright jewel signifying taste, breeding, and class. In Russia, and other parts of Eastern Europe, Pasovic's claim would be met as a familiar one. Aleksandr Solzhenitsyn asserted that values, in his example religious faith, were more precious to the believer than the bread she or he put in their stomach.[2] While these might be extreme forms of attachment to culture, there can be no doubt that, in a broad sense, late tsarist and early Bolshevik Russia considered culture to be almost the essence of political and social life, its meaning and purpose. Though each interpreted this dimension of life in different ways, both before and after 1917 culture was an essential component of the governing systems.

Cultural Policy and Revolution in Russia

The term "cultural policy" can have almost as many meanings and nuances as its chief component, the word "culture" itself. Conventionally, today the term most frequently refers to government policies aimed at enhancing the artistic and intellectual life of a country. It also has echoes in educational policy, an area into which Western industrializing states were beginning to advance in

---

[1] Quoted in Richard Brooks, "Biteback," *The Sunday Times: Culture*, 19 August 2012, 14.

[2] "For the believer, faith is *supremely* precious, more precious than the food he puts in his stomach." Aleksandr Solzhenitsyn, *Letter to the Soviet Leaders*, trans. Hilary Sternberg (London: Collins, 1974), 44.

Russian Culture in War and Revolution, 1914–22, Book 1: Popular Culture, the Arts, and Institutions. Murray Frame, Boris Kolonitskii, Steven G. Marks, and Melissa K. Stockdale, eds. Bloomington, IN: Slavica Publishers, 2014, 1–22.

the mid- and late 19th century. In many cases this meant replacing traditional ecclesiastical involvement in the upbringing of children and young people. However, in 19th- and early 20th-century Russia we are presented with a fundamentally different situation. Here the separation of religion, state, and political culture had taken a very different course from that of Western Europe, where a degree of secularization had been the consequence of great processes such as the Renaissance, the Scientific Revolution, the Enlightenment and a series of democratic, or at least anti-monarchical, revolutions. Russia, on the other hand, had seen the mobilization of national religious culture in the cause of the autocracy. The adoption of Official Nationality and the triad of "Orthodoxy, Autocracy, Nationality" in the reign of Tsar Nicholas I (1825–55) confirmed the close linking of autocracy and religion at the same time as religion was receding, though not disappearing, from the political culture of Western nation-states. Education, such as it was, also bore a strong religious imprint at school level. In these senses, under tsarism, religion was an integral part of imperial legitimacy and of the political system. Not only that, it remained there until the very end and provides us with one of the most important components of tsarism's own peculiar form of cultural policy. By comparison, the Provisional Government in 1917 had little time to develop a cultural, or even an educational, policy and we will have only brief suggestions and fleeting glimpses of its approach which has not attracted very much attention.[3] However, it is with respect to the Soviet regime that cultural policy has been most widely seen as an important, though sometimes peripheral, component of its portfolio of policies. While many will easily accept that Bolshevism had a cultural aspect in its earliest years, testified to by the great experimental artists of the time—Kandinskii, Malevich, Goncharova, Tatlin, Chagall, and so on—far fewer will recognize that Bolshevism, in the eyes of its leaders in general and Lenin in particular, was, ultimately, a cultural project. Its aim was to change human nature. Not only that, a key mechanism for reaching that goal, raising class consciousness, was also, primarily, cultural.

These considerations also remind us that, by undertaking the infrequently attempted task of examining cultural policy through the three regimes of the revolutionary period[4] we will encounter not only the differences one would largely expect but, more surprisingly, certain continuities and similarities, not the least of which is that cultural policy was much more significant to the leaders of all three regimes than was the case elsewhere in the developed industrial world. For Bolsheviks as much as tsarists, despite their deeply ingrained philosophical differences, culture was not the icing on the cake, it was the cake itself.

---

[3] The chief exception to this is the work of Boris Kolonitskii. See, for example, Orlando Figes and Boris Kolonitskii, *Interpreting the Russian Revolution: The Language and Symbols of 1917* (New Haven: Yale University Press, 1999).

[4] An interesting exception is Peter J. S. Duncan, *Russian Messianism: Third Rome, Holy Revolution, Communism and After* (London: Routledge, 2000).

The Cultural Strategy of Late Tsarism

In his path-breaking work on Nicholas I, written more than 50 years ago, Nicholas Riasanovsky made a number of brilliant judgments which have not only stood the test of time but are as relevant to the era of Nicholas II as they were to that of his great-grandfather. Riasanovsky stated that

> the steadfast monarch governed his vast empire and participated in the destinies of the world on the basis of a few simple principles which he held with passionate conviction. The ideology of the reign ... deserves more attention than it has hitherto received. Far from being mere propaganda or empty talk, it represented the conscious orientation of the Russian government.[5]

In analyzing Nicholas I, many historians have tried to attribute "realistic" motives to his policies rather than accept the importance of "the emperor's stubborn loyalty to his convictions" which produced his "extremely rigid and doctrinaire policies." As with Nicholas II, the resulting "extreme regimentation and repression of Nicholas I's reign have to be considered in the light of the emperor's convictions and of the aims which he attempted to achieve."[6] Indeed, Riasanovsky implicitly links the two by contending that Nicholas I's legacy was to make adaptation to change so difficult that "it was still largely the old order of Nicholas I, the antiquated ancien regime, that went down in the conflagration of 1917."[7] Not surprisingly, Riasanovsky's final judgment applies equally to both Nicholases:

> The system of Emperor Nicholas I demonstrated a remarkable coordination between thought and action, a dedication to a set ideal, a determination to mould reality according to an ideological blueprint.... But, in the last analysis, the student of Nicholas I ... in Russia leaves his subject with a sense of the power, not the weakness, of ideas in history, of the importance, not the insignificance, of man's purpose in the shaping of human destiny.[8]

Riasanovsky's comments support the conclusion that tsarism, like its Soviet successor, was at heart a cultural project and saw its cultural policies as shapers of its "material" and "realistic" policies rather than the other way round. In

---

[5] Nicholas Riasanovsky, *Nicholas I and Official Nationality in Russia 1825–1855* (Berkeley: University of California Press, 1959), 266–67.

[6] The comments apply to Stalin, too, in many respects.

[7] Riasanovsky, *Nicholas I*, 269.

[8] Ibid., 271–72.

addition, an examination of the cultural policies, institutions and framework of late tsarism shows that the components of Nicholas I's cultural policy—Orthodoxy, Autocracy, Nationality—remained at the heart of Nicholas II's policies though the detail was very different.

The turning point in late-imperial policies toward reform and revolution came, as is widely agreed, in the wake of the assassination crisis of March 1881. The violent death of the "reforming tsar," Alexander II, confirmed the antireformists even more firmly in their ideas. Two major initiatives emerged from the crisis. In 1882 a set of "Temporary Regulations" retracted limited pre-1881 political concessions. The second was a drive to unify the empire against its enemies by developing a policy of "russification." Both of these were dragon's teeth from which greater revolutionary problems grew. Both also had profound cultural consequences. The unqualified choice of reaction over reform increasingly limited the legitimate space not only for political discussion and political action but for freedom of expression in general. The main practical means for enforcement included law, censorship, political imprisonment and a comparatively small but effective political police service, the Okhrana. The reactionary policies of the early 1880s, which were enthusiastically endorsed at the time of his coronation by Nicholas II, who dismissed reformist ideas as "senseless dreams," were a major cause of revolutionary activity by making it impossible to engage in legal protest or even free speech. "Russification" also rebounded. The central notion of russification was not so much about citizenship, since there was no such thing in any real sense, but about religious affiliation. A certificate of baptism in the Orthodox Church was sufficient for a person to be accepted as a fully-fledged Russian, reminding us that official Russian discrimination at this time was more cultural than racist. However, relatively aggressive policies of russification in the last decades of the 19th century meant that deep antagonisms were stirred up by, for example, building large Orthodox cathedrals in prominent sites in capital cities of minority nationalities. Anyone who has visited Helsinki or Tallinn will have seen the results.[9] One of the most resented was the Aleksandr Nevskii Cathedral opened in the center of Warsaw in 1912, a structure which gave a new meaning to the term imposing. So much so that, once it was independent, the Polish authorities soon demolished it because of its negative connotations (1924–26). Even the imperial capital itself saw assertive cathedral construction in the form of the Cathedral on the Spilt Blood, built between 1883 and 1907 on the actual site where Alexander II had been fatally injured. These were imposing, if frequently ugly, assertions of the supremacy of Russia in the empire. However, it was another associated cultural policy which had more immediate effect in creating greater unrest among ethnic minorities. National languages were

---

[9] The Uspenski Cathedral in Helsinki was built between 1862 and 1868. The Aleksandr Nevskii Cathedral in Tallinn was constructed between 1894 and 1900. Its dedication to a great Russian conqueror of the region was not accidental.

systematically downgraded and the Russian language was imposed to an ever greater extent. The fact that it seems to have been protests against this that brought the young Stalin into the revolutionary movement is enough, in itself, to cause regret for the ill-thought-out and counterproductive policy. Taken together, retreat into authoritarianism and aggressive russification of minorities meant a changing and modernizing Russian society and economy were being forced into narrower and narrower political confines.

The peculiar blend of politics, religion, and repression was not lost on contemporary observers. Writing in 1907, when the failure of the 1905 Revolution had become apparent and reasons were being sought to explain the outcome, a group of intellectuals led by the poets Dmitrii Merezhkovskii and Zinaida Gippius produced a book of essays entitled *Le Tsar et la Révolution*, published in Paris in response to the worsening intellectual environment in their home city of St. Petersburg.[10] One of Merezhkovskii's key ideas was that the revolutionary movement had failed because it had been outside the religious envelope which surrounded the autocracy and fed into mass culture. Tsarism, he argued, was not just a secular autocracy but a kind of theocracy. Its claim to power extended even beyond divine right and into the deepest realms of the religious consciousness. It claimed the plenitude not only of political power, but also spiritual power. The tsar was monarch and pope. It matters less to our current concern to note that Merezhkovskii concluded that, to be successful, revolutionaries had to challenge tsarism as a spiritual entity as well as a secular one, than to note his identification of religious and secular power. Slavophile defenders of tsarism acknowledged the same thing. For them, the tsar was not only the political arbiter of the Russian Empire, he was its moral guardian and its patriarch (in two senses—the father of the Russian family and, effectively, the head of its church since the actual office of patriarch had been in abeyance since 1721). He was the *batiushka* (little father) of his people. A particularly oily expression of monarchist belief was captured in the memoirs of a sycophantic courtier, A. A. Mosolov, at the turn of the century:

> The Tsar can do no wrong; he stands above classes, party politics and personal rivalries.... He seeks nothing for himself; he has a profound love for all those whom God has confided to his supreme care. There is no reason why he should not be the benefactor of each and all.... [The Tsar is] beneficence personified.[11]

Without doubt, the mystique of tsarism was still tied up with carefully constructed cultural policies. In the forefront were the public rituals and

---

[10] D. S. Merezhkovsky, Z. N. Gippius, and D. V. Filosofov, *Le Tsar et la Révolution* (Paris, 1907).

[11] A. A. Mossolov [Mosolov], *At the Court of the Last Tsar* (London: Methuen, 1935), 128.

ceremonies of state. Mosolov himself was a functionary within the sprawling Ministry of the Imperial Court, which was responsible for conducting many aspects of the monarch's business. Tasks ranged from overseeing the royal domains to supervising the Imperial Theaters and arranging official ceremonies. This last implied what today would be called promoting the monarch's "image." Clearly, Mosolov had what it took to be successful in the not-yet-invented sphere of public relations and his department, the Court Chancellery, was, effectively, fulfilling that function for the tsar. In anachronistic language, Mosolov and his associates were promoting the cult of personality of the tsar.[12]

This was done through a variety of "scenarios of power."[13] In the winter season lavish balls which reflected the "greatness" of the monarch's predecessors were held in the Winter Palace. Perhaps the most expensive and elaborate were held between 7 and 11 February 1903. Courtiers were instructed to appear in 17th-century costume. The result was a brilliant spectacle, though perhaps more reminiscent of a Mariinskii or Bolshoi Theater opera production than a court festivity. Life and art seemed to be imitating each other, not least since Fedor Shaliapin sang excerpts from *Boris Godunov*.[14] Semiotically, the event appeared to invoke a return to a pre-Petrine, Muscovite, "traditional" Russia, and, perhaps coincidentally, this reflected Nicholas's distaste for Peter the Great. This became more explicit in May of the same year when the bicentenary of the city of St. Petersburg was celebrated. The outcome was less overwhelming than Mosolov had hoped for, not least because the tsar himself "indicated that he liked Peter less than his other forebears because of his 'infatuation with western culture and destruction of all purely Russian customs.'"[15]

Although the influence of events like the court balls spread beyond the immediate circle of participants—through, in this case, the publication of a luxurious three-volume album of photographs of the occasion and the invitation to the city's diplomatic corps to attend and wonder at one of the

---

[12] The phrase, of course, is normally associated with Lenin and, even more so, Stalin. However, although it falls outside our immediate chronological remit, it is tempting to speculate that the cult of the Soviet leaders fitted comfortably into the leadership niche created around the cult, myth, and mystique of monarchy. See, for example, Nina Tumarkin, *Lenin Lives!: The Lenin Cult in Soviet Russia* (Cambridge, MA: Harvard University Press, 1983; enlarged paperback edition, 1997); Jan Plamper, *The Stalin Cult: A Study in the Alchemy of Power* (New Haven: Yale University Press, 2012); and Maureen Perrie, *The Cult of Ivan the Terrible in Stalin's Russia* (Houndmills, UK: Palgrave, 2001).

[13] Richard Wortman, *Scenarios of Power: Myth and Ceremony in the Russian Monarchy*, 2: *From Alexander II to the Abdication of Nicholas II* (Princeton, NJ: Princeton University Press, 2000).

[14] For an excellent description, see Wortman, *Scenarios of Power*, 377–78.

[15] Ibid., 378.

"performances"—it did not penetrate much beyond the social elite. That was why mass occasions, like the anniversary of the founding of St. Petersburg, were organized in order to pass the message on to the wider population. Nicholas's waning enthusiasm for mass ceremonies was also partly attributable to the disaster of his coronation in May 1896. It had rebounded by turning into a tragedy when some 1400 or so people were crushed in the crowds. Two other special ceremonies of his reign also illustrated key aspects of the monarchy's fortunes, one of which was much more to the tsar's liking. In 1903 one of Russian Orthodoxy's most holy elders of the 19th century, Starets Serafim of Sarov (1754–1833), was canonized. "Although one canonization had already been held during Nicholas's reign and others would come later, none were so laden with symbolic intensity and a self-conscious fusion of politics and piety. It was high politico-religious theatre, similar to that staged in 19th-century Europe, but with a cast that included the emperor, who personally participated at every stage of its planning and performance."[16] As a popular holy man and monastery elder to whom many had turned for spiritual advice, Serafim's cause had long been put forward by many cult followers. However, the decisive impulse came from above, from the tsarina herself. In July 1902 she insisted that he be canonized in six days. Konstantin Pobedonostsev, the procurator of the Holy Synod (secular supervisor of the Orthodox Church), was aghast, as were the church authorities, suspicious of any religious impulse that did not originate with them. They also pointed out that Serafim did not meet the first criterion of Orthodox sainthood—incorruptibility of his corpse.[17] Nonetheless, the tsarina insisted and the metropolitan of Moscow lent his support. Her timescale was unrealistic, but the following year the canonization took place at Sarov, in the deepest provinces.

A great pilgrimage to Serafim's shrine in Sarov was organized. Hundreds of thousands of peasants and workers, as well as members of the elite, joined their tsar in venerating the new saint. Here was an event which warmed the tsar's heart and created the impression that all was well in the Russian world. The occasion became a symbol of apparent unity between tsar and people. "The ceremony of canonisation represented a spiritual and symbolic union of three elements—the 'people,' symbolized by the pilgrims; the church, represented by the participating clergy and the volunteer gonfalon-bearers; and the monarch, with his family and entourage."[18] The event was widely publicized, including photos, in the monarchist press and there is little doubt it had a profound effect on the tsar himself, who began to believe he was brought closer to his people through his developing simple piety. Together with the birth of his son and heir around the same time, Sarov "confirmed his

---

[16] Gregory L. Freeze, "Subversive Piety: Religion and Political Crisis in Late Imperial Russia," *Journal of Modern History* 68, 2 (June 1996): 314.

[17] Wortman, *Scenarios of Power*, 385.

[18] Ibid., 387.

sense of divine communion shared by tsar and people."[19] Consoling it may
have been for the tsar, but nothing better illustrates the illusory nature of this
"communion" than the fact that Sarov is in the province (*guberniia*) of Tambov,
one of the most rebellious regions for peasant unrest in both the 1905 and 1917
revolutions.[20]

For the moment, however, in the eyes of the tsar, he and his peasants stood
as one in their communion with God and the saints. Problems, it followed,
could only come from "outsiders" who did not share that faith—secular,
westernizing intellectuals; Catholic Poles; the national minorities in general
and, specially singled out, Jews. Their collective enmity would be battered to
pieces against the rock of true Russian tsarist theocracy. Gangs of "patriotic,"
"true Russians" emerged as the revolution welled up to physically attack
and intimidate the outsider groups. However, even monarchist thugs could
not prevent the precipitous decline in affection for the Romanovs through
the 1905 Revolution. A conscious, post-1905 attempt to reverse the trend was
implemented in 1913 in the form of celebration of the tercentenary of the
dynasty. The lukewarm response from the masses and tales of ill omen, such
as that of the blackening of the face of Our Lady of St. Theodore, the patron
icon of the family, told their own story.

Much of the Slavophile mystique had been carefully nurtured by culturally oriented policies since 1881. Most important, the tutor of Nicholas II,
Pobedonostsev, had turned his position and influence towards establishing
what he thought was a survival strategy for the idea, mystique, and legitimacy
of autocracy through a series of nationalist and religious policies. In addition
to the direct imposition of Russian-oriented policies, "russification" fed into
and expanded a rising tendency to glorify and mythologize the Russian past
which had already become evident, by the mid-century, in music and art. The
magnificent series of operas on Russia's past, such as *Boris Godunov* (Musorgskii
1869 and 1872), *Khovanshchina* (Musorgskii 1886), *Prince Igor* (Borodin 1890),
A Bride for the Tsar, and *Sadko* (Rimskii-Korsakov 1899 and 1901) are the best
known and enduring examples. While a full account of this is beyond our
scope, we should note certain features. First, there was a "conservative" wing
creating a new national "tradition" as well as a more radical breakaway wing
intent on promoting reform and even revolution. The clearest break here occurred in the split between "official" academy art and dissident groups, of
whom the most well known are the Peredvizhniki (Wanderers), who emerged
in the 1870s. As far as cultural policy is concerned, our interest is in the
former group. While much of this was "spontaneous," personal tsarist and
state sponsorship pushed elements of it into the realm of cultural policy. In

---

[19] Ibid., 390.

[20] In fact, Freeze argues that, despite the best efforts of their impresarios, such ceremonies undermined rather than reinforced the mystique of monarchy. See Freeze,
"Subversive Piety."

particular, in our period, the rise of the Mariinskii Theater in St. Petersburg and the Bolshoi Theater in Moscow would have been inconceivable without such support.[21] Equally significant, the Imperial Theaters projected nationalist and russifying themes and have been appropriately described as "schools for citizens," a title applied to them with respect to tsarist, Provisional Government, and Soviet periods.[22]

Not all high cultural initiatives concerned the performing arts. One of the most significant aspects of cultural policy in the classic sense is provided by the establishment, in April 1895, of the Russian Museum. It opened on 7 March 1898, in the immense Mikhailovskii Palace in St. Petersburg, as a testament to Russian painting, sculpture, and other fine arts since the early icon painters. While the items on exhibition have changed with the regimes, the Russian Museum has remained a steadfast representative of Russian artistic genius. In 1902, an ethnographic section was added which extended the veneration to the wider empire, in particular, by focusing on the multitude of diverse cultures within the confines of the imperial boundary.[23] Its political significance is underlined by the fact that it was originally set up to house gifts to the tsar from the peoples of the empire. The tsar also purchased items for the exhibition from his personal funds since state funding was insufficient for the purpose. In its prerevolutionary years, the museum linked up with the remarkable outburst of exploration undertaken by Russians. While the very foundation of the Russian Empire had arisen from exploration and expansion into the vast, uncharted territories of Siberia as well as Central Asia and the Caucasus, in the mid- and late 19th century, innumerable scientific expeditions, often sponsored by the Academy of Sciences,[24] set out to the four corners of the empire and beyond into Mongolia and China. The Arctic was also a source of interest, and one of the last major global discoveries—of Severnaia Zemlia and its associated archipelago by Boris A. Vilkitskii—resulted from an expedition

---

[21] Their full names were the Imperial Mariinskii Theater and the Imperial Bolshoi Theater, reflecting their official status.

[22] See Murray Frame, *The St. Petersburg Imperial Theaters: Stage and State in Revolutionary Russia, 1900–20* (Jefferson, NC: McFarland and Company, 2000); and Murray Frame, *School for Citizens: Theatre and Civil Society in Imperial Russia* (New Haven: Yale University Press, 2006).

[23] In 1934, the Soviets split it off into an equally impressive and immense separate collection eventually renamed as the State Museum of Ethnography of the Peoples of the USSR.

[24] Again, the full title in these years, the Imperial St. Petersburg Academy of Sciences, reveals its official links. Its continuity down to the present as one of Russia's most prestigious institutions also testifies to the enduring significance of culture in the successive regimes.

in 1913.[25] The host of expeditions studied flora, fauna, geology, natural geography, and anthropology. They returned with artifacts of all kinds, from whale-bone carving to geological samples. Oddly, the most sensational event in the natural world at that time, the Tunguska meteorite, source of the most powerful earth impact event of modern times (17 [30] June 1908), evoked little scientific interest until the 1920s, probably because its immense significance was not appreciated, as it had occurred in a remote and barely inhabited area of eastern Siberia, north of Lake Baikal. Nonetheless, the activities of Petr P. Semenov (1827–1914)—leading geographer, explorer, statistician, and radical who earned the nickname Semenov-Tian-Shanskii from his pioneering exploration and study of the Tian-Shan mountain range—and others like him made a profound impact on Russian culture and, often inadvertently, nurtured its sense of imperial superiority.[26]

However, both tsarist and Soviet cultural policy shared another characteristic. They both failed to win over the population. Tsarist cultural aims, notably russification, brought it into conflict with minority nationalities and with the intelligentsia, including the majority Russian component. As we will see, Soviet cultural construction fared little better, and it has been argued that cultural failure—the failure to win over the population to its values—was a primary cause of the Soviet system's final collapse.[27] With respect to tsarism, it was more or less despite the ruling regime and its ideology that Russia produced a multitalented and vibrant intelligentsia in areas of mathematics, science, biology, literature, art, and music. Talents as diverse as Mendeleev, Vernadskii, Tolstoi, Dostoevskii, Gor'kii, Vrubel', Repin, Chagall, Kandinskii, Chaikovskii, and Stravinskii became internationally famous. There were a host of others. The present volume gives many examples. However, one does not have to look very far into their lives and achievements to see that much of what they stood for contradicted official policy. Scientists were almost universally Darwinian and often atheist rather than Christian. Even religiously inclined writers such as Dostoevskii and, to a greater extent, Tolstoi repudiated or, at least, had ambiguous relations with the tsarist state and the official church. Tolstoi, of course, was excommunicated. The brilliance of Russia's intellectual

---

[25] Like Darwin's association with the expeditionary force of the Royal Navy, which enabled him to make the studies around the globe on which he based his theory of natural selection, Russian scientific interest in the Arctic and the associated sea passages owed a debt to important military-strategic concerns, which helps to explain the state's readiness to fund such enterprises.

[26] There is a relatively recent edition of Semenov's memoirs in English: Petr Petrovitch Semenov, *Travels in the Tian'-Shan' 1856–1857*, trans. Liudmila Gilmour, Colin Thomas, and Marcus Wheeler; ed. and annotated Colin Thomas (London: The Hakluyt Society, 1998).

[27] For an interpretation of Soviet history focused on this issue, see Christopher Read, *The Making and Breaking of the Soviet System: An Interpretation* (Houndmills, UK: Palgrave, 2000).

creativity in these years did not redound to the advantage of either tsarist or Soviet rulers. Indeed, given their own cultural prescriptions, neither could tolerate much diversity and both fell easily into controlling the cultural life of the country. They used the same instruments. Censorship was endemic in both regimes. Only for a brief period around the 1905 Revolution and in 1917 and 1918 was it absent or weak. State patronage was crucial. For the tsars it funded and supported activities and artifacts from cathedrals and monuments to theaters and schools which embodied, reflected, and/or instilled official values. For the Soviet regime, state- and party-controled patronage of arts, education, newspapers, publishing, music, theater, film, museums, schools, and galleries quickly became practically universal, stifling countercurrents at least as effectively as censorship. In other words, culture became an area of contestation between government and society, with culture-makers of varying talents arrayed on either side. Even in a prewar Europe of the Dreyfus Affair and the postwar Weimar Republic, no other great European power had anything quite comparable to Russia in the importance and consequences of its culture wars, not least because, as has been frequently pointed out, censorship in Russia displaced much political discourse into "Aesopian" cultural forms. Solzhenitsyn famously wrote that a great writer was "like a second government."[28]

The Provisional Government Interlude: February–October 1917

The brief interlude of the Provisional Government in 1917 stands in stark contrast to tsarist and Soviet cultural objectives and control. The new authorities had no conscious cultural project of their own. Rather, they promised to "normalize" the cultural situation, that is to adopt liberal toleration characteristic of France and Britain, its chief role models. It did not last long enough to have very much effect. Its general approach symbolizes the work of the Provisional Government more widely. By and large, it devoted itself to nurturing and protecting what it considered the healthy tendencies and institutions of autocratic Russian culture, whether it be the art market, schools, museums, or religions. Its mission was to free such tendencies from attachment to the unhealthy elements of the previous system—Russian chauvinism, illiteracy, absence of rights, censorship, and so on—which were holding back Russia's intellectual and cultural development. It showed little sign of having a revolutionary cultural agenda of its own. It did have some cultural weight, however, embodied in, for example, the Orientalist Sergei Ol'denburg, who became minister of education from July to September in the Second Coalition Government. His eminent career as a scholar and administrator continued long after 1917. As Permanent Secretary of the Academy of Sciences from 1904

---

[28] Alexander Solzhenitsyn, *The First Circle*, trans. Michael Guybon (London: Collins, 1970), 436.

until 1929, he resisted Bolshevik encroachments on its independence until the Stalinist cultural revolution of 1929.[29] Among his deputy ministers were Academician Vladimir Vernadskii and the redoubtable "Krupskaia of the Kadet Party," Countess Sof'ia Panina.

It is possible to grasp the fleeting essence of the Provisional Government approach to culture by looking at Panina's career around this time.[30] Like her Bolshevik counterpart, before the Revolution Panina engaged in adult and secondary-level education. She was involved especially in opening educational paths for young and adult women. She was best known for the Narodnyi dom (People's House), an institution she founded in 1903 in Ligovskii, a working-class district on the outskirts of St. Petersburg, which she directed and financed on her own. Its effect, as one participant wrote in 1913, was that: "Before entering the classes I lived only my own life without noticing what was going on around me. Now in the classes I encountered and clearly saw the turbulent flow of life, which carried me off as well."[31] However, the toughening influence of war had wrought changes. In the words of Panina's biographer,

> almost three years of war, hardship, and revolutionary rhetoric had transformed these women. The working-class wives and mothers who filed into the People's House in 1914 to register for state assistance, Sofia recalled, were "helpless creatures," like "blind moles emerging for the first time from their burrows." But by the spring of 1917, she insisted, that helplessness had disappeared. Soldiers' wives now "were holding mass meetings on the street around the People's House, amid the piles of dirty melting snow, accusing us of stealing their aid packets, and of building the People's House itself on money stolen from the people."

Panina's description was an ominous warning of the limitations of the liberal project itself in Russia. Her students were becoming Krupskaia's students. In a sense, Panina was like Krupskaia, but with her aim calibrated at a target one class higher.

In her first ministerial post, for welfare, she tried to get the Smolnyi Institute out of the hands of the Bolsheviks and return it to its earlier use as a school,

---

[29] Perhaps surprisingly, although it fits in with much of our present argument, the Academy of Sciences was the last tsarist-era institution to be Bolshevized, not least because the old Bolsheviks maintained a respect for reason and culture and hoped to win it over.

[30] I am very much indebted to Adele Lindenmeyr, who allowed me to see the draft of her excellent biography of Countess Panina. The following account is based on her upcoming book.

[31] Extracts from Panina's writings are taken from her memoirs, "My Writings," in the V. D. Lehovich Collection. Translated and supplied by Adele Lindenmeyr.

though not solely for young ladies but also for the training of daycare and kindergarten teachers. Not surprisingly, she lost the battle with the Petrograd Soviet, which had commandeered the building as its headquarters, and resigned from the government as a consequence but returned as an assistant minister for education in the Second Coalition. She remained in government into the Third and final coalition, but much of the focus of her later activity was through the Petrograd City Council, where she occupied herself with tasks such as setting up clubs for children and buying books for libraries.[32]

Underlying Panina's work was a cultural preoccupation which gave many liberals nightmares. She believed, once again according to her biographer, "that Russia's 'dark,' uneducated working men and women needed guidance and leadership." Curiously, the Provisional Government, like its Soviet successor, identified the army as the key point at which to apply its cultural educational policy, the obvious aim being to bolster the morale of the troops by educating them in national values, civic culture, and the aims of the war. Also like the Soviet government, the Provisional Government was intent upon exerting political-revolutionary control over the army as a whole and began to make moves comparable to the soviet utilization of political commissars. They had a dual purpose—to instill the new values in the peasant soldiers and control the politically hostile officers still needed under both regimes.[33] While Krupskaia and the Bolsheviks shared such preoccupations they were prepared to work more closely with the masses, to lead them rather than change them first. Fear of the "dark people" was very much part of the liberal (and conservative) psyche, and the consequent lack of confidence in the masses was one of the considerations leading to the constant postponement of national elections. For the liberal mind, only a long period of mass education could offer any hope of turning "backward" peasants into modern, democratic citizens. One thing the Provisional Government certainly did not have was time.

Bolshevism and Culture

The first, tentative steps in evolving a Bolshevik cultural policy began even before the October Revolution. In Petrograd, a small number of party intellectuals set up the first organized branch of the Proletarian Cultural-Educational Association, which soon became known as Proletkul't. Its chief inspiration was Aleksandr Bogdanov, a one-time leading light of the party

---

[32] *Zhurnaly Petrogradskoi Gorodskoi dumy* (Petrograd, 1917), no. 77 (zasedanie 11 sentiabria 1917 goda): 9; no. 90 (zasedanie 20 oktiabria 1917): 2.

[33] For an excellent brief account of Provisional Government work in this respect, see the sub-chapter entitled "Sociopolitical Enlightenment" in Peter Holquist, *Making War, Forging Revolution: Russia's Continuum of Crisis 1914–1921* (Cambridge, MA: Harvard University Press, 2002), 211–22. The remainder of this excellent chapter, on the Whites and their cultural-educational-propaganda policy, carries the story into the Civil War.

around 1905 but, thereafter, a bitter critic of Lenin, who, unsurprisingly, returned the favor. Because of this enmity Bogdanov maintained an organizational back seat in Proletkul't, but his ideas reigned supreme. He started out from the unexceptionally Marxist premise that a crucial part of the ability of a class to dominate society arose from imposition of its cultural values on that society. For Marx, and for Bogdanov, the European bourgeoisie had been preparing its cultural path, through, for instance, challenging the medieval papacy and church and promoting the rebirth of reason in the Renaissance, long before it had acquired political and economic power. The end result of the process was the "naturalization" of values favorable to their interests, meaning that they were assumed to be absolute and unchanging rather than relative and self-interested. Their values were transmuted into "common sense" and supposed fixed features of "human nature" such as a propensity to selfishness, competition, conflict, aggression, and violence. It therefore followed that, if it were to establish its hegemony over society, the working class had to assert its own culture. However, this was easier said than done. It created, above all, two sets of problems. First, could one define the values on which proletarian culture should be based? Assuming that could be done there was a second stage, how could one develop and propagate them? A serious complication to both of these processes was the existing dominance of bourgeois culture. Not only did the currently ruling class use every means at its disposal to assert its values, it also did everything it could to disrupt the formation of a rival set of proletarian values. So successful had it been that, even at the moment when (as the Bolsheviks thought) the working class was on the verge of seizing power, its cultural development had barely begun. The tiny group of people who set up the first Proletkul't certainly had a job on their hands if they were going to change this situation.

Of the two sets of tasks the former was much the easier. While agreement among intellectuals is notoriously difficult, it was possible to reach a consensus about what values were associated with socialism. The bourgeois capitalist world revolved around core values such as rationalism, individualism, competition, private property, the market, and endless material growth. Philosophical idealism, which supposedly opened the way to mysticism, and religion, at least to befuddle the masses and interrupt the process of forming proletarian consciousness, also featured. Marxism shared some of these—it was, in its own eyes, rational and it also posited unlimited material growth and an abundance of products. However, it claimed to understand these things very differently from the capitalists for whom, for example, economic "rationality" was built on false values of market production, profit, and ownership rather than the concept of "need" which was fundamental to socialist economic priorities. But shared values were the exception. Rather, according to Bogdanov, the fundamental values were in total conflict. For socialists, collectivism, co-operation, communalism, and community were the key underlying concepts. Science and materialism were the philosophical underpinnings. The fundamentals were shared across a wide spectrum of socialist intellectuals.

The luminaries of Proletkul't, including Bogdanov's brother-in-law, the future commissar for enlightenment Anatolii Lunacharskii, the novelist Maksim Gor'kii, and, later and more marginally, Nadezhda Krupskaia, party specialist on adult education, were well aware that their ideas were, as yet, half-baked at best. Given the existing bourgeois dominance of education and the recently expanded mass press and the paucity of proletarian resources, it was no surprise that the gestation of a sound proletarian culture was in its earliest stages. The working class, given the intensity of its working week and its meager recompense, in most cases, had little time or energy to do anything but struggle to survive. Nonetheless, there is evidence that many Russian workers exhibited a great appetite for learning, reading, and self-improvement. In the words of one observer at the time, there was a great thirst among workers for "facts, facts, facts."[34] Better-off workers in more prosperous trades like printing and tailoring were able to enjoy greater cultural development. But it was nothing compared to the resources and achievements of the ruling class, and spontaneous generation of proletarian culture was in its infancy. This created a problem for the Proletkul't leadership. Where were the workers who would develop this culture? The Proletkul't leaders were unhappy about their own involvement in the process since most of them only had the most tenuous claim to be working class themselves. Would their influence taint the purity of any evolving, truly proletarian culture? They got around it by facing up to the fact that there was no alternative and, to mitigate any potentially negative consequences, they promoted genuine workers to the most important positions that they were capable of holding down, though it has to be said that intellectuals dominated the leadership of the movement throughout the period. However, their priority was to end their own domination and hand over the process to actual workers as soon as possible.

In order to define and promulgate proletarian culture Bogdanov had come up with two projects. One was the production of a proletarian encyclopaedia, the other a proletarian university. By and large, the encyclopaedia project remained theoretical. The concept of the proletarian university was also more theoretical than real, although a small party school was set up in Capri in 1909, using funds mostly provided by Gor'kii. Lenin set up a rival school in Longjumeau near Paris (1910).[35] In 1919, a party school was set up in Moscow which was related in terms of ambitions, curriculum, and class-based recruit-

---

[34] L. M. Kleinbort, *Ocherki rabochei intelligentsii*, 1: *1905–1916* (Petrograd: Nachatki znanii, 1923), 10. The pioneering secondary study in this field—Jeffrey Brooks, *When Russia Learned to Read: Literacy and Popular Literature 1861–1917* (Princeton, NJ: Princeton University Press, 1985)—is still very valuable. There is a 2003 edition (Northwestern University Press).

[35] For an account of the party schools, see Christopher Read, *Culture and Power in Revolutionary Russia: The Intelligentsia and the Transition from Tsarism to Communism*

ment to the two small-scale models. Needless to say, Bogdanovite ideas were still officially banished from the new institution, which became known as the Sverdlov University, though the concept of such an institution was inspired by Bogdanov's precedent.

The Sverdlov University was the peak of a developing network of party educational institutions set up to spread fundamental principles and to win over the population to Bolshevik values. It was one of the most important institutions established to teach basic party principles to party members who would take middle-ranking and provincial posts of responsibility in and beyond the party itself. However, few of them were, in any deep sense, Marxists. Party membership peaked at 350,000 to 400,000 between 1917 and 1919 and even the members were largely neophytes whose knowledge of Marxism and the nuances of Bolshevik ideology often consisted of scraps gleaned from slogans, decrees, and policies. One of the prime objects of persuasion and mobilization was the party itself. In order to facilitate the process of winning over party and society, in 1919 the party not only produced a new programme it also commissioned two leading party intellectuals, Nikolai Bukharin and Evgenii Preobrazhenskii, to write an explanation of the programme which was entitled *The ABC of Communism*.[36] The programme and the *ABC* were the focus of reading groups in party cells, especially in factories and military units. The party monopoly on power and its urge to establish a leading position across the economic, political, social, and cultural spectra, put enormous pressure on its manpower. The greatest shortage of all in early Communist Russia was Communists, especially those with much-needed practical skills. Enormous efforts were put into plugging this gap through worker education and a kind of positive discrimination allowing rapidly educated workers to reach university level through so-called workers' faculties (*rabfaki*). It is obvious, of course, that even the process of educating specialists was severely hampered by lack of specialists. Many of the army ideological watchdogs, the political commissars, were not Communists,[37] and as late as the mid-1920s there were teachers of party ideology in provincial *rabfaki* who were not Marxists.[38]

Proletkul't believed it was contributing to this wider process and even had dreams of being in charge of it. However, its actual influence was more

---

(London: Macmillan, 1990), 115–18. There is also an account of Proletkul't as a whole (111–32 and 145–56) and of the Sverdlov University (133–41).

[36] There is an English translation: N. Bukharin and E. Preobrazhensky, *ABC of Communism* (London: Penguin, 1969). It is also available at the Marxist Internet Archive (www.marxists.org/archive/bukharin/works/1920/abc/index.htm).

[37] Christopher Read, *War and Revolution in Russia 1914–1922* (London: Palgrave, 2013), 185.

[38] Read, *Culture and Power*, 225. For an account of the *rabfaki*, see Read, *Culture and Power*, 220–29.

modest. The enterprise was fraught with many practical and theoretical difficulties. Among the former was Leninist distrust, which came to a head in 1920 when Lenin demanded that Proletkul't abandon its claims to autonomy in the cultural sphere and submit to party discipline. To add spurious weight to his campaign, Lenin also charged them with an iconoclastic attitude to the culture of the past. There was no foundation to Lenin's charge in this respect, since Bogdanov argued for preserving all that was of value in the "treasure-chest of past culture" as he called it, but Lenin was right to see that Proletkul't had ambitions to autonomy. The action against Proletkul't coincided with action to end trade union autonomy and prefigured the final Leninist resolution of cultural policy which accompanied the adoption of the New Economic Policy (NEP).

In his last active years, from 1920 to 1922/3 (he died in January 1924), Lenin spent a considerable amount of time pondering cultural issues. While the economic collapse and Civil War dominated the agenda there was little time for him to take up the cultural aspects of revolution. However, as the tide of civil war receded it uncovered a beach covered in curiosities. Like a beachcomber Lenin began to pick through the flotsam and jetsam. Some of it was useful, much was harmful. During the Civil War cultural control had been inconsistent and unsystematic. The nationalization of cultural institutions, such as museums, schools, most of the art market, and publishing, not to mention the education system, censorship, and state control of supplies such as paper, made independent cultural activity difficult, but not impossible. In cracks and crevices, independent thought continued. The philosopher Nikolai Berdiaev (Nicholas Berdyaev) and others ran a small Free Philosophical Academy within the bosom of Moscow University. Small publishers and a few independent publishers eked out a constrained existence. Beyond that, there was an explosion of revolutionary art and artists who colonized whatever state patronage was available. Key sources were the Commissariat of Enlightenment, under the relatively indulgent and tolerant reign of Lunacharskii, and a project to translate classics of world literature into Russian under the control of Maksim Gor'kii. Through these means, and also the provision of a meager special state ration (*paek*) to a number of lucky scientists, writers, artists, and other intellectuals, some basic income, which barely guaranteed survival, was provided. Nonetheless, there was an explosion of experimental art. Its roots went back to the pre-October and pre-1917 period, but its early Soviet-era energy was derived from revolutionary enthusiasm and opportunity. Radical artists of all kinds associated themselves with the revolutionary project, believing, naively as it turned out, that all revolutionary roads led to the same destination. They also, equally naively, fought each other for intellectual domination of the opportunities which existed. The main art school, Vkhutemas (the Higher State Art and Technical Workshop), was taken over by Malevich and Tatlin, and artists they considered insufficiently revolutionary, like Chagall, were banished to the provinces. Many artists in a variety of fields contributed to the new cultural explosion. Tatlin designed objects appropriate to the new way of life, including furniture for reading clubs, clothing for workers, and a vast revolving skyscraper monument and conference building dedicated to the Communist International (never built). The poet Vladimir Maiakovskii produced graphic morality stories illustrating propaganda themes. The artists El (Lazar') Lisitskii and Dmitrii Moor produced, in vastly different styles, propaganda posters. Brilliant pioneers of film, like Dziga Vertov, began to shape Soviet cinema.[39]

There were also controversies over what to do with remnants of tsarist cultural expression. What was to be done with monuments? Some were simply pulled down, like the statue of Alexander III, memorably captured in Sergei Eisenstein's film *October* (1928), creating a symbolic archetype emulated in recent times with the tearing down of statues of Dzerzhinskii in Moscow and Saddam Hussein in Baghdad. However, an uncontrolled wave of statue-smashing was not what the party wanted. Monuments which had artistic value were to be preserved. New street iconography appropriate to the new regime and new values were to be commissioned. Characteristic of the time, a list of approved figures for whom monuments could be constructed was drawn up.[40] There was also the issue of what to do with the institutions of tsarist and nationalist cultural expression. Some, like the art galleries and museums, such as the ethnography museum, could simply be converted to Marxist-Leninist values by changing the interpretative gloss on the artifacts within, though it was only in the 1920s that this was done systematically. One crucial controversy revolved around the apparent quintessence of tsarist culture, the opera and ballet of the Bolshoi Theater. Radicals like Maiakovskii called for its closure. However, the party, with Lenin in the forefront, agreed to pay large subsidies, even in the straitened times of civil war, to keep it functioning and to open it up to the masses. At the height of the Civil War period, tickets for theaters, concert halls, and cinemas were free. A third set of problems revolved around what to do with church buildings. Again, those with artistic value were preserved. Some were converted, sooner or later, into museums like the Kazanskii and Isaakevskii cathedrals in Petrograd.[41] Nonetheless many were either officially or spontaneously closed or demolished.

---

[39] There are many books on the art and artists of the period, including Matthew Cullerne Brown and Brandon Taylor, eds., *Art of the Soviets: Painting, Sculpture and Architecture in a One-Party State 1917–92* (Manchester: Manchester University Press, 1993); and Abbott Gleason, Peter Kenez, and Richard Stites, eds., *Bolshevik Culture: Experiment and Order in the Russian Revolution* (Bloomington: Indiana University Press, 1985).

[40] Christina Lodder, "Lenin's Plan for Monumental Propaganda," in *Art of the Soviets*, 16–32.

[41] They were closed after 1917 and reopened as museums in 1932 and 1931 respectively.

The Leninist Cultural Settlement 1920–22

We cannot know for sure what Lenin was thinking as he surveyed this complex cultural scene, but we do know that the steps he took in response resounded through the cultural life of the country for the entire Soviet period. One of the ironies of Soviet-era culture was that a regime claiming to be revolutionary excelled at the most bourgeois and conservative forms of artistic and cultural activity. Symphony orchestras in formal dress, the aristocratic arts of opera and ballet, realist forms of painting resembling the aesthetic values of Academy art dominated the scene and, at their best, gained global recognition. One of the least proletarian of games, chess, achieved great prestige, not least because it was one of Lenin's favorites. A well-known photo shows him playing against Bogdanov on Capri during his visit to the "heretical" party school. Even everyday life reverted to "bourgeois" norms of, for example, the nuclear family. The party eventually frowned on libertinism and divorce among Communists almost as strongly as the Vatican did among Catholics. Conservatism of artistic forms remained the norm throughout the Soviet period. Khrushchev famously complained that a painting by Ernst Neizvestnyi looked as though it had been produced by a donkey's tail.[42] Brezhnev ordered the bulldozing of an open-air exhibition of abstract and experimental art. Stalin, of course, had his impact on creating this situation, but its origins go back to Lenin, and not just in the matter of chess.

Between about 1920 and 1922 a series of cultural measures tightened the party's grip. They included making the censorship apparatus permanent and extending it to all forms of art, literature, performance, and publishing. Private publishing was practically eliminated. All cultural institutions and patronage were in state hands, notably under the jurisdiction of the Commissariat of Enlightenment. University autonomy was brought to an end in 1921.[43] Some 250 non-Marxist intellectuals were summarily exiled in 1922.[44] A new attempt to shackle the church and to split it through encouraging a pro-regime so-called Living Church was undertaken.[45] There were parallel political developments—the attack on diversity within the party at the expense of the Workers' Opposition and the Democratic Centralists leading to a ban on factions in the party; the trial of leading Socialist Revolutionaries still left in the country; the confirmation that the party should lead in every sphere; the establishment of

---

[42] Khrushchev and Neizvestnyi were reconciled later to the extent that the artist produced a magnificent tombstone for the politician's grave.

[43] See Read, *Culture and Power*, 156–85.

[44] See Stuart Finkel, *On the Ideological Front: The Russian Intelligentsia and the Making of the Soviet Public Sphere* (New Haven: Yale University Press, 2007).

[45] Arto Luukkanen, *The Party of Unbelief: Bolshevik Religious Policy 1917–1929* (Helsinki: SHS, 1994).

the supposedly temporary Cheka on a permanent basis; the establishment of the party Agitation and Propaganda apparatus; the emergence of party Control Commissions. All pointed in the same direction. The socioeconomic defeat inflicted on the party by the peasantry had led to the "retreat" of NEP. NEP was, in some ways, a partial restoration of capitalism. It followed, especially to the Marxist mind, that economic interests inimical to socialism would emerge and try to take advantage of the situation to re-establish capitalist values and politics. Therefore, for Lenin and the party leaders, the tightening of political and ideological control was a necessary preventive measure to ensure there would be no capitalist restoration. It was the corollary to economic "liberalization" which had to be accompanied by intellectual control, not toleration. While control became much more extensive under Stalin, that is no reason for underestimating the degree to which Lenin was establishing a cultural dictatorship.[46] It also linked to the twin cultural foundations of Leninism—winning over the population to socialist values and developing proletarian class consciousness. Where the autocracy had been almost a theocracy, the new Soviet system was becoming a kind of secular equivalent. The status and legitimacy of the new system lay in its ideological rectitude, not the votes of its citizens. Its fundamentalist hold on "truth" gave it the right to marginalize all heresies and use every means of the state to create conditions favorable to the establishment of the new "religion" of socialist ideals and proletarian class consciousness. None the less, the twenties were more tolerant than the thirties for a number of reasons. In the earlier period, more latitude was given to fellow-travelers in the hope they would join the great task of socialist construction and also, perhaps, because the party was led by intellectuals. Although, like Bukharin and Trotskii, for instance, they differed in many ways, they shared a respect for culture and ideas. Such an attitude was much less prevalent among the rapidly educated former workers turned engineers and managers who were the backbone of the party and its apparatus under Stalin.

A glance at Lenin's writings and speeches confirms the basic principles of the cultural-political settlement of his last years. Like Proletkul't, Lenin wanted to establish and develop proletarian culture, but his understanding of the content of that culture was more dogmatic and less experimental. As far back as 1910 he had underlined to Gor'kii that "we know now of only one proletarian science and that is Marxism."[47] He returned to this in the first clause of the draft of his resolution on Proletkul't: "Not special ideas,

---

[46] There is a collection of 844 pages of documents relating to repression in the early 1920s which underlines its depth and breadth. A. N. Artizov et al., eds., "Ochistim Rossiiu nadolgo...": Repressii protiv inakomysliashchikh konets 1921–nachalo 1923 g. (Moscow: Mezhdunarodnyi fond "Demokratiia"; Materik, 2008).

[47] V. I. Lenin, "Notes of a Publicist," in Lenin on Culture and Cultural Revolution (Moscow: Progress, 1966), 25.

but Marxism."[48] In many ways, he shared Proletkul't's view that "Proletarian culture must be the logical development of the store of knowledge mankind has accumulated under the yoke of capitalist, landowner and bureaucratic society," but he prefaced that comment with a quite different spirit: "proletarian culture ... is not clutched out of thin air; it is not an invention of those who call themselves experts in proletarian culture. That is all nonsense."[49] Again this was expressed in pithy form in his rough draft resolution on Proletkul't: "Not the invention of a new proletarian culture, but the development of the best models, traditions, and results of the existing culture" from the point of view of Marxism and the experience of the working class.[50] In his last published article Lenin maintained a similar stance, saying, perhaps surprisingly, "We hear people dilating at too great length and too flippantly on 'proletarian' culture. For a start, we should be satisfied with real bourgeois culture."[51]

Indeed, in his article "On Co-operation" he argued that, where NEP had created the conditions for a rolling transfer of resources from the remaining private sector to the public sector, it only needed to be supplemented by a cultural revolution for socialism to be constructed. The emphasis, Lenin argued, was now on educational and cultural work, especially among the peasants. The pamphlet concludes:

> In our country the political and social revolution preceded the cultural revolution that now confronts us. This cultural revolution would now suffice to make our country a completely socialist country; but it presents immense difficulties of a purely cultural (for we are illiterate) and material character (for, to be cultured, we must achieve a certain development of the material means of production, must have a certain material base).[52]

The second, equally emphatic, element in Lenin's views was that the party should control the process. The rough draft decree on Proletkul't once more: "Not apart from the People's Commissariat for Education [i.e., the Commissariat

---

[48] V. I. Lenin, "Rough Draft of a Resolution on Proletarian Culture," in *Lenin on Culture and Cultural Revolution*, 150.

[49] V. I. Lenin, "The Tasks of the Youth Leagues," in *Collected Works*, 2nd English ed. (London: Lawrence and Wishart; Moscow: Progress Publishers, 1966), 31: 287; also in *Lenin on Culture and Cultural Revolution*, 128.

[50] Lenin, "Rough Draft of a Resolution on Proletarian Culture," 150. Emphases in original.

[51] The quotation can be found in the opening paragraph of V. I. Lenin, "Better Fewer but Better," in *Collected Works* (1965), 33: 487.

[52] V. I. Lenin, "On Co-operation," in *Lenin on Culture and Cultural Revolution*, 210. For Lenin the term culture as used here had a mainly anthropological meaning but did not entirely exclude the intellectual and artistic meaning.

of Enlightenment] but as part of it since RCP[53] + Commissariat for Education = Σ Proletkul't."[54] Even more sharp was the reprimand to Bukharin around the same time when he was dallying with Proletkul't:

1. Proletarian culture = communism
2. The RCP (Russian Communist Party) takes the lead
3. The proletarian class = the RCP = Soviet power
About this we are in complete agreement?[55]

Nothing could be further from the niceties of Proletkul't and its scruples about polluting the proletarian purity of the future culture. For Lenin the class was the party was Soviet power. End of story.

Conclusion

Comparing tsarist and Soviet culture and cultural policy has shown up the expected differences between a system founded in the depths of medieval, aristocratic, religious characteristics and one derived from reason, science, industry, and modernity. However, it has also shown a continuing difference from Western cultures, notably the high priority given to culture and the fundamental importance of cultural issues to the legitimacy, self-perception, and objectives of the tsarist and Soviet systems. The comparison confirms the view that, while institutions can be subjected to rapid revolutionary change, even large and fundamental ones such as armies, the justice system, banks, finance, property, governance, and so on, the hold of cultural norms and notions can be much more tenacious. The remainder of this volume bears this out. Going beyond its immediate scope, one could also conclude that the ultimate collapse of both systems can be attributed in significant part to cultural failure. Tsarism stuck too rigidly to the inflexibilities of official nationalism, damagingly reinforced by the influence of Pobedonostsev. The Soviet system's failure owed a great deal to its defeat on the cultural front. In the battle between socialist values and the traditional petty-bourgeois mentality, the latter won hands down, albeit in modernized form. In evaluating Russian history, one ignores the cultural dimension at one's peril.

---

[53] Russian Communist Party.

[54] Lenin, "Rough Draft of a Resolution on Proletarian Culture," 150.

[55] V. I. Lenin, "Letter to Bukharin," 11 October 1920, in *V. I. Lenin o kul'ture*, 2nd ed. (Moscow: Izd-vo politicheskoi literatury, 1985), 293. Emphases in original.

Popular Culture

Mass Culture and the Culture of the Masses in Russia, 1914–22

Vladimir P. Buldakov

Due to the all-encompassing nature of the First World War, Russian social space needed to be reorganized on the basis of common values. The path to this reorganization lay in cultural initiatives capable of overcoming both the elitist isolation of the upper social strata and the traditionalist reserve of the lower. Aimed at the unification of Russia's spiritual and intellectual space, these initiatives were able to intensify the socialization of the masses on a common basis. In wartime conditions, this could play a decisive role in patriotic mobilization.

Popular culture, in the modern sense of leisure culture, was present in prewar Russia only to a small extent. Here, the very concept took on a rather different meaning than in the West. In a paternalistic social space, popular culture could not exist purely for relaxation. It had to be "public" culture, including actively spiritual and didactic elements and providing "healthy" entertainment. Nevertheless, all "culture" existed in Russia almost entirely independently of the lower classes, which were called upon, at most, to provide decorative material for "high" culture. Behind the facade of rising modernity, poverty and backwardness ruled.[1] In reality, the upper and lower strata existed on entirely different cultural levels. "Urban" culture was isolated from rural; the "populist" intelligentsia inhabited a particular cultural—or, rather, subcultural—niche. Tourism developed only among the wealthy, reflecting the cosmopolitan aspirations of some and the conservative and patriotic attitudes of others.[2] The lower classes had no possibility of travel, beyond pilgrimage or the search for work.

Of course, as everywhere, the development of "lower-class culture" in Russia was linked to consumerism.[3] Moreover, elements of genuine popular

---

[1] Richard Stites, *Russian Popular Culture: Entertainment and Society since 1900* (Cambridge: Cambridge University Press, 1992), 9.

[2] Louise McReynolds, *Russia at Play: Leisure Activities at the End of the Tsarist Era* (Ithaca, NY: Cornell University Press, 2003), 155.

[3] M. L. Hilton, *Selling to the Masses: Retailing in Russia, 1880–1930* (Pittsburgh: University of Pittsburgh Press, 2012).

Russian Culture in War and Revolution, 1914–22, Book 1: Popular Culture, the Arts, and Institutions. Murray Frame, Boris Kolonitskii, Steven G. Marks, and Melissa K. Stockdale, eds. Bloomington, IN: Slavica Publishers, 2014, 25–52.

(public) culture were able to emerge on the tide of wartime patriotism. The Bolsheviks tried to "tame" the culture of the masses by way of the folklore tradition, but revolutionary poetry is more accurately considered propaganda, which was hardly in demand among the population at large.[4] Traditional urban folklore genres developed entirely independently of this.[5]

In summary, the growing "mass culture" of the town and the dominant peasant "culture of the masses" (co)existed according to their own particular logic. However, there was an active interchange between cultural strata.

ఆ ಓ

"The objective conditions of war have changed so much that it can no longer be a source of artistic 'rapture,' and forces the painting muse to fall silent," wrote one eminent art critic. "This 'labyrinth' of a war cannot be accommodated within the aesthetic framework of art, and in modern warfare even the tragedy of death has lost the grandeur of its former agony."[6] A "relaxation culture" was needed that would also play a role in mobilization and morale-building. The search for the "new culture" intensified.

What we might call "mass culture" was socially stratified: *lubki* (colorful popular prints in a traditional style) were produced for the "people," while numerous cabarets and miniature theaters served the "bourgeois" public. "Moscow's entertainment life, which was in decay on the eve of 1914, flourished during the war years with unprecedented strength." The "happy assortment" fit in with this very well.[7] And yet the cultural space did become somewhat unified, at the expense of "urban" (entertainment) culture. Some authors observe that interest in sport increased in connection with the war.[8] But, above all, the formation of mass culture in the modern sense favored the cinema, as well as the so-called urban love song, distributed on gramophone records. Objectively, the town was obliged to repay its debt to the country, as the primary provider of manpower to the front. But Europeanized "simplification" at the expense of technological innovation barely affected the rural environment.

All social strata felt the urgency of restructuring the cultural space on both national and civic grounds. However, "high" culture could not find a suitably

---

[4] James von Geldern and Richard Stites, eds., *Mass Culture in Soviet Russia: Tales, Poems, Songs, Movies, Plays and Folklore 1917–1953* (Bloomington: Indiana University Press, 1995), 3–69, 85–113.

[5] Ibid., 70–73.

[6] Ia. Tugenkhol'd, *Problema voiny v mirovom isskustve* (Moscow, 1916), 159–61.

[7] L. I. Tikhvinskaia, *Povsednevnaia zhizn' teatral'noi bogemy Serebrianogo veka: Kabare i teatry miniatiur v Rossii, 1908–1917* (Moscow: Molodaia gvardiia, 2005), 423.

[8] McReynolds, *Russia at Play*, 112.

general (*obshchegrazhdanskii*) approach. Conservative-minded individuals proposed to cleanse Russian culture of its "alien" elements. "For half a century, neither our pseudo-liberals nor our conservatives have lamented their separation from the people, the Church, and our ancestors; not until the last year," stated Metropolitan Antonii (Khrapovitskii). "But now the war has begun ... a fearfully strong need has emerged to identify their own Russian culture ... its deep opposition to the European way of life based in Roman law, that is to say, paganism...." He also acknowledged that Orthodox civic consciousness, "compatible with an unimpaired understanding of Christianity, we do not have...."[9] Some liberal publications expressed similar ideas: "Now, schooled by bitter experience, we will not seek happiness abroad, when it lives within us and is poured out to us abundantly by our Mother the Orthodox Church: in her walls dwell our salvation, our comfort, and our joy."[10] However, the popularization of "national" principles was understood in various ways. One provincial liberal, the cooperatives activist Georgii I. Fomin, wrote: "The people did not seek, and did not attempt to seek, new outlets for their creativity... In order to shake up popular art, to resurrect it, we needed a brilliant new epoch, which the current great war against 'the Germans' has created."[11]

Amateur artists were also involved in the production of patriotic *lubki*. The most prolific was the Moscow "worker-poet" P. A. Travin (in reality, a private entrepreneur and cabinet-maker). Leaving aside his scribblings about the lives of passionate Italians and Spaniards, he published a whole series of "patriotic" leaflets, the names of which speak for themselves: *The Pig-Beauty, or the Germans Fooled*; *Why Dream of Wilhelm?*; *Sultan Mohammed Sells His Harem*; *How Did a Russian Boot Scare Off a Whole German Regiment?*; *Roasted Wilhelm*; *The Tears of Monsters: The German Crocodile*; *Catastrophe: The Fall of Three Empires*. These works are striking in their blending of genres: the line between the realistic and the fantastical can hardly be seen. Travin also published war songs of his own composition, and descriptions of the great feats of military heroes.[12] Other amateur propagandists also emerged, offering their own variety of folktale parodies.[13] The same could be seen in

---

[9] Nikon (Rklitskii), *Mitropolit Antonii [Khrapovitskii] i ego vremia, 1863–1936*, bk. 2 (Nizhnii Novgorod: Sviato-Troitskaia dukhovnaia seminariia, 2004), 410–11.

[10] *Drug pakharia: Dvukhnedel'nyi zhurnal po sel'skomu khoziaistvu i zemleustroistvu* (Saratov), no. 1 (15 January 1915): 4.

[11] G. Fomin, "Voina i narodnoe tvorchestvo," *V dni voiny: Vestnik voronezhskikh organizatsii voennogo vremeni*, no. 1 (3 July 1916): 28.

[12] Cf. P. A. Travin, *Russkie voennye pesni 1914 g.* (Moscow, 1914); P. A. Travin, *Geroi iz naroda: Riadovye chudo bogatyri. Voennye rasskazy. Stikhi i karikatury* (Moscow, 1914).

[13] Cf. A. V. Prokhorovich, *Novye pesni o Vil'gel'me* (Moscow, [1914]); A. Petrov, *Krovavyi prizrak ili kak Vil'gel'm delal smotr chertiam* (Moscow, 1914); Kh. Shukhmin, *Kak Vil'gel'm*

the provinces. *Saratovskaia pochta* (The Saratov Post) published the following parodies: *The Fat Man and the Skinny Man: Germany Before and After the War; The Kaiser Carefully Sows Iron Crosses among his Troops, but Only Wooden Crosses Grow from These Seeds.*[14] It was persistently suggested that the Germans suffered from insufficient industry and a lack of resources. Hindenburg supposedly received the following telegram: "Will exchange field-marshal's rank for pair of warm boots."[15] By 1916, this kind of "patriotic" pathos had become entrenched.

At the start of the war, notes of optimism could be heard. Some journalists even stated that "the world war … has erased all class boundaries … destroyed all differences between … nationalities…. This is the New Russia, united, strong; feeling its own cultural power, and with all its strength defending it against German dominance…."[16] It is unlikely that the Russian peasantry felt anything of the kind. For this bearer of traditional consciousness, the war was something like a natural disaster to which they reacted "with all their being." Nonetheless, liberals were in a very warlike mood. Some felt that "the world war will create the conditions in which Russia will be able to take its place at the head of an all-European cultural organization."[17] In reality, there were no internal resources for this; the Russian cultural space remained stratified.

The elitism of the Silver Age was by no means past. The eminent poet Konstantin Bal´mont traveled all over the country with his lectures on "Love and Death" and "Woman and the Great Religions," which attracted their own grateful audience.[18] In contrast, some felt uncomfortable with the inadequacy of "high" culture in the face of the wartime prose of life. The painter Il´ia Repin was ashamed of his "patriotic" painting *The Sister Leading the Soldiers to Attack.*[19] Meanwhile, reports of enemy excesses occupied pride of place in print. Appeals on the topic of German brutality were signed by the writers Maksim Gor´kii, Aleksandr Serafimovich (Popov), and Stepan Skitalets, the artists Konstantin Korovin and the Vasnetsov brothers (Apollinarii and Viktor), the sculptor Sergei Merkulov, and the singer Fedor Shaliapin.

---

prisnilsia korobochniku Nikite (Moscow, 1914); N. A. Ratomskii, *Kak Vil´gel´m bral Varshavu* (Petersburg, 1915).

[14] E. Iu. Semenova, *Kul´tura Povolzh´ia v gody Pervoi mirovoi voiny (1914–nachalo 1918 gg.). Po materialam Samarskoi, Simbirskoi, Penzenskoi i Saratovskoi gubernii* (Samara: Samarskii gosudarstvennyi tekhnologicheskii universitet, 2007), 93.

[15] *Velikaia voina. Voennyi iumoristicheskii al´manakh* (Moscow, 1915): 1.

[16] *Ozdorovlenie Rossii: Zhurnal, posviashchennyi voprosam gigieny i sanitarii*, no. 1 (1915): 1.

[17] M. I. Tugan-Baranovskii, ed., *Voprosy mirovoi voiny* (Petrograd: Pravo, 1915), 19.

[18] E. A. Andreeva-Bal´mont, *Vospominaniia* (Moscow: Izd-vo imeni Sabashnikovykh, 1996), 396–97, 399–401.

[19] K. Chukovskii, *Dnevnik, 1901–1929* (Moscow, 1991), 75.

In the meantime, the "popular" commodity—the *lubok*—"moved briskly." Numerous specialized publishers sprang up. "Hundreds of thousands of war *lubki* were released onto the market, if not millions," reported one newspaper in the capital. "Among the artists, along with representatives of the 'old school,' are innovators, even including futurists and cubists..."[20] However, some believed the "futurist *lubok*" to be an absurdity, and there was a grain of truth in this. Artists such as Aristarkh Lentulov, Kazimir Malevich, Il'ia Mashkov, Dmitrii Moor, and others also produced *lubok* posters. Jingoism predominated. Vladimir Maiakovskii produced texts such as these: "Austria surrendered L'vov to the Russians; rabbits cannot win against lions!"; "The enemy is hacked to pieces, and then he may swim in the blue Neman"; "A coarse red-headed German flew away to Warsaw / For the Cossack Danilo Dikii ran him through with a pike/ And his wife Polina makes trousers from Zeppelins."[21] The liberal press claimed that *lubki* such as *The Battle on the River Vistula*, *The Russians Capture a German War Train*, *The Battle of the Neman River*, *The Heroic Feat of Kuz'ma Kriuchkov*, *The Flight of the Austro-Hungarian Troops from Rava-Ruska*,[22] and so on, were widely distributed among the peasantry. However, it is doubtful that they were capable of drumming up genuinely patriotic feeling.

The craze for *lubki* also captivated part of the cultural elite. However, far from all were in favor of it. In a letter of 16 October 1914, the poet and literary historian P. S. Sukhotin confessed: "I cannot read the newspapers, because everything in them is revolting... The patriotism that reigns over every printed character instils horror at what we are teaching the multitudes, and what disgraceful outcome we can expect."[23] In October 1914, Colonel A. Prozorov sent an "Open Letter to Certain People in the Film Industry." "Be ashamed," it said,

> for you deliberately aim to destroy our beautiful Russian cinema, which has barely flowered... It aims to use the silver screen to complement the information printed in the papers, and you feed it a horrible, ignorant, vile concoction ... you mock our heroes... If you, sirs, will speculate about our enemies, leave aside their atrocities and their baseness and do not outrage Russian souls...

---

[20] Cited in A. V. Krusanov, *Russkii avangard, 1907–1932: Istoricheskii obzor*, 1: *Boevoe desiatiletie* (Moscow: Novoe literaturnoe obozrenie, 2010), 487.

[21] I. V. Lebedeva, ed., *Russkii voennyi lubok: Iz kollektsii otdela redkikh knig*, pt. 1, *Pervaia mirovaia voina* (Moscow: Gosudarstvennaia publichnaia istoricheskaia biblioteka Rossii, 1995), 53, 78, 85, 93.

[22] G. Fomin, "Narodnye razvlecheniia," *V dni voiny: Vestnik voronezhskikh organizatsii voennogo vremeni*, no. 2 (10 July 1916): 37.

[23] S. G. Blinov, et al., eds., *Rossiiskii arkhiv: Istoriia otechestva v svidetel'stvakh i doku-mentakh, XVIII–XX vv.*, no. 9 (Moscow: Studia Tritè, 1999), 512.

According to his observations, such films corrupted the youth destined for the front.[24] Whatever the case, according to the press, by the spring of 1916 the *lubok*—designated, meanwhile, as a creation of "sickly lyrical goo and triumphant pathos"—had begun to wither away.[25]

Whatever the case, the combination of cheerful doggerel and pictorial propaganda retained its significance until the end of the Civil War, especially among the Reds. In the first six months of the Great War, almost 600 different prints were released, with a cumulative circulation of 11 million copies.[26] Most of them belonged to the popular culture genre. *Ogonek* was pleased to announce that the "first popular *lubok*" about the war, *The First Hand-to-Hand Fight between the Cossacks and the Prussian Dragoons*, was already being sold on the streets of Moscow and Petersburg at the start of August.[27] Gradually, the *lubok* style came to permeate the art of book illustration. The general artistic standard was low. Some critics saw it as an "inadmissible affectation," while others found "youth and ardour" in it, remarking that "the masses live and breathe" in contemporary caricature.[28] In 1916, Aleksei Kruchenykh published the illustrated album *War* (*Voina*), with a style of illustration referred to as *rez'ba* (fretwork). Some researchers consider this the model for Maiakovskii's famous "satirical windows."[29]

The "visualization" of cultural life found its expression in the satirical publications of the tabloid class. Caricatures of the kaiser became their trademark. But these were hardly convincing: the German emperor was depicted either with a broken helmet, or as Don Quixote.[30] Meanwhile, the magazines produced long lists of "Russian prisoners in Berlin," thickly populated with Germanic surnames.[31] Their "letters" from Berlin were printed: "Oh, I am now so ashamed that I hated the Germans, that I spoke badly of them, that I did not go willingly to prison."[32] Turkey's entry into the war broadened the remit of chauvinistic mockery: one amateur artist published a caricature in which a fez-wearing Turk dragged a pig after him, on the side of which was

---

[24] *Vestnik kinematografii*, no. 100 (15 October 1914): 10.

[25] Tikhvinskaia, *Povsednevnaia zhizn'*, 374.

[26] I. V. Vladislavlev, *Russkaia literatura o voine 1914 g. (Bibliograficheskii ukazatel')* (Moscow, 1915), 5.

[27] *Ogonek*, no. 32 (10 [23] August 1914): 13.

[28] Krusanov, *Russkii avangard*, 488–89.

[29] S. Buriukov, *Poeziia russkogo avangarda* (Moscow: Izd-vo Ruslana Ilinina, 2001), 116.

[30] *Teatr v karikaturakh*, no. 16 (21 September 1914): 1; ibid., no. 17 (9 October 1914): 3.

[31] *Voina i geroi*, no. 3 (1914): 2.

[32] *Dzhigit* (Baku), no. 4 (31 January 1916): 3.

written "Germany."[33] The provinces had their own peculiarities: a humorous magazine in Baku mercilessly mocked the kaiser's ally, the "Turk," depicting him as a "poisonous and malignant specimen" who yearned to fall prisoner in Russia, where "they feed you shish kebabs."[34]

This was just one aspect of the chauvinistic vulgarization of culture. In Moscow, restaurant owners immediately renamed Hamburg steak and Viennese schnitzel to Slavic steak and Serbian schnitzel.[35] One satirical magazine scoffed at the "patriotic" husband reproaching his wife for making Hungarian goulash.[36] The government proposed removing all German-produced films from circulation. These films were subsequently released as American or Dutch.[37]

The press lauded Russia's allies to the utmost. In the Korsh Theater, Moscow, the 1914 season opened with *Matrena the General's Wife* (*General'sha Matrena*). Before the start of the show, Russian, French, English, Serbian, and Montenegrin soldiers each carried their national flag across the stage to the sound of their respective national anthems.[38] Over time, the playing of the Allied anthems became a tradition. At the end of 1914, a series of 12 stamps was released, depicting "Figures from the Great War of 1914." The stamps depicted the commanders in chief of the allied armies: General John French, General Joseph Joffre, Petr I of Serbia, Nikolai of Montenegro. The selection of Russian figures was less successful. Apart from Grand Duke Nikolai Nikolaevich, General I. V. Nikitin, and A. A. Brusilov, there also appeared Adjutant-General Paul von Rennenkampf, whom popular opinion later accused of all but outright treason. In early 1916, at Moscow's Malyi Theater, the famous actor A. I. Sumbatov-Iuzhin proclaimed from the stage: "Take Erzurum!" The audience burst into applause and cries of "Hurrah!"[39] But incidents such as these became rarer and rarer.

From 1915 onwards, the anthems of the allied powers were released on record, as well as heroic and patriotic compositions: *The Hero's Return to the Homeland; The Sufferings of Serbia; The People's Wrath; Sleep, Fighting Eagles; Dream in the Trenches; Night on the Vistula; The Patriotic Seagull; The Warrior's*

---

[33] N. A. Ratomskii, *Kak Vil'gel'm bral Varshavu* (St. Petersburg, 1915), cover.

[34] *Dzhigit* (Baku), no. 2 (17 January 1916): 5; ibid., no. 10 (13 March 1916): 8.

[35] P. D. Dolgorukov, *Velikaia razrukha* (Madrid: n.p., 1964), 117.

[36] *Voina i geroi*, no. 8 (1914): 6.

[37] A. A. Khanzhonkov, *Pervye gody russkoi kinematografii: Vospominaniia* (Moscow–Leningrad: Iskusstvo, 1937), 90.

[38] G. G. Dadamian, *Teatr v kul'turnoi zhizni Rossii (1914–1917)* (Moscow: Izd-vo Rossiiskoi Akademii teatral'nogo iskusstva OOO "Dar-Ekspo," 2000), 12.

[39] M. M. Bogoslovskii, *Dnevniki (1913–1919): Iz sobraniia Gosudarstvennogo istoricheskogo muzeia* (Moscow: Vremia, 2011), 141.

Farewell. A series of posters was published, illustrating the victories of the Russian "magical heroes" (*chudo-bogatyri*): for example, in East Prussia, "the Death Hussars—the favourite cavalry of Emperor Wilhelm, who wore a death's head on their caps"—were routed by the Cossacks. *Lubki* showed the Don Cossack Koz'ma Kriuchkov (who was wounded 16 times) physically mowing down German infantrymen, and the supreme commander in chief, Nikolai Nikolaevich, belaboring the kaiser about the head with a frying pan. Wilhelm II was depicted either as the Antichrist, a cockroach (in Russian, the word *prusak*—a colloquial term for cockroach—is very similar to the word for a Prussian: *prussak*), a pig, or a black dog; sometimes his "stupid sausage-maker" face appeared on a fig.[40] The circus and the cinema, for their part, placed the emphasis on the kaiser's infernal nature.[41] Historical and patriotic initiatives developed with the active support of right-wing politicians. Actors were especially eager to play Suvorov and Kutuzov, and patriotic pantomimes played out in circus arenas.[42]

The "weaknesses" of the enemy were presented in contrast to the "strength and solidarity" of the Russian people. On the cover of one popular magazine, a soldier in down-at-heel boots cheerfully tells his general that he will soon put on the new boots, hanging over his shoulder, in Berlin.[43] The image of Kriuchkov appeared on cigarette packets sold in Rostov-on-Don. The liberals believed that a sort of sociocultural revolution was taking place in the countryside. They had particular hopes of its "sobering up": data were produced about the decline in hooliganism and criminality in connection with the "dry law."[44] Indeed, it was reported from the countryside that "women give their blessings to sobriety," but conversations were also recorded to the effect that "no doubt the gentlefolk drink." At the same time, it was emphasized that "few believed the newspapers," and that the rural intelligentsia and clergy were not doing enough to raise the spiritual level of the population. As a result, communications from the front were "interwoven with the oddest fabrications, fantastical tales, and legends."[45] Over time, bootlegging developed in the countryside, continuing until the 1930s.

The liberal community called for the organization of leisure culture in the countryside and for the making of educational films, insisting that no film must be released without the approval of the zemstvos. Film critics also

---

[40] Cf. *Russkii voennyi lubok.*

[41] S. S. Ginzburg, *Kinematografiia dorevoliutsionnoi Rossii* (Moscow: Iskusstvo, 1963), 199.

[42] Stites, *Russian Popular Culture*, 34–35.

[43] *Voina* (Petrograd), no. 5 (1914): 1.

[44] *Trezvaia zhizn'*, no. 10–11 (October–November 1914): 262–63.

[45] *V dni voiny: Vestnik voronezhskikh organizatsii voennogo vremeni*, no. 23–24 (4 December and 11 December 1916): 2–6.

reacted strongly. They observed that life had fallen too quickly into the usual rut: the average citizen once more was seeking amusement, the film industry was ruled by the "ignorance of the street," and scriptwriters were "turning out scripts about German brutality." Subsequently even this "low sensationalism" became dull, and filmmakers began the search for "new topics": screens were filled with "scenes from the bloody adventures of a famous female outlaw, or a young robber: the heroes of our slums." As a result, the "poor inexperienced parents, who believed the publicity about the irreproachable silver screen, gave way to despair." They thought that "it is now impossible to repair the corrupting effect of watching such abominable scenes, which pollute the child's mind."[46]

Ultimately, however, the cinema—absorbing the traditions of urban "light entertainment" (operetta, farce, variety theater, slapstick, satirical song, cabaret)—steadily entrenched its position. Vsevolod Meierkhol'd made his mark with screen adaptations of Oscar Wilde's *The Portrait of Dorian Grey* (1915) and Stanisław Przybyszewski's novel *The Strong Man* (*Mocny człowiek*, 1916).[47] "The power of the cinema is growing... Proud disdain for the cinema has suddenly vanished," wrote one Russian magazine. "The best writers have begun to write for the screen, and the best actors to act for it."[48] The film industry also stimulated the growth of music as an applied art.[49]

The cinema reflected a general tendency towards the commercialization of art. In Russia in 1916, there were 164 production and distribution companies; around 30 companies produced newsreels, scientific, and artistic films. The most famous example in Petrograd was the Pikkadilli "electric theater," which was patronized by an average of 915 customers per day.[50] At the start of the war, there were 17 cinemas in Saratov and 16 in Samara. On 23 August 1914, the "Slava" cinema in Saratov sold 1010 tickets.[51] By 1917, Moscow had 71 cinemas with a total seating capacity of 23,782.[52] Demand exceeded supply: there were 514 films in circulation, of which almost half were released before 1917.[53] In

---

[46] P. Raevskii, "Kustari i kinematografii," *Vestnik kinematografii*, no. 106 (1915): 10.

[47] Richard Taylor, "Ideology and Popular Culture: The Kiss of Mary Pickford," in *The Red Screen: Politics, Society, Art in Soviet Cinema*, ed. A. Lawton (London: Routledge, 2002), 47.

[48] *Kino* (Riga), no. 1 (1915): 2.

[49] McReynolds, *Russia at Play*, 256.

[50] *Vedomosti petrogradskogo gradonachal'stva*, 25 February 1917.

[51] Semenova, *Kul'tura Povol'zhia*, 141, 142.

[52] *Izvestiia komiteta moskovskikh obshchestvennykh organizatsii*, 7 June 1917, 5.

[53] V. S. Rosolovskaia, *Russkaia kinematografiia v 1917 godu: Materialy k istorii* (Moscow-Leningrad: Iskusstvo, 1937), 100.

the films themselves, the patriotic theme was rather strangely interwoven with the romantic.[54] A similar practice could be seen among cabaret singers.[55]

Eroticism was a steadily growing presence. The particular apotheosis of this development was the film *Nanny Goats... Kids... Billy Goats... (Kozy... kozochki... kozly...)*, about the amorous adventures of a merchant woman on holiday in the Crimea. Needless to say, critics branded it "pornographic" and noted the "excessive vulgarity" of the captions and the "inartistic acting," but the popularity of erotic film did not diminish.[56] *Venus Violated (Oskorblennaia Venera)*, a film adaptation of Anna Mar (A. Ia. Brovar)'s novel *The Woman on the Cross (Zhenshchina na kreste)*, caused a considerable stir. The film tells the story of a young woman attracted to a much older man, who initiates her into sadomasochistic pleasures. Such was the critical response that the 29-year-old author committed suicide in March 1917.[57] *Nelli Raintseva*, a 1916 film by the prominent director Evgenii Bauer, was also popular. The basis of the plot was the story of a girl from a wealthy family who broke away from her surroundings and fell victim to a deceiver.[58] Over time, this theme of "woman as victim" became widespread, together with the figures of the "femme fatale" and the "avenging woman." The combination of the "female theme" with espionage was also typical.[59]

Through the medium of cinema, "high" art began to resonate to the pulse of popular carnivalesque culture. The following genres were especially prominent: the "extravaganza" (allegorical or mythological plots, incorporating ballet); aristocratic or bohemian tragedy; drama claiming a revolutionary perspective on marriage and family life; decadent religious and mystical drama; horror-adventure drama featuring murders and criminal investigations; adventure drama about robber gangs; patriotic drama; family drama; masked farce. In 1917, revolutionary agitational films were added to the list.

The participation of "stars" usually determined a film's success.[60] Prominent Russian film actors included Vera Kholodnaia (*For the Sake of Happiness* [*Radi schast'ia*] and the serial *Son'ka Golden Hand* [*Son'ka Zolotaia Ruka*]), Elena Makovskaia (*Fatal Passion* [*Rokovaia strast'*]), Ol'ga Preobrazhenskaia (*The Kite*

---

[54] Khanzhonkov, *Pervye gody*, 153–54.

[55] Cf. S. Sokol'skii, *Pliashchushchaia lirika: Stikhotvoreniia i pesni* (St. Petersburg, 1916).

[56] *Velikii kinemo: Katalog sokhranivshikhsia igrovykh fil'mov Rossii 1908–1919 gg.* (Moscow: Novoe literaturnoe obozrenie, 2002), 381.

[57] A. M. Gracheva, "Mistika pola i religiia liubvi (Tvorchestvo Anny Mar)," in A. Mar, *Zhenshchina na kreste: Roman, povesti, rasskazy* (Moscow: Ladomir, 1999), 16.

[58] *Pegas*, no. 2 (1917): 11.

[59] Stites, *Russian Popular Culture*, 36.

[60] Ginzburg, *Kinematografiia*, 319.

[*Korshun*]), V. A. Maksimov (*The Chalice of Forbidden Love* [*Chasha zapretnoi liubvi*]), Vitol'd Polonskii (*The Woman's Execution* [*Kazn' zhenshchiny*]) and Ivan Mozzhukhin. The best-known among Western actors were Francesca Bertini (*Lacrymae rerum*), Else Frölich (*The Avenging Woman* [*Zhenshchina-mstitel'nitsa*], and Lyda Borelli (*The Moth* [*La Falena*]), as well as the comic actors Max Linder and Charlie Chaplin.[61] In imitation of the latter, the Liutsifer production company began to make the Antosha films (*Antosha the Thief* [*Antosha-vor*], *Antosha the Mother-in-Law Tamer* [*Antosha—ukrotitel' teshchi*], *Antosha the Bigamist* [*Antosha-dvoezhenets*], etc.), with Anton Fertner in the principal role. The film *Son'ka Golden Hand*, by the A. O. Drankov production company, was developed into a serial.[62]

Later, some critics would designate 1914–17 as "the most fruitful period in Russian cinema"; Russia's isolation from the global film market contributed to this fruition. One writer stated that Russian film studios were producing "pictures, each one better than the last … and the number of theaters is rising, not by the day, but by the hour."[63] The educational role of the cinema was emphasized: "The Russian rural masses have now almost all seen an aeroplane in flight … on the cinema screen."[64]

Two social strata emerged among the most active cinema consumers: the so-called *soldatki* (wives of men serving in the army), who received a relatively high stipend allowing them to lead a comparatively "idle" lifestyle; and the mass of former peasants who filled the towns, either as "proletarians" or as soldiers. The cinema supplied material to satisfy "the cravings of the taste and the cravings of the heart," as the saying went. However, there were notable exceptions, such as the innovative films *Child of the Big City* (*Ditia bol'shogo goroda*, 1914) and *Child of the Age* (*Ditia veka*, 1915) released by Bauer. It was clear that Russian films could compete with Western ones. It soon emerged that there were not enough screenwriters, so that adaptations of Russian literary classics flooded the screen. Critical reception was mixed: alongside praise for individual adaptations came warnings that the genii of Tolstoi and Turgenev might be demoted to the level of "pulp fiction."[65] Wittingly or unwittingly, the cinema contributed its share to the erosion of traditional ideas about marriage; its favorite themes revolved around money and adultery.

---

[61] R. P. Sobolev, *Liudi i fil'my russkogo dorevoliutsionnogo kino* (Moscow: Iskusstvo, 1961), 140.

[62] Khanzhonkov, *Pervye gody*, 91.

[63] S. V. Lur'e, "Polozhenie russkoi kinematografii s 1914 po 1922 god," *Kinematograf dlia Rossii* (Berlin), no. 2 (1922): 3.

[64] *Kino* (Riga), no. 1 (1915): 3.

[65] *Iuzhanin: Zhurnal, posviashchennyi interesam kinematografii Iuga Rossii* (Khar'kov), no. 5 (1 March 1915): 16.

Philanthropy became a matter of patriotic ritual. Charity performances were staged, for example, in the Volga region; in 1915, 25 percent of proceeds from artists' exhibitions in Samara were donated to the All-Russian Zemstvo Union for Aid to Sick and Wounded Soldiers.[66] In 1915, for Palm Sunday, an exhibition of Easter eggs opened in Moscow, with all proceeds destined for the All-Russian Union of Cities. The Moscow committee of the Russian Red Cross staged a benefit concert in the great hall of the Moscow conservatory, in aid of "tobacco for the soldiers for Holy Easter."[67] The writer Aleksandr Kuprin joined the army; a popular magazine put his photograph on the cover, in officer's uniform.[68] Sending gifts to the troops became a widespread activity. To this end, a Ladies' Committee formed in Tver', the members of which also participated in "work for the manufacture of gas masks,"[69] while the Muslim Committee organized women to sew underwear for the troops.[70] A kind of competitive spirit arose. It was reported that, in Moscow, Princess O. P. Volkonskaia had organized a benefit show and collected 12,000 rubles for her field hospital. Countess Witte also put on a show, making 30,000 rubles in all.[71]

The liberal community undertook a series of initiatives in order to raise the general cultural level. In Tver' province, primary school teachers organized readings for the wounded, from Pushkin, Lermontov, Mamin-Sibiriak, Tolstoi, and others, some of which were accompanied by a "magic lantern" show.[72] Concerts were staged in field hospitals. Sacred compositions from the Russian and Italian schools were performed at a concert in Rzhev on 14 December 1914, organized by teachers from the diocesan girls' school and the boys' and girls' gymnasia.[73] The representatives of educated society were looking for "ways" to the people. Of course, no genuine mass culture resulted from these efforts.

---

[66] E. Iu. Semenova, *Blagotvoritel'nye uchrezhdeniia Samarskoi i Simbirskoi gubernii v gody Pervoi mirovoi voiny (1914–nach. 1918 gg.)* (Samara: Izd-vo "Nauchno-tekhnicheskii tsentr, 2004), 34, 40, 41.

[67] A. N. Kazakevich, "Moskva v paskhal'nye dni 1915 g.," in *Moskovskii arkhiv: Vtoraia polovina XIX—nachalo XX v.* (Moscow: Mosgorarkhiv, 2000), 493, 495.

[68] *Ogonek*, no. 48 (30 November [13 December] 1914): 13.

[69] Gosudarstvennyi arkhiv Tverskoi oblasti (GATO) f. 103, op. 1, d. 2881, l. 99.

[70] *Ogonek*, no. 32 (10 [23] August 1914): 3.

[71] "'My poidem po puti vsevozmozhnykh sotsial'nykh eksperimentov': Fevral'skaia revoliutsiia 1917 g. v semeinoi perepiske P. P. Skoropadskogo," *Istoricheskii arkhiv*, no. 4 (2002): 75.

[72] GATO f. 11, op. 1, d. 6046, ll. 5–5ob.

[73] *Tverskie eparkhial'nye vedomosti*, no. 3 (19 January 1915): 58–59.

A Slavophile tendency became noticeable in cultural life. In connection with Russia's military successes in Galicia, V. Korablev wrote that "with a courageous blow of the Russian sword, the yoke has shattered into tiny pieces which for almost six centuries gripped the neck of the Carpathian slave," and that "a great, united Rus' has emerged."[74] It was enthusiastically reported that the Czechs of the capital were converting to Orthodoxy.[75] Certain cabaret singers declared that "now is not the time for jokes."[76] All social classes strove to show their patriotism.

The Society for the Revival of the Art of Russia was formed in March 1915. Its founder was Prince A. A. Shpirinskii-Shikhmatov, who argued—entirely in the spirit of the fight against "German dominance"—that Petersburg was, and remained, an "un-Russian" city and that it was therefore necessary to fight for "our native antiquity" by disseminating knowledge about Russian history and art among the populace.[77] The members of the society were largely aristocrats and high-ranking officials. They proposed to bring the history of art into schools, to undertake the collection of Russian arts and crafts, and to adjudicate competitions, particularly in the area of traditional Russian-style furniture for public institutions.[78] Of course, no truly mass character could be expected of this kind of "populism."

A trend emerged for creating museums of contemporary war. On 18 November 1914, the governor of Penza addressed the local archival commission about one such initiative. In Samara and Saratov, a similar plan came from the archivists themselves.[79] There was an evident tendency towards a cultural unification of the upper and lower strata.

Despite the good intentions of the upper classes, however, the war revealed the true heterogeneity of Russian culture. Meanwhile, popular culture was becoming increasingly vulgar. "The monotonous and often rather silly chastushka [traditional four-line folk poem] has come to replace the previous vivid, colorful products of popular creativity," the liberal magazines declared.[80] Indeed, this popular creativity was becoming steadily more hackneyed.[81] To judge by the cinema playbills, the urban lower classes reveled in sentimental

---

[74] V. Korablev, "Chervonnaia Rus'," *Slavianskie izvestiia*, no. 13 (1914): 196.

[75] *Ogonek*, no. 32 (10 [23] August 1914): 14.

[76] McReynolds, *Russia at Play*, 251.

[77] Rossiiskii gosudarstvennyi istoricheskii arkhiv (RGIA) f. 793, op. 1, d. 2, ll. 1, 10, 217, 240, 249–53.

[78] Ibid., l. 214; ibid., d. 16. ll. 1–18.

[79] Semenova, *Kul'tura Povolzh'ia*, 73.

[80] Fomin, "Voina i narodnoe tvorchestvo," 27.

[81] Cf. V. I. Simakhov, *Chastushki pro voinu, nemtsev, avstriisev, Vil'gel'ma, kazakov, monopoliu, rekrutchinu, liubovnye* (Petrograd, 1915).

themes, as if in a great outburst of self-pity. The educated public, meanwhile, turned their noses up at the "vulgarity" of the cinema.

Researchers and contemporaneous sources agree: the broad mass of the populace understood neither the causes nor the aims of the war. While official propaganda attributed the war to Germany's aspiration to global hegemony,[82] the favored explanation among the lower strata was founded either on a fairytale dynastic scenario (Nicholas II could not forgive Franz Josef his matrimonial deception) or in pragmatism: this was a territorial conflict.[83] The arguments for the liberation of "our Slavic brothers" did not penetrate the rank and file. As the failures of the Russian army grew, the authority of the tsar declined.

CB BO

The Revolution posed anew the question of the relationship between mass culture and the culture of the masses. The relevant sections of "high culture," the revolutionaries acknowledged, should "go to the people"; and some intellectuals genuinely tried to do just that. On 2 March 1917, the right-liberal *Utro Rossii* published Bal'mont's poem *Spring Cry* (*Vesennii klich*), which compared the Revolution to the drifting of ice on a river. The poet wrote that "now, all Russia is set alight by the free spring," calling "Advance, o soul! O sword, advance!" Alas, while sentiments like this were characteristic of the intelligentsia, the people simply took no notice of revolutionary versifying.

The idea of cultural "simplification" was received among the intelligentsia in widely differing ways. "In times of revolution, when the direction and administration of society are democratized, it is entirely normal to speak of the aristocratization of the arts," stated Maksimilian Voloshin. "On the contrary, the principle of the 'democratization' of the arts, 'accessibility,' 'art for all' … is a flagrant absurdity and entirely opposed to the revolutionary idea, i.e., that of liberation." He proposed that "Russia must go towards a religious, and not a social, revolution," as "the transformation of the individual" was the order of the day.[84]

Meanwhile, the Revolution took an imperious hand in the process of artistic creation. "Workers from the plants and factories came to us at the Academy, bringing with them slogans and Red materials," remembered the artist A. N. Samokhvalov, who then taught at the Academy of Arts. "We painted these slogans, making the effort to decorate them with the emblems

---

[82] *Al'bom geroev voiny*, no. 1 (1914): 5.

[83] V. B. Aksenov, "Voina i vlast' v massovom soznanii krest'ian v 1914–1917 godakh: Arkhetipy, slukhi, interpretatsii," *Rossiiskaia istoriia*, no. 4 (2012): 138–39.

[84] M. Voloshin, *Stikhotvoreniia. Stat'i. Vospominaniia sovremennikov*, ed. Z. D. Davydov and V. P. Kupchenko (Moscow: Izd-vo Pravda, 1991), 304–05.

of production: anvils, cogwheels, hammers, sickles, and so forth."[85] Of course, by no means all artists were pleased with this development. The Futurists tried to assert themselves as the leaders of "revolutionary" art. This was impossible: creative life was shooting off in every possible direction, and rival artistic associations began to form.

The Revolution unexpectedly stimulated yet another aspect of cultural life. Actors in Kiev saw the Revolution as an exit to "the open road," a possibility of freeing themselves from the "Moscow turnpikes." Suggestions for the "Ukrainianization" of the theater began to be heard. In the Crimea, the Interim Crimean Tatar (Muslim) Executive Committee began a campaign to turn the Bakhchisarai Palace, which had already been attacked by revolutionary sailors, into "their" museum.[86]

During the period from February to October, Russia's cultural elite underwent a whole cycle of spiritual evolution: from bliss at the prospect of "liberty" to the rejection of the revolutionary politics of the masses. The Provisional Government tried to make use of writers and artists in order to shape democratic consciousness; however, culture became not so much democratic as catering to the lowest common denominator. A wide variety of picture postcards slandering the deposed tsar and his household passed from hand to hand. "When I read the denunciations of the House of Romanov, my hair stands on end," was the response of one provincial inhabitant.[87] Paradoxically, the cinema clung passionately to the image of the imperial couple in defeat.

The intelligentsia quickly began to direct waves of scorn at the Revolution. The magazine *Novyi satirikon* (New Satyricon) parodied the typical demands of the day: the workers supposedly declared that "the pay rises promised by management should be backdated to the start of the liberation movement, that is to say, 14 July 1789"; the "blonds of the fourth company of musketeers" demanded a sofa, stool, and guitar to be delivered from HQ; high school students had achieved the removal of their hated mathematics instructor. A bestial figure with a wooden club graced the cover of one issue; the caption ran: "The Bolsheviks have set the good Russian people on their feet." Another sketch parodied a favourite occupation of the post-February days, "the denunciation of counterrevolutionaries," which turned into mocking passers-by on the street. In the magazine *Bomba* (The Bomb), a Bolshevik was defined as "the mother-in-law of freedom."[88]

The relationship between the various performing arts changed; the people flooded into the theaters. The audience demanded that the "Marseillaise,"

---

[85] A. N. Samokhvalov, *Moi tvorcheskii put'* (Leningrad: Khudozhnik RSFSR, 1971), 44.

[86] A. N. Eremeeva, *"Pod rokot grazhdanskikh bur'…"* (*Khudozhestvennaia zhizn' Iuga Rossii v 1917–1920 godakh*) (St. Petersburg: Nestor, 1998), 43, 49–50.

[87] *Pis'ma viatskogo obyvatelia*, ed. R. Ia. Lapteva (Viatka [Kirov]: O-Kratkoe, 2009), 244.

[88] Cf. *Novyi satirikon* (Moscow), no. 39 (1917): 1, 3, 4; *Bomba*, no. 1 (1917): 5.

"Dubinushka," and "In Memoriam" be played before each performance.[89]
However, the soldiers also warmly welcomed the performances of the former
Grand Duke's favorite, the ballerina Matil´da Kshesinskaia, whose palace was
first ransacked during the revolutionary uprising and then converted into
Bolshevik HQ.[90] Cultural life became not so much "popular" as (even more)
chaotic. Naturally, the revolutionary lower strata instigated their own cultural
practices. The eminent director Konstantin Stanislavskii had to circulate
among the rows of spectators during performances, issuing reprimands to his
new audience members.[91] Within theater collectives, stagehands demanded
equal rights with soloists, and unpopular directors were fired; sometimes
actors would address the audience during a performance with complaints
about the administration; the chorus might go on strike mid-performance.[92]
A. K. Tolstoi's play *The Death of Ivan the Terrible* (*Smert´ Ioanna Groznogo*) was
removed from the repertoire of the Aleksandrinskii Theater (Petrograd) at the
insistence of the actors, on the grounds of its "counterrevolutionary content."[93]
By May 1917, theater attendance had fallen, necessitating some renewal of the
repertoire. The Mikhailovskii Theater (Petrograd) production of *Flavia Tes-
sini*—the sentimental story of the dizzying career of an impoverished Jewish
singer—was especially popular.[94] The Nikol´skii Theater (Moscow) filled
its repertoire with a host of "topical" plays, including the ballet *Free Russia*
(*Svobodnaia Rossiia*) and dramas about the lives of exiles; the Palace Theater
(Petrograd) presented *The Red Banner* (*Krasnoe znamia*): a slapdash work in
which the most odious representatives of the old regime sang vulgar comic
songs.[95]

Plays about the life of Rasputin were a real commercial goldmine, even
if some of them were booed by the public and reviled by the critics.[96] Over
time, "pornographic" plays—such as Ivan Kocherga's *The Girl with the Mouse*
(*Devushka s myshkoi*), at the Nevskii Farce (Petrograd), or Anatolii Kamenskii's
Leda, at the Kamernii Theater (Moscow)—became firmly established in the
repertoire. A mass of imitations arose, of which the apotheosis was the staging

---

[89] V. F. Bezpalov, *Teatry v dni revoliutsii 1917 goda* (Leningrad: Akademiia, 1927), 41.

[90] M. Kshesinskaia, *Vospominaniia* (Moscow: Tsentrpoligraf, 2004), 266–68.

[91] K. S. Stanislavskii, *Moia zhizn´ v iskusstve* (Moscow: Academia, 1926), 645.

[92] *Obozrenie teatrov*, 16 March 1917; *Birzhevye vedomosti*, 8 April 1917.

[93] *Petrogradskie vedomosti*, 24 September 1917.

[94] *Moskovskii listok*, 5 May 1917; *Petrogradskie vedomosti*, 24 September 1917.

[95] *Petrogradskii listok*, 18 March 1917; *Obozrenie teatrov*, 11 April 1917.

[96] *Moskovskii listok*, 8 April 1917; *Strekoza*, no. 28 (July 1917): 5; *Petrogradskii listok*, 13
May 1917; *Obozrenie teatrov*, 2 June 1917.

of naturist beauty contests.[97] In contemporary opinion "the great theaters in no way reflected the revolution—the small theaters cultivated erotic filth."[98] Only in the autumn of 1917 did the leading Moscow theaters enter a period of classic theatrical premieres.[99]

In 1917, there were 514 films in circulation. Attendance at the cinema began to rival that of the theater.[100] The audiences consumed both the old, "bourgeois" films and the new, among them the four-part drama *Grigorii Rasputin*. The particular pinnacle of cinematic tastelessness was the film *Satan Triumphant* (*Satana likuiushchii*). The diabolical theme became so widely employed that the government endowed local commissars with the right to ban the most scandalous films.[101] Meanwhile, the erotic tendency grew ever stronger.[102] In such a context, Bauer's film *The Revolutionary* (*Revoliutsioner*) constituted a notable exception. The director aimed to stimulate the fading patriotic mood: in the final scene, a veteran of the 1905 Revolution sets off for the front together with his son. In July 1917, *The Life and Death of Lieutenant Shmidt* (*Zhizn' i gibel' leitenanta Shmidta*) was filmed in Odessa, with the cooperation of the local soviet.[103]

Mass culture tried to reach its public by way of politics. Famous poets wrote verses to Kerenskii. Nikolai S. Tikhonov portrayed him as a "Russian Gracchus with the soul of a Garibaldi," "captain and brother" to all the country, in whom "alone dwells the great, free Russia." Kuprin used Kerenskii's example to argue that "in all times and all peoples can be found, in times of trial … a divine resonator … of the popular will." In the newspaper *Svobodnaia Rossiia* (Free Russia), the writers B. Mirskii (Boris S. Mirkin-Getsevich), Mark Krinitskii (Mikhail V. Samygin), and Arkadii S. Bukhov, the lawyer Nikolai P. Karabchevskii and the academics Fedor D. Batiushkov and Semen A. Vengerov seconded his opinion.[104] Stanislavskii and Vladimir Nemirovich-Danchenko eulogized Kerenskii in the name of the Moscow Art Theater: "In you we see incarnate the ideal of the free citizen, whose soul shall be prized by humanity in

---

[97] *Obozrenie teatrov,* 19–20 March 1917; *Moskovskii listok,* 29 April 1917; *Petrogradskii listok,* 20 April, 13 May, 15 June, 28 June 1917; *Teatr i iskusstvo,* no. 23 (5 June 1917).

[98] A. N. Voznesenskii, *Moskva v 1917 godu* (Moscow: Gosudarstvennoe izd-vo, 1928), 71.

[99] V. P. Lapshin, *Khudozhestvennaia zhizn' Moskvy i Petrograda v 1917 g.* (Moscow: Sovetskii khudozhnik, 1983), 403.

[100] N. P. Okunev, *Dnevnik moskvicha 1917–1924* (Moscow: Voennoe izd-vo, 1997), 1: 61.

[101] Cf. Rosolovskaia, *Russkaia kinematografiia,* 120—22.

[102] *Obozrenie teatrov,* 8 June 1917.

[103] Ginzburg, *Kinematografiia,* 360.

[104] Cf. *Svobodnaia Rossiia,* 12 June 1917.

centuries to come...."[105] Nevertheless, after the State Conference, intellectuals began to speculate that Kerenskii was simply unwell.[106] The old revolutionary ecstasy was supplanted by worried anticipation. It was recognized that "revolution is a good thing when it throws off the yoke," but that it had now mutated into "a satanic vortex of destruction." Arkadii Averchenko argued that "the world lives in evolutions," rather than revolutions.[107]

The relationship of intellectuals to the people at large was always an ambivalent one: a particular, bookish sort of worship of its potential energy coexisted with an instinctive fear of that energy's uncontrolled release.[108] Some, like Aleksandr Blok, became fixated on the idea of "how best to serve the Russian people." In contrast, the critic R. Ivanov-Razumnik wrote to Gor´kii after the July Days that "a time of unhealthy malice" was approaching, and complained of the "triumph of the many-headed petit bourgeoisie."[109] On the whole, the "intensification" of the revolutionary movement sat badly with elite culture. For Marina Tsvetaeva, freedom appeared as a "wanton girl, clutched to a savage soldier's breast";[110] Zinaida Gippius was haunted by the disgrace of "the ribaldry of sailors."[111] Some members of the intelligentsia suffered the consequences of revolutionary self-will. Peasants burned down Blok's rural estate, Shakhmatovo,[112] which did not stop him from poeticizing similar incidents in the spirit of "vengeance"; whereas the composer Sergei Rakhmaninov, who had invested his entire wealth in his Tambov estate, gave way to despair.[113]

The unbridled activity of the "lower" genres—caricatures, jokes, *chastushki*—corresponded to the elementalism of the revolution. The tabloid press behaved outrageously. This likely reflected a growing cultural division at work. Vladimir Korolenko was obliged to speculate that the "class self-

---

[105] B. I. Kolonitskii, "Kul´t A. F. Kerenskogo: Obrazy revoliutsionnoi vlasti," *The Soviet and Post-Soviet Review* 24, 1–2 (1997): 57.

[106] *Svoboda i zhizn´*, 21 August 1917.

[107] A. Averchenko, *Trava, primiataia sapogom* (Moscow: Druzhba narodov, 1991), 319.

[108] Z. N. Gippius, *Zhivye litsa* (Tbilisi: Merani, 1991), 2: 30.

[109] I. S. Zil´bershtein and N. I. Dikushina, eds., *Gor´kii i russkaia zhurnalistika nachala XX veka: Neizdannaia perepiska*, Literaturnoe nasledstvo 95 (Moscow: Nauka, 1988), 723, 724.

[110] M. I. Tsvetaeva, *Sobranie sochinenii v semi tomakh*, 1: *Stikhotvoreniia* (Moscow: Ellis Lak, 1994), 351.

[111] Z. Gippius, *Poslednie stikhi: 1914–1918. Moskva: "Ogonek"* (Moscow: Terra-Knizhnyi klub, 2008), 25.

[112] M. A. Beketova, *Vospominaniia ob Aleksandre Bloke* (Moscow: Pravda, 1990), 569.

[113] S. V. Rakhmaninov, *Pis´ma* (Moscow: Muzgiz, 1955), 486.

interest" of the revolution had "deadened conscience."[114] Gor'kii wrote of the "beastly stupidity" of the masses and their "bestial instincts."[115] It was more and more difficult to make art "for the people." In the autumn of 1917, Bal'-mont stated that he "deeply loathe[d] all that is taking place in Russia now," comparing the events of the time with the epoch of Stenka Razin and the Time of Troubles, and asserting that "Russians have always been the same, and foulness is the very air they breathe."[116]

Moreover, the "popularization" of cultural life turned out to be inextricably linked with retrogressive ideology. *Groza* (*Thunderstorm*), the organ of the Black Hundreds organization Holy Rus' (Sviataia Rus'), began publication on the Romanian front in 1917. Here the continuation of the hated war was blamed on the English, the French, and the Jews; it was claimed that it would end only with the restoration of autocracy.[117] Apparently, cultural "populism" could most easily be achieved on a basis of xenophobic paranoia.

cs so

The Bolsheviks genuinely strove to create a popular culture for the revolutionary masses. This found an echo among artists on the left. In September 1917, Proletkul't was formed, an association of artists and writers with a bellicose attitude towards "bourgeois" culture. Between 1918 and 1920, the bearers of "proletarian" culture published over 30 separate journals. According to some sources, in 1920 Proletkul't's membership included up to 400,000 workers.[118] Cultural actors tried to make good use of the new aesthetic situation. It was true that, as Sergei Esenin remarked, "these hard times have brought literary sergeant-majors onto the field, who render service to the proletariat, but none at all to art."[119]

Moreover, shock at the "Red Time of Troubles" led some artists to reject the "people." Boris D. Grigor'ev, the author of the "anti-peasant" painting cycle *Raseia*, wrote that in times of revolution people "shamelessly strip

---

[114] V. G. Korolenko, *Zemli, Zemli! Mysli, vospominaniia, kartiny* (Moscow: Sovetskii pisatel', 1991), 125.

[115] M. Gor'kii, *Nesvoevremennye mysli: Zametki o revoliutsii i kul'ture* (Moscow: Sovremennik, 1990), 101.

[116] Andreeva-Bal'mont, *Vospominaniia*, 493, 499, 500.

[117] *Evreiskaia nedelia*, 30 July 1917.

[118] V. V. Gorbunov, *V. I. Lenin i Proletkul't* (Moscow: Politizdat, 1974), 125.

[119] S. A. Esenin, *Polnoe sobranie sochinenii: V semi tomakh, 5: Proza*, ed. Iu. L. Prokushev (Moscow: Golos-Nauka, 1997), 242; *Sergei Esenin v stikhakh i zhizni: Poemy, 1912–1925; Proza, 1915–1925* (Moscow: Respublika, 1995), 287, 290.

humanity right down to the beast within."[120] The conditions of the Civil War worsened matters. The cruelty of the "beast" was supplemented by the "animal" cowardice so necessary to survival. Against such a background, the statements of White Guard propagandists to the effect that "the Church has always been the savior of the Russian people at critical moments of history" looked unconvincing, as did their attempts to organize a "crusade" against the "godless" Bolsheviks.[121]

Cultural figures on the left were thinking not about the proletariat but about the revolution; and the latter was more imagined than real. They probably did not notice that the chaos of the world war had left its mark on their creation.[122] The first Proletkul't members praised the "new Messiah," Lenin, in verse that was highly expressive and just as clumsy.[123] In one war propaganda journal, the poet Vladimir T. Kirillov proclaimed: "It is time, it is time, sons of the people, / Saddle your fiery horses, / Red Freedom calls to you: / Strike down the vicious hangmen!" It is unlikely that the Russian peasant could be inspired by borrowings from the "Marseillaise." The same could be said of Nikolai Kliuev's lines claiming that "the goblet of blood is a global communion / We are fated to drain it!"[124] The "Red Army" poems of the well-known versifier Dem'ian Bednyi (pseudonym of Efim A. Pridvorov) were more popular.

Bolshevik agitational literature, which emphasized the cruelty of the enemy and his "lordly" ways, is unlikely to have enjoyed particular success. Propaganda culture—both Red and White—existed largely in isolation from the masses, who were entirely consumed by the fight for survival. They poured their various emotions into *chastushki*. In this context, the song form gathered strength; this included, to a considerable degree, amateur composition. It is remarkable that the melodies of some songs and marches "migrated" from the Reds to the Whites, or vice versa; only the words changed.

Throughout the Civil War, Soviet film led a pitiful existence. The majority of contemporary film studios relocated to the Crimea. A decree on the nationalization of the film industry was issued in November 1919. Directors and screenwriters were obliged to switch to agitational work, which was con-

---

[120] B. Grigor'ev, *Liniia: Literaturnoe i khudozhestvennoe nasledie* (Moscow: Fortuna EL, 2006), 106.

[121] *Velikaia Rossiia* (Tomsk), no. 3 (3 October 1919).

[122] Characteristically, this also included those who had gone to the front as volunteers. Cf. V. L. Lidin, ed., *Pisateli: Avtobiografii i portrety sovremennykh russkikh prozaikov*, 2nd ed. (Moscow: Sovremennye problemy, 1928), 16, 176, 393.

[123] Iu. A. Andreev, *Revoliutsiia i literatura: Oktiabr' i Grazhdanskaia voina v russkoi sovetskoi literature i stanovlenie sotsialisticheskogo realizma (20–30-e gody)* (Moscow: Khudozhestvennaia literatura, 1987), 74–75.

[124] *Tovarishch. Illiustrirovannyi ezhenedel'nyi zhurnal*, no. 1 (1919): 2–3.

ducted—in the opinion of émigré critics—"on a microscopic scale"; although such figures as Iosif Ermol'ev and Iakov Protazanov easily transitioned from prerevolutionary to Soviet film.[125] There is a myth that the film industry immediately set to work for the new government. In fact, this was by no means the case.[126] Only towards the end of 1921 did the leaders of Bolshevik cinema production begin to think about "reviving the corpse."[127] In the process, they were forced to admit that "the cinematic front turned out to be unprepared not only for an offensive on the broad front of the economic regeneration of the country, but also ... for the struggle to preserve and develop its own living, skilled workforce."[128] Nonetheless, film critics bolstered themselves by declaring that the "triumphal procession of the 'Great Silent' has only begun its struggle against the artistic culture of the past" and that "a curious process of passionate involvement of the entire artistic culture of the cinema is taking place before our eyes."[129]

Cultural figures on the left had concerns of their own. In March 1920, Anatolii Lunacharskii warned Nikolai N. Krestinskii, the secretary of the Bolshevik Central Committee, that "he might soon be approached by young 'green Communists,' impassioned by the theater, who do not recognize the leadership of the State Theatrical Center and consider themselves part of the TsK RKP(b)."[130] Young ideological warriors for the world revolution recognized no authority, apart from that of the supreme party organ. From this platform, they tried to "filibuster," addressing those who did not wish to hear them. Meanwhile, the group of avant-garde cultural figures known as LEF or Levyi front (Left Front of the Arts) assured the government that it was "its right hand in the matter of cultural construction." The government answered that LEF was "not needed in the slightest, and did more harm than good."[131]

On 3 January 1921, in the public debate "The Artist in Contemporary Theater," Maiakovskii stated: "You see, this volcano, this explosion which

---

[125] Denise J. Youngblood, *The Magic Mirror: Moviemaking in Russia, 1908–1918* (Madison: University of Wisconsin Press, 1999), 30–31.

[126] Kristin Thompson, "Government Policies and Practical Necessities in Soviet Cinema of the 1920s," in *The Red Screen: Politics, Society, Art in Soviet Cinema*, ed. A. Lawton (London: Routledge, 2002), 19.

[127] Lur'e, "Polozhenie russkoi kinematografii," 4.

[128] *Kino: Dvukhnedel'nik obshchestva kinodeiatelei* (Moscow), no. 1 (20 October 1922): 1.

[129] V. Turkin, "Kinematograficheskaia revoliutsiia," *Kino* (Moscow), no. 1 (20 October 1922): 9–10.

[130] Rossiiskii gosudarstvennyi arkhiv sotsial'no-politicheskoi istorii (RGASPI) f. 17, op. 84, d. 128, l. 3ob. "State Theatrical Center" is a reference to the Central Theatrical Committee (Tsentroteatr) that regulated theater affairs between August 1919 and November 1920.

[131] L. Ginzburg, *Chelovek za pis'mennym stolom* (Leningrad: Sovetskii pisatel', 1989), 38.

the October Revolution brought with it, requires new artistic forms. At every moment of our agitational activity, we have to ask: where are these artistic forms? We see slogans telling us that 150 million of Russia's population must advance towards electrification. We, too, need the impulse to work, not out of fear, but for the sake of the approaching future...["][132] This corresponded to the desire to create a new theatrical avant-garde, which would be "an artistic agitator and a propagandist of Communist ideology; a creator of a new everyday life."[133] Critics also took up these aims. They saw the "tragedy of drama" in weak repertoires and stagnant productions, calling for "a theater closer to October!"[134] Meierkhol'd imposed a "revolutionary" theatrical trend. Meanwhile, ideology was submerged in the depths of—by no means left-wing—feeling. Some elements of "bourgeois" mass culture remained, despite the genuine efforts of poets of the old school to adhere to "popular revolutionary" culture. It is noteworthy that Boris Pasternak declared himself a Communist in 1922, since, in his opinion, so were "both Peter and Pushkin."[135]

The idea of unifying revolution and tradition was subject to different interpretations. Original projects for the "popularization" of culture sometimes emerged from the lower social strata. In September 1921, Emel'ian M. Iaroslavskii received a visit from a certain person calling himself an "average citizen of, and active participant in, the revolution." In his tract *On the Influence of the Court, the School and the Church on the People*, he proposed to create an Executive Committee of the Clergy (Ispolkomdukh), responsible for "the artistic side of religious worship." While Trotskii was calling for the cinema to divert the population from "the tavern and the church," this amateur idealist suggested that, insofar as "Orthodoxy preaches Communism," it was necessary to make use of the confessional aspects of the old culture. He advised *"placing churches, as buildings of artistic substance, on an equal footing with theaters* [emphasis in the original text—V.B.]," and that the service of worship should be "treated, from a governmental point of view, as a special kind of theatrical performance; a mystery play in which, symbolically and figuratively, to the sound of mysterious, centuries-old motifs and canticles, the same drama is performed, magnificent in its humanity: the tale of how the idealist Jesus Christ, a Jew and an amateur preacher, a communist, was crucified together with robbers, killed by the representatives of power and

---

[132] V. Katanian, *Maiakovskii: Khronika zhizni i deiatel'nosti* (Moscow: Sovetskii pisatel', 1985), 194.

[133] *Kommunisticheskii trud*, 25 August 1921.

[134] *Teatr i kino* (Baku), no. 3 (1925): 4.

[135] B. L. Pasternak, *Sobranie sochinenii v 5-ti tomakh* (Moscow: Khudozhestvennaia literatura, 1992), 5: 125.

capital ... by the Pharisees and the Roman aristocracy." This, he suggested, would transform the Communist idea into culture.[136]

In fact, the renewal of culture was a slow process. Only the Bolshevik "carnivals," which parodied the old rituals, enjoyed a certain success. Thus, Christmas holidays were used to promote Bolshevik farces, which included the practice of "the burning of the gods," in imitation of the Mardi Gras tradition. The "Komsomol Christmas" was staged on an especially lavish scale.[137] However, the Bolshevik leadership banned these and similar practices in 1923, fearing provocative action on the part of amateur "atheists."[138]

Critics wrote that, "after the unprecedented chaos caused by the ... upheavals of war and revolution, we in the artistic field found ourselves ... confronted by an empty space." In the process, "the actual baggage of our art did not increase ... on the contrary, it shrank excessively."[139] Émigré critics remarked that "the beautiful lady 'Nep' treats the theater badly," and "the state does not give one kopeck to the theater." As a result, "at the Mariinskii Theater, opera lies fallow; only the ballet makes much work for the box-office cashiers." On the other hand, many historical plays had begun to appear, in which Tsars Nicholas I, Alexander I, Paul, and the tsarevich Aleksei were all represented.[140] The situation on the operatic stage was the most dispiriting. "All attempts to find a new way to stage old operas ... ended in deplorable failure," stated the critics.[141]

Meanwhile, the trade unions attempted to organize a proletarian film cooperative—Proletkino—intending to use the cinema to "satisfy the cultural requirements of the laboring masses" and, accordingly, to act as a "front in the fight against bourgeois culture."[142] Left cultural figures stubbornly continued to associate the "populism" of culture with its "class nature." Representatives of LEF announced that their ideas had "reached an audience of workers"; however, they admitted that "proletarian art has partly degenerated into state-

---

[136] Cited in A. I. Shapovalov, *Fenomen sovetskoi politicheskoi kul'tury (Mental'nye priznaki, istochniki formirovaniia i razvitiia)* (Moscow: Prometei, 1997), 281.

[137] V. I. Sokolov, *Istoriia molodezhnogo dvizheniia Rossii (SSSR) so vtoroi poloviny XIX do XXI veka* (Riazan': Uzorech'e, 2003), 228–30.

[138] Cf. N. N. Pokrovskii and S. G. Petrov, eds., *Arkhivy Kremlia. Politbiuro i tserkov', 1922–1925* (Novosibirsk: Sibirskii khronograf; Moscow: Rossiiskaia politicheskaia entsiklopediia, 1997), bk. 1, 358–62.

[139] *Teatr: Ezhenedel'nyi zhurnal zrelishchnykh iskusstv,* no. 1 (1922): 7.

[140] N. Mishin, "Teatr v Peterburge," *Teatr i zhizn'* (Berlin), no. 10 (1922): 19.

[141] Iu. Sakhnovskii, "Opera v revoliutsionnoi mechte i deistvitel'nosti," *Teatr: Ezhenedel'nyi zhurnal zrelishchnykh iskusstv,* no. 1 (1922): 11.

[142] *Kino: Dvukhnedel'nik obshchestva kinodeiatelei* (Moscow), no. 4 (25 December 1922): 1.

sponsored literature, and partly fallen under the influence of academicism."[143] Declarative class-based leftism, it emerged, was far removed from the tired masses.

Meierkhol'd pursued the idea of "popularizing" revolutionary culture in his own particular way, performing theater on a larger scale and sometimes in rather improbable forms. On the occasion of the fifth anniversary of the Meierkhol'd Theater (Teatr imeni Meierkhol'da),[144] an airplane was presented to the Red Army in the name of the theater, at the Trotskii aerodrome. At a conference of theater workers, Meierkhol'd declared: "We must fight against the pseudo-revolutionary hackwork often peddled by dramaturgists."[145] Paradoxically, the representatives of the "conservative" theater considered Meierkhol'd himself a revolutionary hack.

Within high literature, certain authors were fixated on one particular idea: to make poetic meter fit the rhythms of the social movement. The poet Andrei Belyi, in the spring of 1917, was still enchanted with the way in which the February uprisings had chimed with the "rhythmic movement" of poetry.[146] He, in turn, attempted to bring his own poetic work into sync.[147] Similarly, as late as 1918, Osip Mandel'shtam published the article *Rhythm and the State* (*Gosudarstvo i ritm*), in which he urged "the reorganization of the individual in the name of the collective." "Solidarity and rhythmicality: these are the quality and quantity of social energy," he claimed. "The masses are solidary. Only the collective is rhythmical."[148] At times, the search for a "rhythm of the masses" found entirely prosaic expression. In Petrograd in 1920, an Institute of Rhythmics was created, resurrecting the Swiss composer and teacher E. Jaques-Dalcroze's system of eurhythmics. Later, adherents of this system claimed it as a weapon of "one of the highest aims of the revolution: to the rebirth of the individual and of humankind." Meanwhile, society itself did not find one united rhythm, nor one conventional form of mass culture.

One émigré journal reported that "a lecture on the *balagan* [a term incorporating traveling circus, fairground entertainment, and low farce] took place at the museum of the Academic Theater," and that a "balagan man" had been invited to serve as "visual material." However, his demonstration of his work

---

[143] *LEF: Zhurnal levogo fronta iskusstv*, no. 1 (March 1923): 4, 6.

[144] *Novyi zritel'*, no. 7 (16 February 1926): 14.

[145] *Novyi zritel'*, no. 8 (22 February 1927): 15.

[146] Cf. S. S. Grechishkin and A. V. Lavrov, "O stikhovedcheskom nasledii Andreia Belogo," in *Struktura i semiotika khudozhestvennogo teksta: Trudy po znakovym sistemam* XII, Uchenye zapiski Tartusskogo gosudarstvennogo universiteta, issue 515 (Tartu, 1981), 133.

[147] Ginzburg, *Chelovek za pis'mennym stolom*, 31.

[148] O. E. Mandel'shtam, "*I ty, Moskva, sestra moia, legka...*": *Stikhi, proza, vospominaniia, materialy k biografii. Venok Mandel'shtamu* (Moscow: Moskovskii rabochii, 1990), 229, 230.

was met with bewilderment. As the critic explained, the problem was that this fairground entertainer had been "inspired" by his previous audiences: "he easily drew his humor, his improvizations, and his models from them." Now, "among the 'masters,' he ... cut all the raciest words from his jokes and catchphrases." Instead of populism, the revolution had created a new, "revolutionary" elitism. As a result, "nothing came of this old-time balagan show."[149]

Purely technical considerations also prevented "revolutionary art" from taking root. "Tattered reels of prerevolutionary film were shown, both Russian and foreign. Sentimental films, such as *Be Silent, Sorrow, Be Silent* (*Molchi grust', molchi*), were especially successful," recalled one memoirist.[150] Theater repertoires remained "bourgeois"[151] and "petit bourgeois" films sustained the popularity of the cinema. Essayists once again began to write about the "morally poisonous dishes" the cinema fed to children.[152] Of course, revolutionary culture did permeate into the cinema. In 1920, a group of Petrograd filmmakers headed by Grigorii M. Kozintsev and Leonid Z. Trauberg published their manifesto, *Eccentrism* (*Ekstsentrizm*), calling for a boycott of the "high genres" in favor of the circus, the music hall, jazz, and the popular poster. "The experiment was directed against tradition," admitted the critic, screenplay writer and author Viktor Shklovskii.[153] But all this remained an experiment.

Meanwhile, the "new" theater suffered from "lack of repertoire." In this context, the greatest theatrical achievement was the staging in Hebrew, in January 1922, of S. An-sky's (S. Z. Rappoport) play *The Dybbuk* at the Habima Theater in Moscow. The Hebrew language had been labeled "reactionary" by the Commissariat of Narkomnats (which contained several Jews amongst its staff) as late as June 1919, but unexpectedly it got through to the audience. Of course, this was a local "celebration of life"; it did not register with the broad mass of the population. The theater was almost shut down in 1921.[154] Revolutionary idealists came to the aid of the struggle against "reaction."

---

[149] *Teatr i zhizn'* (Berlin), no. 10 (1922): 18.

[150] Iu. L. Iurkevich, *Minuvshee prokhodit predo mnoiu...* (Moscow: Vozvrashchenie, 2000), 65.

[151] Sh. Plaggenborg, *Revoliutsiia i kul'tura: Kul'turnye orientiry v period mezhdu Oktiabr'-skoi revoliutsiei i epokhoi stalinizma* (St. Petersburg: Zhurnal "Neva," 2000), 214–15.

[152] L. M. Vasil'evskii, *Golgofa rebenka: Bezprizornost' i deti ulitsy* (Moscow–Leningrad, 1924), 62.

[153] V. B. Shklovskii, *Gamburgskii schet* (St. Petersburg: Limbus Press, 2000), 175.

[154] Attempts to close down the "Zionist Ancient Hebrew theater of the reactionary gourmands," the "speculators' theater," were made by left *Evsektsy* from 1920 onwards. Stanislavskii, Nemirovich-Danchenko, Tairov, Shaliapin and other well-known figures interceded for Habima with Lenin. Cf. RGASPI f. 613, op. 4, d. 52, ll. 3, 5–6, 8–10, 12–13, 16, 19, 50, 64.

In 1921, the Minsk congress of Jewish cultural workers called for a struggle "against clericalism on the Jewish street," "hiding the worst enemies of the proletariat beneath its black cloak…" In 1921–22 there were agitational meetings and so-called "courts" held at heders in more than 70 settlement points.[155]

In the context of an artificially cultivated class divide, of course, there could be no question of popular (public) art: one could only hope that "revolutionary" art would be popular. Its real supporters were found among the youth. In 1922, Kornei Chukovskii set down his impression of the student devotees of Walt Whitman, of whom he was considered a specialist: "They need no aesthetic; they are passionately preoccupied with morality. Whitman interests them as a prophet and teacher…" They thirsted "not for aesthetic enjoyment, but for faith…"[156] In essence, the "new" culture was destined to activate the "judgment complex" characteristic of traditional societies.

Some very significant developments took place in the art world. Exhibitions continued during the Civil War; artistic magazines were published; the prices of paintings remained high: all this was the consequence of typical wartime speculation. And then prices sharply declined. "The traders are full to the back teeth, and now they have no time for us," complained the artist Mikhail Nesterov in September 1922.[157] Nonetheless, the magazine *Among Collectors* (*Sredi kollektsionerov*) continued to appear in Moscow. At the end of 1922, the 17th exhibition of the Union of Russian Artists opened in Moscow, including works by the Vasnetsov brothers, Korovin, Sergei Maliutin, Anna Golubkina, Konstantin Iuon, and Nesterov. Nesterov himself returned to work after a series of artistic disappointments and periods without income, and came to prominence over time with a series of "society" portraits, predominantly of artists and academics.[158]

The Association of Artists of Revolutionary Russia (AKhRR) was established in 1922. It also claimed a monopoly on the leadership of artistic life. Its leaders included such diverse artists as Isaak Brodskii, Maliutin, Nikolai Kasatkin, Vasilii Meshkov, Georgii Riazhskii, Efim Cheptsov and Iuon. Characteristically, their idea of the "birth of the new world" still cohabited with elements of nostalgic lyricism. The artists close to them were concerned not so much with uniting with the "revolutionary people" as with adapting to the Bolshevik government. In July 1922, they organized an exhibition dedicated to

---

[155] A. G. Dalgatov, *Pravitel'stvennaia politika po otnosheniiu k etnokonfessional'nym men'shinstvam: "evreiskii vopros" v zhizni sovetskogo obshchestva (okt. 1917-go–nachalo 1930-x godov)* (St. Petersburg: Nestor, 2002), 98, 93.

[156] Chukovskii, *Dnevnik*, 195.

[157] M. V. Nesterov, *Pis'ma: Izbrannoe*, ed. A. A. Rusakova (Leningrad: Iskusstvo, 1988), 279.

[158] S. A. Pavliuchenkova, ed., *Rossiia nepovskaia* (Moscow: Novyi khronograf, 2002), 251–52.

the everyday life of the Red Army.[159] Iurii Annenkov, who painted the famous portrait of the poet Anna Akhmatova, readily undertook to paint Trotskii. Sergei Chekonin painted Lenin and Zinov'ev on vellum: the portraits were to be presented to them in the name of the Comintern.[160]

Cultural figures on the left believed that, in order to build the society of the future, it was necessary first to "heal the human mind." The "reorganization of the individual" was proclaimed[161] and, accordingly, these figures tried to supplement technocratic ideas with "artistic" content. In 1918, Aleksei Gastev—director of the Central Labor Institute and a proponent of the scientific organization of labour—published works of poetry with characteristic titles: *We Grow from Iron* (*My rastem iz zheleza*), *Rails* (*Rel'si*), *Whistles* (*Gudki*). Now whistles sounded in the conservatories, too: in 1922, the composer Arsenii (Krasnokutskii) Avramov wrote the *Whistle Symphony* (*Simfoniia gudkov*). Meanwhile, in 1920, Gastev openly declared that "Russia is different from the West in that it is lazy, or elementally impulsive; in general, its population shows little tenacity or determination to work."[162] Accordingly, "revolutionary" cultural figures prepared to hammer new ideas into the heads of the masses. In reality, in the urban context, the prerevolutionary song tradition took on a criminal hue: the famous song *Murka* emerged in the early 1920s.[163]

"Left" artists were active everywhere, but in different ways. In Vitebsk, there was the People's Art School, where up to 500 novice artists studied under the direction of Marc Chagall and Malevich. In 1921, Chagall also had occasion to work in Malakhovka (Moscow region) at the Third International Jewish labor school for homeless children.[164] The chaotic times brought forth artistic "provocateurs." "We lived through a very good, very significant and very eventful time in Vitebsk," wrote the artist El (Lazar') Lisitskii to Malevich from Berlin. "Now I see that especially clearly."[165]

The Futurist model of revolution had a mesmerizing effect. Captivated by the idea of building the "highly spiritual and intellectual society," Vasilii Kandinskii was actively involved in the work of the Institute of Artistic Culture, which set the task of creating the monumental art of the future. Its

---

[159] I. N. Golomshtok, *Totalitarnoe iskusstvo* (Moscow: Galart, 1994), 225.

[160] S. V. Iarov, *Konformizm v sovetskoi Rossii: Petrograd 1917–1920-x godov* (St.Petersburg: Evropeiskii dom, 2006), 342.

[161] A. Gol'tsman, *Reorganizatsiia cheloveka* (Moscow: Tsentral'nyi institut truda, 1924), 6.

[162] A. Gastev, "Nashi zadachi: Nasha prakticheskaia metodologiia," *Organizatsiia truda*, no. 1 (1921): 18.

[163] Geldern and Stites, *Mass Culture in Soviet Russia*, 72–73.

[164] M. Chagall, *Moia zhizn'* (Moscow: Ellis Lak, 1994), 170.

[165] Cited in I. Dukhan, "El' Lisitskii i russko-evreiskii avangard," in *Russko-evreiskaia kul'tura*, ed. O. V. Budnitskii (Moscow: RosSPEN, 2006), 454.

aim was "not only the culturing of entertainment forms, but the cult of abstract achievements."[166] These ideas resonated with certain fantasies of the "cultural leadership." Revolutionary speculation disguised the dismal prose of postrevolutionary actuality. But avant-garde abstraction was unsuitable here: easy-to-understand images and symbols were needed, like Iuon's *The New Planet* (*Novaia planeta*, 1921) (see fig. 3 in gallery of illustrations following page 188). Creative utopians tried to look into the "bright future world" with the eyes of the new man. However, life dictated otherwise. If, before the revolution, the avant garde strove to transform the banality of everyday life into phantasmagoria, in order to expose its terrible contradictions, now it longed to escape from the chaos of war to the security of tradition. Moreover, surrealist images of the ordinary clashed with the futurist visions suitable to the state.

The succession of wars and revolutions engendered only individual elements of a mass culture, of an aggressively carnivalesque type. These could not be assembled into a new type of culture. In place of the prerevolutionary cultural hierarchy, a sort of revolutionary elitism arose. Only in the 1930s was something like a mass culture created in Soviet Russia, with the help of music and film.

Translated by Kirsty McCluskey

---

[166] Cf. *Sovetskoe iskusstvo za 15 let: Materialy i dokumentatsiia* (Moscow-Leningrad: OGIZ, 1933), 131.

Worker Culture(s) during War and Revolution, 1914–20

Page Herrlinger

In September 1918, delegates to the first All-Russian Conference of Proletarian-Cultural Enlightenment Organizations laid out a platform for what would be known as the Proletkul't movement, just as it was being unified on the national level. As one delegate later noted:

> The task of the "Proletkults" is the development of an independent proletarian spiritual culture, including all areas of the human spirit—science, art, and everyday life. The new socialist epoch must produce a new culture, the foundations of which are already being laid. This culture will be the fruit of the creative efforts of the working class and will be entirely independent. Work on behalf of proletarian culture should stand on a par with the political and economic struggle of the working class.[1]

Exactly what "proletarian culture" meant would remain a topic of intense debate through the Revolution and Civil War. Nonetheless, Proletkul't generated widespread enthusiasm for its project, and its efforts to forge new cultural paths were paralleled in myriad worker circles and clubs, representing virtually every sphere of art and knowledge.[2] Such a pronounced focus on cultural activity during a devastating time of political conflict and deprivation was not considered odd, much less inappropriate; it was seen rather as a powerful and unprecedented validation of the cultural potential of the working people. At once a liberation from the bonds of bourgeois culture, as well as an overcoming of the "backwardness" of peasant culture, the process of creating a truly "proletarian culture" was considered to be every bit as important to the socialist future as the emancipation of workers from the economic exploitation of capitalists and the political oppression of tsarist

---

[1] V. Kerzhentsev, "Out of School Education and the 'Proletkults,'" in *Bolshevik Visions: First Phase of the Cultural Revolution in Soviet Russia*, ed. W. G. Rosenberg (Ann Arbor, MI: Ardis Publishers, 1984), 343.

[2] Lynn Mally, *Culture of the Future: The Proletkult Movement in Revolutionary Russia* (Berkeley: University of California Press, 1990), xix.

Russian Culture in War and Revolution, 1914–22, Book 1: Popular Culture, the Arts, and Institutions. Murray Frame, Boris Kolonitskii, Steven G. Marks, and Melissa K. Stockdale, eds. Bloomington, IN: Slavica Publishers, 2014, 53–83.

authorities.[3] A primary difference between worker culture and "proletarian culture," explained Proletkul't's main theorist, Aleksandr Bogdanov, was that the latter rested on praxis, the integration of life and art, life and thought.[4] In this sense, proletarian culture could only begin to develop once capitalism was gone; as with socialist society more generally, how theory would translate into practice would only become evident once workers decided to act.

The great optimism shared by the members of Proletkul't about the creative potential of the working classes in 1917 was in direct proportion to the pessimism that observers of workers' cultural tendencies had had before the Revolution. Indeed, for most of the late imperial period, the term "worker culture" had an oxymoronic ring to it: the urban factory environment— metonymically identified with tavern culture—was identified as a site of back- wardness and immorality, of violence, brutality, and sexual depravity. And the larger the urban working class became, as waves of peasant migrants poured into the cities from all over the empire, the more it appeared to degenerate. Clergy, "bourgeois" cultural elites, and the worker intelligentsia alike decried urban factory life as a realm ruled by ignorance, "moral negligence," and the "flourishing of base instincts."[5]

Concerns about workers' general lack of cultural development centered not only on the corrupting influence of the tavern, but also on the lack of healthier ways to spend their limited free time. "The decisive moment and in- fluence in a person's life is not work but the leisure time after work," reflected the progressive Petrograd philanthropist Countess Sof'ia Panina, for "only in the hours of leisure is there a place for love and joy, for that which turns a robot into a human being and a human being into an individual."[6] While some cultural elites stressed the cause of temperance more than the cultivation of healthy leisure, the result was the same: by the start of war in 1914, workers in both Petrograd and Moscow had access to a well developed network of attractions and courses intended to engage them in more "rational" forms of recreation and edification. As Stephen Frank has argued with respect to similar "civilizing" missions in the Russian village, the model at work was primarily colonial in its assumptions and intentions. "With the methods and ideology of Victorian social reform," urban cultural elites sought to "rescue"

---

[3] Mally, *Culture of the Future*, 25.

[4] Ibid., 9–10. Zenovia A. Sochor, *Revolution and Culture: The Bogdanov–Lenin Controversy* (Ithaca, NY: Cornell University Press, 1988), 38–41.

[5] Mark Steinberg, *Proletarian Imagination: Self, Modernity, and the Sacred in Russia, 1910– 1925* (Ithaca, NY: Cornell University Press, 2002), 87.

[6] Quoted in Adele Lindenmeyr, "Building Civil Society One Brick at a Time: People's Houses and Worker Enlightenment in Late Imperial Russia," *Journal of Modern History* 84, 1 (2012): 12.

workers from their "backwardness" by means of their own "enlightened" culture.[7]

The rhetoric of "liberation" that dominated cultural debates in the era of Proletkul't contrasted sharply with the civilizing language of the prerevolutionary period. In addition to holding different estimations of workers' cultural potential, cultural activists before and after 1917 assigned somewhat different meanings to "culture," as well as its ideal relationship to class. While most Proletkul'tists believed that workers' culture and education should reflect their experience and perspectives as laborers, bourgeois culture-builders before 1917 tended to assume that what workers did in their non-working hours could (and should) help to compensate for the (primarily negative) realities of their class. Yet, what linked cultural activists on either side of 1917 was a belief in the transformative potential of culture, in the importance of workers' engagement in art and all forms of knowledge, and in their embrace of "respectable" behaviors or "kul'turnost'." In short, both believed that culture—however they might define it—mattered greatly, and moreover, that the cultural development of the working classes was necessary to the welfare of Russian society as a whole.

The following discussion explores patterns in cultural politics and cultural practice among the working classes of Russia's two most industrialized and politicized cities, Petrograd and Moscow, during the years of war and revolution. Although the working population in both cities was somewhat diverse in terms of ethnic and religious identity, in the interest of addressing the broadest experience and making the most of existing scholarship, the focus here is primarily on the majority of ethnically Russian and (at least nominally) Orthodox workers.[8] The first part surveys secular and religious trends in workers' leisure and daily life (*byt*) during the first years of the war, 1914–16. Drawing on studies of worker identity and popular cultural and educational institutions, as well as my own research on workers' religious identity, it considers a range of factors that influenced workers' leisure practices and behaviors, including the "culturist" agendas of secular and religious elites, commercial forces, state policy, conditions of war, and last but not least, workers' own traditions, tastes, experiences, and beliefs. In a variety of ways,

---

[7] Stephen P. Frank, "Confronting the Domestic Other: Rural Popular Culture and Its Enemies in Fin-de-Siècle Russia," in *Cultures in Flux: Lower-Class Values, Practices, and Resistance in Late Imperial Russia*, ed. Frank and Mark D. Steinberg (Princeton, NJ: Princeton University Press, 1994), 92.

[8] On the ethnic and religious composition of the St. Petersburg population as a whole on the eve of the war, see James H. Bater, *St. Petersburg: Industrialization and Change* (Montreal: McGill-Queen's University Press, 1977), 377–78. For an extensive and helpful discussion of worker identities in both Moscow and St. Petersburg, see Victoria Bonnell, *Roots of Rebellion: Workers' Politics and Organizations in St. Petersburg and Moscow, 1900–1914* (Berkeley: University of California Press, 1982), chap. 1.

it takes into account the diversity and fluidity of urban working identity, especially the impact of gender on the experience of culture and daily life.

The second part of the chapter looks at patterns in workers' cultural activity and cultural debates during the crisis-ridden years of revolution and civil war, 1917–20, the period when Proletkul't made its most inspired attempt to create a truly "proletarian" culture on the ground of the old. While few would dispute that 1917 marked a significant cultural shift, insofar as the Revolution offered workers an unprecedented amount of cultural authority and autonomy, the following will also suggest lines of continuity in cultural practice and belief across the revolutionary divide. It will argue that, even as some workers enthusiastically committed themselves to the challenge of creating a "proletarian culture," the trajectory of cultural behaviors and beliefs among the working class as a whole was towards greater diversity and pluralism, rather than the kind of homogeneity or uniformity the term implied. To the extent that workers stood on common cultural ground as a class in years of civil war, it had far less to do with a shared set of practices, behaviors, or beliefs than with an increasingly widespread commitment to autonomy and self-realization in all spheres of culture.

Workers at Rest and Play

By 1914, the length of the average working day in the Russian factory was ten to eleven and a half hours. Although this meant only a few hours of discretionary time each day, plus Saturday evenings and Sundays, long gone were the days when the worker's options for "leisure" were limited largely to "stewing in their juices" in overcrowded communal apartments or seeking release by going to the tavern.[9] Indeed, myriad opportunities for workers to amuse or enlighten themselves existed in virtually every cultural corner of the city— in People's Conservatories and popular theaters, in People's Universities and evening courses, and in tearooms and libraries. Whether initiated by factory owners, private individuals, clergy, or state-run organizations such as the massive St. Petersburg Guardianship for Public Sobriety, activities associated with the movement for "rational recreation" were informed by three shared assumptions about what workers "needed" in terms of cultural development: first, a healthy physical and social environment in which to relax and enjoy themselves; second, diverse and morally uplifting forms of entertainment to amuse and distract them from their harsh lives; and third, opportunities for enlightenment in all branches of science and the arts. By all accounts, these three goals were best and most fully realized in the institution of the People's House (Narodnyi dom), which brought together under one roof a full menu of cultural and educational opportunities for ordinary working people.

---

[9] Semen Kanatchikov, *A Radical Worker in Tsarist Russia: The Autobiography of Semen Ivanovich Kanatchikov*, ed. and trans. Reginald E. Zelnik (Stanford, CA: Stanford University Press, 1986), 87.

Of the 222 People's Houses already completed in Russia by 1914, the most outstanding model was that on Ligovskaia Street in Petrograd, founded in 1903 by the young and highly progressive Countess Sof'ia Panina. The Ligovskii Narodnyi Dom (the LND) was founded on a widely shared and expressly secular belief in the importance of leisure in the cultivation of the individual, and in Adele Lindenmeyr's words, of "light, knowledge, and modernity as the means to create a new model of sociability and citizenship."[10] In an impressive new building, which stood out against the gray working-class landscape like a "wondrous castle out of a fairy tale, a cathedral of light, a crystal palace,"[11] the workers of Petrograd were invited to explore an especially rich and diverse set of options for relaxation, entertainment, and enlightenment. Enhanced by high-tech amenities such as modern heating, toilets, and electricity, the interior facilities—which included a library for adults and children, classrooms, an auditorium, and even a planetarium—were modern, bright, clean, and warm. The LND also had a cafeteria and a tearoom, intended to function as a "local club," where workers could relax comfortably, reading a newspaper or a book, conversing on contemporary issues, or playing a game of chess.[12] As Sarah Badcock has explained with respect to people's enlightenment projects in the provinces, the importance of these new social spaces lay also in their function as a site of civic interaction, a "new forum for conscious, civilized Russia."[13] In this sense, workers were invited into the People's House not just to unwind but to learn how to be good citizens by socializing with other "respectable" folk, especially those of a higher class.[14]

The LND's enormous auditorium was a space devoted to both amusement and enlightenment; with a capacity of almost 700, it served as the stage for lectures, readings, films, and concerts, some of which were performed by a workers' choir and balalaika orchestra. The LND also housed a theater company. Because productions were financed entirely by Panina, the company did not have to cater to workers' love of spectacle, farce, and melodrama to stay afloat, as so many other People's Houses and commercial stages did.[15] In fact, the Ligovskii repertoire included only Russian and foreign dramatic classics, on the founder's insistence that workers should be exposed to works of literary and artistic quality, and to characters that were psychologically transparent

---

[10] Lindenmeyr, "Building Civil Society," 17.

[11] Ibid., 15.

[12] Ibid., 9, 15.

[13] Sarah Badcock, "Talking to the People and Shaping Revolution: The Drive for Enlightenment in Revolutionary Russia," *Russian Review* 65, 4 (2006): 622–23.

[14] Lindenmeyr, "Building Civil Society," 9–10.

[15] Gary Thurston, "The Impact of Russian Popular Theatre, 1886–1915," *Journal of Modern History* 55, 2 (1983): 257–59.

and accessible.[16] A similar belief in the transformative value of aesthetic experience was at work at the state-sponsored Nicholas II's People's House, where instead of polkas, waltzes, and marches, 2411 opera performances were staged over the course of 15 years, and lower-priced tickets were made available to workers.[17]

The majority of workers who visited the LND came to relax with friends or family, to read newspapers, to listen to a reading with slides, or to go to the cafeteria.[18] A smaller but enthusiastic population of mostly younger workers took advantage of its lectures and evening classes. Intended for both adults and adolescents, male and female, the courses were offered at different levels to accommodate workers' varied backgrounds; separate literacy courses were taught for women. Lectures, always subject to government censorship, covered academic topics like biology and history, as well as issues more directly relevant to workers' lives (such as family relations and alcoholism). Over 1000 adults enrolled in the fall of 1910. Although the attrition rate was high, a committed group of younger workers from the evening courses went on to form a successful literary circle, which produced two anthologies of their own work in 1913–14.[19]

Pursuing knowledge for its own sake was not always universally acceptable in working-class circles,[20] especially those with strong peasant roots. But as the example of the LND suggests, after 1905 workers as a whole began to embrace education in far greater numbers—not only with the aim of gaining more skills or technical training, but also with the conscious intention of becoming more "cultured" in a distinctly bourgeois sense.[21] Education, or "enlightenment," was understood, even if only dimly by some, as more than a way to escape the "dark" conditions of the tavern or communal apartment; it was a means by which to escape the confines of the working-class self.

As much as the LND was able to support the needs of its small circle of worker-intellectuals, it is also the case that some conscious workers rejected the "culturalist" premise that informed it. The problem was not the aim to

---

[16] Lindenmeyr, "Building Civil Society," 25. On debates over the proper repertoire at People's Theaters, see E. Anthony Swift, *Popular Theater and Society in Tsarist Russia* (Berkeley: University of California Press, 2002), 86.

[17] Patricia Herlihy, *The Alcoholic Empire: Vodka and Politics in Late Imperial Russia* (Oxford: Oxford University Press, 2002), 20.

[18] Lindenmeyr, "Building Civil Society," 23.

[19] Ibid., 27–29; Steinberg, *Proletarian Imagination*, 46.

[20] Mark Steinberg, "The Injured and Insurgent Self: The Moral Imagination of Russia's Lower-Class Writers," in *Workers and Intelligentsia in Late Imperial Russia: Realities, Representation, Reflections,* ed. Reginald E. Zelnik (Berkeley: University of California Press, 1999), 322–23.

[21] Steinberg, *Proletarian Imagination*, 36–44; Bonnell, *Roots of Rebellion*, 260–62, 328–38.

"uplift" the working classes by cultural means. On the contrary, conscious workers regularly used the trade-union press to voice concern about the cultural underdevelopment of their class, and were quick to denounce drunkenness and common habits like swearing as inimical to their ideals of selfhood.[22] They also shared the belief that more crass forms of entertainment "posed a danger to the proletariat's psyche." "The acrobats, gymnasts, clowns, etc. give no pleasure to the worker's soul, but on the contrary, develop coarse instincts in him," complained a young worker to a Bolshevik daily in 1913.[23]

At the same time, however, worker-intellectuals rejected the elite assumption that workers' cultural development was as simple or limited as directing them from the tavern to the tearoom, or forcing them to give up fistfights for physics, or *chastushki* for Chaikovskii. Arguing that workers themselves needed to take responsibility for their own behaviors—to become active subjects in the cultural realm, rather than passive objects—they thus questioned the manufacture of cultural institutions for workers by elite actors, and began to organize their own clubs and circles in 1906–07.[24] Run primarily through newly legalized trade unions, the clubs were theoretically for workers *by* workers, although in practice, socialist intellectuals were instrumental to the process as well. Nonetheless, as the Petersburg metalworkers' paper observed, the success of the clubs' lectures, courses, and libraries could be attributed to shared "workerist" goals—that is, not only a desire to acquire a wide range of knowledge about the world and society, but also a need to "work out their world view."[25]

A particularly successful avenue of cultural activism at this time was workers' theater, which was envisioned as an alternative to both theater for the privileged, educated classes, and the commercialism and "vulgarity" (*poshlost'*) of "cheap theater and cinema" produced for workers by the bourgeoisie.[26] While staging performances of Gogol''s *Marriage*, and plays by Hauptmann, Ostrovskii, Tolstoi, and Maksim Gor'kii, worker theater organizers encouraged an unprecedented level of worker participation at all stages of production, with an emphasis as much on the creative process as the cultural

---

[22] Steve Smith, "Masculinity in Transition: Peasant Migrants to Late-Imperial St. Petersburg," in *Russian Masculinities in History and Culture*, ed. Barbara Evans Clements, Rebecca Friedman, and Dan Healey (Houndmills, UK: Palgrave, 2002), 98–99; Steinberg, "The Injured and Insurgent Self," 321.

[23] As translated in Tony Swift, "Workers' Theater and 'Proletarian Culture' in Prerevolutionary Russia, 1905–1917," in *Workers and Intelligentsia in Late Imperial Russia*, 279.

[24] By 1909 in St. Petersburg, 21 new clubs and cultural societies with names like "Knowledge Is Light" had been set up, with a peak membership of 6,830 (Bonnell, *Roots of Rebellion*, 329–30).

[25] *Nadezhda*, 26 September 1908, 8, cited in Bonnell, *Roots of Rebellion*, 332.

[26] Swift, "Workers' Theater," 278.

product. Although performances were often "painfully amateurish" and quite conventional, they reflected the desire on the part of workers to assume cultural authority, and to create an alternative, worker-centered culture, free both from elite aims and oversight.[27]

Worker-writers, like the circle that emerged at the LND, were driven by a similar ambition "not only to consume culture but to create it."[28] By 1916, over 40 collections of workers' writings had appeared in print, many of them published by working-class associations, such as the Moscow-based Surikov Circle. Far from "average," these workers tended to see themselves as separated by a "great ocean of darkness" from the rest of their class, but their poetry and prose nonetheless reflected workers' "enormous need for self-expression" and gave voice to the uniquely working-class experience of oppression and search for humanity.[29] As Mark Steinberg has observed, writing enabled these workers to develop a sense of purpose and self that was not limited to their identity as victims of oppression.[30] And though their talk "of raising the culture of the poor" appeared to echo elite concerns, "the logic was more defiant and transgressive than integrative," and the goal very different—that is, "to make the poor more dangerous to an unequal social order, not less."[31]

Because of their susceptibility to politicization and radical activity, all independent workers' organizations were officially repressed by wartime.[32] Whether or not the many prewar worker-run clubs and circles constituted the kind of "alternative culture" found in Germany is debatable,[33] but they clearly served to enhance the growing subculture of "modern" workers—that is, those mostly skilled and secularized workers who were interested in politics and current events and committed to developing their intellect and various forms of "self-improvement" (including cultivating habits like sobriety, cleanliness, and sexual restraint). And while the repression no doubt slowed the evolution of a specifically "worker" culture during the early years of war, the clubs—as well as the cultural debates that had inspired them—quickly reemerged once the tsarist regime had fallen in 1917.

As independent worker organizations were shut down, more "rational" cultural venues expanded. In 1914, over 80 People's Houses were under construction across the empire, and Moscow authorities made plans in 1915 to

---

[27] Ibid., 277–78.

[28] Steinberg, *Proletarian Imagination*, 44.

[29] Ibid., 32–33.

[30] Steinberg, "The Injured and Insurgent Self," 311–12.

[31] Steinberg, *Proletarian Imagination*, 85. See also Mally, *Culture of the Future*, 21.

[32] Mally, *Culture of the Future*, 20.

[33] Vernon L. Lidtke, *The Alternative Culture: Socialist Labor in Imperial Germany* (Oxford: Oxford University Press, 1985).

increase the city's network considerably, although war-related financial con-
straints soon put their plans on hold.[34] As popular as many elite-sponsored
institutions appeared to be, however, it is clear that their appeal was far from
universal. Efforts at the People's Conservatory to attract workers to its choral
classes had fallen flat, for example, and those workers who did attend evidently
preferred to think of the classes more as entertainment than as a chance to
be "enlightened."[35] Still other evidence suggests that in spite of the multiple
avenues for "rational recreation" in place by 1914, many workers chose to
spend their free time engaged in far less rational ways, at least some of the
time. Even as they aspired as individuals to the goal of "self-improvement,"
they continued to seek out ways to escape their hard lives and to "feel good"
and have fun, especially in the company of friends, whenever they could.

For some workers, drinking alcohol—often to excess—remained a central
preoccupation during the war. In the short run, the introduction of prohibition in 1914 helped to redirect workers away from the tavern, resulting in an
initial decline in evidence of drunkenness and its related problems for the
first year or so of war.[36] But soon it became clear that prohibition had not
stopped workers from drinking entirely, nor had it eliminated the various
reasons they drank.[37] With access to *samogon* (moonshine) widespread,[38]
many workers frequented underground tearooms or pubs, or drank in private
spaces, where they were likely to engage in the same cycle of behaviors found
at the tavern. Even as prohibition forced socializing into private spaces, increasing the likelihood that men and women would socialize together,[39]
drinking nonetheless remained central to the "largely homo-social world"[40]
in which most workers lived. Especially widespread on holidays, name days,
and at weddings, drinking was also part of weekly ritual, enjoyed after work
stopped on Saturday. It was also associated with workplace rituals, male bond-

---

[34] Lindenmeyr, "Building Civil Society," 2; Swift, *Popular Theater*, 67–68.

[35] Lynn M. Sargeant, "High Anxiety: New Venues, New Audiences, and the Fear of
the Popular in Late Imperial Russian Musical Life," *19th-Century Music* 35, 2 (2011):
104–06.

[36] Kate Transchel, *Under the Influence: Working-Class Drinking, Temperance, and Cultural
Revolution in Russia, 1895–1932* (Pittsburgh: University of Pittsburgh Press, 2006), 71.

[37] On reasons for drinking, see Daniel R.. Brower, *The Russian City between Tradition
and Modernity, 1850–1900* (Berkeley: University of California Press, 1990), 145–46; and
Laura L. Phillips, *Bolsheviks and The Bottle: Drink and Worker Culture in St Petersburg,
1900–1929* (DeKalb: Northern Illinois University Press, 2000), especially 60–65.

[38] When *samogon* was not available, lacquer sales went up in working-class areas (as
they did in 1915) (Transchel, *Under the Influence*, 71).

[39] Anne E. Gorsuch, *Youth in Revolutionary Russia: Enthusiasts, Bohemians, Delinquents*
(Bloomington: Indiana University Press, 2000), 146.

[40] Smith, "Masculinity in Transition," 95–96.

ing, and the rite of passage signifying the transformation of adolescent males into "men," liberated from the control of women.[41] Last but not least, alcohol remained a way for workers to relieve themselves from the physical demands of their labor and to forget, temporarily at least, about their hard lives.

With and without alcohol, male workers also regularly sought out opportunities for competition involving displays of luck, strength, and skill. In addition to billiards and skittles, cards and gambling were wildly popular. Among men and boys, the worker Aleksei Buzinov observed, a "passion for cards was almost universal," and it was not uncommon for workers to turn into "red-eyed roaches" after 40 hours of weekend play (and drink).[42] Even swearing could be competitive, a contest in crudeness and cleverness waged with "three-storey" and even "seven-storey" obscenities.[43] Another popular form of competition was the *kulachnyi boi*, or collective fistfight, which involved organized and often brutal contests between several hundred men at a time, playing on teams, typically on holidays. Although sometimes dismissed as a rural import, scholars have also seen them as a vital means of redefining masculinity in the urban context, of male bonding, competition, and entertainment.[44]

For all the attention paid to developing the worker's mind and spirit, very little thought was given to the condition of the body, and thus workers' physical culture remained poorly developed before 1917. Although workers engaged regularly in physical activities—promenading, sledding, and skating on local ponds or rivers, or hunting or fishing on the outskirts of town, for example—organized opportunities to engage in sport and exercise were few. The one exception was the foreign (and "bourgeois") import of football, which was becoming more popular among workers by the war in spite of elite attempts to shut them out of amateur clubs by setting high dues. In the face of continued police surveillance, many younger workers organized street (or "wild") games wherever they could, and workers' clubs had formed in urban areas, including at the massive Putilov and Obukhov ironworks in Petersburg, and in the Presnia district of Moscow, where the team Spartak was born.[45] As

---

[41] Although women drank too, they were associated (in the male imagination) with abstinence and childhood. Laura L. Phillips, "In Defense of Their Families: Working-Class Women, Alcohol, and Politics in Revolutionary Russia," *Journal of Women's History* 11, 1 (Spring 1999): 101.

[42] Steve Smith and Catriona Kelly, "Commercial Culture and Consumerism," in *Constructing Russian Culture in the Age of Revolution: 1881–1940*, ed. Kelly and David Shepherd (Oxford: Oxford University Press, 1998), 127–28.

[43] Smith, "Masculinity in Transition," 98.

[44] Ibid., 96.

[45] The coach of the Presnia Society of Physical Education, Boris Efimovich Evdokimov, apparently used the organization as a cover under which to influence youth with Bolshevik ideas. Robert Edelman, *Spartak Moscow: A History of the People's Team*

Robert Edelman has suggested, football offered young male workers "a different way to prove their manhood in a new public space where they could demonstrate physical strength and stamina."[46]

Attendance at mass entertainment venues such as the amusement park and circus (with all its "acrobats, gymnasts, clowns") was higher among workers in 1915–16 than before the war.[47] Most popular of all were the movie houses.[48] Although certainly a trend before the war, film had really taken off by 1914, and by 1916 audiences would buy 12 times as many tickets for movies as for theater.[49] As in other belligerent countries, wartime spectacles of all kinds were frequently cast with patriotic intentions, not only to "sell" the war or rally support, but also because war themes resonated strongly with the masses.[50] For example, worker audiences responded enthusiastically to show-wrestling spectacles at the circus involving a Russian pitted against a "bad" German, who needed to be brought to justice.[51] They also loved the variety of skits, stories, and images produced about the heroic Cossack Koz'ma Kriuchkov who was said to have killed eleven Germans with a single lance.[52] Already by 1915, however, the heavy emotional toll of the war precipitated a shift towards sentimentalism and escapism.[53] While lower-class audiences still appreciated newsreels connecting them to the front, the most popular films were those that provided some relief from wartime anxieties through comedy and adventure, including detective and crime stories. They also appreciated social melodrama with a clear class message, typically involving an innocent female victimized by a wealthy good-for-nothing.[54] On screen, as on

---

in the Worker's State (Ithaca, NY: Cornell University Press, 2009), 29, 33, 40; James Riordan, *Sport in Soviet Society: Development of Sport and Physical Education* (Cambridge: Cambridge University Press, 1980), 27.

[46] Edelman, *Spartak Moscow*, 40.

[47] Hubertus Jahn, "Patriots or Proletarians? Russian Workers and the First World War," in *Workers and Intelligentsia in Late Imperial Russia*, 333.

[48] Ibid., 333.

[49] Richard Stites, *Russian Popular Culture: Entertainment and Society Since 1900* (Cambridge: Cambridge University Press, 1992), 28.

[50] Ibid., 36.

[51] Jahn, "Patriots or Proletarians?," 338.

[52] Ibid., 339; Stites, *Popular Culture*, 34.

[53] Hubertus Jahn has noted that even as patriotism declined as a popular theme, it still had a working-class audience in some locations, leading him to conclude that workers' views on the war cannot easily be classified as "for" or "against," "patriotic" or "proletarian" ("Patriots or Proletarians?," 343).

[54] Not unlike war movies, Richard Stites has suggested, melodramas like *Be Still, My Grief* (1918) might have helped to sanction acts of collective hatred and indignation, as

stage, workers liked "to see good and evil sharply differentiated, the former rewarded and the latter punished."[55]

With relatively high literacy rates that were steadily increasing (although more for men than women),[56] many workers were avid readers in the early years of the war, and they took advantage of the unprecedented volume of news and pulp made accessible to them by cheaper presses and a wide network of factory and public libraries. The first years of war brought an increase in news, as well as workers' interest in it. Sales of wartime broadsides (*lubki*) were also unexpectedly strong.[57] But beyond the early success of war-related themes, workers' reading habits suggest the difficulty of categorizing their tastes and inclinations. Workers were drawn to the classic Russian poets of the 19th century (including Pushkin, of course) and authors like Tolstoi, Lermontov, and Gogol′, as well as the inspiring "poets of the people," like Nikolai Nekrasov, Ivan Surikov, and Gor′kii.[58] Although religious literature was not as widely consumed as the secular press, Scripture, the lives of the saints, and meditations on various figures and models of true Christian life remained popular.[59] For all but the most "conscious" or religious workers, however, an appetite for crime stories, Cossack tales, and pulp fiction usually won out over a desire to be informed or enlightened. The serialized story about a benevolent thief named Anton Krechet, which ran for seven years from 1909–16, remained one of the all-time most popular pieces of fiction in worker circles.[60]

Faith and Religious Identity before the Revolution

With a proliferation of ways to entertain and amuse themselves, workers were spending more time engaged in secular pursuits early in the war. As

---

in the widespread cases of vandalism in the early revolutionary period (Stites, *Popular Culture*, 33).

[55] Swift, *Popular Theater*, 230.

[56] In 1910, three out of five migrant women to the big city were literate—a much improved statistic over the previous decade, but women still trailed significantly behind male migrants in literacy (87 percent to 60 percent among migrants). Barbara Alpern Engel, *Between the Fields and the City: Women, Work, and Family in Russia, 1861–1914* (Cambridge: Cambridge University Press, 1996), 132.

[57] Hubertus Jahn, *Patriotic Culture in Russia during World War I* (Ithaca, NY: Cornell University Press, 1995), 13.

[58] On reading habits, see Jeffrey Brooks, *When Russia Learned to Read: Literacy and Popular Literature, 1861–1917* (Princeton, NJ: Princeton University Press, 1985), 130–40.

[59] *Otchet o deiatel′nosti Obshchestva dlia rasprostraneniia religiozno-nravstvennogo prosveshcheniia v dukhe Pravoslavnoi Tserkvi za 1906 i 1907 gg.* (St. Petersburg, 1908) [hereafter Otchet 1905], 9–10.

[60] Stites, *Popular Culture*, 24.

generations of Soviet scholars highlighted, many younger, fully urbanized workers were fully secularized in their outlook, and a growing number were committed atheists.[61] In fact, secularism was becoming increasingly a mark of "culture." The "modern worker," A. Zorin had observed in 1910, "is neither for, nor against religion. He has somehow erased the question itself."[62] At the same time, however, other workers, including the many raised as Orthodox in the village, were not so much against faith as they were easily distracted from it: "[the Russian people] run off with light hearts to watch theatrical spectacles," commented a conservative journal, "and find the fulfillment of their Orthodox religious duties onerous, having become completely indifferent to things that are sacred, to the temple of God."[63]

Yet, even as secular concerns became predominant for many workers (especially the more "urbanized"), their lives were regularly—and, I would add, significantly—punctuated by many different types of religious rituals and behaviors. To be sure, workers' religious habits as a whole were far from consistent, especially when it came to devoting their free time on Sunday to worship.[64] Depending on the beliefs and inclinations of their co-workers or roommates, some participation might have been less than completely voluntary. The young migrant worker's sense of duty (or fear) towards the matter of Sunday liturgy, for example, was one of the last vestiges of rural patriarchy to disappear in the city. This was also true in the case of the fulfilling of one's annual Easter confession and communion, which was mandated not only by the church, but also by the state.

Nonetheless, workers' engagement in religious life was often intentional, as well as meaningful. Even if they did not go to church or consider themselves to be especially pious,[65] almost all workers participated to some extent in the

---

[61] L. I. Emeliakh, *Antiklerikal'noe dvizhenie krest'ian v periode pervoi russkoi revoliutsii* (Leningrad: Nauka, 1965); M. M. Persits, *Ateizm russkogo rabochego* (Moscow: Nauka, 1965); V. F. Shishkin, *Tak skladyvalas' revoliutsionnaia moral'* (Moscow: Mysl', 1967).

[62] A. Zorin, "Rabochii mir (Sovremennye nastroeniia)," *Zhizn' dlia vsekh*, no. 2 (1910): col. 105.

[63] Quoted in Iurii I. Kir'ianov, "Mentality of Russian Workers at the Turn of the Twentieth Century," in *Workers and Intelligentsia in Late Imperial Russia*, 85.

[64] For more on patterns of church-going, see Page Herrlinger, *Working Souls: Russian Orthodoxy and Factory Labor in St. Petersburg, 1881–1917* (Bloomington: Slavica, 2007), chap. 2.

[65] In an ethnographic study conducted in the early 1920s, Elena Osipova Kabo found that among a relatively small sample of Moscow workers, only 16 percent of those male workers who admitted to going to church prior to 1918 went regularly, whereas almost half (48 percent) said they went to mass only on major holidays. Among the women, 38 percent claimed to have gone to church every Sunday, while 35 percent attended only on major holidays. Elena Osipova Kabo, *Ocherki rabochego byta: Opyt monograficheskogo issledovaniia domashnego rabochego byta* (Moscow: Kn-vo VTSSPS, 1928), 1: 199–200.

celebration of saints days and holidays—on the factory floor, in their communal apartments, and at church. The very full calendar of church holidays regulated work schedules (and by default, time off), and most workers also participated in sacramental life, annually at Easter and at transitional moments in their lives. The vast majority of workers bowed to the tradition of baptizing their children, and burying the dead with the help of a priest, even though these rituals could be difficult to manage in terms of time and cost.[66] By 1914, the one tradition in decline in worker circles was the religious wedding; for a variety of reasons, including the desire of young workers to break away from the village, the trend was towards civil marriage.[67]

Workers also regularly spent time in prayer, both as individuals and as a group, usually to ask for assistance in negotiating the uncertainties of their lives (illness, unemployment, marital problems), to express gratitude for their blessings, and to remember the dead or to mark an important event (such as Emancipation, or the great cholera).[68] Illness, accidents, and epidemics—all of which were a constant reality in poor urban neighborhoods—continued to motivate workers to turn to the saints for help, even as they began to privilege the advice of medical practitioners, or "science," by the start of the war.[69] Alcoholism was another very good reason to pray; the Aleksandr Nevskii Temperance Society's annual pilgrimages to the Trinity-Sergius and Valaam monasteries were massive events, regularly attracting 60–80,000 people, many of whom were working class.[70] If, for some workers, the traumas of war brought religious doubt,[71] for others, the war added new reasons to turn to the saints. Indeed, belief in miracle-working icons was alive and well in

---

[66] S. Prokopovich, *Biudzhety peterburgskikh rabochikh* (St. Petersburg: Imperatorskoe russkoe tekhnicheskoe obshchestvo, Otdel XII, 1909), 34. During the early Soviet period, baptism was known as the most common religious "stumbling block" to the de-Christianization of workers. This was apparently true even for Party workers, especially females (Kabo, *Ocherki rabochego byta*, 200).

[67] In reference to the decline among workers with respect to the sacrament of marriage (and its high cost), S. G. Strumilin explained that "in general, economic factors influenced our moral judgments significantly." S. G. Strumilin, *Iz perezhitogo, 1897–1917 gg.* (Moscow: Gosudarstvennoe izd-vo politicheskoi literatury, 1957), 102; Engel, *Between the Fields and the City*, 160.

[68] M. Davidovich, *Peterburgskii tekstil'nyi rabochii* (Moscow: Vysshii sovet narodnogo khoziaistva, 1919), 1: 81–82. For more on workers' practices, see Herrlinger, *Working Souls*, chap. 2.

[69] "L. S-ii," "Iz nabliudenii nad sovremennoi religioznoi zhizn'iu," *Tserkovnyi vestnik*, no. 26 (30 June 1911): cols. 797–99.

[70] Rossiiskii gosudarstvennyi istoricheskii arkhiv (RGIA) f. 796 (Chancellery of the Holy Synod), op. 442, d. 2105 (1905), l. 122.

[71] O. N. Chaadaeva, *Rabotnitsa na sotsialisticheskoi stroike: Sbornik avtobiografii* (Moscow: Partiinoe izd-vo, 1932), 137.

working-class circles throughout the war, as reflected in the massive exercise of faith and patriotism on 22 October 1917, a low point only days before the Bolshevik coup, when hundreds of thousands of ecstatic Orthodox from all classes gathered in the center of Petrograd to celebrate the feast day of the miraculous icon of the Kazan' Mother of God, known as the "sword against [Russia's] enemies."[72]

In their own efforts to lure workers from the tavern, Orthodox clergy and missionaries had set up temperance tearooms as well as a network of religious-moral lectures (besedy) in working-class areas.[73] While some lectures dealt with contemporary issues (natural phenomena, alcoholism, and family relations, for example), many workers clearly valued them as an opportunity to immerse themselves in Scripture, prayer, and meditation on models of Orthodox piety. In this way, the lectures were also about self-improvement, in a religious sense. Given the enormous size and perpetual flux of most urban parishes, they were often a starting point for smaller religious communities, sometimes leading to collective acts of self-help and charity,[74] such as organizing aid to war victims. Partly as a result of these efforts at "enlightened piety," by wartime the Orthodox clergy had begun to comment on the emergence of a "new [Orthodox] layperson" who was both more educated about the faith and more conscious and intentional with respect to religious practice.[75] A common tendency among these "modern" believers, who included workers, was a passionate desire both to read Scripture and to interpret it on their own. Significantly, this meant they were more likely to think and debate the meaning of Orthodoxy in everyday life, as well as to question the authority of the clergy and church authorities.[76]

Enabled by new laws on religious toleration and freedom of conscience after 1905, working-class believers began to explore and experiment in the capital's

---

[72] *Vserossiiskii Tserkovnyi obshchestvennyi vestnik,* 25 October 1917, 2.

[73] Otchet 1905, 136. At their peak around 1905, St. Petersburg clergy offered over 6,000 lectures (on average, almost 17 per day) in churches, tearooms, and factories, reaching 2,193,063 people at 73 different locations, primarily in working-class neighborhoods and parishes. RGIA f. 796, op. 442, d. 2046 (1904), ll. 59ob., 97. The numbers would go down by the war, but lectures continued regularly throughout the city.

[74] For examples, see Otchet 1905, 70–71, 133; RGIA f. 796, op. 442, d. 1632, ll. 55–55ob.

[75] *Izvestiia po S.-Peterburgskoi eparkhii,* no. 8/9 (1908): 56; A. S. Pankratov, *Ishchushchie boga* (Moscow: A. A. Levenson, 1911), 9; "Pechat'," *Vserossiiskii Tserkovnyi obshchestvennyi vestnik* 101 (24 August 1917): 3.

[76] Interestingly, these included workers who returned to faith after a long period of alienation, including those who became disillusioned with revolutionary (political) means of change after 1905 (Pankratov, *Ishchushchie boga,* 8–9).

rapidly expanding religious marketplace to an unprecedented extent.[77] While for some this meant identifying more closely with the Orthodox Church, for many other religious workers, it meant breaking away, and embracing alternative beliefs, including evangelical Christianity and Baptism.[78] Others gravitated towards strong charismatic spiritual leaders, like Father Ioann of Kronstadt, Tolstoi, and Brother Ioann Churikov, a lay preacher who regularly attracted thousands of workers to his Sunday afternoon interpretations of Scripture.[79] In this way, the already religiously diverse working population was becoming even more heterogeneous in matters of faith on the eve of the Revolution.[80]

The "Other" Culture of Women before 1917

The individual worker's pattern of engagement in the urban cultural marketplace discussed so far could depend on any number of factors, including age, skill and wage level, factory or shop affiliation, and level of literacy or education. Personal taste and inclination, as well as ethnic or religious background could also matter considerably, as could the state of a worker's "consciousness" (whether political or religious), especially if that worker identified strongly with a particular subculture most or all of the time. But the single most important influence on the nature and degree of cultural engagement was a worker's sex. Indeed, it is fair to say that almost every dimension of working-class life looks different from a female perspective.

Even as the war directed workers away from the tavern and brought more women into the work force, the urban working-class environment remained predominately masculine, and often hostile to women's engagement—even among those considered more "enlightened." The factory was often not a welcoming place, especially as more women came onto the factory floor in the decade after 1905, and even in those industries, such as textiles and chemicals,

---

[77] *Tserkovnyi vestnik,* no. 41 (12 October 1906): col. 1329. V. I. Iasevich-Borodaevskaia, *Bor'ba za veru* (St. Petersburg: Gosudarstvennaia tipografiia, 1912), 351.

[78] Heather Coleman, *Russian Baptists and Spiritual Revolution, 1905–1929* (Bloomington: Indiana University Press, 2005), especially chap. 3.

[79] Herrlinger, *Working Souls,* chap. 5.

[80] In addition to the Russian Orthodox majority, the working population of the capital included small but significant numbers of Protestants (many from the Baltic provinces), Catholics (primarily Poles), and Jews. While Jews and other non-Christians appear to have been largely segregated, Protestants (including converts to various kinds of "sectarianism") and Catholics were integrated into the worker population as a whole (Bater, *St. Petersburg,* 377–78). Although the number of "sectarian" workers is difficult to ascertain, Orthodox clergy were clearly concerned about their growing visibility and influence in working-class circles, especially after 1905 (Herrlinger, *Working Souls,* 73, 226–27).

where they predominated. Both before and after 1917, Diane Koenker has observed, women were regarded as "intruders into the male club" of the shop floor, which was dominated by tavern-like behavior such as "banter, teasing, swearing, practical jokes and even cruelty."[81] Vulgarity was all too often accompanied by multiple forms of sexual harassment, including the expectation of sexual favors in exchange for promotion (sex, as much as skill, often determined a woman's status in the workplace).[82] "The attitude of the [factory] administration to us women is utterly obscene," complained a young female worker in her journal. "They don't see us as people but as cattle. They make advances, grab us unawares, pour abuse and bad language on us and make unseemly hints."[83]

By 1914, marriage in the city (as opposed to the village) was becoming more common among workers, especially among more skilled workers who could afford to support a family.[84] While marriage could provide some degree of financial and even emotional security for a woman, it did not necessarily make her life easier, nor her hours any freer, even if she was lucky enough to have a sober husband who did not beat her.[85] Deeply patriarchal norms about a woman's role in the home (as wife and mother) were one of the most religiously guarded rural imports to the city. While married men might help their wives on occasion—by going to the market, by occasionally watching the children, and by drinking less—the household was her responsibility, even when she worked a full day at the factory.[86] As a female textile worker, A. Il'ina, complained in 1917, "having finished work at the factory, the woman worker is still not free. While the male worker goes off to a meeting, or just takes a walk or plays billiards with his mates, she has to cope with the housework—to cook, to wash, and so on … she is seldom helped by her husband."[87] With so

---

[81] Diane Koenker, "Men against Women on the Shop Floor in Early Soviet Russia: Gender and Class in the Socialist Workplace," *American Historical Review* 100, 5 (December 1995): 1447.

[82] Ibid., 1449.

[83] P. F. Kudelli, ed., *Rabotnitsa v 1905 v Sankt-Peterburge* (Leningrad: Priboi, 1926), as quoted in S. A. Smith, "Workers and Supervisors: St. Petersburg, 1905–1917 and Shanghai 1895–1927," *Past and Present*, no. 139 (May 1993): 140–41.

[84] Evel Economakis and Robert J. Brym, "Marriage and Militance in a Working Class District of St. Petersburg, 1896–1913," *Journal of Family History* 20, 2 (1995): 26.

[85] See the case of a long-time wife-beater and metalworker at the San Galli machine works in Petersburg by the name of Eremeev. Barbara Alpern Engel, "Marriage and Masculinity in Late Imperial Russia: The 'Hard Cases,'" in *Russian Masculinities*, 116–18.

[86] Steve Smith, *Red Petrograd: Revolution in the Factories, 1917–1918* (Cambridge: Cambridge University Press, 1986), 26.

[87] *Tkach*, no. 2 (1917): 7, as translated and quoted in Smith, *Red Petrograd*, 26–27.

few daycare facilities in the city, the working mother routinely struggled to
find someone to care for her children during the day. Many children were
left inadequately supervised and cared for. The intensification of the double
burden of work and family on women during the war would only further
contribute to the neglect of children—and, in turn, to the erosion of the
working-class family.[88]

The home then, more than the workplace or the People's House, served as
the focal point of a female worker's limited leisure time. A 1922 time budget
study suggests that a working woman spent 15.8 hours per month socializing
with friends (compared to 9.8 for men), including 4 hours a month dancing,
5.3 hours singing or playing music, and 1.1 hours playing cards (usually the
fortune-telling kind).[89] Women drank too, but typically only on holidays or
special occasions.[90] With the remainder of their free time, women were more
likely than men to tend to household comforts and aesthetics. When possible,
this could mean shopping in the bustling urban markets for various items,
like a samovar, a clock, icons or cheap prints to hang on the walls, or even
a sewing machine; it also meant working hard to keep their living spaces
clean and well-furnished, with amenities like a lamp, flowers, and regularly
laundered sheets. Given that such concerns were not characteristic of the
village, Barbara Engel has suggested that they might be taken as a sign of
female workers' "rising expectations of life and a growing sense of personal
dignity."[91] Whatever the case, a woman's isolation in the home—even a relatively well kept one—could only serve to reinforce a sense of "otherness" or
marginalization within the factory environment as a whole.

Although many women had little opportunity to take advantage of cultural amusements or engage in a sustained course of "self-improvement"
outside the home, evidence does suggest that by the war some younger women
(especially those without families) were becoming more "modern" in their
leisure time. More than ever before, the new sites of sociability and education
sponsored by the church or the People's Houses offered women places to
spend their time, and provided opportunities for their children to learn and
play in a safe and healthy environment. And indeed, some female workers did
go to the theater, concerts, and cinema—although about half as often as men—
while others attended evening classes, read newspapers, and went to union

---

[88] On the phenomenon of *bezprizornost'*, see Joan Neuberger, *Hooliganism: Crime,
Culture, and Power in St. Petersburg, 1900–1914* (Berkeley: University of California Press,
1993), chap. 4.

[89] Smith and Kelly, "Commercial Culture and Consumerism," 127–28.

[90] Phillips, "In Defense of Their Families," 101.

[91] Engel, *Between the Fields and the City*, 153.

meetings just like men.[92] But even when they found the time and energy to engage intellectually or culturally, their efforts did not always engender respect, let alone support, from male workers. Even "conscious" workers tended to look down on female workers as lesser versions of themselves.[93]

The one cultural corner increasingly dominated by female workers was religion. Especially as a greater number of male workers identified themselves as either hostile or indifferent to any form of religious belief, it became identified as a "woman's issue" (*baboe delo*), meaning both that women spent more time than men engaged in religious life, and that the female worker became "the perpetrator of religious traditions in the family,"[94] making critical choices about her family and children—whether or not to baptize them, to seek medical doctors when they were ill, and how often to take them to church. Part of the explanation, memoirists suggested, related to women's lack of regular access to alternative forms of leisure or escape—thus factory and faith constituted the balance in their lives (whether they liked it that way or not).[95] Yet, many women evidently continued to practice their faith by conscious choice, sometimes in direct defiance of their husbands' efforts to convert them to their own "modern" (secularized) worldview.[96] Although some socialists would try to explain away their decision as a function of women's ignorance or "naturally" emotional nature,[97] it could also be said that a woman's commitment to faith reflected a measure of autonomy and agency not accorded to her in other spheres of her life.

Workers and Culture in Revolution

Until 1916, patterns in workers' leisure habits showed remarkable continuity from before the war. On the one hand, a small but growing number of primarily young male workers defined themselves as advanced or "conscious" by adhering to certain patterns of cultural consumption—foregoing the tavern or the cheap entertainment venues in order to frequent museums, attend evening lectures, and read "thick" journals. On the other hand, the working population

---

[92] Frosina, "Biudzhet semei rabotnits," in *Trudy pervogo Vserossiiskogo zhenskogo s'ezda pri Russkom zhenskom obshchestve v S.-Peterburge, 10–16 dek. 1908 g.* (St. Petersburg, 1909), 330–31.

[93] Steinberg, *Proletarian Imagination*, 43.

[94] Davidovich, *Peterburgskii tekstil'nyi rabochii*, 81.

[95] S. Lapitskaia, *Byt rabochikh Trekhgornoi manufaktury)* (Moscow: Istoriia zavodov, 1935), 73; "Rasskaz rabotnitsy o 9-m ianvarii," *Leningradskaia Pravda*, 22 January 1925, 7.

[96] Davidovich, *Peterburgskii tekstil'nyi rabochii*, 81. These observations were based on statistical materials gathered in 1908 (Chaadaeva, *Rabotnitsa*, 137).

[97] N. Krupskaia, "Rabotnitsa i religiia," *Kommunistka* 3–5 (1922), reprinted in *Antireligioznaia rabota sredi zhenshchin: Sbornik*, ed. L. Stal' (Moscow: Gosizdat, 1926), 12–15.

as a whole expressed a desire not only to learn and "improve" themselves, but also to "escape" in their free time in diverse ways.[98] As Laura Phillips has persuasively argued, it would be wrong to overdraw the "cultural divide" that distinguished the "conscious" from the "rank-and-file" worker, since the line between these two cultural extremes was often very permeable.[99] Moreover, as Catriona Kelly and Steve Smith have observed, the cultural boundaries *around* working-class life were as fluid and porous as those within, at least in the sense that much of "worker culture" was almost impossible to distinguish from the broader category of "lower-class" or "mass" culture.[100] Differences related to religious practice and gender identity further blurred both of these sets of categories.

One clear line of continuity through the early part of the war was the almost complete lack of outlets and sites for workers to express themselves culturally—that is, as laborers with a particular point of view and a unique set of experiences. The collapse of the tsarist regime in 1917 changed this almost immediately. With the lifting of censorship, the introduction of the eight-hour working day, the expansion of workers' control, and the allocation of space and resources to workers' cultural and educational pursuits, the cultural marketplace opened up to workers more than ever, not only allowing them free reign as consumers, but also privileging them as producers. And in spite of the paralyzing fuel shortages and severe lack of food, workers embraced the opportunity to remake their lives and to express themselves culturally; revolutionary utopianism, it seems, helped to feed the soul, even as the war continued to starve the body.

In 1917, workers' clubs emerged throughout the country, through trade unions, factory committees, soviets, cooperatives, and parties, each with its own "cultural-educational" agenda. Under the Provisional Government, some 150 workers' groups formed in Petrograd alone, claiming approximately 100,000 members.[101] Many of them were initiated and run by workers themselves, sometimes with no official affiliation at all, as in the case of the cultural circle at the former Guzhon steel mill, which had a band and brought workers together to talk and write.[102] On the whole, the range of activities was similar to prewar clubs, including circles in drama, art, and music, lectures on science and academic topics, museum excursions, and gender-specific activities, such as sewing and knitting circles for women, and wood-working and boot-

---

[98] Stites, *Popular Culture*, 22.

[99] Laura L. Phillips, "Message in a Bottle: Working-Class Culture and the Struggle for Revolutionary Legitimacy, 1900–1929," *Russian Review* 56, 1 (January 1997): 25–43.

[100] Smith and Kelly, "Commercial Culture and Consumerism," 153.

[101] Mally, *Culture of the Future*, 22.

[102] Steinberg, *Proletarian Imagination*, 54.

making circles for men.[103] Sport societies also emerged, although they would be the first to experience state control during the Civil War, as the development of physical culture was initially the concern of the military.[104]

At the heart of this storm of cultural autonomy and initiative was the Proletkul't, founded in the autumn of 1917. Throughout the country, Proletkul't set up workshops, studios, and clubs dedicated to the fostering of workers' engagement and creativity in art, architecture, music, literature, and theater. Drawing its leaders from a wide range of independent, party, and non-party organizations, its membership totaled over 400,000 by 1920.[105] As with prewar worker clubs, what mattered most for activists was the movement's spirit and the unprecedented approach to awakening what its theorists imagined to be a uniquely "proletarian creativity":

> In the area of work methods "Proletkult" goes its own special way. It strives to create for the proletariat appropriate conditions for facilitating creative work on the new culture. Therefore, it uses a wide system of studios—literary, dramatic, for the fine arts. Studios are not only schools, but a place for the quest of a new path. Studios abandon authoritarianism and build on comradely principles of equality and collegial creativity.[106]

With the deepening of civil war in 1918–19, the conditions for innovative cultural work became increasingly challenging, especially in the major cities. The working populations of Moscow and Petrograd shrank precipitously during this period, due mostly to outmigration to the village and Red Army recruiting.[107] And although subsidized prices increased the accessibility of cultural events, at the same time, those workers who remained in the city were often too desperately engaged in the struggle against illness or starvation to make the most of them. In their spare time, rather than relaxing or going to classes, many workers stood for hours in food queues, tended kitchen gardens, or tried to trade at local markets.

As life overwhelmed art in various ways, material realities derailed some cultural plans and the club movement suffered. With chronic shortages in staff and the restricted allocation of precious resources, all too often club activities existed only on paper, or as one female worker evidently claimed,

---

[103] Diane Koenker, *Republic of Labor: Russian Printers and Soviet Socialism, 1918–1930* (Ithaca, NY: Cornell University Press, 2005), 102.

[104] Riordan, *Sport in Soviet Society*, 68–81.

[105] Stites, *Russian Popular Culture*, 40.

[106] Kerzhentsev, "Out of School Education," 345.

[107] William J. Chase, *Workers, Society, and the Soviet State: Labor and Life in Moscow, 1918–1929* (Urbana: University of Illinois Press, 1990), 31–33.

Potemkin-village style.[108] At the same time, however, when clubs managed to keep the heat on (so to speak), they often served as meaningful centers of both culture and life, especially for the young. According to Gabriele Gorzka, the club served as a "home away from home" for many workers, a place to hang out, to exchange information and supplies, and to experience a sense of community: "sometimes I don't want to go home," reported one worker, "it is so pleasant and cozy in the club; you feel yourself so free here, and the people are all so familiar."[109]

For all the hardship and chaos, those committed to culture-building and experimentation under the umbrella of Proletkul't continued to create and perform during the Civil War period. As before the war, theatrical circles were especially successful, at least in terms of stirring up worker enthusiasm and participation. As Petr S. Kogan observed in 1919, "the future historian will note that during the bloodiest and cruelest of revolutions, all Russia continued to act," with more than a thousand officially registered theatrical groups comprised of workers and peasants and many more unregistered ones.[110] Indeed, Lynn Mally has argued that, "with its peculiar combination of hardship and utopia, devastation and creation, the [civil] war helped to further enthusiastic revolutionary goals."[111] It also meant that local groups had even more autonomy than they might have had otherwise.[112] Innovations encouraged by "cultural bureaucrats" and Proletkul't alike included playwriting competitions, short "agitation plays" (agitki), and improvisations. The "living newspaper," which entailed acting out current events, was a feature of Red Army theater, as were mass revolutionary spectacles; the point of both was "not simply to inform viewers but also to inspire action" in support of the regime.[113]

Yet, it is also clear that even as Proletkul't activists held onto a "transcendent image of the new society," the first few years of Soviet power and cultural experimentation had taught them to scale back expectations: "those who offered a hazy promise of socialist habits and mores recast in the fire of revolution ended up with agitational campaigns to promote sobriety and

---

[108] Koenker, Republic of Labor, 101.

[109] Quoted in Gabriele Gorzka, "Proletarian Culture in Practice: Workers' Clubs, 1917–1921," in Essays on Revolutionary Culture and Stalinism: Selected Papers from the Third World Congress for Soviet and East European Studies, ed. John W. Strong (Columbus, OH: Slavica Publishers, 1990), 41.

[110] P. Kogan, "Socialist Theater in the Years of the Revolution," in Bolshevik Visions, 440–41.

[111] Mally, Culture of the Future, xxviii.

[112] Ibid., 50.

[113] Lynn Mally, Revolutionary Acts: Amateur Theater and the Soviet State, 1917–1938 (Ithaca, NY: Cornell University Press, 2000), 37–44.

punctuality."[114] According to Gor'kii, the presence of so many new workers on the factory floor during wartime further complicated the project of creating a new culture rooted in workers' experience.[115] And as much as Proletkul't benefited from the lack of oversight afforded by the Civil War, the experience of that same war had "significantly muted" its utopianism over the long run. As V. Kirillov explained in 1921 at the second Proletkul't conference, "the severe, cruel facts of life have shown us that those things we hoped and dreamed about in our work are very, very far away."[116]

Whether one chooses to see Proletkul't's cup as half-full or half-empty, there seems little doubt that the movement's efforts had been successful at liberating worker enthusiasm and the proletarian self, or at least some version of one. As a worker explained, her club offered her a welcome break from her "daily labor and cares," and the opportunity to study subjects once unknown to her, such as music and literature. Out of gratitude, she added, "Remember, comrades! Remember that we used to live as oppressed slaves.... Now we understand that we are people like everyone else and that we have even more right to live than others because everything is made by our hands."[117] While Proletkul't's workshops and stages offered workers an unprecedented chance to explore and exercise their creative impulses, its publications offered them a space to express their new commitment to self-realization. "Now, to each one of us is given the possibility of gazing at the light," read a letter by a female garment worker to a journal in 1919. The goal, wrote Proletkul't activists in Kolpino, not far from Petrograd, was to help workers to "feel themselves to be human beings in the most noble and proud meaning of that concept."[118]

As the Civil War was ending in 1920, and peace promised a renewal of vibrant cultural labor, Lenin began to reassess the status of both the workers' club movement and Proletkul't. Personally more inclined towards classics than futurism, he placed Proletkul't under the control of the Commissariat of Enlightenment (Narkompros), marking a first step towards a tightening up of cultural autonomy by the young state. In December 1920, the Central Committee of the Communist Party responded to protests by linking Proletkul't with "anti-Marxist" and "bourgeois" intellectuals, whose aims were different than those of the socialist state. If Proletkul't's demise can be attributed in part to the consolidation of power by the Bolsheviks, Lynn Mally has stressed that Proletkul't activists weakened their own cause because of their difficulties in defining its mission and coming to agreement over issues of cultural authority.

---

[114] Mally, *Culture of the Future*, 191.

[115] Maxim Gorky, *Untimely Thoughts: Essays on Revolution, Culture and the Bolsheviks, 1917–18*, trans. Herman Ermolaev (New Haven: Yale University Press, 1995), 96.

[116] Quoted in Mally, *Culture of the Future*, 255.

[117] Quoted in ibid., 137.

[118] Quotes from Steinberg, *Proletarian Imagination*, 120.

The experience of worker-writers involved in Proletkul't sheds light on the debates that troubled the movement. "Empowered" by the Revolution to write and to create a new proletarian culture, many gave up their former trades and jobs to write full time.[119] By 1920, however, many of the most experienced worker-writers had left Proletkul't, as it became clear that what counted as "proletarian" was not necessarily the same as "created by and for workers."[120] In this sense, they claimed, Proletkul't had "hindered" their "creative capacities" by insisting that they write in an accessible way, addressing issues of importance to workers, in terms they could understand. For them, however, the main issue was not one of accessibility or usefulness to the masses, but rather authority. Dismissing Bogdanov's position that what determines if something is "proletarian" is "not the author but the point of view," they held firm to the idea that the best writing for workers should be done by "an intelligentsia formed among workers themselves," by those who understood the "life-feeling" (zhizneoshchushchenie) of working people.[121] At the same time, Mark Steinberg has observed, their withdrawal from Proletkul't reflected a loss of faith in the movement's mission: "many worker writers, at least implicitly, questioned whether there could, even in theory, be a unified and unambiguous culture of the proletariat." The "insistence on creative freedom" voiced by worker authors at the First Congress of Proletarian Writers in October 1920 similarly indicated "potentially dangerous philosophical doubts about the growing demands for cultural uniformity."[122]

Not unlike the efforts of prerevolutionary cultural activists, the various projects undertaken by Proletkul't and the club movement were far from universal in their reach. For all the creative energy of the first years, in fact, workers' leisure habits had not changed considerably. Although the ban on alcohol was extended beyond the war, for example, drunkenness remained a serious problem in the 1920s, as did the pervasive lack of "cultured" or "respectable" behavior. Workers also continued to thirst for entertainment, not only to create (actively) but to escape (passively) during their free time. As spectators, they still enjoyed "bourgeois" pot-boilers and cabaret-style acts staged by traveling acting troupes, as well as second-rate melodramas about the cruelty of the exploiting classes by the prolific playwright Sof'ia Belaia.[123] As readers, many workers still longed for serial adventure stories, lubok literature, and religious tales or saints' lives. In fact, when state culture-builders attempted to

---

[119] Ibid., 27.

[120] Ibid., 45.

[121] Ibid., 56–62.

[122] Ibid., 61.

[123] John Hatch, "The Formation of Working Class Cultural Institutions during NEP: The Workers' Club Movement in Moscow, 1921–23," *The Carl Beck Papers in Russian and East European Studies*, no. 806 (August 1990): 21; Mally, *Revolutionary Acts*, 36.

replace these more popular genres with "healthier" works more in line with Bolshevik goals, many workers simply stopped reading.[124] Even the Petrograd Komsomol faced resistance when it tried to force workers to study subjects like "material culture" and "political economy" instead of popular activities like art class and choral singing, or to replace dances with "more reasonable entertainment" in their club programs.[125] Not surprisingly, then, when the young state tried to convey "proper" values and tastes to workers through the large network of union-sponsored clubs at the end of the Civil War, it met resistance too.[126]

By 1920, belief in the transformative power of culture and knowledge remained strong, but bitter was the realization that people's habits were difficult to shape and transform, especially in times of great need. As Bolshevik culture-builders realized quickly, one of the most effective ways to influence popular patterns of cultural activity and consumption was to meet workers where they were culturally, as with the successful hybrid genres of the revolutionary adventure story and the *agitka*, which used melodrama in the service of socialist enlightenment.[127] The fact that the Ligovskii People's House continued to offer workers a similar menu of leisure and enlightenment options long after socialists took control of it reflects deep strains of continuity through the revolutionary years—in terms of workers' tastes and desires, as well as the goals and methods of those in charge.[128] While it was one thing to accommodate workers' love of spectacle or cabaret, however, it was quite another to accept their tendency towards abusive behaviors, such as swearing or the ill treatment of women. As Trotskii would remark in 1923, the Revolution did not deserve its name if it could not eliminate behaviors that insulted the personal dignity of another individual.[129]

Religious Culture(s) after 1917

Initially at least, many Christian believers welcomed the Revolution as a new "Easter," especially those who had suffered persecution as "sectarians" under the tsar. The first years of official atheist rule were for them—paradoxically,

---

[124] Stites, *Russian Popular Culture*, 41–42.

[125] Quoted in Isabel A. Tirado, *Young Guard: The Communist Youth League, Petrograd, 1917–1920* (New York: Greenwood Press, 1988), 136.

[126] Steinberg, *Proletarian Imagination*, 53. On this point, see John Hatch, "Hangouts and Hangovers: State, Class and Culture in Moscow's Workers' Club Movement, 1925–1928," *Russian Review* 53, 1 (January 1994): 98.

[127] Elizabeth Wood, *Performing Justice: Agitation Trials in Early Soviet Russia* (Ithaca, NY: Cornell University Press, 2005), 85.

[128] Lindenmeyr, "Building Civil Society," 38.

[129] Leon Trotsky, "The Struggle for Cultured Speech," in *Bolshevik Visions*, 185–86.

perhaps—a time of spiritual and religious awakening. As contemporary observers noted, not unlike the period after 1905, the Revolution of 1917 gave way to "a wider and wider outpouring throughout Russia of the streams and rivers of free-religious, extra-church, and 'sectarian' movements."[130] Although religious belief did not necessarily preclude support for the (atheistic) regime or the goals of socialism, the search for God was fundamentally very personal and individualistic, and in this sense, would serve to contribute to the diversification of worker culture as a whole.

Many Orthodox also celebrated the Revolution in early 1917, grateful for the liberation of their church from tsarist state control, and hopeful that the Revolution would empower them as believers. For example, in mid-1917, as other workers rallied around their unions and clubs, a Petrograd brotherhood of Orthodox workers actively petitioned to democratize the church, to increase lay influence, and to refocus the clergy's attention away from politics towards matters of the spirit.[131] For the most part, however, believers in the working-class areas of Petrograd were silent for most of 1917, content to retreat from the much-contested political sphere in the interest of pursuing—both as individuals and communities—their newly gained religious freedom.

Matters changed dramatically in January 1918, when the new Bolshevik authorities made clear their disregard—indeed, contempt—for the faithful. In the context of the Bolshevik decree separating church and state and the closing of the synodal press, authorities in Petrograd attempted an armed requisitioning of Orthodox valuables at the Aleksandr Nevskii Monastery, allegedly in the interest of raising funds to help the war wounded. To the apparent surprise of the authorities, believers were outraged by this clear violation of sacredness. Almost immediately, hundreds of thousands of Orthodox (many working class) took unprecedented collective political action, emboldened by the patriarch's declaration of anathema against the godless leadership. In addition to organizing a "union to defend the sacred objects" and writing letters of protest, their boldest act of defiance against the government was a massive icon and cross procession on 21 January, during which the faithful sang Easter songs to signify their "resurrection."[132]

During this first of many confrontations to come, the working faithful, including a large proportion of women, made their commitment to their faith, as well as their fear of Bolshevik intentions, very clear. A letter from a semiliterate "Orthodox laywoman" spoke for many others as it bitterly denounced Bolshevik actions, following the forced requisitioning of sacred

---

[130] *Istinnaia svoboda*, no. 1 (April 1920): 2, as quoted in Steinberg, *Proletarian Imagination*, 252.

[131] Protoierei N. Drozdov, "O tserkovnykh lenintsakh," *Izvestiia po Petrogradskoi Eparkhii*," 30, 1 (1917): 11.

[132] "Bratstvo zashchity A. N. Lavra," *Pribavlenie k Tserkovnym Vedomostiam*, no. 5 (7/20 February 1918): 200.

church valuables. Refusing to die a "spiritual death," it began, the Orthodox would refuse to allow the authorities to dispossess them of their rights to their rites, to force them to leave children unbaptized like "dogs," to get married outside the church, or "to be buried like a [piece of] putrefying flesh, closed up in a pit without the blessing of the church."[133] Similar protests sparked by the campaign in 1919 to exhume Orthodox saints also made it clear that, even in the highly politicized context of the Civil War, the Orthodox would not allow the state to challenge their notions of the sacred, and the right of the individual believer to cultivate his or her religious self. Robert Greene's finding that "popular support for the campaign did not always fall in line with neatly demarcated Marxist categories of class," suggests a deepening of the divide between believers and atheists among the working population as a whole.[134]

Bolshevik authorities quickly denounced the January protests as the beginning of the "counterrevolution," and in the months to follow continued their efforts to dismantle and disempower the church as an institution, including the execution of well-known clergy. In part because of popular protests, however, Bolsheviks slowed down the process of de-Christianization for most of the Civil War. A full-blown, organized assault on the faith would not resume until 1921.

Although the Bolsheviks would never waver in their association of religious belief with cultural "backwardness," the first years of Soviet rule were in many ways ambiguous with respect to the future place of religion—and the religious—in the new cultural order. The case of the Petrograd factory worker Ol'ga Bogdanova raises important questions in this regard.[135] Bogdanova was a devoted follower of the popular lay preacher Brother Ioann Churikov; when her atheistic co-workers eventually learned of this, they mocked her and tried to cure her of her "delusion" by forcing her to study political literacy. Bogdanova eventually quit her job, in effect surrendering her class identity instead of her faith. She then happily moved out of the "maelstrom of secular life" to Churikov's agricultural commune outside Petrograd, where she "found satisfaction for the demands of [her] soul."

---

[133] Ibid.

[134] Robert Greene, *Bodies Like Bright Stars: Saints and Relics in Orthodox Russia* (DeKalb: Northern Illinois University Press, 2010), 193. On the exhumation campaign, see chaps. 4–6.

[135] Given that the only record we have of Bogdanova comes from a piece of spiritual testimony she recorded for her religious mentor, Brother Ioann Churikov, in 1926, the kinds of details one might expect to find in a worker's vita are not available—for example, where she was born and in what year, or where she worked, and in what capacity. Her brief autobiography can be found in Gosudarstvennyi muzei istorii religii (GMIR) f. 2 ("Sekta trezvenniki" Bonch-Bruevich, V. D.), op. 17, d. 363, ll. 16–16ob.

Bogdanova's case was unique in some ways, and probably more so in the first years of the Revolution, when religious norms remained highly fluid as before 1917. Nonetheless, the conflict that Bogdanova felt between her spiritual life and the often militant secular culture of the early Soviet period was an indication of things to come, as was her resistance to her co-workers' attempts to force her to conform to socialist norms. Instead of renouncing God, she left work and disengaged from society. In this way, her conscious commitment to her faith, rather than her class or society as a whole, posed questions of everyday life and cultural authority every bit as important as those of the Proletkul'tists. When attempts to educate, threaten, and ridicule the religious failed to convert them, what more could be done? Would individuals like Bogdanova be granted accommodation for their religious beliefs in the new society? Would they be allowed to withdraw from secular life? Instead of unifying on the basis of a notion of proletarian culture, would the working class continue to fracture along cultural lines? If not, what was to be done? By what means, and on whose authority?

Working Women and Gender in the Revolution

In theory, of course, the Revolution promised to empower working women, legally emancipating them not once but twice, as workers and as females. Promising to liberate them from the demands of bourgeois home and family, the Bolsheviks were firm in the belief that women's inequality was primarily the product of economic relations (capitalism) and poor social environment. Through education and labor, and new institutions like communal dining halls and daycare, the proletarian family would embrace both men and women equally. In practice, however, progress towards these goals was understandably slowed by the war and a serious lack of resources. But even more so, the first few years of Soviet rule would reveal the significant extent to which the "women's question" was fundamentally cultural, a question of power and identity, which could not be addressed by bricks and mortar alone. If religion challenged not only the secular basis of proletarian culture, the deeply engrained gender perspectives revealed during the Civil War period called into question the proletariat's ability to build a new culture on the basis of the old. At the very least, it raised the question of timing, and the length of the transition from the old order to the culture of the future.[136]

There is no doubt that some working women took immediate advantage of the new possibilities the Revolution offered them, even assuming new roles on the battlefield. Women were also much more vocal in standing up to oppression, and embracing new expectations of themselves. For all the new

---

[136] On female workers in the early Soviet period, see Wendy Z. Goldman, *Women, the State and Revolution: Soviet Family Policy and Social Life, 1917–1936* (Cambridge: Cambridge University Press, 1993); and Elizabeth A. Wood, *The Baba and the Comrade: Gender and Politics in Revolutionary Russia* (Bloomington: Indiana University Press, 1997).

opportunities and promises, however, evidence of women's emancipation was hard to find in the factory environment. Diane Koenker's study of women in the printing industry (where women comprised 35 percent of the workforce in 1923) convincingly shows that negative attitudes towards female workers did not easily disappear after 1917—in fact, they might have intensified as women's participation in the workforce increased, as did their claims to full equality. Moreover, stereotypes about women's "innate inferiority," based on their comparative lack of physical strength, their inability or unwillingness to learn skills, and their general "disorderliness" not only persisted after the Revolution, but were compounded by accusations that women resisted "calls to consciousness" because "they preferred shopping over factory meetings and gossip over Lenin study circles."[137] Female activists as well as men criticized women for resisting the new order, and frequently described female workers as "a stagnant swamp, impossible to budge."[138]

Anne Gorsuch has found powerful stereotypes based on gender difference at work even among the Komsomol youth—that is, precisely where one might expect more openness to gender equality. The obstacles young women faced when trying to become active on behalf of their class were many: while what "counted" was what workers did in the public sphere, many families still insisted that daughters work at home, and made it difficult for them to attend classes or meetings. Thus young women (wives as well as daughters) were forced to find a workable balance between their duties to family, and their desire to be part of the Communist culture.[139] Young males, they pointed out, were free to do whatever they wanted with their free time. Moreover, they were given greater opportunities to gain worldly experience (for example, through the army, by going to lectures, by doing seasonal work), which prepared them for work in the Komsomol. Female workers' lack of the same experiences left them feeling inadequate and unprepared.

Even those extraordinary young females who managed to overcome the barriers to Komsomol membership had to struggle against a predominately masculine culture. They encountered not only the persistence of patriarchal notions of gender difference—as when their male "comrades" chided them for doing "women's work," which they forced them to do but did not count as "serious"—but also new norms of revolutionary masculinity, rooted in the shared experience of men at war. Young men enjoyed a new bond of "fraternity," from which young women were excluded. At the same time, the ideal of the young Communist as "a warrior and a rebel" was essentially a male model (in spite of the fact that some women had successfully played both roles).[140]

---

[137] Koenker, "Men Against Women," 1441.

[138] Ibid., 1443.

[139] Gorsuch, *Youth in Revolutionary Russia*, 99.

[140] Ibid., 101–02.

Thus the female experience of the Komsomol suggested that the challenge of gender equality did not stem simply from the "backwardness" of women who refused to "budge," nor from the stubborn persistence of patriarchal men (though both remained factors). A new source of their marginalization was tied to the fact that emergent proletarian identity—that is, those beliefs and traits defined as "proper" working-class behaviors—were predominately masculine, and thereby inherently alienating to women. The militant atheism of the new regime reinforced this. And even in the proletarian imagination, women were marginalized. "Proletkult artistic products reinforced this image of the working class and its institutions as an adult male sphere," Lynn Mally has observed, and "women and children were minor, almost missing, themes in the factory-centered thematic of Proletkult creation."[141]

Conclusions

Before and after 1917, workers' cultural practices and aspirations remained highly diverse, and resist simple categorization. As discussed, this was true with respect to every dimension of culture from music and books to thoughts on God and alcohol. Different perspectives and behaviors relating to gender, faith, and education suggested deep divisions within the working-class population as a whole; yet, at the same time, worker cultural identities remained fluid, as workers themselves routinely crossed over these multiple fault-lines. As Laura Phillips has suggested, even as the Revolution deepened the intensity of debates over worker culture because of its widely assumed political importance, it did not dramatically alter workers' tendencies to behave or believe in ways that challenged the dominant discursive categories of "conscious" or "backward."[142] Thus, by the end of the Civil War at least, the proletariat's "unified, harmonious view of the world" anticipated by Proletkul't theorists was nowhere to be found.[143]

To the extent that there was a common trajectory to workers' cultural tendencies in the years 1914–20, it was towards self-improvement through enlightenment, broadly conceived—not in the complete absence of amusement (as political or religious radicals might expect), but as a complement to it. Even more fundamentally, however, the trend was towards greater cultural autonomy, agency, and accessibility, a right both to create and consume culture as workers themselves saw fit. In certain circles before the Revolution, but increasingly after 1917, workers resisted efforts to tell them what was "good" for them. In cultural matters (as in politics), they embraced the idea that the Revolution had given them (not only as workers, women, and religious believers, but as individuals) the right and freedom to create their own lives,

---

[141] Mally, *Culture of the Future*, 176.

[142] Phillips, "Message in a Bottle," 38–39.

[143] Mally, *Culture of the Future*, 8.

turning them overnight from objects of cultural elites into active subjects. While the material conditions of civil war made cultural life difficult, those same conditions allowed for an unprecedented number of grassroots cultural initiatives, empowering workers who wanted to learn, to create, and to believe in their own way. Even as culture-builders in the new Soviet state began to seek greater control over the tastes and impulses of the working masses in the interest of a more unified notion of "proletarian" morality and culture, the conditions of war and revolution reinforced workers' expectations of autonomy and self-realization.

In cultural terms, then, the Civil War was less a war, than a period of peace. And the Revolution as a cultural process was less a transformation than a period of transition and liberation, marked equally by experimentation and conservatism (of tastes, of assumptions). For workers and the Bolshevik state, the war in the cultural realm—over issues of authority, identity, and everyday behavior[144]—still lay in the future.

---

[144] On the struggle for *kul'turnost* under Stalin, see Vadim Volkov, "The Concept of *Kul'turnost'*: Notes on the Stalinist Civilizing Process," in *Stalinism: New Directions*, ed. Sheila Fitzpatrick (London: Routledge, 2000), 210–30.

Fade to Black: The Russian Commercial Film Industry during War and Revolution

Denise J. Youngblood

By the time the lights went out on the Russian "bourgeois" film industry at the end of 1920, as the last boats carrying White Russian refugees left the Black Sea ports, a remarkably rich and original body of work had been created, of which little, sadly, survives. Russian cinema came to maturity during war and revolution and bore the marks of this tumultuous period. Even though Russian producers quickly lost interest in making pictures about the war itself (at least before the mid-1920s; see the chapter by Alexandre Sumpf in book 2 of this volume), their fascination with lurid and apocalyptic themes surely reflected popular unease with the societal destabilization caused by war and then revolution. This chapter shall explore the rise and fall of the Russian commercial film industry before turning to a brief discussion of the phoenix that arose from the ashes of revolution: the Soviet agitational film.

Early History

The era of moving pictures in Russia began on 4 May 1896 in St. Petersburg's Aquarium amusement park, with a screening arranged by Lumière. Until 1908, with the screening of the first film made by a Russian studio—Aleksandr Drankov's *Stenka Razin*—the French dominated the film business in Russia. Despite the rapid and impressive growth of the Russian film industry—in 1913, 129 films were made—foreign films continued to dominate Russian screens before World War I, but after 1908, the French had to compete not only with Russian films, but also with those from Germany, Sweden, Denmark, and Italy.[1]

---

[1] For a complete discussion of the prerevolutionary film industry, see Denise J. Youngblood, *The Magic Mirror: Moviemaking in Russia, 1908–1918* (Madison: University of Wisconsin Press, 1999). In Russian, see S. S. Ginzburg, *Kinematografiia dorevoliutsionnoi Rossii* (Moscow: Iskusstvo, 1963).

Russian Culture in War and Revolution, 1914–22, Book 1: Popular Culture, the Arts, and Institutions. Murray Frame, Boris Kolonitskii, Steven G. Marks, and Melissa K. Stockdale, eds. Bloomington, IN: Slavica Publishers, 2014, 85–99.

As was the case elsewhere in Europe, native Russian production sky-rocketed after the outbreak of war in 1914.[2] German imports were banned (although they were sometimes retitled to disguise their origin),[3] and other foreign films became increasingly rare as the war deepened and land routes became difficult to traverse.[4] As a result, Russian production nearly doubled in the period 1913–14, from 129 to 230 titles, and by 1916, to 500 titles annually. (More than 1,200 native films were released during the war.)[5] Russia's war-time movie business was, therefore, an island of prosperity in the midst of a national economy in collapse. Movie theaters were packed; it is possible, as Hubertus Jahn suggests, that the wartime ban on alcohol helped draw people to the movies.[6] However, there were signs of trouble despite the boom. During the war, taxes on moving pictures increased dramatically as the government frantically searched for new sources of revenue.[7] Some theaters were requisitioned as hospitals, and there were restrictions on the use of electricity at night.[8] Fuel for heating the theaters was in short supply, as was film stock. Speculators and black marketeers flourished.[9]

Exhibition

Given the explosion of the film industry after the war began, it is not surprising that exhibition sites increased as well. In 1913, the empire had counted 1,500 movie theaters, but by 1916, there were about 4,000 movie theaters in

---

[2] See, e.g., Ramona Curry, "How Early German Film Stars Helped Sell the War(es)," in *Film and the First World War,* ed. Karel Dibbets and Bert Hogenkamp (Amsterdam: Amsterdam University Press, 1995), 143.

[3] Hubertus F. Jahn, *Patriotic Culture in Russia during World War I* (Ithaca, NY: Cornell University Press, 1995), 152.

[4] In Germany, the ban on French films meant that there were actual shortages on German screens; see Rainer Rother, "The Experience of the First World War and German Film," in *The First World War and Popular Cinema: 1914 to the Present,* ed. Michael Paris (Edinburgh: Edinburgh University Press, 1999), 219.

[5] N. A. Lebedev, *Ocherk istorii kino SSSR: Nemoe kino,* 2nd ed. (Moscow: Iskusstvo, 1965), 49.

[6] Jahn, *Patriotic Culture,* 152. However, the same was true in European countries that did not ban alcohol. See, e.g., Nicholas Hiley, "The British Cinema Auditorium," in *Film and the First World War,* 160.

[7] Jahn, *Patriotic Culture,* 152. Other European governments also found movie theater taxes especially lucrative. See, e.g., Hiley, "The British Cinema Auditorium," 166.

[8] Jahn, *Patriotic Culture,* 153.

[9] V. R. Gardin, *Vospominaniia,* 1: *1912–1921* (Moscow: Goskinoizdat, 1949), 112.

Russia serving over two million viewers daily.[10] In 1916, Petrograd had 229 movie theaters (up from 130 in 1913), with 15 on Nevskii Prospekt alone. By this time the cinema outsold the stage 10 to 1, a significant shift in audience preferences.[11]

Before the war, movie-theater programs had followed a format laid out in the trade journals, generally consisting of five titles lasting no more than an hour, in the belief that audience attention spans were short. During the war, however, as audience sophistication grew, the five-film format was abandoned in favor of one full-length contemporary melodrama (60–90 minutes) accompanied by a newsreel and a short comedy. With the growth of a respectable urban audience that viewed an evening at the movies as a special event, theater owners realized the importance of investing in amenities. By the outbreak of the war in 1914, the number of large theaters (seating at least 1,000) was on the rise. These theaters advertised their ability to separate social classes on the basis of space and ticket price. Other amenities were important, too, especially music. As competition among the big city theaters increased during the war, orchestras became more common, both to accompany the films and to entertain during the intermissions. Heating, ventilation, and electrical lights were also promoted, along with the quality of food and drink at the buffet, café, or restaurant connected to the theater. As the movie-going experience became more luxurious, there was little to indicate that there was a war going on, which was precisely the point.

Patriotic Films

One of the most interesting aspects of Russian cinema during the Great War is the relative absence of patriotic films from the repertory after 1914, particularly as the war dragged on with little success and faith in the government of Nicholas II plummeted.[12] Initially Russian studios responded with the same degree of cheerful jingoism as did the studios of the other combatant nations. Filmmakers were at first pleased to have new subject matter—and new villains. For the first time, not only was it politically safe to make movies about a modern war, it was encouraged as a patriotic duty.

---

[10] N. A. Lebedev, *Ocherk istorii kino SSSR*, 1: *Nemoe kino* (Moscow: Goskinoizdat, 1947), 5. In Britain, by way of comparison, there were 5,400 in 1915. See Hiley, "The British Cinema Auditorium," 160.

[11] Ginzburg, *Kinematografiia dorevoliutsionnoi Rossii*, 46.

[12] In France, disillusionment with the war was apparent somewhat later, by 1916. See Pierre Sorlin, "The Silent Memory," in *The First World War and Popular Cinema*, 120. Hollywood was never particularly interested in war as a theme, even after the U.S. entered the conflict in 1917; see Leslie Midkiff DeBauche, "The United States Film Industry and World War One," in *The First World War and Popular Cinema*, 140–41.

From 1 August 1914 to the end of the year, nearly half the films made (50 of 103) concerned the war, but two years later, in 1916, the figure was only 13 titles out of 500.[13] In 1917, there was one, which focused on the war only in part.[14] Part of this shift can be attributed to moviegoers' understandable desire for escapist entertainment as the brutal war dragged on. However, it probably also illustrates the public's disaffection from the tsarist government and the disastrous war effort—as well as the government's difficulty in organizing cinema propaganda effectively (the impact of which the Bolsheviks surely noted).

The failure of the government's efforts at political persuasion were not, of course, limited to cinema. But the government's inability to mine cinema's propaganda potential is particularly noteworthy, given the tsar's well-known personal interest in film and photography. In fact, Nicholas II seriously considered nationalizing all film production to create a state cinema that, unlike Western cinema, would be firmly situated on moral ground.[15]

However, the sole government-funded studio was run by the nominally independent Skobelev Committee, which was founded during the Russo-Japanese War.[16] Until December 1916, the Committee held a monopoly on footage from the frontlines.[17] Even so, battle scenes in its newsreels were almost always staged.[18] Its first World War I film—*Holy War*, compiled from prewar clips—appeared on 30 August 1914.[19] In 1914–15, the Committee produced nine series of Russian war chronicles, several special episodes not part of any series, and a major documentary titled *Under the Russian Banner*.[20] Its chief production in 1916 was another feature documentary titled *The Second*

---

[13] Ginzburg, *Kinematografiia dorevoliutsionnoi Rossii*, 191–92.

[14] Evgenii Bauer's *The Revolutionary*, discussed below.

[15] Viktor Listov, "Early Soviet Cinema: The Spontaneous and the Planned, 1917–1924," trans. and ed. Richard Taylor and Derek Spring, *Historical Journal of Film, Radio, and Television* 11, no. 2 (1991): 22.

[16] Jahn, *Patriotic Culture*, 40. Also see Peter Kenez's discussion of the Skobelev Committee in *The Birth of the Propaganda State: Soviet Methods of Mass Mobilization, 1917–1929* (Cambridge: Cambridge University Press, 1985), 105.

[17] Kate Betz, "As Tycoons Die: Class Struggle and Censorship in the Russian Cinema, 1917–1921," in *Art, Society, Revolution: Russia, 1917–1921*, ed. Nils Ake Nilsson (Stockholm: Almqvist and Wiksell, 1979), 209.

[18] Jahn, *Patriotic Culture*, 155. The only genuine war footage shown was the taking of Przemysl in Galicia and the fall of Erzurum, Turkey (156).

[19] Ginzburg, *Kinematografiia dorevoliutsionnoi Rossii*, 178.

[20] Ibid., 182.

Fatherland War, 1914–1915.[21] Under the Provisional Government, the Committee's contributions to the war effort declined dramatically, and it began producing newsreels on "social" and "educational" themes.[22] Commercial producers were not pleased to have state-financed competition from the Skobelev Committee, but it quickly became clear that they had no reason to worry. The state fared no better at filmmaking than it did at war-making.

Russian producers made films on patriotic themes when they felt so inclined, and only as long as war movies would attract paying customers to the theaters. Studio head Aleksandr Khanzhonkov, Russia's most successful producer, recounted in his memoirs that in October 1914, he "had to give in" to pressure to make a movie supporting the war effort, despite the fact that he was "not a supporter of tendentious war films, lacking in art and unconvincing."[23] The result was *King, Law, and Freedom*, which was based on a play by the popular writer Leonid Andreev. This movie was better received critically than the play itself, in part because Khanzhonkov re-enacted a dramatic flooding of the fields of Belgium, which obviously could not be re-created on a stage in a traditional theater.[24]

Few of the patriotic films made during the Great War survive. According to Jahn, who has done the most research on patriotic propaganda during the war, through fall 1914, all of the patriotic films were in the *lubok* style, and "vulgarity, incoherence, and cheap laughs" reigned.[25] After that, the focus was on love stories, espionage, treason, and films on Orientalist themes.[26] They were produced for their entertainment value, and patriotism was an afterthought.

Based on their titles and descriptions, we can imagine that they were, as Khanzhonkov suggested, "lacking in art and unconvincing." As Peter Kenez dryly notes, "The Germans in Russian films committed extraordinary atrocities before they had time to do so in real life."[27] For example, the film *By Fire and Blood* (1914) also went by the more descriptive title *The Atrocities of the German Major Preisker*. The best of the extant specimens of wartime patriotism

---

[21] Ibid., 183. In Britain, interest in the feature-length documentary quickly faded after the surprising success of *The Battle of the Somme*. See Nicholas Reeves, "Official British Film Propaganda," in *The First World War and Popular Cinema*, 31.

[22] Betz, "As Tycoons Die," 209.

[23] Quoted in Yuri Tsivian et al., *Silent Witnesses: Russian Films, 1909–1919* (Pordenone: Edizione Biblioteca dell'Imagine; London: BFI Publishing, 1989), 224.

[24] Tsivian et al., *Silent Witnesses*, 224.

[25] Jahn, *Patriotic Culture*, 159, 168.

[26] Ibid., 160–63.

[27] Peter Kenez, "Russian Patriotic Films," in *Film and the First World War*, 40. ·

in cinema are the over-the-top melodrama *Glory to Us—Death to the Enemy* (1914) and the charming "trick" film *The Lily of Belgium* (1915).

Glory to Us—Death to the Enemy, directed by one of early Russian cinema's most gifted filmmakers, Evgenii Bauer, falls below the aesthetic and dramatic standards of his finest work. It is, however, noteworthy in prefiguring the violent woman of the Soviet war film. The picture starred Dora Chitorina as a woman who joins the Red Cross to avenge herself upon the Germans for the death of her husband, played by the Russian screen idol Ivan Mozzhukhin. The idea of a nurse as a murderous avenging angel might strike those familiar with the conventions of American cinema of this period as strange, but the strong, independent, even murderous heroine was a recurring motif in prerevolutionary Russian film melodramas, the genre in which Bauer excelled.

The Lily of Belgium provides a sharp contrast. This propaganda film, sponsored by the Skobelev Committee, renders the "rape of Belgium" suitable for viewing by children and the tenderhearted, through the magic of Władysław Starewicz's stop-motion animation of insect puppets. In *Lily*, the rape of Belgium is portrayed through a battle between gentle winged insects and loathsome, ugly German beetles. A single battered lily escapes the treacherous onslaught of the murderous beetles.

By 1916, however, producers no longer felt that they "had to give in" to any demands the government might make to produce patriotic films. The audience ruled, and audiences were apparently no longer feeling particularly patriotic. Studios returned to the production of the contemporary melodramas, historical costume dramas and literary adaptations, often on apocalyptic themes, that drew spectators to the movies in droves.[28]

The "Boulevard" Melodramas

At least three versions of *War and Peace* appeared during the war, but most of the production from 1915 on was the "boulevard" melodrama, more often than not sizzlingly erotic and violent, showing a society in extreme disarray, particularly in terms of its gender relations. Bauer's films are the exemplar of this trend. *Children of the Age* (1915) is a chilling portrait of sexual guile, exploitation, and violence that ends in a man's suicide after his wife is raped by a wealthy banker. *Daydreams* (also 1915), which focuses on a man's obsessive love for his dead wife, smacks of necrophilia, which concerned film critics of the time. Viktor turns an actress, Tina, into a mannequin of his late wife, then strangles the soubrette with a long shank of his wife's hair, lovingly preserved in a glass box, when she mocks him.

These themes continued into 1916, with Bauer's outstanding films *A Life for a Life* and *The Dying Swan*. *A Life for a Life* stars the queen of the Russian

---

[28] The melodrama was the favorite genre everywhere in Europe during the war. See, e.g., Marguerite Engberg, "Nordisk in Denmark," in *Film and the First World War*, 46.

screen, Vera Kholodnaia, as a woman married to one man, but having a torrid affair with her adoptive sister's husband, an affair that began before their respective marriages. This affair ends in murder, as the factory owner mother kills her daughter's faithless husband. It is unclear, however, whether she does this because of his sexual misconduct or his financial misconduct, which threatens to bring ruin upon the family. One suspects it is the latter. Notably, Kholodnaia's character, Nata, is not punished for her sins, an ending that is typical for Russian films of this genre

The Dying Swan is even more remarkable for its portrayal of a society in decline, as epitomized by its fraught gender relations. The well-known ballerina Vera Karalli (Coralli) stars as Gisella, a mute ballerina who is caught between three men: her loving and overprotective father, her handsome and tender lover, and a deranged artist. After seeing Gisella dance her signature role, the artist, Count Glinskii, who has been suffering from painter's block, is inspired to paint the ballerina in her final pose as the Dying Swan as a way of capturing death on canvas. Everyone save Gisella is fearful of Glinskii's increasing obsession. One day, after her lover Viktor has proposed to her, she arrives at Glinskii's for her sitting in a light-hearted mood. Joy has transformed her. Outraged, Glinskii calmly breaks her neck, returns her to the unnatural pose of the Dying Swan, and continues painting. Perhaps Bauer punishes Gisella as an example of the "new woman." Despite her handicap, she is markedly independent in all her activities, and of course, has a career. She even wears a wristwatch, another sign of her liberation from stuffy conventions.

1917

Movie producers rejoiced when the autocracy fell in February 1917. The overthrow of the Romanov dynasty in February ended media censorship, which naturally pleased filmmakers. Their joy was, however, short-lived. It soon became clear that the democratic Provisional Government, which was determined to continue the war, could not provide political, economic, or social stability to a country on the brink of total anarchy. Film production dropped calamitously.

After the February Revolution, only studio head Iosif Ermol'ev seemed to recognize the danger the mounting chaos presented to the film industry. He formed the first producers' association in March 1917, and distributors, creative workers, theater owners, projectionists, and the trade press quickly followed, all forming their own association in the spring and summer. Strikes broke out, and the tensions between the owners and the workers were high. Even the state-run Skobelev Committee was subject to riots and strikes.[29]

Yet films continued to be made in the turbulent months from February to October 1917, the majority of which were melodramas. The most notable was

---

[29] Betz, "As Tycoons Die," 208.

Iakov Protazanov's *Father Sergius* (which was not, however, released until 1918 due to the temporary closure of movie theaters after the October Revolution). Protazanov had long wanted to adapt Tolstoi's story of a naïve and self-centered young officer who becomes a monk and faith healer but could not until the censorship lifted. (The story had been considered too incendiary to film because of the highly negative portrayal of Nicholas I and Father Sergius's inability to control his sexual desires.) The picture earned its place in film history primarily due to Mozzhukhin's brilliant portrayal of the title character, whose sexual obsession ultimately proves to be his salvation. Despite Sergius's ambitious, narcissistic attempts to become the holiest of all monks, he cannot escape his sexual impulses and memories of his beautiful fiancée, who had been the tsar's mistress, which Protazanov renders in flashbacks. The film's most famous scene, when the glamorous and frivolous Madame Makovkina (played by Mozzhukhin's real-life wife, Natal'ia Lisenko) attempts to seduce Sergius, is deeply erotic. Although she fails, Sergius's battle with fleshly desires is not over. Twenty years later, his reputation as a faithhealer brings him into contact with a merchant's lascivious, mentally unbalanced daughter. Sergius rapes her (or in a charitable interpretation, is seduced by her). As he is looking for an axe to murder her, he is stopped by a fellow monk who offers to chop wood for him. This is Sergius's epiphany. He leaves the monastery to become a pilgrim. Eventually he is arrested and deported to Siberia, where he lives out his days as a truly humble man.

There were also films rushed into production between February and October 1917 to capture revolutionary themes, like Drankov's *Grandmother of the Russian Revolution*, about Ekaterina Breshko-Breshkovskaia, which celebrated the Socialist Revolutionary leader in a hagiographical portrait. A much better film was Bauer's *The Revolutionary*, which was strongly pro-war and anti-Bolshevik in its orientation. The film begins in 1907, with the arrest of the fictitious revolutionary known as "Granddad." After ten years of exile in Siberia, Granddad returns home after the February Revolution to find that his son is a defeatist and a Marxist. Believing that "the salvation of the revolution lies in a victorious end to the war," Granddad persuades his son and his son's comrades to abandon their evil ways; father and son go off together to win the war. Although *The Revolutionary* was of higher quality than most "revolutionary" films, it was still well below the standards of Bauer's finest work.

But Protazanov's full-scale, two-part blockbuster *Satan Triumphant* (1917) was in a class by itself, and for Soviet film historians epitomized the "decadence" of commercial cinema and the marked turn toward apocalypticism. It also reflected late imperial Russia's fascination with Satanism.[30] In this film, the great Mozzhukhin, plays both a fire-and-brimstone pastor and his son Sandro. A lost traveler arrives, and it quickly becomes clear that he is Satan. Sex-

---

[30] See Kristi A. Groberg, "The Shade of Lucifer's Dark Wing: Satanism in Silver Age Russia," in *The Occult in Russian and Soviet Culture*, ed. Bernice Glatzer Rosenthal (Ithaca, NY: Cornell University Press, 1997), 99–133.

ual strife threatens to destroy the household, as the pastor sleeps with his married sister-in-law. The child that is born from this unholy union, Sandro, becomes a famous pianist, eventually selling his soul to the devil. All manner of shocking behavior, including sexual misadventure, results. Although critics were divided on the merits of this film, Mozzhukhin received kudos for his acting, one critic describing him as "virtually the most exciting screen actor in the Moscow pléiade."[31]

The industry faced other problems in addition to the lack of quality films. By the fall of 1917, shortages of electricity left theaters dark most of the week, and the Bolsheviks closed them altogether in November and December. Problems with the supply of electricity for movie theaters continued into 1918.[32] After the capital moved from Petrograd to Moscow in 1918, producers were particularly alarmed. In summer 1918, fearing possible nationalization as the "sword of Damocles,"[33] production companies in Moscow, the center of the film industry, began evacuating their studios and personnel to the Crimea, where the counterrevolutionary White forces were marshaling strength. By late 1919, it was obvious to most filmmakers that the Reds would win the Civil War, and they began to leave the country in droves. As the fighting wound down in 1920, most of the Russian film industry's leaders were in foreign exile, primarily in Paris, Berlin, and Prague. A few even made their way to Hollywood. Some, like Protazanov, eventually returned to Soviet Russia and reestablished their careers.[34]

Commercial Cinema after the October Revolution

It is commonly supposed that only Bolshevik-sponsored organizations made films after October 1917. In fact, private studios continued producing, making 352 films in the period 1917–21, with most appearing 1918–19.[35] This was far from the 500 films produced in 1916 alone, but considering the political and economic tumult, the number is impressive. The Bolsheviks were concerned enough to restore film censorship in June 1918.[36]

---

[31] Tsivian et al., *Silent Witnesses*, 422–26.

[32] Richard Taylor, "Agitation, Propaganda, and the Cinema: The Search for New Solutions," in *Art, Society, Revolution*, 241.

[33] Taylor, "Agitation, Propaganda, and the Cinema," 238.

[34] See Denise J. Youngblood, *Movies for the Masses: Cinema and Soviet Society in the 1920s* (Cambridge: Cambridge University Press, 1992), chap. 6.

[35] See *Sovetskie khudozhestvennye fil'my: Annotirovannyi katalog* (Moscow: Iskusstvo, 1966), 3: 248–306; 42 of these are extant either in whole or in part.

[36] Betz, "As Tycoons Die," 217. Taylor notes that some censorship existed in Moscow as early as March 1918 ("Agitation, Propaganda, and the Cinema," 242). Prerevolutionary censorship in cinema was haphazard; see Kenez, "Russian Patriotic Films," 38.

From 1918 to 1921 Bolshevik film censorship broke down into four categories: 1. Recommended and approved (only 8 films fell into this category); 2. Allowed into distribution (35); 3. Allowed but not recommended (89); 4. Banned (32).[37] Interestingly, most of the Satan films and erotic melodramas were not banned but fell into categories 2 and 3; examples are *Aziade*, a Sheik melodrama, and the Satan film *Scherzo of the Devil*.[38] Most of the films that were banned outright were prohibited for moral, not political, reasons, particularly as pornography. *Little White Slaves* and *Ladies of the Sanatorium* are examples of "pornographic" banned titles. Only 6 of the 32 banned films were prohibited for political content; an example is *Power to the People*, which purportedly presented Socialist Revolutionary and Menshevik views on the Constituent Assembly.[39]

The problem was not, therefore, that the studios were making explicitly anti-Bolshevik films. In fact, they continued to produce sensational melodramas of four basic kinds: the Satan genre, the "God Seekers" genre (about the occult, mysticism, and the sexual shenanigans of monks and nuns), historical pictures, and the sex-and-suicide melodrama.[40]

However, the best of the post-October films from the commercial cinema focused on sex and suicide, and the greatest of these is Protazanov's *Little Ellie* (1918), a psychological melodrama about a child rapist-murderer, starring Mozzhukhin as the perpetrator. This film took the preoccupation of Russian cinema with sexual degradation to a new extreme, but was also an extremely intricate work, constructed with multiple flashbacks. Mozzhukhin plays Norton, an unnamed town's mayor, who in the opening scene is examining his bruised arm and torn shirtsleeve.

Next we learn that a young girl has been found murdered in the woods. This is Ellie, the little sister of Clara, soon to become Norton's fiancée. Her murder remains unsolved, but Norton, stricken with panic attacks, starts acting very strangely. He is disturbed enough to decide to commit suicide, but as he sits down to write the note, he writes a confession to the murder instead. Surprised by Clara as he is writing, he manages to hide the incriminating letter.

After that his psychological condition is in a downward spiral. Here Protazanov inserts flashbacks, first of the history of his relationship with Clara and Ellie; second, the image of the dead child lying on the path; and third, the chilling recreation of the crime. Here Protazanov and Mozzhukhin penetrate the mind of a pedophile. He had, after all, turned to Ellie for "love," when he believed that Clara was not responding to his affections. The little girl was

---

[37] Betz, "As Tycoons Die," 219.

[38] Ibid., 220–21.

[39] Ibid., 221–22.

[40] Ibid., 212–13.

flattered by his grown-up attentions and in Norton's mind flirted with him at a party he escorted her to. On the day of the murder, Norton had been drinking heavily. He meets Ellie on her way home from school and persuades her to take a path through the woods. He begins kissing and caressing her; she bites his arm and breaks away. As he chases the terrified child, he is caught in blurred closeup, the camera tracking him as he runs. Norton tells Clara that Ellie's death was an accident, that she tripped and fell while running away from him. Clara goes to the police station with the confession, but changes her mind and burns it. Norton commits suicide.

Rather than focusing on the victim, *Little Ellie* provides a chilling psychological portrait of the perpetrator. It is sensational, but not exploitative and still has the power to shock nearly a century later. One *Cinema Gazette* reviewer claimed it to be a conventional melodrama without "interesting and vivid moments," although he did note that the final flashback produced an "unpleasant sensation" of "excessive tension and intensity."[41]

Another noteworthy film, which was a major box office success in 1918, was Petr Chardynin's *Be Still, Sadness, Be Still*.[42] The Soviet-era print that I viewed claimed that the film promoted the "values of the bourgeoisie," and indeed, it epitomizes the notion that anything can be bought and sold, even a human being, and that the most important things in life are surface appearance and material possessions. The inimitable Kholodnaia plays Pola, a circus performer, whose partner, the clown Loria (played by the director himself), becomes crippled in a drunken accident, leaving the pair destitute. "Salvation" comes in the form of four gentlemen (including the matinee idols Vladimir Maksimov and Vitold Polonskii) who invite Pola to perform at their private bachelor party. They try to buy her from Loria; outraged, Pola refuses and returns to the streets, but when Pola and Loria are truly destitute she offers herself to Volyntsev, an artist (Maksimov), leaving Loria to sink ever deeper into poverty. Pola quickly tires of Volyntsev, and he of her, so that he tries to sell her to Telepnev, a younger rival (Polonskii). Angered, she turns pridefully to yet another man in this incestuous circle. When her new lover loses an astronomical sum gambling he plans to rob his friend Telepnev, with Pola serving as a decoy. However, the robbery plot fails, and her lover commits suicide with a revolver he has stolen from Pola's dresser. A more optimistic conclusion would have been out of place in a society in the midst of civil war.

Coda: The Early Years of Soviet Filmmaking

As the commercial film industry continued to churn out lurid melodramas, the Bolsheviks began making their first films, called agit-films. The difference

---

[41] Tsivian et al., *Silent Witnesses*, 466–70.

[42] Neia Zorkaia, "Les stars du muet," in *Le cinéma russe avant la révolution* (Paris: Editions Ramsay, 1989), 41.

between the quality and topics of Soviet cinema with Russian cinema was, not surprisingly, striking. Agit-films were short, simple agitational movies designed to propagandize Bolshevik programs and policies, primarily during the period of the Russian Civil War (1918–21), when it was the dominant cinema form. The length of the typical agit-film was 250–700 meters, or less than 30 minutes running time. It was feared that longer propaganda films would bore and thereby alienate audiences, which consisted of city-dwellers, peasants, soldiers, and especially children.

Another reason for the short running time of the films was the shortage of film stock.[43] Although the Bolsheviks immediately seized control of the studios of the Skobelev Committee, the amount of film stock available legally through an agreement with Kodak, and illegally through the black market, fell far below the demand. The Bolsheviks were so desperate for film stock that they sought to reuse it through a re-emulsification process. Re-emulsified stock was, however, of low quality.

Because most movie theaters were closed for much of the Civil War, agit-films were shown at agit-points, which were stationary exhibition centers usually set up at train stations, special political houses, traveling agit-trains,[44] and even agit-steamboats. Agit-trains and agit-steamers were extremely important given the shortage of film copies; sometimes only one or two copies were made, which made the traveling shows even more necessary. All exhibition sites were colorfully decorated with political paintings (often by avant-garde artists like Maiakovskii and El [Lazar'] Lisitskii, although realist paintings came along later) and political slogans. These were multimedia agitational venues for propagandizing the citizenry by all available means, not just cinema. For example, the political houses offered theater, music, books and pamphlets, education, and even food, as well as cinema.

Of English-language scholars, Richard Taylor has written the most about the agit-trains. His research has shown that the agit-trains traveled around the country, including the fronts in Ukraine and Siberia. Indeed, the first agit-train tour was to the Eastern Front, to Kazan', where troop morale was considered to be especially low. A tour of duty was typically three months, with two-day stops at each location. The Party Central Committee assigned specially trained agitators, the most famous of whom were M. I. Kalinin on the agit-train *October Revolution* and V. M. Molotov on the agit-steamer *Red Star*, to discuss the films with the audience. Political instructors from the various commissariats were also on board the agit-trains. Audiences were impressive considering the circumstances and the crude qualities of the films: 1.3 million in 753 meetings in 1919 alone.[45]

---

[43] Taylor, "Agitation, Propaganda, and the Cinema," 245.

[44] See ibid., 248–53, for a detailed discussion of the agit-trains.

[45] Richard Taylor, *The Politics of the Soviet Cinema, 1917–1929* (Cambridge: Cambridge University Press, 1979).

The agit-films were always the major draw at political meetings, especially in the countryside, which had been poorly served by the prerevolutionary film industry. The films were the first item of business at a meeting, followed by propaganda and other activities for the literacy and agricultural campaigns. People who enjoyed the films, and the little evidence available indicated that many did, would stay for the rest of the program and become involved with the activities.[46]

Over the course of the Civil War, based on my analysis of the annotated catalogue *Soviet Fiction Films,* 69 agit-films were made (out of a total of 104 films), comprising the majority of Soviet film production.[47] The height of agit-film production was 1919, when 39 agit-films were produced. There were 3 in 1918, 20 in 1920, and 7 in 1921. Most agit-films came from the studios of the Moscow and Petrograd Cinema Committees, sometimes acting in partnership with one of the new collective studios, like Neptune and Rus'. Shortly after cinema was nationalized in August 1919, the Moscow Cinema Committee became a section of the Commissariat of Enlightenment and was known by the acronym VFKO, the All-Russian Photo-Cinema Section. VFKO took over production of agit-films, some of which were made in its newly established film school.[48] Often the directors were well-known figures from the tsarist cinema or soon to become well-known in Soviet cinema, like Vladimir Gardin, Lev Kuleshov, Aleksandr Ivanovskii, Aleksandr Panteleev, Ivan Perestiani, Aleksandr Razumnyi, and Iurii Zheliabuzhskii. Script-writers included Demian Bednyi, Aleksandr Serafimovich, and Anatolii Lunacharskii. Dziga Vertov worked as an editor.

Little has been written about the agit-films themselves, probably because only 10 have survived, some of them missing a reel or two.[49] All of the surviving films, except for *Overcrowding,* are military-themed or have the Civil War as an explicit backdrop. Indeed, in 1919, arguably the most crucial year of the Civil War and the height of the agit-film, 25 of the 39 agit-films made were on military themes.[50] In addition to military themes, agit-films promoted campaigns against religion, illiteracy, and various social conditions, like hunger or the seizure of private property.

---

[46] Taylor, *Politics of the Soviet Cinema,* 58–59.

[47] *Sovetskie khudozhestvennye fil'my: Annotirovannyi katalog,* 1: *Nemye filmy (1918–1935)* (Moscow: Iskusstvo, 1961).

[48] Taylor, *Politics of the Soviet Cinema,* 49–50.

[49] Based on my analysis of *Sovetskie khudozhestvennye fil'my,* vol. 1, these are: *Overcrowding* (1918), *Deserters* (1919), *For the Red Banner* (1919), *Smelchak* (1919), *Taras's Dream* (1919), *Comrade Abraham* (1919), *Two Poles* (1920), *Children Teach the Elderly* (1920), *On Peasant Land* (1920), *Hunger* (1921).

[50] Based on my analysis of *Sovetskie khudozhestvennye fil'my.*

Despite the fact that only a very few titles have survived, the catalogue *Soviet Fiction Films* provides brief plot descriptions for almost all of the agit-films that were made, based on archival materials.[51] What distinguishes the true agit-film from the "cinema poster" is that the agit-film actually tells a story, however crude and simplistic. As Peter Kenez has pointed out, the agit-films can be divided into different genres. A few were comedies, like *The Frightened Bourgeois* (1919), in which an insomniac capitalist finds his condition cured by hard labor. Most, however, were melodramas, like *Father and Son* (1919), in which a captured Red Army soldier is guarded by his father, whom the Whites had drafted; the son persuades his father of the rightness of the Red cause and induces him to free all the Red prisoners and join the Red Army. *Peace to the Shack and War to the Palace* (1919) is another example of the Red Army film. A World War I veteran, a poor peasant, returning to see his landlord living in wealth and comfort, joins the Red Army to fight for the Bolshevik cause. This film was part of the Red Army recruitment campaign in Ukraine. *Comrade Abraham* (1919) appeals to Jews to join the Red Army by focusing on the travails of a man who has suffered through pogroms and World War I.[52]

The popularity of military agit-films notwithstanding, *Overcrowding* (1918) is the most famous of the agit-films, a true prestige project. The film script was written by the Commissar of Enlightenment, Lunacharskii; the movie begins with a shot of Lunacharskii grinning boyishly at the camera. It is the story of a pampered professor, played by VFKO head D. I. Leshchenko, who is forced to give up some rooms in his large house to workers. After a rough start, all turns out well. The professor begins teaching science at a workers' club, and his son falls in love with a proletarian girl who has moved in with them. *Overcrowding* is a perfect example of an agit-film, for it has a rudimentary plot, a simple message supporting a regime goal, and limited character development. Its poster shows the professor standing beside a worker, their arms draped over each other's shoulders, with the slogan "Workers of the World Unite!" above them. The cinematic style can be charitably described as primitive; despite the simplicity of the plot and the limited cast of characters, the actions and relationships of the characters are often confusing. A political instructor or agitator really would have been necessary to explain the film.

The primitiveness of the production sharply divides the agit-films from the fiction films of the rest of the 1920s—and from the Russian commercial cinema that preceded it. As Richard Taylor has noted, however, the filmic style of the agit-films became the foundation for important filmmakers like Sergei Eisenstein, Kuleshov (who taught at the film school), Vsevolod Pudovkin, Esfir'

---

[51] See also N. M. Iezuitov, "Agitki epokhi grazhdanskoi voiny," *Iskusstvo kino*, no. 5 (May 1940): 47–51.

[52] Peter Kenez, *Cinema and Soviet Society, 1917–1953* (Cambridge: Cambridge University Press, 1992), 34–35.

Shub, and Dziga Vertov. Especially important to the success of the agit-films were their concise and dynamic style, achieved by skillful editing. He writes, "Without the challenge of the Civil War it is unlikely that the Soviet cinema would have developed the forceful, distinctive and revolutionary visual style of the 1920s..."[53] The Civil War agit-films also influenced the "fighting cinema anthologies" of World War II.[54]

○3 ○○

After 1914, Russian commercial cinema during the war reflected the deep-seated anxieties of a society in crisis. Women as well as men are depicted as sexual predators, and the typical male in prerevolutionary Russian cinema was weak, obsessed, or downright deranged. Women suck men dry in classic "vamp" fashion out of anger and revenge at their ill treatment—or even kill them. Most of the male sexual predators are upper-class, exploiting maids and clerks, but also women of their own class, an unpardonable transgression. Punishment for sins is rare with the exception of self-punishment in the form of suicide. As we have seen, the trajectory of commercial filmmaking did not alter substantially with the coming of revolution in 1917 and continued through 1920, when many of the most influential members of the industry had emigrated.

The agitational films of early Soviet cinema represent a sharp rupture with the Russian heritage. The urbane sophistication of commercial movies gave way to crudely political films that were as poorly made as they were openly propagandistic. Not until the mid-1920s would "boulevard" melodramas and comedies return to Soviet screens, under the influence of the NEP, as some directors began to return to their roots in the prerevolutionary cinema.

---

[53] Taylor, *Politics of the Soviet Cinema*, 63.

[54] Kenez, *Cinema and Soviet Society*, 36.

Hypnosis in Russian Popular Culture during the Era of War and Revolution

Julia Mannherz

Hypnosis was a hot topic in Russian mainstream publishing throughout the era of war and revolution, but it was never a simple phenomenon which allowed contemporaries to agree in their assessments of it. Precisely because of its contentious character, the technique lends itself for an analysis of continuity and change across the political caesuras of 1914, 1917, and 1921. Throughout the period, hypnosis was advertised as a practice that offered entertainment; it was also recommended as a means of personal self-advancement; and furthermore it was part of scientific enquiry and medical practice. Doctors championed hypnosis as an infallible treatment, i.e., as a method that worked reliably and which was able to heal bodily ailments and social ills which had befallen the tsarist empire or which had not (yet) vanished in the young socialist state. Hypnosis also appealed to contemporaries because it offered an explanation for the social and political upheavals they were witnessing: the technique, it seemed, accounted for the stellar rise of some political leaders.

The phenomenon of hypnosis itself was not new in 1914.[1] Since the late 18th century, men and women had observed with amazement that slow movements of the hands or steady oscillations of shining objects transported subjects into a state of mind that resembled neither waking nor sleeping. In this condition, participants frequently behaved out of character, seemingly becoming the willing fulfillers of the hypnotist's authoritative commands. Hypnosis had also been used as a medical cure. Indeed, the technique first became notorious in the late 18th century when Franz Anton Mesmer, a Viennese doctor, received significant public attention for employing it in Parisian high society. Mesmer believed hypnosis to be an occult force, a fluid that flowed from the hypnotist to his object. This "magnetic fluid" acted on the nerves of his patients and called forth the astonishing phenomenon he termed "animal magnetism." Mesmer used his technique to cure patients whose illnesses, he

---

[1] On the history of hypnosis, see Alan Gauld, *A History of Hypnotism* (Cambridge: Cambridge University Press, 1995). A general, although slightly unreliable, overview of the history of hypnosis in Russia is provided by Ludmila Zielinski, "Hypnotism in Russia, 1800–1900," in *Abnormal Hypnotic Phenomena: A Survey of Nineteenth-Century Cases*, ed. Eric J. Dingwall (London: Churchill, 1968), 1–105.

Russian Culture in War and Revolution, 1914–22, Book 1: Popular Culture, the Arts, and Institutions. Murray Frame, Boris Kolonitskii, Steven G. Marks, and Melissa K. Stockdale, eds. Bloomington, IN: Slavica Publishers, 2014, 101–17.

argued, were caused by "obstacles" in the fluid's movement through the body. A panel of scientists, however, concluded in 1784 that mesmerism was a fraud. Mesmer had to flee Paris and the fame of animal magnetism declined. In 1831, however, a new scientific commission in Paris published a favorable report and the technique became fashionable again among doctors and laypeople; by the next decade it was widely appreciated across Europe for its anesthetic, curative and entertaining features. In 1842, the British surgeon James Braid termed the phenomenon of mesmerism "hypnosis" after the Greek god of sleep. Braid's move was partly motivated by an attempt to rid the technique of the supernatural aura that had always surrounded mesmerism, and in the last quarter of the 19th century, hypnosis began to engage the attention of numerous esteemed scientists all over Europe.

In order to conquer hypnosis for scholarly professions, academics had to propose scientific explanations about its workings. Mesmer's ideas of "nervous fluids" and later theories about electromagnetic forces ceased to convince the scientifically educated from about 1850, when experimental results showed that the nervous system was not powered by some quasi-electrical energy.[2] During the last decades of the 19th century, when neurologists, anatomists and histologists developed a strong interest in hypnosis, they commonly explained the phenomenon in physiological terms. In the 1880s, the most authoritative figure on the subject was the Parisian neurologist Jean-Marie Charcot, who viewed hypnosis as a distinct nervous state. According to Charcot, hypnosis resembled hysteria, to which it was etiologically linked, and both were brought about by a biological predisposition. Charcot's view was prominently challenged in the late 1880s by Hippolyte Bernheim in Nancy, who argued that hypnotic trances were instances of extraordinary psychological, not physiological, states that were neither abnormal nor a sign of illness such as hysteria. Although contemporary researchers were increasingly drawn to Bernheim's psychological suggestion, physiological and psychological explanations continued to coexist. The Russian neurologist Vladimir Bekhterev described suggestion in a lecture series delivered at the Military-Medical Academy in St. Petersburg in 1897 as a form of irrational reasoning. In Bekhterev's view, hypnosis was a psychological state, but one which could affect groups of people in ways akin to the spread of contagious microbes.[3]

The increasing scientific interest in hypnosis notwithstanding, the technique remained closely associated with magic by society at large, and physiologists and medical doctors frequently bemoaned that it was prac-

---

[2] Gauld, *History*, 265–66.

[3] V. M. Bekhterev, "Priroda gipnoza," *Vestnik znaniia*, no. 1 (1926): 35–40; Bekhterev, *Suggestion and Its Role in Social Life* (New Brunswick, NJ: Transaction Publishers, 1998).

ticed by "charlatans."[4] When the famous spiritualist medium Stefan Sambor realized in 1900 that he too could heal hypnotically, his feats were reported in the mainstream press and confirmed a long-established connection: the medium, who earned his living through the rather dubious profession of communicating with the spirits of the departed, was described by *Peterburgskaia gazeta* as a plausible candidate for a successful hypnotist.[5]

Because of its mysterious qualities, hypnosis was a highly popular topic in early 20th-century mass publishing. In this sphere, the terms mesmerism, (animal) magnetism, suggestion, hypnotism, and hypnosis were used synonymously, a linguistic practice which underlines the ambiguous position of hypnosis within and outside established science. Particularly successful with customers were instruction manuals, which taught readers how to hypnotize and to impose their will upon others, and they frequently went into numerous editions.[6] Journals too serialized courses on suggestion, while newspapers advertised pamphlets and reported the feats of powerful hypnotists.[7] Fascination with the topic continued from the later years of imperial Russia right into the first decade of the young Soviet republic. In 1925, for example, in the popular science journal *Vestnik znaniia*, zoologist and professor at the university of St. Petersburg Petr Iu. Shmidt recommended the hypnotization of animals. "Hypnotizing a frog is easiest," Shmidt explained. This kind of experiment was highly entertaining, as the scientist knew from personal experience, having recently used two grass frogs in "a rather amusing experiment." Shmidt made one hypnotized frog "sit cross-legged and put one of its hands to its heart, the other I stretched out to the front. I made another frog sit opposite the first one in exactly the same position and thus obtained a scene in which two frogs confessed their love. This scene lasted for a few minutes and greatly entertained my children and acquaintances."[8]

---

[4] See, for example, P. Rozenbakh, "Gipnotizm," *Entsiklopedicheskii slovar'* (St. Petersburg, 1893), 8A: 726–34.

[5] "Mediumy progressiruiut (Iz besedy s g. Stano)," *Peterburgskaia gazeta*, 22 November 1900, 3.

[6] For example, Kh. M. Shiller-Shkol'nik, *Novyi kurs gipnotizma: Nasha sila vnutri nas* (Warsaw: Miss Hasse, 1910), reprinted in 1911 in St. Petersburg, Saratov, and Warsaw; and again in 1914.

[7] Bell, "Gipnotizm: Kurs prakticheskikh metodov ukrepleniia v sebe sily voli i dukha dlia razlichnogo roda vnusheniia," *Spiritualist*, no. 8 (1906): 365–74; no. 9 (1906): 424–29; no. 10 (1906): 469–76; no. 11 (1906): 523–26; no. 12 (1906): 584–87; A. A. Likhanov, "Skrizhali maga: Rukovodstvo k razvitiiu psikhicheskikh sposobnostei cheloveka," *Izida*, no. 1 (1913): 3–5; no. 4 (1914): 3–7; no. 5 (1914): 4–12; no. 7 (1914): 3–7; no. 8 (1914): 4–9; no. 9–10 (1914): 5–9; no. 11 (1914): 6–14; no. 12 (1914): 3–7; no. 6 (1915): 1–6; "Lichnoe vliianie," *Gazeta-kopeika* (Moscow), 20 April 1909, 6; A. Dn-ov, "L. L. Onore i ego lechenie vnusheniiami na iavu," *Peterburgskii listok*, 28 February 1910, 3.

[8] P. Iu. Shmidt, "Kak gipnotizirovat' zhivotnykh," *Vestnik znaniia*, no. 3 (1925): 243–46.

Hypnosis in Peacetime: Self-Advancement and the Occult

One striking characteristic of prerevolutionary hypnosis was the promise that it could be used by everyone for personal self-advancement, as authors enthusiastically recommended hypnosis to their readers as a way of improving their individual lives. The ultimate aim of this program was to become a self-assured and assertive person with a strong will that was free from dithering. Once a student of hypnosis had acquired this personal confidence, he could quickly learn how to read the minds of others, but more importantly, he could acquire the skill to exert influence upon others through his psychic power.

How to achieve the authoritative character required for suggestion was the subject of numerous tracts. According to A. A. Likhanov, trainee hypnotists first had to subjugate the physical functions of their own bodies to the power of their minds. This was to be achieved through strict dietary regimes and exercises inspired by yoga. Only once the adept was able to control his body with his will could he turn to the "production and accumulation" of "fluid." Gaining control of this fluid enabled him to develop a commanding gaze and confident gestures. Hypnosis was a highly gendered practice according to this and other instruction manuals. Men, Likhanov noted, were most likely to turn the "fluid" into an active "temperament" that would enable them to "capture the thoughts of others" and to influence those around them. Women, in contrast, developed "passive, mediumistic abilities," i.e., the ability to receive communications from supernatural beings.[9]

The personal gains of masculine hypnotic ability were great indeed: manuals promised supreme knowledge, success in business and triumph in love. Descriptions of the successful hypnotist portrayed him as a vigorous and aggressive man, while the rare women who practiced the technique grew into meek communicators of edifying wisdom. Catriona Kelly has suggested that late imperial advice literature about how to cultivate aggressive manliness was addressed at white-collar workers who had to make an impression upon subordinates, superiors, and colleagues in large organizations and whose status was not determined by the rigid table of ranks that dominated state service.[10] In following her interpretation, hypnosis courses can be seen as reflecting both the experience of social change and the personal aspiration with which some contemporaries drove this transformation.

---

[9] Likhanov, "Skrizhali maga," no. 1 (1913): 4–5.

[10] Catriona Kelly, "The Education of the Will: Advice Literature, Zakal, and Manliness in Early Twentieth-Century Russia," in *Russian Masculinities in History and Culture*, ed. Barbara Evans Clements, Rebecca Friedman, and Dan Healey (Houndmills, UK: Palgrave, 2002), 136. On page 134 of that article, Kelly suggests that before the Revolution programs to develop an aggressive masculinity were directed towards bodily strength only, whereas after 1917 muscle building was combined with education of the will. The sources cited here suggest that the education of the will was already prominent in late tsarist Russia.

Likhanov's instructions also illustrate how popular instruction literature explained hypnosis. His claims combined Mesmer's fluids, Eastern practices such as yoga, contemporary concerns about self-advancement, and spiritualist communications with the beyond. Other authors added science to the mix. A. Khrapovitskii, for example, claimed that mental power resided in the celiac plexus, and his exercises consequently taught readers how to enable communication between the brain and this abdominal network of nerves.[11] A different "scientific" explanation was advanced by A. V. Segno, whose course on strengthening the will went into its 47th edition in 1912 and was addressed to "all who seek truth and power." Segno asserted that all thoughts left physical traces in the forms of ethereal waves. It was these vestiges which his technique enabled users to read and utilize. Like many similar practices, Segno's method was acquired through ritual repetition of firm resolutions, which included "I will control my behavior and actions; I will never worry nor dither," and "I will be successful."[12]

The incorporation of scientific metaphors notwithstanding, early 20th-century ideas concerning hypnosis remained inextricably linked to the occult. Likhanov in his instructions, for instance, claimed that his own innovative method was a "rational combination of yoga"—then universally seen as an exotic, esoteric practice—"with the methods of Western practical occultism."[13] Indeed, many guides to hypnosis were printed in what could be described as the occult press.[14] Zerkalo tainykh nauk, a popular and much advertised compendium of all things magical, for example, discussed hypnosis alongside demons, black magic, dreams, hallucinations, doppelgänger, fortunetelling, spiritualism, haunted houses, chiromancy, astrology, and stage magic.[15]

This close association between hypnosis and the supernatural, however, was contested by doctors who strove to explain hypnosis scientifically and who laid claim to hypnosis as a technique that only the medical profession should be allowed to practice.[16] They were particularly opposed to traveling practitioners of hypnosis, who lacked medical training, such as the medium Sambor or Osip I. Fel'dman, Russia's undisputed star hypnotist and hero of the

---

[11] A. Khrapovitskii, *Magneticheskoe pis'mo* (Moscow: Tip. Mamontova, 1907).

[12] A. V. Segno, *Zakon mentalizma: Prakticheskoe nauchnoe ob"iasnenie mysli i dushevnoi sily, zakon upravliaiushchii vsemi myslennymi i fizicheskimi deistviiami i iavleniiami, sushchnost' zhizni i smerti* (Moscow: A. A. Levenson, 1912), 66, 125.

[13] Likhanov, "Skrizhali maga," no. 1 (1913): 5.

[14] "Kurs lektsii o gipnotizme," *Lektsii okkul'tnykh znanii* (1911): 1–48.

[15] *Zerkalo tainykh nauk ili otrazhenie sud'by cheloveka: Polnyi kurs gipnotizma* (Moscow: Aviator, 1914).

[16] On similar developments in Germany, see Heather Wolffram, "'An Object of Vulgar Curiosity': Legitimizing Medical Hypnosis in Imperial Germany," *Journal of the History of Medicine and Allied Sciences* 67, 1 (2012): 149–76.

popular broadsheet *Peterburgskii listok*. Doctors convinced Russian lawmakers that hypnosis was a dangerous tool in the hands of laymen. From 1890, the law was changed repeatedly and either required medical doctors to be present whenever hypnosis was conducted, or stipulated that only doctors were allowed to practice it.[17] The frequent legal changes and the repeated passing of the same stipulation, however, indicate that official regulations were largely ignored. Indeed, the press published numerous accounts about lay hypnotists valiantly defying state regulation and ridiculed official "hypnocrats."[18]

In attempts to claim hypnosis either for lay practitioners or for science, authors elaborated upon the benefits the technique could bring to society as a whole. Laymen stressed the healing potential of hypnosis and referred to hopeless medical cases, in which their "passes"—i.e., hand movements—finally relieved patients from long suffering.[19] Lay healers claimed to be treating not only individual afflictions, but also the social ills that had befallen society, such as alcoholism, wayward behavior in teenage girls, the breakdown of marriages, irresponsibility, and rebelliousness more generally.[20] Scientists also promised social progress through the advance of rational knowledge that hypnotic experiments would provide. Bekhterev, moreover, hoped that suggestion could be harnessed to influence groups that were not easily convinced by reformers' rational arguments. In 1897 he argued that "there are far more numerous and various ways of transferring psychic states with the help of suggestion than there are ways for transferring thoughts through argument." Reason, he claimed, "can mainly affect persons with a soundly logical mind, whereas suggestion affects not only these persons, but, to a greater extent, persons possessing insufficient reasoning capacity as, for example, children and the popular mass."[21] In Bekhterev's eyes, hypnosis could serve as a tool in

---

[17] P. Rozenbakh, "Gipnotizm" and "Gipnoz," *Bol´shaia sovetskaia entsiklopediia*, ed. S. I. Vavilov and B. A. Vvedenskii, 2nd ed., 51 vols. (Moscow: Gosudarstvennoe nauchnoe izd-vo, 1952), 11: 403–05.

[18] "Mediumy progressiruiut (Iz besedy s g. Stano)"; "Intsident s L. L. Onore," *Peterburgskii listok*, 8 August 1911, 4.

[19] "Eshche izlechenie gipnotizmom," *Rebus* 5, 16 (1886): 170–71; "Gipnoz i vnusheniia," *Peterburgskii listok*, 30 July 1895, 3; L. L. Onore, *Gipnoticheskaia sanatoriia* (Tomsk, 1907); A.-ov, "Na seansakh u L. L. Onore," *Petrogradskii listok*, 12 January 1914, 8.

[20] Nadezhda Nikolaevna (vdova podpolkovnika) Anton´eva, "Izlechenie dushevno-bol´noi," *Rebus* 7, 35 (1888): 315; "U O. I. Fel´dman," *Russkii listok*, 4 February 1893, 3; L. L. Onore, *Gipnoticheskaia sanatoriia*; "Na seansakh u L. L. Onore," *Petrogradskii listok*, 30 October 1914, 14. For the larger significance of such seemingly private disputes, see Barbara Alpern Engel, *Breaking the Ties that Bound: The Politics of Marital Strife in Late Imperial Russia* (Ithaca, NY: Cornell University Press, 2011).

[21] Bekhterev, *Suggestion*, 18–19.

an enlightened professional mission to reform Russia, which would overcome the stubbornness of its backward-looking elements.[22]

While hypnosis was enthusiastically embraced by readers of instruction manuals who strove for personal betterment and by physiologists who enlisted it in their research, the technique also gave rise to anxieties. If it was plausible that everybody could achieve absolute power over another person through mental suggestion, then the practice that offered such opportunities to some was simultaneously a possible threat to others. In the 1890s, the press frequently reported hypnotic abuse and hypnotic experiments gone awry. The latter included cases of subjects who, once hypnotized, could not be woken afterwards, or patients who repeatedly fell asleep at the time a dilettante hypnotic experiment had first been conducted.[23] Other victims of hypnosis were said to have committed crimes that had been suggested to them by a hypnotist.[24] With the help of hypnosis, numerous women and young girls were allegedly made to marry men they did not love, while other women were reportedly raped while in a hypnotic trance. A third group of women, consisting mainly of mature wives, was made to commit suicide.[25] So great was the apprehension of being under someone's malevolent hypnotic influence that Bekhterev named a new illness after this fear: *paranoia suggestio-delira*.[26]

Doctors exploited these anxieties in their attempts to restrict the practice of hypnosis to qualified medics. Pavel Ia. Rozenbakh, distinguished psychiatrist and author of the entry on hypnotism in the eminent *Entsiklopedicheskii slovar'*, echoed concerns raised in the mass media by warning that suggestion administered by unworthy hypnotists could lead subjects to commit crimes against their will or could turn the hypnotized into victims of fraudsters and rapists.[27] V. Sukhova-Osipova claimed in 1904 in *Vestnik psikhologii, kriminal'noi antropologii i gipnotizma*, the organ of the Psychoneurological Institute in St. Petersburg—edited by, among others, Bekhterev—that Fel'dman had harmed

---

[22] Daniel Beer has shown that such authoritarian approaches in the name of social progress were common among those who described themselves as progressives acting in the interests of the people. Daniel Beer, *Renovating Russia: The Human Sciences and the Fate of Liberal Modernity, 1880–1930* (Ithaca, NY: Cornell University Press, 2008).

[23] "Kratkie zametki," *Rebus* 9, 2 (1890): 20.

[24] Rozenbakh, "Gipnotizm," 726–34.

[25] "Gipnoticheskoe prestuplenie," *Rebus* 16, 26 (1897): 219; "Zhertva gipnoza," *Russkii listok*, 24 February 1901, 3; V. M. Bekhterev, *Bred gipnoticheskogo ocharovaniia ili Paranoia suggestio-delira* (St. Petersburg, 1913).

[26] Bekhterev, *Bred gipnoticheskogo ocharovaniia*.

[27] Rozenbakh, "Gipnotizm," 726–34.

the internal organs of some of his patients.[28] The image of hypnosis in prerevolutionary Russia thus presents a contradictory picture of a practice drawn between magical connotations and medical analysis, as a technique that could possibly heal the ills of society, or aggravate these if practiced by dilettantes or with evil intent.

Hypnosis in War and Revolution

Anxieties about the possible abuse of hypnosis were intensified by internal conflict and civil war. The previously anonymous hypnotist, who could have been any reader of one of the numerous cheap instruction manuals, was now associated with political leaders. During the tumultuous years following Russia's entry into the Great War, hypnosis was frequently described in the mass media as a technique mastered and employed by powerful schemers in order to manage either psychologically weaker, impressionable men who held positions of power; or to steer whole masses into action. Thus, during the war some suggested that the German enemy was employing hypnosis as a weapon. At the same time, numerous publications directed at a mass readership depicted in great detail the weak willpower of Nicholas II and surmised that he had become a puppet in the hands of dangerous machinators.[29] Grigorii Rasputin was the prime suspect for such a manipulative role, and hypnosis was frequently mentioned when commentators tried to explain the exceptional position of the Siberian peasant at the center of imperial power. In 1917, S. P. Beletskii, erstwhile director of the police department, argued in front of the extraordinary inquiry of the Provisional Government that he had received intelligence reports in 1913 which suggested that Rasputin was taking lessons in hypnosis. Beletskii had been so concerned by this that he inquired more closely into the activities of Rasputin's teacher and blackmailed him into leaving the capital.[30] Numerous memoirists and commentators have later claimed that Rasputin hypnotized a significant number of powerful people, including the tsar and his wife, Empress Aleksandra, and Bishop Feofan (Bystrov). Rasputin was allegedly less successful with some prominent men

---

[28] V. Sukhova-Osipova, "Gipnotizm," *Vestnik psikhologii, kriminal'noi antropologii i gipnotizma* 1, 8 (1904): 614–16.

[29] O. S. Porshneva, *Mentalitet i sotsial'noe povedenie rabochikh, krest'ian i soldat Rossii v period pervoi mirovoi voiny (1914–mart 1918 g.)* (Ekaterinburg: UrO RAN, 2000), 229–30; B. I. Kolonitskii, *"Tragicheskaia erotika": Obrazy imperatorskoi sem'i v gody pervoi mirovoi voiny* (Moscow: Novoe literaturnoe obozrenie, 2010), 197–223.

[30] P. E. Shchegolev, ed., *Padenie tsarskogo rezhima: Stenograficheskie otchety doprosov i pokazanii, dannykh v 1917 g. v Chrezvychainoi Sledstvennoi Kommissii Vremennogo Pravitel'stva* (Leningrad: Gosudarstvennoe izdatel'stvo, 1925), 4: 501.

such as Prime Minister Petr Stolypin.[31] These failures notwithstanding, Rasputin's hypnotic influence, these authors suggested, explained not only his success at court, but also the political blunders of the hapless tsar.

German generals and Rasputin were not the only political figures who were suspected of having obtained power through hypnosis in revolutionary Russia. During the Civil War, the political enemy was frequently charged with having resorted to the use of suggestion. At times, this was a metaphorical allegation, expressed, for example, when Bolsheviks accused the propertied classes of employing the hypnotic power of money in the suppression of the proletariat, or when Communists claimed that the bourgeoisie used nationalism as a form of "political hypnosis" to estrange non-Russian workers from the Soviet cause.[32] The metaphorical use of hypnosis became an important and ubiquitous ingredient in the political language of the early Soviet Union. Ten years after the October Revolution, *Pravda* celebrated Lenin's unique revolutionary achievement by noting that he had "freed the masses from [their] historical state of hypnosis."[33] The metaphor would not have evoked such a powerful image had the technique itself not been known as a powerful tool with quasi-magic qualities.

And indeed, the allegation that hypnosis was a tool in politics was not always merely employed in a figurative manner in revolutionary Russia. The charismatic socialist Aleksandr Kerenskii was rumored to possess, quite literally, mesmeric powers capable of inducing states of hysteria in his listeners.[34] When *Pravda* claimed in an article about political enemies that "all these Kerenskiis, Chernovs, Vinnichenkos, Petliuras, Martovs, [and] Gegechkoris ... suppress the proletariat and the peasantry through the hypnosis of pretty socialist slogans" (*pri pomoshchi gipnoza krasivykh sotsialisticheskikh fraz*) the borders between metaphorical and literal speech became blurred.[35] In the context of rumors about Kerenskii, it seemed possible that either he, the Menshevik Martov, leaders of the Socialist Revolutionary Party, Ukrainian or Georgian revolutionaries were indeed employing those hypnotic techniques which instruction manuals had long advertised as powerful tools of persuasion. A similar ambiguity existed in relation to the Bolshevik leader.

---

[31] René Fülop-Miller, *Der Heilige Teufel: Rasputin und die Frauen* (Leipzig: Grethlein & Co., 1927), 4–5, 64; Bernard Pares, *The Fall of the Russian Monarchy: A Study of the Evidence* (London: J. Cape, 1939), 138–42; M. V. Rodzianko, "Krushenie imperii," in *Grigorii Rasputin: Sbornik istoricheskikh materialov*, ed. V. Kriukov and I. Saiko (Moscow: Terra, 1997), 153–56, 263.

[32] "Iz slovaria burzhuazii," *Pravda*, 6 June 1918, 1; "Gipnoz deneg," *Izvestiia*, 31 December 1921, 2.

[33] "Fevral'—etap k oktiabriu," *Izvestiia*, 3 November 1927, 1.

[34] Orlando Figes and Boris Kolonitskii, *Interpreting the Russian Revolution: The Language and Symbols of 1917* (New Haven: Yale University Press, 1999), 81–83.

[35] L. Sosnovskii, "Ili Getman—ili Sovety," *Pravda*, 9 May 1918, 1.

Some contemporaries explicitly attributed Lenin's success to his extraordinary willpower, the prerequisite of imposing one's will upon others through hypnotic means, and to his "hypnotic power."[36] In 1920, *Izvestiia* published an article entitled "Why Does Lenin Influence the Masses?"[37] In the first paragraph, its author rejected the proposition that Lenin's charisma was due to "hypnosis or an authoritative personality, his intense political will, [or his] steadfastness." Yet this statement implied that such suggestions were voiced by some and needed to be rebutted by the government newspaper. In the second section of his piece, however, the author himself could not refrain from suggesting that Lenin possessed some form of hypnotic power. "The special quality of [Lenin's] slogans [*formuly*]," he wrote, "brings about hypnosis." This was "the hypnosis of precise, clear and basic slogans which Vladimir Il'ich throws out incessantly." Lenin's formulas were based on a superhuman understanding of the present, which gave the Bolshevik leader "foresight" (*predvidenie*). Both the importance of short authoritative commands and Lenin's ability to foresee the future echo occult ideas about hypnosis, such as the similarity of hypnotic commands to magic spells and its link to clairvoyance.

Most frequently, the claim that someone exerted hypnosis on unsuspecting followers was voiced by political opponents, thus portraying hypnosis as an illicit tool of persuasion. Sometimes, however, even political allies were described as possessing some form of hypnotic ability. The success of prerevolutionary instruction manuals had clearly prepared the ground for the image of hypnosis at times of political upheaval.[38] If absolute power over others could be obtained through its practice, then hypnosis became a plausible explanation of the sudden rise and fall of political figures.

The Russian attitude towards hypnosis during the Great War and its aftermath compares tellingly to German opinions during the same period. As Paul Lerner has shown, hypnosis was celebrated during the war by German doctors, who promoted it as an almost magical technique that could cure the most disconcerting ailment of the time: shell shock. During the social and political upheavals that followed the country's defeat of 1918, however, the restorative qualities of hypnosis that had been hailed before by medics, patients, and social commentators alike, turned into an imminent threat. As contemporaries witnessed the revolutionary upheaval and political instability of the Weimar Republic, they began to see hypnosis as implicated in the un-

---

[36] Figes and Kolonitskii, *Interpreting the Russian Revolution*, 102.

[37] N. Podvoiskii, "Pochemu Lenin vliiaet na massy?" *Izvestiia*, 23 April 1920, 2.

[38] Russians were by no means alone in their suggestion that a mass following was somehow created through hypnosis. In an essay written in 1920, Sigmund Freud suggested that the relationship between charismatic leaders and their followers was brought about by a bond of hypnotic identification. Sigmund Freud, "Massenpsychologie und Ich-Analyse," in *Massenpsychologie und Ich-Analyse. Die Zukunft einer Illusion* (Frankfurt am Main: Fischer, 2007), 31–105.

settling of traditional authority. Instead of the trustworthy doctor who healed suffering defenders of the fatherland during the Great War, hypnosis after 1918 was described as being practiced by scheming charlatans and unreliable elements.[39] Hypnosis in Germany and Russia, it seems, mirrored contemporary attitudes towards figures in power and social authority. As long as there was social stability and agreement about where legitimate power and authority lay, hypnosis was a generally-acclaimed cure. When social and moral authorities were disintegrating, however, the technique acquired a threatening quality. As we shall see below, the development from cure to threat that Lerner describes in the case of Germany was, to some degree, reversed in Russia.

While war and revolutionary upheaval turned hypnosis into a powerful topic of political discourse in Russia, the technique also retained its visible prerevolutionary role in entertainment and science. Yet this role experienced a number of adjustments. In Soviet popular culture, hypnosis was no longer the "democratic" discipline that could potentially be learned and employed by anyone. Instead, hypnotists were portrayed in the 1920s as an exclusive group, consisting of political leaders, a few exceptional entertainers and most significantly medical doctors. As far as the previously contested question of who could explain and legitimately practice hypnosis was concerned, the press was now securely on the side of doctors in general and on that of academician Bekhterev in particular. When hypnosis appeared in the listings of Soviet newspapers, it was almost exclusively employed to advertise the therapeutic services of doctors' surgeries.[40] Training courses open to the public or teach-yourself manuals, which had previously been prominent, were no longer promoted.

The monopoly doctors enjoyed when it came to the legitimate practice of hypnosis was underlined by a number of articles in the Soviet press that highlighted the scientific nature of the technique. *Izvestiia*, for example, noted the prominence of hypnosis at the Second International Congress of Psychical Research held in Warsaw in 1923.[41] A year later, the same newspaper reported how at the All-Russian Congress of Psycho-neurologists, "enormous interest was sparked by the presentations in the section about hypnosis, which described the recent medical successes of hypnosis."[42] These medical achievements were closely followed by newspapers which published

---

[39] Paul Lerner, "Hysterical Cures: Hypnosis, Gender and Performance in World War I and Weimar Germany," *History Workshop Journal* 45 (1998): 79–101.

[40] See, for example, "Dr. Ia. I. Shalyt," *Izvestiia*, 2 December 1922, 5. Over the course of one month, the advertisement was repeated on 6, 9, 16, and 23 December; it was also printed in the following years. Dr. Shalyt was joined by numerous colleagues who also referred to their hypnotic qualifications when advertising their surgeries. One of them was Dr. Markovnikov. See "Dr. Markovnikov," *Pravda*, 14 December 1922, 6.

[41] "Kongress psikhicheskikh issledovanii," *Izvestiia*, 17 August 1923, 4.

[42] "Vserossiiskii s'ezd psikho-nevrologov," *Izvestiia*, 1 July 1924, 4.

celebratory reports about the use of hypnosis during operations and difficult births. This reporting also included news items about the role of hypnosis in the research projects of famous scientists, most prominently in the work of Bekhterev.[43]

Sensationalist titles such as "Operations under Hypnosis" not only stressed the medical monopoly of the technique but simultaneously preserved its old scandalous flair. The press also advertised talks about "Hypnosis and the Will" and "Books on Hypnosis," which further underlined the thrilling appeal of hypnosis, even though these presentations were now given by qualified medics.[44] In some instances, such announcements were printed under the heading "Lectures, Talks and Concerts," suggesting that the link between hypnosis and entertainment had not been severed altogether.[45] Occasionally, hypnosis was indeed still used to advertise theater productions, circus stunts, and documentary or foreign films, although officially sanctioned reviews were frequently highly dismissive of the superficial and obscurantist character of such productions.[46]

As the upheavals of the First World War and the Civil War subsided, hypnosis turned into a purely medical technique. In stark contrast to prerevolutionary lay-magnetizers such as Fel'dman, the Soviet hero-hypnotist was an established academic, and most prominently this role was fulfilled by the acclaimed neurologist Bekhterev. But Bekhterev too altered his view on hypnosis. Whereas he had described suggestion as a psychological process in his 1897 lecture, in the 1920s he emphatically advanced the view that hypnosis was a physiological state in which the workings of the reflexes in the brain were suppressed. This explanation was the undisputed exegesis in early Soviet publications, not least because opponents of materialist explanations were deprived of the opportunity to express their views in print.[47] Bekhterev's disciples now proclaimed confidently that "the further science progresses, the more and more secure the triumph of the materialist approach becomes."[48]

---

[43] "Operatsii pod gipnozom," *Izvestiia*, 2 July 1923, 5; "Operatsii pod gipnozom," *Izvestiia*, 1 February 1924, 3; "Operatsii i rody pod gipnozom," *Pravda*, 1 July 1924, 7; A. A. Sukhov, "Iubilei akademika V. M. Bekhtereva," *Izvestiia*, 19 September 1925, 3; "Novaia kniga Pavlova," *Izvestiia*, 15 March 1927, 5.

[44] "Gipnoz i volia," *Pravda*, 20 February 1920, 8; "Knigi po gipnozu," *Pravda*, 13 April 1928, 8.

[45] "Gipnoz i volia."

[46] "Indiiskaia grobnitsa," *Izvestiia*, 3 March 1923, 5; "Kino: 'Gipnoz i vnushenie,'" *Pravda*, 18 August 1924, 8; "Tsirk miuzik kholl," *Izvestiia*, 22 October 1926, 7.

[47] Bekhterev, "Priroda gipnoza."

[48] A. V. Dubrovskii, "Novoe v izuchenii chelovecheskoi lichnosti," *Vestnik znaniia*, no. 6 (1926): 392.

Doctors also approached hypnosis with more optimism than before the Revolution. Reports about hypnotic treatments gone awry or articles about victimized women vanished from postwar Soviet newspapers. Instead, doctors now recommended hypnosis for use in child-rearing and education. The use of hypnosis as an investigative tool in criminology was also acceptable to Soviet doctors, whereas prerevolutionary practitioners of hypnosis had strongly rejected such proposals.[49] Doctors moreover advanced hypnosis as a potent tool against social ills. First and foremost, this was still related to alcoholism, but it also concerned smoking, kleptomania, bedwetting, and aberrations from what Bekhterev saw as normal sexual behavior.[50] To rid workers of a shameful bourgeois heritage, Bekhterev administered mass hypnosis and taught his patients how to use autosuggestion so as to prevent future relapses.[51] While hypnosis was still used to transform subjects and to turn them into more perfect members of the human race, this transformation was now done with a collective goal in mind, not individual self-advancement. Bekhterev, it seems, grasped the opportunity to carry through his prerevolutionary agenda of transforming the dark masses that threatened to hold back Russia. By doing so, he embraced and furthered the goals of the Soviet state in ways that were not uncommon among Soviet psychologists, as Martin Miller shows in his chapter in book 2 of this volume.[52]

Linked to this optimism regarding hypnosis was the conviction, or at least the claim, that the technique was now fully understood by scientists. Neurologists usually mentioned in the introductions to their texts that hypnosis had in the past been associated with magic or spiritualism, but that these connections were now no longer accepted by intelligent people. Instead, hypnosis could be explained physiologically as a braking process that affected cerebral reflexes. Some of the explanations advanced in the Soviet press revived older 19th-century notions about the workings of hypnosis. Passes were

---

[49] "Narodnoe obrazovanie," *Izvestiia*, 1 November 1922, 4. On the rejection of hypnosis in child-rearing by prerevolutionary doctors see, for example, Rozenbakh, "Gipnotizm."

[50] "Dr. Markovnikov"; V. M. Bekhterev, "Samovnushenie i kueizm, kak istseliaiushchii faktor," *Vestnik znaniia*, no. 17–18 (1925): 1121–30; Bekhterev, "O lechenii gipnozom," *Vestnik znaniia*, no. 2 (1926): 85–96; Bekhterev, "Perspektivy refleksologii cheloveka," *Vestnik znaniia*, no. 6 (1927): 323–26. According to Bekhterev, hypnosis could be used against pain during menstruation, masturbation, onanism, and unspecified "sexual perversion." See also Patricia Herlihy, *The Alcoholic Empire: Vodka and Politics in Late Imperial Russia* (Oxford: Oxford University Press, 2002), 9.

[51] Bekhterev, "Samovnushenie i kueizm"; Bekhterev, "Sotsial'noe nasledie starogo byta," *Vestnik znaniia*, no. 9 (1927): 351–538.

[52] See Martin A. Miller, "Psychiatric Diagnosis as Political Critique: Russia in War and Revolution," in book 2 of this volume, 245–55.

now painstakingly rationalized as a way of dispersing electromagnetic waves from one organism onto another.[53]

Portraying hypnosis as a scientific technique was furthermore achieved by the increased reference to animals on which hypnotic experiments were conducted. Reports about such tests were published, and detailed instructions taught readers not only how to hypnotize frogs, mice, rabbits, lizards, snakes, birds, dogs, or fresh-water crabs, but also how to dissect these organisms and how to conduct other neurological experiments.[54] Hypnosis was thus portrayed as a method akin to other, long established forms of laboratory practice.

Instructions on how to hypnotize animals moreover firmly established hypnosis as a technique for which medical expertise was vital. Whereas in prerevolutionary Russia manuals on how to hypnotize other men and women abounded, no such instructions for laypeople were printed in the 1920s. If scientifically interested Soviet citizens wanted to try the technique at their leisure, they had to use reptiles or small mammals for their experiments, that is, the common objects of amateur biological studies. Trials with other humans were restricted to the medical profession. The same development took place in popular entertainment. When the circus magician To-Ramo advertised his feats in the 1920s, he promised to hypnotize "lions, crocodiles, constrictor snakes, and eagles" but no people.[55]

Doctors' emphatic claims that they fully understood the workings of hypnosis expressed social progress in the Marxist sense in a further respect, that of religion. Religious miracles, so the argument went, represented nothing else than hypnotic cures. By exposing religious events as scientifically explicable phenomena, doctors strove to undermine the authority of belief. In 1925, Bekhterev, for example, wrote that "in biblical times, the possessed were healed everywhere." These are cases "which science now recognizes as hysterical psychoses" and which it would cure with hypnosis.[56] Hypnosis not only explained stories in the gospels, it also provided the clue to medieval

---

[53] V. M. Bekhterev, "Gipnoz," *Vestnik znaniia*, no. 16 (1925): 1057–64; L. L. Vasil'ev, "Novoe o gipnoticheskikh passakh," *Vestnik znaniia*, no. 1 (1927): 27–38.

[54] R. Gabrieliants, "K voprosu o gipnoze zhivotnykh," *Vestnik znaniia*, no. 21–22 (1925): 1293–98; Shmidt, "Kak gipnotizirovat' zhivotnykh"; G. N. Sorokhtin, "Prakticheskaia fiziologiia liubitelia," *Vestnik znaniia*, no. 5 (1925): 387–94; L. L. Vasil'ev, "O peredache mysli na rastoianie," *Vestnik znaniia*, no. 7 (1926): 457–68. Hypnotic experiments with animals were not unknown before the Revolution. However, they were reported far less frequently and usually were not set in the broader context of neurology. Cf. "Kratkie zametki," *Rebus* 7, 47 (1888): 423.

[55] "Tsirk miuzik kholl." This seems to have changed in the 1930s, when the magician Ornal'do entertained circus audiences by hypnotizing the front row. Muzei Tsirkogo Iskusstva (St. Petersburg), R_vyr/154.

[56] V. M. Bekhterev, "Vnushenie i chudesnye istseleniia," *Vestnik znaniia*, no. 5 (1925): 322–31.

and modern visions of Mary or the Holy Cross and to the ecstatic behavior of Old Believers and other sectarians.[57] Hypnosis was thus not only a technique which could rid Soviet citizens of paralysis, sadness, and bourgeois leftovers like alcoholism; it also provided a rational explanation for religious emotions and alleged miracles.

That early Soviet descriptions of hypnosis made use of materialist explanations will not come to anyone as a surprise. That occult notions also found their way into Bekhterev's laboratories and those of his colleagues might be a little less expected, however. In an article about the many uses of hypnosis and autosuggestion, Bekhterev echoed prerevolutionary occult practices for the strengthening of one's willpower. He recommended repeating resolutions regularly, such as "from now on, I have freed myself from my [harmful] habits." This should be done in bed, just before going to sleep and immediately after waking in the mornings.[58] These techniques mirror religious practices like prayers, and quote prerevolutionary courses on how to hypnotize almost literally.[59] Bekhterev himself was aware of this. He noted that "autosuggestion has so far not received much attention from doctors. In the past it has either served moral aims (the attainment of Nirvana in the East) or, in the hands of healers, the strengthening of the will along the formula 'the power is within ourselves.'"[60]

Early Soviet scientific approaches to hypnosis also echoed earlier occult ideas when it came to the application of the technique. By proposing to heal Soviet citizens both from physical and psychological ailments, hypnosis became a tool in the creation of the New Soviet Man. As Professor Birchevskii wrote in *Vestnik znaniia*, neurology and hypnosis were part of "contemporary eugenics—i.e., the science of the improvement of man's nature." According to him, this science would "strive towards the inner perfection [of man] and his emotional functions."[61] Birchevskii had prominent support for this view. In *Literature and Revolution*, a work written in 1922–23 and published in 1924, the Bolshevik leader Lev Trotskii described the "psycho-physical self-education" required in the process of creating the new Soviet man in a manner that is strongly reminiscent of prerevolutionary occult instructions of self-perfection

---

[57] V. M. Bekhterev, "Vzaimovnushenie v soobshchestve liudei i kollektivnye galliutsinatsii," *Vestnik znaniia*, no. 6 (1926): 361–66.

[58] Bekhterev, "Samovnushenie i kueizm," 1123.

[59] Compare, for example, Segno, *Zakon mentalizma*.

[60] Bekhterev, "Samovnushenie i kueizm," 1126. The formula was a direct quotation from the many occult publications on hypnosis that appeared in fin-de-siècle Russia, for example, Shiller-Shkol'nik's *Novyi kurs gipnotizma*.

[61] I. Birchevskii, "Nauchnoe dal'novidenie i, tak naz., 'iasnovidenie,'" *Vestnik znaniia*, no. 23 (1927): 1409–14. According to Bekhterev, hypnosis could improve the rational abilities of man. V. M. Bekhterev, "Perspektivy refleksologii cheloveka," *Vestnik znaniia*, no. 6 (1927): 323–26.

through meditative practice and hypnosis. The new man, Trotskii wrote, "will try to master first the semi-conscious and then the subconscious processes in his own organism, such as breathing, the circulation of the blood, digestion, reproduction, and within necessary limits, he will try to subordinate them to the control of reason and will." Eventually, these exercises would allow him to conquer the "nature of man himself ... hidden in the deepest and darkest corner of the unconscious, of the elemental, of the sub-soil."[62] Trotskii's work, in which he lambasted the mysticism of the prerevolutionary intelligentsia, simultaneously smoothly translated prerevolutionary occult programs into a Soviet plan of action.[63]

ଓ   ଚ

Throughout the revolutionary period, hypnosis remained a practice that raised difficult questions about its scientific workings and about why some men held power over others. Before the war, hypnosis held out the promise that the opportunities for social change could be enjoyed by ordinary people. When seminal political events followed in quick succession, hypnosis gained traction because it seemed to explain what was going on at court, at the frontline, and why society was becoming so polarized along ideological lines. It short, hypnosis seemed to provide the answer to the disconcerting question of why traditional authorities were being toppled by new ones, whose source of power remained (in the eyes of some) in need of explanation.

In the sphere of science, hypnosis challenged neurologists throughout the period to come up with models of the brain that could explain the functioning of suggesting. In many ways, this was more difficult before the Revolution than afterwards, since from 1900 until 1917, esoteric freethinkers enthusiastically published accounts in which they claimed hypnosis for themselves and creatively adapted explanations advanced by academics. They thereby challenged doctors' understanding of science and academics' view about who was allowed to make use of its insights. These voices, which tried to advance a worldview that had not received the academic seal of approval and was not securely based on materialistic assumptions, were silenced after 1917. In the mid-1920s, when doctors had firmly established their authority with regard to hypnosis, scientists like Bekhterev could repeat—mantra-like and without fear of remonstration—the assertion that neurologists had found a way of dealing with hypnosis scientifically, even when the explanations they offered remained sketchy. At the same time, and with their rivals silenced, Bekhterev and his colleagues were now freer to take up occult notions themselves and incorporate them into their experiments and theories. By doing so, Soviet

---

[62] Leon Trotsky, *Literature and Revolution* (Ann Arbor: University of Michigan Press, 1971), 255.

[63] On Trotskii's criticism of intelligentsia mysticism, see ibid., 21–23.

neurologists showed remarkable open-mindedness in their scientific research, a flexibility which is easily overlooked in light of the Marxist language doctors employed and which included vehement rejections of religion, unwavering support of scientific materialism, and references to Lenin, the Great October Revolution, and the class struggle.[64] Yet as Trotskii's vision of the Soviet superman illustrated, even Bolshevik politicians could not entirely escape the allure of "bourgeois mysticism" and one of its favorite obsessions: hypnosis.

---

[64] See, for example, Bekhterev, "Perspektivy refleksologii cheloveka"; A. A. Sukhov, "Akademik Bekhterev, kak svetoch znanii i geroi poluvekovogo nauchnogo truda," *Vestnik znaniia,* no. 6 (1926): 441–42; S. Gruzenberg, "V. M. Bekhterev na obshchestvennom postu," *Vestnik znaniia,* no. 6 (1926): 443–46.

The Arts

The Feast in the Time of Plague: The Russian Art World, Easel Painting, and the Experience of War and Revolution, 1914–22

Aaron J. Cohen

Artists in Russia faced a new world with the outbreak of World War I. In the decades after the Great Reforms of the 1860s, imperial Russian artistic life had kept pace with the steady unfolding of civil society.[1] Russian painters of this time understood well the effects of social, political, and cultural change on themselves and their art, for they had experienced both the turmoil of high culture and politics in fin-de-siècle Europe and a revolution in Russia in 1905. No one, however, was prepared for the personal and professional challenges of the massive war that began in August 1914. The idea that cultural life could continue amidst such great destruction of economic capacity, cultural heritage, and human life seemed incredible, and many believed artistic life would immediately stop. For them, a classical proverb expressed the incompatibility of art and war: *When the cannons roar, the muses are silent.* The publicist and poet Dmitrii Merezhkovskii conveyed the problematic position of the creative artist during the Great War in two short sentences: "Two lines of a war bulletin are more important than the works of Goethe and Pushkin. Culture in the time of war is a feast in the time of plague."[2]

Yet not only did art life continue in war and revolution, it thrived, and sometimes in unexpected ways. The scale of mass violence experienced by individuals, increase in social and economic instability, and accelerated pace of change in the art world between 1914 and 1922 was a sharp departure from the prewar era, but the great majority of artists in Russia seem to have been disengaged from war and revolution, if one judges by the small number of

---

[1] For more details and sources on the art world here and throughout this chapter, see Aaron J. Cohen, *Imagining the Unimaginable: World War, Modern Art, and the Politics of Public Culture in Russia, 1914–1917* (Lincoln: University of Nebraska Press, 2008). I do not claim to cover all aspects of the art world or supply the most authoritative readings of any work of art or artist's life in this essay, for there are many ways to find meaning in art. The expert reader in art history should be ready for some oversimplification as well as a focus on historical analysis and interpretation.

[2] D. S. Merezhkovskii, *Nevoennyi dnevnik, 1914–1916* (Petrograd: Ogni, 1917), 207.

Russian Culture in War and Revolution, 1914–22, Book 1: Popular Culture, the Arts, and Institutions. Murray Frame, Boris Kolonitskii, Steven G. Marks, and Melissa K. Stockdale, eds. Bloomington, IN: Slavica Publishers, 2014, 121–38.

easel paintings in this period that actually depicted these dramatic events. But war, revolution, and civil war left their mark on Russian painting in other, and often subtle, ways. Demand for art reached record levels during World War I, and changes in the market led to important structural changes inside the art world. Far from retreating into isolation, painters of all genres began to engage in broader social activism, a practice that continued after the Revolution. Even the radical avant-garde, previously ridiculed in the press and deprived of professional respect from other artists, rethought their public rejection of engagement with broader society. The particular political values of the Bolshevik government, collapse of the money economy, and disintegration of familiar public institutions during the Civil War wrecked the old system, but artists nonetheless found new and creative ways to explore the meaning of the revolution in art and life. Indeed, the influence of Russian paintings and ideas created in the time of intense creative activity between 1914 and 1922 continues to this day.

The imperial Russian art world had well-known rhythms and predictable institutions before 1914. These included the official Academy of Arts, several large, prominent artistic groups with fairly consistent aesthetic views, a number of important large museums and smaller galleries, and a patronage system based on rich merchants, interested aristocrats, and the broader public. This art culture was intertwined with the broader public sphere and civil society, for painters made connections to many of their customers through institutions like the print media, exhibitions, and museums. Major groups put on annual shows at the end of December in Moscow and in mid-February in St. Petersburg, often opening their exhibitions in the same week (or even on the same day) in the same exhibition space year after year. Daily newspapers released reviews of these exhibitions within a few days of opening, and prominent painters made their art available to the reading public through popular illustrated weeklies. In these ways, visual artists formed an overarching occupational group that shared public institutions and practices even though they were divided into different milieus with different aesthetic values, audiences, and personalities. Painters in the Russian avant-garde were notorious for their rejection of this mainstream art culture, and their works destabilized formal conventions by emphasizing the sensory qualities of light, color, motion, and texture in art. Vasilii Kandinskii was working on abstract art in Germany, while Mikhail Larionov and Natal'ia Goncharova exhibited rayism, another early form of abstraction, in Russia. But the mass media and more conventional artists despised, ignored, or ostracized the radical artists and their art. Art life in Russia seemed stable, to many critics even boring, as most painters focused on the mundane professional matters of their craft.

After August 1914 this system seemed to be on the verge of dissolution. Conscription took millions of people from their regular lives, while material difficulties and public distractions weakened institutions and made professional life difficult. The art market slumped, journals closed, and visitors avoided museums, while painters who were working abroad, like Kandinskii and Marc Chagall, found themselves back home, forced to adjust to new personal and professional conditions. What could an artist do when familiar audiences, institutions, and culture seemed to be collapsing? Many no longer felt like painting as mobilization, excitement, and uncertainty reigned. "I am no longer a painter" wrote V. V. Perepletchikov, a landscape artist in the Union of Russian Artists who served on six war committees. "I have almost forgotten that I used to paint."[3]

But the first wartime art season was not a disaster, just different, and in 1915 and 1916 the art world adjusted to a new situation. The prewar growth in art groups leveled off in Moscow and Petrograd (and dropped slightly in the empire), but the overall number of groups did not collapse. In fact, one reason that regular exhibitions were so disorganized was that the war became a focus for new institution building. War charity exhibitions and auctions appeared as artists blended patriotic social activism and professional self-interest to meet the sudden need for social mobilization, and these new institutions competed for space, artists, and customers with traditional group exhibitions. Special war-related exhibitions and charities became routine fixtures instead of one-off events as painters, dealers, and buyers took advantage of a heightened interest in painting that appeared among some segments of the population. The war's second art season in the winter of 1915–16 exceeded all expectations, and the market boomed during the 1916–17 season, even as economic ruin loomed across the land. Far from shrinking or falling apart as the destructive war raged, the art world continued to develop as wartime conditions channeled people's interest in paintings and their wealth into the market.

A new public structure for art emerged during the war, an art world linked to the war directly through the mass mobilization of public patriotism or indirectly as a byproduct of economic change and internal migration. Control over painting was passing from established authorities toward artistic outsiders, painters from the established groups bypassed traditional art structures, and genre and aesthetic boundaries blurred as paintings from all milieus appeared in charity, inter-group, and open exhibitions. Exhibition activity began earlier, and major groups, individual artists, and exhibitions that did not have a specific affiliation existed side-by-side. Established and new painters could avoid the scrutiny of juries who approved submissions at the traditional exhibitions in new inter-group, individual, and specialty institutions. The First Summer Exhibition, for example, was organized in 1916 specifically to be a profitable way for artists to get their work to the public without intermediaries.[4] The critic Abram M. Efros implied in late 1916 that the old art world was dying: "To find the living flow of art we must look not in 'societies,' not in 'groups,' but in separate artists of diverse groups."[5]

---

[3] Stephen Graham, *Russia and the World* (London: Cassell, 1917), 19–20.

[4] *Novoe vremia*, 24 July 1916, 5.

[5] *Russkie vedomosti*, 19 November 1916, 5.

The political, cultural, and institutional distance between the most radical modernist painters and wider public also shrank in this wartime mobilization.[6] Common cause in wartime allowed for reconsideration of the avant-garde's place. In 1914 several newspapers, for example, dropped their attacks on futurism after several young artists were wounded at the front.[7] "In peacetime they used to call you and me crazy, mentally ill," wrote the futurist poet Velimir Khlebnikov sarcastically to a friend in mid-1916, "as a result most government jobs were closed to us. But now in wartime, when every action is especially crucial, I become a full-fledged citizen."[8] Many of these artists responded to this new opening, and the existence of avant-garde war charity activity demonstrates in concrete terms that radical artists remained embedded in the general public mobilization.[9] This new avant-garde engagement with society continued after the February Revolution, when radical modernists joined public institutions alongside other painters to defend the legitimacy of their art and support their place in the art world.

The heightened institution-building of the war years expanded as freedom brought by the revolution in February 1917 gave artists the ability to form institutions outside the traditional art world and to organize their profession without state interference.[10] As in 1914, they used new institutions to protect their interests in a time of political instability, economic disruption, and institutional confusion. The academic milieu and its aesthetic supporters were discredited, newly-formed unions, advocacy groups, and special commissions took organizational power away from the major art groups, and there were new public tasks that needed to be undertaken (such as the protection of monuments from vandalism). A national Union of Artists emerged as an umbrella organization to unite the local professional unions that popped up to represent the economic interests of artists and the art world. The difference between 1914 and 1917, however, was that political restrictions and social conventions broke down to a greater degree in 1917 as the state and traditional art institutions fell into deeper disarray, which in turn opened public space for individuals and groups to mobilize more completely. After February 1917, the number of art groups spiked in Moscow and Petrograd, when more than 100 groups existed throughout the country, a record. Twenty-eight new art

---

[6] A. V. Krusanov, *Russkii avangard, 1907–1932: Istoricheskii obzor. V trekh tomakh,* 1: *Boevoe desiatiletie: 1907–1917* (St. Petersburg: Novoe literaturnoe obozrenie, 1996), 253.

[7] *Utro Rossii,* 25 January 1915, 5; *Ranee utro,* 22 January 1915, 4.

[8] Charlotte Douglas, ed., *Collected Works of Velimir Khlebnikov,* 1: *Letters and Theoretical Writings* (Cambridge, MA: Harvard University Press, 1987), 109.

[9] Cohen, *Imagining the Unimaginable,* 124–25.

[10] For details, see V. P. Lapshin, *Khudozhestvennaia zhizn´ Moskvy i Petrograda v 1917 godu* (Moscow: Sovetskii khudozhnik, 1983), 85–100.

groups appeared in that year alone, more than twice as many as in 1909 and three times more than in 1914.

In the early Bolshevik period, the art world faced massive disorder caused by a collapsing civic society, economic chaos, and uncertain public culture. These problems diverted people's attention from painting as society became preoccupied with political and economic questions.[11] The art season of 1917–18 did continue after the Bolshevik takeover in October 1917, but public attendance at exhibitions was down. The Hermitage was closed and prepared for evacuation as the Germans approached, and museums faced a new round of deep financial and administrative problems. The number of art groups dropped sharply in 1918, 1919, and 1920, artists stopped painting, and many established groups did not exhibit. The painter Mikhail Nesterov noted how different public space had become by 1920: "Moscow has changed greatly in two years, there is no trade, and everything that accompanies it: advertising, stores, markets, and the rest do not exist."[12]

Painters lost much of their traditional bases for support as civil society contracted. In 1919 a writer in the newspaper *Zhizn' iskusstva* noted that the art public had changed: "There are days when museums have almost no visitors. This is explained by the fact that the educated public stopped coming to Petrograd to see the sights of the capital, including museums. It is more or less lively in museums on Sundays and Thursdays when tours of students and workers visit."[13] The private art market became unstable and at the peak of the Civil War largely collapsed. The first big art exhibition after the Revolution drew some 40,000 visitors in 1919, but sales (100,000 rubles) were "sluggish due to the current situation."[14] Nesterov had been a very successful artist but found it difficult to restore his position in face of the material hardship. "I am slowly returning to work … but working is hard: there is no paint."[15] Art prices were high in Moscow in 1921, but he was not rushing to sell paintings due to tremendous inflation.[16]

Art institutions under the Bolsheviks were in a state of flux, a condition that the government addressed with state activism and aesthetic toleration for artists who did not engage in counter-revolutionary activity. Before 1917 Bolshevik leaders did not have an official aesthetic, nor did they have experience in art administration. To support a teetering system after October, they moved quickly to nationalize existing private art collections and institu-

---

[11] *Moskovskie vedomosti*, 21 April 1917, 2.

[12] M. V. Nesterov, *Pis'ma: Izbrannoe*, ed. A. A. Rusakova (Leningrad: Iskusstvo, 1988), 273.

[13] *Zhizn' iskusstva*, 4 March 1919, 3.

[14] "Zakrytie vystavki," *Zhizn' iskusstva*, 28 June 1919, 1.

[15] Nesterov, *Pis'ma izbrannye*, 273.

[16] Ibid., 274.

tions and to set up new state institutions. The Department of Fine Arts (IZO) of the People's Commissariat of Enlightenment became the first official state department in Russian history designed to administer art policy and artistic affairs; it organized art exhibitions open to all forms of art, ran art education, and produced art publications. By 1919 juries at state exhibitions were abolished, entrance was made free, and IZO was given "rather large sums" to acquire paintings.[17] Official demand could also substitute for the loss of private demand for art in more indirect ways. In late 1918, for example, the Russian Museum had money to spend "widely" on acquisitions, and its buyers took advantage of market weakness: "Many collectors in the grip of events are ready to sell valuable works of art at rather moderate prices."[18] Lenin himself, according to Anatolii Lunacharskii, viewed his program for monumental propaganda in part as a way to occupy the "not small number of artists" who lived in "extreme poverty."[19] As the art market shrank and institutions wobbled, only the state could prevent collapse.

The art world in the early revolutionary years was not its imperial counterpart; it contained a heightened role for the state, a mishmash of ideas and institutions, a new, politicized public culture, and an unstable economic environment. But it did have elements that existed before 1914 or had emerged during World War I. Important painters from imperial Russian groups such as the World of Art, the Wanderers, and the Union of Russian Artists continued to exhibit, if sporadically, as individuals. With the New Economic Policy (NEP), the private art market showed signs of revival. Many of imperial Russia's major groups reemerged in 1922–23, and in 1922 a large charity exhibition was organized to raise money for famine victims.[20] Nesterov showed two paintings at the Union of Russian Artists exhibition, which was visited by "a lot of people" and had "good work" from old and new artists.[21] The structural characteristics that united the period of war, revolution, and civil war continued, especially the destabilization of familiar institutions, weakening of the traditional authority of the art group, and increased public engagement. These conditions of cultural life in a time of public mobilization led to important changes in the form and content of paintings.

Ironically, war and revolution brought changes to public life that made it difficult for Russian artists to depict those events in their painting. The general mobilization of patriotic culture in 1914 and 1915 inspired some genre

---

[17] *Moskva*, no. 2 (1919): 16.

[18] *Zhizn' iskusstva*, 19 November 1918, 5.

[19] V. N. Perel'man, ed., *Bor'ba za realizm v izobrazitel'nom iskusstve 1920-kh godov: Materialy, dokumenty, vospominaniia* (Moscow: Sovetskii khudozhnik, 1962), 89.

[20] Brandon Taylor, *Art and Literature under the Bolsheviks*, 1: *The Crisis of Renewal 1917–1924* (London: Pluto, 1991), 163.

[21] Nesterov, *Pis'ma izbrannye*, 279.

painters to take up war themes, and even several avant-garde artists found the war a compelling topic.[22] On occasion, professional and amateur painters at the front depicted the war to pass the time or at the request of comrades, and in 1915 an official unit of war illustrators was formed to go to the front.[23] But few painters put images of battle into their work, and fewer still produced works that made it into public art exhibitions. Major exhibition groups like the Union of Russian Artists and the World of Art showed little interest in the war as a subject, and in 1916 only 10 or 15 of 500 paintings at the academic Salon reflected "contemporary life."[24] This lack of war art was not unusual in the European context. Artists in Germany, for example, produced war paintings early in the war but soon returned to conventional themes, and war genre was a tiny portion of painting at the British Royal Academy.[25]

Several factors limited the direct representation of the world war in easel painting. There was little intellectual appetite for war art among most artists, and painters and collectors in milieus where such ideas were widespread were encouraged to avoid it. War images that did appear at exhibitions were often met with hostility from critics and colleagues. Il´ia Repin's *Nurse Ivanova* (1915), for example, was "the worst canvas at the whole exhibition," according to one writer.[26] "A dry, official report of Nurse Ivanova's death." The painter Konstantin Somov attacked Kuz´ma Petrov-Vodkin's *In the Firing Line* (1915) (see fig. 1 in the gallery of illustrations following page 188) so harshly that Petrov-Vodkin felt "it would be better now to shoot or hang me."[27] The public was also broader than the official and courtly audience that patronized battle painting in the 19th century. Those who engaged the market had to match the expectations of buyers who did not want canvases that depicted events

---

[22] For more on the Russian avant-garde art of the war, see Richard Cork, *A Bitter Truth: Avant-Garde Art and the Great War* (New Haven: Yale University Press, 1994), 18–20, 37–41, 48–54, 122–25; Dzhon E. Boult [John E. Bowlt], "Khudozhestvennaia novatsiia i voennaia strategiia: Russkii avangard i Pervaia mirovaia voina," in *Avangard 1910-kh– 1920-kh godov: Vzaimodeistvie iskusstv*, ed. G. F. Kovalenko (Moscow: Iskusstvoznanie, 1998), 25–35.

[23] Irina Kuptsova, *Khudozhestvennaia intelligentsiia Rossii v gody pervoi mirovoi voiny* (Moscow: ITRK, 2007), 95.

[24] *Petrogradskaia gazeta*, 25 February 1916, 3.

[25] Jost Hermand, "Heroic Delusions: German Artists in the Service of Imperialism," in *1914/1939: German Reflections of the Two World Wars*, ed. Reinhold Grimm and Hermand (Madison: University of Wisconsin Press, 1992), 98; Thomas Noll, "Zur Ikonographie des Krieges," in *Die letzten Tage der Menschheit: Bilder des ersten Weltkrieges*, ed. Rainer Rother (Berlin: Deutsches Historisches Museum, 1994), 270; Angela Weight, "Kriegsgenrekunst," in *Die letzten Tage*, 283.

[26] *Novoe vremia*, 22 February 1916, 5.

[27] Iu. N. Podkopaeva and A. N. Sveshnikova, eds., *Konstantin Andreevich Somov: Pis´ma, dnevniki, suzhdeniia sovremennikov* (Moscow: Iskusstvo, 1979), 156.

too close to home. Painters could not use the heroic conventions of history painting or cheerful patriotism of the media to represent something that people knew was destructive, violent, and ugly. One refugee, for example, wept before a beautiful landscape in an art exhibition, which was her refuge from the outside world. "Blood, blood, everywhere blood," she cried, *"but here it is so nice."*[28] Finally, painters who served in the army were busy doing other things, not to mention physically separated from studios and galleries. The oeuvre of I. S. Efimov shows such a gap: "1916 and 1917 were the years of military service for Efimov. These years are therefore missing from the list of art."[29]

The mobilization of visual culture during the war was much more pervasive in the mass media, not the art exhibition, and this phenomenon redirected artistic interest away from easel painting. Many painters created images for postcards, caricatures, and popular prints that extolled Russian soldiers and denigrated the enemy. Famous images by L. O. Pasternak, V. M. Vasnetsov, N. K. Rerikh, and S. A. Vinogradov appeared in newspapers and on street posters, while A. O. Sharleman, G. I. Narbut, and several World of Art painters created war *lubki* (popular prints), as did avant-garde artists like Kazimir Malevich. Academic battle artists capitalized on increased demand in the public for war images in magazines and newspapers. Such war illustrations, one journalist argued, did not "count as pearls of Russian art" but were "as necessary as the newspaper page" since they provided a "fast, immediate response to events that were interesting to everyone."[30] In this way, the public mobilization that began with the war tended to dislocate any depiction of current events from the art exhibition to a broader public of illustrated weeklies and local kiosks (fig. 2). These types of images did not belong to traditional painting culture; they existed in the culture of the mass media with its postcards, posters, and popular prints that depicted heroic warriors, evil Germans, and proud generals.

This pattern of cultural mobilization continued after February 1917, but the object of cultural mobilization and public engagement shifted from war to revolution. Artists, illustrators, and publicists resurrected the visual culture of the early part of the war to reflect the Revolution as patriotic agitation and enthusiastic propaganda revived. The revolution in 1917, like the war in 1914, suddenly appeared in postcards and posters, and the agitprop trains and traveling exhibitions of the Provisional and early Bolshevik governments continued a tradition of wartime trophy tours. Battle painters and illustrators also transferred the culture of war to the Revolution when they sketched il-

---

[28] Iakov Tugendkhol'd, "V zheleznom tupike," *Severnye zapiski*, no. 7–8 (July–August 1915): 102. Emphasis in the original.

[29] N. Ia. Simonovich-Efimova, *Zapiski khudozhnika* (Moscow: Sovetskii khudozhnik, 1982), 259.

[30] *Iskry*, no. 37 (1914): 296.

lustrations of street battles and revolutionary activity. But as in wartime some newspapers complained that Russian painters still could not capture the reality of the Revolution in their art.[31]

In early Soviet Russia, conventional topics overwhelmed the number of paintings that depicted revolutionary themes at the regular art exhibitions.[32] Critics in *Izvestiia* and *Pravda* took figurative and abstract artists to task for their apparent inability to exhibit major paintings that portrayed the Revolution (the exceptions were sometimes noted to confirm the rule).[33] Political agitation in easel painting did not have a high priority in official policy, since most Bolsheviks believed that art exhibitions could only reach a very narrow audience compared to the mass media. Lenin himself admitted that he was "more gratified by the setting up of two or three elementary schools in some out-of-the-way villages than by the most magnificent exhibit at some art show."[34] By 1927, the critic Iakov Tugendkhol'd argued that October still had not produced an "epochal" or "perfectly synthetic" work of art, and he used language that echoed wartime discourse, a sign that similar personal and public dynamics were at work in both war and revolution: "We still don't have such grand canvases and perhaps they are not possible. The old Latin proverb 'When the cannons roar, the muses are silent' is still true."[35]

Later Soviet critics argued that the most important paintings of this period employed allegory and symbolism to communicate ideas about the revolutionary experience.[36] Canvases like Arkadii Rylov's *Blue Expanse* (1918), Boris Kustodiev's *Bolshevik* (1920), and Konstantin Iuon's *The New Planet* (1921) entered the Soviet art canon as effective depictions of the Revolution from this time.[37] Iuon's representation of dawn on a distant planet in *The New Planet* (fig. 3) depicts this dramatic and dynamic moment in time through narrative

---

[31] *Petrogradskaia gazeta*, 5 April 1917, 6; *Petrogradskii listok*, 9 April 1917, 2.

[32] As a Soviet art historian once observed, "revolutionary events scarcely existed in the work of the overwhelming majority of artists" at early Soviet exhibitions. M. S. Lebedianskii, *Stanovlenie i razvitie russkoi sovetskoi zhivopisi: 1917– nachalo 1930-kh gg.* (Leningrad: Khudozhnik RSFSR, 1983), 86.

[33] See, for example, *Izvestiia*, 9 February 1919, 6; 10 May 1919, 4; 19 January 1922, 3; 12 May 1922, 3; *Pravda*, 13 August 1922, 5; 30 November 1922, 5; 16 January 1923, 5. The Association of Artists of Revolutionary Russia did contribute war paintings, portraits, and sketches to a special exhibition that marked the fifth anniversary of the creation of the Red Army (*Izvestiia*, 27 December 1922, 6).

[34] V. I. Lenin, *On Literature and Art* (Moscow: Progress, 1978), 279.

[35] Ia. A. Tugendkhol'd, *Iz istorii zapadnoevropeiskogo, russkogo i sovetskogo iskusstva* (Moscow: Sovetskii khudozhnik, 1987), 225.

[36] Lebedianskii, *Stanovlenie i razvitie russkoi sovetskoi zhivopisi*, 99.

[37] See, for example, D. V. Sarab'ianov, ed., *Istoriia russkogo i sovetskogo iskusstva* (Moscow: Vysshaia shkola, 1989), 336–39.

(the reactions of human figures) and form (the strong colors and heavy lines), an approach that stands in stark contrast to the bucolic Russia found in his usual impressionist and lyrical landscapes. The use of allegory and symbolism allowed artists to show ideas about the Revolution indirectly, with room for ambivalence. In Iuon's vision, the Revolution looms as a violent force of nature that evokes devotion in some but fear in others (if indeed it depicts the Revolution at all). Aesthetic realists, by contrast, appear to have had more difficulty finding a compelling visual language to show events. One critic saw the aesthetic realist Wanderers in 1922 as hopelessly mired in a mentality of the 19th century that could not depict what was going on without outside guidance. Only "strong ideological leadership and organization," he argued, could bring them to paint images relevant to Soviet reality, but "until then our life, our revolution remains unrepresented."[38]

The main arena for revolutionary art was in open spaces, not the art exhibition. The Soviet state prioritized public mobilization in ways that tried to bring the Bolshevik Revolution to a population who did not understand it and to organize violence against internal enemies who did. One of the new government's earliest decrees on cultural policy thus concerned the removal of tsarist monuments and the protection of cultural heritage, a sign that the communication of ideas in public space would be the main focus of early Bolshevik culture. Direct government propaganda focused on agitprop trains and boats, outdoor movies, and posters. Central, too, were public festivals and celebrations, street decorations, industrial products, and the creation of new monuments to historical figures that reflected revolutionary ideals (fig. 4). As Efros wrote in 1922, the process of art creation moved from the inner-looking individual artist to the demands of the extra-artistic world: "The more art shrank in intensiveness, the more it rose in extensiveness: the *creation* of art turned into the *use* of art; 'creative activity' replaced by 'outside the school behavior.'"[39]

The experience of Mitrofan Grekov shows how changing institutional and cultural conditions helped determine the production of successful war painting. Grekov (born Martyshchenko) studied at the Academy of Arts under the battle artist F. A. Rubo. In 1914 he was sent to the front, where he spent much of the war until released in 1917. Grekov admitted that this war service "deprived him of the opportunity to paint," but he did find the time to complete many sketches and drawings.[40] These were not formal war paintings but genre paintings of life at the front (fig. 5); few depicted actual

---

[38] *Izvestiia*, 12 March 1922, 4.

[39] Abram Efros, "Kontsy bez nachal: Iskusstvo v revoliutsii," *Tvorchestvo*, no. 3 (1990): 15. Emphasis in the original.

[40] Quoted in G. A. Timoshin, *Mitrofan Borisovich Grekov: Zhizn' i tvorchestvo* (Moscow: Sovetskii khudozhnik, 1961), 57; Kh. A. Ushenin, ed., *M. B. Grekov v vospominaniiakh sovremennikov* (Leningrad: Khudozhnik RSFSR, 1966), 31.

combat.[41] None appear to have been exhibited or made public at the time. During the Civil War, Grekov painted images of the steppe and the lives of Cossacks for a new audience, the local Cossack museum, while living in his native Don region under White control. In 1920 the artist turned to Red Army themes after falling in with the First Cavalry, where he met K. E. Voroshilov and S. M. Budennyi. His career took off with such patrons, and after 1923 he went to the capital and began to participate in major exhibitions (fig. 6). Soviet critics considered some of Grekov's Civil War-era paintings to be precursors of socialist realism, but they held up only his later work as mature representatives of socialist war painting. His public success in painting war depended on the professional opportunities he found as he moved from personal visions of World War I and the Civil War to officially-sanctioned Soviet battle painting.

In several ways, a sharpened artistic concern with the problem of reality, realism, and the representation of reality emerged in the new political, cultural, and economic conditions that emerged between 1914 and 1922. Painting changed as artists sought to stabilize their personal and professional lives through more narrative or traditional art forms, a trend that took place even among modernist artists who eschewed conventional aesthetics. When P. N. Filonov, for example, painted realistic portraits during the war, he did so certainly at the wish of patrons for "purely worldly reasons."[42] This search for stability in times of crisis, ironically, also led to the opposite response: some dispensed with the depiction of reality altogether. In 1915 Vladimir Tatlin, Malevich, and their friends and associates were perhaps the first modern artists to abandon the objective in art, an idea of tremendous significance in European intellectual history.[43]

Wartime changes in the art market, for one thing, encouraged painters to adopt conventional styles. Aristocrats, entrepreneurs, and ordinary people found more rubles in their pockets as limits on alcohol, foreign travel, and imported goods expanded personal budgets, and inflation spurred investment in hard assets. Many Poles fled to the Russian hinterland after the Germans took Poland, and anti-Semitic tsarist policies and Cossack behavior in the western borderlands forced Jews to seek refuge in large cities. These new buyers who entered the market flexed their power with conservative preferences, as they sought out, in the words of one critic, clear, simple, and "understandable" pictures.[44] Purchases from traditional patrons and connoisseurs also showed

---

[41] Timoshin, *Mitrofan Borisovich Grekov*, 62.

[42] Iu. P. Markin, *Pavel Filonov* (Moscow: Izobrazitel'noe iskusstvo, 1995), 26–27.

[43] V. B. Mirimanov, *Russkii avangard i esteticheskaia revoliutsiia XX veka: Drugaia paradigma vechnosti* (Moscow: RGGU, 1995), 25; Jeannot Simmen, *Kasimir Malewitsch. Das schwarze Quadrat* (Frankfurt: Fischer, 1998), 6.

[44] *Birzhevye vedomosti*, morning edition, 26 September 1916, 4.

a historicist and conservative bent.[45] Conservative artists did not rule the market, for modernist artists experienced an upswing in popularity. Yet the taste of art buyers at war-related exhibitions appalled Somov: "At the auction for refugees where I donated three things the prices were: 500 rubles for a marquise with a devil-shaped beauty spot, a monstrous price for such junk, a vignette of yellow roses 250! A study 150! All three trifles."[46] The British Russophile and travel writer Stephen Graham noted the prosperity among merchants and rich refugees who had started new businesses. One made a fortune selling boots in Archangel, joined the city council, and bought art with his profits.[47]

There was a psychological aspect to this war that led some artists to return to conventional aesthetics. Its stark and unpleasant reality challenged those at the front and the millions left at home to consider existential questions, and thinking about it fostered an atmosphere of sobriety and reflection. The writer Boris Zaitsev, for example, observed that his colleagues felt war's inner pressures, which led them to consider life more seriously and to feel tragedy with greater sensibility.[48] Traditional motifs allowed viewers and artists to comprehend the trauma of mass war and the mystery of mortality, and the presence of familiar classical, Romantic, or religious images in the popular culture of the war in Europe attests to the universality of sorrow and bereavement.[49] Russians could also express feelings of nostalgia and grief through symbols that echoed the past in content and form. A saleswoman at a monastic bookshop linked the war to the popularity of pictures of the Last Judgment: "There is a great demand for this particular subject and the sale of this picture has gone up. The war is making people think of death."[50]

The war's emotional impact was important in changing the art of Marc Chagall. Chagall resided in Paris but became trapped in his hometown, Vitebsk, while visiting in the summer of 1914. There he began to drop the cubist and expressionist leanings of his Parisian work for a series of pictures that used more conventional perspective, color, and composition.[51] The critic Fannina Halle later observed that Chagall's work became "somewhat more

---

[45] John E. Bowlt, "The Moscow Art Market," in *Between Tsar and People: Educated Society and the Quest for Public Identity in Late Imperial Russia*, ed. Edith W. Clowes, Samuel D. Kassow, and James L. West (Princeton, NJ: Princeton University Press, 1991), 128.

[46] Podkopaeva and Sveshnikova, *Konstantin Andreevich Somov*, 155.

[47] Stephen Graham, *Russia in 1916* (London: Cassell, 1917), 26–27, 127.

[48] *Utro Rossii*, 10 December 1916, 5.

[49] Jay Winter, *Sites of Memory, Sites of Mourning* (Cambridge: Cambridge University Press, 1995), 5.

[50] Sonia E. Howe, *Real Russians* (London: Sampson Low, Marston and Co, 1917), 198.

[51] Aleksandr Kamensky, *Chagall: The Russian Years, 1907–1922* (New York: Rizzoli, 1989), 153, 156–57.

accessible, clearer, quieter" in wartime.[52] She explained this shift in "the joy of the Prodigal Son," home again after a long separation. The great conflict itself attracted his eye and inspired him to engage war through his art. In a striking series of ink sketches, the artist memorialized wounded soldiers whom he saw around him. His painting literally helped him to protect Jews from forced evacuations (fig. 2): "I felt like having them all put on to my canvases, to keep them safe."[53] In Petrograd, the war, through his imagination, continued to influence his art practice. "The poisonous gases choked me even at Lyteiny [sic] Prospect 46, the headquarters of my military office," he wrote in his autobiography.[54] "My painting lost its edge."

A new understanding of painting as the creation of a new reality emerged during the war in the work of Malevich, Tatlin, and associated artists.[55] Modern painting, even if abstract, was always understood to represent something outside itself. Larionov and Goncharova presented rayism as the depiction of light rays reflected from everyday objects, and Kandinskii's famous abstract works were said to be expressions of various inner feelings and sensations. In the non-objective conception that emerged during World War I in Russia, however, painters argued that art creation no longer lay in a representation of external objects, but in the form, artistic execution, and reality of the physical artifact. Malevich argued that in the practice of this kind of art, which he called Suprematism, only the painter, who worked with pure intuition, could exercise the power of creation: "*Objects have vanished like smoke; to attain the new artistic culture,* art advances toward creation as an end in itself and toward domination over the forms of nature."[56] Malevich's *Black Square* (1915) (fig. 7) was thus not a representation of a black square or of anything else. It was a black square, a reality in itself fully under control of the artist. Around this same time, Tatlin abandoned frame, canvas, and paint altogether to create "corner counter-reliefs," three-dimensional sculpture-like objects that stretched across walls and corners. He explained his wartime work in terms that we now recognize as formalist: "Now I am not interested in anything except form and surface."[57]

For these artists and their advocates, non-objective art stabilized a reality that had been made unstable by war and its effects on life. Malevich emphasized how Suprematism gave him the power to restore a disintegrated world. Prewar cubists, he argued, had "destroyed objects together with their

---

[52] Fannina W. Halle, "Marc Chagall," *Das Kunstblatt* (1922): 514–15.

[53] Marc Chagall, *My Life* (Oxford: Oxford University Press, 1989), 132.

[54] Ibid., 131.

[55] Cohen, *Imagining the Unimaginable*, 131-47.

[56] John E. Bowlt, ed. and trans., *Russian Art of the Avant-Garde: Theory and Criticism, 1902–1934* (New York: Viking, 1988), 119. Emphasis in the original.

[57] Tugendkhol'd, "V zheleznom tupike," 110.

meaning, essence, and purpose."[58] Suprematism, in contrast, promised an art culture that made the world whole. "Our world of art has become new, nonobjective, pure," he declared, where "forms will live, like all living forms of nature. These forms announce that man has attained his equilibrium."[59] Similarly, one of Tatlin's advocates suggested that the artist's work was a way to give the artist power over reality, and the militarized language he invoked suggests that the reality this art opposed was the destructive and violent war.[60] The critic Nikolai Punin remembered later that artists around Tatlin used these non-painterly materials to find a way to save reality from violent destruction. "We weren't searching for a new method," he wrote, "we were looking for a means to seize reality, devices, by means of which it would be possible to grasp reality with an iron grip, without tearing it up or being torn up by it, by its convulsions and moans, its agony, and put it on canvas."[61]

The existence of public conditions that favored conventional figurative and narrative representation at art exhibitions continued into the revolutionary period. Private art collectors continued to provide a conventional market for art when economic conditions allowed, although in some years and some places this market ceased to exist, and the museums, although nationalized, continued to collect art mostly as their directors saw fit. The Bolshevik government's lack of focused attention on the production of revolutionary content in easel painting (as opposed to the mass media) meant that artists and collectors had the capability to continue their previous work as long as it was not deemed counterrevolutionary. Many people, including most Bolshevik politicians, assumed that the public could only understand conventional painting anyway. Punin admitted in 1919 that "realists enjoy greater success with the broad masses than the left artists. That is because their paintings are understandable to them."[62] Chagall later claimed that his Vitebsk street decorations in 1918 were met with smiles from workers and confusion from Communists: "Why is the cow green and why is the horse flying through the sky, why? What's the connection with Marx and Lenin?"[63]

The presence of traditional landscape, portrait, and genre painting in early Soviet art exhibitions can in part be seen as a reaction to institutional and personal instability, similar to what artists had experienced during the war years but in a different political context. As the Soviet art historian V. S. Manin put it, artists had the "desire to return to usual activity, interrupted

---

[58] Bowlt, *Theory and Criticism*, 127.

[59] Ibid., 133.

[60] See Cohen, *Imagining the Unimaginable*, 143.

[61] Sidney Monas and Jennifer Greene Krupala, eds., *The Diaries of Nikolay Punin, 1904–1953*, trans. Krupala (Austin: University of Texas Press, 1999), 26.

[62] I. I., "Disput ob iskusstve," *Zhizn' iskusstva*, 6 May 1919, 1.

[63] Chagall, *My Life*, 137.

and destroyed by the revolution" as a way to survive hard and unpredictable times.[64] Around the time of the Bolshevik Revolution, Petrov-Vodkin started to "tamp down" and "bring order" to his affairs.[65] A work like *Petrograd in 1918* (1920) (fig. 8) represents one way in which artists could create that order through art. Petrov-Vodkin's use of color, flat composition, and fine lines present this simple picture of a young woman with infant as a modern icon, a Madonna from whom one can seek peace and consolation. Both form and content of this painting offer reassurance and succor; the artist felt a calming effect in person when he saw it hanging on a museum wall in 1921: she was "so meek, and had so much depth in her, that her success in Moscow is completely understandable."[66] From this perspective, Rylov's *Blue Expanse* (1918) (fig. 9) might also be understood as a reassuring image in an uncertain time. With its abstract location, bright lighting, and moving action, the picture gives an impression of dynamism, adventure, and exploration.[67] It is a voyage into the unknown, but one that seems sunny, bright, and optimistic, not the unpleasant reality and fear of the future that others felt (fig. 3).

For the engaged artists of the avant-garde, new uses and locations for art counteracted the weakness of traditional institutions and helped stabilize professional activity. "Into this chaos," as Aleksandr Rodchenko described the role of the avant-garde in the new time, "came suprematism [sic] extolling the square as the very source of all creative expression. and [sic] then came communism and extolled work as the true source of man's heartbeat."[68] Constructivists, Suprematists, production artists, and others hoped to re-make life through art, which in the era of the proletarian revolution meant to fuse technology and art to produce objects that would be aesthetic and functional.[69] The Higher State Art and Technical Workshop (Vkhutemas), for example, became a school of design that combined art education and a guild-like atmosphere in a curriculum designed to create the "artist-constructors" who could help construct a new socialist culture.[70] Socialism, for the politi-cized avant-garde, would be realized when the differences between art and artifact, between creation and labor, were broken down. They brought art

---

[64] V. S. Manin, *Iskusstvo v rezervatsii: Khudozhestvennaia zhizn' Rossii 1917–1941 gg.* (Moscow: Editorial URSS, 1999), 16.

[65] E. N. Selizarova, ed., *K. S. Petrov-Vodkin: Pis'ma, stat'i, vystupleniia, dokumenty* (Moscow: Sovetskii khudozhnik, 1991), 323.

[66] Ibid., 212.

[67] Sarab'ianov, *Istoriia russkogo i sovetskogo iskusstva*, 339.

[68] Bowlt, *Theory and Criticism*, 153.

[69] Christina Lodder, *Russian Constructivism* (New Haven: Yale University Press, 1983), 75–76.

[70] Lodder, *Constructivism*, 109.

into factories, workshops, and design schools and merged it with the material world as dishware, books, clothing, furniture, and other objects of daily life.

Avant-garde art, however, could also become more conventional in response to public needs. Suprematists continued to work after 1917, and non-objective art remained the truest form of radical culture for some critics and artists. But the need to address the new political and representational tasks of the 1920s required the abandonment of the idea of non-objectivity even if its forms were kept intact. El (Lazar') Lisitskii's iconic *Beat the Whites with the Red Wedge* (1919) (fig. 10), for example, owes much to the visual language of Suprematism, but the artist used it to represent a story of revolutionary violence in which the red power of proletarian force splits white counterrevolutionary resistance, and written text was added to anchor this meaning. The non-objective work of art became objective in a poster designed to communicate with audiences outside the art world, and it became undesirable as the state began to develop an official aesthetic based on figurative art and political engagement. As Tugendkhol'd later argued, "Narrow professional formalism is a legacy of prerevolutionary culture, of the epoch of the war."[71]

The importance of the war as a moment when artistic form could change dramatically can be seen in the work of Petrov-Vodkin, a noted symbolist with connections to the World of Art. The figures in his famous painting *Bathing a Red Horse* (1912) thus exist in an ideal, abstract golden age outside time and space; as subjects "far removed from everyday reality," they represent nothing in the real world.[72] Petrov-Vodkin turned to a narrative depiction of Russian reality during the war, which, as the artist later said, "roused us" and inspired his "first political answer to the history of the moment."[73] His personal patriotism and concern for Russian soldiers are clear in *In the Firing Line* (1915) (fig. 1), and it was a direct experience in the external world that inspired it: "I only had this sincere wish to paint exactly this picture. I saw in Samara how the echelons left for war and felt the indestructible, black earth Russian power, a force bashful, not knowing itself, and unbounded."[74] The canvas, however, was a clear break with the World of Art's disdain for narrative painting and for sociopolitical engagement in art, and the harsh criticism it evoked was a form of "iron discipline" from a group seeking to uphold aesthetic boundaries.[75] Its iconography, in essence, reflected popular patriotic culture, not modernist aesthetic values: as Russian infantry struggle to advance over a small hill, a young soldier in the lead is shot in the chest, taking a sacrificial pose as the

---

[71] Tugendkhol'd, *Iz istorii zapadnoevropeiskogo, russkogo i sovetskogo iskusstva*, 230.

[72] Dmitri V. Sarab'ianov, *Russian Art from Neoclassicism to the Avant-Garde, 1800–1917* (New York: Abrams, 1990), 246.

[73] Selizarova, *K. S. Petrov-Vodkin*, 323.

[74] *Petrogradskii listok*, 23 February 1917, 2.

[75] *Birzhevye vedomosti*, evening edition, 23 October 1916, 3.

shells fly and fires burn in the background. *In the Firing Line* might have later been canonized as a great Russian war painting if not for the problematic place of the World War I experience in the Bolshevik view of history.

Petrov-Vodkin found a different way to combine war, painting, and politics in the context of Bolshevik victory. After 1917, the artist admitted that he felt, "like many," a "great obligation" to use art for the public good in the face of "all the masses moving into life."[76] In *After the Battle* (1923) (fig. 11), he believed he had for the "first time succeeded in communicating an archetype of that time and of the events when the Red Army was being built."[77] Visually, *After the Battle* is a kind of sequel to *In the Firing Line*, for we see a dying soldier similar to one in the earlier painting.[78] But the narrative has shifted in time, and while *In the Firing Line* presents a snapshot of battle, *After the Battle* shows fighting men who remember their fallen comrade. The worth of the Red Army men is demonstrated by their actions during and after combat, while the consequences of the soldier's sacrifice in *In the Firing Line* are not resolved. Petrov-Vodkin later recognized that the depiction of remembrance in victory made for a more successful painting. "If I compare *In the Firing Line* and the second painting, then you see that they have nothing in common," the artist recalled, "For five years there were no more soldiers except Red Army men, Red guards, that is something different."[79] His spouse likewise saw imperial Russian failure in the disjointed action in *In the Firing Line*; in it, she wrote, "we can understand the confusion from which will emerge the future disorganization which will finally bring the collapse of tsarism."[80] *After the Battle* shows the human cost behind a well-earned Red victory, not the deadly mess of combat where the ultimate reason for fighting remains obscure. In the aftermath of the Civil War, order was restored.

From 1914 to 1922, Russian public institutions became unstable as unprecedented economic, social, and political changes wracked the country. World War I altered the structure of the public sphere to produce more and more kinds of artistic participation, and painters became engaged in unprecedented levels of social and political activism. Some produced war images for the mass media, while a return to a more figurative visual style was one clear response to personal stress or to changes in the market. The participation of the avant-garde in the formation of early Bolshevik culture had its roots in this wartime public mobilization, as did their radical new vision of art: non-objectivity. After 1917, cultural mobilization in Russia focused on the Revolution, and

---

[76] Selizarova, *K. S. Petrov-Vodkin*, 323.

[77] Ibid., 329.

[78] V. I. Kostin, *K. S. Petrov-Vodkin* (Moscow: Sovetskii khudozhnik, 1966), 82.

[79] Selizarova, *K. S. Petrov-Vodkin*, 323.

[80] Rossiiskii gosudarstvennyi arkhiv literatury i iskusstva (RGALI) f. 2010, op. 2, ed. khr. 57, reel 2.

the state took on a more important role as a direct shaper of art culture. The expansion of space for mobilized visual culture from exhibitions and news media to the physical space of the city was also new in the revolutionary period. But the underlying conditions of personal and public instability remained the same, and in many respects the war, not the revolution, was the instigator for the most important changes. The poems of Sassoon and Owen, paintings of Nevinson and Dix, and novels of Remarque and Hemingway have defined the strangeness, ugliness, and tragedy of modern warfare for generations, but where are the great works of the Great War in Russia? They lie not in any great antiwar or prorevolutionary canvas but in Malevich's *Black Square* and the other paintings of this vital period that have entered the canon of modern art history in Russia and the West.

Press Photography in Russia's Great War and Revolution

Christopher Stolarski

On the eve of the Great War, press photography in Russia appeared primarily in weekly magazines. Most of these publications first hit news stands around 1900 as literary supplements to daily newspapers. But as readers grew more interested in current events, magazine editors increasingly replaced essays and short fiction with pictures of the news. Photo-reportage quickly became central to the commercial appeal of the illustrated press. And starting in 1914, riveting images of war and revolution, as well as everyday reports on celebrities, technical innovations, and exotic destinations around the world informed and entertained millions of readers throughout the Russian Empire. With portraits and scenic views—familiar genres associated with family and the passage of time—press photographers established meaningful connections between the private lives of readers and the public "world outside."[1] Through these pictures, magazines offered a carefully-framed window that looked out into the world and made ordinary people feel engaged in the progress of history as citizens, soldiers, patriots, victims, and revolutionaries.

Photographers worked with publishers and editors to create the visual landscape of photojournalism. They combined images with headlines, captions, and short articles to communicate the topical news of the day. Magazines catered to a broad middle class, composed of urban professionals, provincial gentry, school teachers, and homemakers, as well as skilled workers and migrant peasants.[2] The illustrated press was also quite partisan. The politics of publishers and civil society, which were typically liberal and opposed to autocracy, shaped the narrative ebb and flow of photographic news coverage in Russia's most popular magazines—this despite censorship statutes that forced magazines to contend with the state's ever-changing official policy on the press. But press photography itself, more than the content it carried, determined the immense popularity of magazines in this period. It raised the status of Russian periodicals as consumer objects, while offering publishers a

---

[1] Walter Lippman, *Public Opinion* (New York: Harcourt, Brace, 1922), chap. 1; on family and photography, see Pierre Bourdieu, *Photography: A Middle-Brow Art*, trans. Shaun Whiteside (Stanford, CA: Stanford University Press, 1990).

[2] Jeffrey Brooks, *When Russia Learned to Read: Literacy and Popular Literature, 1871–1917* (Princeton, NJ: Princeton University Press, 1985), 111.

Russian Culture in War and Revolution, 1914–22, Book 1: Popular Culture, the Arts, and Institutions. Murray Frame, Boris Kolonitskii, Steven G. Marks, and Melissa K. Stockdale, eds. Bloomington, IN: Slavica Publishers, 2014, 139–63.

cheap, efficient, and seemingly objective means of reporting on current events. Objectivity and fact-based reporting, rather than editorial opinion, defined the "new journalism" at the end of the imperial era.[3] Photo-reportage allowed spectators to interpret what they saw according to their own politics, social perspectives, and life experiences. By providing a transparent and widely accessible picture of reality, the illustrated press included the reading public in the act of telling the news.

Between 1914 and 1922, magazines captured a complex and often chaotic portrait of war and revolution.[4] Publishers used photography to report the news, and they used the news to advance specific political, social, and cultural agendas. During the Great War these agendas were counterbalanced by the commercial interests of publishing houses. On the one hand, magazine publishers strongly supported progressive politicians in the State Duma and the continued prosecution of the war, especially when those politicians took charge of foreign affairs in February 1917. On the other hand, they published a broad range of pictures, hoping to attract a large and diverse public regardless of readers' political views. This diversity diluted the politics of the illustrated press and allowed readers to pick and choose among the pictures on the page— to craft their own narrative of the news. After the Revolution, Soviet photo-reportage inherited the propagandistic tendency without the moderating influence of commercialism. For the Bolsheviks, the calculation was simple: just as the bourgeois press bolstered the bourgeois state, so too should the Soviet illustrated press champion the Communist state.[5] Soviet publishers faced constant material shortages, which diminished the production of photo-reportage and of magazines. Less photography appeared in fewer weeklies, and the centralization of press affairs in Soviet Russia ensured that the few pictures taken during the Civil War captured a portrait of society that was firmly in line with the Bolshevik worldview. The Revolution did not radically alter the function of photo-reportage, at least not immediately. But the pictured "world outside" was smaller and less diverse, and provided readers with fewer options for individual interpretation.

---

[3] Louise McReynolds, *The News Under Russia's Old Regime: The Development of a Mass-Circulation Press* (Princeton, NJ: Princeton University Press, 1991), 113–22.

[4] For this study, I examined a handful of magazines closely, namely *Ogonek, Iskry, Niva, Sinii zhurnal, Solntse Rossii,* and *Plamia.* I also examined a number of other weekly publications more broadly, including *Letopis' voiny 1914 goda, Priroda i liudi, Zhurnal-kopeika, Zerkalo zhizni, Vsemirnaia panorama,* and *Russkaia illiustratsiia.*

[5] "Dekret o pechati," in *Lenin o pechati* (Moscow: Gosudarstvennoe izd-vo politicheskoi literatury, 1959), 691; Robert Service, *Lenin: A Biography* (Cambridge, MA: Harvard Belknap, 2000), 318.

Photographers and News Magazines

A relatively small group of photographers supplied most of the pictures for news magazines during the Great War and Revolution. This included, among others, Aleksei I. Savel'ev, Iakov V. Shteinberg, Petr A. Otsup, Aleksandr Bulla, and Karl Bulla. Together, this group represented the first generation of photographers in Russia to dedicate their careers to photo-reportage. They were all based in Petrograd or Moscow; they covered the city news and worked closely with the local "capital" (*stolichnye*) press.[6] Savel'ev, for example, reported on current events from Moscow and worked primarily with Ivan Sytin's Moscow-based *Iskry*.[7] Likewise, pictures taken by Shteinberg, Otsup, and the Bullas covered the news from Petrograd and appeared in magazines published from the imperial capital. This arrangement ensured regular communication between editor and photographer and a quick turnover of topical news stories. Publishers, however, did not own the exclusive rights to the work of any single photographer. Most press photographers were independent, providing images regularly for a specific publication but also free to sell photos to other magazines. Savel'ev's pictures of Moscow, for example, appeared throughout the Russian illustrated press, and not just in *Iskry*.

Other news coverage was supplied by provincial photographers, special correspondents, international news agencies, and amateurs. Photographers with access to the frontlines included Z. M. Shubskii, A. V. Martynov, S. A. Korsakov, A. D. Dalmatov, V. A. Bystrov, and a few others. Again, these photographers worked primarily with specific magazines, but also sold images to other publishers. Editors often printed photographs anonymously, that is, without credit or with reference to "our special war correspondent." Publishers placed a high value on their "own" photographers in the field and highlighted access to wide networks of correspondents in subscription advertisements. Photographs from abroad, usually purchased from news agencies such as Underwood & Underwood, were also printed anonymously, as were photographs taken by amateurs. Armed with easy-to-use hand-held cameras, amateurs offered editors a cheap source of news information. Regular advertisements in *Ogonek* solicited the public to send pictures of "local events related to the war," including hospitals, infirmaries, wounded soldiers, charities, and prisoners of war.[8] In the theater of war, this sort of recruitment ensured access to pictures that otherwise were difficult to obtain. Covering the

---

[6] P. E. Esperov, *Chto dolzhen trebovat' chitatel'-intelligent ot organa pechati?* (St. Petersburg: Samoposhch', 1904), 18.

[7] Rossiiskii gosudarstvennyi arkhiv literatury i iskusstva (RGALI) f. 595 (Editorial papers of the newspaper *Russkoe slovo*), op. 1, ed. khr. 22, l. 30 (Letter to the Moscow Committee on Print Matters).

[8] These appeared regularly throughout the war and 1917 Revolutions, for example: *Ogonek*, no. 42 (19 October [1 November] 1914): 2.

frontlines required extra manpower and permission from military authorities. By relying on amateurs, editors could circumvent bureaucracy, obtain images cheaply, and perhaps convey the sense that the public's perspective was truly represented in the press.[9]

During the war, the most popular magazines were illustrated supplements to daily newspapers. This included *Ogonek*, which was attached to the Petrograd business daily *Birzhevye vedomosti*, and *Iskry*, the illustrated weekly to Sytin's Moscow-based *Russkoe slovo*.[10] From Monday to Friday, the dailies reported on current events and on the weekends the supplements provided photos, fine art, and short fiction. Other magazines, such as *Niva, Solntse Rossii*, and *Sinii zhurnal*, were freestanding publications.[11] These weeklies prioritized photo-reportage, but they also preserved a distinctly literary character. *Niva*, for example, was a respected family magazine, which offered essays and literature alongside a variety of illustrated material. *Solntse Rossii* published a similar balance of image and text, while catering to more refined aesthetic sensibilities. By contrast, *Sinii zhurnal* offered a distinctly ironic perspective on the news, featuring satire and political cartoons alongside photo-reportage. A few magazines, such as *Letopis´ voiny 1914 goda*, were devoted exclusively to the Great War. This weekly was exquisitely produced and presented an official, government-approved chronicle of the war. Photo-reportage also appeared in books, art journals, and other media, such as postcards and stereographs. Weekly magazines, however, offered readers the best source of photo-reportage on a regular basis.

Magazines peaked in popularity during the war as editors cut down on written material in favor of more photo-reportage. They were available by annual subscription or sold individually in bookstores and city kiosks. Prices varied greatly and fluctuated when publishers were forced to offset the rising

---

[9] Camera manufacturers, such as Eastman Kodak, targeted soldiers with equipment made specially "for soldiers" to "capture scenes experienced during the Great War." *Liubitel´ kodakist*, no. 36, advertisement.

[10] Another example: Mikhail Gorodetskii's daily newspaper *Gazeta-kopeika* offered subscribers a choice of two different illustrated weeklies, namely *Zhurnal-kopeika* and *Zerkalo zhizni*. Gorodetskii also published the magazine *Vsemirnaia panorama*. Other newspapers, such as *Novoe vremia, Moskovskii listok, Peterburgskaia gazeta*, and *Novosti*, all published weekly or biweekly illustrated supplements. For a comprehensive index of the prerevolutionary press, see Esperov, *Chto dolzhen trebovat´ chitatel´-intelligent*, 18–19.

[11] These were among the most popular freestanding publications. Other examples include *Rodina, Priroda i liudi*, and *Vokrug sveta*. On weekly magazines, see A. S. Voronkevich, "Russkii ezhenedel´nik v nachale XX v.," in *Iz istorii russkoi zhurnalistiki nachala XX veka*, ed. B. I. Esin (Moscow: Izd-vo Moskovskogo universiteta, 1984), 140–59.

cost of paper and ink.[12] In 1914, *Ogonek* was among the cheaper publications, costing 5 kopecks per issue or 2.50 rubles per year. High-quality magazines, such as *Niva*, *Solntse Rossii*, and *Letopis' voiny*, cost considerably more.[13] In terms of weekly circulation, the leading magazine was *Ogonek*, which reached 700,000 subscribers per week and an estimated 6 million readers nationwide.[14] Magazines were enjoyed over the long term and among multiple readers. The editors of *Ogonek* estimated that a single copy of their periodical reached 10 people on average. The same report described the typical reader as someone sitting "in the warmth and comfort of home," flipping leisurely through an issue over a cigarette.[15] This domestic fantasy was made available to business travelers and seasonal vacationers who purchased magazines along train routes.[16] Publishers also offered special premiums, such as art albums and complete works of Russian authors. More expensive publications included images and maps intended for framing. In fact, the graphic design (and premium price) of *Solntse Rossii* marked the periodical as a luxury item worth preserving and exhibiting—a sign of the consumer's elite tastes. The illustrated press was thus a rich source of information and an object of conspicuous consumption.

After 1917, the Bolsheviks shut down the imperial press, and magazines such as *Ogonek* and *Iskry* ceased to exist. The flagship Soviet magazine during the Civil War was *Plamia*. Edited by Anatolii Lunacharskii, this weekly was first published in Petrograd in May 1918. *Plamia* offered readers essays, short fiction, and poetry, as well as photography, fine art, and other illustrated material. Another magazine dedicated to photo-reportage was the Moscow-based *Khronika*. In its first issue, the editor N. F. Preobrazhenskii wrote, "[W]e owe it to history to photograph everything we can, and to preserve this for future generations."[17] He also stressed the need for alternative accounts of

---

[12] *Ogonek*, no. 40 (4 [17] October 1915): 1; *Sinii zhurnal*, no. 50 (12 December 1915): 2. The editors of *Ogonek* and *Sinii zhurnal* reported that shortages also affected the magazines *Strekoza*, *Novaia vsemirnaia illiustratsiia*, *Zhizn' i sud*, *Dvadtsatyi vek*, *Vsemirnaia panorama*, *Vsemirnaia nov'*.

[13] In 1914, *Niva* cost 20 kopecks per issue and 8 rubles per year. *Solntse Rossii* cost 25 kopecks per issue and 6 rubles per year. *Letopis' voiny* cost 35 kopecks per issue and did not offer an annual subscription because, of course, the publishers could not predict the length of the war.

[14] For figures provided by the editors in subscription advertisements, see *Ogonek*, no. 43 (26 October [8 November] 1914): 19 and *Ogonek* no. 51 (21 December [3 January] 1914): 20. By contrast, in 1914, the weekly circulation of *Iskry* was about 100,000, of *Sinii zhurnal*, 86,000, and of *Letopis' voiny*, 35,000.

[15] *Ogonek*, no. 43 (26 October [8 November] 1914): 19.

[16] On magazine distribution, see Brooks, *When Russia Learned to Read*, 110.

[17] Quoted in L. F. Volkov-Lannit, *Istoriia pishetsia ob"ektivom* (Moscow: Planet, 1971), 48.

the news, in order to oppose the "printed lies" of anti-Bolshevik propaganda. These Soviet periodicals overlapped briefly with remnants of the "bourgeois" illustrated press. Both *Niva* and *Sinii zhurnal* appeared well into 1918.[18] The postrevolutionary version of *Sinii zhurnal* lacked its characteristic satirical bite, but the photo-reportage remained fundamentally unchanged in form and content. However, chronic shortages of paper and trained personnel suffocated the illustrated press, perhaps more so than Bolshevik policy, and amidst additional distribution problems and falling circulation, *Niva* and *Sinii zhurnal* folded in September 1918.[19] *Khronika* suffered a similar fate soon after. Although photographs also appeared in books and other types of periodicals, *Plamia* was the only magazine to publish them on a weekly basis throughout the Civil War.

Press photographers of the imperial era continued to work in the Soviet press infrastructure. Many of them contributed to the photo-reportage of the Civil War and to Soviet mass media for decades after. Savel'ev, for example, became head of the Narkompros section of photo-reportage and newsreel (VFKO) in 1918. He was joined by a few other prerevolutionary photographers, but mostly he oversaw the work of documentary filmmakers, such as Dziga Vertov, Petr K. Novitskii, and Eduard K. Tisse.[20] Around the same time, Otsup was made head of photography at the All-Russian Central Executive Committee (VTsIK). He organized photographic exhibitions and participated in the work of the most important Soviet agitational train, the *October Revolution*.[21] Although Karl Bulla retired in 1917, his two sons, Aleksandr and Viktor, remained in Petrograd, where they continued to produce press photography and to operate their father's portrait studio on Nevskii Prospekt.[22] Likewise, Shteinberg remained a productive photojournalist throughout the Civil War, providing almost all the pictures for *Plamia* in its first few years of publication. Although a new generation of photographers came of age in this period, the old guard, trained and tested in tsarist Russia, continued to produce photo-reportage well into the 1920s.

The paucity of the early Soviet illustrated press forced photographers to find other venues in which to exhibit news images. Photo-reportage was thus also distributed through postcards, pamphlets, placards, and photographic

---

[18] For *Niva*, see Ia. I. Dodzin and A. B. Velizheva, *Periodicheskaia pechat' SSSR 1917–1949: Bibliograficheskii ukazatel'* (Moscow: Izd-vo vsesoiuznoi knizhnoi palaty, 1958), 46.

[19] Peter Kenez, *The Birth of the Propaganda State: Soviet Methods of Mass Mobilization, 1917–1929* (Cambridge: Cambridge University Press, 1985), 44–45.

[20] Gosudarstvennyi arkhiv Rossiiskoi Federatsii (GARF) f. 2306 (People's Commissariat of Enlightenment), op. 27, d. 7, l. 28 (Payroll of the Cinema-News Section).

[21] Volkov-Lannit, *Istoriia pishetsia ob"ektivom*, 91.

[22] Iu. N. Sergeev, *Fotografii na pamiat': Fotografy Nevskogo prospekta 1850–1950* (St. Petersburg: Lenfilm, 2003), 397.

albums. Prints of Lenin and other prominent Bolsheviks, of party congresses and meetings, and of Red Army frontline encounters, were available for free at agitational stations (*agitpunkty*).[23] These were kiosks where propaganda material was stored, displayed, and distributed. In 1920, the Moscow section of Narkompros organized weekly showcases of photo-reportage at 60 such "points" in the city and in train stations throughout the Soviet Union.[24] Press photographers also traveled on board agitational trains, which were equipped to develop film and to produce prints for distribution on the frontlines.[25] These trains were inspired originally by similar mobile propaganda stations used to boost morale during the Great War.[26] In addition, the new regime commissioned photographic albums, which were intended to describe Soviet "reality" to foreigners and to dispel the rumors of disorder disseminated by White propaganda.[27] In the absence of a robust illustrated press, these older, antecedent forms of press photography, many of which originated in the 19th century, offered photographers an alternative venue for publication. The small scope and centralization of the distribution of photo-reportage during the Civil War also ensured that Soviet censors retained control of the ideological content of the news.

Censorship of Press Photography

A number of different censorship statutes governed press photography during the war. First, there was the statute on wartime correspondents ("Polozhenie o voennykh korrespondentakh v voennoe vremia"), which regulated the activities of press photographers working in the theater of war.[28] Written by the general staff in 1912, this document paid special attention to photographers, including their exact numbers, nationality, and freedom of movement, and to the use of hand-held cameras in general.[29] Directives

---

[23] G. M. Boltianskii, *Ocherki po istorii fotografii v SSSR* (Moscow: Goskinoizdat, 1939), 97–98.

[24] Ibid., 98; Kenez, *Birth of the Propaganda State*, 58–59.

[25] On agitational trains, see Richard Taylor, "A Medium for the Masses: Agitation in the Soviet Civil War," *Soviet Studies* 22, 4 (April 1971): 562–74.

[26] Hubertus F. Jahn, *Patriotic Culture in Russia during World War I* (Ithaca, NY: Cornell University Press, 1995), 81.

[27] Volkov-Lannit, *Istoriia pishetsia ob"ektivom*, 51.

[28] For a transcript of the "Statute on War Correspondents in Wartime," see M. K. Lemke, *250 dnei v tsarskoi stavke (25 sentiabria 1915–2 iiulia 1916)* (St. Petersburg: Gosudarstvennoe izd-vo, 1920), 125–32.

[29] Almost all the articles in the statute applied to press photographers and journalists equally, and a number of them concerned only war photography.

regarding the content of photography were laid out in the general statute on war censorship ("Vremennoe polozhenie o voennoi tsenzure"), established in July 1914.[30] Attached to this document was a list of proscribed subjects, which included the size, location, and preparedness of land and naval forces, the construction of railways, the conditions of telegraph lines, and other information on weapons, fortifications, and military strategy.[31] Furthermore, all photographs of the imperial family had to be approved by the Ministry of the Imperial Court before publication, and publishers were subject to additional scrutiny by various local committees and officials for press affairs.[32] Although preliminary censorship had not been enforced since 1905, editors were required to submit copies of magazines for review and could be prosecuted if the content violated the criminal code.[33]

Military censorship came under intense criticism in the first year of the war. In his memoirs, the general staff officer Mikhail K. Lemke recalled publishers complaining about the lack of coordination between military and civil authorities, the arbitrary application of censorship statutes, and the difference between censorship in the theater of war and outside this zone.[34] Periodicals in Petrograd, for example, were subject to strict military regulations, while in Moscow and the provinces censors were more relaxed. Publishers, angered by wartime statutes, often expressed their disapproval by leaving "white spaces" in magazines.[35] Protests of this kind led the authorities to enact regulation more uniformly throughout the empire, which loosened censorship at the front but brought about more stringent oversight everywhere else. Furthermore, the reformed statutes often overstepped their legal bounds. In a letter to the general staff, Prime Minister Ivan Goremykin stressed the need for censors

---

[30] "Vremennoe polozhenie o voennoi tsenzure (20 iiulia 1914 g.)," in *Vlast' i pressa: K istorii pravovogo regulirovaniia otnoshenii 1700–1917. Khrestomatiia* (Moscow: Izd-vo RAGS, 1999), 204–13.

[31] This list was amended a number of times in July 1914 (Lemke, *250 dnei v tsarskoi stavke*, 364–73).

[32] S. I. Grigor'ev, *Pridvornaia tsenzura i obraz verkhovnoi vlasti 1831–1917* (St. Petersburg: Aleteiia, 2007), 219–20.

[33] Caspar Ferenczi, "Freedom of the Press under the Old Regime, 1905–1914," in *Civil Rights in Imperial Russia*, ed. Olga Crisp and Linda Edmondson (Oxford: Clarendon Press, 1989), 195–201.

[34] Lemke, *250 dnei v tsarskoi stavke*, 426.

[35] Ibid., 391, 403. For examples of these gaps on the page, see *Ogonek*, no. 14 (5 [18] April 1915): 6–7; *Sinii zhurnal*, no. 13 (26 March 1915): 7; *Russkaia illiustratsiia*, no. 13 (3 May 1915): 8–9.

to assess material "not only from a narrow military point of view, but also regarding more general political matters."[36]

Magazine editors, however, found creative ways to protest against this overreach. In November 1916, censors prevented Pavel Miliukov's speech, which criticized the government's handling of the war, from being printed in the press. In retaliation, newspaper editors left gaps in news columns. *Sinii zhurnal*, though unlikely to publish the speech in normal circumstances, also printed a blank page in one issue. But to drive the point home, and perhaps to clarify what was being censored, the editors included a small portrait of Miliukov in the corner of the page.[37] (See fig. 12 in the gallery of illustrations following page 188.) The photograph thus substituted for the speech symbolically. This display presumed prior knowledge of the situation, whether from newspapers, which reported the censorship, or from other non-press sources. Nonetheless, the simple use of a picture demonstrated the power of an image to circumvent official censorship, while still complying with the letter of the law.

Tsarist censorship came to an end in April 1917 when the Provisional Government issued a directive that officially sanctioned the dismantling of the Chief Administration of Press Affairs. However, this unprecedented level of freedom ceased abruptly when the Bolsheviks took power six months later. Lenin was by no means an advocate of unchecked press freedoms.[38] He believed that the bourgeois capitalists had attained ideological dominance by monopolizing the press before the Revolution and wished to achieve something similar in Bolshevik Russia.[39] A monopoly over the periodical press was necessary in order to preserve the Revolution and, furthermore, to prevent the publication of counterrevolutionary material.

The Bolsheviks did not single out press photography in documents relating to censorship. Like prewar imperial statutes, they approached censorship broadly, using legal institutions to punish offenders, rather than listing specific prohibitions. In January 1918, the Bolsheviks set up a three-man Revolutionary Tribunal for the Press charged with prosecuting publishers and editors for crimes such as presenting "false or distorted information

---

[36] Quoted in G. V. Zhirkov, *Istoriia tsenzury v Rossii XIX–XX vv.* (Moscow: Aspekt Press, 2001), 196.

[37] *Sinii zhurnal*, no. 48 (26 November 1916): 6.

[38] See Peter Kenez, "Lenin and the Freedom of the Press," in *Bolshevik Culture: Experiment and Order in the Russian Revolution*, ed. Abbott Gleason, Kenez, and Richard Stites (Bloomington: Indiana University Press, 1985), 131–50.

[39] Jeffrey Brooks, *Thank You, Comrade Stalin! Soviet Public Culture from Revolution to Cold War* (Princeton, NJ: Princeton University Press, 2000), 3.

about the phenomena of societal life."[40] A guilty verdict would subject the offender to fines, public censure, confiscation of property, imprisonment, exile, and the deprivation of "all or some political rights."[41] Later that year, Trotskii reinstated the practice of wartime censorship ("Polozhenie o voenno-revoliutsionnoi tsenzure"). This statute required all printed matter "in which information of a military nature is reported" to be submitted for preliminary review.[42] In practice, censors interpreted this document broadly and excised any news that threatened the revolutionary spirit of the people. Guilty parties were tried before a military tribunal. But, according to historian Arlen Blium, the lack of coordination between military authorities, the Revolutionary Tribunal, the Cheka, and various press commissars in Petrograd and Moscow prevented wartime censorship from being applied consistently for another two years.[43]

The Visual World of Photo-Reportage

Wartime press photography focused on the frontlines. This included pictures of soldiers, weaponry, mobilization, prisoners, trophies, leisure activities, and military successes, and they appeared in regular photographic layouts, typically called "At the Front" or "Army in the Field," which reported from all the war zones.[44] The coverage of the Eastern Front, mired in trench warfare, military encampments, and burning villages, differed greatly from the Southern or Caucasian Front, which offered readers epic vistas of mountainous terrain. *Niva*, in particular, luxuriated in the region's exotic geography, where Russian soldiers scaled hills and craggy rocks. Frontline news also included reports from Russia's allies in the West. Magazines, such as *Solntse Rossii*, arranged extensive profiles on Britain, France, and Belgium, which established a sense of kinship among the allies, based equally in military and cultural affairs.[45] Throughout the conflict, the Russian effort was integrated visually into the

---

[40] "O revoliutsionnom tribunale pechati: Dekret soveta narodnykh komissarov," in *O partiinoi i sovetskoi pechati: Sbornik dokumentov* (Moscow: Pravda, 1954), 175–76.

[41] Ibid., 176.

[42] Quoted in A. V. Blium, *Za kulisami "ministerstva pravdy": Tainaia istoriia sovetskoi tsenzury 1917–1929* (St. Petersburg: Akademicheskii proekt, 1994), 44–45.

[43] Ibid., 45–47.

[44] For example, *Ogonek*, no. 46 (16 [29] November 1914): 7; *Sinii zhurnal*, no. 5 (31 January 1915): 7; *Niva*, no. 9 (28 February 1915): 170–71; *Iskry*, no. 15 (10 April 1916): 116–17.

[45] Starting with *Solntse Rossii*, no. 29–30 (August 1914), the editors published a series of "war numbers" which included entire issues dedicated to photographs about Russia's allies in the West. Other magazines offered less extensive overviews of the West, typically featuring a series of portraits of politicians and royalty or landscapes of iconic national landmarks.

pan-European war; pictures of French battlefields, for instance, appeared alongside similar scenes in Galicia. Stories of camaraderie among allies flattered Russia's accomplishments in the eyes of the West. In 1916, a series in *Iskry* underlined the "special warmth" of Parisians towards Russian troops, who marched down the Champs-Élysées.[46] Like tourist photos, these pictures captured the landmarks of the French capital, where Russia's representatives abroad were welcomed symbolically into the Western European fold.

Photography was also used to commemorate heroes and victims. The sacrifice of soldiers was personalized in portraits and biographical sketches. Editors solicited their readers for portraits of loved ones killed or wounded in battle.[47] The most striking tributes appeared in *Ogonek*, where the editors honored Russian casualties with five or six pages of small portraits[48] (fig. 13). Coverage of refugees, typically women and children in makeshift camps, revealed the national dimension of a humanitarian disaster. Captions identified Latvian, Armenian, Polish, and Jewish refugees. By contrast, displaced Ukrainians, Belorussians, and Germans were not singled out. The cause of their homelessness, that is, whether they suffered at the hands of the German military or as a result of deportations enacted by Russian troops, was not revealed.[49] Nonetheless, drawing attention to nationality allowed editors to connect these images to the publicized efforts of civil society to organize relief. The most emotionally compelling reports, however, elided the national question. *Solntse Rossii*, for example, featured intimate portraits with captions that spoke through the experience or universal sense of what it means to be hungry, uprooted, and alone. The caption below a picture of an infant and two desperate-looking women simply read "Homeless."[50] In a series called "Refugees on the Road," a photo of a baby is captioned "Left behind" and another of children eating read "They are hungry."[51] Photo-reportage generalized the plight of refugees, thus allowing spectators, irrespective of nationality, to feel more connected to the photographed subjects.

---

[46] *Iskry*, no. 30 (31 July 1916): 236–37; another story covering the Russian army in the west appeared in *Iskry*, no. 5 (1 February 1917): 33, 36–37.

[47] *Ogonek*, no. 40 (5 [18] October 1914): 11; *Letopis' voiny 1914 goda*, no. 3 (6 September 1914): table of contents, inside cover.

[48] For example, *Ogonek*, no. 40 (5 [18] October 1914): 10–13; for similar tributes, see *Iskry*, no. 47 (30 November 1914): 375; *Niva*, no. 29 (18 July 1915): 569; *Letopis' voiny 1914 goda*, no. 11 (1 November 1914): 183; *Sinii zhurnal*, no. 8 (21 February 1915): 7.

[49] Peter Gatrell, *A Whole Empire Walking: Refugees in Russia during World War I* (Bloomington: Indiana University Press, 1999), chap. 1.

[50] *Solntse Rossii*, no. 47 (302) (November 1915): 1.

[51] *Solntse Rossii*, no. 43 (298) (October 1915): 1–3. Other magazines were also unspecific about the national make-up of refugees: *Iskry*, no. 31 (9 August 1915): 244–45; *Russkaia illiustratsiia*, no. 18 (7 June 1915): cover.

News from the home front captured the work of doctors and nurses in hospitals, as well as the activities of celebrities, academics, businessmen, and various civilian politicians contributing patriotically to the war. Enlisted members of the Duma were profiled extensively, as were those deputies who coordinated relief efforts on the home front. Group photos of charities, zemstvo committees, and national congresses also appeared. Artists were captured by photographers at the front, visiting with soldiers to boost morale and deliver gifts of books and cigarettes. The opera star Fedor Shaliapin, in particular, publicized his philanthropic work, including the founding of a hospital, where the singer was shown conversing with amputees.[52] Publishers also wrote themselves into their own magazines. In *Iskry*, a photo-story of a workshop established to teach new skills to maimed soldiers mentioned that Sytin had donated books and charts to aid this education.[53] Likewise, *Niva* included photos of a hospital named in honor of patron and publisher A. F. Marks.[54] These stories reinforced the role of the press in civil society and highlighted the vital efforts of Russians working outside the tsarist bureaucracy.

The imperial family played a central role in wartime press photography. This included photos of the tsar, his wife Aleksandra, their children, the Grand Duke Nikolai Nikolaevich, and a few other relatives.[55] Russia's declaration of war was accompanied by full-page portraits of the tsar, whose image symbolically embodied (and unified) the Russian nation.[56] In general, the representations of the imperial family were divided along gender lines. The tsar fulfilled ceremonial duties on the frontlines or at headquarters; he reviewed troops, awarded medals, and inspected trenches, often in the company of his son Aleksei or the Grand Duke, who towered physically over the monarch.[57] When Nicholas adopted a more active role in the day-to-day conduct of the war, the photo-reportage showed the "crowned toiler," dressed in a simple

---

[52] *Sinii zhurnal*, no. 5 (30 January 1916): 12; *Iskry*, no. 2 (11 January 1915): 10.

[53] *Iskry*, no. 11 (15 March 1915): 86.

[54] *Niva*, no. 5 (31 January 1915): 84.

[55] For representations of the imperial family during the war, see B. I. Kolonitskii, *"Tragicheskaia erotika": Obrazy imperatorskoi sem'i v gody pervoi mirovoi voiny* (Moscow: Novoe literaturnoe obozrenie, 2010).

[56] *Letopis' voiny 1914 goda*, no. 1 (23 August 1914): 1; *Iskry*, no. 29 (27 July 1914): 225; *Ogonek*, no. 30 (27 July [9 August] 1914): 1; *Vsemirnaia panorama*, no. 31 (276) (1 August 1914): cover.

[57] For example: *Vsemirnaia panorama*, no. 32 (8 August 1914): 1–3; *Sinii zhurnal*, no. 37 (12 September 1915): 3; *Ogonek*, no. 52 (25 December [3 January] 1914): 2; *Ogonek*, no. 18 (3 [16] May 1915): 1; also see Kolonitskii, *"Tragicheskaia erotika,"* 444–63.

field uniform, laboring over reports and strategizing with generals.[58] By contrast, the Tsarina Aleksandra and her daughters appeared in hospitals and Red Cross barracks, visiting and aiding wounded soldiers. Aleksandra cultivated an image of the "most august nurse." Along with the princesses Ol'ga and Tat'iana, she posed in nurses' garb for official portraits and among the wounded in the officers' hospital at Tsarskoe Selo.[59] Ironically, the royals played these roles just as magazines publicized the widespread breakdown of traditional divisions of labor in photo-stories of women working in factories and of female fighting units.

Starting in February 1917, the old regime was eclipsed in magazines by prominent members of the Duma and the Petrograd Soviet. These figures took center stage in Russia's political life, and photographic portraits introduced the public to the major *dramatis personae*. Miliukov, Mikhail Rodzianko, and Prince Georgii L'vov were the Revolution's symbolic heads. Photographers captured these politicians working in government and performing ceremonial duties, such as honoring the "victims of the Revolution" on 23 March. This public funeral was a media spectacle featuring thousands of people gathered along Nevskii Prospekt. In *Niva*, the editors combined wide panoramic views of the procession with portraits of politicians near the burial site. Rodzianko and key members of the Provisional Government were shown standing alongside soldiers and ordinary citizens, who waved banners with slogans such as "Land and Freedom" and "Freedom for the Arts."[60] Not focused (yet) on a central charismatic figure, these pictures captured and disseminated the political performance of the new revolutionary order allied with the masses.[61] Though ostensibly leading the revolution, members of the Provisional Government drew legitimacy from and were fundamentally branded by the slogans of the street.

In 1917, the streets of Petrograd and Moscow were the main stages of political theater. Photographers captured officers, infantrymen, and sailors; factory workers, waiters, seamstresses, and typographers; various national delegations; and women demanding equality and suffrage. These groups stated their demands clearly on flags and banners as they marched through the streets. Orators addressed the crowds, and the news coverage in *Solntse Rossii* showed anonymous speakers shouting from makeshift tribunes. Though

---

[58] Richard S. Wortman, *Scenarios of Power: Myth and Ceremony in Russian Monarchy*, 2: *From Alexander II to the Abdication of Nicholas II* (Princeton, NJ: Princeton University Press, 2000), 487–92.

[59] *Ogonek*, no. 43 (26 October [5 November] 1914): 1 ; *Letopis´ voiny 1914 goda*, no. 8 (11 October 1914): 122; *Iskry*, no. 35 (11 September 1916): 273. On Aleksandra's image as a nurse, see Kolonitskii, "*Tragicheskaia erotika*," 246–89.

[60] *Niva*, no. 14 (8 April 1917): 205–11.

[61] Richard Stites, *Revolutionary Dreams: Utopian Vision and Experimental Life in the Russian Revolution* (Oxford: Oxford University Press, 1989), 81–82.

prominent figures, such as Aleksandr Kerenskii, also addressed the people in the streets, in general the speakers were not politicians. Photographers moved in close enough to reveal soldiers and workers dressed in tattered clothes. They spoke outside the offices of the Provisional Government, around the Skobelev monument, and near the Mariinskii Palace, where the monument of Nicholas I stood in the background.[62] The masses occupied these spaces, which symbolized moments of "political, social, and cultural contestation" of the past and present.[63] Visually captured in these meaningful locations, the orators and the masses gave these spaces new historical meaning, which was preserved in iconic images for decades to come.[64] These photographs invited the reading public onto the political stage, legitimized their demands, and validated the masses as participants in revolutionary struggle.

In mid-1917, no figure dominated photo-reportage like Kerenskii. A gifted lawyer with a flair for the theatrical, Kerenskii played well to the cameras as photographers traced his rise from civilian minister to quasi-military leader. The photographs in Solntse Rossii, in particular, captured his leadership cult and reinforced his close personal bond with the military[65] (fig. 14). In one photo, the war minister accepted a bouquet of red roses from a transfixed crowd of soldiers.[66] Images of this kind of intimacy were common. While touring the front, he was shown being carried off by soldiers and even receiving a kiss on the cheek.[67] Photography transmitted the scenarios of power enacted by Kerenskii, who struck a balance between the image of people's politician and the image of military leader reminiscent of Russia's past. Frontline tours offered a mix of modern "photo-ops," with Kerenskii glad-handing soldiers, while he also participated in traditional displays of power which recalled the pomp of the imperial era. In Niva, a series of photographs captured the traditional representation of the imperial military review at Tsarskoe Selo.

[62] Solntse Rossii, no. 10 (368) (1917): 7; Solntse Rossii, no. 12 (370) (1917): 5.

[63] William G. Rosenberg, "Visualizing 1917," in Picturing Russia: Explorations in Visual Culture, ed. Valerie A. Kivelson and Joan Neuberger (New Haven: Yale University Press, 2008), 143.

[64] For example, two iconic photographs, originally published in Solntse Rossii, of orators addressing crowds in front of the Skobelev monument and the Mariinskii Palace, respectively, were later reused on multiple occasions in the Soviet illustrated press: Solntse Rossii, no. 12 (370) (1917): 5; Solntse Rossii, no. 18 (376) (1917): 8–9; Krasnaia panorama, no. 11 (11 March 1927): 8–9; Krasnaia panorama, no. 11 (11 March 1927): 12–13; Ogonek, no. 11 (207) (13 March 1927): 1; Prozhektor, no. 4 (98) (28 February 1927): 11.

[65] On the cult of Kerenskii, see Orlando Figes and Boris Kolonitskii, Interpreting the Russian Revolution: The Language and Symbols of 1917 (New Haven: Yale University Press, 1999), 76–89.

[66] Solntse Rossii, no. 12 (370) (1917): 8–9.

[67] Solntse Rossii, no. 16 (374) (1917): 6; Solntse Rossii, no. 22 (380) (1917): 2.

However, instead of sitting on a horse, as Tsar Nicholas had done, Kerenskii stood in a large automobile.[68] In essence, Kerenskii adopted the tsarist model of personal power, traditionally linked to the Russian army, and adapted it to the revolutionary moment in the age of photographic publicity.[69]

During the Civil War, photo-reportage in *Plamia* was sparse and of poor quality. The basic categories, however, did not change. Portraits, group photos, and views remained the dominant "genres," and news reports focused on culture, political meetings, and current events, such as funerals and public holidays. Of course, news coverage orbited around the politics and ideology of the new Soviet order. The state-sponsored Proletkul't, for example, monopolized cultural news.[70] Large group photos captured the meetings of various Soviet organizations. The deaths of V. Volodarskii, Moisei Uritskii, and Iakov Sverdlov allowed the editors to memorialize and to educate the public about important contributors to the new Soviet way of life. Also, pictures of kindergartens, schools, and children's camps reflected "the spirit of collectivism" while serving as an indicator of Soviet Russia's cultural growth and successful drive toward modernization.[71] International news appeared rarely between 1918 and 1922. Instead, the editors published reports of Russian reactions to events abroad, such as the public demonstrations held in protest at the deaths of Rosa Luxemburg and Karl Liebknecht. Photographs from the German revolution in 1918 were the only pictures taken abroad in *Plamia*'s first year of publication.[72]

News coverage in *Plamia* expanded slightly during the Civil War. Portraits, views, and vignettes of the Red Army appeared in small photographic collages. One of these ("On the Perm' Front") filled an entire page and included a portrait of two soldiers, a large piece of artillery, a downed plane, a snow-covered town, a military telephone post, and a small frigate[73] (fig. 15). Brief captions identified prominent Bolsheviks who visited the frontlines. The editors also printed images of war atrocities committed by White commanders. In one issue, three small photos showed half-naked bodies piled on top of each other. The same caption appeared below each picture: "On the Borisoglebsk Front:

---

[68] This photograph was taken by the firm C. E. fon Gan & Co, which for a time enjoyed the status of official court photographers under Tsar Nicholas. *Niva*, no. 24 (17 June 1917): 371.

[69] On tsarist display of personal power, see Wortman, *Scenarios of Power*, 9, 131.

[70] *Plamia*, no. 7 (16 June 1918): 16; *Plamia*, no. 21 (22 September 1918): 13; *Plamia*, no. 42 (23 February 1919): 9.

[71] Catriona Kelly, *Children's World: Growing Up in Russia, 1890–1991* (New Haven: Yale University Press, 2007), 70.

[72] *Plamia*, no. 34 (29 December 1918).

[73] *Plamia*, no. 30 (1 December 1918): 11.

Victims of Krasnov's Whiteguard raid."[74] No article or headline accompanied these pictures, and the small size of the photos and rough grain of the paper further obscured the details.[75] In the absence of more information, the reading public was aware presumably of the picture's operating context from other propaganda.

Unique to *Plamia*, and to the Soviet illustrated press more generally, was the coverage of historical commemorations, socialist "holidays," and other significant dates in the Soviet calendar. This included, among others, the February Revolution, the October coup, May Day celebrations, and, to a lesser degree, the July Days (1917) and Bloody Sunday (1905). In 1920, *Plamia* printed a special double issue for the Congress of the Third International, which featured striking visual layouts that translated the spectacle for the reading public.[76] The cover featured the iconic image of Lenin standing on the steps of the Uritskii Palace (formerly the Tauride Palace) with a group of delegates. Two photographic collages, each laid out symmetrically over two pages, showed various scenes from the congress. The second collage included four pictures of the theatrical spectacle called "Toward the Worldwide Commune," which recreated the "cycle of revolt and repression" in history, beginning with the 1871 Paris Commune and ending with the October Revolution.[77] The actors performed against a set of thick classical columns and large red banners, which draped down like a curtain above a proscenium arch. The editors of *Plamia* did not so much report on these spectacles as much as they created a photojournalistic analog of the events for the reader at home. Looking at the photo-reportage was the next best thing to actually attending the congress. The news coverage was a mass media extension of the represented event.

The Politics of Photo-Reportage

The politics of magazine publishers during the imperial era were aligned closely with the progressives in the Duma. Publishers and civilian politicians were ambitious, wishing to exert greater influence over public opinion, and they shared a common history rooted in Russia's defeat in the Russo-Japanese War.[78] The 1905 Revolution gave birth to the Duma, and the commercial press, which had stoked revolutionary fervor, managed to secure greater freedom from censorship. War had been a catalyst for revolution, which translated into more influence in public affairs. To some degree, publishers and progressive

---

[74] *Plamia*, no. 45 (16 March 1919): 4–5.

[75] At the end of 1918, the editors of *Plamia* reduced the dimensions of the publication.

[76] *Plamia*, no. 13–14 (August 1920).

[77] Stites, *Revolutionary Dreams*, 96.

[78] Terrence Emmons, *The Formation of Political Parties and the First National Elections in Russia* (Cambridge, MA: Harvard University Press, 1983), 73.

politicians alike hoped that history would repeat itself. In the words of one Duma member, the war "will give us opportunity to defeat not only the external enemy, but will also open up joyful hopes for solving the problems of internal construction and reform."[79]

Before the Revolution, magazine editors used press photography to construct a visual narrative in support of war. Echoing the Duma, the illustrated press argued for intervention in the Balkans on patriotic grounds. The people of Russia had a historical responsibility to Serbia—reasoning that "created a climate of opinion wherein war against Germany and Austria appeared an acceptable and indeed necessary instrument of policy."[80] Photo-reportage encouraged readers to identify with Serbia. Like pictures in a family album, the coverage reminded the Russian public that they belonged to a community of Slavs. The story of Radko Dmitriev presented a living symbol of the spirit of Pan-Slavism. In *Iskry*, the editors printed a full-page portrait of the Bulgarian general under the headline "Slavic Hero."[81] The short article described how Dmitriev had joined the Russian army in protest at his government's failure to condemn Austrian aggression. This tribute offered a heroic example of personal (and national) sacrifice and served to flatter Russians, who could take pride in their nation's leadership. However, the story also implied that failing to support the war meant betraying Dmitriev's faith in Russia and rejecting his sacrifice made on behalf of Slavic brotherhood.

Photo-reportage reinforced the perception of national consensus about the war. Coverage of prowar rallies, for example, universalized the enthusiasm for war, masking the reality of people's reactions, especially among the peasant population.[82] In *Iskry*, the photo-story "Nation and War" reported on a series of Slavic prowar marches in Moscow, but gave the impression of the entire Russian nation up in arms. Seven photographs showed crowds at different stages of the rally: listening to speakers, standing at the Skobelev monument, gathering en masse on Red Square, etc. Taken from elevated vantage points, the pictures emphasized the anonymous masses and encouraged the reader to view the marchers collectively. This was reinforced by the headline and short article, both of which used collective terms such as "nation" (*narod*) and "Russian society" to describe the participants. Furthermore, the monuments of Minin and Pozharskii and General Skobelev placed the rally in the context of Russia's past, defending Slavs and the homeland from foreign invaders. By

---

[79] Quoted in Geoffrey A. Hosking, *The Russian Constitutional Experiment: Government and Duma, 1907–1914* (Cambridge: Cambridge University Press, 1973), 240–41.

[80] Ibid., 215.

[81] *Iskry*, no. 36 (14 September 1914): 281; *Niva*, no. 32 (9 August 1914): 640b; *Zhurnal-kopeika (SPb)*, no. 39 (297) (September 1914): 2.

[82] On peasant reactions to the war, see Corrine Gaudin, "Rural Echoes of World War I: War Talk in the Russian Village," *Jahrbücher für Geschichte Osteuropas* 56, 3 (2008): 391–414, and Corrine Gaudin's chapter in book 2 of this volume.

foregrounding these symbols and obfuscating the Slavic character of the rally, the editors invited readers to immerse themselves in what appeared to be, at first glance, a spontaneous evocation of Russian patriotism. The arrangement of images and words reframed the story, breathing symbolic meaning into the news and thus equating the specific concerns of the Slavic demonstrators with the general feelings of the reading public.

Support for the war in the illustrated press intensified in 1917. Photographs of refugees and casualties continued to underline the stakes of defeat, but more alarming were the reports of mass desertion.[83] In light of this, editors set out to remind Russians of their patriotic duties. Magazines such as *Ogonek* and *Iskry* launched heavy-handed campaigns to shame those who shirked their military obligations. In one issue of *Iskry*, the headline "Shame!" appeared above a picture of "faithful soldiers" reading about the "escape of cowards from the front, who disgraced the Russian army."[84] Another issue printed a "leaflet of shame" (*pozornyi list*), which could be used to report deserters to military authorities.[85] Though typically framed in nationalistic terms, magazines also implied that deserters brought shame to their families. The cover of *Ogonek*, for instance, featured an illustration of a deserter returning home, only to be turned away by his furious wife.[86] In fact, desertion was often inspired by concerns for family, especially amidst stories of landowners burning villages and grabbing land in the absence of peasant men-folk.[87] By condemning antiwar sentiment, this type of coverage served to flatter patriotic sensibilities and precluded nuanced debate in the public sphere.

These feelings were reinforced by pictures of Russian soldiers expressing a desire to win the war. This coverage appeared almost in defiance of the February Revolution. In mid-March, when mass demonstrations in Petrograd and Moscow dominated headlines, the cover of *Iskry* featured a full-page photograph of soldiers with a banner that read "War to a Victorious End."[88] Posing sternly and looking into the camera, the soldiers addressed readers directly with their petition. In *Niva*, photo-reportage of the April Crisis showed soldiers carrying signs in support of a victorious conclusion to the war.[89] The grievances and demands of soldiers listening to speeches, occupying

---

[83] Allan K. Wildman, *The End of the Russian Imperial Army*, 1: *The Old Army and the Soldiers' Revolt (March–April 1917)* (Princeton, NJ: Princeton University Press, 1980), 364–65.

[84] *Iskry*, no. 30 (6 August 1917): 233.

[85] *Iskry*, no. 28 (23 July 1917): 223.

[86] *Ogonek*, no. 23 (18 June [1 July] 1917): cover.

[87] Wildman, *End of the Russian Imperial Army*, 235.

[88] *Iskry*, no. 11 (19 March 1917): 81.

[89] *Niva*, no. 17 (29 April 1917): 254, 256; *Niva*, no. 18 (6 May 1917): 268.

buildings, and partaking in other revolutionary action were not captured in general, and those who supported the Bolsheviks were branded as traitors, as was evidenced during the July Days. Despite the great diversity of social and political perspectives on the streets, the illustrated press focused on the soldiers' eagerness to fight the Germans. Their support for the war offered an antidote to the defeatism of socialist movements, the waning enthusiasm of the public, and the reports of mass desertion at the frontlines.

Photo-reportage during the Civil War reflected and advanced the politics of the Bolshevik regime. In particular, *Plamia* promoted the specific utopian aims of Narkompros, while presenting Narkompros as essential to the new socialist order. Under Lunacharskii, this publication was both an instrument of education and a means of promoting an image of an enlightened society. The high-brow literary and visual material offered readers great "culture" and was evidence of the regime's high valuation of art and literature. Early issues included poems by Dem'ian Bednyi and Aleksandr Blok, as well as reproductions of paintings by Cézanne, Picasso, and Van Gogh.[90] Russian prerevolutionary artists, such as Il'ia Repin (a staple of the imperial illustrated press), were rarely featured. Rather, *Plamia* introduced readers to the works of avant-garde painters associated with the art department (IZO) of Narkompros, such as David Shterenberg and Natan Al'tman.[91] The only reference to the paintings of the old regime was a parody of Viktor Vasnetsov's *Bogatyrs*, which replaced the medieval knights with caricatures of a thug, a priest, and a diminutive Tsar Nicholas II.[92] The caption ("three bogatyrs at the crossroads looking to see if they can return") playfully suggested that the old regime, in both art and politics, had no future in Soviet Russia.

Lunacharskii used culture and history to frame the Soviet Union in a grander European and world-historical context. Written and visual material drew tacit parallels between the Russian and French Revolutions. In one issue of *Plamia*, the editors published a series called "People and Facts of the Great French Revolution," which included illustrations of historical scenes amidst the week's photo-reportage.[93] Other issues included a biography of Maximilien Robespierre and a short story about the "Marseillaise." One week, the cover featured Delacroix's *Liberty Leading the People*; in another, it was David's revolutionary allegory *Oath of the Horatii*. The magazine also covered the public unveiling of monuments dedicated to Robespierre and other French revolutionaries in Moscow and Petrograd. Like those statues, the contents of

---

[90] *Plamia*, no. 2 (12 May 1918): 15; *Plamia*, no. 3 (19 May 1918): 5.

[91] Shterenberg was the head of the IZO and Al'tman published in *Art of the Commune*, the official journal of IZO Narkompros. Matthew Cullerne Bown, *Art under Stalin* (New York: Holmes & Meier, 1991), 21–22.

[92] *Plamia*, no. 14 (4 August 1918): 13.

[93] *Plamia*, no. 22 (29 September 1918).

Plamia were important touchstones in a new revolutionary school.[94] For Lunacharskii, the history, fine art, and literature reminded the reading public of the great figures in the history of socialism and connected the struggles of these historical agents to the lives of ordinary Russians.

The editors of *Plamia* also used photography to publicize schools and the reformed Soviet educational system. The magazine reflected a society that prioritized education and in which Narkompros played a central role in bringing enlightenment to the masses. News reports focused on early childhood education, especially when connected to manual labor. In 1918, a profile of a kindergarten for proletarian children showed boys and girls in workshops—the younger children working with clay and building toys and the older children learning to become joiners.[95] Reports on adult education showed Soviet engineering courses and lectures at the "peasant university," and the magazine also publicized various polytechnic conferences and meetings of the "workers' intelligentsia."[96] Throughout this photo-reportage, the commissar of enlightenment was a seemingly ubiquitous presence. Lunacharskii was shown lecturing, participating in conferences, unveiling monuments, chairing meetings, recording his voice for posterity, and even posing with a string quartet named in his honor. Lunacharskii and Narkompros were central to the culture and education of early Soviet Russia, and photo-reportage served to promote and legitimize these activities, which, by extension, promoted and legitimized the Soviet regime overall.

Narratives and Counternarratives

Photographers, editors, and publishers created photo-reportage with specific intentions, but ultimately no one could anticipate how readers responded to the news. War atrocities, for example, were traditionally used to galvanize the embattled population. The graphic portrayals of wounded soldiers in *Iskry* seemed to offer visual evidence of German barbarity.[97] Each picture confronted the viewer, like a forensic photo taken at a crime scene, and the attached article provided more horrific details. However, the meaning of these photographs was deeply contested. Intended to harden soldiers and to stiffen the resolve of civilians, these images could also serve to sap morale and discourage fighting. In fact, during the war, the most shocking pictures

---

[94] Stites, *Revolutionary Dreams*, 89.

[95] *Plamia*, no. 22 (29 September 1918): 13–15.

[96] *Plamia*, no. 5 (2 June 1918): 6; *Plamia*, no. 26 (27 October 1918): 5–6; *Plamia*, no. 43 (2 March 1919): 3–4.

[97] *Iskry*, no. 25 (28 June 1915): 200; *Iskry*, no. 29 (26 July 1915): 227.

were used by pacifists to induce revulsion.[98] Pacifist propaganda was a real concern for the Russian military, and graphic depictions of wartime violence were a common means to express antiwar sentiment before and after the Revolution.[99] The only fact offered by atrocity photography was that Russians suffered greatly in battle. Otherwise readers were free to use the photographic evidence in support of any number of personal or patriotic agendas.

Pictures that "lived" on both sides of the Revolution revealed the elasticity of press photography. In commemorating the past, Soviet magazine editors re-interpreted images created for the imperial illustrated press. For example, the iconic picture of Rodzianko standing among soldiers in the Tauride Palace reflected two different historical narratives about the February Revolution. In 1917, reproductions in *Niva* and *Ogonek* highlighted the leadership of the Duma in February.[100] Rodzianko was visible among the soldiers, and in *Ogonek* the editors demarcated his exact position with an "x." The captions underneath both images singled him out: "Representative of the State Duma Mikhail Rodzianko among the ranks of the army and navy, who crossed over to the side of the Provisional Government" (*Niva*). However, in 1919, the caption under a smaller version in *Plamia* simply read, "Revolutionaries in the Ekaterina Hall of the Tauride Palace."[101] There is no mention of the barely visible Rodzianko. Even more striking was the caption in *Krasnaia niva* in 1925: "The military delegates in the State Duma (in the Ekaterina Hall of the Tauride Palace) who crossed over to the side of revolution."[102] Mirroring the caption in *Niva*, the editors not only purged Rodzianko, they also made "revolution" the primary agent of political change. In Soviet Russia, this iconic image was evidence of the masses aligning themselves not with a person or party, but with the progress of history.

Another image that inspired competing historical narratives was Viktor Bulla's iconic photograph of the July Days. Shot from an elevated perspective, the photo showed a crowd fleeing gunfire on a wide boulevard. (fig. 16). The image vividly captured the instant of panic and confusion as people ran for

---

[98] John Taylor, "Atrocity Propaganda in the First World War," in *Shadow and Substance: Essays on the History of Photography*, ed. Kathleen Collins (Bloomfield Hills, MI: Amorphous Press, 1990), 307.

[99] On pacifism, see Joshua Sanborn, *Drafting the Russian Nation: Military Conscription, Total War, and Mass Politics, 1905–1925* (DeKalb: Northern Illinois University Press, 2003), 186. On graphic representations of war, see Karen Petrone, *The Great War in Russian Memory* (Bloomington: Indiana University Press, 2011), chap. 4.

[100] *Ogonek*, no. 10 (19 March [1 April] 1917): 2; *Niva*, no. 11–12 (25 March 1917): 172.

[101] *Plamia*, no. 44 (9 March 1919): 5. A slightly more detailed caption appeared below the photograph in the 1927 issue of *Ogonek*, but still there was no mention of Rodzianko: *Ogonek*, no. 11 (207) (13 March 1927): 3.

[102] *Krasnaia niva*, no. 10 (8 March 1925): 225.

cover.[103] In 1917, *Solntse Rossii* offered a seemingly detached perspective. The headline read "Nightmares of the July Days" and the caption provided only basic information: "4 July 1917 in the afternoon on Nevskii Prospekt near the Public Library." But, in fact, this photograph was published following weeks of anti-Bolshevik propaganda in connection with this incident. Pictures of those blamed for the shooting appeared in a "retributive" issue that reported on the sacking of the offices of the Bolshevik newspaper *Pravda*. In addition, all the major weekly publications covered the public funeral held for the Cossacks killed on that day. In the illustrated press, the July Days symbolized the treachery of antigovernment (and thus antirevolutionary) elements. And when *Iskry* reprinted Bulla's image in October, the connection was made explicit; the headline read "Bolsheviks in Petrograd" and a short article listed the exact number of casualties.[104] Just days before the October coup, the editors drew on the memory of the July Days massacre and the well-established narrative, triggered and symbolized by the photograph, of Bolshevik treachery.

Years later, the photograph was re-contextualized as evidence of reactionary violence perpetrated by the Provisional Government. Blame was leveled at the Cossacks, who previously had been mourned as victims. In 1923, a cropped version of the photograph appeared on the cover of *Krasnaia panorama*.[105] Inside the issue, the July Days massacre was framed as a trap; the bourgeoisie had provoked the masses to demonstrate and the shooting had "been prepared long in advance." Sergei Eisenstein's film *October* reinforced this narrative. Inspired by Bulla's image, he recreated the massacre on film and showed the peaceful marchers approaching the Public Library, where the "reactionaries" waited with machine guns. In 1928, the photograph was featured in a landmark exhibition celebrating ten years of Soviet photography. Here, Bulla's photograph was entitled "Shooting at the demonstrators in front of the Public Library" and was credited to the Museum of the Revolution.[106] The picture was thus enshrined in the visual canon as a historical document that commemorated the sacrifice of those who opposed the bourgeois government. Decades later, the historian Leonid F. Volkov-Lannit again reinforced the Bolshevik interpretation. He claimed that Kerenskii had censored the image, presumably to conceal evidence of the Provisional Government's complicity in the massacre, and his analysis ended with a rhetorical flourish that summarized the Soviet narrative: "In 1905, the workers were gunned down

[103] *Solntse Rossii*, no. 23 (381) (1917): 8–9.

[104] *Iskry*, no. 41 (22 October 1917): 326.

[105] *Krasnaia panorama*, no. 8 (26 July 1923): cover, 2–3.

[106] *Sovetskoe foto*, no. 6 (June 1928); the Museum of the Revolution was recognized by the exhibition jury for it contributions to "agitation and propaganda" and specifically for "elevating the use of historical photos to the highest levels."

by the tsar—in 1917, by the bourgeois government."[107] In his account, Volkov-Lannit thus not only confirmed the accepted Soviet version of the July Days massacre, but also linked the event to a history of government repression in the imperial era.

Photographs taken during the October coup had a contested legacy as well. This included a set of widely circulated pictures taken by Otsup around the Smol'nyi Institute, the most famous of which showed two Red Guard soldiers standing outside Lenin's office.[108] This picture played into the master narrative of hidden "dark forces" who opposed the war, worked for the Germans, and conspired to overthrow the legitimate Russian government. In 1917, Lenin and the Bolsheviks had virtually no photographic presence in magazines. The only pictures of Lenin appeared in *Iskry*: two mug shots of the "hidden head of the Bolsheviks" suggested a criminal past. The two guards, dressed in soft caps and dark overcoats, evoked the dominant caricature of the Bolsheviks as a band of criminals and thugs.[109] Of course, after the coup was rechristened the October Revolution, the Smol'nyi pictures became iconic images of the Soviet regime's origins.[110] In interviews, Otsup contributed to the narrative of a truly popular revolution, rather than one orchestrated by Lenin. He recalled how the Red Guardists, who defended Smol'nyi, were simple workers who could barely handle their weapons.[111] According to the photographer, one of the soldiers was Nikolai Riabov, who later became a celebrated Red Army general. Pictures of the October coup thus illustrated a story of rebirth, wherein a worker began his new life of great achievement. In the words of Otsup, "All the Red Guardists, sailors, soldiers, and all of the Russian people began a new life on that day."[112]

Finally, iconic photographs from the Civil War era also were retouched and cropped in magazines. By altering the image, magazine editors often denied readers the freedom to interpret the original photograph and, by extension, the denoted historical event. This process, however, testified more to the convergence of avant-garde practices and photojournalism, and less to an organized conspiracy to reshape historical memory. For example, Viktor Bulla's photo of Lenin at the congress of the Third International was published originally in *Plamia* in 1920, and later altered for a memorial issue of *Krasnaia*

---

[107] Volkov-Lannit, *Istoriia pishetsia ob"ektivom*, 131.

[108] *Niva*, no. 46–47 (18 November 1917): 721; *Solntse Rossii*, no. 28 (386) (1917): 13.

[109] *Iskry*, no. 42 (29 October 1917): 330; also see *Sinii zhurnal*, no. 43–44 (December 1917): 5.

[110] For example: *Krasnaia panorama*, no. 45 (4 November 1927): 4; and *Krasnaia niva*, no. 45 (6 November 1927): 22.

[111] Quoted in Volkov-Lannit, *Istoriia pishetsia ob"ektivom*, 87.

[112] Ibid., 87.

niva[113] (fig. 17). Specifically, the crowd in the original was replaced by a larger crowd in order to visually "boost Lenin's popularity."[114] As a photograph of Lenin on a certain day, from a certain angle, this altered version indeed misrepresented a historical event. However, in the context of *Krasnaia niva*, the photograph was a component of a modernist collage, which featured other images of Lenin, also cropped and restructured. In fact, beginning in 1924, Soviet magazines often featured collages, many of which took similar liberties with photography. Much like the photomontages of Raoul Hausmann and Max Ernst, these Soviet collages "combined separate and disparate pictures to form a new visual entity."[115] One such collage published in *Krasnaia panorama* even credited the "montage" designer rather than the original photographers.[116] In the context of an evolving Soviet illustrated press, the altered version of Bulla's photograph thus existed somewhere between deliberate falsification and artistic license.[117] As new avant-garde trends exerted greater influence on Soviet magazines, the very meaning of photojournalism shifted, from reporting the news to a process of constructing a new reality.

Conclusion

The falsification of photographs in magazines such as *Krasnaia niva* represented a radical attempt by Soviet editors to control interpretation. Editors on both sides of the "revolutionary divide" tried to shape the meaning of press photography with captions, headlines, and articles, but the Bolsheviks took this process one step further. By altering the photographic object itself, they interfered with the ontological authenticity of photo-reportage—what Roland Barthes called the "analogical perfection" of photography.[118] Commercial imperatives and the fundamental ambivalence of the photographic medium prevented publishers

---

[113] *Plamia*, no. 13–14 (August 1920): 9; *Krasnaia niva*, no. 7 (17 February 1924): 167.

[114] David King, *The Commissar Vanishes: The Falsification of Photographs and Art in Stalin's Russia* (New York: Metropolitan Books, 1997), 78.

[115] Beaumont Newhall, *The History of Photography from 1839 to the Present* (New York: The Museum of Modern Art, 1982), 210.

[116] *Krasnaia panorama*, no. 3 (7 February 1924): 8–9.

[117] On Soviet photomontage, see Victor Margolin, *The Struggle for Utopia: Rodchenko, Lissitzky, Moholy-Nagy, 1917–1946* (Chicago: The University of Chicago Press, 1997); Margarita Tupitsyn, *The Soviet Photograph, 1924–1937* (New Haven: Yale University Press, 1996); Andrei Fomenko, *Montazh, faktografiia, epos: Proizvodstvennoe dvizhenie i fotografiia* (St. Petersburg: Izd-vo S.-Peterburgskogo universiteta, 2007); V. T. Stigneev, "Poetika fotomontazha (v dokomp'iuternuiu epokhu)," in *Fotografiia: Problemy poetiki*, ed. V. T. Stigneev (Moscow: Izd-vo LKI, 2008).

[118] Roland Barthes, "The Photographic Message," in *Image, Music Text*, trans. Stephen Heath (New York: Hill and Wang, 1977), 17.

and editors in tsarist Russia from systematically imposing a political agenda. After the October coup, the Bolsheviks eliminated the commercial imperative, and material shortages during the Civil War narrowed the range of available pictures. In both periods, captions and other texts allowed editors to craft a narrative about press photography, but viewers were still relatively free to interpret the photographic news images. Politics shaped the original message, but the evidentiary power, and thus the possibility of alternate interpretations, remained. So, when Soviet editors altered images of the Civil War, they crafted a narrative around the photographs and tampered with the picture's documentary worth. And if "analogical perfection" defined the photographic medium, as Barthes would have us believe, then Soviet magazine editors were not only eliminating the threat of alternate interpretations, they were also eliminating the threat of the photography itself.[119]

---

[119] Leah Dickerman, "Camera Obscura: Socialist Realism in the Shadow of Photography," *October* 93 (Summer 2000): 142–44.

Russian Architecture and the Cataclysm
of the First World War

William C. Brumfield

The Russian architectural profession during the decade before the First World War had entered a period of remarkable growth and development. Despite substantial structural and social problems in the Russian Empire's rapid economic expansion, architects and engineers looked toward an energetic future of construction in major industrial centers such as Moscow and St. Petersburg, as well as in important regional satellites such as Omsk, Samara, and Saratov. The increase in building activity involved professional development on all levels, from institutions for highly qualified technical training to professional societies that set standards and propagated achievements in architecture and civil engineering.[1]

The beginnings of cohesion in the profession date from the 1860s, when architects in both St. Petersburg and Moscow realized the need to create an association that would rise above narrow, commercial interests to address problems confronting architects as a group. Commercialism had provided the major financial impetus for a professional organization, as the economic forces of nascent capitalism led to the replacement of the older patronage system of architectural commission with a more competitive, contractual approach to the business of building. Yet in order to promote the interests of professional development and to regulate the practice of architecture, a form of organization that transcended the individual architect or architectural firm was essential.

The Great Reforms of the 1860s facilitated the economic progress necessary for the expansion of architecture beyond the commissions of the state, the court, and a few wealthy property owners, and they also created the legal conditions for the foundation of private associations. Although certain Petersburg architects had begun to explore the prospect of founding a professional group as early as 1862, the first formal organization was the

---

[1] See William C. Brumfield, *The Origins of Modernism in Russian Architecture* (Berkeley: University of California Press, 1991).

Russian Culture in War and Revolution, 1914–22, Book 1: Popular Culture, the Arts, and Institutions. Murray Frame, Boris Kolonitskii, Steven G. Marks, and Melissa K. Stockdale, eds. Bloomington, IN: Slavica Publishers, 2014, 165–88.

Moscow Architectural Society, chartered in October 1867.[2] From the outset this organization disseminated new technical information and served as a center for the establishment of standards in building materials and practices. In addition to its advisory function in technical matters, the society initiated a series of open architectural competitions as early as 1868, thus establishing a precedent to be followed in the awarding of major building contracts during the latter half of the century. An ambitious attempt by the society to sponsor a general conference of architects in 1873 failed for bureaucratic reasons, and it was not until 1892 that the First Congress of Russian Architects took place.[3]

In the meantime, architects in the capital obtained imperial approval to found the Petersburg Society of Architects, chartered in October 1870, whose functions paralleled those of the Moscow Architectural Society. At the beginning of 1872, the Petersburg group published the first issue of the journal *Zodchii* (Architect), which appeared monthly, and later weekly, through 1917. For 45 years this authoritative publication not only served as a record of the architectural profession in Russia but also provided a conduit for information on technical innovations in Western Europe and the United States. It would be difficult to overestimate the importance of *Zodchii* in supporting professional solidarity among architects and establishing a platform from which to advance ideas regarding architecture's "mission" in the creation of a new urban environment.[4] Although there were other architectural publications in Russia, *Zodchii* remained the major source for information on architecture and civil engineering in Russia and abroad. During this period architectural design was largely a matter of eclectic facade decoration.

Varieties of Early Modernism

The appearance of the "new style"—or style moderne—in Russia's major cities at the turn of the century has many obvious influences but no clear point of origin.[5] There were no programmatic statements like Otto Wagner's Moderne Architektur or harbingers like Joseph Olbrich's Secession House in Vienna. At the turn of the century, however, there were signs of an awareness of new

---

[2] For a history of the foundation of the Moscow Architectural Society, see Iu. S. Iaralov, ed., *100 let obshchestvennykh arkhitekturnykh organizatsii v SSSR 1867–1967: Istoricheskaia spravka* (Moscow: Soiuz arkhitektorov, 1967), 6–11.

[3] Ibid., 12.

[4] The complex publishing history of *Zodchii* and its supplement *Nedelia stroitelia* is presented in ibid., 103–04.

[5] Among the Russian publications that examine the style moderne, two of the most authoritative and comprehensive are E. A. Borisova and T. P. Kazhdan, *Russkaia arkhitektura kontsa XIX–nachala XX veka* (Moscow: Nauka, 1971); and E. I. Kirichenko, *Russkaia arkhitektura 1830–1910-kh godov* (Moscow: Iskusstvo, 1978). On the appearance of the terms *new style* and *style moderne* as applied to Russian architecture, see Brumfield, *Origins of Modernism*, 47–48.

developments in Western and Central Europe that would stimulate a major aesthetic and technological redirection of Russian architecture. The speeches delivered at the Third Congress of Russian Architects, held in Petersburg in 1900, made no substantial reference to architectural innovation, yet the speakers had finally abandoned the debate over the relevance of medieval Russian architecture for the creation of a "national" style. Indeed, this was the first major conference in which engineering topics clearly predominated over the aesthetic.[6]

The greater attention given to building technology at the turn of the century did not imply that aesthetic issues had been neglected in favor of pragmatism. The frequent references in architectural journals to John Ruskin, William Morris, the English Arts and Crafts movement, and the work of artists associated with the Abramtsevo community demonstrated that aestheticism in both design and architecture enjoyed great vigor in an era of commercial development.[7] Yet the actual creation of a "new style" seems to have filtered into Russian architecture. The style moderne, whose realization in Moscow and Petersburg displayed considerable differences, assumed and maintained a protean character that reflected its varied sources of inspiration, from Vienna to Paris to Glasgow.

The essential precondition for the new style was the continued expansion not only of the population of large cities such as Moscow and Petersburg, but also the rise of a class of private patrons whose wealth derived from capitalist, entrepreneurial activity. The decades preceding World War I formed an unprecedented period of private initiative and investment in the construction of Russian cities. The results were correspondingly varied in both style and taste as architects of greater or lesser talent strove to accommodate the deluge of work involved in the creation of an urban infrastructure under social and economic conditions that were still far from modern.[8]

Toward the end of the century's first decade, the style moderne as a decorative system for commercial architecture yielded to a more rectilinear design. In some instances this led to the use of classicizing elements within a modern tectonic system, exemplified in St. Petersburg by the Building of the Guards Economic Society. (See fig. 18 in the gallery of illustrations following

---

[6] The only reference to medieval monuments at the Third Congress occurred in Nikolai Sultanov's plea for the preservation of Russia's ancient architectural heritage: "O neobkhodimosti sokhraneniia nashikh drevnikh pamiatnikov," *Trudy III s'ezda russkikh zodchikh* (St. Petersburg, 1905), 1: 58.

[7] On Russian critical response to the new aestheticism and the Arts and Crafts movement, see Brumfield, *Origins of Modernism*, 47–62.

[8] One of the main economic issues in the creation of a new infrastructure was the development of private financing for such projects—a topic that still awaits adequate study. An account of means of financing new apartment buildings in the late 19th century is contained in D. A. Zasosov and V. I. Pyzin, *Iz zhizni Peterburga 1890–1910-kh godov: Zapiski ochevidtsev* (Leningrad: Lenizdat, 1991), 47–48.

page 188.) Built in 1908–09 by a team of architects that included Ernest F. Virrikh, Stepan S. Krichinskii, and Nikolai V. Vasil'ev, the building served as a department store that catered to the upper strata of elite Petersburg Guards regiments, and was at the time of its completion the city's most modern facility for retail trade, a symbol of economic and social status. Like Roman I. Klein's building for the Muir and Mirrielees department store in Moscow, the Guards building was a ferro-concrete structure with extensive use of plate glass and surfaced with natural stone. Although the classical motifs are particularly evident in the rotunda above the corner of the building, the facade is shaped by the alternation of structural elements and a ferro-vitreous membrane.

The interior of the Guards Economic Society demonstrated Virrikh's reputation as a specialist in the use of ferro-concrete.[9] The main hall, rising the full height of the building, was surrounded by three gallery levels (fig. 19). The reinforced concrete arches over the hall are decorated with coffers and rosettes; yet the classical details do not distract from the central space and its arched roof of glass in an iron frame.

Modern rationalism was capable of a more "romantic" interpretation, exemplified in the Passage on Liteinyi Prospekt (fig. 20). Designed in 1911 by Nikolai Vasil'ev, the project represents an evolution of style moderne architecture after the superficially decorative features of the style had disappeared.[10] Constructed in 1912–13, the Passage has no obvious decorative elements of any provenance. In this extended facade—plate glass within a two-story masonry grid—Vasil'ev introduced an element characteristic of the moderne in Petersburg and in Finland. The ferro-concrete piers that separate the window bays are surfaced with rusticated, gray granite that is reminiscent of the new style's emphasis on the texture of material, and of Eliel Saarinen's use of red granite for the Helsinki railway station. Within the profiled arches is a highly abstracted, modern design for grid on the second floor above each main entrance. The grid is of bronzed iron, as are the simple, functional window transoms.

One source for the reduced, "stripped" classicism after 1910 can be found in the monumental design by Peter Behrens for the new German Embassy in St. Petersburg (1911–12). Behrens received less attention in the Russian press than his Viennese contemporaries, whose designs would have been more amenable for commercial architecture in Russia; yet this leading representative of the Werkbund was undoubtedly known to Petersburg architects through German architectural journals. His contribution to this key site in central Petersburg is all the more remarkable for the difficult, trapezoidal site on which the embassy is situated. Behrens's solution was to create in effect two

---

[9] The Building of the Guards Economic Society was described and illustrated in *Zodchii*, no. 47 (1910): 471–73, and plates 48–50. The cost of the original structure was listed as 1,200,000 rubles.

[10] Vasil'ev published a description of the Passage in *Zodchii*, no. 10 (1913): 119, and plate 5.

independent, yet joined, structures, surfaced in rough-hewn red granite (fig. 21). The main part, facing St. Isaac's Square and containing the embassy's state and reception rooms, is defined on the exterior by a horizontal frame of pilasters, attic, and base. By eliminating the acute corner angle, Behrens attached a second rectangular structure—extending along the side street and containing consular offices and staff quarters—at an angle to the main facade (fig. 22). This arrangement joined the two parts, and yet left each a discrete unit. In contemporary criticism on the building, its integrity of design and unity were associated with an absence of architectural ornamentation.[11]

Whatever the impact of Behrens's monument on Petersburg architecture, the stylistic gamut of Vasil'ev's work—from the florid style moderne to stripped classicism and functional commercial architecture—is repeated in the careers of many of his contemporaries, such as Fedor I. Lidval, Vladimir P. Apyshkov, Andrei A. Ohl, and Marian S. Lialevich. Lialevich, who studied with Leontii Benois and graduated from the Academy of Arts in 1901, became one of the leading proponents of stripped neoclassicism for apartment and commercial architecture.[12] In 1911–12 he constructed a building on Nevskii Prospekt for the trading firm of F. Mertens (furriers), whose clarity of design illustrates the merging of modern functional architecture with classical details (fig. 23).

The advances in construction technology and design that had been introduced as part of the style moderne continued in commercial construction with new stylistic markers. For architects such as Vasil'ev and Lialevich, and Ivan S. Kuznetsov in Moscow, the opposition between the moderne and neoclassicism was largely irrelevant. In 1910, for example, Lialevich and Marian M. Peretiatkovich designed an expressionistic, freeform project for the Sytnyi Market (fig. 24), and Iakov G. Gevirts adapted ancient forms from Middle Eastern architecture for a strikingly modern prayer house at the

---

[11] Early responses to the German Embassy building include an unsigned article in *Moskovskii arkhitekturnyi mir*, no. 1 (1913): 103–07; and Marian Lialevich, "Dom germanskogo posol'stva," *Peterburgskaia gazeta*, 19 January 1913. A critique of the embassy—with favorable commentary on Behrens's rough-hewn interpretation of neoclassicism, but with no mention of his name—appeared in an article signed with the initial "G.": "Dom germanskogo posol'stva," *Arkhitekturno-khudozhestvennyi ezhenedel'nik*, no. 2 (1914): 5–7. After the beginning of the war, another article in the same journal showed a predictable nationalist reaction against the embassy building and its symbolic projection of German might: Martell, "Razgadannyi rebus," *Arkhitekturno-khudozhestvennyi ezhenedel'nik*, no. 26 (1914): 253–55. For a more detailed analysis of reaction to the embassy design, see Brumfield, *Origins of Modernism*, 227–28.

[12] For a survey of Lialevich's work, see B. M. Kirikov, "Marian Lialevich," in *Zodchie Sankt-Peterburga: XIX–nachala XX veka*, ed. V. G. Isachenko and Iu. V. Artem'ev (St. Petersburg: Lenizdat, 1998), 912–24.

Preobrazhenskoe Jewish Cemetery (figs. 25, 26) on the southern outskirts of Petersburg.[13]

Classical Architecture and the Attack on "Bourgeois" Modernism

There were, however, architects and critics for whom the neoclassical revival in architecture formed not simply an aesthetic movement but an essential part of a cultural and ideological platform to revive a sense of national direction during the instability of the prewar decade. Neoclassicism, criticized during the reign of Nicholas I and neglected thereafter during the 19th century, reappeared as an expression of nobility and imperial grandeur, in opposition to the questionable, bourgeois values of the style moderne.[14] The development of the neoclassical revival is illuminated by the work of the architect and designer Ivan A. Fomin. In 1894 he entered the Imperial Academy of Arts, but interrupted his studies in 1896 following a political protest, after which he left for a year in France and returned to Moscow as an architectural assistant. His mentors at the turn of the century included modernists such as Fedor O. Shekhtel´ and Lev N. Kekushev, and Fomin himself made a significant contribution to the new style with his interior designs and project sketches for houses.[15]

The seminal influence on Fomin was the aesthete and critic Aleksandr Benois, who in 1902 published an article entitled "Picturesque Petersburg" in *Mir iskusstva*. Benois defended the capital's classical architectural heritage and proclaimed that one must "save [Petersburg] from destruction, stop the barbarous deformation, and preserve its beauty from the encroachments of crude

---

[13] On the Sytnyi Market, see Borisova and Kazhdan, *Russkaia arkhitektura*, 113, 130–31. The Preobrazhenskoe Cemetery prayer house designed by Gevirts has been neglected in the critical literature, although his work is listed in B. M. Kirikov, ed., *Arkhitektory-stroiteli Sankt-Peterburga serediny XIX–nachala XX veka* (St. Petersburg: Pilgrim, 1996), 86. See Brumfield, *Origins of Modernism*, 232–35.

[14] The primary forum for neoclassical aestheticism in the arts was the elegantly-produced journal *Apollon*, founded in 1909 by the poet Sergei K. Makovskii. Although literary in its orientation, *Apollon* published frequent commentary on architecture, and certain issues contained lavishly illustrated surveys of neoclassical architecture— particularly in Petersburg, which, appropriately, served as the center of the movement. The relation between style and ideology in the movement are analyzed in William C. Brumfield, "Anti-Modernism and the Neoclassical Revival in Russian Architecture, 1906–1916," *Journal of the Society of Architectural Historians* 48 (1989): 371–86.

[15] This aspect of Fomin's early career is examined in V. G. Lisovskii, *I. A. Fomin* (Leningrad: Lenizdat, 1979), 10–11. Fomin's designs for houses in both the modern and neoclassical styles appeared in *Ezhegodnik Obshchestva arkhitektorov-khudozhnikov* 1 (1906): 116–19. His work in subsequent issues of the architectural annual was devoted to variations on the classical theme.

boors who treat the city with such incredible carelessness."[16] The implications of Benois's statement were immediately clear to his contemporaries: Petersburg was being destroyed by entrepreneurs whose new buildings violated the spirit of the imperial architectural ensemble.[17] To those who criticized his attack on modern architecture, Benois responded with another critical essay, "The Beauty of Petersburg," in *Mir iskusstva*:

> The quest for profit and the reconstruction of buildings is entirely natural, but it is unforgivable when buildings are disfigured in the process.... Unfortunately our architects ... prefer pathetic parodies in the deutsche Renaissance, in French Rococo, in the gothic (the Fabergé building), or more recently—oh horrors!—the absurdly interpreted *style moderne*.[18]

In 1904 Fomin published his own panegyric, also in *Mir iskusstva*, to the neoclassical architecture of early 19th-century Moscow, contrasted to the sterility of urban architecture: "By some strange stylistic act of a trivialized species of people and their talentless artists, multi-story buildings are already replacing these amazing structures from the epoch of Catherine II and Alexander I. There remain so few of them. All the more valuable are they."[19]

In 1905–09 Fomin studied at the Academy of Arts in the architectural studio of Leontii Benois, where he not only produced impressive neoclassical project sketches, but also engaged in scholarly and archival work for a major exhibition of 18th-century Russian art and architecture. Although originally scheduled for 1908 at the Academy of Arts, the Historical Exhibition of Architecture did not open until 1911, at which point it celebrated the critical reappraisal of neoclassicism that had been brought about so largely by Fomin, whose work now included a number of neoclassical revival mansions.

Yet as an alternative to the moderne in shaping the urban environment, the neoclassical revival had to justify itself with large developments. An early example of modernized classicism can be found in the work of Fedor Lidval' (1870–1945), who built two banks in the latter style between 1907 and 1909: the Second Mutual Credit Society and the Azov-Don Bank (fig. 27).[20] Both exploit the texture and color of granite as well as the sculptural qualities of natural stone in the decoration of the facade (fig. 28). And both made extensive use

---

[16] Aleksandr Benua [Benois], "Zhivopisnyi Peterburg," *Mir iskusstva*, no. 1 (1902): 1–5.

[17] The response to Benois on the part of architectural critics who supported the style moderne was predictably negative. See Brumfield, *Origins of Modernism*, 51.

[18] Aleksandr Benois, "Krasota Peterburga," *Mir iskusstva*, no. 8 (1902): 138–42.

[19] Ivan Fomin, "Moskovskii klassitsizm," *Mir iskusstva*, no. 7 (1904): 187.

[20] A basic study of Lidval''s work is V. G. Isachenko and G. A. Ol', *Fedor Lidval'* (Leningrad: Lenizdat, 1987).

of iron structural components on the interior to support the transaction halls and adjoining office space. Lidval´ had established that essential connection between neoclassicism and modern, "bourgeois" architecture by melding a functional commercial structure and an aesthetic system derived from the monumental architecture of Petersburg.

Another neoclassicist, Marian Peretiatkovich, turned to the Italian Renaissance, which he had studied as a pupil of Leontii Benois at the Academy and seen during his diploma trip to Italy in 1906.[21] His design for the Vavelberg Building (fig. 29), which contained the Petersburg Trade Bank, combined features of the Florentine quattrocento, such as the rusticated stone work of Michelozzo's Palazzo Medici, with the double arcade of the Palace of Doges in Venice. On a narrower facade, Peretiatkovich repeated the style of the Renaissance palazzo in his design for the Russian Bank of Trade and Industry (1912–14), which incorporated elements of 16th-century Italian palaces. A more severe form of late imperial neoclassicism characterizes Lidval´'s Hotel Astoria on St. Isaac's Square (1911–12), a six-story building with a few highly visible decorative elements, such as the classical urns and channeled pilasters along the austere granite facade (fig. 30). Lidval´ also created a number of prominent apartment buildings with a sensitive yet sparse application of classical and Renaissance detail.

The most ambitious attempt to apply classical elements to city planning occurred on Golodai Island, an undeveloped area to the north of Vasil´evskii Island in the northwest part of the city. In view of the Russian interest in English concepts of town planning, it is revealing that in 1911 an English investment firm initiated a project, called "New Petersburg," for a community occupying much of the western part of the island (about one square kilometer).[22] The general design for the project was entrusted to Fomin, who intended to create a monumental housing development for the city's middle class. Yet very little of the New Petersburg project ever materialized. In 1912 he constructed one of the five-story apartment blocks, whose "Roman" facades followed the curve of the semicircular entrance park. For Georgii K. Lukomskii, the leading proponent of the neoclassical revival, the New Petersburg project gave hope for the creation of a "part of the city with a truly European appearance and a strict unity of classical architectural ensembles, situated on the shores of an

---

[21] A survey of the career of Peretiatkovich is contained in the obituary by G. Kosmachevskii, *Zodchii*, no. 23 (1916): 219–20. See also I. E. Gostev, "Marian Peretiatkovich," in *Zodchie Sankt-Peterburga*, 723–45.

[22] The information on the New Petersburg project is contained in a technical report by the noted Petersburg civil engineer Aleksandr Montag, "Izmenenie plana ostrova Golodaia," *Zodchii*, no. 49 (1915): 510; and from Georgii Lukomskii, "O postroike Novogo Peterburga," *Zodchii*, no. 52 (1912): 519–21.

open sea."[23] Financial limitations and the onset of the First World War halted construction after the initial stages of the project.

Despite the failure of "New Petersburg," Kamennoostrovskii Prospekt flourished as it had since the beginning of the century, when the tramline appeared and Lidval' completed his first major apartment complex in the style moderne. Foremost in this development was Vladimir A. Shchuko, who graduated from the Academy of Arts in 1904 and, like Fomin, was awarded a diploma trip to Italy. The early careers of the two architects contain significant parallels: the effect of Italian architecture on their work, and their appreciation for the varieties of Russian neoclassicism, so brilliantly reinterpreted in Shchuko's pavilions for the 1911 Rome and Turin exhibitions.[24]

Shchuko's first apartment house on Kamennoostrovskii Prospekt, No. 63 (1908–10), was constructed for Konstantin V. Markov, a military engineer and real estate developer who had done the initial structural design. The building, whose fifth story is situated above the profiled cornice, represents a variation on the Italian Renaissance style, with loggias, ionic pilasters, and carved ornamental panels. His subsequent, and adjacent, apartment house for Markov (No. 65; 1910–11) adopted a more forceful display in its massive articulation of the classical order.[25]

At the Fourth Congress of Russian Architects, held in Petersburg in January 1911, Lukomskii gave the most forceful advocacy of the neoclassical revival as the proper style of the times. Having dismissed the style moderne as a rootless invention of "a little decade-long epoch of individualism," the critic noted the return to basic principles in architecture.[26] Yet the very cult of individualism that both Fomin and Lukomskii had criticized in their commentary on the demise of the style moderne now flourished within the varieties of the neoclassical revival—whether in Petersburg or in Moscow.

---

[23] Lukomskii, "O postroike Novogo Peterburga," 520–21. On Lukomskii's work as a standard-bearer of the neoclassical revival, see Brumfield, "Anti-Modernism and the Neoclassical Revival."

[24] A number of Shchuko's sketches appeared in *Ezhegodnik Obshchestva arkhitektorov-khudozhnikov* 2 (1907): 142–45, as well as in other issues of this annual. Although Shchuko's Italian exhibition pavilions did not have a strong impact on his domestic work, they were among the most finely conceived of his neoclassical revival projects. The standard monograph on Shchuko is T. A. Slavina, *Vladimir Shchuko* (Leningrad: Lenizdat, 1978).

[25] Despite his praise for the loggias and the subtlety in detail of Shchuko's first building, Lukomskii was even more impressed by the hypertrophied forms of the second, which proved that the classical system of orders could be applied on a scale commensurate with the demands of a modern city. See Lukomskii, "Novyi Peterburg (Mysli o sovremennom stroitel'stve)," *Apollon*, no. 2 (1913): 25.

[26] Georgii Lukomskii, "Arkhitekturnye vkusy sovremennosti," *Trudy IV S"ezda russkikh zodchikh* (St. Petersburg, 1911), 28. A similar attack against "excessive" individualism appeared in Lukomskii's "Novyi Peterburg," 9.

Whatever the ideological implications in the transition from the style moderne to the classical model, the economic, entrepreneurial basis of apartment construction remained the same.

This idiosyncrasy is particularly evident in the two Italianate apartment houses that Andrei E. Belogrud built between 1912 and 1915 for the developer Konstantin I. Rozenshtein, at the intersection of Kamennoostrovskii and Bol'shoi Prospekt on the Petersburg Side (figs. 31, 32). Designers of neoclassical buildings, no less than those of the moderne, used stylistic identity as an advertisement for the amenities that justified the cost of living at a fashionable address. In praising the return to monumentality for modern housing Lukomskii was imposing an architectural ideal of the Renaissance within an environment created by and for private financial interests. Yet the inability to achieve a coherent urban environment in the imperial capital could not be resolved by an appeal to nostalgia. As Lukomskii noted, "Fomin's art does not at all correspond to the contemporary economic spirit of calculation and triviality, of contemporary cheapness and bad workmanship; and this, of course, makes it difficult for him to work on the construction of apartment houses."[27]

The Neoclassical Revival and Imperial Ideology

On the eve of World War I, the ideological pronouncements of architectural critics were directed, implicitly or explicitly, against the bourgeoisie and the current political malaise. Proponents of a new, rational era in architecture dismissed both the moderne and the neoclassical revival, yet Lukomskii and Lialevich remained influential advocates of classical aestheticism, even as they wrote vaguely of the coming of a new era.[28] For Lukomskii, architecture's mission was to restrain the future and its attendant chaos in favor of aesthetic principles representative of moral strength. There could be no clearer statement of this position than the introduction to his 1913 article "New Petersburg." Taking a monarchist position in the year of the Romanov tercentenary, the critic insisted that great architecture must derive from the power of the state and church:

> Therefore, all efforts to present a "New Petersburg" only on the basis of proposed conditions in economy and hygiene can lead to nothing other than pale, gray facades. For just this reason, the entire epoch of bourgeois and democratic modernism has given Petersburg *nothing*. Only the restoration of previous architectural canons can increase the beauty of our city.... A completely ideal [solution] is unthinkable. We

---

[27] Lukomskii's comment on Fomin's work is from his 1913 survey of contemporary neoclassical architecture in *Apollon*, "Novyi Peterburg," 22.

[28] On these ideological pronouncements, see Brumfield, *Origins of Modernism*, 289–95.

do not have the conditions to create it. It is necessary to limit ourselves to retrospectivism.[29]

Indeed, retrospective sentiments in Russian architecture displayed a resurgence during the decade before World War I. The neo-Russian style that had formed part of the modern aesthetic movement at the beginning of the century turned toward a more insistent, "escapist" form of architectural fantasy, as demonstrated in Aleksei V. Shchusev's winning design for the Kazan' Railway Station in Moscow (1913–26)—an elaborate 17th-century stylization based on fortress towers in Moscow and Kazan' and located opposite Shekhtel''s style moderne masterpiece, the Iaroslavl Station.[30] In Moscow, Ivan Kuznetsov adopted the teremok design for the Savvinskoe Podvor'e office building and hostel (1907), with a polychrome ceramic facade.

As architects pursued their modernist or retrospective visions, the antidemocratic sentiments of much architectural criticism before and during World War I revealed a lack of faith in the viability of the bourgeoisie as a source of governance—social, political, or cultural. The ultimate ramifications of this line of thought appeared in Lukomskii's book *Contemporary Petrograd* (*Sovremennyi Petrograd*), published a few months before the first, so-called "bourgeois," revolution in February 1917:

> It is more and more evident that contemporary Petrograd is losing its national, noble character; is becoming more trivial, European. Only a common, amicable effort in matters of construction, only an artistic dictatorship in the distribution of building sites and the attraction of the best resources will save the capital and give it an even more powerful and beautiful appearance than it had during its best days in the epoch of Alexander I.[31]

The nostalgic reference to Petersburg during the golden age of Alexander I, a century earlier, represented an attempt to revive the glorious myth of the imperial capital and of Russia itself during a time of military defeat and national crisis. A stunning reversal: after almost a century of criticism

---

[29] Lukomskii, "Novyi Peterburg," 10.

[30] Shchusev's winning proposal for the Kazan' Railway Station was the subject of detailed reports in *Arkhitekturno-khudozhestvennyi ezhenedel'nik*: no. 4 (1914): 46–48; no. 19 (1915): 217–19. Shekhtel himself had submitted a similar historicist proposal for the station in 1911, and turned to a skillful blending of medieval elements in a number of projects in Nizhnii Novgorod. See Brumfield, *Origins of Modernism*, 167–69.

[31] *Sovremennyi Petrograd* (Petrograd, n.d.), 30. Subtitled "A Sketch of the History of the Appearance and Development of Neoclassical Construction," the volume represents a compendium of Lukomskii's major writings on the neoclassical revival—including the 1913 and 1914 issues of *Apollon*—with an expanded preface, in which the above quotation appears.

directed against neoclassicism as an alien, monotonous style bureaucratically imposed to the exclusion of vibrant national traditions, Russia's neoclassical architecture was proclaimed by Lukomskii and other critics as the purest expression of national culture.

It is ironic that Lukomskii's solution for controlled urban design would become, in basic terms, the accepted practice in the Soviet period. Even the neoclassical revival proved easily transferable to the heroic enthusiasm of the early period of Soviet power, when architects such as Fomin, Belogrud, and Shchuko produced numerous designs for public buildings in the so-called "Red Doric" or "proletarian classical" manner.[32]

In its final phase the neoclassical revival produced exquisitely refined buildings, even as the old order moved toward collapse during the war. It is perhaps fitting that one of the most accomplished of these neoclassical buildings was a burial shrine, architecture in memoriam. At the grand Iusupov estate of Arkhangel'skoe near Moscow, Roman Klein constructed in 1909–16 a mausoleum for the Iusupovs in the Palladian style, with a domed chapel and curved, double colonnade extending from either side.[33] The design and materials (including gray granite and marble for the structure) were of the highest quality, and the ensemble has been preserved in its cold magnificence (fig. 33). The interior decorative work was created by Ignatii I. Nivinskii, who had also directed the wall painting for Klein at the Museum of Fine Arts in Moscow.

As would be expected, Petrograd, that summation of empire, also had monumental statements of the neoclassical revival. In the center of the city the most visible example was Ivan Fomin's palatial town house built in 1913–15 for Prince Semen S. Abamalek-Lazarev on Moika Quay, No. 23 (fig. 34). The design is faithful to the spirit of the Empire style; but within the constricted space of a Petersburg town house, the details acquire an exaggerated prominence that serves to comment on, rather than reproduce, the old style. When completed in the middle of the war, the house and its lavish interiors (fig. 35) represented an egregious statement of social disparity in a setting of national crisis.[34]

The greatest concentration of the capital's neoclassical revival was on the more isolated Stone Island, with its assembly of mansions for the most

---

[32] Two remarkable examples of the Red Doric style are project sketches, dating from 1919, by Fomin and Belogrud for a palace of workers, reproduced in A. M. Zhuravlev, A. V. Ikonnikov, and A. G. Rochegov, *Arkhitektura sovetskoi Rossii* (Moscow: Stroiizdat, 1987), 56, 59.

[33] Klein's sketches for the Iusupov mausoleum appeared in *Ezhegodnik Moskovskogo arkhitekturnogo obshchestva*, no. 1 (1909): 35–37. His assistant in the project was Grigorii Borisovich Barkhin, later a leading Constructivist architect.

[34] Several photographs of the Abamalek-Lazarev house and its grand interiors appeared in *Ezhegodnik Obshchestva arkhitektorov-khudozhnikov* 11 (1916): 110–16.

wealthy. Here too, Fomin took a leading role in his design for the elegant palace—called a "dacha"—for the prominent diplomat Aleksandr A. Polovtsov (Polovtsev; 1832–1909). The site was the most desirable on the island: directly situated across the expanse of the Middle Nevka River from Rossi's magnificent Elagin Palace. The original plan for the project was conceived in 1909 by Karl Shmidt, who like many other "modernists" had adopted the new fashion of neoclassicism. After the death of the senior Polovtsov, his older son—Aleksandr A. Polovtsov, Jr. (1867–1944)—hired the more talented Fomin to produce a new design. As before, Fomin drew upon motifs of the Russian Empire style, yet applied them on a much larger scale—as though the reaffirming of classical values required their amplification.

The extensive interior decoration of the Polovtsov dacha—more appropriate to a museum than a dwelling—involved the work of Roman F. Meltser and the painter Usein A. Bodaninskii. The interior was not completed until 1916, at which point the house had less than a year to serve as a monument to a statesman instrumental in Russia's expansionist policy in the Far East and in the construction of the Chinese-Eastern Railway through Manchuria. The importance of the Polovtsov mansion as the summa of the neoclassical revival was reflected by its extensive photographic coverage in the major journals.[35]

Despite the seeming dominance of neoclassical aestheticism in architectural polemics before the Revolution, there were others who rejected the exuberant experiments of the moderne as well as an adherence to retrospective styles in favor of a sober rationalism. A signal statement of this position appeared in the critical essay "The Parthenon or St. Sophia," published by the architect Oskar R. Munts in January 1916.[36]

Munts had received a thorough grounding in classical architecture during his study at the Academy of Arts, from which he graduated in 1896 with the gold medal; and for his article he chose the two great monuments of Greek civilization as opposite principles in architecture: the Parthenon, a statement in pure form perfect in detail and unmitigated by utilitarian demands; and St. Sophia, imperfect in detail and the ultimate expression of the purposeful, utilitarian logic of construction. Despite the creative adaptations of ancient classicism by the Romans and their Renaissance successors, the only possible

---

[35] Lukomskii's "Novyi Peterburg" (in *Apollon*) included four photographs of the house; fourteen more, including many views of the interior, appeared in *Ezhegodnik Obshchestva arkhitektorov-khudozhnikov* 11 (1916): 95–109; and *Zodchii* published a lyrical view in the illustrated supplement to its 1916 volume.

[36] O. R. Munts, "Parfenon ili Sv. Sofiia? K sporu o klassitsizme v arkhitekture," *Arkhitekturno-khudozhestvennyi ezhenedel'nik*, no. 2 (1916): 19–22. The essay appeared in response to an article in praise of neoclassicism by Aleksandr Benois, who had an unfailing ability to arouse the opposition of "modernist" critics. The Benois article appeared in installments during November and December in the newspaper *Rech'* and took as its point of departure the neoclassical, retrospective trend in a recent show of student projects at the Academy of Arts.

choice for the modern age is the constructive principle symbolized by St. Sophia. Having reviewed the familiar explanations for the neoclassical revival—as a reaction against the "unceremonious moderne" and a reflection of the creative stagnation of the age—Munts rejects the application of a supposedly eternal stylistic system over an unrelated, modern structure:

> It is both significant and horrible that this [contemporary] neoclassicism, just as much as the infatuation with free decorative forms [the moderne] threatens a general catastrophe: the complete separation of so-called artistic architecture from construction itself, with its technical, engineering innovations....
>
> In order to avoid the catastrophe, it is necessary to return architecture to its eternal source—to purposeful, intelligent construction, the principle of which is so imposingly expressed in the temple of St. Sophia.[37]

The American Alternative

Even as Russian critics debated the merits and significance of modernist and retrospective styles within the European context, yet another direction—the American experience—gained increasing attention within Russian architectural circles. For Russian commentators American architecture was something of a curiosity, remote from the centers of European culture that had influenced Russian architecture since the founding of St. Petersburg. Nonetheless, the extraordinary growth of American cities during the late 19th century exerted a fascination on observers who traveled to America and wrote about the scale of construction for the Russian architectural press.[38]

This interest in American architecture and building technology only intensified at the beginning of the 20th century, as is indicated in the number of articles on American developments in the Russian architectural press, and particularly in the journal of record, *Zodchii*. For example, during most of its final decade of publication (1907–17), *Zodchii* reported regularly on technical innovations in the construction of American skyscrapers. Articles appeared on the Singer Building in 1906, on the Metropolitan Life Building in 1907, and on buildings by Francis Kimball in 1908. There were also reports on the completion of other major structures, such as New York's Penn Station and the New York Public Library. A brief notice in 1908 commented on the "gigantomania" of Ernest Flagg, probably the most active builder of skyscrapers in New York: Flagg "dreams of constructing a building as high as one thousand feet.... Even the Yankees have had second thoughts about this.

---

[37] Munts, "Parfenon ili Sv. Sofiia?" 22.

[38] For a survey of prewar Russian perceptions of American architecture, see U. Brumfild [William Brumfield], "Russkoe vospriiatie amerikanskoi arkhitektury," *Arkhitekturnoe nasledstvo*, no. 45 (2003): 246–57.

There are reasonable people thinking of raising the question of a law to set limits on the flights of artists beyond the clouds."[39]

After 1908, for no clear reason, the number of articles on America in *Zodchii* underwent a temporary decline. In 1909, the only item on America dealt with air pollution in Chicago; in 1910, there was a single report on a new bridge in Philadelphia; and in 1911, R. Bernhard reviewed R. Vogel's book *Das amerikanische Haus*, reflecting a growing curiosity about the American design of the detached house and its suitability as a model for suburban development around Moscow.

The reappearance of articles on American architecture and technology in *Zodchii* was due, in large measure, to the Sixth International Congress on Materials Testing, held at New York's Engineering Societies Building in 1912. Given the standards of the time, it is noteworthy that the journal's correspondent was a woman, Maria Koroleva, about whom regrettably little is known. Her dispatches provide detailed and highly technical accounts of the proceedings, as well as an analysis of the construction of New York's Woolworth Building by Cass Gilbert.[40] To Russian observers, the Woolworth Building represented an extreme example of the American mania for the office tower—a mania that went beyond the limits of economic feasibility, according to the writer of an article on the building, who also noted that its primary function was to serve as a trademark for the Woolworth firm.[41] In a series of postcards entitled "Moscow in the Future," dating from 1913, visionaries in Russia were producing fanciful sketches of a "new Moscow," which bore a distinct resemblance to midtown Manhattan." Indeed, the first tentative steps in this direction had already been taken with the completion of Ivan Ivanovich Rerberg's modest tower for the Northern Insurance Company (figs. 36, 37) in central Moscow in 1911.[42]

The increasingly specific technical descriptions of the engineering involved in the construction of skyscrapers and their skeletal steel frames indicate that Russian builders were prepared to undertake such projects. World War I and subsequent events, however, postponed the large-scale application of this technology until the late 1940s. The most significant statement of this convergence between American and Russian goals in civil engineering appeared in Nikolai Lakhtin's two-part survey of the latest techniques for the use of steel and reinforced concrete in New York's skyscrapers.[43] For Lakhtin,

---

[39] *Zodchii*, no. 40 (1908): 375.

[40] *Zodchii*, no. 46 (1912): 455–59; no. 47 (1912): 467–70; and no. 48 (1912): 479–81.

[41] *Zodchii*, no. 52 (1912): 522.

[42] The tower has survived quite well in contemporary Moscow and is now the headquarters of the Constitutional Court of Russia. See photograph in Brumfield, *Origins of Modernism*, 284.

[43] *Zodchii*, no. 18 (1913): 203–11; and no. 19 (1913): 215–21.

Russia's economic future clearly pointed toward the American model in urban architecture:

> Industry, trade, and technology are developing, prices for land parcels are growing, telephones and other communications cannot always satisfy demand; in short, circumstances analogous to those in America are gradually arising in our urban centers. These circumstances make it necessary to construct tall buildings, which must be erected on a steel frame.[44]

With this imperative in mind, Lakhtin analyzed the tall building from foundation to wind braces and made detailed drawings of key points in the steel column and girder structure. The same message, regarding the convergence of Russian and American architectural conditions, was propagated at the Fifth Congress of Russian Architects in 1913 by Lakhtin and Edmond Perrimond, both of whom had recently attended conferences in America and returned to Russia convinced of the relevance of the new American architecture.[45]

With the onset of war, visions of growth, progress, and technical development receded, and with them the possibilities of an American-style construction boom in Russia. These visions were undoubtedly unrealistic or premature; Lakhtin once went so far as to compare the subsoil of St. Petersburg with that of New York to assess whether it could support tall buildings. During the war years, references to America dwindled, with the exception of a series of detailed articles written in 1916 by Roman Beker on small community library buildings in America. Beker presented a highly favorable view of these structures because of their design, and also because they seemed to express the democratic belief in education for the people.[46] In 1917, America's entry into the war on the side of the Entente produced renewed interest in the United States; but at the end of 1917, *Zodchii* ceased publication. Ironically, the last article published in the journal bore the title "American Engineers and the War."[47]

The Housing Problem before the War

The rapid expansion of apartment construction in Moscow and Petersburg during the decade before the First World War produced many projects with

---

[44] *Zodchii*, no. 18 (1913): 204.

[45] Cf. Koroleva's report on papers read at the technology section of the Fifth Congress (*Zodchii*, no. 3 [1914]: 27).

[46] *Zodchii*, no. 46 (1916): 412–16, and the three subsequent issues, with floor plans, photographs, and a bibliography.

[47] *Zodchii*, no. 47–52 (1917): 226–29.

claim to architectural distinction—almost all of which remained beyond the reach of a majority of the population. Advances in building technology, along with a concern for functionalism, comfort, and hygiene, sustained the new style as well as the neoclassical revival; yet these improvements could not adequately address the larger problems of housing availability.[48] The economics of speculative apartment construction remained untouched by social reform. Indeed, unscrupulous property owners gained more profit per square meter in overcrowded, substandard buildings for transients and the lumpenproletariat than did the builders of apartments for the prosperous.

Even large segments of the middle class, such as office workers and much of the intelligentsia, were faced with prohibitive rents. One solution, used increasingly after 1905, was the organization of housing cooperatives that provided the funds for a number of large apartment complexes, such as that in central Petersburg for the Third Basin Society for the Construction of Permanent Apartments (i.e., for permanent residents, as opposed to transients). Built in 1912–16 on a site that covered some four city blocks, the Basin apartments were among the last and most ingeniously designed of such complexes (fig. 38). Its architects included Aleksei I. Zazerskii, Ernest Virrikh, Aleksei F. Bubyr', and Nikolai Vasil'ev, all of whom had much experience in apartment design.[49] Zazerskii in particular designed a number of developments for cooperative apartment societies between 1910 and the Revolution.

It must be emphasized, however, that the Basin project, as well as ventures such as the complex for the Second Petrograd Society for Apartment Construction near the upper reaches of Kamennoostrovskii Prospekt (1912–13; also by Zazerskii), were still beyond the means of most people, including the lower middle class. As cooperative, not-for-profit institutions, their advantage lay in an ability to apply relatively more capital to attractive site planning, and to more comfortable and hygienic apartment design in comparison with the crowded, noisy, and overpriced apartment blocks typical of the urban milieu. The efforts of such cooperative or benevolent societies, although impressive in themselves, had little impact on the general housing situation. The lower levels of the "middle class" in both Moscow and Petersburg generally lived in less favorable conditions.

At the lower end of the scale was the working class, which was itself divided into several segments. Many— perhaps most—workers had no permanent residence at all, particularly those in the cities on a seasonal basis. Others, including families, were crammed into subdivided apartments. With

---

[48] A detailed analysis of patterns of housing development in St. Petersburg is contained in James H. Bater, *St. Petersburg: Industrialization and Change* (Montreal: McGill-Queen's University Press, 1976).

[49] For a study of the work of Vasil'ev and Bubyr', see V. G. Lisovskii and V. G. Isachenko, *Nikolai Vasil'ev. Aleksei Bubyr'* (St. Petersburg: Beloe i Chernoe, 1999), with illustrated commentary on the Basin Cooperative project, 132–50.

the industrial development of the latter half of the 19th century, many large enterprises established workers' housing on or near the premises for purposes of convenience. For factories located in the suburbs or the country, primitive "villages" of clustered one-story houses (similar to peasant huts) predominated, while large enterprises in an urban area would provide multistoried "barracks" housing with stacked bunks for workers and rooms for families. Such buildings generally provided only the most rudimentary facilities, and the obvious problems with hygiene led to frequent outbreaks of infectious diseases such as cholera and typhus.

Humane considerations aside, these conditions made it difficult to maintain the stable work force needed for the more advanced industrial concerns, and some of them attempted at the end of the 19th century to create more tolerable housing called "workers' colonies." Among the first and most notable of such projects were the two large multistoried brick buildings designed by Robert A. Gedike for the Russian-American Rubber Company. Constructed in 1897–98, the buildings represented a simplified version of a proposal that the company had presented in a widely publicized architectural competition. Indeed, the competition itself served to bring much attention to the issue of workers' housing, even though the winning entries were rejected in favor of the simpler design, with fewer amenities, commissioned from Gedike.[50] (The simplified version allowed a higher return on investment—7.7 percent per annum, derived from rent and from shops on the first floor of one of the buildings. Although Moscow workers generally did not have to pay for factory-provided housing, workers in Petersburg were assessed rent in such cases.)

In addition to company-sponsored housing for workers, there were a very few projects sponsored by philanthropic societies such as the Company for the Struggle with Housing Needs, which built the Harbor Workers Village (Gavanskii rabochii gorodok) at the western end of Vasil'evskii Island. The main architect, Nikolai V. Dmitriev, had expended much effort in a comparative study of approaches to urban housing—particularly for workers and their families—throughout Europe. This project, launched in 1904 with support from influential segments of society, was intended as a model for further progress in this area. Architecturally, the five buildings of the complex were solidly designed, with modest decoration in a vernacular style. For all of the attention placed on its design, however, the project had difficulty attracting its proposed working-class tenants, since even their modest rents (from 4.30 rubles per month for a room to 7.40 rubles for a small apartment) were beyond

---

[50] A detailed report on the competition for the workers' housing project at the Russian-American Rubber Company was published in *Stroitel' (Vestnik arkhitektury, domovladeniia i sanitarnogo zodchestva),* 3, 9–10 (May 1897): 321–54. It should be noted that this journal included an extensive section devoted to the development of inexpensive housing.

the ability of most wage-earners to pay. Thus the project only highlighted larger structural problems in the prevailing economic and social system.[51]

These well designed and praiseworthy efforts met only a small fraction of the housing need and did very little to address the question of workers' housing. Indeed, the construction of even private, speculative housing became less attractive as expectations rose among the middle class for amenities in apartment design that considerably increased the cost of construction. By 1910 large-scale apartment construction became largely the business of cooperatives, professional societies, and insurance companies.

Yet the call to impose order on a free market that operated within severely limited city services and a primitive infrastructure was by no means limited to the retrospective ideals of Lukomskii. A number of critics advocated a more coherent, regulated system of urban planning and development (including the right of eminent domain for city authorities) with the return to normal housing construction after the war. In the event, such ameliorist approaches were never implemented, for the worsening chaos of the war and ensuing revolutions destroyed the economic base that had supported private apartment construction.

The War Economy and the Collapse of Architectural Practice

The beginning of the war in August 1914 unleashed economic pressures that would reveal the vulnerability of Russia's already volatile economy. Yet for the first half of the war projects continued to be built and developed on a substantial scale, as demonstrated in a survey of professional publications such as *Zodchii, Ezhegodnik Obshchestva arkhitektorov-khudozhnikov,* and *Ezhegodnik Moskovskogo arkhitekturnogo obshchestva.* This continued activity was true not only in Moscow and St. Petersburg, but also in major provincial centers such as Nizhnii Novgorod, Omsk, and Krasnoiarsk.

Inevitably, however, the prolongation of the war caused ever greater dislocation and damage to the Russian economy.[52] The ceaseless drain of mo-

---

[51] The Harbor Workers Village was extensively discussed at a special meeting of the Petersburg Society of Architects at the beginning of 1907. Detailed reports of the discussion and further commentary by participants were published in *Zodchii* throughout 1907, including an initial article in no. 4: 30. Dmitriev himself was the author of a book on the topic, *Bor'ba s zhilishchnoi nuzhdoi* (St. Petersburg, 1903).

[52] For an overview of the economic situation in Russia during the First World War, see Vincent Barnett, *The Russian Revolutionary Economy, 1890–1940* (London: Routledge, 2004), 49–55. See also James H. Bater, "Modernization and Municipality: Moscow and St. Petersburg on the Eve of the Great War," in *Studies in Russian Historical Geography,* ed. James H. Bater and R. A. French (London: Academic Press, 1983). For a discussion of the problems of Russian society during the two decades before the Revolution, see Arthur Mendel, "On Interpreting the Fate of Imperial Russia," and Theodore von Laue, "The Problems of Industrialization," in *Russia under the Last Tsar,* ed. Theofanis

bilization had a growing impact on the available labor force, both for construction and for factories. Perhaps nowhere was this crisis more evident than in housing, which became one of the country's most explosive social issues. New construction was curtailed at the very time the populations of Moscow and Petersburg were experiencing still greater pressures as a result of the influx of refugees, transient labor, and troops. The rapid inflation introduced by the war and its overheated, distorted economy placed additional pressure on housing prices, as did dwindling credit for new construction.[53] In recognition of the potential social chaos stemming from spiraling rents, the government imposed rent controls in 1915, and in 1916 forbade the eviction of tenants. Under these circumstances building owners abandoned basic services and repairs, which were no longer covered by rent.

By the autumn of 1917 the financial structure for rental apartments had essentially collapsed, as had most authority elsewhere in society. At the same time the growing discontent with the continuing war and a catastrophic economy fueled radical demands for a redistribution of housing—demands that the Bolsheviks readily accepted by expropriating both private houses and apartment buildings. Those who still had apartments in 1918–19 were forced to endure the horrors of winter in structures with no basic services, no water, no heat, no sanitation, and usually no electricity. These conditions have been vividly described in memoirs and works of Russian literature such as Evgenii Zamiatin's story "The Cave," in which the inhabitants of a Petersburg apartment building are reduced to a Stone Age level of existence (an ironic extension of a visual metaphor used by Ippolit A. Pretro in his Putilova apartment design). Boris Pasternak's novel *Doctor Zhivago* portrays similarly harrowing conditions in Moscow.

By the end of the Civil War in 1921, the population of Petrograd had been reduced to little over 700,000, approximately a third of its number at the beginning of the war.[54] Many had perished from cold, hunger, disease, and violence; others from the middle and upper classes had emigrated; and the largest number—workers with village connections—had gone back to the countryside. To some degree this migration facilitated a resettlement from substandard workers' districts to better housing, where apartments (still scarce)

George Stavrou (Minneapolis: University of Minnesota Press, 1969), 13–41 and 117–53, respectively. A comprehensive analysis of the social crisis is Teodor Shanin's two-volume study *Russia as a "Developing Society,"* and *Russia, 1905–07: Revolution as a Moment of Truth* (New Haven: Yale University Press, 1986).

[53] An account of economic factors in the housing crisis from the perspective of apartment owners in St. Petersburg is presented in I. Pretro, "Obshchestva kvartirovladel'tsev," in *Arkhitekturno-khudozhestvennyi ezhenedel'nik*, 3, 42 (1916): 403–04. This journal ceased publication at the end of 1916.

[54] For a detailed analysis of census data in St. Petersburg, see Bater, *St. Petersburg*, 309–21ff.

were subdivided by communal living arrangements. Nonetheless, the solidity of prewar housing construction had provided a serviceable physical base that could accommodate large numbers of residents, while the new authorities devised their own plans to meet the seemingly intractable problems of living space in Russia's major cities.

From the perspective of the innovators of the 1920s, Russian architecture of the early 20th century—whether moderne or neoclassical—had achieved little as the expression of the values and the requirements of the modern age. Within the relatively short time and limited economic resources available to it, Russian capitalism had provided architects with a means to approach the problems of the modern urban environment, but not to solve them. Had the late imperial social and economic order enabled a more rational use of resources, architects could have shown a greater sense of purpose in meeting social needs such as urban housing. The inability to address immediate issues was compounded by the lack of a coherent theoretical system that would have guided architecture to a union of technology and design.[55]

Recreating Architecture after the War: Change and Continuity

"October 1917 marked the beginning of the Russian Revolution and the opening of a new page in the history of human society. It is to this social revolution, rather than to the technological revolution, that the basic elements of Russian architecture are tied."[56] In 1930, when the above passage appeared in El (Lazar') Lisitskii's essay *Russia: An Architecture for World Revolution*, little remained of the ferment that had motivated the radical experiment in Russian architecture in the 1920s.

With unintended irony Lisitskii had stated a truth that would acquire a new dimension in the Stalinist era, as the Communist Party erected its monuments with little concern for the technological revolution and the experimental, at times utopian, quests of the preceding decade. But for the 15 or so years of its existence, the great postrevolutionary experiment in its many manifestations endeavored to alter conceptions of architectural space, to create an environment that would inculcate new social values, and at the same time to utilize the most advanced structural and technological principles.

---

[55] It is on this point that the leading theoretician of Russian Constructivist architecture, Moisei Ginzburg, dismissed prerevolutionary modernism. See Moisei Ginzburg, *Style and Epoch* (1924), trans. and ed. Anatole Senkevitch (Cambridge, MA: M.I.T. Press, 1982), 42.

[56] From El Lisitskii's essay, originally published in Austria in 1930 as *Russland: Die Rekonstruktion der Architektur in der Sowjetunion*, and republished, with supplementary material, in 1965 in Germany as *Russland: Architektur für eine Weltrevolution*. The English translation, by Eric Dluhosch, draws its title from the German edition. See El Lissitzky [Lisitskii], *Russia: An Architecture for World Revolution* (Cambridge, MA: M.I.T. Press, 1970), 27.

The assumption that a revolution in architecture (along with the other arts) would inevitably accompany a political revolution was soon put to the test by social and economic realities. Russia's rapidly developing industrial base lay in a shambles after a war, a revolution, and a civil war; technological resources were extremely limited in what was still a predominantly rural nation; and Moscow's population—poorly housed before the war—increased dramatically as the city became in 1918 the administrative center of a thoroughly administered state. One of that state's earliest edicts, in August 1918, repealed the right to private ownership of urban real estate.

To be sure, the prerevolutionary building boom had established a viable foundation, in both architectural theory and practice, for urban development on a large scale. Furthermore, the Russian architectural profession was relatively intact after the emigration that decimated other areas of Russian culture after the Revolution. And the most prominent art and architectural schools in Moscow and Petrograd were capable of providing a base for the development of new cadres, despite sometimes sweeping changes in the composition of the faculty. Nonetheless, the task of resuscitating these institutions, of allocating resources for new construction, and of devising a plan for coordinating further development could only have been Herculean.

Even as the country plunged into civil war, groups of architects in Moscow and Petrograd designed workers' settlements that represent an extension of the "garden city" movement that had already tentatively appeared in Russia during the decade before the First World War.[57] More monumental designs drew upon massive, archaic forms of neoclassicism (reminiscent of the heroic architectural visions of the French Revolution), such as projects by Ivan Fomin and Andrei Belogrud for a Palace of Workers in Petrograd.[58] Indeed, with the collapse of commercial architecture, many designs of the first years of Soviet power consisted of classically-inspired monuments to revolutions and revolutionary thinkers, European as well as Russian. Two prominent examples to be implemented were the Freedom Obelisk (1918–19; not extant) by Dmitrii Osipov and the sculptor Nikolai A. Andreev; and the monument

---

[57] A survey of new plans for workers' communities is contained in V. E. Khazanova, *Sovetskaia arkhitektura pervykh let oktiabria* (Moscow: Nauka, 1970), 51–71. More generally on early planned communities in Russia, see S. Frederick Starr, "The Revival and Schism of Urban Planning in Twentieth-Century Russia," in *The City in Russian History*, ed. Michael F. Hamm (Lexington: University Press of Kentucky, 1976), 222–42; and Brumfield, *Origins of Modernism*, 295, 321 n. 95.

[58] For reproductions of the Fomin and Belogrud submissions, see A. M. Zhuravlev et al., *Arkhitektura sovetskoi Rossii*, 56, 59. The Belogrud design was modeled on the Castel Sant'Angelo in Rome, with additional components in the Florentine style. For a detailed, annotated analysis of the projects for this competition, see Khazanova, *Sovetskaia arkhitektura pervykh let oktiabria*, 125–27.

on Mars Field in Petrograd to those who perished in the Revolution (1919) by Lev Rudnev and Ivan Fomin.[59]

Other projects were built of wood—cheap, still readily available, and technologically undemanding. In 1920 Ivan Fomin used wood, with gypsum details, for rostral columns and a triumphal entrance to newly-converted rest homes for workers on Stone Island, earlier the site of elegant suburban mansions.[60] The most impressive such exercise, with a combination of both modernist and traditional designs, was the 1923 All-Russian Agricultural and Cottage Industry Exhibition, situated to the north of central Moscow. From Ivan Zholtovskii's monumental double-arched entrance to Konstantin Melnikov's pavilion for the Makhorka tobacco factory and the futuristic open-frame tower of the *Izvestiia* pavilion (Boris Gladkov, Vera Mukhina, Aleksandra Ekster), the variety of wooden pavilion designs served as a symbol of a society re-emerging toward prosperity and development in the countryside.[61] For more prosaic purposes, the old Russian technique of building from standardized, precut wooden components was refined for workers' housing in provincial industrial towns.[62]

Paradoxically, the poverty and social chaos of the early revolutionary years propelled architects and artists toward radical ideas on design, many of which were related to an already thriving modernist movement in the visual arts. For example, Lisitskii's concepts of space and form, along with those of Kazimir Malevich and Vladimir Tatlin, played a major part in the development of an architecture expressed in "stereometric forms," purified of the decorative elements of the eclectic past. The experiments of Lisitskii, Vasilii Kandinskii, and Malevich in painting and of Tatlin and Aleksandr Rodchenko in sculpture had created the possibility of a new architectural movement, defined by Lisitskii as a synthesis with painting and sculpture.[63]

---

[59] A survey of revolutionary monuments (including the early variants of Shchusev's Lenin Mausoleum) is contained in Khazanova, *Sovetskaia arkhitektura pervykh let oktiabria*, 151–67.

[60] On Fomin's Rostral columns, see Zhuravlev et al., *Arkhitektura sovetskoi Rossii*, 66–67. His contribution to the design of the workers' rest zone on Stone Island is described in V. A. Vitiazeva, *Kamennyi ostrov* (Leningrad: Lenizdat, 1991), 222–24.

[61] The 1923 Agricultural Exhibition is examined in Khazanova, *Sovetskaia arkhitektura pervykh let oktiabria*, 167–73. On Melnikov's Makhorka pavilion, see S. Frederick Starr, *Konstantin Melnikov: Solo Architect in a Mass Society* (Princeton, NJ: Princeton University Press, 1978), 59–63; and S. Kazakov, "Promyshlennaia arkhitektura Konstantina Melnikova," *Arkhitektura SSSR*, no. 4 (1990): 82.

[62] See N. P. Bylinkin, V. N. Kalmykova, A. V. Riabushin, and G. V. Sergeeva, *Istoriia sovetskoi arkhitektury (1917–1954 gg.)* (Moscow: Stroiizdat, 1985), 48.

[63] Lissitzky, *Russia: An Architecture for World Revolution*, 28–34. An English survey of these developments is contained in Camilla Gray, *The Russian Experiment in Art: 1863–1922* (New York: Thames and Hudson, 1986), 240–41 and passim.

Yet this revolutionary vision would soon be replaced by a return to the "eternal values" of the Italian Renaissance and neoclassicism. Some of the major proponents of these values had left Russia: Lukomskii emigrated to France, and Lialevich and Peretiatkovich returned to Poland. Yet there were others, such as Fomin and Ivan Zholtovskii, who were well equipped to apply the stylistic markers of late imperial architecture to the burgeoning Stalinist prestige projects in Moscow and Leningrad during the 1930s and beyond. Thus did Soviet architecture return to the ideology of empire and hierarchy proclaimed on the eve of the First World War.

Figure 1. K. S. Petrov-Vodkin. *In the Firing Line* (1915–16). © 2013, State Russian Museum, St. Petersburg.

Figure 2. Marc Chagall. *The News Vendor.* 1914. © 2013 Artists Rights Society (ARS), New York / ADAGP, Paris.

Figure 3. Konstantin Iuon. *The New Planet*. 1921. Courtesy of the Tretiakov Gallery, Moscow.

Figure 4. Petrograd. Mariinskii Palace. May Day, 1918.

Figure 5. M. B. Grekov. *Cossack Patrol on Recon Duty.* 1915.

Figure 6. M. B. Grekov. *In Group To Budennyi*. 1923. Courtesy of the Tretiakov Gallery, Moscow.

Figure 7. K. S. Malevich. *Black Square.* 1915.
Courtesy of the Tretiakov Gallery, Moscow.

Figure 8. K. S. Petrov-Vodkin. *Petrograd in 1918.* 1920. Courtesy of the Tretiakov Gallery, Moscow.

Figure 9. A. A. Rylov. *Blue Expanse.* 1918. Courtesy of the Tretiakov Gallery, Moscow.

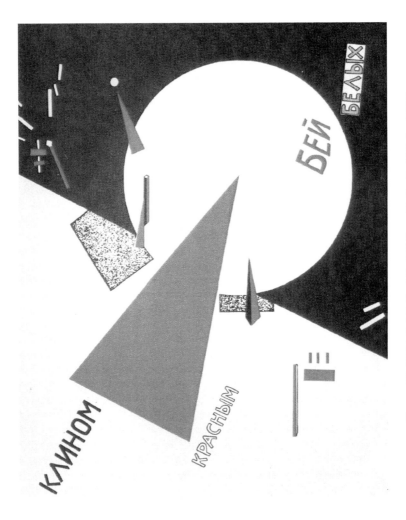

Figure 10. El Lisitskii. *Beat the Whites with the Red Wedge* (1919).

Figure 11. K. S. Petrov-Vodkin. *After the Battle.* 1923.

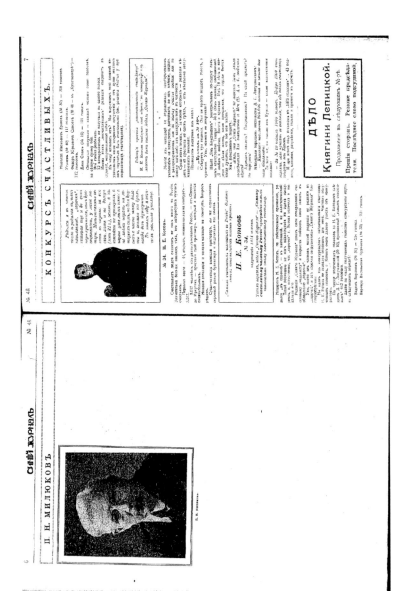

Figure 12. A portrait of Pavel Miliukov alongside "white spaces." *Sinii zhurnal*, 1916.

Figure 13. "Heroes and Victims of the Patriotic War of 1914." Photographs "kindly delivered to Ogonek." *Ogonek*, 1914.

Figure 14. "The war and naval minister A. F. Kerenskii gives a speech in front of soldiers of the Semenovskii Guards regiment." Photograph by K. Bulla. *Solntse Rossii*, 1917.

Figure 15. "On the Perm Front." Photographs by
Iakov Shteinberg. *Plamia*, 1919.

Figure 16. "Nightmares of the July Days. 4 July 1917 in the afternoon on Nevskii Prospekt at the Public Library." *Solntse Rossii,* 1917.

1) В. И. Ленин произносит речь на 1-ом Конгрессе Коминтерна; 2) В. И. среди членов Президиума II-го Конгресса; 3) В. И. среди представителей восточных народов на II-м Конгрессе; 4) В. И. среди членов II-го Конгресса; 5) В. И., сидя на полу, записывает во время заседания II Конгресса; 6) митинг на площади Урицкого; В. И. произносит речь перед трудящимися Ленинграда.

Figure 17. "Meeting on the Uritskii Square: V. I. gives a speech to workers in Leningrad." *Krasnaia niva*, 1924.

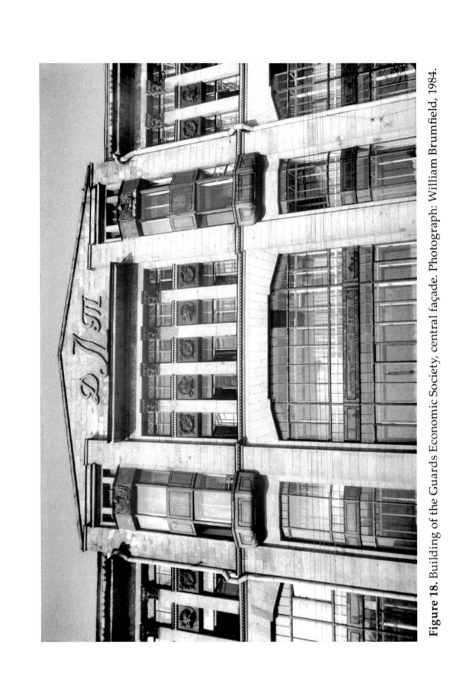

Figure 18. Building of the Guards Economic Society, central façade. Photograph: William Brumfield, 1984.

Figure 19. Building of the Guards Economic Society, interior. Photograph: William Brumfield, 2002.

Figure 20. Passage on Liteinyi Prospekt. Photograph: William Brumfield, 2003.

Figure 21. German Embassy, St. Isaac's Square. Photograph: William Brumfield, 1972.

Figure 22. German Embassy, St. Isaac's Square, main façade.
Photograph: William Brumfield.

Figure 23. F. Mertens Building, Nevskii Prospekt.
Photograph: William Brumfield, 1997.

Figure 24. Sytnyi Market project drawing. *Ezhegodnik 1910 Obshchestva Arkhitektorov-Khudozhnikov* .

Figure 25. Prayer house, Preobrazhenskoe Jewish cemetery. Photograph: William Brumfield, 2009.

Figure 26. Prayer house, Preobrazhenskoe Jewish cemetery, back façade. Photograph: William Brumfield, 2009.

Figure 27. Azov-Don Bank, Bol'shaia Morskaia Street. Photograph: William Brumfield, 1971.

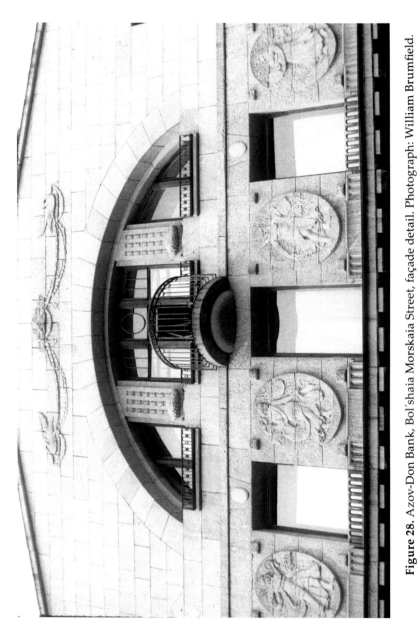

Figure 28. Azov-Don Bank, Bol'shaia Morskaia Street, façade detail. Photograph: William Brumfield.

Figure 29. Vavelberg Building, Nevskii Prospekt. Photograph: William Brumfield, 1971.

Figure 30. Hotel Astoria, St. Isaac's Square. Photograph: William Brumfield, 1991.

Figure 31. Rozenshtein apartment house, Kamennoostrovskii Prospekt, no. 35. Photograph: William Brumfield, 2013.

Figure 32. Rozenshtein apartment house, Bol'shoi Prospekt, no. 77.
Photograph: William Brumfield, 2013.

Figure 33. Iusupov mausoleum, Arkhangel'skoe (near Moscow). Photograph: William Brumfield, 1992.

Figure 34. Abamalek-Lazarev house, Moika Quay 23. Photograph: William Brumfield, 1971.

Figure 35. Abamalek-Lazarev house, Moika Quay 23, interior. Photograph: William Brumfield.

Figure 36. Northern Insurance Company, Moscow.
Photograph: William Brumfield, 1979.

Figure 37. Northern Insurance Company (left) and Delovoi Dvor, Moscow. Photograph: William Brumfield.

Figure 38. Third Basin Society for the Construction of Permanent Apartments. Photograph: William Brumfield, 1997.

Figure 39. Marc Chagall. *Vitebsk. Train Station.* 1915. © VG Bild-Kunst, Bonn 2012.

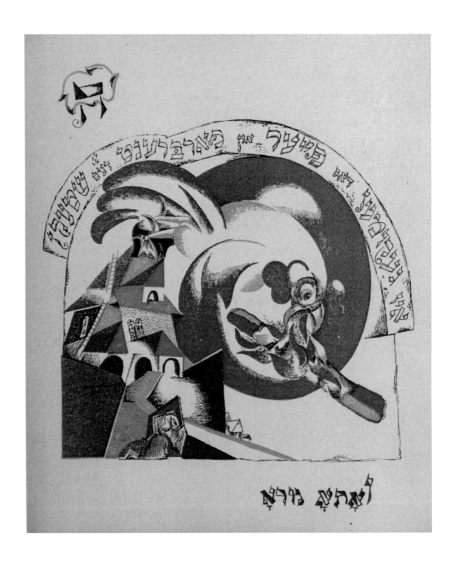

Figure 40. El Lisitskii. Illustration to *Chad Gadya* (1919). http://www.wikipaintings. org/en/el-lissitzky/illustration-to-chad-gadya-1919

ВОЙНА ВЪ РУССКОЙ ПОЭЗІИ

Составила АНС. ЧЕБОТАРЕВСКАЯ.

Съ предисловіемъ ѲЕДОРА СОЛОГУБА.

Figure 41. Cover design by Nikolai K. Kalmakov for
Anastasiia Chebotarevskaia's *War in Russian Poetry* (1915).

Center and Periphery in Russian Jewish Culture during the Crisis of 1914–22

Anke Hilbrenner

Most avant-garde art around the turn of the century was Russian, and from there it was transferred abroad and "shaped the modern world."[1] This leading role was especially true for Russian Jewish art. Even though the Jews in the Russian Empire were heavily discriminated against, Russian Jewish culture flourished in the early 20th century, especially after 1915. In many texts about the world of Russian Jewish artists such as Marc Chagall, El (Lazar') Lisitskii, or Natan Al'tman, to name only a few, their contributions appear remarkably remote from the fate of the Jewish masses, from disfranchisement, pogroms, and deportations. This perception gap sheds light on one of the main problems of Russian history, namely center and periphery: the tension between the two and their interactions are at the core of not only Jewish history in late imperial Russia. *Beyond the Pale* was the title of an important study of Russian Jewish history published in 2002 that analyzes the politics and culture of the Jews of St. Petersburg, who set themselves apart from the Jewish "masses" in the so-called "Pale of Settlement."[2] They perceived themselves as modern, while they regarded the Jews at the periphery as backward, but at the same time they reached out to them as benefactors and intellectuals in search of their roots within an imagined community. "The Pale of Settlement" in this context refers not only to the territories where Jews were allowed to settle before 1915 (mainly the western provinces of the tsarist empire stretching from the Baltic to the Black Seas). It also serves as a metaphor symbolizing the legal restrictions and discriminations experienced by the vast majority of the five million Jewish subjects of the last tsars.

The tension between center and periphery reached a climax between 1914 and 1921. This period was experienced as a great crisis for the Jews of the empire. The Pale of Settlement existed until 1915—its territories did not only turn into a theater of war, but later became the scene of mass expulsions,

---

[1] Steven G. Marks, *How Russia Shaped the Modern World: From Art to Anti-Semitism, Ballet to Bolshevism* (Princeton, NJ: Princeton University Press, 2003), 176–274.

[2] Benjamin Nathans, *Beyond the Pale: The Jewish Encounter with Late Imperial Russia* (Berkeley: University of California Press, 2002).

Russian Culture in War and Revolution, 1914–22, Book 1: Popular Culture, the Arts, and Institutions. Murray Frame, Boris Kolonitskii, Steven G. Marks, and Melissa K. Stockdale, eds. Bloomington, IN: Slavica Publishers, 2014, 189–207.

bloodshed, Civil War atrocities, and violent pogroms until 1921. At the same time, in St. Petersburg/Petrograd and Moscow, Russian and Soviet Jews claimed a leading role in modern and avant-garde culture and, after 1917, also in politics. Nevertheless, the importance of the Jews at the center cannot be understood without reference to the situation at the periphery. This chapter will discuss the interaction of center and periphery[3] in Russian Jewish cultural history during the years 1914 to 1922 in the broader context of modern Jewish history in the Russian Empire, seven years that witnessed crisis and success simultaneously. It was a time of "great expectations and rude awakenings."[4]

Emancipation Undone[5]

Before the partitions of Poland very few Jews lived under tsarist authority. It was one of the outcomes of the three partitions (1772-95) that the mainland of Jewish settlement in Eastern Europe became incorporated into the Russian Empire. Settlement regulations were enforced in 1804, and from that time onwards the Pale of Settlement became an infamous topos of the Russian Jewish historical narrative. In 1804 any regulation with regard to the Jews was equaled by similar approaches to other subjects of the tsars. Mobility, for example, was also restricted for the great majority of Russians—most importantly the peasants. The modernizing efforts of Alexander II (1855–81) improved the situation for a number of so-called "productive" Jews. The turning point of tsarist policy towards the Jews came in 1881. A wave of violent anti-Jewish pogroms took place in the southwestern periphery of the empire. The government blamed the Jews. "Jewish exploitation" of Russian and Ukrainian peasants was held structurally responsible for the outbreak of unrest and rioting. Alexander III (1881–94) promulgated the May Laws, a number of regulations directed against the Jews. The pogroms of 1881 were thus the

---

[3] For the relativity of center and periphery, see Arkadi Zeltser, "Imaginary Vitebsk: The View from the Inside," *East European Jewish Affairs* 43, 3 (2010): 225–31.

[4] As Ezra Mendelsohn put it with regard to Charles Dickens. Ezra Mendelsohn, "Zwischen großen Erwartungen und bösem Erwachen: Das Ende der multinationalen Reiche in Ostmittel- und Südosteuropa aus jüdischer Perspektive," in *Zwischen grossen Erwartungen und bösem Erwachen: Juden, Politik und Antisemitismus in Ost- und Südosteuropa 1918–1945*, ed. Dittmar Dahlmann and Anke Hilbrenner (Paderborn: Schöningh, 2007), 13.

[5] For a deeper investigation of "emancipation undone," see Manfred Hildermeier, "Die jüdische Frage im Zarenreich: Zum Problem der unterbliebenen Emanzipation," *Jahrbücher für Geschichte Osteuropas* 32 (1984): 321–57; Heinz-Dietrich Löwe, *The Tsars and the Jews: Reform, Reaction, and Anti-Semitism in Imperial Russia, 1772–1917* (Chur, Switzerland: Harwood Academic Publishers, 1993).

starting point of anti-Jewish legislation and politics in the Russian Empire.[6] The measures remained in effect until World War I. State anti-Semitism, the expulsion of Jews from Moscow in 1891, and the brutal pogroms of 1903–06 added to the notion of the "pogrom era." The revered dean of Russian Jewish historiography Simon Dubnov labeled the period from 1881 to 1917 "one long war by the authorities against the Jews."[7] This long war reached a climax during World War I. Even though 500,000 Jews served in the army, they were heavily discriminated against. Most of the Jewish soldiers were denied entry into the officer corps. Discrimination also intensified in the civil sphere. Yiddish and Hebrew publications were banned and the majority of the Jewish population were thus cut off from their media.[8]

When the Pale of Settlement turned into a theater of war, the Russian army took hostages from Jewish communities in order to extort loyalty from Jewish subjects. In 1915, when Russian troops were retreating, Jews, collectively suspected to be spies, were expelled from certain areas of the Pale. Hysteria and fear of espionage were part of the Russian experience during World War I. But rumors about Jewish spying—including their use of modern devices like telephones and light signals—were highly absurd in the face of the alleged premodern living conditions in the Pale, where in most *shtetls* neither telephone wires nor electricity existed in Jewish homes. Nevertheless, about one million Jews were deported between 1914 and 1917.[9] Moreover the libel of Jewish espionage led to brutal atrocities by Russian military and civilians against the Jewish population of the Pale, in the Kingdom of Poland, and in Galicia. Historians estimate that the number of Jews killed in the wartime

---

[6] The pogroms of 1881-82 have recently been covered in John Klier, *Russians, Jews, and the Pogroms of 1881–1882* (Cambridge: Cambridge University Press, 2011).

[7] Avraham Greenbaum, "Bibliographical Essay," in *Pogroms: Anti-Jewish Violence in Modern Russian History*, ed. John Klier and Shlomo Lambroza (Cambridge: Cambridge University Press, 1992), 377; Anke Hilbrenner, *Diaspora-Nationalismus: Zur Geschichtskonstruktion Simon Dubnows* (Göttingen: Vandenhoeck & Ruprecht, 2007), 159–64.

[8] Jan Kusber, "Zwischen Duldung und Ausgrenzung: Die Politik gegenüber den Juden im ausgehenden Zarenreich," in *Jüdische Welten in Osteuropa*, ed. Annelore Engel-Braunschmidt and Eckhard Hübner (Frankfurt am Main: P. Lang, 2005), 45–64, here 45–47.

[9] Estimates range from 500,000 to 1 million. Eric Lohr, "The Russian Army and the Jews: Mass Deportation, Hostages, and Violence during World War I," *Russian Review* 60, 3 (2001): 404. For published source material, see Maksim Vinaver, "Iz chernoi knigi rossiiskogo evreistva: Materialy dlia istorii voiny 1914–1915," *Evreiskaia starina*, no. 10 (1918): 231–96. On accusations of Jewish espionage, see the local examples in S. Pivovarchik, "Tragedii Pervoi mirovoi voiny: "Evrei-shpiony" (po materialam Natsional'nogo istoricheskogo arkhiva Belarusi v Grodno)," in *Mirovoi krizis 1914–1920 godov i sud'ba vostochnoevropeiskogo evreistva*, ed. Oleg V. Budnitskii (Moscow: ROSSPEN, 2005), 71–83.

pogroms reached 100,000 or even 200,000.[10] It has to be emphasized that these mass killings were committed by the Russian army (chiefly Cossacks) against Russian subjects.[11] This dark chapter in Russian Jewish history has not yet been fully recognized and its memory is overshadowed by the violent pogroms of the Civil War.[12]

The census of 1897 counted 5.2 million Jews in the Russian Empire. "Russian Jews"[13] thus comprised half of the Jewish population worldwide at the turn of the century. A total of 4.8 million Jews lived in the Pale of Settlement, whilst the others were part of the elite, living "beyond the Pale." Many young people tried to move from the Pale to the center in order to enroll in institutions of higher learning. Admittance to secondary schools and universities was restricted for Jews inside and outside of the Pale, but the center of the empire still remained attractive for those who wanted to reach "beyond the Pale" intellectually or culturally. Jews at the center often provided young migrants with money, food, or shelter, and even more importantly with residency permits via fictional employment. Moreover, the "productive" and often wealthy Jews who lived in St. Petersburg tried to lobby for their remote "brethren" in the Pale. For a long time, migration and such politics of intercession (*shtadlanstvo*) were the main interaction between center and periphery.

Towards the Center: Jewish Artists from Pale to St. Petersburg/Petrograd

The relationship between center and periphery changed gradually during the early years of the 20th century. While in the second half of the 19th century the cultural ideal of Jews beyond the Pale was the universal ideal of modern civilization, after the turn of the century modern Jews strove for their cultural roots in national art, history, language, and folklore, to be found precisely in the Pale. But this turn to roots was a long and sometimes twisted process.

---

[10] S. An-ski, *The Enemy at His Pleasure: A Journey through the Jewish Pale of Settlement during World War I*, ed. and trans. Joachim Neugroschel (New York: Metropolitan Books/Henry Holt and Co., 2002), x.

[11] On the Cossacks and the pogroms, see John Klier, "Kazaki i pogromy: Chem otlichalis' 'voennye' pogromy?" in *Mirovoi krizis 1914–1920 godov*, 47–70.

[12] On the pogroms during the Civil War, see Anke Hilbrenner, "Pogrome im Russischen Bürgerkrieg (1917-1921)," in *Handbuch des Antisemitismus: Judenfeindschaft in Geschichte und Gegenwart*, 4: *Ereignisse, Dekrete, Kontroversen*, ed. Wolfgang Benz (Munich: Saur, 2011), 296–98; Peter Kenez, "Pogroms and White Ideology in the Russian Civil War," in *Pogroms*, 293–313.

[13] For the problem of the notion of "Russian Jews," see Eli Lederhendler, "Did Russian Jewry Exist prior to 1917?" in *Jews and Jewish Life in Russia and the Soviet Union*, ed. Yaacov Ro'i (London: Frank Cass, 1995), 15–27. Nevertheless, contemporaries such as Simon Dubnov used the term to refer to Russian Jews as an imagined community. See Hilbrenner, *Diaspora-Nationalismus*, 73–76.

The education of the famous artist Marc Chagall is a striking example of this shift of cultural values and ideals. He was born in 1887 as the eldest son of nine children in a rather poor, observant Chassidic family. His hometown became Vitebsk in the Belorussian part of the Pale. After some years of traditional Jewish education in the *kheder,* his mother tried to integrate him into a Russian institution of higher learning. Simon Dubnov (born in 1860) had rebelled against the Jewish tradition of the Belorussian *shtetl* Mstislavl in order to enter a Russian secondary school.[14] In the case of Chagall, who was born into the next generation, his mother took 50 rubles and bought his way into the Russian school. But Chagall's school career was not successful.[15] His school years were a time of social unrest and violent riots in Vitebsk. The city experienced a pogrom during the military mobilization for the Russo-Japanese War in October 1904, and there was another pogrom in the same year. Forty-eight Jews were severely injured. Another pogrom took place in November 1905, after the declaration of the October manifesto: 80 Jews were killed.[16] Chagall does not mention those events in his memoirs but recalls that he went to the drawing school of the Russian Jewish realist artist Jehuda Pen in Vitebsk at that time.[17] Pen's drawing school was the stepping stone for a number of promising artists born in the 1880s and 1890s. In addition to Chagall, El Lisitskii trained there.[18] The educations and careers of Chagall and Lisitskii were strongly interrelated. Even though their friendship ended in bitter conflict, there is some evidence that they were very close in their early years as artists.[19] Another pupil of Pen was Shlomo Yudovin, the ethnographic photographer.[20] Pen himself was a classical example of a Russian Jewish artist of the older generation, closer to the generation of Dubnov. For Pen the universal ideal was reached by acculturation into Russian high culture. He was born in the 1870s near Kovno into a traditional Jewish family who at first prohibited painting as a sinful activity. After many struggles Pen was

---

[14] Semen M. Dubnov, *Kniga zhizni: Vospominaniia i razmyshleniia. Materialy dlia istorii moego vremeni* (St. Petersburg: Peterburgskoe Vostokovedenie, 1998).

[15] Marc Chagall, *Mein Leben* (Stuttgart: Hatje, 1959), 46–53.

[16] Shlomo Lambroza, "The Pogroms of 1903–1906," in *Pogroms*, 214–18, 231.

[17] Chagall, *Mein Leben*, 54–66.

[18] Seth L. Wolitz, "El Lissitzky," http://www.yivoencyclopedia.org/article.aspx/Lissitzky_El (accessed 1 February 2012).

[19] Ziva Amishai-Maisels, "Chagall and the Jewish Revival: Center or Periphery?" in *Tradition and Revolution: The Jewish Renaissance in Russian Avant-Garde Art, 1912–1928,* ed. Ruth Apter-Gabriel (Jerusalem: Israel Museum, 1987), 84–85.

[20] Anke Hilbrenner, "Invention of a Vanished World: Photographs of Traditional Jewish Life in the Russian Pale of Settlement," *Jahrbücher für Geschichte Osteuropas* 57 (2009): 176–77; Ruth Apter-Gabriel, *The Jewish Art of Solomon Yudovin (1892–1954): From Folk Art to Socialist Realism* (Jerusalem: Israel Museum, 1991).

accepted into the Academy in St. Petersburg. He became part of the movement of the Peredvizhniki (Itinerant Artists) that included Il'ia Repin, Isaak Levitan, Valentin Serov, and other realist painters who were opposed to the aesthetics nurtured by the Academy.[21] Gertrud Pickhan has shown recently how much the realist art of the Peredvizhniki is perceived as a genuine part of the Russian cultural heritage, notwithstanding the Jewish origins of some of the Itinerant artists, such as Levitan and Pen.[22] This testifies to the creative merger of Russian and Jewish artist in the 19th century. Close to the Itinerants was the famous Russian art critic Vladimir Stasov, who advocated various national styles within the Russian artistic empire. He therefore urged his friend, the famous Russian Jewish sculptor Mark Antokolski, to search for a Jewish art,

> because the highest achievement in art derives from the depth of a people's soul. What the artist is born with, impressions and images that surrounded him, among which he grew to manhood, to which his eye and soul were riveted, only that can be rendered with deep expression, with truth and genuine force.[23]

According to Stasov, Jewishness was supposed to be the motif, not the style, of Jewish artwork. Famous Russian Jewish realist artists, such as Antokolski or Pen, therefore chose a number of specifically "Jewish" topics for their realist works. Pen was perceived in this way—i.e., as an artist who used Jewish themes—by the *narodnik* and folklorist S. An-sky (Shloyme Zaynvl Rappoport, 1863–1920) in a row with the realist Yiddish writers Mendele Moicher Sforim and Sholem Aleichem.[24]

The realist school in painting was nevertheless rejected by the next generation of artists. Even though Pen and Antokolski had occasionally chosen Jewish topics, young artists rejected the realist style as "dated" and rather fit for literature or photography.[25] Antokolski, in particular, who was admired in the 19th century as the embodiment of Jewish art, was judged in 1919 as "a sickness which has to be overcome."[26] Boris Aronson and Issachar Ryback, as representatives of the Russian Jewish avant-garde, depicted him as

---

[21] See, for example, S. An-ski, "Jurij Päen," *Ost und West*, no. 8 (1912): 733–36.

[22] Gertrud Pickhan, "Levitan – Gottlieb – Liebermann: Drei jüdische Maler in ihrem historischen Kontext," *Osteuropa* 58, 8–10 (2008): 247–63.

[23] Cited in Avram Kampf, *Chagall to Kitaj: Jewish Experience in the Art of the Twentieth Century* [exhibition catalogue], rev. ed. (London: Barbican Art Gallery, 1990), 16.

[24] An-Ski, "Jurij Päen," 737.

[25] Kampf, *Chagall to Kitaj*, 16.

[26] Issachar Ryback and Boris Aronson, "Di vegen fun der yiddisher malerei," *Oyfgang* (1919): 120.

a rootless and formalistic individual torn between Russian society and the Jewish community. Their harshest judgment was that Antokolski's art needed symbols for the embodiment of ideas, while the avant-garde artists believed in the expressiveness of form: "Form is the essential and necessary element of art and content is harmful."[27]

Generational Conflict

This rejection of the naturalistic movement was part of the general dissatisfaction with modernity, common among artists of the Russian Silver Age.[28] This conflict was not visible between the young Chagall and Pen, his admired teacher and fatherly friend in Vitebsk, but it surfaced in 1906, when Chagall moved to St. Petersburg. This confrontation was due not only to a clash of artistic approaches, but also to the social situation. Like many other Jews from the Pale, Chagall was confronted by many problems in the city, notably staying there—despite the settlement regulations—and entering one of the famous art schools. In 1909 Lisitskii tried to enter the Art Academy in St. Petersburg and was rejected. Instead he went to study architecture in Darmstadt in Germany. Chagall did not have the means to go abroad at that time, but St. Petersburg was remote enough for the poor young Jew from the *shtetl*. In the capital Chagall was confronted with the omnipresent artistic ideal of the previous generation, the Peredvizhniki. For Chagall, this generation of artists was symbolized by Antokolski, who is mentioned in his memoirs over and over again. He recalls his mentor, the sculptor Il'ia Gintsburg,[29] who also represented the influence of Antokolski:

> His [Gintsburg's] studio was located in the academy and crammed with souvenirs, recalling his teacher Antokolski, and with busts of all kinds of prominent people of his age. This studio seemed to me to be the place of the chosen few, who have found their way in life. Indeed this little man was directly connected to Lev Tolstoj, Stasov, Repin, Gorki, Shalyapin and others.[30]

Chagall recalls Gintsburg with grateful empathy. This remains an exception to the other members of the established art circles in the capital. In order to

---

[27] Ibid.

[28] Marks, *How Russia Shaped the Modern World*, 232.

[29] For Il'ia Gintsburg, see Isidore Singer and Cyrus Adler, eds., *The Jewish Encyclopedia: A Descriptive Record of the History, Religion, Literature, and Customs of the Jewish People from the Earlist Times to the Present Day*, 12 vols. (New York: Funk & Wagnalls, 1901–06), 6: 112.

[30] Chagall, *Mein Leben*, 79.

help Chagall, Gintsburg wrote a letter of recommendation to Baron David Gintsburg (who was not related to him despite the name). Baron Gintsburg was a famous art patron in St. Petersburg and especially supported young and unknown Jewish artists. He sponsored Jewish courses of higher learning and was known as an important orientalist.[31] Chagall recalls Baron Gintsburg with critical irony and the bitterness of a rejected artist: "He recognized a future Antokolski in every young man he was introduced to (how many lost hopes!), and he supported me with a monthly grant of 10 rubles, albeit only for a couple of months."[32] After four or five months, Chagall was given his last grant by a servant of Baron Gintsburg, who told him not to come back for more. To the young Chagall the monthly grant was a question of survival, and after his rejection by Baron Gintsburg he had to work the corridors of the various art patrons of St. Petersburg. Because of his shyness he perceived this situation as an unbearable imposition.

In 1905 Baron Gintsburg had published, with Stasov, a collection of illuminated pages from medieval Jewish manuscripts, L'Ornement hébraïque. This publication influenced the invention of a Jewish calligraphy that was heavily used by avant-garde artists from that time onwards. But Chagall did not recall this important contribution, stating rather that Gintsburg lacked artistic knowledge and competence.[33]

Without Gintsburg's grant, Chagall lived a life of poverty and without valid papers in St. Petersburg. He was hungry, and he shared rooms and beds with other members of the underprivileged milieux. Sharing beds was not uncommon among the urban poor, especially among the workers in the industrial centers of the empire. Being a Jew, Chagall also went to prison because of his illegal status until the wealthy advocate Grigorii A. Goldberg employed him as a servant.

In 1908 Chagall attended the art class of Leon Bakst (1866–1924). Bakst was also of Jewish origin and born in the Pale, but he represented the World of Art movement (Mir iskusstva) and thus the initiatory phase of the Russian avant-garde.[34] Chagall was eager to impress Bakst for a long period, but in his memoirs he emphasizes his remoteness from Bakst's artistic concept and criticizes the sophisticated mannerism of the World of Art's aesthetics.[35] Bakst inspired him to go to Paris, where Chagall developed his style and was first recognized by avant-garde poets and later by artists such as Robert Delaunay and Fernand Léger. The influential Russian Jewish politician Maksim Vinaver

---

[31] "Gintsburg, David Gorachievich," in Rossiiskaia evreiskaia entsiklopediia, ed. Herman Branover, 2nd ed., 4 vols. (Moscow: Epos, 1994), 1: 315–16.

[32] Chagall, Mein Leben, 80.

[33] Ibid.

[34] Marks, How Russia Shaped the Modern World, 176.

[35] Chagall, Mein Leben, 89.

financed Chagall's trip to Paris.[36] He was among the first people who bought Chagall's work, and in times of trouble he allowed the young artist to take shelter in the rooms of the Jewish Historical and Ethnographic Society (JHES). The JHES was just starting to search for the roots of the Russian Empire's Jews by planning ethnographic exhibitions in the southern areas of the Pale.[37]

When Chagall returned to Russia in 1914 on the eve of the war, he was already a promising avant-garde artist who had exhibited in one of the cutting-edge galleries in Germany, Herwarth Walden's Galerie Der Sturm (an offshoot of his art magazine *Der Sturm*). This one-man show in a gallery that also presented the works of Vasilii Kandinskii marked his arrival on the international avant-garde art scene.[38] His return to Russia in order to marry his future wife, Bella, is interpreted by Ziva Amishai-Maisels in an interesting way:

> He undoubtedly saw himself as the "new Antokolski," the established modern artist, returning home, as Antokolski had done, to claim the reward for his success—the hand of the daughter of the *gvir*, the wealthy and important community leader.[39]

After the humiliation and rejection he experienced at the hands of Antokolski's generation while he was still in St. Petersburg before the war, this self-assurance must have been a delayed compensation. Yet Chagall was already renowned before the revolution of 1917, not only in Paris and Berlin but also in Russia. He exhibited 25 paintings from Vitebsk in Moscow at the show *The Year 1915*. Other exhibitions followed in Petrograd and Moscow.[40] Chagall, therefore, had finally made it into the center.

But at the time of his triumph there was also a bitterness about his situation and about the situation of Russian Jews during the war. This bitterness is found in his drawing as well as his writing. The situation of Jews in the Pale and in Galicia, where the Russian Army was at war with German and Austrian troops, was terrible. An-sky, who traveled throughout the Pale try-

---

[36] For Vinaver, see Christoph Gassenschmidt, *Jewish Liberal Politics in Tsarist Russia, 1900–14: The Modernization of Russian Jewry* (Basingstoke, UK: Macmillan /St. Antony's College, 1995).

[37] See, for example, Amishai-Maisels, "Chagall and the Jewish Revival," 73; Kerstin Armborst, "Wegbereiter der Geschichtsforschung: Über den Vorstand der Jüdischen Historisch-Ethnographischen Gesellschaft in St. Petersburg," *Jahrbuch des Simon-Dubnow-Instituts* 6 (2007): 411-40; Hilbrenner, "Invention of a Vanished World."

[38] Marks, *How Russia Shaped the Modern World*, 231.

[39] Amishai-Maisels, "Chagall and the Jewish Revival," 79.

[40] Sidney Alexander and Kurt Schwob, *Marc Chagall: Eine Biographie* (Munich: Kindler, 1984), 142–43.

ing to help the Jews after the pogroms, describes the fate of Jewish civilians in his wartime memoirs:

> Mass violence was launched. When the Russian army passed through many towns and villages, especially when there were Cossacks, bloody pogroms took place. The soldiers torched and demolished whole neighborhoods, looted the Jewish homes and shops, killed dozens of people for no reason, took revenge on the rest, inflicted the worst humiliation on them, raped women, injured children.[41]

During the first months of the atrocities, nobody knew what was happening close to the frontline. News and letters from the frontline were censored, and information about the pogroms only passed as singular rumor. But in 1915 the word was out and everybody interested knew what was going on.[42] The deportation of Jews from the Pale, in particular, was a topic among political circles in the capital, and thus it became familiar to the reading public as well. In a Duma debate in August 1915, the parliamentarian N. Friedman blamed the Russian government for fighting a war against its own subjects:

> Jews are deported in freight cars as if they were cattle. The freight cars were labeled: Goods: 350 Jews deported to.... In times when every car is needed for the transport of ammunition and lamentation about the lack of means of transportation is everywhere—what is the government doing? What is the minister of transport doing? A train with 110 cars loaded with deported Jews waits several days at a train station.[43]

Chagall's drawing *Vitebsk. Train Station*, dated 1915, can be read as a commentary on this debate. In the center of the picture are two soldiers in a farewell scene, promenading with their spouses, one woman carrying a baby. The sad atmosphere caused by the departure of the soldiers is augmented by the sight of a wounded soldier being carried away on a stretcher. At the train station in the background, a train with five freight cars is visible. The cars are crammed with people and labeled with the number 814. (See fig. 39 in the gallery of illustrations following page 188.) Most probably the train represents the deportation freight wagons that transported Jews from the northern

---

[41] An-ski and Neugroschel, *The Enemy at His Pleasure*, 6.

[42] In 1915 Maksim Vinaver also published details from the "Black Book of Russian Jewry" ("Iz chernoi knigi rossiiskogo evreistva"). Simon Dubnov was also active in publicizing wartime atrocities committed against the Jews. See Semen M. Dubnov, "Inter Arma," *Evreiskaia nedelia*, no. 4 (1915): 31–32; Semen M. Dubnov, *Istoriia evreiskogo soldata: Ispoved' odnogo iz mnogikh* (Petrograd: Razum, 1918).

[43] Salomon Kalischer, *Die Lage des jüdischen Volkes in Russland: Reden, gehalten in der Duma* (Berlin: Schwetschke, 1916), 15.

Pale. Vitebsk was a way station for tens of thousands of Jews expelled from Lithuania.[44] Beginning on 8 May 1915, the Jews of Kovno and Kurland were deported in boxcars going through Vitebsk. The trains were crammed with 40 to 60 people in each car, typhus broke out, and mortality was high.[45] Expulsion of Jews from the Pale was not only a topic of public debate, but a reality experienced regularly at the train station in Vitebsk. In a letter to Aleksandr Benois written in 1915, Chagall underlines this constant threat of deportation: "Proclamation after proclamation impose deportation upon me (where to? To Kamchatka)."[46] In his memoirs Chagall noted that he wanted to save and rescue Jewish refugees with his paintings.[47] This is only one example that shows how, with Chagall's art, the *shtetl* was brought into the galleries of the center; not only through his famous airy and colorful Jewish types, but also in his depictions of the traumas of the violent reality in the Pale.

The world of the Pale was represented not only by the content of Chagall's art, by his topics, figures, and types, even though they were definitely Jewish. His artistic style was also Jewish, as Aronson and Ryback noted:

> In Chagall's painting his indebtedness to the *shtetl* is manifest, enabling him to poetically recreate Jewish folk creations.... [B]eing a product of Jewish culture, Chagall has also demonstrated his national form. That is his great merit, and he is thus the first one entitled to bear the name "Jewish artist."[48]

Consequently Chagall's art was not only displayed in the broader context of the Russian avant-garde; he was also active in the institutionalization of Jewish art. In Petrograd Chagall was in close contact with Natan Al'tman, who, with David Gintsburg, established the Society for the Encouragement of Jewish Art in January 1916.[49] Because of the growing fame of Al'tman as well as Chagall, they established contact with Jewish artists in Moscow, among them Chagall's old friend from Vitebsk, El Lisitskii. Together they founded the Union of Moscow Jewish artists and organized the First Exhibition of Jewish

---

[44] See, for example, the wartime memoirs of An-ski and Neugroschel, *The Enemy at His Pleasure*, 6.

[45] Lohr, "The Russian Army and the Jews," 411.

[46] Marc Chagall, "Marc Chagall and A. N. Benois: 1915," in *Marc Chagall: Die russische Jahre 1906–1922* [catalogue], ed. Christoph Vitali and Marc Chagall; trans. Jörn Brunotte et al. (Frankfurt am Main: Schirn Kunsthalle Frankfurt, 1991), 148.

[47] Chagall, *Mein Leben*, 132.

[48] Ryback and Aronson, "Di vegen fun der yiddisher malerei," 122.

[49] Amishai-Maisels, "Chagall and the Jewish Revival," 83.

Artists in 1916.[50] This was proof of the fact that Jews had arrived culturally at the center of the empire.

Towards the Pale: The Jewish World of the Pale in a Museum in Petrograd

While a young generation of Jewish artists made their way into the center of the empire, Jewish intellectuals from the center reached out to the periphery. During the first two decades of the 20th century An-sky—a Russian *narodnik*, secretary to Petr Lavrov in Paris, co-founder of the Socialist Revolutionary Party, and writer—turned to the ethnography and folklore of the Jews in the Russian Empire.[51] He was a member of the JHES, together with Simon Dubnov, Maksim Vinaver, and other leading Russian Jewish intellectuals of the time. The JHES was unable to provide the money for An-sky's ambitious plans. Already in 1908 he had outlined an agenda for Jewish folklore studies in the empire and started trying to raise funds for an ethnographic expedition. In 1912 he received a considerable sum of money from the Jewish patron Baron Vladimir Gintsburg of Kiev. Vladimir was the brother of David Gintsburg, who was decisive for the renewal of Jewish culture in St. Petersburg.[52] Vladimir Gintsburg asked An-sky to name the exhibition after their father, Baron Horace Gintsburg, the patron of the St. Petersburg Choral Synagogue.[53] The headquarters of the expedition thus were removed from Vilna to Kiev, and therefore the field trip began in Volhynia and Podolia.[54] Even though the JHES was not involved in its creation, An-sky's expedition took place under the auspices of the society.[55] The expedition was intended to last three years, but the war brought it to an earlier end.[56] In 1914 An-sky recalled that their

> aim was to visit the most important cities and towns of the Pale of Settlement and collect everything that is left of our past both spiritually and materially: to write down stories, historical facts, songs,

---

[50] Ibid., 84.

[51] See for biographical detail Gabriella Safran et al., eds., *The Worlds of S. An-sky: A Russian Jewish Intellectual at the Turn of the Century* (Stanford, CA: Stanford University Press, 2006).

[52] "Gintsburg, Gorachi Osipovich," 315–16; Chagall, *Mein Leben*, 80.

[53] Anke Hilbrenner, "Orte des jüdischen St. Petersburg," in *Sankt Petersburg: Schauplätze einer Stadtgeschichte*, ed. Karl Schlögel, Frithjof B. Schenk, and Markus Ackeret, 77–94 (Frankfurt am Main: Campus, 2007), 80–84.

[54] For the founding of the expedition, see also Gabriella Safran, *Wandering Soul: The Dybbuk's Creator, S. An-Sky* (Cambridge, MA: Harvard University Press, 2010), 186–224.

[55] For the JHES, see Armborst, "Wegbereiter der Geschichtsforschung."

[56] Safran, *Wandering Soul*, 186–224.

allegories, to notate old Jewish melodies, to take photographs of old synagogues, gravestones, Jewish types, and scenes of Jewish life, to collect manuscripts, documents, and old ritual objects for a national Jewish museum.[57]

On 19 April 1914 an exhibition opened in St. Petersburg at No. 50 on the Fifth Line of Vasil'evskii Island. The building was the Jewish almshouse, the headquarters of the Jewish Historical and Ethnographic Society, and it became the site of the Jewish museum from that day onwards.[58] On display were about 800 items collected during the An-sky expedition. The museum closed after the outbreak of war and An-sky returned to the Pale, not to collect folkloric material but to raise money to help people, to try to save lives in the midst of wartime atrocities. He followed on the coattails of the Russian army. An-sky later remembered the first stage of his mission:

> During my first tour of Galicia, I had virtually followed the trail blazed by the combat. I had wandered through places still warm from fires; I had seen the fresh signs of pogroms. The fear of death lurked in every corner. Every town, every house, every article spoke of dramatic events, and there was even more tragedy in the people, who had survived recent mortal terror and were shocked and nearly crazy with despair.[59]

Although An-sky did not continue his studies, Jewish communities occasionally gave him their valuables in order to rescue them from destruction in the pogroms. An-sky brought the items as folk art to the museum in Petrograd.[60]

It was not only items of Jewish folk art that went from the *shtetls* to the museum. It also provided shelter for refugees from the Pale. Dubnov, who was on the board of the JHES, remembers meeting the people who fled the pogroms

> in the almshouse here on Vasilyevsky Island, next to the archive of our Historical Society. Enervated men and women told me monstrous experiences hitherto unheard of. Inhabitants of Zareba-Koscielna were ordered by the army to leave before a given date. Those who did not

---

[57] S. Ansky, "The Jewish Ethnographic Program, Petrograd 1914," cited in *S. Ansky (1863–1920): His Life and Works. Exhibition Catalogue* (New York: YIVO Institute for Jewish Research, 1980), 21.

[58] Hilbrenner, "Orte des jüdischen St. Petersburg," 87–89.

[59] An-ski and Neugroschel, *The Enemy at His Pleasure*, 250.

[60] Ibid., 166.

manage to leave in time were locked up by the Cossacks and the *shtetl* was set on fire.[61]

Refugees were an important channel of information while information about the atrocities in the Pale was censored. Moreover, they proved by their very existence at the center the violent fate of the Russian Jews at the frontlines of the war.

When the museum opened its doors again after the revolution in May 1917, a new exhibition was organized by Yitzhak Lurie and contained over 600 objects gathered during the An-sky expedition. An-sky's field trip had several results. First of all, it gave him intimate knowledge of life in the Pale, and therefore he knew what to do and did not hesitate to come to the aid of the Jewish people helplessly confronted with the outraged Russian troops. It also brought items of folk art and culture into the center, to be displayed in the museum, as well as information about life at the periphery. Last but not least, he brought people from the Pale to Petrograd, testifying to the violent reality threatening the lives of a great number of Russian Jews. The example of An-sky underlines the interrelation of the catastrophe in the Pale and the Jewish cultural renaissance in the center. But this was true not only for An-sky himself, but also for the Jewish artists of the younger generation, familiar with periphery and center alike.

An-sky's expedition encouraged other Jews of the center to go to the Pale, not to help, but to research their roots. Al'tman, who had been accepted already for the World of Art exhibition in St. Petersburg in 1912, went to his Ukrainian *shtetl* Vinnitsa in 1913 to copy reliefs of old Jewish tombstones.[62] The traditional symbols of the deer and the lion proved to be especially important. Combined with a distinctive Jewish calligraphy inspired by *L'Ornement hébraïque* of Gintsburg and Stasov, Al'tman introduced an avant-garde Jewish style to drawings, lettering, and illustration. Seth L. Wolitz perceives Al'tman as Chagall's chief rival in the Jewish art renaissance in Russia.[63]

In 1916 El Lisitskii and Issachar Ryback[64] also went to the Pale. They took part in another expedition of the JHES, traveled down the Dnieper, and documented the architecture and the decoration of the wooden synagogues along the river. An-sky had already recognized ethnographic collection as the task of saving a culture in decline. When he went to the Pale for the field trip

---

[61] S. M. Dubnow, *Buch des Lebens: Erinnerungen und Gedanken. Materialien zur Geschichte meiner Zeit (1903–1922)* (Göttingen: Vandenhoeck & Ruprecht, 2005), 2: 183.

[62] Mark G. Etkind, ed., *Nathan Altman: Mit Beiträgen von Nathan Altman und seinen Zeitgenossen* (Dresden: VEB Verlag der Kunst, 1984).

[63] Seth L. Wolitz, "Al'tman, Natan Isaevich," http://www.yivoencyclopedia.org/article.aspx/Altman_Natan_Isaevich (accessed 1 February 2012).

[64] Seth L. Wolitz, "Rybak, Yisakhar Ber," http://www.yivoencyclopedia.org/article.aspx/Rybak_Yisakhar_Ber (accessed 1 February 2012).

in 1912, the culture of the *shtetl* was endangered by modernization and migration. After 1914, in the turmoil of wartime atrocities, he realized that the danger was much more violent and direct. Lisitskii and Ryback had the same experience. In 1916 they set out to explore the synagogue of Mogilev and to document architecture and decoration. On their way, they stopped in Kopys, a small town on the banks of the Dnieper. Kopys was a center of the Hasidic movement Chabad and well known for its synagogue, which was supposedly painted by the same master as the Mogilev synagogue, Hayyim b. Isaac Segal of Slutsk. Master Segal was so famous for his decorations that Chagall claimed him to be his biological ancestor.[65] But when Lisitskii and Ryback arrived in Kopys, they found only the ruins of another burned-down *shtetl*:

> All we found in Kopys were bits of charcoal and charred bricks from the foundation, and some rotted logs which someone had planned to use for a new synagogue. The old one had burned down. In fact, the entire town had gone up in flames, and not the slightest trace of its past remained. We pressed on and arrived in Mogilev.[66]

Kopys had been hit by a pogrom already in April 1905 and was rebuilt afterwards, so it must have been destroyed sometime during the war. Thus Lisitskii and Ryback had arrived at a place "still warm from fire" and saw "fresh signs of pogroms," just as An-sky had in Galicia. But Lisitskii reported the destruction of Kopys in very succinct terms. His focus remained on the task of documenting folk art in the face of its decline. They hurried onwards, because they did not want to face the same kind of destruction in Mogilev. But Mogilev was the headquarters of the Russian high command during the war, following the German advance in 1915. The Russian high command was notorious for its anti-Semitism, but still it seems as if the commanders in chief spared the Jewish community in the town, where they had their headquarters.[67] At least the synagogue was still in existence when Lisitskii and Ryback finally found it: "The synagogue stands on the banks of the Dnieper, but set so that it is completely hidden. It is remarkable!"[68] The architecture as well as the interior decoration was a great inspiration: "This is something entirely contrary to the laws of primitivism: rather, this is the fruit of a great culture."[69] With their means as artists Lisitskii and Ryback turned to this great culture and took

---

[65] Amishai-Maisels, "Chagall and the Jewish Revival," 71–72.

[66] Lazar M. Lisickij, "Vegn der moglever shul," *Milgroim*, no. 3 (1923): 10.

[67] For anti-Semitism in the Russian army, see Simon Goldin, "Russkoe komandovanie i evrei vo vremia Pervoi mirovoi voiny: Prichiny formirovaniia negativnogo stereotipa," in *Mirovoi krizis 1914–1920 godov*, 29–46.

[68] Lisickij, "Vegn der moglever shul," 12.

[69] Ibid.

part in the Jewish art renaissance in Russia. Ryback, moreover, contributed a number of disturbing paintings about his experience of pogroms in 1919. His own father died in a pogrom.[70]

After the Revolution

Lisitskii remembers the Jewish art renaissance in Russia as having grown out of the periphery and traveled to the center:

> It was all worked out in a few towns in Lithuania, Belorussia, and the Ukraine. From there it circled around to Paris and came to an end— at that time we thought it was the beginning—when this movement arrived in Moscow for the "First Exhibition of Jewish Artists in 1916."[71]

Even though Lisitskii perceived 1916 as marking the end of the development of Jewish art in Russia, the revolution of 1917 was a turning point for the Jews of Russia, politically and culturally. After the collapse of tsarism in February 1917 the Provisional Government abolished all anti-Jewish legislation. Jews were emancipated at once. But from 1918 until 1921 they were again victims of anti-Semitic violence, and pogroms were committed by almost every party in the Civil War. In this period about 1,000 pogroms occurred and somewhere between 50,000 and 200,000 people died. Culprits were the Ukrainian national forces, the White Army, the Polish Army, detachments of the Makhno movement, or other hordes of carousing soldiers. Anti-Semitic assaults were also committed by units of the Red Army, but its leadership prohibited pogroms and it was the only side that Jews could turn to in the midst of the violence and destruction.[72] The Jewish experience of violent anti-Semitism in late tsarist Russia and during the Civil War transformed many Jews into allies of the new regime, even though this honeymoon lasted only for a short time.[73]

In the centers of the new Russia a number of Jewish cultural institutions emerged, such as the Jewish University established in Petrograd in December 1918.[74] The *kulturlige* was founded by Ryback, Boris Aronson, Lisitskii, and

---

[70] Susan T. Goodman and Ziva Amishai-Maisels, eds., *Russian Jewish Artists in a Century of Change, 1890–1990* (Munich: Prestel, 1995), 219.

[71] Lisickij, "Vegn der moglever shul," 9.

[72] Anke Hilbrenner, "Pogrome im Russischen Bürgerkrieg," 296–98.

[73] Gerhard Simon, "Juden in der Sowjetunion: Von der Emanzipation in den 1920er Jahren zur Verfolgung in der späten Stalinzeit," in *Jüdische Welten in Osteuropa*, ed. Annelore Engel-Braunschmidt and Eckhard Hübner (Frankfurt am Main: P. Lang, 2005), 94–100.

[74] Valery Gessen, "The Jewish University of Petrograd," *East European Jewish Affairs* 22, 1 (1992): 73–79.

others in Kiev in the same year.[75] The Habima Theater was set up under the auspices of the Moscow Art Theater in 1918 and Aleksei Granovskii's Jewish theater workshop in Petrograd in 1919.

This studio moved to Moscow two years later and became the State Jewish Theater.[76] But while the cultural situation was promising in the centers of the new Russia, life became unbearable. Famine and terror threatened everybody in the big cities. In Petrograd the same Yitzhak Lurie who was in charge of the Jewish museum and the exhibition of An-sky's folkloristic findings was sent into forced labor: "As a 'bourgeois' he had to do compulsory labor: loading artillery shells into freight cars. He worked with a group of 'intellectuals' without food or even drink and thus returned seriously ill."[77] Food and heating were scarce for everybody, especially "intellectuals." They were starving and freezing, and consequently they spent their last money in the black market. Everybody who had the chance left the big cities and went to the countryside, where life was supposed to be easier. Leaving the cities was especially urgent for those who had small children, such as Chagall.

Chagall was appointed Art Commissar of Vitebsk in August 1918 and planned an academy and museum for a new revolutionary era of art at the periphery. In this period of his life he was eager to institutionalize his understanding of art, to form a school, to find disciples and to contribute to the project of the new Soviet state. His enthusiasm for the new regime became very clear by his planning of the first anniversary celebrations for the October Revolution. Chagall organized an opulent festivity in times of scarcity. The cloth used for his colorful street decorations was needed everywhere, but he used it for huge banners greeting the Revolution in the streets of Vitebsk with flying green cows. Moreover, he employed the best teachers for an avant-garde art school, and almost every artist that he wanted to employ as a teacher came to Vitebsk, because living conditions were much easier than in Moscow or Petrograd. For a short time, therefore, the small town of Vitebsk in the former Pale of Settlement became the center of avant-garde art. Chagall appointed Lisitskii and Shlomo Yudovin, both of whom had taken part in prerevolutionary ethnographic expeditions to the Jewish Pale. Robert Falk and Ivan Punin were also teachers at the academy, as well as the old realist artist and teacher of many of the young avant-garde artists, Yehuda Pen. One of the few artistic companions of Chagall who preferred to stay in Petrograd was Natan Al'tman, who was a member of the Department of Fine Arts and

---

[75] G. Kazovskii, *Khudozhniki Kul'tur-Ligi* (Moscow: Mosty kul'tury; Jerusalem: Gesharim, 2003); Markus H. Lenhart, *Du sollst dir ein Bild machen: Jüdische Kunst in Theorie und Praxis von David Kaufmann bis zur Kultur-Lige* (Innsbruck: StudienVerlag, 2009).

[76] Jeffrey Veidlinger, *The Moscow State Yiddish Theater: Jewish Culture on the Soviet Stage* (Bloomington: Indiana University Press, 2000).

[77] Dubnow, *Buch des Lebens*, 272.

thus busy with the introduction of "proletarian art."[78] A new branch of art was represented by Kazimir Malevich, who introduced Suprematism to the Vitebsk school and finally drove Chagall out of his own project in 1920.

Nevertheless, between 1918 and 1922 Vitebsk became a modern metropolis, "the first town of the new world."[79] Avant-garde art again related to the experience of the violent Jewish reality during the Civil War. It was not only the need for food, heating, and housing that brought the artists to Vitebsk; they also wanted to transform the topic of anti-Jewish violence into the iconic language of modernity. With his 1919 poster *Beat the Whites with the Red Wedge*, Lisitskii relates his paintings inspired by Jewish folk art—such as the *Chad Gadya* illustrations—to his contributions to Constructivism. Alan C. Birnholz has argued that *Chad Gadya*, as interpreted by Lisitskii, was a parable of the victory of the Red Revolution.[80] Lisitskii transformed the color, design, and content of his folkloric book illustrations into a painting closely related to the contemporary works of Malevich and Tatlin. The text of the "Red Wedge" was introduced by Il'ia Erenburg (Ehrenburg). The Russian "Bei Belykh" ("Beat the Whites") is reminiscent of the infamous "Bei zhidov" ("Beat the Jews") that was notorious in the anti-Jewish pogroms in Russia from 1881 until the Civil War.[81] (See figs. 40 and 10.)

While in the periphery Vitebsk became the "the first town of the new world," in Moscow the Jewish theater brought several branches of artists together for a Jewish national avant-garde art. This facet of the Jewish art renaissance related to the initiatory phase of the Russian avant-garde: the World of Art movement.[82] Like his early teacher Bakst, Chagall was now painting decorations for a Jewish "Gesamtkunstwerk." Granovskii, the director, had worked in Germany with Max Reinhardt. The leading actor was the famous Solomon Mikhoels. They opened the theater with plays by the Yiddish writer Sholem Aleichem. Chagall not only painted the stage decorations and designed the costumes, he also refurbished the whole theater with tableaux in a constructivist manner which also included his typical Jewish types and his

---

[78] Etkind, *Nathan Altman.*

[79] Karl Schlögel, "Die erste Stadt der neuen Welt: Wie Witebsk in Weißrussland für einen historischen Moment zur Metropole der Moderne wurde," *Die Zeit*, 19 January 2006, available at http://www.zeit.de/2006/04/A-Witebsk/komplettansicht; Claire LeFoll, *L' école artistique de Vitebsk (1897–1923): Eveil et rayonnement autour de Pen, Chagall et Malevitch*, Collection Biélorussie (Paris: L'Harmattan, 2002). Vitebsk was known not only for its artistic tradition but as an important center for a variety of imagined communities. See Zeltser, "Imaginary Vitebsk."

[80] Alan C. Birnholz, "El Lissitzky and the Jewish Tradition," *Studio International* Bd. 186, no. 959 (1973): 131.

[81] Avram Kampf, *Jüdisches Erleben in der Kunst des 20. Jahrhunderts* (Weinheim: Quadriga, 1987), 52.

[82] Marks, *How Russia Shaped the Modern World*, 176.

beloved animals.[83] At the same time, Al'tman designed the scenery for An-sky's play *The Dybbuk* at the Habima Theater. *The Dybbuk* is a dramatic legend about a demon, inspired by the folk legends that An-sky collected during his expeditions in the Pale.[84]

Jewish communities in the former Pale of Settlement were at a historical turning point. The violent reality of the Civil War killed thousands of Jews, Jewish folk art was destroyed in pogroms, and Jewish life was severely re-stricted by antireligious legislation as well as by the Sovietization of everyday life. At that time the artistic representation of the Jewish culture of the Pale in the center was a secular construction of Jewishness in the circumstances of Soviet modernity. Theaters transformed old Jewish legends into modern tales and thus integrated their own artistic activity into the centuries-old legacy of Jewish culture.[85]

ଔ ଓ

In 1921 the Civil War finally came to an end. Together with the catastrophe at the periphery, the flourishing of Jewish culture also decayed. In 1922 Chagall, Lisitskii, Ryback, and Aronson left the Soviet Union.[86] In the subsequent years, the Jews of the former Pale departed for Soviet cities.[87] The division between center and periphery began to blur. Russian Jewish life would never be the same again.

---

[83] See, for example, Kampf, *Jüdisches Erleben in der Kunst des 20. Jahrhunderts*, 46–47.

[84] Safran, *Wandering Soul*, 186–224.

[85] Kampf, *Jüdisches Erleben in der Kunst*, 49.

[86] Marina Dmitrieva, "Traces of Transit: Jewish Artists from Eastern Europe in Berlin," in *Impulses for Europe: Tradition and Modernity in East European Jewry*, ed. Manfred Sapper (Berlin: BWV, Berliner Wiss.-Verl., 2008), 143–56.

[87] Gabriele Freitag, *Nächstes Jahr in Moskau!: Die Zuwanderung von Juden in die sowjetische Metropole 1917–1932* (Göttingen: Vandenhoeck & Ruprecht, 2004).

In Search of the Truth about the Great War:
The Theme of War in the Works of Five Russian Writers

Ben Hellman

"The first victim of war is truth." This saying, initially attributed to Aeschylus, became topical in connection with the First World War. Key roles in the "killing" of the truth were attributed not only to the statesmen and the generals, but also to the intelligentsia. The repressed truth about the Great War, as seen retrospectively, is that it was nothing but "a festival of mud and blood," a universal tragedy of "madness, massacres, and mutinies."[1] It could be summed up as a "mechanised slaughter," with a rotting corpse on barbed wire as its most pregnant symbol.[2] Nameless millions met a meaningless death in long-drawn-out trench warfare, broken only by desperate, already doomed attempts at breakthroughs. In the Soviet Union the war was retrospectively renamed from "Second Patriotic War," with its connotation of being a follow-up to the Napoleonic War, to "imperialist war." Fooled by noble sounding patriotic slogans, the people had been drawn into a war with goals foreign to its prime interests.

Generalizations and simplifications like these are usually formulated post factum, when the consequences of events are there for everyone to see. Obviously the situation was more complicated during the war. When in 1914 the war theme almost completely took over Russian literature, be it poems, short stories, novels, or plays, a general acceptance of the war reigned. A few major motives stood out, such as the revitalizing force of the war on the individual and the nation, the Russian heroic soldier and his depraved opponent, Russia's noble allies, and the war as the ultimate struggle against German militarism and imperialism.[3] Among philosophers, the events gave

---

[1] Back cover text for A. J. P. Taylor, *The First World War: An Illustrated History* (London: Penguin Books, 1977).

[2] Phillip Knightley, *The First Casualty: The War Correspondent as Hero and Myth-Maker from the Crimea to Kosovo* (Baltimore: Johns Hopkins University Press, 1975), 88–89.

[3] For the treatment of the main themes of the war in Russian culture, see Richard Stites, "Days and Nights in Wartime Russia: Cultural Life, 1914–1917," in *European Culture in the Great War: The Arts, Entertainment, and Propaganda, 1914–1918*, ed. Aviel Roshwald and Stites (Cambridge: Cambridge University Press, 1999), 16–28.

Russian Culture in War and Revolution, 1914–22, Book 1: Popular Culture, the Arts, and Institutions. Murray Frame, Boris Kolonitskii, Steven G. Marks, and Melissa K. Stockdale, eds. Bloomington, IN: Slavica Publishers, 2014, 209–31.

birth to a wave of Neo-Slavophile thinking according to which Russia was finally to fulfil its historical mission through the war.[4]

Soon, however, the critics and, presumably, also the readers had had enough: the "truth" about the war was evidently not to be found in this mass of literature. "Please stop writing about the war," the writers were told. Your speculations on the theme of war are totally out of place; they are annoyingly weak artistically, and—worst of all—you disgrace and profane essentially tragic events while hurting the feelings of the victims of the war. "You cannot invent something lifelike at a time when life itself speaks, cries out with a deafening roar," wrote Zinaida Gippius.[5] The Futurist poet Vladimir Maiakovskii accused the Symbolist Valerii Briusov of applying a totally out-of-place view of the modern war with his anachronistic images taken from antiquity.[6] And Dmitrii Merezhkovskii branded those who used the events to instigate hatred for the enemy and create flattering myths concerning their own national essence as "nightingales above the blood."[7]

A "wise silence" is the most decent response to the war, Gippius advised in a poem,[8] implicitly referring to the old saying *Inter arma silent Musae* ("When the arms talk, the muses fall silent"). Not everyone, however, was willing to accept this appeal. The famous writer Leonid Andreev answered with an article with the defiant title "The Poets Should Not Be Silent."[9] At a moment when everyone was concerned by the war and reacted in his or her own way, why should writers not be allowed to use their talent for expressing their thoughts and feelings? Andreev's belief in the power of fiction was unshaken. A cannon shot sounded louder when described by a good writer than it did in reality, and the myths that writers consciously or unconsciously produced

---

[4] See Ben Hellman, "Kogda vremia slavianofil'stvovalo: Russkie filosofy i Pervaia mirovaia voina," in *Vstrechi i stolknoveniia: Stat'i po russkoi literature. Meetings and Clashes: Articles on Russian Literature*, Slavica Helsingiensia 36 (Helsinki: Department of Slavonic and Baltic Languages and Literatures, Helsinki University, 2009), 9–29.

[5] Z. N. Gippius, "Voina, literatura, teatr," in *Chego zhdet Rossiia ot voiny: Sbornik statei* ([Petrograd]: Prometei, [1915]), 98.

[6] V. V. Maiakovskii, "Voina i iazyk," in *Polnoe sobranie sochinenii: v trinadtsati tomakh* (Moscow: Gosudarstvennoe izdatel'stvo khudozhestvennoi literatury, 1955), 1: 327.

[7] D. S. Merezhkovskii, "Solov'i nad krov'iu," in *Nevoennyi dnevnik 1914–1916* (Petrograd: Ogni, 1917), 197–204.

[8] Z. N. Gippius, "S liubov'iu (Tishe)," in *Otrazheniia. Okolo voiny. Literaturnyi al'manakh* (Moscow: Mysl', 1915), 4. Also in Z. N. Gippius, *Stikhi: Dnevnik 1911–1921* (Berlin: Slovo, 1921), 39. The poem, dated 7 (28) August 1914, was a reaction to an early, triumphant war poem by Fedor Sologub.

[9] L. N. Andreev, "Pust' ne molchat poety," *Birzhevye vedomosti*, 18 October 1915, utrennii vypusk, 2–3.

were at bottom truer than the newspapers' reports.[10] In the eyes of Andreev the campaign against war literature was an expression of a petty bourgeois wish to forget about the conflict. What he refused to understand was that writers were primarily taken to task for not understanding the very essence of the ongoing war. No matter whether they wrote about life in the rear or at the front, they only produced black-and-white pictures, missing all the endless nuances, and revealing a fatal blindness to the inherent personal and national calamitous prospects of events.

Only a few of the writers who turned war into fiction, or the thinkers who hastened to give their view of events, had any firsthand experience of front life. On the other hand, there were a great number of Russian war correspondents who were allowed to enter the war zone, especially during the first year of the war.[11] Every newspaper had temporarily at its disposal several journalists and writers, who sent in reports from Poland, Galicia, or the Caucasus, sometimes even straight from the frontlines. Briusov, Evgenii Chirikov, Aleksei Tolstoi, Mikhail Prishvin, Aleksandr Serafimovich (Popov), Vasilii Nemirovich-Danchenko, Viktor M. Muizhel', Fedor D. Kriukov, and Aleksandr M. Fedorov can be mentioned. Even in faraway France there were Russian war correspondents, such as, for instance, V. Ropshin (the literary pseudonym of Boris Savinkov) and Il'ia Ehrenburg.

Did these Russian war correspondents tell the truth about the war or did they assist in its "killing"? Naturally, war censorship aggravated publication of unpleasant facts and antiwar sentiments, and, undoubtedly, part of the "truth" about the war is to be found in the empty pages and the missing paragraphs, lines, and words that wartime books, magazines, and newspapers are full of. But what was left did not convince the actual participants of the Great War. In his *From the Letters of an Ensign-Artillerist*, Fedor Stepun tells how he and the other officers, sitting in the trenches somewhere at the Hungarian Front, laughed out loud when they read what the Russian newspapers and magazines wrote about the war.[12] To read the stories and reports about the war was both "amusing and annoying," writes the private Iakov Okunev. It is nothing but "fabrications," a soldier tells him.[13] To the writer and war correspondent Stepan Kondurushkin, a Russian officer declared that what the

---

[10] L. N. Andreev, "Dve letopisi," *Den'*, 21 January 1914, 3.

[11] In his book on the work of modern war correspondents, Phillip Knightley dedicates a substantial chapter to the First World War. He is concerned mainly with British and American war journalism, and Russia is mentioned only in passing: "Russia had only a few war correspondents—M. Lebeder at the Moscow newspaper *Russkoye slovo* and M. Sukhovich of *Kievskaya muysel* [sic!]—but they were not allowed near the front while fighting was in progress" (*First Casualty*, 90). The statement is erroneous in all aspects.

[12] F. A. Stepun, *Iz pisem praporshchika-artillerista* (Tomsk: Vodolei, 2000), 74.

[13] Iakov Okunev, *Na peredovykh pozitsiiakh: Boevye vpechatleniia* (Petrograd: Knigoizdatel'stvo byvsh. M. V. Popova, 1915), 75, 37.

newspapers wrote about the war was just "naïve rubbish."[14] And the nurse Sof'ia Fedorchenko was moved to publish her *The People at War* to contradict all the "shameful lies" that had been written about the war. What she wanted to give was "the truth about the war, and only the truth, even if I could not succeed in writing the whole truth."[15] Implied is the assertion that only those who participated in the fighting, lived under continuous danger, and were ready to kill or get killed had a true notion of the conflict. The writers who came to the front zone to gather firsthand information and impressions during a brief sojourn only saw the surface and never fully grasped the realities of the war. It was not only a question of factual errors; it was also an ignorance concerning the psychology of the soldier and the prevailing mood in the army.

If we look for the "truth" about Russia in the Great War, we are left with just a few works that were written or edited by actual participants and published while the war was still in progress. The genres are not those of fiction, but notes (*zapiski*), letters, sketches (*ocherki*), and collections of soldiers' stories and utterances. To this category belong Sergei Krechetov's *With Iron in Our Hands and the Cross in Our Hearts*, Nikolai Gumilev's "Notes of a Cavalryman," Okunev's *At the War Zone: Battle Impressions* and *The Toil of War: Battle Impressions*, Stepun's *From the Letters of an Ensign-Artillerist*, and Fedorchenko's *The People at War*.[16] The writers' personal experience of front life gives these works an aura of authenticity and reliability. True, their works are also marred by censorial cuts, but in some cases the author was able later to restore the authentic text. Of importance is that they published during the ongoing conflict, without any insight into the outcome of events. Stepun, in his memoirs *What Happened and What Did Not Happen* (1956), confirmed the principal value of firsthand, spontaneous comments. When rereading his published wartime letters 25 years later, he was astonished by their tone of anger and bitterness. The October Revolution and the Civil War, with all their horrors, might not have justified the Great War, but they had definitively "purified" it in the memory of an anti-Bolshevik Russian émigré, making him look at it in a new, almost positive light.[17]

---

[14] S. S. Kondurushkin, *Vsled za voinoi: Ocherki velikoi evropeiskoi voiny* (Petrograd: Izdatel'stvo tovarishchestva pisatelei, 1915), 39.

[15] V. I. Glotser, "K istorii knigi S. Fedorchenko 'Narod na voine,'" *Russkaia literatura*, no. 1 (1971): 153.

[16] Lev Voitolovskii, *Po sledam voiny: Pokhodnye zapiski 1914–1917* (1931; Leningrad: Gosudarstvennoe izdatel'stvo khudozhestvennoi literatury, 1991) could also have been added to the group, as the doctor's notes appear to have genuinely been written during the war, but as they were published only in 1925–27, and therefore could have been influenced by contemporary attitudes to the war, it has not been included.

[17] Fedor Stepun, *Byvshee i nesbyvsheesia* (Moscow: Progress–Litera, Aleteia, 1995), 279.

CR   BO

Sergei Krechetov's (1878–1936) *With Iron in Our Hands* covers only a few months of the early stage of the war. A minor Symbolist poet and critic, Krechetov joined the war as a volunteer and participated in two offensives on East Prussian territory as an ensign in the autumn of 1914. His notes from the campaigns beyond the Russian border appeared as a book in the summer of 1915, at a time when the author was actually a POW in Germany, having been wounded in battle during the second retreat from East Prussia.

The truthfulness of Krechetov's book comes out in the many pages written in the present tense, partly even coming close to a stream-of-consciousness style. The author does not look for conflicts or scenes of cruelty and violence, but mostly depicts the everyday life of an officer on enemy ground. Riding around in East Prussia, Krechetov's main concern is to find food and lodging for the night for his soldiers. There are actually more contacts with the civilian population than with the German army. The retreats are not commented upon, and, not surprisingly, at no point does Krechetov appear to have a general view of the situation.

Krechetov's notes are from the initial period of the war, when rhetorical devices and standard phrases had not yet been deprived of their value. The associations are linked to high culture, starting from Xenophon's historical writings, and individual war deaths are still recorded and lofty words bestowed upon them: "What a glorious death! [...] He died a hero, giving his last sigh, his last drop of blood, his last flicker of thought to his fatherland. [...] his name will serve as an unforgettable example of the highest military valour."[18] According to Krechetov, this was a war in which heroes were born and legends created.

The dream of "universal brotherhood" is buried under the "roar of guns and frenzied cries," but this is only something temporary, Krechetov declares.[19] In a Neo-Slavophile fashion he sees the war as the turning point in history: Russia is now to fulfil its historical mission and finally become the Third Rome, an all-Slavic Christian empire. The first sign of this process Krechetov detected in the change in Polish attitudes to Russians: thanks to the High Commander's Appeal to the Poles (1/14 August 1914), they now looked upon their former antagonists as friends. The war also appeared to unite Russia internally: "Yes, this war is something special. It has made a divided Russia one body, and this body is of the same blood."[20] Krechetov wrote these lines after witnessing how soldiers divided the bloody shirt of the mortally wounded Prince Oleg Konstaninovich among themselves, treating

---

[18] S. Krechetov, *S zhelezom v rukakh, s krestom v serdtse: Zapiski ofitsera* (Petrograd: Prometei, [1915]), 62–63.

[19] Ibid., 13.

[20] Ibid., 82.

the pieces of cloth with reverence, almost as relics. Krechetov found the same feelings of solidarity within the Russian army too. The soldiers adored their officers and they in turn took a fatherly care of those under their command, in contrast to the situation in the German army: "By us the officer is loved, on the other side he is feared."[21] Germany was marked by "spiritual emptiness" and "intoxicated conceit."[22]

In the war the best Russian features come out, Krechetov insisted. Civilians on the conquered soil had been frightened with stories about the Russians as "barbarians," but what they actually met was respect for the local culture and the rights of the individual. In Krechetov's notes, the Russian officers and soldiers stand out as good-natured, helpful, and supportive. Even when dealing with prisoners, among them clear cases of espionage, the Russians find it difficult to show the necessary severity. In the hospitals everybody is treated alike, and all are viewed as unhappy victims of the war. After witnessing yet another scene of mercy, Krechetov exclaims: "This is how you are, you Russian soul! The German cannot understand it. He would only laugh at the 'Slavic sentimentality.' But it is because of this very sentimentality that God will pardon Russia."[23]

The Great War as experienced by a Russian ensign in the autumn of 1914 was a blessing; it was a war that the individual and Russia could only benefit from. That this was only the prelude to a war of quite another character Krechetov could not see. Among critics *With Iron in Our Hands* was praised for its sincerity, poetic language, and sober tone, in spite of the military catastrophes and changes in the general mood that had befallen Russia since the appearance of Krechetov's book. I. Dzhonzon in *Utro Rossii* admitted that readers had grown tired of reports from the front, but he still thought that the diary narrative of *With Iron in Our Hands* and the author's status as a participant in the war gave this work a special value.[24] The fact that Krechetov became a POW—an unwritten but well-known epilogue to his book—also strengthened his position as a witness.

CЗ　Ю

Among the Russian writers of the period, Nikolai Gumilev (1886–1921) stands out as the exemplary "poet-warrior." In all, he spent around one and a half years at the front, was twice decorated for bravery, and promoted to ensign.

---

[21] Ibid., 114.

[22] Ibid., 74.

[23] Ibid., 28.

[24] I. Dzhonzon, "Novye knigi," *Utro Rossii*, 26 September 1915, 5. See also V. Ermilov, "Pevets voiny," *Rampa i zhizn'*, 25 October 1915, 3–4; and V. Iu. B., "Dykhanie voiny," *Novoe vremia (Literaturnoe prilozhenie)*, 12 December 1915, 10.

As a poet he produced a cycle of war poems in which the war is treated in solemn, rhetorical terms. The war is a valuable, mystical experience, a "festival of the spirit," and, in addition, it constitutes a challenge for the Acmeist poet, the adventurous romantic, who is drawn to a life of danger.[25]

When Gumilev volunteered for the frontline as a hussar at the outbreak of the war, he accepted simultaneously the role of "special war correspondent" for the newspaper *Birzhevye vedomosti*. Under the title "Notes of a Cavalryman" ("Zapiski kavalerista") 17 sketches were published during a period of one year, from February 1915 to January 1916. In reality, Gumilev did not qualify for the task of a war correspondent, as his articles were written or appeared with great delays, sometimes up to five or six months, and were thus of little, if any, topical interest. His notes are highly subjective, dealing mostly with the feelings and thoughts of a cavalryman during fighting and periods of inactivity. The title pays homage to Nadezhda Durova, the heroine of the Napoleonic Wars, who, disguised as a man, participated in battles, and later published her war memoirs under the title *Notes of a Woman Cavalryman* (*Zapiski kavalerist-devitsy*, 1836–39). By choosing a historical figure as his muse, Gumilev revealed that he did not expect the nature of war or the cavalry's role to have undergone any significant changes during the last hundred years.

"Some people are born exclusively for war," Gumilev thought, when looking around him in his regiment in the summer of 1915.[26] These are words that he could have used about himself. With an almost shocking frankness, he expresses his enthusiasm about participating in the conflict. At the East Prussian border in August 1914, ready to step onto enemy ground, he is gripped by "a sweet thirst for striving forward." He identifies himself with conquerors from Russian history as he advances, filled with an overwhelming feeling of victory, pride, and curiosity about the unknown ahead.[27] In Gumilev's notes we do not find any information about the disastrous outcome of the East Prussian campaign. The poet-cavalryman probably did not know about the debacle, as military censorship blocked such distressing news, but on the other hand, he does not show much concern for the general situation. Words like "Russia" and "fatherland" do not appear in his sketches, and never does he ponder the meaning of the war. Only once, in passing, does Gumilev say

---

[25] On Gumilev's war poetry, see N. Elaine Rusinko, "The Theme of War in the Works of Gumilev," *Slavic and East European Journal* 21, 2 (1977): 204–13; Ben Hellman, "A Houri in Paradise: Nikolai Gumilev and the War," *Studia Slavica Finlandensia* (Helsinki) 1 (1984): 22–37; Iu. Zobnin, "Stikhi Gumileva, posviashchennye mirovoi voine 1914–1918 godov," in *Nikolai Gumilev: Issledovaniia. Materialy. Bibliografiia* (St. Petersburg: Nauka, 1994), 123–42.

[26] N. Gumilev, *Sobranie sochinenii v chetyrekh tomakh* (Washington, DC: Victor Kamkin, 1968), 4: 528.

[27] Ibid., 450.

that the goal is "a lasting peace,"[28] but he does not define the conditions for such a peace.

An unfailingly cheerful mood reigns in Gumilev's notes. The cavalrymen are "a happy, rambling artel," a team that does its "job" singing.[29] To see them advance is a "remarkable" sight. Even the general retreat from Poland in the summer of 1915 does not have a depressive effect upon Gumilev, as "in the blessed cavalry service, even a retreat can be joyful."[30] The withdrawal is just an order among other orders which you have to obey. Occasionally Gumilev mentions the cold and the hunger, the strenuous periods of passivity, but again these are outweighed by the purely physical delight he can take in small, unexpected treats like tobacco, a glass of milk or tea, fried potatoes with bacon, an apple given from the hands of a Polish woman, heavy sleep after a tough day or a move to a new part of the front. Also a service of worship in the open air is an uplifting experience: "We prayed intensively on that day."[31] The sight of corpses or wounded soldiers, be they enemies or Russians, does not affect the prevailing mood.

A central feature of Gumilev's "Notes" is their poetic language. The tropes employed serve to free the events from a harsh reality and give them a romanticized aura. The machine guns "prattle something incomprehensible in their childish and strange language";[32] the airplanes soar in the sky like hawks. The bullets buzz like bees, collecting bright-red honey. The rhetorical climax of the "Notes" is the exclamation "On that day the fire-bright bird of victory lightly touched also me with its enormous wings."[33] The war is turned into pure poetry, distancing the reader from its reality.

One explanation for Gumilev's ability to remain unconcerned by the dreariness of the war and its destructive and tragic face is that, during the initial part of the conflict, he served in the cavalry, which had not yet lost its glamor. What he experienced at the front corresponded to his expectations. There was room for deeds of bravery and adventures, as when the hussars fulfilled reconnaissance tasks, tracked down the enemy, or succeeded in taking prisoners. The initiative and courageous spirit of the individual was of decisive importance. Gumilev's war is not a never-ending battle between big armies; it consists of numerous skirmishes and dangerous situations into which the individual soldier is thrown. It is a succession of duels, where you "live on tenterhooks" and have to show readiness to accept all challenges. Face to face with the enemy, Gumilev has only one thought in mind, "alive and powerful,

---

[28] Ibid., 445.

[29] Ibid., 443.

[30] Ibid., 525.

[31] Ibid., 467.

[32] Ibid., 444.

[33] Ibid.

like passion, like fury, like ecstasy: it's him or me!!"[34] There is no room for moral considerations. The notorious passage where Gumilev compares the war with the big-game hunting that he had experienced in Africa is revealing: "Only when hunting big-game animals, leopards, buffalos, have I had the same feeling when the fear for one's own life suddenly changes into fear of losing a magnificent quarry."[35] He also associates the experience with the childhood reading of adventure books by writers like Thomas Mayne Reid and Gustave Aimard and the games they inspired.

In the long run, the cavalry proved to be of limited military value in a modern war. It delayed transport to the front, it was slow and inaccurate in its reporting and, even worse, the new long-range weapons made it extremely vulnerable.[36] Nothing of this is to be found in Gumilev's front sketches, but it is clear that, when the war on the Eastern Front became bogged down in trench warfare, he could not but feel distressed. The new situation was expressed in a letter to a friend in January 1917: "I found myself in the trenches, shot at the Germans with a machine gun, they shot at me, and two weeks passed by this way."[37] Nothing of the initial romantic glamor is left as the modern weapons take over, changing the very nature of warfare. As an officer Gumilev endured, but not as a writer. After the autumn of 1915 no new war sketches were published.[38]

In his "Notes" Gumilev mentions meetings with Cossacks, Polish civilians, women, and estate owners, but he does not take much interest in their thoughts and feelings. It is as if he is fighting his own, separate war; the "we" that he occasionally uses stands for his army unit, where everyone is united by the same feelings. Where others, in spite of an initial enthusiasm, at least occasionally could admit that at bottom war was a human tragedy, Gumilev did not express such doubts, and he appears to have come out of the ordeal with an unbroken spirit. "You think it is horrible?" he told an English

---

[34] Ibid., 464.

[35] Ibid., 523. Gumilev's frank confession of his feelings at the sight of the enemy appearing in front of him, the awakening of instincts similar to that of the hunter, has led Karen Petrone to claim that he "celebrated the Russians' appetite for killing," a rather pessimistic and, at bottom, unfair generalization. Karen Petrone, *The Great War in Russian Memory* (Bloomington: Indiana University Press, 2011), 133.

[36] Norman Stone, *The Eastern Front 1914–1917* (London: Hodder and Stoughton, 1975), 50.

[37] N. S. Gumilev, *Neizdannye stikhi i pis'ma* (Paris: YMCA Press, 1980), 139.

[38] The lack of new front sketches has been explained either as a lack of material or as the result of prohibition by officers in command. See P. N. Luknitskii, *Trudy i dni N. S. Gumileva* (St. Petersburg: Nauka), 442–43.

journalist around New Year 1915, "no, at war it is gay."[39] In his "Notes" Gumilev presented his "truth" about the war, recording his private feelings and
exposing the psychology of an exemplary hussar officer.

CB Ω

Iakov Okunev (1882–1932) published his first book, a collection of short stories,
in 1914. In the same year, as war broke out, he was called up for military service.
As a private soldier he participated in the Galician campaign until Easter 1915,
being awarded a George Cross for his service, while simultaneously writing
front sketches for *Rech´*, *Birzhevye vedomosti*, and the magazine *Sovremennyi
mir*. In the middle of 1915, two collections of his sketches appeared: *At the War
Zone: Battle Impressions* and *The Toil of War: Battle Impressions*.

Okunev's war is mostly grey, everyday life and simple routine, but it is
also "a nightmare of brutalization and devastation."[40] He writes about aimless
marches back and forth under hard conditions and about the depressing
sights of refugees and demolished villages. There are scenes straight out of
the battles, filled with the sound of roaring guns and cries from the wounded.
Okunev records the sight of "a mountain of human flesh," a field filled with
wounded and dying soldiers, yellowish brains splattered in the grass, entrails
pouring out of stomachs and the rotting corpse of a child with its face blown
away. Still, he points out, in the war zone you get used to everything; there
is no room for compassion and concern, not even for feelings of fright and
horror. When asked the same question as Gumilev, "Isn't it terrible?" Okunev
gave a more nuanced answer than his colleague: "It is both terrible and good,
it is both horror and rapture, something which reason cannot grasp and the
heart forget."[41]

Okunev came to the army as a Jewish intellectual with a firm belief that
war as such could on no account be accepted or defended. He overcame the
problem of acting against his inner conviction by asserting that this particular
war essentially differed from war in general: "War is horror, war cannot be
justified from any point of view, but what we are doing, that is not war."[42]
At bottom it was a "job" that just had to be done. For the intelligentsia it was
a war of liberation, a struggle against "force and oppression,"[43] as Okunev
says, while the Russian soldiers with their religious attitude to events saw it
as "God's war." Their sense of community and the collective courage they got

---

[39] C. E. Bechhöfer, "Letters from Russia," *The New Age* (London) 16, 13 (28 January
1915): 344.

[40] Okunev, *Na peredovykh pozitsiiakh*, 82.

[41] Ibid., 67.

[42] Ibid., 110.

[43] Ibid., 98.

from "the one big truth" gave them and Okunev a certainty in a final victory of justice, that is, of Russia.[44]

For Okunev, just as for the few other intellectuals in his regiment, it was essential to become an integrated part of his military unit. This meant getting used to the hard life, forgetting your private opinions, suppressing the inclination for analysis and reflection, and starting to feel and think like the rest. The individual had to become part of the whole, so that everyone alike— officers and soldiers, students and peasants, Jews and Russians—would form one body. The ideal figure is the Russian peasant-soldier, "solid and simple, endlessly patient and steadfast."[45] Having closely identified himself with this soldier, Okunev set out to portray his comrades at the front. He sometimes watches them from the outside, but occasionally employs a "we," a sign indicating that the identification process is successful. The true heroes are not the few individual soldiers who out of free will seek danger and perform daring deeds; instead Okunev pays tribute to "the simple and grey private" who conscientiously, seriously, efficiently fulfilled his duty. For the common soldier, war was just a job, and reasoning "that's how it should be, that's what they ask us," he attacked or defended, all according to given orders. Dangers were met with the response "it's all the same to us." The Russian soldier knows about the enemy's exploding bullets and jagged bayonets but calmly comments that "this is war." He wants to live, but he is not afraid of dying.

The Russian soldier, as Okunev sees him, feels no enmity towards the enemy. He kills without hatred, because once you had got involved in the war, killing was no longer murder, but "a necessary and important task."[46] Okunev confirms Krechetov's words about the Russian good nature. For the prisoners, the private feels pity. Okunev overheard a Russian soldier explaining to a German soldier, whom he called, in a friendly way, "Karl Ivanovich": "You pray Christ and me pray him too. We're not animals, we're human beings. Nothing bad shall happen to you. I pity you."[47] The Russian side was also prepared to assist the enemy across the front line with medicines and bandages. Scenes like these make Okunev amazed and overwhelmed by "the simple, but great beauty and grandness of the Russian spirit."[48] They appeared to show that the Russian good nature and mild heart were untouched by the cruelties of the war.

The Russian soldier did not know much about his mother country, and he was not inspired by any high-flying ideals. All reasoning about the war and its verbal justification were superfluous, as in the Russian soul you could find

---

[44] Ia. Okunev, *Voinskaia strada: Boevye vpechatleniia* (Petrograd: Prometei, 1915), 32.

[45] Ibid., 7.

[46] Ibid., 40.

[47] Ibid., 73.

[48] Ibid., 77.

a "spontaneous instinct for truth and justice."[49] The sight of the soldiers' calm faces and endless patience revealed that their cause was "just and fair."[50] As can be seen, Okunev, unlike the other private soldiers, did not shy away from big, abstract phrases. In the name of necessity the soldiers accepted suffering and possible death: "Our death is needed, just like the death of the autumn leaves, falling to the ground and fertilizing the earth for a new magnificent harvest."[51] The individuals could die, but the whole of which they formed a part could never die. The sacrifices would lead to a better Russia, Okunev reasoned, implicitly speaking for the Russian soldier in general.

Okunev did not deny the strength of the German army. The enemy was a serious and worthy opponent, he was cunning and cultured, technically superior, but even so he would be defeated by "the grey man from the backwoods of some small village in Simbirsk."[52] In a war where the machine was confronting the living man, Russia's weapon was "the patience, endurance, and steadfastness" of the simple soldier.[53] A private put it plainly: "He fights with his brain, but we give him an uppercut."[54]

When writing about the inner feelings of soldiers during a battle, Okunev echoed some of Gumilev's observations, but the image that he created of the Russian private came close to myth-making. He took a critical stand on what the writers in the rear wrote about the frontline soldier and the enemy, and with the authority of a participant and an eyewitness he set out to correct the picture. Romanticizing the Russian muzhik, Okunev nevertheless confirmed much of what was said in the bulk of war literature. His soldier is a superior figure, expressly because of his simplicity. The genuinely national features secured Russia a victory in the Great War and a bright future, while simultaneously hindering the people from being affected by the cruelties of modern war, the excesses of which Okunev did not hesitate to describe. But his front sketches from the first four months of 1915 are still full of hope. Russian armies approach Hungary and the Carpathian mountains; behind them they have "historical victories." The demoralized Austrian army is retreating, and panic-stricken enemy soldiers surrender of their own free will. This was Iakov Okunev's "truth" about the Great War in the spring of 1915.

---

[49] Okunev, *Na peredovykh pozitsiiakh*, 109.

[50] Ibid., 98.

[51] Ibid., 46.

[52] Okunev, *Voinskaia strada*, 113.

[53] Okunev, *Na peredovykh pozitsiiakh*, 52.

[54] Okunev, *Voinskaia strada*, 114.

☙ ❧

On one point Fedor Stepun (1884–1965) was sure: the majority of those who wrote about the war did not know it; to know it, you had to see it with your own eyes. Experiencing the war, however, did not mean that you understood some simple "truth" about it. On the contrary, to see the war meant accepting the impossibility of grasping its essence: "He who has not seen and experienced the war will never understand anything about it, that is, he will not refrain from understanding, explaining, and justifying it." There were no words to do justice to the war experience: "Everything that we who have stayed alive and kept our mind sound can say about it is, if not absolutely untrue, then deeply insufficient."[55]

Stepun, a philosopher and doctor of science, was called to arms at the outbreak of the conflict. As a younger officer, an ensign, initially in the 12th Siberian Riflemen-Artillery brigade, he came to spend about a year and a half at the front or in its vicinity, in Galicia, Hungary, Poland, and Latvia. His service was broken only by an eleven-month treatment for a wound. From the war zone, Stepun wrote extensive letters to his wife and mother, giving detailed information not only about his own thoughts and feelings but also concerning the situation at the front. By using chance opportunities to have his letters delivered straight to Moscow by travelers, he managed to avoid the military censorship.

In the autumn of 1916 Stepun was persuaded by the literary critic and historian of ideas Mikhail Gershenzon to publish parts of the letters. The first two installments, published in the summer of 1916 under the pseudonym N. Lugin in the magazine *Severnye zapiski*, covered the period from December 1914 to March 1915. When the book *From the Letters of an Ensign-Artillerist* came out in 1918, letters from the autumn of 1914, and from 1916 and 1917, had been added and the previously censored passages restored. The work has been called an "epistolary novel"[56] and a "philosophical novel"[57] with a fictional letter-writer as its persona, something which naturally would decrease the work's documentary value. This view cannot, however, be verified. In his later memoirs, Stepun treats the letters as genuinely personal documents, quoting them as reliable sources about his experiences, thoughts, and moods during the First World War. Neither is there any reason to doubt Stepun's claim that it was only on the insistence of Gershenzon that he decided to publish private letters.

---

[55] Stepun, *Iz pisem praporshchika-artillerista*, 190.

[56] Petrone, *The Great War*, 156. S. M. Polovinkin, "Filosof na voine," in Stepun, *Iz pisem praporshchika-artillerista*, 191.

[57] Kvon Ki Be, "Romany F. A. Stepuna: Filosofiia. Poetika" (Candidate diss., Sankt-Peterburgskii gosudarstvennyi universitet, 2003), http://www.dslib.net/russkaja-literatura/kvon2.html (accessed 10 May 2013).

Just as in the case of Okunev, there is a paradoxical dualism in Stepun's attitude to the war. His was a "conditional pacifism," which eventually meant both denying and accepting the conflict. At bottom he was strongly disgusted by it on all levels: "As a material fact the war is terrible—it is only a line of groans, grinding of teeth, millions of open bleeding wounds."[58] Equally revolting was the collective effect of the war on the minds of people: "Everything utterly evil, sinful and stinking, prohibited by elementary consciousness when it concerns the relationship between two persons, is now the truth and heroism when it concerns two nations. Both sides without hesitation curse and deny everything great that has been created by the spirit and the genius of the side that it is waging war on."[59] Stepun felt depressed by the senseless destruction, the sight of fallen soldiers, the activity of the marauders, the Russian soldiers' submissiveness but also occasional cruelty, the impudence and stupidity of the officers in command, and the way the Jews were treated both in the army and in the occupied territory. In one sense, the war was the "truth" about the lies in which Europe had lived prior to 1914, but on the other hand, mixed with all these lies, Stepun also found some positive results, another "truth": a growing love for your own people and country, victory over stagnation, egotism and self-interest, and the creation of "a sober, mature, and unselfish atmosphere." When lives were sacrificed for some higher idea, war could simultaneously be both tragic and holy.

Stepun also observed a split in his own feelings. In principle he accepted Dostoevskii's idea, expressed by the Elder Zosima in *The Brothers Karamazov*, that "everyone is guilty for everything and for everyone," but simultaneously he had to admit that what he actually felt was a total moral irresponsibility. The enemy in the trenches in front of you was not a human, but just a faceless "he," whom you killed without hesitation, filled with "a feeling of sporting competition." You gave commands and fired grenades without any feelings of remorse. Like Okunev, Stepun noticed that the soldiers killed without hatred. Hatred was felt only by those in the rear and by the war correspondents, who sought an outlet for their inner conflicts in the war. Those involved in the actual fighting, on both sides of the front line, were united by another feeling. By some "mysterious will" they were placed face-to-face with death and forced to do something essentially foreign to them, that is killing a fellow man. The "feeling of the war" was not just an awareness of being under deadly danger, but mainly a sense of participation in an event of mutual killing.

In the midst of the fighting and the destruction of nature, the beauty of which he frequently stops to admire, Stepun is often filled with a cheerful mood, an unexpected gaiety. In his letters there are passages that are reminiscent of some of Gumilev's lines: "The moment when I galloped to the positions and saw how rose-colored puffs of smoke from exploding grenades

---

[58] Stepun, *Iz pisem praporshchika-artillerista*, 5.

[59] Ibid.

rose to the right and left of me was one of the brightest and happiest moments of my life."[60] During the battle he felt happy, his mind at ease; all sense of personal danger was lost, as he was raised above life and death.

The letters from the spring of 1915 bear witness to a change of mood in Stepun and the Russian army in general. On top of the personal painful losses of fallen friends came revelations of Russia's lack of military preparedness. While Stepun himself still submissively accepted the war, he observed that the privates had started to wait for its end. In his memoirs, he claims that the Russian soldiers during the first period of the war looked upon it as a "crusade"; ready to obey the emperor's command, they showed "a firm, sober, responsible attitude" to the war and displayed a "victorious spirit."[61] There are slight echoes of Krechetov's and Okunev's claims here. But by now, the soldiers' thoughts were already back home. The work on their land was something real, while the war had become a fraud, a kind of delusion. In Stepun's battery a somber atmosphere reigned: "The longer the war lasts, the more it loses all likeness with something that, although tragic, is nevertheless big and important."[62]

Stepun saw the major retreat of the summer of 1915 as one of the most tragic pages in Russia's military history. In six days the army gave up what it had conquered during six months. The possibilities to stop an enemy, numerically bigger and better equipped and organized, appeared to be next to nonexistent. In the Russian army stupidity and irresponsibility were exposed, and lives were lost, "endlessly, senselessly and uselessly." Nothing was left of the soldiers' willingness to sacrifice their lives for some instinctively felt "truth"; on the contrary, by now the majority fought only because refusing meant the death penalty. A war which brought "madness and suffering" to the world could not be holy and righteous, Stepun concluded. From a Christian point of view it was more honorable to deny the war than to accept it. Tolstoi was right after all, he admits: "It is impossible to be a Christian and kill Christians in the name of Christ!"[63] Yet Stepun's dialectical inner dialogue continued with an imposing honesty. He maintained that falsehood and truth still existed side by side in the war. While hating the war, he still managed to see something beautiful, important, and valuable in it. In the war zone you kept up a dialogue with eternity, and there were those, after all, who still consciously gave their lives to save their fatherland and the prestige of Russia.

After one year at the rear as a result of a leg injury, in November 1916 Stepun returned to the army, this time joining the infantry on the Galician front. He had longed for army life and battles, but reality brought him quickly

---

[60] Ibid., 26. Repeated in Stepun, *Byvshee i nesbyvsheesia*, 286.

[61] Stepun, *Byvshee i nesbyvsheesia*, 273, 285.

[62] Stepun, *Iz pisem praporshchika-artillerista*, 79–80.

[63] Ibid., 71.

back to earth. The disastrous situation at the front could no longer be denied. During the one year Stepun had been away, "some not very happy change in the psychology of the army seems to have occurred," he wrote to his wife.[64] On the one hand there was the "pitch-dark boorishness of Russian state power,"[65] and on the other an army which had lost all interest in the war. Materially the situation was better than before, but the spiritual power had been broken. The moral degradation of the rear had reached the front, as the initial courage had been replaced by a total indifference. There were disturbing rumors about the killing of officers, and fears of mutiny and desertion were widespread.

In January 1917 Stepun calls the situation utterly alarming: the spirit in the army had fallen to a level from where soon it would be impossible to continue the war. Nobody—not even Stepun—now saw the war as something imposed upon mankind by fate, something which you just had to endure; anger and wrath were now turning towards those in power.[66] The war stopped interesting Stepun; instead of enriching him spiritually, it made him feel an "instinctive and almost physiological disgust."[67] Nevertheless, in discussions he could still argue for a continuation of the war, despite his insights into the disastrous state of things. "I am not a defeatist," he declared. A German defeat was needed, but not in the name of culture, peace, and freedom, as the Russian intelligentsia had initially thought. A military victory would save Russia from becoming economically dependent on Germany, which in all aspects was foreign to the Russians. Along the lines of Neo-Slavophile thinking, Stepun now defined the task of the Russian army as helping the true Germany, the spiritual Germany, to overcome its modern evil double. A Russian victory would in fact be a service to Germany. The problem was that, just as Germany had two faces, so did Russia: a shameless and helpless empirical Russia and a spiritual Russia, the carrier of truth.

Stepun was hopelessly entangled in his "conditional pacifism." The war had to be continued until a "decent peace" was achieved, but even so he was upset by rumors that the tsarist regime planned a separate peace with Germany. Overthrowing the tsar would only mean that a continuation of the war would become impossible, Stepun declared, but when rumors about a revolution in Petrograd in February 1917 reached the front line, he nevertheless exclaimed: "Oh if it only was true!"[68] The same dualism continued under the new regime; while Stepun clearly saw that the soldiers had lost all interest in the war—a reaction he fully understood—he accepted an invitation to appear

---

[64] Ibid., 141.

[65] Ibid., 139.

[66] Stepun, *Byvshee i nesbyvsheesia*, 301.

[67] Stepun, *Iz pisem praporshchika-artillerista*, 153.

[68] Ibid., 190.

in front of the same soldiers as Head of the Political Board by the Ministry of War, agitating for a continuation of the war.

Stepun's search for the "truth" about the war stretched over a longer period than it did for Krechetov, Gumilev, and Okunev, and as a result his position is more dynamic and contradictory. The "truth" appears to lie in the incompatibility of the diverging views which he expressed. Parallel to the attempts at an objective observation of the ever-changing situation at the front, there is the unsolvable inner conflict between denial and acceptance of the war. Stepun found a solution in abstaining from intellectual analysis. In 1914 he had wondered how it was possible to see the horrors of the war without losing one's mind, to calmly continue normal life without remorse and nightmares. When, with three years' experience of the war, he returned to the thought, "madness" appeared to be the only "sound" explanation and answer: "The war is madness, death, and destruction, since it can only be fully understood by madmen and corpses, mentally or physically cracked."[69] In his enthusiastic review of Stepun's book, the critic Iulii I. Aikhenval'd praised this attitude: "Stepun must be praised for refraining from understanding the war, that is, from embracing madness with your intellect."[70]

cs so

Here we have "the real truth about the war, about the Russian people," Iakov Tugenkhol'd wrote in his review of Sof'ia Fedorchenko's (1888–1959) *The People at War* in 1918.[71] The military doctor Lev N. Voitolovskii, who was to publish his own "campaign notes" in the mid-1920s, called it an "encyclopaedia of the people's soul."[72] And three years later, in 1921, Aleksandr Blok characterized the book as "grey, dirty, disgusting, full of hatred, darkness, but good, truthful, and scrupulous."[73]

Fedorchenko went to the front at the outbreak of the war to work as a nurse, and she returned to Kiev one year and eight months later, after falling seriously

[69] Ibid. Also, in Stepun, *Iz pisem praporshchika-artillerista*, 305, it is said that everyone at the front saw it as madness.

[70] Iu. Aikhenval'd, "Novye knigi o voine," *Nash vek*, 28 April 1918, 5.

[71] Iakov Tugenkhol'd, "Sof'ia Fedorchenko: Narod na voine," *Ponedel'nik*, 23 April 1918. Quoted in N. Trifonov, "Nespravedlivo zabytaia kniga o russkom narode," in Sof'ia Fedorchenko, *Narod na voine* (Moscow: Sovetskii pisatel', 1990), 4.

[72] *Kievskaia mysl'*, 16 August 1918. Quoted in Trifonov, "Nespravedlivo zabytaia kniga o russkom narode," 4.

[73] A. Blok, *Sobranie sochinenii v 8-mi tomakh* (Moscow–Leningrad: Goslitizdat, 1963), 7: 411.

ill.[74] While at the front, she perpetually recorded overheard conversations among the soldiers,[75] publishing the first of seven fragments under the title "What I Heard" in *Severnye zapiski* shortly before the February Revolution. The rest followed in 1917 in *Narodopravstvo*, a Kadet publication, under the title "Soldiers' Conversations: Notes." In the same year the Committee of the South-West Front under the All-Russian Country [*zemskii*] Union published, in Kiev, Fedorchenko's collection of soldiers' stories and thoughts in the form of a book entitled *The People at War: Notes from the Front.*

The air of truthfulness and reliability in *The People at War* is based to a high degree upon the work's exceptional literary form and language. The narrative point of view is that of the soldiers, and their speech appears to be exactly reproduced. The book's documentary status was questioned in the 1930s, partly because of Fedorchenko's own contradictory statements concerning her role in the compilation of the material, but later research has testified to its authenticity.[76] The work's validity was not doubted, for example, by Stepun, who quotes *The People at War* in his memoirs, unhesitatingly accepting the words as those of the soldiers,[77] or by Il'ia Erenburg (Ehrenburg), who found Fedorchenko's book to be of exceptional interest among all Russian works dealing with the war.[78]

Fedorchenko's own views are not explicitly expressed, but as the editor, she naturally had to make a choice between the recorded utterances and

---

[74] "Piat' desiat let S. Z. Fedorchenko," *Literaturnaia gazeta*, 1 May 1939, 6. The article can be seen as an official rehabilitation of Fedorchenko's reputation, because the veracity of her *The People at War* is here unanimously accepted. See also Glotser, "K istorii knigi S. Fedorchenko," 153. In one book it has been claimed that Fedorchenko made her way "secretly" to the war zone in 1914, and upon returning after one year and eight months, she was "totally overwhelmed by what she had witnessed." See B. P. Koz'min, ed., *Pisateli sovremennoi epokhi: Bio-bibliograficheskii slovar' russkikh pisatelei XX veka* (1928; Moscow: DEM, 1991), 1: 252.

[75] In the foreword to the first publication in *Narodopravstvo* (no. 3 [1917]: 6), Fedorchenko says that conversations had been recorded in 1915–16, a claim repeated in the 1917 volume. On the other hand, among the vignettes there are many which could belong to the initial period of the conflict, as Fedorchenko opens with the soldiers' remembrances of their reactions to the outbreak of war and the call-up.

[76] For the controversy about *The People at War*, see Petrone, *The Great War*, 237–38, 332 n. 109.

[77] Stepun, *Iz pisem praporshchika-artillerista*, 298.

[78] I. Erenburg, *Sobranie sochinenii v deviati tomakh* (Moscow: Khudozhestvennaia literatura, 1966), 8: 293. Ehrenburg also singled out Stepun's book for "showing the war without the obligatory gilt" (221). Both books were among the few works that managed to avoid a dualistic attitude to the war, either for or against, but saw the war's "innumerable faces." I. Erenburg, *Lik voiny: Vo Frantsii* (Sofia: Rossiisko-Bulgarskoe izdatel'stvo, 1920), 3.

decide about the overall structure. The final result is a truly polyphonic work, a chorus of voices, where the totality of the diverging opinions seems to correspond with the nurse's own inner division. The initial feelings vary from fear to joy. Some saw the war as a disastrous intruder in their personal life, while others greeted it as a welcome break in a monotonous, hard existence. One soldier felt that life in the army was easier than back home: you were given food, clothes, and shelter, and the only thing that was asked of you was to obey orders.[79] Attempts to explain the background of the war and its goals are few; for a people with a high percentage of illiteracy, official explanations remained unclear. It is the attitude that Okunev formulated as "We are ignorant." One soldier suspects that it is a lack of living space which lies behind the war, while another explains it by reference to the merchants' hunger for profit. The majority seem to accept everything submissively: "There are too many people in the world. The world doesn't need them all. And that's why the war started."[80]

No patriotic feelings are expressed in *The People at War*. Just like Gumilev, the soldiers refrain from using words like "Russia" and "mother country." To religion, a cynical attitude is taken, quite unlike Okunev's observation. Before the war the church taught you to love your neighbor, that killing was a sin, and that God's name should not be misused, but the war had changed everything. Nothing was a sin anymore, as peace-loving people turned into "animals." Life had become cruel and gruesome. Stepun's insight that there was no room for feelings of personal responsibility is echoed in the words of Fedorchenko's soldiers: the individual's own role in the war is reduced to obeying and killing.

The actual battles are recalled and commented upon in a callous tone. The notion, also expressed by Okunev, that you gradually become used to everything—the dangers, the pains, the hunger, the lack of sleep, and the killing—is a recurring one. Everything is met with the same persistence. With a revealing lack of remorse, Fedorchenko's soldiers also recall offences against women and children in the occupied areas, and the brutality and contempt with which local Jews could be treated by the Russians. Many incidents of officer misconduct are also retold. *The People at War* includes gruesome details about the warfare of the Russian army—marauding, rape, violence, murder, and abuse of civilians. Soldiers are beaten up for no apparent reason ("Whatever you say to him, he will beat you up... Even for 'yes, sir,' he'll punch you on the jaw").[81] The rough treatment leads to a bitter insight into the nature of a divided Russia: "They don't understand us simple people."[82] The feared

---

[79] S. Fedorchenko, "Chto ia slyshala," *Severnye zapiski*, no. 1 (1917): 139.

[80] Ibid., 135.

[81] Fedorchenko, *Narod na voine*, 47.

[82] Ibid., 52.

officers despise the people, while the soldier finds good and trustworthy comrades only among his equals in the army. The enemy is commented upon with respect, often with a feeling of inferiority. The Germans are clever people, they are literate, and at home they live a much better life than the Russians. This could paradoxically turn the war to the advantage of the Russians: "I think we'll beat the German. I've heard that he even now changes underwear every week. Soon he'll get tired of a life without any comfort and just leave."[83] The Russian soldiers could even feel a kind of solidarity with the German private: just like them, he had been sent to the front to participate in a war which essentially was foreign to him.

In a few cases, the bitterness gives rise to voices of protest. There are some scattered threats and comments that changes might be on their way and that another sort of war is yet to be fought. Still, the author of the article on Fedorchenko in *Literaturnaia entsiklopediia* (1939) criticized *The People at War* for not reflecting truthfully the deep ideological changes that occurred among soldiers during the war, eventually taking the form of Bolshevism.[84] This criticism only further enhances the truth value of Fedorchenko's first volume. It was composed without any thoughts about current political and ideological expectations.

After the February Revolution, Fedorchenko went to the Austrian front in order to organize workshops in aid of Russians and Austrians who had suffered from the war.[85] She kept up her interest in the stories and thoughts of the soldiers, continually taking notes.[86] The result was a second volume of *The People at War*, published in 1925, illustrating life at the front between the two revolutions of 1917. As a postwar publication, this book does not fulfil the requirements asked from the other publications analyzed here, but, on the other hand, the negative response received by the 1925 book in Soviet Russia confirms that it was not written to order. Fedorchenko shows that the February Revolution was met with the same attitude of submission, bewilderment, and distrust as the outbreak of war in 1914. No regrets at the tsar's abdication are recorded. Revolution means, above all, freedom from authority. Even the belief in God is crumbling: if the tsar could so easily be removed, perhaps God, too, is superfluous, being just something that the upper class had invented to keep the people humble. The revolutionary "freedom" also includes freedom to think independently about the war. The recurrent thought is "let's go back home." There the future—primarily the decision on the "land question"—is

---

[83] Fedorchenko, "Chto ia slyshala," 137.

[84] "Fedorchenko Sof'ia Zakharovna," in *Literaturnaia entsiklopediia* (Moscow: Khudozhestvennaia literatura, 1939), 11: 680.

[85] Koz'min, *Pisateli sovremennoi epokhi*, 252.

[86] An item in *Rech'* (9 March 1917) with the title "V eti dni" records conversations overheard in Petrograd (in the streets, in lines, and in the Duma) shortly after the February Revolution. Only a few of the utterances are connected with the ongoing war.

taking shape. A typical comment is "Well, you no longer play a hero at the front. Your comrades will only laugh at you. Let's take our fearlessness back home, there it is needed."[87] As for the Russian "heroism" at war, one soldier explains it with the lack of alternatives. Had there been any choice, only "idiots" would have risked their lives.[88]

One soldier, on the brink of deserting, feels remorse at the thought of those who still go on fighting,[89] but the general feeling is that the war is over. The officers and those who come to the front to speak for its continuation—like Stepun, for instance—and all the talks about the fatherland being in danger are met with distrust. These are the worries only of those who belong to the alien upper class. And is it possible to achieve peace through war? a soldier asks.[90] The deserting soldiers hope that the Germans will refuse to continue the war and create a revolution just like the Russians. The German soldiers are now perceived as being much closer than the Russians' own officers, as they have one enemy in common, that is, those who chased them like sheep out into the war.[91]

Fedorchenko experienced the Civil War in Ukraine and Southern Russia (Novorossiisk, the Crimea and the Northern Caucasus), witnessing, as she says, 21 coups in the period 1917–22.[92] Now she was also perpetually collecting material for a planned third volume of *The People at War*. In the late 1920s Fedorchenko managed to place some extracts in the periodical press, but the full volume could come out only in 1983, long after the death of the author. Many of the fragments bear witness to how the process of demoralization that started during the Great War had now reached a point where human life had lost all value. Violence and killing rule, most often without any reason or objective justification. Occasionally a soldier may add a statement like "Afterwards people will live a better life" to his shocking story, but without much conviction.

Fedorchenko claims to have recorded utterances by "all kinds of rebels, bandits, greens, reds, whites and all the rest"[93] for her third volume, but understandably most of the voices belong to Bolsheviks and Red Army soldiers. Many like to compare the World War and the Civil War, claiming that the present war is "their war," a war they participate in of their own free will, a war which is waged not abroad, but on Russian soil, a war which you understand

---

87 Fedorchenko, *Narod na voine*, 106.

88 Ibid., 107.

89 Ibid., 105.

90 Ibid., 107.

91 Ibid., 106.

92 Ibid., 253.

93 Sof'ia Fedorchenko, "Narod na voine," *Novyi mir*, no. 3 (1927): 82.

and accept, a war for "freedom." The word "freedom" has been given a completely new meaning, far from that which Okunev and others gave it in 1914. No one seems to be troubled by the thought of Russians fighting against Russians; on the contrary, for the Red Army soldier, the other side, that is, the Volunteer Army and the White Army, is regarded as the arch-enemy against whom it is a "pleasure" to fight.[94] It is difficult to decide whether these voices are representative of the majority, but in any case they belong to the side that came out of the war years as a winner.

03   80

Writing from their own experience at the front, the Russian writers treated in this chapter avoided the fallacy of "inventing something life-like" alongside the real war. Their position as participants in the events gave their publications a special dignity, even if at times they appeared to repeat many of the myths and beliefs of the rear. From their notes, sketches, and letters no unambiguous, simple "truth" about the Great War emerges. All of them wrote from his or her position and background and, even more important, the time of writing left clear marks on the text. The summer of 1915, with its military setbacks and heavy losses of human life, destroyed most of the initial optimism and enthusiasm. The war record of Sergei Krechetov and Iakov Okunev does not go beyond the spring of 1915 and thus they never publicly lost their "innocence." While their experiences, just like those of Nikolai Gumilev, met their expectations to a high degree, Fedor Stepun could not close his eyes to the general change in mood that had occurred as he returned to the army in late 1916. If the common characterization of the Russian soldier at the early stage of the war was "mildness, long-suffering, submissiveness and even a kind of sense of being doomed,"[95] very little of this was left in 1916, not to speak of 1917, the year of revolutions. The hardships and dangers at the front were no longer met with a passive, unreflective acceptance.

Sof'ia Fedorchenko's method of recording the words of soldiers without any authorial comment provides a deeper insight into the process that turned the Great War into a civil war. Her will to listen to the common soldier, the "atom" of the Russian army, was based on an understanding that here was the decisive force in the outcome of events. As she started to write down the soldiers' words only in 1915, the frank cynicism and the signs of growing dissent are more prominent than in Krechetov's and Okunev's observations.

The February Revolution sanctioned a revolt against all authority, but it could also strengthen the will to wage the war until a victorious end. The war was madness, a universal slaughter—that was one of Fedor Stepun's

---

[94] Fedorchenko, *Narod na voine*, 165.

[95] A. I. Ivanov, "Oblik russkogo soldata v otechestvennoi literature perioda pervoi mirovoi voiny (1914–1918 g.g.)," *Vestnik SamGU*, no. 4 (38) (2005): 91.

"truths"—but when the very existence of Russia appeared to be under threat, the forces of war had to be used for national advantage. As a spokesman for the Provisional Government, he felt a responsibility for bigger issues more than did the ordinary soldier, but ultimately it was interests of personal and class character that finally decided the fate of Russia.

Contemplating War, Caught Up in Revolution:
A Survey of Russian Poetry, 1914–22

J. Alexander Ogden

> All we had were compelling songs of the future;
> and suddenly these songs are no longer part of
> the dynamic of history.... When singers have
> been killed and their song has been dragged into
> a museum and pinned to the wall of the past, the
> generation they represent is even more desolate,
> orphaned, and lost—impoverished in the most
> real sense of the word.
> —Roman Jakobson, "On a Generation That
> Squandered Its Poets" (1931)[1]

Soon after the outbreak of war in 1914, the poet Zinaida Gippius—a Symbolist known up to that point for her apocalyptic mysticism and provocative style—started writing letters in verse to soldiers at the front. Written in a sing-song, pseudo-folk style, such as that used for *lubok* broadside prints, these poems were then wrapped up as little presents in the drawstring pouches used for tobacco. Seeking a folksy touch, Gippius often signed them with the names of her household servants rather than her own name. They had such an impact that, a year into the war, Gippius was able to publish a collection entitled *How We Wrote to the Soldiers, and What They Wrote Back to Us* (1915), selected from among the roughly 400 letters that came back in response from the front. Often these responses included ditties of their own, such as one beginning, "Получив мы пакет / Посылаем ответ / Из далекой страны / Из театра войны" (Having received your packet / We send a reply / From a distant land / From the theater of war).[2]

---

[1] Roman Jakobson, "On a Generation That Squandered Its Poets," trans. E. J. Brown in his *Major Soviet Writers: Essays in Criticism* (London: Oxford University Press, 1973), 32.

[2] Z. N. Gippius, comp., *Kak my voinam pisali i chto oni nam otvechali* (Moscow: Sytin, 1915), 23. On the quantity of responses, see I. V. Zobnin, *Dmitrii Merezhkovskii: Zhizn´ i deianiia* (Moscow: Molodaia gvardiia, 2008), available at http://royallib.ru/book/ zobnin_yuriy/dmitriy_meregkovskiy_gizn_i_deyaniya.html. Unless otherwise credited, all translations are my own.

Russian Culture in War and Revolution, 1914–22, Book 1: Popular Culture, the Arts, and Institutions. Murray Frame, Boris Kolonitskii, Steven G. Marks, and Melissa K. Stockdale, eds. Bloomington, IN: Slavica Publishers, 2014, 233–59.

Gippius's publication, in some ways one of the more unusual poetic responses to war, nevertheless exhibits several features typical of literary reactions early in the conflict. For many writers at the time, a civic-minded approach became common; this was true even on the part of writers not always previously known for their civic-mindedness. Patriotism in tone and theme was the norm, whether writers fully supported the war or, like Gippius, believed it to be tragically misguided. A pervasive folk influence shaped imagery, vocabulary, and poetic form. And many poets showed an inclination to seek an understanding of their times and their own place in them by way of dialogue, whether with the troops, with the nation, or with fellow poets. As the war continued, and then was followed by revolutions and civil war, these features evolved and were supplemented by others, including a growing strain of escapism, but a continuity of response can be traced even through the many abrupt breaks and shifting priorities of these years of war and revolution.

One of Russia's most gifted and prolific generations of poets lived through—and wrote about—the years from 1914 to 1922. Given this fact, it seems particularly surprising that, summing up his contemporaries' response to the Great War, noted historian of Russian literature D. S. Mirsky wrote that "the War is much less interestingly reflected in Russian literature than in that of the Western nations. The little there is (with the exception of Gumilev's lyrics and with the exception of young writers who made their appearance after the War) is the work of war correspondents, not of soldiers."[3] Subsequent studies of Russian literary history have tended to follow Mirsky's line, ignoring the poetry of the war years as a coherent period and often focusing instead on literature reflecting the Bolshevik Revolution and Civil War in isolation from what immediately preceded it.[4] But responses to revolution did not emerge from a vacuum; they continued in important ways the poetry of the war

---

[3] D. S. Mirsky, *Contemporary Russian Literature* (New York: Knopf, 1926), 241.

[4] Only a handful of works focus on World War I, including Ben Hellman's *Poets of Hope and Despair* on the Symbolist poets in 1914–18 (Helsinki: Institute for Russian and East European Studies, 1995); a themed double issue of the journal *The Silver Age* (vols. 3–4, 2000–01) entitled "World War I: The Poetic Response in Russia" (edited by Maria Basom); and Anatolii Ivanov's study *Pervaia mirovaia voina v russkoi literature, 1914–1918 gg.* (Tambov: Izd-vo Tambovskogo gosudarstvennogo universiteta, 2005). One short monograph worth returning to, although one not focused solely on Russia, is C. M. Bowra's *Poetry and the First World War* (Oxford: Oxford University Press, 1961), delivered as "The Taylorian Lecture" for 1961. Bowra, an Oxford classicist, literary critic, editor of a bilingual anthology of Russian poetry, and friend of the poet Viacheslav Ivanov, was one of the few people equipped to write a truly international study of poetic responses to the war. Bowra considers Blok, Briusov, Maiakovskii, Khlebnikov, and Gumilev, quoting poetry in the original beside Cavafy in Greek, Rilke and others in German, as well as French, Italian, and British poets.

period, and both must be seen in the context of the vibrant culture of Russia's early 20th-century "Silver Age."[5]

ය ෨

Art of all kinds flourished in turn-of-the-century Russia—visual art, music, ballet, theater, and the full range of literature—but poetry occupied a central place.[6] In the years preceding the war, the era's best-known poets were celebrities, and poetry was everywhere: on stage, in newspapers and magazines, and in innumerable chapbook publications and anthologies. Symbolism, which as a grouping and aesthetic approach had dominated Russian poetry in the first decade of the 20th century, had suffered a decisive crisis in 1910. However, all the major Symbolist figures were still active: both the "first generation" Symbolist writers (Dmitrii Merezhkovskii, Gippius, Konstantin Bal'mont, Fedor Sologub, and Valerii Briusov) and the "second generation" (Aleksandr Blok, Andrei Belyi, and Viacheslav Ivanov) would remain central to the poetic environment throughout the years of war and revolution, and many continued to write well into the 1920s and beyond. Meanwhile, new movements and individual talents emerged in the immediate prewar years. Members of the Poets' Guild (and its offshoot Acmeism, including Nikolai Gumilev, Sergei Gorodetskii, Osip Mandel'shtam, and Anna Akhmatova) were particularly active in these years. Marina Tsvetaeva published her first verse collections in 1910 and 1912. And at the end of 1912 David Burliuk, Aleksei Kruchenykh, Vladimir Maiakovskii, and Viktor (Velimir) Khlebnikov issued their Futurist manifesto "A Slap in the Face of Public Taste," claiming that only *they* were the face of their era and famously casting "Pushkin, Dostoevskii, Tolstoi, etc. etc. off the ship of modernity."[7] Poets of the period

---

[5] While no comprehensive survey focuses on Russian literary output of 1914– 22 as a whole, a number of works of biography, memoir literature, and literary analysis trace the evolution of individual writers through this period. It is in these works, through the microcosm of individual lived experience in these years, that the period has most extensively been treated as a cohesive whole. See, for example, Steven Broyde, *Osip Mandel'štam and His Age: A Commentary on the Themes of War and Revolution in the Poetry, 1913–1923* (Cambridge, MA: Harvard University Press, 1975).

[6] In this sense early 20th-century Russia was the polar opposite of England. As one literary historian of British war poetry notes, "It is one of the ironies of English literary history that the years immediately preceding the first great modern war—the war that brought to trial the fundamental premises of Western civilization—coincided with what C. Day Lewis calls 'a period of very low vitality' for poetry." John H. Johnston, *English Poetry of the First World War: A Study in the Evolution of Lyric and Narrative Form* (Princeton, NJ: Princeton University Press, 1964), 3.

[7] D. D. Burliuk et al., "Poshchechina obshchestvennomu vkusu," in *Literaturnye manifesty: Ot simvolizma do "Oktiabria,"* ed. N. L. Brodskii and N. P. Sidorov (1924, Moscow: Agraf, 2001), 129. While there has been a tendency recently to back away from the

were not writing alone or in isolation, but instead were contributing to artistic collaborations that sought a synthesis of the arts. Blok, Briusov, Ivanov, and Mikhail Kuzmin all made major contributions to the theater. Burliuk, Maiakovskii, and many other Futurists brought poetry and visual art closer together. Some of the era's most representative venues for the arts were its salons, cabarets, and other social gatherings.[8]

The vast majority of writers associated with these movements were multilingual, internationally aware, and unusually well educated. Truly cosmopolitan and with a deep and intimate appreciation for wider European cultural traditions, many had spent significant time in Western Europe (Bal'-mont, Belyi, and Maksimilian Voloshin all spent the first year or two of the war abroad). They viewed contemporary events through prisms as varied as folk belief and ancient Rus', 19th-century Slavophilism and pan-Slavism, theosophy, utopianism, and apocalypticism.

Given the cultural prominence of poetry at the time, it was natural for Russians to attempt to understand the war that broke out in the summer of 1914, place it in context, and show their support for the national cause by means of poetry. A significant number of collections of war poetry were published in the first year of the war. Often, these were explicitly put out to raise money for wounded soldiers, for Poland, or for other war-related causes (or causes that could be linked to the war).[9] Thus, for example, the nearly 300-page *The Current War in Russian Poetry* (1915), compiled by Boris Borisovich Glinskii, collected immediate responses to the war—poems from the first three months of the conflict—and included both known poets and beginners in a somewhat undiscriminating selection. Divided thematically, the book starts with a section on "Slavdom," followed by sections on Galicia and Poland, the Slavic areas affected directly. The 16 sections of the book include everything from "Homeland," "Cossacks," and "Heroes," to "Mother," "Belgium," and "Enemies." A section simply titled "War" is striking for how few of its 33

---

importance of schools in literature in reaction to Soviet criticism's oversimplified and categorical classification of writers by ideology, the fact remains that in the period leading up to the war most writers themselves acutely sensed their affiliation with a particular group, as evidenced by their fondness for programmatic statements, manifestos, journals, anthologies, and even publishing houses reflecting individual and exclusive approaches.

[8] For a wealth of memoir accounts of Silver Age literary and social gatherings, see T. F. Prokopov, ed., *Moskovskii Parnas: Kruzhki, salony, zhurfiksy Serebrianogo veka (1890–1922)* (Moscow: Intelvak, 2006).

[9] Every few weeks saw a new collection of this sort, which sometimes grouped causes together somewhat haphazardly. Thus, for example, net income from the 1915 literary almanac *V tylu* (1915) was to be split evenly between aid to war victims and "needy students of Riga Polytechnic Institute"; contributors included Sologub, Akhmatova, Gumilev, Teffi, Briusov, Gippius, and others. See *Biulleteni literatury i zhizni*, no. 21–22 (1915): 582.

poems actually focus on battle. Prince Fedor Kasatkin-Rostovskii's "From the War" ("S voiny") is a vigil and a prayer in a calm and quiet setting.[10] In Nikolai Minskii's "Colors of War" ("Tsveta voiny"), the colors have nothing to do with any battlefield colors other than those of the flags, and all symbolic associations that Minskii links to the tricolor take us far away to what the soldiers are fighting for and what is inspiring them, not what their senses perceive in battle.[11] Briusov's "An Old Question" ("Staryi vopros"), a poem that was reprinted in several different collections of war verse, greets the war eagerly as an opportunity to answer the "Old Question" of Russia's identity, stature, and reputation in the world.[12]

Other collections took a historical approach to the topic. Of the 23 poets featured in *War in Russian Lyric: An Anthology* (1915), 18 were poets of the 18th and 19th centuries. In a note "From the Compiler," written during the first month of the war, poet Vladislav Khodasevich sought to justify a collection of poetry in the midst of war, a time when the peaceful "voice of lyres" seems drowned out by the din of the battlefield. But, in a war fought in the name of peace and in defense of culture, Khodasevich writes, poetry can express our noblest thoughts. Seeking to include the best of Russian war poetry from its beginnings to the present (the collection opens with Vasilii Zhukovskii's 1812 poem "The Singer in the Camp of Russian Warriors"), Khodasevich rejects verse with a political focus and instead selects "poems about the process of war itself, about its beautiful and repulsive aspect, and about the feelings aroused by it."[13]

War in Russian Poetry (1915) was similar in its historical survey: nearly half the poems included dealt with wars prior to the current conflict, starting with works by Zhukovskii, Petr Viazemskii, and Aleksandr Pushkin. The collection was compiled by minor poet and translator Anastasiia Chebotarevskaia, wife of the writer Fedor Sologub, and included a foreword by the latter. Poets given greatest space were Sologub himself (9 poems), Mikhail Lermontov (7 poems), and Briusov (4 poems). Unlike the half-apologetic justification offered by Khodasevich for his collection, Sologub in his short foreword to this volume forcefully claims a central place for war poetry. Noting its similarity to love poetry—both are full-voiced and complete expressions of the hidden soul of the poet and of the Russian people—he finds a particularly Russian attitude to war in the poems' simplicity, generosity, and burning sense of fairness. Such

---

[10] B. B. Glinskii, comp., *Sovremennaia voina v russkoi poezii* (Petrograd: Tip. t-va A. S. Suvorina, 1915), 59. Accessed online at http://hdl.handle.net/2027/mdp.39015063082807.

[11] Ibid., 55–56.

[12] Ibid., 89–90.

[13] V. F. Khodasevich, comp., *Voina v russkoi lirike* (Moscow: Pol'za, 1915), 4.

poems, in his view, will envelop a reader in feelings of "joy, strength, and hope."[14] (See fig. 41 in the gallery of illustrations following page 188.)

Anthologies of war poetry received mixed reviews. In a January, 1915, review for *Apollon* titled "War Verse" ("Voennye stikhi"), poet and critic Georgii Ivanov dismissed several recent anthologies as "ridiculous war collections," and he scorned Glinskii's *The Current War* as a "thick, watered-down volume."[15] Other reviews of Glinskii's book, while praising its worthy fundraising goal ("in aid of ravaged Poland") and, at times, its contents ("exclusively that which is truly literary"), often highlighted the dangers for poetry when it became too narrowly topical or too jingoistic.[16] Thus, one reviewer, impressed by all the major poets represented, nevertheless found the poems marred by "one common feature: pure journalese [*gazetnost'*].... No passion, no creative fire, no beautiful reconstructions...."[17] Another noted that the poems often exhibited patriotism of "an unbearably shrill character" and observed, "when real poets resort to a *lubok* writing style ... it becomes frightening for Russian poetry."[18]

Some of the most characteristic and most anthologized poems from early in the war were written before the outbreak of major hostilities. Thus, Briusov's "The Last War" ("Posledniaia voina"), anthologized in all three collections discussed above, was written 20 July 1914 (2 August in New Style), the day after Germany's declaration of war on Russia but before battles had been fought on any front.[19] Briusov's poem presents the war as a long-due conflict that, while bloody and destructive, will sweep away a tired old world and offer new life and a new world. He ends the poem:

---

[14] A. N. Chebotarevskaia, comp. *Voina v russkoi poezii,* with a foreword by Fedor Sologub (Petrograd: M. V. Popov, 1915), 6.

[15] G. V. Ivanov, *Tretii Rim: Khudozhestvennaia proza, stat'i,* ed. Vadim Kreid (Tenafly, NJ: Hermitage, 1987), 186. The other recent collections dismissed by Ivanov were those compiled by A. Rakshitar and E. Minaeva; he found Khodasevich's "much more interesting."

[16] The review quoted is from *Izvestiia knizhnogo magazina t-va M. O. Vol'f,* no. 1 (1915). Excerpted in *Biulleteni literatury i zhizni,* no. 21–22 (1915): 573.

[17] Al. Ozhigov, *Sovremennyi mir,* no. 2 (1915). Excerpted in *Biulleteni literatury i zhizni,* no. 21–22 (1915): 573.

[18] V. Evgen'ev in *Zhurnal dlia vsekh,* no. 3 (1915). Excerpted in *Biulleteni literatury i zhizni,* no. 21–22 (1915): 573.

[19] While Archduke Franz Ferdinand had been assassinated on 28 June and Austria-Hungary began shelling Belgrade and other locations in northern Serbia on 29 July, the Austro-Hungarian army did not cross into Serbia until 12 August. The Battle of Liège, in Belgium, beginning 5 August, was the first significant battle of the war. See Martin Gilbert, *The First World War: A Complete History* (New York: Henry Holt, 1994), 30–37; Randal Gray, comp., *Chronicles of the First World War, 1: 1914–1916* (New York: Facts On File, 1990), 10–20.

Пусть рушатся былые своды,
Пусть с гулом падают столбы,—
Началом мира и свободы
Да будет страшный год борьбы![20]

[Let the vaults of old be destroyed, / Let pillars fall with a roar, — / May a terrible year of struggle / Be the beginning of peace and freedom!]

Poems written by contemporary poets about earlier conflicts—even much earlier ones—took on a new light when republished in the war years. Thus, Blok's cycle "On the Field of Kulikovo" ("Na pole Kulikovom"), taking Dmitrii Donskoi's 1380 battle against the Mongols as its focus although very much reflecting Blok's current concerns about Russia when he wrote it in 1908, was reprinted several times early in the war, including in Khodasevich's *War in Russian Lyric*. As Blok scholar Avril Pyman notes, these poems, "published without the date of writing, read very differently in 1915 than they had in 1908."[21]

Even as multiauthor anthologies presented readers with a range of Russian poetic responses to war, both historical and contemporary, the current authors included in these volumes also were publishing their own individual works on the war. As already seen, Briusov and Sologub were particularly active in shaping the literary response to war. The poet associated most directly with World War I, however, was Gumilev, who volunteered for the Imperial Army, served proudly at the front, and wrote about it in several poems dating mostly from the first year of the conflict. These poems were not numerous—fewer than ten—and are not generally considered among his best work; Gumilev himself included only half of them in any of his collections.[22] But they capture both the immediate experience of war—the whistle of bullets, shrapnel exploding overhead, and an awareness of imminent death—and the rhetoric of honor, glory, and religious mission surrounding a noble cause, as in these lines from 1914:

И воистину светло и свято
Дело величавое войны.

---

[20] Valerii Briusov, *Sobranie sochinenii v semi tomakh* (Moscow: Khudozhestvennaia literatura, 1973), 2: 141. The poem first appeared in *Russkaia mysl'*, no. 8–9 (1914), as one of five poems in the cycle *Sovremennost'* (which also included "Staryi vopros") and was subsequently much anthologized.

[21] Avril Pyman, *The Life of Aleksandr Blok, 2: The Release of Harmony, 1908–1921* (Oxford: Oxford University Press, 1980), 219.

[22] Barry Scherr, "Of Death and the Poet: Nikolai Gumilev and World War I," in "World War I: The Poetic Response in Russia," ed. Maria Basom, special issue, *The Silver Age* 3–4 (2000–01): 57–58.

Серафимы, ясны и крылаты,
За плечами воинов видны.

[And, verily, the majestic vocation / Of war is radiant and sacred; /
Winged and bright seraphim appear / Behind the warriors' shoulders.][23]

While the war as a significant theme mostly disappears from Gumilev's
poetry after 1914–15, the poet remained "tremendously in love with adventure
and battle" (in the words of revolutionary and writer Victor Serge, who met
him at the Russian military mission in Paris in the summer of 1917).[24] Looking
back from 1920 in his poem "Memory" ("Pamiat'"), Gumilev describes his
earlier selves in the third person, in an extended apostrophe to Memory personified. Of the war years, both their hardship and his decorations for bravery
in combat, he writes:

Знал он муки голода и жажды,
Сон тревожный, бесконечный путь,
Но святой Георгий тронул дважды
Пулею не тронутую грудь.

[He knew the agonies of thirst and hunger, / Knew troubled dreams,
an endless journey, / But twice his chest, untouched by bullets, / was
touched by the Cross of St. George.][25]

Gumilev spent a year in Europe (spring 1917 to spring 1918), and a packet
of documents from Paris and London attests to his continuing military involvement there.[26] In spite of his monarchist sentiments, Gumilev returned
to revolutionary Petrograd, even as "the White armies are said to have
memorized his poems and recited them in battle."[27]

---

[23] "Voina," text with translation by Scherr, in "World War I: The Poetic Response in
Russia," 156–57. See also the selection of poems included here both in the original and
in Scherr's translations.

[24] Victor Serge, *Memoirs of a Revolutionary, 1901–1941* (London: Oxford University
Press, 1963), 59.

[25] Gumilev, "Pamiat'," text with translation by Scherr, in "World War I: The Poetic
Response in Russia," 170–71.

[26] "Posluzhnoi spisok N. S. Gumileva," "Drugie dokumenty, otnosiashchiesia k
voennoi sluzhbe N. S. Gumileva," in N. Gumilev, *Sobranie sochinenii v chetyrekh tomakh*,
ed. G. P. Struve and B. A. Filippov (Washington, DC: Victor Kamkin, 1962), 1: xlv–lvi.

[27] Sidney Monas, "Introduction. Gumilev: Akmê and Adam in Saint Petersburg,"
in *Selected Works of Nikolai S. Gumilev*, trans. Burton Raffel and Alla Burago (Albany:
SUNY Press, 1972), 14.

Gumilev was such an exception as a poet with combat experience that sources often refer to him as the only Russian poet who fought in World War I. While not quite true—Benedikt Livshits, for example, was drafted and then severely wounded during the army's attack on the Vistula River in August 1914, and the peasant poet Petr V. Oreshin wrote antiwar verse while serving at the front[28]—the larger fact remains that, as Mirsky noted, very little of the Russian poetry about the war was written by soldiers. Unlike in Britain, whose army consisted of young men of all classes, including many with classical educations and literary ambitions, in Russia exemptions and other forms of service meant that few poets saw frontline action; many soldiers at the front were at best semiliterate—although, as responses to Gippius from the front reveal, a number were willing to try their hand at verse.[29] With few exceptions, poets remained at least a little removed from the front, even though many of them did experience some form of military service, whether as draftsmen (Maiakovskii, Kruchenykh), hospital workers (Khlebnikov, Sergei Esenin), or accountants (Blok). Others had significant careers as war correspondents (Briusov, Gorodetskii).

For many, the war became a catalyst sparking greater civic engagement. Gippius began sending her verse missives to the troops. Akhmatova, who had established herself in her earlier verse as a master of refined, intimate, and minute observation of mood, word, and gesture, consciously remade her lyric persona to become the chronicler and prophet of Russian suffering. Looking back at July 1914 from two years into the war, she wrote:

Из памяти, как груз отныне лишний,
Исчезли тени песен и страстей.
Ей – опустевшей – приказал Всевышний
Стать страшной книгой грозовых вестей.

---

[28] Other poets who saw active service during the war include Nikolai Aseev, Konstantin Bol'shakov, and Vsevolod Rozhdestvenskii. On Livshits, see Eugenia Afinoguénova, "Benedikt Konstantinovich Livshits," in *Russian Writers of the Silver Age, 1890–1925*, ed. Judith E. Kalb, J. Alexander Ogden, and I. G. Vishnevetsky, Dictionary of Literary Biography 295 (Detroit: Thomson-Gale, 2004), 269. On Oreshin, see K. G. Petrosov, "Oreshin, Petr Vasil'evich," in *Russkie pisateli: 1800–1917. Biograficheskii slovar'*, 4: *M–P*, ed. P. A Nikolaev (Moscow: Bol'shaia rossiiskaia entsiklopediia, 1999), 445.

[29] Even in Britain the immediacy of Great War poetry was something new. As Edmund Blunden (himself a Great War poet) notes, "[W]hether in acceptance of war as inseparable from the scheme of things, or possibly as a form of international law and order, or in protest against its ingenious and often tremendous brutalities, few war poets in England in Cowper's days [late eighteenth century] could claim any more direct experience of it than Cowper in his unsacrificed greenhouse. The same may be said of his nineteenth-century followers. *They were professional authors composing at a distance from the soldier in the field.*" Edmund Blunden, *War Poets, 1914–1918* (London: Longmans, 1958), 11–12 (bracketed clarification and emphasis added).

[From my memory, like a weight henceforth superfluous, / Disappeared the trace of songs and passions. / The Almighty commanded it [memory], emptied out, / to become an awesome book of terrifying tidings.][30]

The change in Akhmatova's perspective was gradual, and love lyrics still had a significant place in her 1917 collection *White Flock* (*Belaia staia*), but already the ground was laid for her later role as voice of the Russian people, to culminate years later in spare, powerful verse such as *Requiem* (*Rekviem*, 1935–40).

Since relatively little of the war experience was firsthand for Russian writers, portrayals of the war and the people who fought it had less concrete detail. Instead, soldiers in much of the poetry take on an idealized anonymity, as in a poem titled "To Russia's Soldiers" ("Russkim voinam") dated November 1914, in which the addressees are seen as "unknown brothers, nameless and numberless."[31] Many poems in the anthologies published early in the war use words like *tam* (there) and *daleko* (far away), emphasizing the distance between the actual battles and the creation and consumption of verse. Khodasevich, in the editor's preface to his anthology, captures that distance well when he asks rhetorically, "Why should it be surprising if, being there on the battlefield in our thoughts, we take from the shelf a book of poems and, in it, too, search for echoes of the thing that insuperably torments us?"[32] Maiakovskii, typically provocative and with much less sympathy for those safely at home reading newspaper accounts of the war's casualties while "lasciviously humming Severianin," confronts these "talentless masses, thinking only / of stuffing your faces" in a poem entitled "For You!" ("Vam!" 1915), which begins:

Вам, проживающим за оргией оргию,
имеющим ванную и теплый клозет!
Как вам не стыдно о представленных к Георгию
вычитывать из столбцов газет?!

---

[30] A. A. Akhmatova, "Pamiati 19 iiulia 1914," translated as "In Memory of 19 July 1914" by Sonia Ketchian, in "World War I: The Poetic Response in Russia," 137 (translation slightly revised).

[31] "За вас, неведомые братья / без имени и без числа...." Sergei Rafilovich, "Russkim voinam," in Chebotarevskaia, *Voina v russkoi poezii*, 112.

[32] Что же удивительного, если мысленно присутствуя там, на полях сражений, мы берем с полки книгу стихов и в ней тоже ищем отголосков того, что томит нас неодолимо? (Khodasevich, *Voina v russkoi lirike*, 3–4).

[You, wasting away from orgy to orgy, / owning a bathtub and heated toilet, / aren't you ashamed, scanning through St. Giorgy's / Awards in the columns of newspapers?][33]

In the previous year, from August to October of 1914, Maiakovskii had produced verses for more than 50 *lubok* prints and postcards.[34] These ditties are interesting as a commentary and for their collaboration with other major Futurists—illustrated as they were by artists including Kazimir Malevich, Aristarkh Lentulov, Mikhail Larionov, Burliuk, and Maiakovskii himself—but they also highlight some of the pitfalls of war verse, providing neither strong examples of Maiakovskii's verse nor a nuanced view of war:

В славном лесе Августо́вом
Битых немцев тысяч сто вам.
Враг изрублен, а затем он
Пущен плавать в синий Неман.[35]

[In the famed Augustów forest / Are a hundred thousand dead Germans for you. / The foe was hacked up, and thereupon / Sent to float the dark-blue Neman.]

Too fixed a focus on contemporary events, civic themes, and patriotism had the potential to flatten out the richness and complexity of Silver Age poetry, and it is true that much of the war verse early in the conflict, based as it was specifically on immediate civic and political concerns, was not of enduring significance, even when produced by some of the era's great poets (Gumilev, Sologub, Kuzmin). As Nikolai Bogomolov and John Malmstad note, writing about the literary environment once the war began, "Russian literature of this time yielded not a single even somewhat serious work tied to contemporary events (although individual poems could somewhat stand out against the general background). The reason for this, of course, was not the imperialist character of the war, but rather the primitively propagandistic character of the ideology that was earmarked for wide distribution."[36]

---

[33] V. V. Maiakovskii, *Polnoe sobranie sochinenii v 13 tomakh* (Moscow: Khudozhestvennaia literatura, 1955), 1: 75. Maiakovskii read this poem at the Stray Dog on 11 February 1915, and, in his autobiography, claimed that the cabaret venue was nearly closed down due to his reading of the poem (*Polnoe sobranie sochinenii*, 1: 432). Translation by Katya Apekina in *Night Wraps the Sky: Writings by and about Mayakovsky*, ed. Michael Almereyda (New York: Farrar, Straus and Giroux, 2008), 76.

[34] Maiakovskii, *Polnoe sobranie sochinenii*, 1: 451.

[35] Ibid., 356.

[36] N. A. Bogomolov and Dzhon E. Malmstad [John E. Malmstad], *Mikhail Kuzmin: Iskusstvo, zhizn´, epokha* (Moscow: Novoe literaturnoe obozrenie, 1996), 191.

As seen above, in the charged environment of the war's beginning it was almost impossible not to write cheerleading patriotic verse. One of the few to counter this current was Tsvetaeva, who, writing during the fraught month of July 1914, noted and rejected the rush to a religious-tinged militarism:

Война, война! – Кажденья у киотов
И стрекот шпор.
Но нету дела мне до царских счетов,
Народных ссор.

[War, war! – Censing near the icons / And the jangle of spurs. / But I have no business with tsars' accounts, / With nations' quarrels.][37]

Early in the war, Tsvetaeva was very much the exception; a strain of nationalism can be found even in the poetry of Boris Pasternak and Mandel´shtam, poets not given to patriotic outbursts.[38] In most of their poetry about the war, though, all three of these poets displayed a notable pacifism, a feature that became more and more prevalent the longer the war went on. It was particularly painful for poets like Pasternak and Tsvetaeva, both steeped in German culture and more particularly in German romanticism, to see the stark and simplistic rejection of everything German that was part of wartime patriotism. Mandel´shtam, who had a thorough background in the literature and culture of France and Germany, including university studies in both countries, and who also had a fascination with classical civilization, brought the full weight of this heritage to bear in his poetic portrayal of the barbaric tragedy of war. His poem "The Menagerie" ("Zverinets," January 1916), for example, is a statement about the futility of the war's nationalistic struggles, personified in the confrontations of animals: France's rooster, England's lion, Germany's eagle, and Russia's bear. Mandel´shtam ends, though, on a hopeful note and a return to a peaceful age:

В зверинце заперев зверей,
Мы успокоимся надолго,
И станет полноводней Волга,
И рейнская струя светлей, —
И умудренный человек
Почтит невольно чужестранца,
Как полубога, буйством танца
На берегах великих рек.

---

[37] Dated "Moscow, 16 July 1914." Marina Tsvetaeva, *Sobranie sochinenii v semi tomakh* (Moscow: Ellis Lak, 1994), 1: 210.

[38] Lazar Fleishman, *Boris Pasternak: The Poet and His Politics* (Cambridge, MA: Harvard University Press, 1990), 84; Broyde, *Osip Mandel´štam and His Age*, 200.

[Having locked the beasts up in the menagerie / We will rest content for a long time, / And the Volga will become deeper, / And the Rhenish water brighter— / And man, having become wiser / Will involuntarily honor the foreigner, / Like a demigod, with the turbulence of dance / On the shores of the great rivers.]

During the course of 1915, the initial patriotic surge in Russian verse waned overall, mirroring a more general, increasingly negative, sentiment about the war, and by 1916 war-themed poetry was almost uncommon. As one scholar writes, "the theme of war disappears from the pages of the majority of literary almanacs. And the very number of almanacs with war-themed works declined from 21 in 1915 to 5 in 1916."[39] Of course numbers for all almanacs and other publishing venues declined as book and serial publishing became more difficult, a feature both of scarce wartime resources and of increased wartime censorship. But significant collaborative publications of the period included *The Archer* (*Strelets*, also translated as *Sagittarius*, with issues in both 1915 and 1916), noteworthy because it united the Symbolists and Futurists under one cover.

To the extent that the war did figure in the poetry of 1915 and 1916, it was seen less and less as a patriotic mission tinted with shades of nobility and glory; instead, the focus increasingly became the death and senseless destruction of the conflict and the suffering both at the front and of those left behind. This change in tone mirrored, of course, that of British and other poets as the war progressed—the difference being that for British poets the disillusionment and "realization of the horror of war" came by way of "soldiers' assimilation of combat conditions," experienced firsthand, whereas for Russian poets the horror was experienced at a distance.[40]

---

[39] A. S. Fedotov, "Pervaia mirovaia voina v russkikh literaturno-khudozhestvennykh al'manakhakh i sbornikakh (1914–1916)," *Russkaia kul'tura v usloviiakh inozemnykh nashestvii i voin: X–nachalo XX v. Sbornik nauchnykh trudov*, vyp. 2 (Moscow: Institut istorii SSSR AN SSSR, 1990), 275; quoted in Ivanov, *Pervaia mirovaia voina v russkoi literature*, 369.

[40] Quotations on British war poetry come from Philippa Lyon, ed., *Twentieth-Century War Poetry* (Houndmills, UK: Palgrave Macmillan, 2005), 22. See also Paul Fussell, *The Great War and Modern Memory* (London: Oxford University Press, 1975). On the evolution from heroism and patriotism to disillusionment: "It has become a tradition when assessing English poetry of the First World War to see a fairly clear division in the output of poetry. The claim is that the early poetry, written before the Battle of the Somme in 1916, was concerned with the struggle in a righteous cause and the chivalric and heroic aspect of military service, stressing the virtue of sacrifice and dwelling on the image of St. George of England versus the dragon of the Central Powers; and that the later poetry represents a sense of disillusionment brought on by involvement in a senseless war of attrition, and by the shattering cost of modern warfare in human terms.... There is plenty of evidence to support this view, but signs of disquiet exist in

Perhaps for that reason, Russian war poems, with rare exceptions, convey little intimate sense of the details of battlefield life and instead are more ready to jump from the present to historical comparisons, as in Maiakovskii's narrative poem "War and the World" ("Voina i mir"), written in late 1915 and 1916. [41] Maiakovskii found that the bloodshed of the current war spectacularly outpaced even the bloodiest historical eras:

Нерон!
Здравствуй!
Хочешь?
Зрелище величайшего театра,
Сегодня
бьются
государством в государство
16 отборных гладиаторов.

Куда легендам о бойнях Цезарей
перед былью,
которая теперь была! [42]

[Nero! / Hello! / Want it? / A spectacle of theater most supreme, / Today / are fighting / as state against state / 16 hand-picked gladiators. / What are the legends of the Caesars' butchery / before the reality / that now was!]

Velimir Khlebnikov captured the deadening effect on a poet of army life even when not serving at the front: "Again the hell of the transformation of a poet into an animal bereft of sense, addressed in the language of stable men.... Marches, orders, the murder of my rhythm drive me mad by the end of evening exercises.... Thanks to the monotonous, severe cursing, the feeling for language in me is dying." [43] Aleksandr Blok, who "since the 1905

---

much of the poetry written in the earliest days of the war." Robert Giddings, *The War Poets* (New York: Orion, 1988), 8.

[41] In keeping with the Futurists' irreverent attitude toward the past, Maiakovskii here is "improving on" Tolstoi. In modern orthography, the titles of Maiakovskii's poem and that of Tolstoi's *War and Peace* are identical. Before the orthographic reform of 1918, however, Maiakovskii's "мір" was distinct from Tolstoi's "мир." Maiakovskii's title is variously rendered in English as "War and the World" or "War and the Universe."

[42] Maiakovskii, *Polnoe sobranie sochinenii*, 1: 220.

[43] Letter to Nikolai Kul'bin, in Khlebnikov, *Sobranie proizvedenii*, ed. Iurii Nikolaevich Tynianov and N. Stepanov (Leningrad: Izd-vo pisatelei v Leningrade, 1933), 5: 309–310; translated in N. A. Bogomolov, "Velimir Khlebnikov (Viktor Vladimirovich Khlebnikov)," trans. Curtis Ford, in *Russian Writers of the Silver Age*, 227.

Revolution … had anticipated a historical cataclysm that would purge Russia of its old structures and leave it ripe for renewal,"[44] increasingly sensed an impending crisis, as is clear in the ominous circling bird of prey in his poem "The Kite" ("Korshun," 1916):

Чертя за кругом плавный круг,
Над сонным лугом коршун кружит
И смотрит на пустынный луг. –
В избушке мать над сыном тужит:
«На хлеба, на, на грудь, соси,
Расти, покорствуй, крест неси».

Идут века, шумит война,
Встает мятеж, горят деревни,
А ты всё та ж, моя страна,
В красе заплаканной и древней. –
Доколе матери тужить?
Доколе коршуну кружить?[45]

[Marking circle after circle, / Over the sleepy meadow a kite circles / And watches the deserted meadow. / In an *izba*, a mother laments over her son: / "Take bread, take it, take the breast, suck, / Grow, be submissive, bear the cross." / The ages pass, war dins, / Rebellion rises, villages burn, / And you're still the same, my country, / In your tear-stained, ancient beauty. / How long must the mother grieve? / How long shall the kite circle?]

Russian society shared Blok's anticipation of crisis and renewal, and the February Revolution, with the abdication of the tsar and the establishment of the Provisional Government, bore out this widespread expectation. "Is this the beginning of life?" asked Blok, continuing, "I have no clear opinion of what is going on, and this when, by the will of fate, I have been set to be witness to a great epoch."[46] Pasternak told a colleague, "Just imagine … if the sea of blood and filth begins to radiate light."[47] The sense of possibility expressed by both

---

[44] Andrew Kahn, "Poetry of the Revolution," in *The Cambridge Companion to Twentieth-Century Russian Literature*, ed. E. A. Dobrenko and Marina Balina (Cambridge: Cambridge University Press, 2011), 41.

[45] A. A. Blok, *Polnoe sobranie sochinenii i pisem v dvadtsati tomakh* (Moscow: Nauka, 1997), 3: 188.

[46] A. A. Blok, *Zapisnye knizhki, 1901–1920* (Moscow: Khudozhestvennaia literatura, 1965), 316 (entry for 14 April 1917), quoted in Pyman, *The Life of Aleksandr Blok*, 2: 241.

[47] K. Loks, "Povest' ob odnom desiatiletii (1907–1917)" (unpublished manuscript), quoted in Fleishman, *Boris Pasternak: The Poet and His Politics*, 89.

these poets was typical, and Pasternak was also not unusual in that, "It was not individual parties or political slogans that attracted him, but the general spirit of freedom and unanimity, which he saw as uniting not only inimical groups and classes of society but even the trees and the land—nature itself."[48]

One noticeable sign of this newfound spirit of freedom was the prevalence of the "Marseillaise," which served the function of a national anthem under the Provisional Government. It was very much in the air in 1917, both in its French original and, especially, in its 1875 Russian variant, with a simplified and even more stirring melody and words by the 19th-century revolutionary and philosopher Petr Lavrov.[49] Numerous poets evoke the mood of the time with allusions to the hymn. It shows up in Maiakovskii's "poetochronicle" of the February Revolution, written in April 1917:

Как в бурю дюжина груженых барж,
над баррикадами
плывет, громыхая, марсельский марш.[50]

[Like a dozen loaded barges in a gale, / over the barricades / swims, rumbling, the Marseille march.]

One of the more unusual appearances of the "Marseillaise" in the poetry of 1917 is the rousing "Red Song" ("Krasnaia pesnia") by the peasant poet Nikolai Kliuev. First published in the newspaper *Zemlia i volia* in May 1917, signed simply "Krest′ianin" (A Peasant), later that year it came out as a separate two-page leaflet, this time under Kliuev's name.[51] The connection to the "Marseillaise" was explicit: in the first appearance thanks to a subtitle, "Russian Marseillaise," and in the second in a note beneath the title that it could be sung like the "Marseillaise."[52] The poem's opening imagery is

---

[48] Fleishman, *Boris Pasternak: The Poet and His Politics*, 89.

[49] On the role played by the "Marseillaise," see B. I. Kolonitskii, *Simvoly vlasti i bor′ba za vlast′: K izucheniiu politicheskoi kul′tury rossiiskoi revoliutsii 1917 goda* (St. Petersburg: D. Bulanin, 2001), 287–89; N. A. Soboleva, "Iz istorii otechestvennykh gosudarstvennykh gimnov," *Otechestvennaia istoriia*, no. 1 (2005): 3–21, available at http://www.hymn.ru/ paper-soboleva-200501.pdf; and S. M. Khentova, *Melodii velikogo vremeni: Marsel′eza. Internatsional* (Moscow: Muzyka, 1986), available at http://www.norma40.ru/articles/ marselyeza-v-rossii.htm.

[50] "Revoliutsiia: (Poetokhronika)," in Maiakovskii, *Polnoe sobranie sochinenii*, 1: 137.

[51] The leaflet publication is typical of 1917 in the unlikely juxtapositions surrounding its publication (which echo the unlikely juxtapositions of Kliuev's text itself): the printer (Synod), the publisher (the Artistic Commission for the Organization of Spirit), and the larger sponsoring organization (the Committee for Technical War Aid).

[52] Kliuev reprinted the poem in later collections but omitted explicit reference to the French anthem, and also, in the later publications, ended the refrain with just one call

unsurprising: clichéd images of chains sundered and oppression overcome, and an evocation of Russia's expanses through an enumeration of far-flung geographic locations that echoes a trope common in national songs the world over. But the poem gets more interesting starting in the second verse:

> Пролетела над Русью жар-птица,
> Ярый гнев зажигая в груди.
> Богородица наша Землица,
> Вольный хлеб мужику уроди.

> Сбылись думы и давние слухи—
> Пробудился народ-Святогор,
> Будет мед на домашней краюхе
> И на скатерти ярок узор.[53]

[A firebird has flown over Rus', / Igniting a raging anger in the breast. / O dear land of ours, Mother-of-God, / Bring forth free bread for the peasant. / Meditations and ancient rumors have come true—the Sviatogor-folk has awakened. There will be honey on the fat wedge of bread, / And the tablecloth's pattern is bright.]

Particularly interesting in Kliuev's poem is how insistently it grounds Russia's revolutionary present in the country's past. Folk legends (the Firebird, the sunken city of Kitezh), *byliny* (two references to the *bogatyr* Sviatogor), and folk religion (icons of the Mother-of-God and of a "peasant Savior") are mixed together with contemporary events, knowledge, and science. When compared to its acknowledged model—Lavrov's "Marseillaise," which is unequivocal in its rejection of the past ("We will renounce the old world, / And shake its dust from our feet!")[54]—Kliuev's poem seems almost polemical, welcoming the new order but insisting that it offers the fulfillment of age-old peasant utopian dreams.

Unlike the poetic response to World War I, for which there had been a more or less set patriotic narrative to subscribe to, the revolutionary events of 1917 were sensed as something categorically new and unprecedented, stoking poets' imaginations and leading them in multiple directions. This was true both of works directly inspired by revolutionary events, and of works in which the Revolution was only a background, such as Pasternak's poems in *My Sister, Life* (*Sestra moia—zhizn'*, 1922), subtitled "Summer 1917." What was

---

"to battle," unlike the five in the first publication, likely because, if not actually being sung, they risk appearing somewhat ridiculous.

[53] Nikolai Kliuev, *Krasnaia pesnia* (Petrograd: Khudozhestvennaia komissiia po organizatsii dukha, pri Komitete voenno-tekhnicheskoi pomoshchi, 1917), n.p.

[54] "Отречёмся от старого мира, / Отряхнём его прах с наших ног!"

revolutionary in Pasternak's collection had little to do with politics. While Pasternak later linked the book explicitly to concepts of revolution, saying that it "expressed everything that can be learned about a revolution of the most unprecedented and elusive things," the revolutionary transformations reflected in the book were personal ones—of personal relationships, style, and language use.[55]

The sense of possibility and freedom widely expressed in poetry of the spring and summer of 1917 continued with the October Revolution and the Bolsheviks' assumption of power. We find a huge range of interpretations, narratives, and symbols; the Revolution functioned as an empty signifier, full of potential, ready to be filled with whatever content a poet desired. It could be anything from a Futurist revolution to a revolution fulfilling the age-old prayers of the Russian peasantry. Even poets with disparate views, however, often shared an unrestrained revolutionary enthusiasm. Andrei Siniavskii and A. N. Men'shutin identify a spirit of romanticism that unites poets as different as Maiakovskii, Briusov, Esenin, Aleksei Gastev, and Vladimir T. Kirillov.[56]

As with February, not only was there no established interpretation to cramp poets' imaginations, there was also much more direct experience of the revolutionary events, as opposed to the events of the World War. The revolutions were not experienced at a distance, "over there," but in the streets of Petrograd and elsewhere, encountered directly in the daily lives of the poets. Thus Blok's famous poem *The Twelve* (*Dvenadtsat'*, completed in January 1918) was written in direct response to events unfolding outside his windows, and featured among other images, portrayed in stark black and white, a banner lauding the recently defunct Constituent Assembly and an old woman bemoaning the waste of fabric the banner represented in a period of want. In keeping with the conflicting interpretations of Russia's revolutionary events, Blok ended the poem with the surprising image of Jesus Christ, holding a flag in revolutionary red and thus suggesting—controversially—divine sanction for the bloody revolution:

Так идут державным шагом –
Позади – голодный пес,
Впереди – с кровавым флагом,
И за вьюгой невидим,
И от пули невредим,
Нежной поступью надвьюжной,

---

[55] Pasternak makes the comment in an afterword written for (but not published with) his *Okhrannaia gramota*. Boris Pasternak, *Polnoe sobranie sochinenii s prilozheniiami v odinnadtsati tomakh*, ed. E. B. Pasternak and E. V. Pasternak (Moscow: Slovo, 2004), 3: 524.

[56] A. D. Siniavskii and A. N. Men'shutin, *Poeziia pervykh let revoliutsii, 1917–1920* (Moscow: Nauka, 1964), 122–23.

Снежной россыпью жемчужной,
В белом венчике из роз –
Впереди – Исус Христос.[57]

[And so they keep a martial pace, / Behind them follows the hungry
dog, / Ahead of them – with bloody banner, / Unseen within the bliz-
zard's swirl, / Safe from any bullet's harm, / With gentle step, above the
storm, / In the scattered, pearl-like snow, / Crowned with a wreath of
roses white, / Ahead of them – goes Jesus Christ.][58]

Similarly evoking the immediacy of events, Maiakovskii's "Order to the
Army of Art" ("Prikaz po armii iskusstva," 1918) characterized the streets of
revolutionary Russia as artists' brushes and the squares as their palettes.[59]
The explosion of poetic inspiration that came with revolution was something new, but it was rooted in poets' previous experiences and orientations.
This was evident both in individual poetic responses and in the stances of
various groupings. Thus both workers and peasants, in whose name the
Soviet transformation of Russia was underway, had their participants in the
era's poetry. Proletarian poetry, represented in the revolutionary period by
figures such as Gastev, Kirillov, Mikhail P. Gerasimov, and Il'ia I. Sadof'ev,
had been a feature of the literary scene since the late 19th century. These
poets—often writing while they worked a full-time position as a metalworker, fitter, or other factory job—frequently had early ties to the Russian
Social Democratic Workers Party (either the Bolsheviks or the Mensheviks),
and many had become quite politically involved, had been involved in labor
activism, and had been sent to foreign or internal exile at some point in their
careers. Their themes centered on modern working life: the world of cities,
factories, machines, and tremendous power. Maksim Gor'kii had helped
encourage and organize proletarian writers, working during the World War
on coediting an anthology of their poetry. The untrammeled enthusiasm
and imagination of a poet like Gastev was clear from a collection such as his
Poetry of the Worker's Blow (*Poeziia rabochego udara*, 1918), which "progressed
from factory-floor documentaries to fantasies on an interplanetary scale, and
from sensitive prose renderings of the living worker to radical experiments in
machine verse."[60] With the October Revolution, proletarian writers responded
enthusiastically to the Bolshevik push for a collective identity and culture. But

---

[57] Blok, *Polnoe sobranie sochinenii*, 5: 20.

[58] Blok, *Twelve*, trans. Maria Carlson, Russia's Great War and Revolution website, http://
russiasgreatwar.org/media/culture/twelve.shtml, last updated 10 September 2012.

[59] "Улицы — наши кисти. / Площади — наши палитры" (Maiakovskii, *Polnoe
sobranie sochinenii*, 2: 15).

[60] Rolf Hellebust, *Flesh to Metal: Soviet Literature and the Alchemy of Revolution* (Ithaca,
NY: Cornell University Press, 2003), 48.

belonging to a privileged group in the new Soviet state, complete with their own organization, Proletkul't, was a mixed blessing, since measuring up to an abstract proletarian and collective culture proved difficult. As Mark Steinberg notes, in the discussions around proletarian culture, "actual proletarian voices were among the most troubled and ambivalent."[61]

Of the peasant poets, Esenin began his most productive creative years with the Revolution, moving from the blasphemous peasant paradise of "Inoniia" (1918) to a series of narrative poems about the Revolution, to, by 1919, his new stance as Imaginist and "tender hooligan." The peasant poets contributed one of the first portrayals of Lenin in poetry, found in Kliuev's poem "Lenin Has the Spirit of Kerzhenets" ("Est' v Lenine kerzhenskii dukh...," 1918), in which the poet—continuing the integration of the Revolution into peasant legend and tradition seen in "Red Song"—casts the new leader as an Old Believer hegumen. Peasant poets—Esenin, Kliuev, and Oreshin—also contributed substantially to the Scythian group and its two almanacs (one appearing in August 1917, the second in 1918). Centered around the critic R. V. Ivanov-Razumnik and a Left Socialist Revolutionary ideology that gave the peasantry a central role in Russia's revolutionary transformation, the Scythians also included Andrei Belyi and Blok. As Victor Terras writes, Scythianism, or Eurasianism, "believed to have discovered Russia's Asian roots in the past and pointed toward the menace of a new Asian invasion (literal or symbolic) in the future."[62] Although Blok's work did not appear in the two Scythian volumes, his poem "The Scythians" ("Skify"), written immediately after *The Twelve* in 1918 during the Brest-Litovsk negotiations meant to end Russia's participation in the war, is often seen as emblematic of the group's vision of the Eastern roots of Russian national identity:

Мильоны – вас. Нас – тьмы, и тьмы, и тьмы.
Попробуйте, сразитесь с нами!
Да, Скифы – мы! Да, азиаты – мы, –
С раскосыми и жадными очами![63]

---

[61] Mark D. Steinberg, *Proletarian Imagination: Self, Modernity, and the Sacred in Russia, 1910–1925* (Ithaca, NY: Cornell University Press, 2002), 103. On collectivist discourse, see Steinberg, chap. 3, "The Proletarian 'I'"; Donald Loewen, *The Most Dangerous Art: Poetry, Politics, and Autobiography after the Russian Revolution* (Lanham, MD: Lexington Books, 2008); and Siniavskii and Men'shutin, *Poeziia pervykh let*, 155ff.

[62] Victor Terras, *Poetry of the Silver Age: The Various Voices of Russian Modernism* (Dresden: Dresden University Press, 1998), 4.

[63] Blok, *Polnoe sobranie sochinenii*, 5: 77.

[You are millions. We are hordes and hordes and hordes. / Try and take us on! / Yes, we are Scythians! Yes, we are Asians— / With slanted and greedy eyes!][64]

Challenging "old-world" Europe to recognize and join in Russia's revolution, Blok concluded,

В последний раз – опомнись, старый мир!
  На братский пир труда и мира,
В последний раз – на светлый братский пир
  Сзывает варварская лира![65]

[Come to your senses for the last time, old world! / Our barbaric lyre is calling you / One final time, to a joyous brotherly feast / To a brotherly feast of labor and of peace!][66]

Of all literary groupings, the years following the Revolution belonged first and foremost to the Futurists; as Valerii Briusov wrote retrospectively in his "The Yesterday, Today, and Tomorrow of Russian Poetry" ("Vchera, segodnia i zavtra russkoi poezii," 1922): "[P]roletarian poetry is our literary 'tomorrow,' as Futurism for the period 1917–22 was our literary 'today,' and as Symbolism was our literary 'yesterday.'"[67] The first People's Commissar for Enlightenment, Lunacharskii, made a conscious decision to favor avant-garde artists in his new ministry, since, "even relatively left-wing artists would have been frightened at the time by the need to struggle with the almost age-old foundations of artistic life. In this connection, a great deal of fervor, faith and, perhaps, youthful zeal were necessary."[68] That the Futurists, adopting a consciously confrontational stance, were ready to struggle with tradition, was clear in lines such as these (from Maiakovskii's "Order No. 2 to the Army of the Arts" ["Prikaz No. 2 armii iskusstv," 1921]):

Бросьте!
Забудьте,

---

[64] Blok, "Scythians," trans. Tatiana Tulchinsky, Gwenan Wilbur, and Andrew Wachtel, in *From the Ends to the Beginning: A Bilingual Anthology of Russian Verse,* http://max.mmlc.northwestern.edu/~mdenner/Demo/texts/scythians_blok.html

[65] Blok, *Polnoe sobranie sochinenii,* 5: 80.

[66] Blok, "Scythians," trans. Tulchinsky et al.

[67] Briusov, *Sobranie sochinenii v semi tomakh,* 6: 532.

[68] "Iz literaturnogo nasledstva A. V. Lunacharskogo," *Novyi mir,* no. 9 (1966): 238. Quoted in Vahan D. Barooshian, *Russian Cubo-Futurism 1910–1930* (The Hague: Mouton, 1974), 117.

плюньте
и на рифмы,
и на арии,
и на розовый куст,
и на прочие мелехлюндии
из арсеналов искусств.[69]

[Give it up! / Forget it. / Spit / on rhymes / and arias / and the rose bush / and other such mawkishness / from the arsenal of the arts.][70]

Maiakovskii ended the poem with a summons to practitioners of the new art:

Товарищи,
дайте новое искусство —
такое,
чтобы выволочь республику из грязи.[71]

[Comrades, / give us a new form of art— / an art / that will pull the republic out of the mud.][72]

Pasternak, who in 1918–19 had links to groups ranging from the Futurists, to the Scythians, to the Imaginists, put considerable energy into prose writing in this period but also focused on revising and adding to the poem cycles that would be published in 1922 as *My Sister, Life*.[73] While consciously apolitical, Pasternak felt himself in tune with the Revolution and the new Soviet government.[74] For Marina Tsvetaeva, on the other hand, the new order was unnatural and was doing violence to Russia, as she asserted in these lines from late spring 1918:

---

[69] Maiakovskii, *Polnoe sobranie sochinenii*, 2: 87.

[70] Translated by George Reavey in Vladimir Mayakovsky, *The Bedbug and Selected Poetry*, ed. Patricia Blake (Bloomington: Indiana University Press, 1975), 147.

[71] Maiakovskii, *Polnoe sobranie sochinenii*, 2: 88.

[72] Translated by Reavey in Mayakovsky, *The Bedbug*, 149.

[73] Pasternak published several of his first postrevolutionary works in the Socialist Revolutionary organ *Znamia truda*, the literary section of which was edited by Ivanov-Razumnik. See Fleishman, *Boris Pasternak: The Poet and His Politics*, 97–98.

[74] Fleishman, *Boris Pasternak: The Poet and His Politics*, 110.

Народ обезглавлен и ждет главы.
Уж воздуху нету ни в чьей груди.[75]

[The *narod*, beheaded, awaits a head. / There's no more air in anyone's chest.]

During the years of revolution and war communism, Tsvetaeva matured as a poet and wrote a huge amount of verse, which would make up the collections *Mileposts* (*Versty*, 1921), *Craft* (*Remeslo*, 1923), *Swans' Demesne* (*Lebedinyi stan*, unpublished during her lifetime), and *Separation* (*Razluka*, 1922).

Velimir Khlebnikov, who wrote 16 epic poems and much else between 1918 and his death in 1922, traveled widely in this period despite serious illness and presented a sympathetic and nuanced picture of war-torn Russia in his writings.[76] Khlebnikov's narrative poem *Night in the Trenches* (*Noch′ v okope*, 1919) demonstrates his ability to portray the current conflict as rooted in Russia's past and its landscape. The poem opens with snatches from the nighttime musings of Red Army soldiers, talking in the presence of primordial stone statues:

Семейство каменных пустынниц
Просторы поля сторожило.
В окопе бывший пехотинец
Ругался сам с собой: Могила!

Объявилась эта тетя,
Завтра мертвых не сочтете,
Всех задушит по немножку.
Ну, сверну собачью ножку![77]

[Statues of women, stony sisterhood, / stood like sentries in the open field, / watched over stretches of flatland. / A man who was once a tsarist draftee / crouched in the trenches cursing: "Christ! / Those weird old women! Where did they come from? / Too many dead men tomorrow to count— / they'll roll us under, one by one." / "Well, one last chance to roll your own."][78]

---

[75] From the poem "Orel i arkhangel! Gospoden′ grom!…," dated "7 May 1918, the third day of Easter," in *Lebedinyi stan* (Tsvetaeva, *Sobranie sochinenii v semi tomakh*, 1: 398).

[76] Bogomolov, "Velimir Khlebnikov," 229.

[77] V. Khlebnikov, *Noch′ v okope* (n.p.: Imazhinisty, 1921), n. pag. [1]. Facsimile edition available at http://www.bibliophika.ru/book.php?book=3214.

[78] Translated by Paul Schmidt in *Collected Works of Velimir Khlebnikov*, ed. Ronald Vroon (Cambridge, MA: Harvard University Press, 1997), 3: 160. Schmidt notes that

Khlebnikov allows readers to eavesdrop on trench life in a way that simultaneously captures its quotidian and its existential aspects—something missing from Russian poetry of the World War. Throughout the poem, the age-old setting makes itself felt, including references to the Scythian Chertomlyk burial mound and "the animal face of the steppe-goddess" (*zhivotnoe litso stepnoi bogini*).[79] As Ronald Vroon notes, "This juxtaposition of contemporary and ancient reality is particularly significant in light of Khlebnikov's cyclical theory of time, transforming a political tableau into a meditation on the tragedy of historical recurrence."[80]

Other poets for whom the Civil War years were particularly productive included Akhmatova, whose poems went into *Plantain* (*Podorozhnik*, 1921) and *Anno Domini MCMXXI* (1921); Mandel'shtam, whose *Tristia* appeared in 1922; Gumilev, who, even while supporting himself by editing the poetry series for Vsemirnaia Literatura (World Literature) and translating everything from Coleridge's *Rime of the Ancient Mariner* to the epic of *Gilgamesh*, also managed to write his best original verse in these years; and the Futurist Aleksei Kruchenykh, who produced several dozen short books and manuscripts in the Civil War years.[81]

The literary profusion of these years is particularly remarkable given the difficulty of daily life under war communism. Mandel'shtam was arrested first by the Reds, then by the Whites; Tsvetaeva experienced privations so dire that she placed her daughters in an orphanage, where one died. Publishing was very difficult.[82] Writers were affected by moves, separation, and—increasingly—emigration. Nevertheless, most poets, unlike the majority of their fellow Russians, were cosmopolitan, mobile, and well-connected, able to move to the Crimea or Prague or Berlin and to continue to find audiences for their work. And as long as the Soviet state was focused first and foremost on its survival, writers had considerable artistic freedom. As Robert Maguire explains, during war communism, "the Party consistently refused to articulate an official policy toward literature, in other words, to demand or sanction an official way of writing, and it also refused to allow any of the numerous literary groups to speak in its name. Diversity and competition were encouraged.... [W]riters

---

some of his translations, as here, are "very free—variations, if you will, on the theme of the original" (viii).

[79] This image occurs eight lines from the end of the poem.

[80] *Collected Works of Velimir Khlebnikov*, 3: 254.

[81] Denis Akhapkin, "Aleksei Eliseevich Kruchenykh," in *Russian Writers of the Silver Age*, 244.

[82] "By 1921, only 66 journals were coming out in Moscow—a decline of 85 per cent from 1918—and a mere 116 in all of Russia. The production of books followed a similar curve: from over 26,000 titles in 1913, it declined to 4,500 between 1920 and 1921." Robert A. Maguire, *Red Virgin Soil: Soviet Literature in the 1920s* (Ithaca, NY: Cornell University Press, 1987), 6–7.

were expected to be more or less sympathetic to the new order of things, but beyond making openly counterrevolutionary statements, they could write pretty much what and how they wished."[83]

In some crucial ways, the new state helped struggling writers. As conditions worsened, official organizations arose in response, such as Obshchestvo vzaimopomoshchi literatorov i uchenykh (Writers' and Scholars' Mutual Aid Society), Dom literatorov (Writers' House), Dom iskusstv (House of the Arts), and Dom uchenykh (Scholars' House). There was a direct relationship between aid organizations and publishing, as the organizations published their own newspapers and journals, while publishers like Vsemirnaia Literatura and Gosizdat, the new state publishing house, had a philanthropic as well as a commercial aim; the latter "had been set up specially to provide employment for penurious intellectuals, as translators, editors, and copyreaders."[84] Central to such initiatives was Maksim Gor'kii, who created or contributed to numerous organizations through a combination of an assiduous work ethic, direct access to Lenin and other key figures, and a steadfast desire to help fellow writers.[85]

As a huge Russian diaspora established itself abroad, the boundaries between émigré and Soviet life were sometimes fluid, as numerous writers spent considerable time abroad without emigrating (Pasternak and Belyi are two examples). While the intellectual life of the emigration and Soviet Russia were closely tied, there was also a strong sense of rivalry, as it became a priority of both Soviet writers and émigrés to assert their intellectual weight and their right to claim the heritage of Russian literature. Both the Soviet publishing industry and the émigrés pushed to overcome the difficult economics of publishing in the early 1920s and start up new "thick" journals in the 19th-century tradition. Within a year of each other *Contemporary Annals* (*Sovremennye zapiski*) started in Paris (1920) and the first issue of *Red Virgin Soil* (*Krasnaia nov'*) appeared in Soviet Russia (1921). But for their literary sections these journals had markedly different resources to draw on. While the émigrés included a crowd of authors well-known to readers—Merezhkovskii and Gippius, Viacheslav Ivanov, Bal'mont, Igor' Severianin, and many more—Aleksandr Voronskii's *Red Virgin Soil* was left scrambling for talent, and the literature section of the first issue was "filled with unfamiliar names and, with one exception, seemed dedicated to the service of mediocrity."[86] *Red Virgin Soil* made a virtue of necessity, however, giving wide exposure and a prominent backdrop to new literary talent and leading many to proclaim a rebirth of

---

[83] Robert Maguire, "Introduction," in *Russian Literature of the Twenties: An Anthology*, ed. Carl R. Proffer et al. (Ann Arbor: Ardis, 1987), ix.

[84] Maguire, *Red Virgin Soil*, 3–4.

[85] On Gor'kii's contributions, see Barry P. Scherr, "Maksim Gor'ky (Aleksei Maksimovich Peshkov)," in *Russian Writers of the Silver Age*, 162–63.

[86] Maguire, *Red Virgin Soil*, 10.

literature in Soviet Russia, whereas a problem for *Contemporary Annals* and most other émigré publications for much of the 1920s was their tendency to feature primarily "older" writers who had established a reputation before leaving Russia.[87] As John Glad writes about the decline in energy in émigré publishing efforts, "Although the appearance abroad of so many prominent writers in the early post-revolutionary years created an exhilarating new environment, in time stagnation began to replace excitement."[88]

Several milestones in the early 1920s stood out for contemporaries as marking the passing of a generation. In mid-October of 1921 Gor'kii went abroad, exhausted and discouraged. Two months earlier, the Cheka had arrested Gumilev on suspicion of participation in a monarchist conspiracy. He was condemned to death and shot by the end of that month. The émigré writer Nina Berberova had spent time with Gumilev before his arrest and recalled in her memoirs how she visited the Writers' House in Petrograd several days later hoping to find out more about his fate. What she learned instead was that Blok had died. "A feeling of sudden and sharp orphanhood, which I never again experienced, seized me. The end is near.... We will remain alone... The end is coming. We are lost... Tears spurted out of my eyes," she wrote.[89] At Blok's funeral, attended by a number of leading poets, Berberova had the impression, she later wrote, that Blok's death marked the end of an era: "Probably there was not a man in this crowd who did not think—if only for a moment—that not only Blok had died, but that this city was dying with him, that its special power over people was coming to an end, that a historical period was closing, that a cycle of Russian destinies was being completed, that an epoch was stopping to turn and rush off to other predicaments."[90]

Berberova's impressions echoed those expressed by Roman Jakobson in 1931. Looking back over a decade marked not only by the deaths of Gumilev and Blok but by Khlebnikov's death "amid cruel privations and under circumstances of inhuman suffering" (1922) and the later suicides of Esenin (1925) and Maiakovskii (1930), Jakobson wrote, "And so it happened that during the third decade of this century, those who inspired a generation perished between the ages of thirty and forty, and each one of them shared a sense of doom so vivid and sustained that it became unbearable."[91]

In his famous poem "Born in the close, unechoing years..." ("Rozhdennye v goda glukhie..."), begun in 1913 but finished in September of 1914, Blok

---

[87] Maguire, *Red Virgin Soil*, 11–12; John Glad, *Russia Abroad: Writers, History, Politics* (Tenafly, NJ: Hermitage; Washington, DC: Birchbark Press, 1999), 250.

[88] Glad, *Russia Abroad*, 250.

[89] Nina Berberova, *The Italics Are Mine*, trans. Philippe Radley (New York: Harcourt, Brace & World, 1969), 125.

[90] Ibid, 128.

[91] Brown, *Major Soviet Writers*, 8.

called his generation "the children of Russia's frightful years" and soberly confronted the toll those years, up to the present ones, had taken:[92]

Есть немота — то гул набата
Заставил заградить уста.
В сердцах, восторженных когда-то,
Есть роковая пустота.

И пусть над нашим смертным ложем
Взовьется с криком воронье, —
Те, кто достойней, Боже, Боже,
Да узрят Царствие Твое![93]

[If we are dumb, it is the tocsin / Has taught us how to hold our peace. / In hearts, once eagerly exalted, / There is a fateful emptiness. / Then let above our deathbed hover / The crows—a raucous, swirling scum. / They who are worthier—Father, Father, / May they behold Thy Kingdom come.][94]

Like Blok, many of his contemporaries would again go through both exhilaration and despair during the years of war, revolution, and civil strife. Some, like Berberova, Jakobson, and Akhmatova, would survive and document this period retrospectively. But, as the survivors would observe and mourn, for many those years were ultimately fatal.

---

[92] While there were certainly generational differences in poets' responses to war and revolution, Blok speaks here more broadly of his contemporaries. The authoritative voice among poets of the period, he also was one of the most consistent in his welcoming of the new era, even as he knew it would destroy him. At the same time, among younger poets, the revolutionary enthusiasm of the Futurists was countered by the doubts of Tsvetaeva and many others. As Sidney Monas notes, "Whatever the relationship of individual artists to the political upheaval of 1917–1921, the art of the period as art tended to be radical, innovative, and extreme and therefore in a real sense revolutionary" (Monas, "Preface," in *Selected Works of Nikolai S. Gumilev*, x).

[93] Blok, *Polnoe sobranie sochinenii*, 3: 187.

[94] Translated by Avril Pyman in her *The Life of Aleksandr Blok*, 2: 225.

Russian Theater and the Crisis of War and Revolution, 1914–22

Murray Frame

Most histories of Russian theater portray the 1917 Revolution as a major turning point, and the reasons for this historiographical consensus are not difficult to fathom: the Revolution radically altered the political context in which all the arts functioned, particularly after the October Revolution. For some observers, the events of 1917 inaugurated a period of unprecedented creative achievement and international renown for the Russian stage, whilst for others it led to debilitating state regulation and the eclipse of artistic freedom.[1] Divergent assessments like these are conditioned partly by the perspectives of individual historians, and inevitably they conceal a more complex reality. Both are underpinned, however, by a recognition that the political context in which the theater functioned after 1917 was tangibly different, and no amount of emphasis on continuities across the revolutionary divide can eliminate that salient fact. In this sense, the year 1917 is hardly an arbitrary chronological marker in theater history; but nor is it an entirely adequate one

---

For helpful comments on an earlier draft of this chapter, I am grateful to Boris Kolonitskii, Adele Lindenmeyr, and Steve Marks, and to the participants in the Clemson Conference on Russian Culture during the First World War and Revolution, 1914–1922 (Clemson University, South Carolina, October 2011). The Carnegie Trust for the Universities of Scotland generously supported the research.

[1] Soviet theater historians naturally depicted the October Revolution as a positive event for the stage and its development. Among the myriad studies, see, for example, Iu. A. Dmitriev and G. A. Khaichenko, *Istoriia russkogo i sovetskogo dramaticheskogo teatra* (Moscow: Prosveshchenie, 1986); N. G. Zograf et al., eds., *Ocherki istorii russkogo sovetskogo dramaticheskogo teatra v trekh tomakh*, 1 (Moscow: Izd-vo Akademii nauk SSSR, 1954); D. I. Zolotnitskii, *Akademicheskie teatry na putiakh Oktiabria* (Leningrad: Iskusstvo, 1982); Konstantin Rudnitsky, *Russian and Soviet Theatre, 1905–1932*, trans. Roxane Permar (London: Thames and Hudson Ltd., 1988). Several non-Soviet writers have also emphasized the creative vitality of Russian theater during the decade after 1917. An early example is Huntly Carter, *The New Spirit in the Russian Theatre 1917–1928* (New York: Brentano's, 1929). See also Robert Leach, *Revolutionary Theatre* (London: Routledge, 1994). For a more hostile account, see Nikolai A. Gorchakov, *The Theater in Soviet Russia*, trans. Edgar Lehrman (New York: Columbia University Press, 1957).

Russian Culture in War and Revolution, 1914–22, Book 1: Popular Culture, the Arts, and Institutions. Murray Frame, Boris Kolonitskii, Steven G. Marks, and Melissa K. Stockdale, eds. Bloomington, IN: Slavica Publishers, 2014, 261–82.

for understanding what happened in the theatrical realm during the early years of Soviet power, not least because several notable developments that occurred after 1917 had deep roots in the prerevolutionary period.

Nor is it any more satisfactory to begin a study of Russian theater in 1914. The outbreak of the Great War is widely regarded as a seminal moment in modern history, marking a boundary between distinct eras, but the meaningful dates in cultural history rarely coincide neatly with major political or military landmarks. This is not to suggest that the war exerted little influence upon culture—clearly it did—but not all aspects of culture experienced prominent turning points or iconic moments during the conflict. In the case of Russian theater it could be argued that—with the key exception of the altered political context after 1917—relatively little happened between 1914 and 1922 that had not already started to take shape from the early years of the 20th century. This is particularly evident with regard to the artistic history of the theater. Despite some momentary fusion of avant-garde experimentation and political radicalism after the October Revolution that created the impression of a sudden transformation, the crisis of war and revolution did not alter fundamentally the artistic interests of the time, which built upon longer-term creative trajectories. In artistic terms, therefore, 1914–22 is an unnatural periodization for the theater.

Nevertheless—and bearing in mind these introductory caveats—insofar as historians regard the years from 1914 to 1922 as a discrete period of extended crisis in Russia, it seems reasonable to ask the question: how did that crisis affect the theater? This chapter will suggest that, if we view the eight-year period of upheaval as a unified whole, two particular themes stand out. First of all, professional and organizational matters were a central concern for the theater industry. This was manifested in the efforts of performers and associated personnel to protect their interests during the war, and in the state's more interventionist approach to entertainment culture after 1917. Secondly, the period was characterized by an intensification of theatrical "democratization," broadly defined as making the stage more accessible to ordinary workers and peasants in order to spread enlightenment and raise the "cultural level" of the population. From 1914, advocates of people's theater were optimistic that the war would provide an opportunity to advance their aims, and from 1917 those aims blended almost seamlessly with the concept of proletarian theater. Underlying both of these themes—organization and democratization—was the notion that theater was not simply an idle amusement but a vital public force. Indeed, the Bolshevik regime's interest in the utility of the stage drew upon a long-standing conviction among Russian cultural activists that theater had the power to influence the masses if carefully guided and adequately resourced. In that sense too, 1917 served to accelerate trends that had been gathering pace for some years.

The following discussion is divided chronologically by 1917 simply because the Revolution's impact on theater was undeniably significant. Yet the sense of sudden rupture should not be exaggerated, not least because many aspects of theatrical life remained largely impervious to the political maelstrom. In the repertoire, for instance, despite some bold revolutionary experiments, there was a remarkable degree of continuity. Oliver Sayler, an American drama critic who visited Russia during the winter of 1917–18, remarked upon the ostensible normality of the theater: "On it went, undisturbed, through pillage and murder and anarchy."[2] Nor should it be assumed that all theater people were consumed by questions of organization and democratization. For most, the routines of rehearsal and performance were punctured only by the gradual encroachment of food and fuel shortages; otherwise the crisis of 1914–22 affected their creative work less directly than might be imagined. The chapter's focus on the themes of organization and democratization is therefore intended to highlight the distinctive ways in which the crisis of war and revolution affected the theater industry, rather than to draw a comprehensive picture of theatrical life. For this reason artistic matters—notably the experimental productions of Vsevolod Meierkhol'd, arguably the greatest achievements of Russian theater during these years—will remain largely in the background, although the chapter will conclude with some brief consideration of the repertoire.

Russian Theater and the Great War

In 1914 Russia possessed a rich and varied theatrical landscape. Its theaters can be classified into four types. First, there were the state-subsidized Imperial Theaters in the capitals: three in St. Petersburg (the Aleksandrinskii, the Mariinskii, and the Mikhailovskii) and two in Moscow (the Malyi and the Bolshoi). Many of the empire's most renowned performing artists, such as Mariia Ermolova, Fedor Shaliapin, and Vatslav Nizhinskii, were associated at one time or another with these institutions, attracted by their prestige and resources. Secondly, there were artistically accomplished private commercial theaters, often backed by wealthy individuals, including the Moscow Art Theater and the Korsh Theater. Thirdly, there were people's theaters (*narodnye teatry*), intended to provide rational recreation for the urban masses and often run by temperance societies or factory owners. Finally, there was an array of smaller club theatricals, including estrada (a cross between nightclub and music hall) and cabaret venues, such as the Crooked Mirror in St. Petersburg and the Bat in Moscow.[3] It is difficult to quantify the number of theaters with

---

[2] Oliver M. Sayler, *The Russian Theatre* (New York: Brentano's, 1922), 6.

[3] On the Imperial Theaters, see Murray Frame, *The St. Petersburg Imperial Theaters: Stage and State in Revolutionary Russia, 1900–1920* (Jefferson, NC: McFarland, 2000). For a discussion of the leading private commercial theaters, see E. Ia. Dubnova, "Chastnye teatry Moskvy i Peterburga," in *Russkaia khudozhestvennaia kul'tura kontsa XIX–nachala XX veka (1908–1917)*, bk. 3, *Zrelishchnye iskusstva, muzyka*, ed. A. D. Alekseev et al. (Moscow: Nauka, 1977). On people's theater, see G. A. Khaichenko, *Russkii narodnyi*

any accuracy, partly because many were short-lived. It has been estimated that by 1900, in addition to the five Imperial Theaters, St. Petersburg and Moscow were home to 14 commercial stages plus 21 "summer enterprises" with theatrical performances. Elsewhere the empire possessed 2,134 entertainment venues, including 216 theaters, 32 concert halls, 42 circuses, and hundreds of clubs and amateur societies. By 1904 there were 150 people's theaters, and by 1909 they had been joined by 420 government-subsidized temperance theaters.[4] We can be certain, therefore, that Russia possessed an extensive network of theatrical venues in 1914, probably employing somewhere in the region of 30,000 people.

When war broke out most theater people—broadly defined to include actors, *régisseurs*, designers, and critics—argued that the Russian stage should continue to function normally. One theater journalist, Ia. L. Rosenstein ("L'vov"), summarized the rationale for normality: "The theater must help us to forget the nightmare of war. The theater must give us tears and laughter."[5] In this way, it would serve a useful purpose on the home front. In a reflection of that sentiment, the standard repertoire remained largely unchanged. Patriotism was expressed in renditions of the national anthem before performances and in the banishment of German works from the repertoire, but there were relatively few attempts to stage explicitly patriotic works. The small number produced, such as Leonid Andreev's *King, Law and Freedom* (about the German invasion of Belgium), were poorly received and soon dropped from playbills, especially by the summer of 1915. With the exception of such productions that related "to the moment," audience numbers remained buoyant.[6] This did not mean that theater people were indifferent to the war, but they tended to express their patriotism by engaging in charity work, notably by helping to care for injured soldiers, and by arranging special performances to raise war

---

teatr kontsa XIX–nachala XX veka (Moscow: Nauka, 1975); E. Anthony Swift, *Popular Theater and Society in Tsarist Russia* (Berkeley: University of California Press, 2002); Gary Thurston, *The Popular Theatre Movement in Russia, 1862–1919* (Evanston, IL: Northwestern University Press, 1998). On estrada and cabaret, see Louise McReynolds, *Russia at Play: Leisure Activities at the End of the Tsarist Era* (Ithaca, NY: Cornell University Press, 2003), chaps. 6 and 7, and H. B. Segel, *Turn-of-the-Century Cabaret* (New York: Columbia University Press, 1987), chap. 6.

[4] *Rossiiskii gosudarstvennyi arkhiv literatury i iskusstva* (RGALI) f. 641, op. 1, ed. khr. 2587 (list of theaters in Russia); V. R. Leikina-Svirskaia, *Russkaia intelligentsia v 1900–1917 godakh* (Moscow: Mysl', 1981), 186; T. P. Korzhikhina, *Izvol'te byt' blagonadezhny!* (Moscow: Rossiiskii gosudarstvennyi gumanitarnyi universitet, 1997), 30; Swift, *Popular Theater*, 69; Thurston, *Popular Theatre Movement*, 125; Gary Thurston, "The Impact of Russian Popular Theatre, 1886–1915," *Journal of Modern History* 55, 2 (1983): 238.

[5] *Rampa i zhizn'*, 12 October 1914, 2.

[6] *Apollon*, nos. 4-5 (1915): 109; E. G. Kholodov et al., eds., *Istoriia russkogo dramaticheskogo teatra* (Moscow: Iskusstvo, 1987), 7: 398.

funds. Prominent among these were the "patriotic evenings" organized by the Mariinskii soprano Mariia Dolina at the Cinizelli Circus in Petrograd, concerts which included renditions of the national anthem and readings of telegrams from the front.[7] Such performances, however, had largely—if not entirely—disappeared by the summer of 1915 and the repertoire was characterized by a fundamental continuity.

The theater was affected more directly by material rather than artistic pressures during the war. The professional interests of theater people were represented formally by the Russian Theater Society (Russkoe teatral'noe obshchestvo, or RTO), founded in 1894 to promote the development of theater throughout the empire. One of the society's most important functions was to provide material assistance for actors, whose vocation entailed a great deal of economic uncertainty. The RTO provided financial assistance to individual actors and troupes, organized insurance for sick and elderly performers, and endeavored to put the relationship between impresarios and troupes on a quasi-legal footing, amongst many other things.[8] From the start of the Great War, the RTO's routine activity intensified. It began to receive a larger number of requests than usual for financial assistance as mobilization disrupted life in the western provinces.[9] The growing demands placed upon the society led by November 1915 to a budget deficit of 40,000 rubles, and in order to raise more funds it organized a "Day of the Russian Actor" on 22 November 1916. Performances and concerts were held all across Russia, and all the proceeds—120,000 rubles—were donated to the RTO.[10] In this way the society was able to sustain its core activity at that time.

Other wartime pressures tested the RTO's capacity to defend the theater industry's interests, and they led to a more urgent articulation of what was regarded as the public value of the theatrical arts. Two particular developments strained the industry's resources. The first was a new tax on tickets for entertainments, including theatrical performances, introduced at the beginning of February 1916 and amounting to an average of 30 per cent of gross box-office revenues.[11] The RTO petitioned the government for a reduction in the rate of the new tax, arguing that it particularly threatened people's theaters and other enterprises accessible to lower-income audiences. The RTO explained that the stage was prepared to make appropriate wartime sacrifices

---

[7] *Novoe vremia*, 25 August (7 September) 1914, 5; ibid., 26 August (8 September) 1914: 6. For some other examples, see Frame, *St. Petersburg Imperial Theatres*, 138–40.

[8] Further on the RTO, see Murray Frame, "Commercial Theatre and Professionalization in Late Imperial Russia," *Historical Journal* 48, 4 (2005): 1025-53.

[9] *Rampa i zhizn'*, 3 August 1914, 5.

[10] *Teatral'naia gazeta*, 29 November 1915, 3; *Rampa i zhizn'*, 27 November 1916, 5–6; *Teatr i iskusstvo*, 4 December 1916, 988; *Rampa i zhizn'*, 19 February 1917, 4.

[11] *Rampa i zhizn'*, 17 January 1916, 10.

but that the new tax was "disproportionate" and should not be allowed to undermine the theater's good work: "The entire future of our country depends upon the development of cultural and educational forces. In the history of Russian self-consciousness the Russian theater has played a considerable role; it shall play an even greater role in the future."[12] Remarkably, in response to persistent lobbying by the RTO, the Finance Ministry agreed in July 1916 to reduce the tax rate on tickets, citing what it had been persuaded was the "important cultural significance for the population, in particular the growing generation, of theatrical shows."[13]

The second development that threatened to drain resources from the theater industry was conscription. Although precise figures are unavailable, large numbers of theater people were drafted during the war, as attested by the theatrical press, which reported on call-ups and often featured photographs of artists in their military garb. One side effect was that, by the end of 1915, unemployment among actors had all but vanished, although this meant that the stage was on the verge of a critical shortage of qualified personnel. A new military levy of theater workers in 1916—aimed at more experienced stage professionals because younger ones had already been conscripted—provoked criticism from a number of quarters. The critic Aleksandr Pavlov feared that the theater would be ruined by the absence of its "main talents" and called for wider recognition of its public role: "Theater is not an amusement and not for fun.... Theater is a school, a temple of art, whence we derive the spiritual strength to serve humanity," something all the more necessary during the European conflagration. Actors were not afraid of the front, Pavlov insisted, but they were also necessary at the rear.[14] In October 1916 the RTO petitioned the Ministry of Internal Affairs and the General Staff for an exemption from conscription for theater people. In the view of one leading theatrical journal, this would be a "necessity" not a "privilege" because "the cultural business of theater has its great mission in the preservation of the living reserves of mental courage."[15] These efforts failed to persuade the authorities that theater was essential for the defense of the motherland. An exception was made, however, for the Imperial Theaters: whilst large numbers of their staff had been drafted since the start of the conflict, they received assurances that personnel levels would remain sufficiently high to enable them to continue working.[16]

---

[12] *Rampa i zhizn'*, 10 January 1916, 11; *Teatr i iskusstvo*, 20 March 1916, 237–38.

[13] *Rampa i zhizn'*, 24 July 1916, 3; G. G. Dadamian, *Teatr v kul'turnoi zhizni Rossii (1914–1917)* (Moscow: Izd-vo Rossiiskoi Akademii teatral'nogo iskusstva OOO "Dar-Ekspo," 2000), 37–38.

[14] *Rampa i zhizn'*, 14 August 1916, 3–4.

[15] *Teatr i iskusstvo*, 16 October 1916, 839.

[16] *Rampa i zhizn'*, 11 December 1916, 5.

In these ways a discourse about the public value of the stage, which had its longer-term roots in the 18th century, was invoked in an effort to protect the basic professional interests of theater people from wartime demands.[17] The RTO in this respect enjoyed only modest success, and a certain level of dissatisfaction with the society contributed to the formation of an alternative organization to support theater people. Established on the initiative of the impresario A. A. Narovskii during spring 1915, the new association became known as Theatrical Mutual Aid (Teatral'naia krugovaia poruka). Its guiding principle was mutual obligation amongst actors, and its practical work would include the provision of loans, pensions, an orphanage, a hospital, and organizational support for theatrical enterprises.[18] The initiative was further testimony to the organizational energy that characterized the theater industry during the war as it confronted material challenges.[19]

The second broad feature that characterized Russian theater from 1914 to 1922 was "democratization." The term was used by contemporaries to describe the interrelated phenomena of audience expansion and greater accessibility of the stage to ordinary people, a process that had developed steadily since the late 19th century, particularly as a result of the people's theater movement. After 1914, however, theatrical democratization entered a new phase. The huge population displacements that transferred large numbers of people to the empire's political and cultural centers created a much broader audience base for the entertainment industry. The dramatist, *régisseur*, and critic Aleksandr Kugel' was struck by the changing nature of the audience, as "new classes of patrons" were ushered in by "the process of inevitable democratization which is accompanying the war."[20] Moreover, the introduction of temperance legislation at the start of the conflict was regarded as a golden opportunity by advocates of people's theater, because didactic entertainment might fill the leisure vacuum created by restrictions on alcohol sales.[21] The general climate of mobilization further emboldened people's theater activists to pursue their ambitions with greater energy.

Efforts to advance people's theater were most evident in a Congress of People's Theater Activists held in Moscow during late 1915 and early 1916. The majority of the 373 delegates were not theater personnel as such, but rather

---

[17] On the longer-term development of the notion of theater's public value in Russia, see Murray Frame, *School for Citizens: Theatre and Civil Society in Imperial Russia* (New Haven: Yale University Press, 2006).

[18] *Teatral'naia gazeta*, 29 November 1915, 3–4.

[19] For a more detailed discussion of these developments, see Murray Frame, "Cultural Mobilization: Russian Theatre and the First World War, 1914–1917," *Slavonic and East European Review* 90, 2 (2012): 288–322.

[20] *Teatr i iskusstvo*, 30 August 1915, 649–51.

[21] Thurston, *Popular Theatre Movement*, 253–54.

representatives of the provincial intelligentsia and cooperative movement who regarded theater as a means of promoting literacy and improving the morals of ordinary people.[22] The central issue at the congress was whether the repertoire of the people's theater should have an "all-national" or "class" character, a debate that reflected rival conceptions of the movement's fundamental purpose. The liberal intelligentsia regarded such theaters as a means to bring "high culture" to the masses and thereby to help bridge the gulf that separated the people from the privileged classes. It was in this sense that theater would be "democratized." Radical delegates, by contrast, argued that the repertoire should reflect the political interests of the people, with an emphasis not only on aesthetics but on ideological content. The final congress resolutions reflected a measure of compromise between these two positions. It was agreed that, in principle, the main criteria for determining a play's suitability for the people's stage should be "richness of ideological content and artistic merit."[23]

Whilst the people's theater movement had been active for several decades and had achieved a great deal, the general climate of mobilization from 1914 appears to have inspired its activists, who sensed a new opportunity to advance their agenda. Perhaps the clearest expression of this was the articulation of political demands at the congress, which explicitly linked the aims of theater activists to a perceived need for wider reform. Congress resolutions called not only for an end to theatrical censorship, which had survived the 1905 Revolution and was deemed contrary to the principles of "freedom of speech and artistic creativity." They also demanded greater decentralization of the zemstva and municipal administrative system, and the full implementation of freedoms promised in the October Manifesto of 1905, which would enable them to extend the network of people's theaters more widely.[24] These aspirations were long-standing—they echoed similar demands made by theater people during the 1905 Revolution[25]—but their ardent reiteration during the war pointed to a renewed expectation of reform.

During 1916, expectations of a fundamental reorganization of Russia's theaters gathered pace. Two alternative models for change appear to have circulated. The first one emphasized the role of the zemstva and the importance of local initiative. For example, Nikolai N. Bogoliubov, an opera *régisseur* and member of the RTO's governing council, argued that after the war, in order to ensure that theater is a "stimulus of national development, a realm where the spirit of the people participates in the lofty humanitarian achievements

---

[22] *Rampa i zhizn'*, 3 January 1916, 4; *Teatr i iskusstvo*, 3 January 1916, 16–18.

[23] Swift, *Popular Theater*, 201–02; *Teatr i iskusstvo*, 3 January 1916, 19–20; *Rampa i zhizn'*, 3 January 1916, 3–4; *Teatr i iskusstvo*, 10 January 1916, 41. For further discussion of the congress, see Thurston, *Popular Theatre Movement*, 258–64.

[24] *Teatr i iskusstvo*, 10 January 1916, 40–41; *Rampa i zhizn'*, 10 January 1916, 3–5.

[25] See Frame, *School for Citizens*, 189–92.

of culture ... a radical reorganization of theater affairs is imperative." This should take the form, he suggested, of the "municipalization of theatrical enterprises," in other words, the creation of self-governing town theaters at the initiative of public bodies like the zemstva.[26] The other model envisaged a greater role for the state. In September 1916 the theatrical press reported on unattributed plans to create an organization of "All-Russian State [*kazennyi*] Theaters." According to the plan new drama, opera, and ballet theaters would be created in all the major towns and cities of Russia, including the capitals, and their purpose would be "to cultivate all branches of contemporary stage art," including people's theater. The new state theaters would be subordinate to a central organ in Petrograd, but crucially this would not be the Imperial Court Ministry, which already had responsibility for the Imperial Theaters.[27] In this way the plan embraced a role for the state and its resources in the future development of theater, whilst clearly attempting to circumvent what many regarded as the restrictive traditions of the existing state theaters.

Russian Theater and the Revolution, 1917–22

The Revolution ensured that issues of organization and democratization continued to preoccupy the theater industry between 1917 and 1922. The major organizational question was the relationship between theater and state, now open, like most spheres of politics, society, and culture, to redefinition and readjustment. This was manifested under the Provisional Government in two ways. First of all, preliminary censorship for all stage productions was abolished. This had been a long-standing aim of the cultural intelligentsia, and it was a key reason why the February Revolution was welcomed by most theater people. It created a triumphant sense of artistic freedom, and plays that the tsarist authorities had banned or abridged, such as Dmitrii Merezhkovskii's *Paul I* and A. K. Tolstoi's *Death of Ivan the Terrible*, were staged in full for the first time.[28] Secondly, the Provisional Government moved quickly to confirm the status of the Imperial Theaters in the new state structure. Since the 18th century these prestigious, largely conservative institutions had been financed by the government and managed directly by court officials, most of whom possessed little practical experience of the stage.[29] During the 1905 Revolution

---

[26] *Iskusstvo i zhizn´*, no. 4 (1916): 8–10.

[27] *Teatr i iskusstvo*, 25 September 1916, 790. It is not clear where this plan emanated from, or how advanced it was by September 1916. It may well have been a rumor, but one that nevertheless expressed a strand of thinking in theatrical circles.

[28] Gorchakov, *Theater in Soviet Russia*, 100.

[29] The last director of the Imperial Theaters, Vladimir A. Teliakovskii, for instance, had served as an officer in the Horse Guards regiment. Teliakovskii was "director" (*direktor*) in the sense of manager, not artistic director (*régisseur*). See Frame, *St. Petersburg Imperial Theaters*, 28–30, 44-64.

some Imperial Theater artists had endeavored to assert institutional autonomy from the authorities—in terms of recruitment of personnel, selection of the repertoire, and the allocation of performance parts—but without success. The Provisional Government retained the Imperial Theaters as state-sponsored institutions, but it renamed them State Theaters and granted them full autonomy over artistic affairs. General management would be exercised by the government's chief representative of State Theaters, the Kadet and professor of the history of literature Fedor D. Batiushkov. This situation suited the theaters' personnel because it meant that artistic freedom was accompanied by a guarantee of resources, including salaries and pensions, and it partly explains why the State Theaters adapted quickly to the new political circumstances. Their symbolic paraphernalia was transformed in order to express their support for the Revolution—the gilded double-headed eagles in the auditoria, for instance, were either removed or draped in red cloth, and gala performances were staged in honor of the Provisional Government, including a special performance of Gogol''s satire on tsarist local government, *The Government Inspector*, at the Aleksandrinskii on 9 April.[30]

In contrast to the Provisional Government, the Bolshevik regime pursued a cultural policy that ultimately entailed the subjugation of all theaters to the state, not only the former Imperial stages. This process was gradual and *ad hoc* rather than sudden and systematic, and it emanated from a complex and fundamentally pluralistic approach to Russia's theatrical heritage. Two broad positions on theater coexisted within Bolshevik circles, reflecting the wider debate about the prerevolutionary cultural heritage. The first position argued for the complete destruction of "bourgeois" culture and its replacement by a new "proletarian" one. The second advocated a pragmatic assimilation of the finest artistic achievements of prerevolutionary culture into the new society. Lunacharskii, who as head of Narkompros had overall responsibility for theater, carefully balanced these competing tendencies, promoting the construction of a new proletarian theater whilst protecting the traditional stage—notably the State Theaters—from the designs of the "theatrical left." His reasoning was simple: "I believe that well-produced drama and opera performances in the best theaters, created by old Russia, are a hugely important element in the work of creating a new theater...."[31] Bolshevik policy towards the theater during the early months and years of Soviet power was shaped consistently by this concern to synthesize artistic tradition and radicalism.

The October Revolution was met initially by resistance from much of the theatrical world. On 27 October the Petrograd Military-Revolutionary Committee appointed Mikhail P. Murav'ev—a former *régisseur* at the Suvorin

---

[30] Frame, *St. Petersburg Imperial Theaters*, 140–52; Meriel Buchanan, *The Dissolution of an Empire* (London: John Murray, 1932), 201–02.

[31] A. V. Lunacharskii, *Sobranie sochinenii, 3: Dorevoliutsionnyi teatr, sovetskii teatr: Stat'i, doklady, rechi, retsenzii (1904–1933)* (Moscow: Khudozhestvennaia literatura, 1964), 93.

Theater in Petrograd—as Commissar for State and Private Theaters, signaling an early intention to bring all theaters under the purview of the new regime. The State Theaters briefly suspended performances in protest at this attempt to replace Batiushkov, still regarded as their legitimate governmental overseer. More fundamentally, the State Theaters already suspected that the Bolshevik regime would erode their autonomy. In early December 1917 the Aleksandrinskii troupe declared that it was apolitical and that a "change of government cannot serve as an occasion for changing the autonomous constitution [of the theater]."[32] Batiushkov echoed that sentiment, claiming that "the artists and the majority of workers in the State Theaters are activated by a feeling of complete solidarity in defense of the independence of art from political parties" and that the use of "force and arbitrariness" was contrary to the spirit of the February Revolution.[33] Lunacharskii responded by dismissing Batiushkov for his "boycott" of the new authorities, clearly unimpressed by his defense of artistic autonomy from political interference. For the Narkom, Batiushkov's appointment by the Provisional Government constituted "political interference" and could hardly be considered a "defense of autonomy." "Whose Chief Representative are you?" asked Lunacharskii. "Kerenskii's government? But that does not exist. Of the new government? But you do not recognize it."[34]

At the same time Lunacharskii sought to reassure the State Theaters that their newfound liberties would not be compromised. In an address to their Petrograd employees he insisted that "the shameful times when you were like servants at the tsar's court are gone forever. You are free citizens, free artists, and no one will encroach upon that freedom." There was a significant caveat, however, that implied a new ideological role for the stage: "The laboring masses cannot support the State Theaters unless it is certain they exist not for the amusement of landowners, but for the satisfaction of the great cultural requirements of the laboring population."[35] This encapsulated Lunacharskii's approach to the traditional theaters—they should be protected by the Revolution, not abolished, but in return for continued subsidies they must serve the interests of the new authorities. In the meantime they would be administered by a Theater Soviet, established in early January 1918, comprising representatives from different theatrical constituencies—actors, singers, dancers, technical personnel, etc.—with broad autonomy.[36] This

---

[32] Quoted in Frame, *St. Petersburg Imperial Theaters*, 160.

[33] V. D. Zel'dovich, "Pervye meropriiatiia Narkomprosa po upravleniiu teatrami," *Istoricheskii arkhiv*, no. 1 (1959): 53.

[34] A. Z. Iufit, ed., *Russkii sovetskii teatr, 1917–1921: Dokumenty i materialy* (Leningrad: Iskusstvo, 1968), 24; Zel'dovich, "Pervye meropriiatiia," 54–55.

[35] Iufit, *Russkii sovetskii teatr*, 37.

[36] Ibid.

was enshrined in March 1918 in a Charter of Autonomous State Theaters that regulated relations between the stage and the authorities. During 1918 autonomy was a functioning reality, and the Aleksandrinskii actor Grigorii Ge even remarked that "Lunacharskii, in the sense of autonomy, gave us more than we wanted."[37] The personnel of the State Theaters were reluctant to distance themselves too far from the authorities, in view of the resources and privileges that—at least formerly—accrued from state patronage. These were all the more valuable in the context of the privations of the Civil War years. In February 1919 Ge described the conditions in which State Theater artists worked: "Weary, hungry, cold, freezing at home, freezing on stage in a torrent of icy air in a poorly heated theater, we try to keep our spirits up and perform eight times a week."[38] Such conditions provided a compelling reason for the theaters to maintain a close connection to the state and its resources, the only potential relief from crippling shortages.

From early 1918 Narkompros developed an apparatus for the administration of all Russia's theatrical enterprises that soon crystalized into a twofold structure: a Department of State Theaters and a Theater Department (known as TEO, from Teatral'nyi otdel) to oversee all other stages. This arrangement was a deliberate attempt to shield the State Theaters from the designs of the radical cultural activists who dominated TEO, notably Ol'ga Kameneva, who ran the department from its inception in January 1918 until July 1919 and who insisted that "the working class should not support the old theater."[39] At a TEO conference in December 1918 Lunacharskii defended the arrangement by insisting that the proletariat would find "its own paths" and that in the meantime it should have access to the "classic repertoire," unimpeded by hasty efforts to politicize the repertoire: "Let the State Theaters renovate their repertoire themselves without unnecessary haste...."[40]

During 1919 the government began to adopt a more interventionist stance. The most significant development for the entire theater industry was nationalization. This issue had been raised initially in early 1919 by TEO radicals who coveted full authority over all the country's theatrical infrastructure, including the State Theaters, in order to maximize the resources that could be devoted to proletarian theater. Its supporters included Kameneva, Meierkhol'd, and Platon Kerzhentsev (see below), all closely connected to the proletarian theater movement; its opponents included the leading Malyi Theater actor Aleksandr Sumbatov-Iuzhin, the founders of the Moscow Art Theater Konstantin Stanislavskii and Vladimir Nemirovich-Danchenko, and the *régisseur* Aleksandr Tairov, each a prominent representative of the traditional

[37] Zolotnitskii, *Akademicheskie teatry,* 37.

[38] Iufit, *Russkii sovetskii teatr,* 234 n. 37.

[39] Quoted in Korzhikhina, *Izvol'te byt' blagonadezhny!* 89.

[40] Iufit, *Russkii sovetskii teatr,* 48.

stage who recognized the potential implications of the proposal. Eventually, on 26 August 1919, Sovnarkom nationalized all theaters on Soviet territory. All resources pertaining to the stage, including buildings, equipment and props, became state property, and the authorities explicitly reserved for themselves the right to guide the repertoire. In the short term, however, this appears to have had little practical impact: the decree affirmed that theaters would remain "autonomous," and the State Theaters retained their protected status within Narkompros. The decree also established a Central Theatrical Committee (Tsentroteatr), a new organ designed to regulate all theatrical affairs, including ticket pricing and the distribution of subsidies that were now available, in principle, to all theatrical enterprises. TEO acted as the executive branch of Tsentroteatr until the latter was disbanded in November 1920 in favor of the situation that had obtained before its creation.[41]

Whilst the State Theaters remained protected from the theatrical left, the government began to encroach more directly on their routine activity. Almost from its inception Narkompros had reserved the right to supervise the artistic work of the State Theaters to encourage ideological conformity, and that role now began to displace the autonomy that had prevailed since the start of the Revolution. In February 1919 new management boards (*direktorii*) were established in the State Theaters, each to include at least one member appointed by Narkompros. Their principal task was to draw up repertoire plans that would be subject to approval by the Department of State Theaters.[42] Then, in April 1920, the boards were replaced by a system of individual (*edinolichnyi*) administration directly controlled by Narkompros. This effectively signaled the eclipse of artistic and administrative autonomy, in the sense understood by the theaters in 1905 and 1917. Why had this occurred? According to Soviet historians, the fundamental reason was the regime's desire to supervise the "bourgeois specialists" who still dominated the cultural professions, whilst non-Soviet scholars have emphasized the incompatibility between autonomy and a nascent totalitarianism. A third explanation has been suggested: closer supervision was intended to protect the State Theaters from other parts of the theatrical administration that would have taken a less tolerant stance than Lunacharskii towards the traditional stage.[43] Whatever the real balance between these arguments, all of which have some validity, the regime certainly remained committed to preserving Russia's theatrical heritage. In December 1919 the State Theaters were renamed State Academic Theaters in order to emphasize their status as the curators of artistic tradition and, moreover, their number was increased: the Moscow Art Theater joined their

---

[41] Iufit, *Russkii sovetskii teatr*, 26-28; Korzhikhina, *Izvol'te byt' blagonadezhny!* 93–94. For an account of the nationalization issue, see A. Iufit, *Revoliutsiia i teatr* (Leningrad: Iskusstvo, 1977), chap. 3.

[42] Iufit, *Russkii sovetskii teatr*, 58 and 80 n. 191.

[43] Frame, *St. Petersburg Imperial Theaters*, 166–67.

ranks in December 1919, followed in 1920 by the Kamernyi Theater and the Moscow Children's Theater.[44]

Underlying all of these developments—from nationalization to closer supervision of the traditional stage—was the conviction that theater was ultimately a powerful cultural weapon in the struggle for a new society. This idea was expressed, for example, by the Proletkul't activist Petr S. Kogan in 1919: "Among the means by which a class illuminates its collective consciousness, sharpens emotions and forges its will, the theater is the most powerful instrument."[45] The notion that theater could play a key role in transforming society was already widespread among the cultural intelligentsia before 1917 and— with the exceptions of the dispute about the State Theaters, and the new emphasis on the proletariat—the discourse about theater's public utility under the Bolsheviks was hardly novel. The core difference arguably resided in the means by which that notion was mobilized and articulated. Before 1917 the RTO had argued for the public value of the stage in its efforts to protect the theater industry; after 1917, the state adopted that discourse, emphasizing the theater's importance for the construction of a new society. The RTO survived the Revolution, but its role was diminished by the appearance of several new organizations designed to represent the industry, including the United Trade Union of Stage Workers, the Dramatic Union, the All-Russian Provincial Union of Artists, the Trade Union of Moscow Artists (chaired by Stanislavskii), and several others. All of these associations, including the RTO, were incorporated gradually into TEO, and most of their functions were assumed later by RABIS (the All-Russian Trade Union of Art Workers, founded in 1919).[46] Through this process the theater industry lost its independent representative associations.

The second distinctive characteristic of theater during the crisis of war and revolution—democratization—accelerated after 1917. A persistent mantra of the Bolshevik regime was that the Revolution had made Russia's cultural treasures accessible to the masses, and for this reason the democratization discourse can sound like an ideological ambition rather than a real accomplishment. In the case of theater, however, there is a considerable degree of truth in the claims. Witnesses consistently testified to the way in which ordinary workers and peasants poured into Russia's playhouses during the Revolution and Civil War. Stanislavskii, for instance, recalled the presence at Moscow Art Theater performances of a new audience that included soldiers and workers, especially during the first 18 months after the October Revolution. "This audience," he claimed, "proved to be extraordinarily suited for theater: it came to the theater not in passing but with trembling and expectation of something important,

---

[44] Iufit, *Russkii sovetskii teatr*, 65; *Teatral'naia entsiklopediia*, 1, col. 105.

[45] P. Kogan, "The Theater as Tribune," quoted in William G. Rosenberg, ed., *Bolshevik Visions: First Phase of the Cultural Revolution in Soviet Russia*, pt. 2, 2nd ed. (Ann Arbor: University of Michigan Press, 1990), 134.

[46] Korzhikhina, *Izvol'te byt' blagonadezhny!* 88.

unprecedented."[47] The lack of experience was reflected in the new audience's unfamiliarity with etiquette: on several occasions Stanislavskii had to request patrons to refrain from talking loudly during performances.[48] According to one report, the new audience watched performances "attentively" and displayed a "refined and receptive" attitude towards the established repertoire, for example, when the Moscow Art Theater staged *The Cherry Orchard* in a local soviet for "the democracy" (i.e., the people); "topical interest or politics" was not its main concern. Consequently, after some initial apprehension, actors regarded the new audience with enthusiasm, and it had become the "issue of the day."[49]

Further testimony to the altered profile of theatrical audiences was provided by two English writers who visited Russia during the period. Arthur Ransome observed the Bolshoi audience during a visit to Moscow:

> It had certainly changed greatly since the prerevolutionary period. The Moscow plutocracy of bald merchants and bejewelled fat wives had gone. Gone with them were evening dresses and white shirt fronts. The whole audience was in the monotone of everyday clothes.... There were many soldiers, and numbers of men who had obviously come straight from their work.... The same people who in the old days scraped kopecks and waited to get a good place near the ceiling [and who] now sat where formerly were the people who came here to digest their dinners.... But, as for their keenness, I can imagine few audiences to which, from the actor's point of view, it would be better worth while to play. Applause, like brains, had come down from the galleries.[50]

And H. G. Wells attended performances in Moscow and Petrograd in October 1920. "When one faced the stage," he wrote, "it was as if nothing had changed in Russia; but when the curtain fell and one turned to the audience one realised the revolution. There were now no brilliant uniforms, no evening dress in boxes and stalls. The audience was an undifferentiated mass of people, the same sort of people everywhere, attentive, good-humoured, well-behaved and shabby...."[51]

Several factors account for the changing audience profile. On one level it was simply an extension of the accelerated democratization that started in 1914. Bolshevik policy also contributed, principally through various

[47] K. S. Stanislavskii, "Moia zhizn' v iskusstve," in *Sobranie sochinenii v vos'mi tomakh,* ed. M. N. Kedrov (Moscow: Iskusstvo, 1954), 1: 375.

[48] Jean Benedetti, *Stanislavski* (London: Methuen, 1988), 231.

[49] *Teatral'nyi kur'er,* 26, 27, 28 November 1918, 4–5.

[50] Arthur Ransome, *Six Weeks in Russia in 1919* (Glasgow: Socialist Labour Press, 1919), 61–62.

[51] H. G. Wells, *Russia in the Shadows* (London: Hodder and Stoughton, n.d. [c.1920]), 36.

free-ticket schemes for soldiers, workers, and peasants, and TEO's efforts to encourage theater for the proletariat. Perhaps the most significant impulse to democratization, however, was the rapid proliferation in the number of theaters and theatrical troupes, especially amateur ones, during the Civil War. The TEO activist and future *régisseur* Pavel A. Markov claimed that "the country had never been attacked by such violent theatre-fever as during the first years of the Revolution."[52] Clubs, factories, and army units organized their own theatricals in a veritable "theater epidemic." It has been estimated, for example, that by the end of 1919 a total of 1,210 trade-union theaters had been organized at the frontlines of the Civil War, partly because from April that year Bolshevik cultural authorities were allowed to conscript performers for this purpose.[53] Precise overall numbers are unavailable, but Russia's professional theaters probably were joined by at least 2,000 amateur enterprises. As a result of this process, supply must have played a role in creating demand for theatrical entertainments, leading to a virtuous circle of creativity.

In 1919 Kogan wrote: "The future historian will note that during the bloodiest and cruelest of revolutions, all Russia continued to act."[54] That prediction, confirmed by several historians, betrayed his own sense that there was something incongruous about the country's evident thirst for theatricals in the midst of civil war. Is there an adequate explanation for the theater epidemic? Elements of an answer would include the use of theater as propaganda by the new regime (*agitprop*), curiosity about a previously inaccessible cultural pastime, and, of course, a need to be distracted and entertained. Yet the widespread enthusiasm for theatricals, especially amateur dramatics, retains a surreal quality because it suggests a light-heartedness that we associate principally with stability and prosperity, not with the horrors of the Civil War. Here we should simply note that theatrical democratization was a largely spontaneous phenomenon that prerevolutionary activists only ever dreamed about.[55]

Finally, to what extent did the gradual assertion of Bolshevik authority over the Russian stage and the appearance of a new audience affect the repertoire? In the case of the traditional theaters, Lunacharskii's protective policy was predicated upon an assumption that they would soon be imbued with the wider revolutionary mood, adapting to the needs of the proletariat: "The Revolutionary atmosphere in which we live and breathe will contrive

---

[52] P. A. Markov, *The Soviet Theatre* (London: Victor Gollancz Ltd., 1934), 137.

[53] Korzhikhina, *Izvol'te byt' blagonadezhny!* 103; Robert Russell, "The First Soviet Plays," in *Russian Theatre in the Age of Modernism*, ed. Russell and Andrew Barratt (Houndmills, UK: Macmillan, 1990), 149.

[54] P. Kogan, "Socialist Theater in the Years of the Revolution," quoted in Rosenberg, *Bolshevik Visions*, 146.

[55] On amateur theater, see Lynn Mally, *Revolutionary Acts: Amateur Theater and the Soviet State, 1917–1938* (Ithaca, NY: Cornell University Press, 2000).

to inspire even the conservative theatre with the spirit of the age."[56] For the most part, this proved to be an overly optimistic prognosis. The repertoire plan submitted by the Malyi—Russia's oldest drama stage—to Narkompros in June 1919, for example, emphasized the theater's commitment to staging only the established classics, justified by reference to a new audience for the old repertoire and the absence of suitable alternatives.[57] The Aleksandrinskii was characterized during the 1918-20 period by "creative prostration."[58] Emma Goldman claimed to have seen most of its productions during her sojourn in Russia (1920–21), "and not one of them gave any hint of the earthquake that had shaken Russia. There was no new note in interpretation, scenery, or method."[59] And between 1918 and 1922, the Moscow Art Theater mounted only one new production, Byron's *Cain*, an unsuccessful effort to stage something that might be considered relevant to the times.[60]

Despite the fundamental continuity of repertoire, however, there is some evidence that the traditional theaters endeavored, where appropriate, to highlight the relevance of older plays to the Revolution. For a new production of A. K. Tolstoi's *Posadnik* in October 1918, for instance, the Malyi distributed a brochure explaining how the play resonated with the revolutionary epoch, insofar as its core theme was a struggle between "people-power and princely despotism."[61] The dominance at the Aleksandrinskii of two works by the dramatist and *régisseur* Petr Gnedich during the Civil War period, *Slaves* (about serfdom) and *The Decembrist* (forbidden by the censors before 1917), possibly reflected an effort to stage dramas that were critical of the old order. In addition, the plays of Aleksandr Ostrovskii—such as *Wolves and Sheep*, his most frequently performed work at the Malyi in the early Soviet period—remained a staple part of the traditional stage repertoire, their critical portrayals of the merchant class enabling the theaters gently to castigate "bourgeois" values without compromising their dedication to the classics.

Moreover, the traditional stage was prepared occasionally to experiment with new dramas that were written expressly to provide theaters with revolutionary content. On the fourth anniversary of the October Revolution the

---

[56] Quoted in R. Fülop-Miller and J. Gregor, *The Russian Theatre: Its Character and History, with Especial Reference to the Revolutionary Period*, trans P. England (Philadelphia: J. P. Lippincott, 1929), 72.

[57] Iufit, *Russkii sovetskii teatr*, 105–07.

[58] Constantine Derjavine, *A Century of the State Dramatic Theatre, 1832–1932* (Leningrad: State Publishing House, 1932), 79.

[59] Emma Goldman, *My Disillusionment in Russia* (Mineola, NY: Dover Publications, 2003), 226.

[60] Benedetti, *Stanislavski*, 239–44.

[61] Iurii Aikhenval'd, *Aleksandr Ivanovich Sumbatov-Iuzhin* (Moscow: Iskusstvo, 1987), 282-83. See also Zolotnitskii, *Akademicheskie teatry*, 74-80.

Malyi became the first State Academic Theater to produce a play from the nascent Soviet repertoire when it staged Lunacharskii's *Oliver Cromwell*, penned by the Narkom specifically to give the traditional theaters a theme suitable to the era. Sumbatov-Iuzhin, who played the title role, wrote that "Oliver Cromwell is an unimpeachable, organic revolutionary, combining in himself the destructive and constructive strength of the fighter for liberty against despotism and the despot."[62] Those on the theatrical left were rather more sceptical of the play's revolutionary credentials, since Cromwell was the hero of a "bourgeois" revolution, whereas the more radical elements of mid-17th-century England, such as the Levellers, might have been a more appropriate theme.[63]

The most obvious and striking influence of the Bolshevik Revolution on the repertoire occurred beyond the traditional stage, in the work of the theatrical left, the cultural activists whose commitment to creating a proletarian theater began to take the people's theater movement in a new direction.[64] Their ideas and projects often overlapped with—but were not entirely synonymous with—the realm of what is broadly known as the avant-garde. This had developed steadily in Russia from the early years of the 20th century, when stage realism was challenged increasingly by the advocates of theatrical conventionality (*uslovnost´*) who included Symbolists and Futurists.[65] In contrast to the theater of realism—represented notably by the Moscow Art Theater, which tried to recreate real life on stage as faithfully as possible—they argued that the essential meaning of a play was conveyed best by a conscious theatricality in

---

[62] Aikhenval'd, *Aleksandr Ivanovich Sumbatov-Iuzhin*, 293.

[63] On the controversy surrounding Oliver Cromwell, see S. E. Roberts, *Soviet Historical Drama: Its Role in the Development of a National Mythology* (The Hague: Martinus Nijhoff, 1965), 33–36, 39–45.

[64] People's theaters generally continued to function during the first few years of Soviet power, but now under the aegis of local soviets, workers' clubs, and municipalities. Some were transformed into Palaces of Culture. See Swift, *Popular Theater*, 241, 246. Many prerevolutionary People's Houses that possessed their own theaters, such as the Ligovskii People's House in Petrograd, similarly were adapted to the new political context. See Adele Lindenmeyr, "Building a Civil Society One Brick at a Time: People's Houses and Worker Enlightenment in Late Imperial Russia," *Journal of Modern History* 84, 1 (2012): 37–38.

[65] On various aspects of the theatrical avant-garde in Russia before the Revolution, see, for example, E. Braun, *Meyerhold: A Revolution in Theatre* (London: Methuen, 1995); S. M. Carnicke, *The Theatrical Instinct: Nikolai Evreinov and the Russian Theatre of the Early Twentieth Century* (New York: P. Lang, 1989); Spencer Golub, "The Silver Age, 1905–1917," in *A History of Russian Theatre*, ed. Robert Leach and Victor Borovsky (Cambridge: Cambridge University Press, 1999), 278–301; J. B. Woodward, "From Brjusov to Ajkhenvald: Attitudes to the Russian Theatre, 1902–1914," *Canadian Slavonic Papers* 7 (1965): 173–88; N. Worrall, *Modernism to Realism on the Soviet Stage: Tairov-Vakhtangov-Okhlopkov* (Cambridge: Cambridge University Press, 1989).

which there was no attempt to conceal the fact that actors were performing in front of an audience. Under the influence of two works—Richard Wagner's *Die Kunst und die Revolution* (1849), published in Russia in 1906, and Romain Rolland's *Le Théâtre du Peuple* (1903), published in Russia in 1910—the avant garde also argued that there was an urgent need to reconnect the theater with the people; this could be achieved by breaking down the barriers between actors and audience in order to unite the community in a kind of cultic ceremony.[66] These ideas inspired a rich tapestry of theatrical experimentation under the leadership of figures like Meierkhol'd, Tairov, Nikolai Evreinov, and Evgenii Vakhtangov. For all its prominence and notoriety, however, the avant garde constituted only a small proportion of the prerevolutionary theatrical landscape. For some of its members, the Bolshevik Revolution, in its open commitment to abandoning the "bourgeois" past and building a new order, signaled an opportunity to advance their ideas in a fusion of political and artistic radicalism. In this way the most innovative theater of the Civil War years was inspired by the Revolution, even though it built upon the achievements of prerevolutionary developments.

The most vocal exponents of the theatrical left emanated from Proletkul't, whose most prominent theoretician of the stage was Platon Kerzhentsev (1881–1940), a history and philosophy student who joined the Bolshevik Party in 1904. His book *The Creative Theater*, published in several editions during the Civil War, articulated the broad aims of the movement and can be considered the most influential theatrical tract of the period.[67] The essence of Kerzhentsev's argument was that, in order to build a new theater, with new form and content, the old one first had to be destroyed. Proletkul'tists were dismayed by Lunacharskii's tolerance of the traditional stage because a proletarian theater could be created only by the proletariat itself, not by the remnants of the bourgeois stage. The physical appearance of the new theater would be radical too: the proscenium arch, the curtain, and the footlights would be banished as symbols of the old theater's emphasis on the separation of actors and audience. Clearly influenced by Wagner and Rolland, both of whose works were republished in Russia during the Civil War, Kerzhentsev insisted that theater could fulfil its potential as a mass art only by creating a collective experience in which actors and audience merged with one another. These ideas found their most dramatic practical expression in mass festivals, the vast open-air theatrical pageants that were organized during the Civil

---

[66] Wagner had taken his inspiration from the theater of ancient Greece, Rolland from the mass pageants of the French Revolution. Lars Kleberg, "'People's Theater' and the Revolution: On the History of a Concept before and after 1917," in *Art, Society, Revolution: Russia 1917–1921*, ed. Nils Åke Nilsson (Stockholm: Almqvist & Wiksell International, 1979), 179–97.

[67] V. [Platon] Kerzhentsev, *Tvorcheskii teatr: Puti sotsialisticheskogo teatra*, 3rd ed. (Moscow: Izd-vo Vserossiiskogo Tsentral'nogo Ispolnitel'nogo Komiteta Sovetov R., S., K. i K. Deputatov, 1919).

War by professional artists but which involved hundreds of ordinary citizens. They were designed as triumphal celebrations of the Revolution. The most celebrated of them was *The Storming of the Winter Palace*, organized to mark the third anniversary of the October Revolution, under the direction of Evreinov in Palace Square, Petrograd. It is reputed to have involved the participation of 8,000 people and 100,000 spectators.[68]

Mass festivals, however, were exceptional spectacles staged mainly for special occasions. The challenge for the theatrical left was the absence of an authentic proletarian repertoire that could be used in the majority of theaters around the country. Several competitions were held to encourage ordinary workers to write plays, but the results were disappointing. One exception was Aleksandr A. Vermishev's *Red Truth*, a widely performed drama about an old peasant whose sympathy for the Whites is eroded when he experiences the brutality of their rule at first hand.[69] Kogan described it as "one of those rare artistic specimens in which aesthetic and civic requirements are combined harmoniously."[70] For the most part, however, until a new repertoire could be created the old one would have to be adapted to meet proletarian needs. A resolution of the first national Proletkul't conference in September 1918— based on an address by Kerzhentsev—confidently expressed the view that "it is possible to select from amongst the world's literature plays discussing themes which are spiritually close to the mood of the revolutionary proletariat."[71] Examples included Gogol''s *The Government Inspector*, Ostrovskii's *The Forest*, Schiller's *The Robbers*, and Shakespeare's *King Lear*.

The most prominent theatrical figure to join the Communist Party during the Civil War was the avant-garde *régisseur* Meierkhol'd. Before the Revolution Meierkhol'd worked at the Moscow Art Theater and the St. Petersburg Imperial Theaters, but their general artistic conservatism—despite Stanislavskii's willingness to try new approaches in his "Theater-Studio"[72]— forced him to confine his experimental work to smaller stages and clubs. After the Revolution he abandoned the old theater altogether to concentrate on revolutionary productions, notably his collaboration with Vladimir Maiakovskii on the latter's influential *Mystery-Bouffe*, initially staged for the first

---

[68] James von Geldern, *Bolshevik Festivals, 1917–1920* (Berkeley: University of California Press, 1993), 199–207.

[69] Robert Russell, *Russian Drama of the Revolutionary Period* (Totowa, NJ: Barnes and Noble Books, 1988), 34–36.

[70] *Vestnik teatra*, no. 38 (October 1919): 4.

[71] Iufit, *Russkii sovetskii teatr*, 331.

[72] Benedetti, *Stanislavski*, chap. 12. The Theater-Studio was conceived as a kind of creative laboratory, supported by—but separate from—the Moscow Art Theater. Its initial incarnation in 1905 was a Symbolist collaboration between Stanislavskii and Meierkhol'd. Stanislavskii was unhappy with the results and none of the Theater-Studio's work was shown to the public.

anniversary of the October Revolution. In certain respects *Mystery-Bouffe* served as a prototype for the theatrical left. Its Cubist costumes and props designed by Kazimir Malevich made it a "cartoon-style piece of agitprop theatre" which developed out of "the extension and realisation of a single metaphor (the Revolution as a flood which will sweep away the old world in its entirety)."[73] It culminated in the depiction of a futuristic technological paradise. For Konstantin Rudnitsky, *Mystery-Bouffe* could be described as Futurist "in the primary and literal sense of the term: focus on the future and hatred of the past, of the old, outmoded system, including, of course, old forms of art."[74]

In September 1920, after a period fighting with the Red Army in southern Russia, Meierkhol'd was invited by Lunacharskii to assume the leadership of TEO, a position that he held only until February 1921. The Narkom justified the appointment as follows: "I can charge Comrade Meyerhold with the destruction of the old and bad or the creation of the new and good. But the preservation of the old and good ... I can not entrust to him."[75] In other words, the iconoclastic *régisseur* could develop a theater for the new era but would not be permitted to interfere with the Academic Theaters. Meierkhol'd began by announcing the advent of "Theatrical October," a policy intended to promote an artistic and political revolutionary theater, and then established its model stage, the RSFSR Theater No. 1 in Moscow. Its first production was a reworked version of Belgian Symbolist poet Emile Verhaeren's *The Dawns* for the third anniversary of the Bolshevik Revolution, but the controversy surrounding the overly aestheticized character of the production, which proved too much even for Lunacharskii, led to Meierkhol'd's dismissal as TEO chief.[76]

The fate of "Theatrical October" indicated the limits to what the regime would tolerate as revolutionary theater. Meierkhol'd continued to experiment with theatrical form throughout the 1920s, showcasing his innovative ideas about constructivism and biomechanics in his iconic production of Fernand Crommelynck's *The Magnanimous Cuckold* (1922).[77] But the general theatrical climate was starting to change. Lenin's growing intolerance of Proletkul't's assertions of independence from the Communist Party led to its emasculation in 1920. As a result the amateur theater epidemic began to wane, and mass festivals largely disappeared. In 1923 Lunacharskii proclaimed the slogan "Back to Ostrovskii!"—it was the centenary of the great dramatist's birth— which effectively called upon the stage to be less concerned with experimental

---

[73] Russell, *Russian Drama*, 45.

[74] Rudnitsky, *Russian and Soviet Theatre*, 43.

[75] Quoted in Russell, *Russian Drama*, 32.

[76] E. Braun, *The Theatre of Meyerhold: Revolution on the Modern Stage* (London: Eyre Methuen, 1979), 157; Rudnitsky, *Russian and Soviet Theatre*, 59–64.

[77] Rudnitsky, *Russian and Soviet Theatre*, 89–94.

forms, more with the kind of realism that was considered accessible to ordinary people. In the same year a theater censorship agency, Glavrepertkom (Glavnyi repertuarnyi komitet), was established to provide greater scrutiny of what Russia's theaters produced, and it gradually assumed a more interventionist role as the 1920s unfolded. A new phase in the development of the Russian theater had begun, and it made the 1917–22 period stand out as an unrivaled moment of genuine enthusiasm for a fusion of avant-garde experimentation and politics in the repertoire, confined though it was to a relatively small segment of the diverse theatrical scene.

03   80

This overview of Russian theater during the crisis of war and revolution has suggested that the predominant issues for the theatrical realm during 1914–22 were twofold. First of all, organizational matters assumed greater importance than ever, as theater people endeavored to protect their interests in the face of material challenges introduced by the Great War, and were then confronted by a more interventionist state after the Revolution. Secondly, the notion and reality of theatrical democratization intensified, initially as a function of mass population displacement after 1914, and subsequently as part of the Civil War theater epidemic and the related drive for a new proletarian theater. It was in these ways that the turmoil of Russia's Great War and Revolution directly affected the theater during the discrete period from 1914 to 1922 as a whole. Whilst the year 1917—and the Bolshevik Revolution in particular—marked an important turning point for the theater because it dramatically shifted the political context for the arts, there was a distinct degree of continuity across the revolutionary divide. Even the blatantly politicized productions of the Civil War years, driven by the enthusiasm of the theatrical left and the avant garde, were as much an acceleration of prerevolutionary artistic (if not political) trends. The revolutionary rupture remains central to explaining the development of Russian theater, but the fundamental continuities, including the repertoire, are a reminder that sudden historical transformations are rarely as disconnected from the past as they can appear.

Institutions: Education, the Orthodox Church, and Museums

Higher Education in Russia during the
First World War and Revolution

Anatolii E. Ivanov

This article treats the theme of science, broadly defined, during the First World War and Revolution. The subject is important because higher education was the keystone of Russia's scientific and intellectual establishment. Its emergent academic institutions, with their infrastructure of experimental laboratories, were not only professional and educational. During wartime they were primarily centers for scientific research that supplemented the military's application of scientific knowledge, and oriented themselves so as to fulfill government defense orders. The "producers" of this knowledge, professors and teachers in universities and national economic institutes, played an outstanding role in working with the state to overcome the scientific and technical backwardness in the defense system that had become evident from the catastrophic situation at the onset of hostilities between Russia and Germany. Moreover the torrent of war immediately engulfed students, who were the main reserve replenishing the rapidly diminishing cadre of junior officers (ensigns and non-commissioned officers) of the Russian army lost in combat. In a word, the "academic population" immediately made itself vital to the defense of the fatherland.

The purpose of this chapter is to reconstruct the many factors involved in the patriotic and military mobilization of the scientific, intellectual, and research resources of the imperial higher education system in its response to the urgent demands of an autocratic government at war. The First World War was the prologue to the collapse of the tsarist regime in February 1917 and to the subsequent Bolshevik coup in October. The epilogue to these revolutionary events provoked by the First World War was the response of the academic community to both the Provisional Government's declaration that it would honor its commitments to its allies, and to the decision of the Bolshevik government to pull out of the war.

The historiography of this topic is at present still inchoate. Its initial beginnings are to be found in works published during the Soviet period on the history of the universities and national economic institutes that arose duing the 19th and early 20th centuries. While providing useful information, this sketchy and ideologically-driven material is not a complete canvas of

Russian Culture in War and Revolution, 1914–22, Book 1: Popular Culture, the Arts, and Institutions. Murray Frame, Boris Kolonitskii, Steven G. Marks, and Melissa K. Stockdale, eds. Bloomington, IN: Slavica Publishers, 2014, 285–313.

historical events and does not adequately portray the mind set, feelings, and collective patriotic actions called forth by wartime conditions and fueled by the desire for victory on the part of the academic community (professors, teachers, and students).

A distinct exception to the fact-based Soviet historiography is an article by B. F. Sultanbekov that portrays the social and political outlook of the faculty of Kazan' University at the beginning of the 20th century.[1] Using documents in the Central State Archive of the Tatar Soviet Socialist Republic (now the National Archive of the Republic of Tatarstan), Sultanbekov was the first to reconstruct the multifaceted defense-related activity of Kazan''s professorial body. His article serves to a certain extent as an initial methodological guide for scholarship on the defense initiatives of the scientific and higher-education community across all national universities during 1914–18.[2] The problems it poses are dealt with in an article by A. Kozhevnikov on the activity of "Big Science," comprising scientific institutes and their faculty during the First World War and the Civil War.[3] These articles initiated the historiography of the field in the post-Soviet era.

In subsequent years, too, the emphasis of scholarship continues to be on the "man of science" as the progenitor of diverse military programs or reform initiatives in the sphere of higher education whose beginnings, according to the accurate observation of A. N. Dmitriev, were, "paradoxically, the war period." Dmitriev's article on state academic politics focuses on the effort of the entire academic community to affirm its corporate prerogatives in the harsh atmosphere of everyday life in a time of war. His work laid the foundation for further research on the impact of the First World War on higher education in late imperial Russia.[4]

---

[1] B. F. Sultanbekov, "Evoliutsiia politicheskikh vzgliadov professorov i prepodavatelei vysshikh uchebnykh zavedenii Povolzh'ia (1905–fevral' 1917 gg), in *Bor'ba KPSS za razvitie narodnogo obrazovaniia i kul'tury Tatarii i Srednego Povolzh'ia* (Kazan': Tatarskoe knizhnoe izd-vo, 1977).

[2] A. E. Ivanov, "Professorsko-prepodavatel'skii sostav rossiiskoi vysshei shkoly v period Pervoi mirovoi voiny," in *Russkaia kul'tura v usloviiakh inozemnykh nashestvii i voin: X–nachalo XX v. Sbornik nauchnykh trudov*, ed. A. N. Kopylov (Moscow: Institut istorii SSSR, 1990), 224–58; Ivanov, "Rossiskoe 'uchenoe soslovie' v gody 'Vtoroi otechestvennoi voiny' (Ocherk grazhdanskoi psikhologii i patrioticheskoi deiatel'nosti)," *Voprosy istorii estestvoznaniia i tekhniki*, no. 2 (1999): 108–27.

[3] A. Kozhevnikov, "Pervaia mirovaia voina: Grazhdanskaia voina i izobretenie 'bol'-shoi nauki,'" in *Vlast' i nauka, uchenye i vlast': 1880–nachalo 1920-kh godov*, ed. Nikolai N. Smirnov (St. Petersburg: Dmitrii Bulanin, 2003), 87–111.

[4] A. N. Dmitriev, "Pervaia mirovaia voina: Universitetskie reformy i internatsional'naia transformatsiia rossiiskogo akademicheskogo soobshchestva," in *Nauka, tekhnika i obshchestvo Rossii i Germanii vo vremia Pervoi mirovoi voiny*, ed. E. I. Kolchinskii and D. Bairau [Dietrich Beyrau] (St. Petersburg: Nestor-Istoriia, 2007), 236–55.

Recent research analyzes the social behavior of the corporate professorial bodies of various regional institutions: Petersburg (by E. Rostovtsev), Kazan' (by I. Giliazov), and Derpt-Iur'ev (by C. Tamul and T. Maurer).[5] Rostovtsev writes that "[d]espite all this professorial 'patriotism' the war was perceived primarily as an instrument for the realization of political as well as corporate values so important to the professoriate."[6] The facts, including those set forth in this chapter, do not corroborate this imperious conclusion and do not justify enclosing the honest patriotism of the professoriate in ironic quotation marks. Such a judgment does not take into consideration the professors' collaboration with the minister of education, P. N. Ignat'ev, minister from January 1915 to December 1916, in preparing postwar liberal university reform: this was a positive response of the academic community to the government's initiative.

Scholars also interpret the social behavior of the student body differently than did the Soviet historiography of higher education. Whereas the latter, for ideological reasons, emphasized the antiwar (defeatist) activity of a minority group of students with a Bolshevik and Left SR orientation, the research of contemporary specialists takes into account the student body as a whole, with its varied responses to the situation at the front ranging from belligerence to pacifism.[7] An example of this new approach is Rostovtsev's work on the extent to which students were drafted into the army—although it must be said that he bases his claim that there was a limited mobilization of students up to the spring of 1916 exclusively on data from St. Petersburg University. Our statistics (see below) paint a different picture for higher education as a whole.[8] One should also bear in mind that from the beginning of the war through the spring of 1916 students volunteered for military service en masse.

Mobilization of Higher Education for Defense

Like Russian society as a whole, the higher education "population" (professors and teachers—approximately 5,000; students—approximately 130,000) regarded the First World War, especially in its early stages, as a patriotic war. This contrasted with the public reaction to the Russo-Japanese War, which only strengthened resentment against the supreme power. The war with Germany took place within the boundaries of the Russian Empire and obviously dis-

---

[5] Trude Maurer and Aleksandr Dmitriev, *Universitet i gorod v Rossii (nachalo XX veka)* (Moscow: Novoe literaturnoe obozrenie, 2009).

[6] E. A. Rostovtsev, "Universitet stolichnogo goroda (1900–1917 gody)," in ibid., 312.

[7] S"iuzen Marasi [Susan Morrissey], "Mezhdu patriotizmom i radikalizmom v gody Pervoi mirovoi voiny," in *Rossiia i Pervaia mirovaia voina: Materialy mezhdunarodnogo kollokviuma* (St. Petersburg: D. Bulanin, 1999); A. R. Markov, *Chto znachit byt' studentom* (Moscow: Novoe literaturnoe obozrenie, 2005).

[8] Maurer and Dmitriev, *Universitet i gorod*, 314.

rupted the lives of its subjects. This immediately evoked a defensive, patriotic response in society.[9] V. M. Bekhterev testified: the "common call" to bring the war to a victorious conclusion was heard in almost all social organizations and meetings in Russia. Even such thinkers as the well-known G. V. Plekhanov made similar declarations. The only exceptions were the so-called "defeatists," who followed the Bolsheviks and the Left SRs.[10]

The First World War effected cardinal changes in the whole make-up of relationships within the teaching staff of Russian higher education. The news about the beginning of military action was met with a burst of patriotism by the professoriate, uniting liberals, conservatives, and the far right. On the eve of the war they had been in a state of inter-party and academic warfare, inflamed to the highest degree by the minister of education, L. A. Kasso, minister from September 1910 to November 1914, whose policy was to apply pressure on the Kadet-leaning liberal professoriate who were, in his opinion, responsible for the endless student disorders.[11]

"People of science" eagerly offered scientific, technical, and intellectual support for the imperial war machine. Like the Russian bourgeoisie, which had greeted the news of Russia's entry into the conflict with the call for "Military mobilization of industry!" the academic community proclaimed the "Military mobilization of higher education!" The prevailing patriotic aspirations in the teaching corps were succinctly expressed by the Council of Moscow University in a resolution of 18 September 1915: "In view of the need to encourage large-scale assistance from the university community to the state and society in connection with the war" the council approached the leaders and institutions in Moscow that were concerned with defense matters, care of the wounded, refugee affairs, and the supply of food and fuel and asked how faculty and students might help them.

The professoriate immediately demonstrated its patriotic sentiments through a series of philanthropic actions such as the resolution of the Council of the University of Petrograd to contribute 3 percent of their salaries for the use of the Red Cross and to help families of reservists.[12] At very short notice the teaching corps of the capital undertook the collection of funds for the cre-

---

[9] See F. A. Gaida, *Liberal'naia oppozitsiia na putiakh k vlasti: 1914–vesna 1917 g.* (Moscow: ROSSPEN, 2003); Erik Lur [Eric Lohr], *Russkii natsionalizm i Rossiiskaia imperiia: Kampaniia protiv "vrazheskikh poddannykh" v gody Pervoi mirovoi voiny* (Moscow: Novoe literaturnoe obozrenie, 2012); Hubertus F. Jahn, *Patriotic Culture in Russia during World War I* (Ithaca, NY: Cornell University Press, 1995).

[10] V. M. Bekhterev, *Moral'nye itogi velikoi mirovoi voiny: Rech' na torzhestvennom zasedanii Psikhonevrologicheskogo instituta 2 fevralia 1915 g.* (Petrograd, 1915), 6.

[11] Tsentral'nyi istoricheskii arkhiv Moskvy (TsIAM) f. 418 (Moskovskii universitet), op. 92, d. 924 (Postanovleniia Soveta Moskovskogo universiteta), l. 100.

[12] *Protokoly zasedanii Soveta imp. Petrogradskogo universiteta za 1914 g.*, no. 70 (Petrograd, 1916): 85.

ation of a military transit hospital which opened in October 1914. Students also made donations to the tune of more than 62,000 rubles.[13]

Yet although they were united in a tumult of concerns for the defense of an embattled government, professors did not forget their personal political concerns about a postwar Russia following the expected victory over Germany: the conservatives with strengthening the autocracy, the liberals with broad constitutional reform and the democratization of academic life.

Students, too, greeted the announcement of war with overt expressions of patriotism. The influx of student volunteers into military institutes for short-term officer training showed their willingness to shed blood for their homeland. During a brief period in the fall of 1914, between 2,500 and 3,000 places for cadet training were taken up by student volunteers.[14]

However, even in the initial period of general patriotic fervor, war did not bring "internal peace" to students. They remained just as divided politically as before the war. While desiring Russia's victory over an external enemy the students did not forget the internal enemy—the autocracy. Their patriotism was of an anti-autocratic, republican character. The reaction to the war sharpened the ideological confrontation between the patriotic majority in the student body and the anti-war minority who followed the Bolsheviks and the Left SRs. Furthermore, while proclaiming their dedication to the defense of the country, the student revolutionaries, democrats, and liberals strove to dissociate themselves from the ultra-patriotism of the Black Hundred wing that demonstrated a zealous, knee-bending devotion to the monarchy.

The military defeats fatally dogging Russia, the ongoing influx of students into the army for military and civilian operations, the daily news from the front reporting the deaths and maiming of their comrades and the hardships of everyday life—all these together tempered the patriotic fervor of students, who were becoming more and more burdened by the common mood of despondency and frustration. In October 1915 a meeting of the representatives to the student economic organizations of Petrograd University maintained that for their peers life "presented a distressing picture of intellectual collapse and moral impoverishment. Students had become isolated attendees of the university and represented a drab mass devoid of any ideological position." Such a mood of decline "is acutely evident now, when the war so relentlessly highlights the country's social and economic ruination."[15] Pacifism grew in this soil, as seen in a letter of 1 March 1915 from a certain Kira, a nurse at a

---

[13] Rossiiskii gosudarstvennyi istoricheskii arkhiv (RGIA) f. 733 (Departament narodnogo prosveshcheniia), op. 156, d. 317 (Ob etapnom lazarete imeni Petrogradskikh vysshikh uchebnykh zavedenii), ll. 11–12.

[14] RGIA f. 1276 (Sovet ministrov), op. 11, d. 1369 (Ob organizatsii zaniatii v evakuirovannykh uchebnykh zavedeniiakh), l. 4.

[15] Gosudarstvennyi arkhiv Rossiiskoi Federatsii (GARF) f. 102.00 (Departament politsii. Osobyi otdel. 1916), op. 17, d. 64, chast´ 57, ll. 1–19.

military hospital, to her friends, students at Moscow's Shaniavskii University: "I am surprised at how you, Arsenii, and also Levin, such fine youths with pure souls, can remain so indifferent to the war, toward these horrors; how even though you are so imbued with antimilitarist ideas you want to shut your eyes to what is going on around you—for after all you have done nothing to help stop the war."[16]

By 1917 the attitude of the democratic student body to the war inclined toward pacifism, whether intellectual or instinctive in nature.[17] Unlike the Bolsheviks, the young intelligentsia did not wish for the defeat of Russia in order to promote a proletarian revolution. They dreamed of an immediate and honorable exit for Russia from the disastrous conflict in the name of civic peace and as a guarantee against a revolutionary catastrophe.

All on the Altar of Victory

The war demonstrated that Russian higher education was a flexible, culturally vital set of institutions capable of reacting to the extreme challenges of state and society, even temporarily waiving its primary academic objectives and functions based on the fundamental postulate of the freedom of science and teaching. Higher education readily transformed its scientific, educational focus into a component of the Russian Empire's military structure.

As the scale of military actions widened, the universities and national economic institutions were drawn deeper into the vortex of emergency wartime measures designed to mitigate the crises affecting the army: the shortfall in command personnel; military, medical, and chemical supplies; and those crises in the rear—rations, fuel, and transport. It may be that never in the history of the Russian Empire had there been so many highly qualified specialists and students working for the support of the defense capability and economic sustainability of the country without a pure scientific purpose. Never before had higher education, with its creative and cultural spirit, bound itself so organically to the urgent needs of the state's defense establishment. Russian higher education became a part of the overall military complex.

However, it was very quick to feel the destructive force of the military Moloch. The militarization of the daily life of universities and economic institutes had a deleterious effect on their ability to fulfill their main function, namely scholarship and teaching. The director of the Petrograd Technical Institute, Professor A. A. Voronoi, recalled:

> The difficult conditions of teaching created by the war were exacerbated still more by the diversion of part of the professoriate and teaching

---

[16] GARF f. 102.00 (1915), d. 9, chast' 46, Litera "B," l. 99.

[17] Rostovtsev, "Universitet stolichnogo goroda," 314; I. A. Giliazov, "Gorod Kazan' i kazanskii universitet v nachale XX v.," in *Universitet i gorod v Rossii*, 556–65.

staff to tasks connected with defense, including trips abroad. Some of the laboratories were also occupied with defense work. The institute assigned rooms for various courses as required by the military.[18]

The already paltry funding for higher education was reduced further.

The approaching front disrupted the sparse "network" of higher education centers located in 23 cities. Those institutions located in the western part of the empire were evacuated eastwards. In 1915 Warsaw University transferred to Rostov-on-Don and was renamed Rostov-on-Don University in 1917. In the same year Warsaw Polytechnic became the Nizhii Novgorod Polytechnic Institute. The Veterinary Institute in Warsaw was likewise transferred to Novocherkassk in 1917 and named the Don Veterinary Institute. The Novoaleksandriiskii Institute for Agriculture and Forestry evacuated to Khar'kov, where it remained after the war.[19] Some institutes of higher education were moved from Kiev to Saratov on a temporary basis: the University of St. Vladimir; the Business Institute; and the Frebelev Women's Institute. They were all housed under the wing of the local university; Kiev Polytechnic was the only one to remain in place.[20]

Substantial material expenditure, organizational expertise, and time were required for the evacuated institutes to adapt to their new academic conditions and everyday activities. This circumstance prompted special sittings of the government on 3 September and 28 October 1915 in order to address the issue, "On Starting Operations in Evacuated Higher Education Establishments." Evidently a definite decision was not made. We only know the position of Minister of Education Ignat'ev, who wanted to shore up admissions to these institutes. In a memorandum of 3 September 1915 to Premier I. L. Goremykin he proposed that students attending them regain the across-the-board privilege of exemption from military conscription they had held before the war. Furthermore, anticipating the situation after the war, Ignat'ev argued for the opening of new universities and institutes "in spite of the State Treasury's current difficulties." The minister suggested that such a policy would also soften "the nervousness and confusion of the man on the street" and become an inspirational factor for young people, including those who had been evacuated, and their families.[21]

---

[18] *Tekhnologicheskii institut im. Leningradskogo soveta rabochikh, krest'ianskikh i krasnoarmeiskikh deputatov* (Leningrad, 1928), 1: 191.

[19] A. E. Ivanov, "Geografiia vysshei shkoly Rossii v kontse XIX–nachale XX v.," in *Istochnikovedcheskie i istoriograficheskie aspekty russkoi kul'tury: Sbornik statei,* ed. L. N. Pushkarev, A. N. Kopylov, and Ivanov (Moscow: Institut istorii SSSR, 1984), 163–64.

[20] V. A. Solomonov, *Imperatorskii Nikolaevskii Saratovskii universitet (1909–1917)* (Saratov: Sootechestvennik, 1999), 184.

[21] RGIA f. 1276, op. 11, d. 1369, ll. 1–4.

In the final analysis it was only the higher educational establishments in Iur'ev (formerly Derpt, now Tartu) (the university; the Veterinary Institute; and the Advanced Courses for Women) and Riga (the Polytechnic Institute) that were occupied by German forces in February 1918. As stated in a "top secret" report by Ignat'ev to Goremykin on 12 December 1915, their evacuation did not take place due to disagreement on this question with the chief commander of the Northern Front, Adjutant-General Ruzskii. Ruzskii was the first person to insist on the immediate evacuation of Iur'ev University "not in view of any threatening circumstances on the front, but chiefly for political reasons ... the presence in the city of German elements concentrated in the colleges and the divinity department of the university [Lutheran] is very harmful militarily." The commander warned that otherwise "broad repressive measures" would be needed.[22] Ignat'ev held a different view, affirming that Latvians and Estonians comprised the majority in the Evangelical Lutheran Confession of the university while there was only a small group of Germans. The minister of education emphasized that the local population considered the university to be "its own cultural property." Referring to the experience of the evacuated Warsaw and Kiev universities, he pointed out how ruinous it was to move such "cumbersome and crowded establishments" hurriedly to other cities. Only 60 percent of the students of Kiev University decided to relocate to Saratov.[23] Settling the 9,500 students and teachers from the higher education institutions of Kiev was an extraordinarily difficult task.[24]

If evacuation became unavoidable, Ignat'ev recommended making Perm' the city for the relocation of Iur'evskii University. But life turned out otherwise. Contrary to the assurances of the command about the reliability of Russian defenses, the first to fall to the invading German forces was Riga, with its ancient Imperial Polytechnic, and in turn Iur'ev, with its higher education establishments. Indeed, the transfer of the property of the local universities of Perm', Voronezh, and Nizhnii Novgorod began only in the fall of 1917. The rest of Iur'evskii University, and more precisely the Russian component of the professoriate and student body, along with certain property, became the basis for the creation of Voronezh University.[25]

---

[22] RGIA f. 560 (Obshchaia kantseliariia Ministerstva finansov), op. 26, d. 1342 (O vysshikh uchebnykh zavedeniiakh (Petrogradskom i Iur'evskom universitetakh i Kievskikh vysshikh zhenskikh kursakh) i ob uchitel'skikh seminariiakh (pechatnoe predstavlenie Ministerstva narodnogo prosveshcheniia; otnoshenie Ministra narodnogo prosveshcheniia po voprosu ob obrazovanii pri Petrogradskom universitete osobogo kabineta gosudarstvennykh nauk; telegrammy po voprosu ob evakuatsii Iur'evskogo universiteta, 1915–17 gg.), ll. 8ob.–9.

[23] RGIA f. 560, d. 1342, ll. 9ob. and 10ob.

[24] V. D. Zernov, *Zapiski russkogo intelligenta* (Moscow: INDRIK, 2005), 206.

[25] See M. D. Karpachev, *Voronezhskii universitet: Vekhi istorii, 1918–2003* (Voronezh: Izdvo voronezhskogo universiteta, 2003), 15–81.

The rapid progress of enemy forces toward Petrograd led to the suspension of higher education in the capital, with the exception of the medical institutes. In other institutes only graduating students pursued their studies. The possibility of having students take courses in universities and institutes in other cities was considered, but these were already overloaded with students.[26] A Perm' branch of Petrograd University was created as an evacuation base; later, by the decision of the Provisional Government, it was reorganized into the independent Perm' University. This increase in the network of domestic universities in no way compensated for war damage to the underdeveloped higher education system of the empire.[27]

"The war years of 1914–1915 placed a heavy burden on the development of science," stated V. I. Vernadskii:

> It deflected resources intended for peaceful cultural and scientific work and removed personnel from their scholarly pursuits for months at a time. Thousands of talented people fell on the field of battle and died in field hospitals; among these were some who would have been major scholars in better life circumstances. Among them would have been some such as are born once in a generation.[28]

The rift in international scientific relations, most of all with Germany, was regarded by scholars as a crushing blow. For the Russian "scholarly class" Germany was viewed as a scientific Mecca, possessing a rich network of well-equipped universities with highly qualified teaching personnel. For Russian professors, teachers, and researchers, frequent scientific trips to Germany from the 18th century onward had been a most important element in academic

---

[26] RGIA f. 1276, op. 11, d. 1369, l. 5.

[27] RGIA f. 741 (Otdel promyshlennykh uchilishch), op. 11, d. 203 (Postanovlenie Komissii o razgruzke Petrograda v otnoshenii vysshikh uchebnykh zavedenii), ll. 1–2. We note, however, that the evacuation of institutes of higher learning had certain positive consequences. For example, for Saratov University, which consisted of one medical department, the connection, even though temporary, with the older Kiev University led to a reinvigoration of scientific and academic life. Professor V. D. Zernov recalled: "When the Kiev people saw our 'spic and span' new buildings and equipment, they were amazed: they saw that being in Saratov was not like being 'in the sticks.' They did not even unpack their own equipment, but used ours. We lived with them in a very friendly fashion. Some of us even took part in teaching and administering examinations. I, for example, gave exams on physics for the State Commission and on meteorology...; I was an official committee member for Masters' dissertations.... Not all the professors came to Saratov from Kiev, and our participation was truly necessary, and in this way 'the guests' 'fed' their 'hosts'" (*Zapiski russkogo intelligenta*, 206).

[28] V. I. Vernadskii, "Voina i progress nauki," in his *Perezhitoe i peredumannoe* (Moscow: Vagrius, 2007), 234.

achievement. From the 18th and into the second half of the 19th centuries German scholars traditionally occupied the most honored places among the foreign teachers and "honorary members" of Russian higher education establishments and the scientific societies associated with them.

The war destroyed this academic harmony. It was obscured by threatening clouds of germanophobia. The Russian professoriate accused its erstwhile colleagues of justifying "militarism," of having "exerted their fatal influence on the whole spiritual culture of Germany, in which the former cult of truth, goodness, and beauty had for some time been changing to a postulate of brute force and an urge to justify violence and vandalism." On 1 September 1914 A. S. Dogel', a professor at Petrograd University, censured the brutal actions against culture by the "barbarians of the twentieth century—the Germans" for their destruction of Leuven University in Belgium and challenged his colleagues to break all scholarly ties with German scholars and to exclude those who "shame and humiliate science" from the register of honorary membership in Russian universities.[29] After long and animated discussions, on 24 November 1914 the professorial body of Petrograd University removed the name of a professor at the University of Berlin, von List, from its register of honorary members. Only the professor of zoology, V. M. Shimkevich, voted against the motion. This measure was taken in response to a legislative decree by the Council of Ministers on 31 October 1914 on the exclusion of all German subjects from the staff of research institutions and universities. This action caused a chain reaction. Higher education in Russia excluded representatives of German science. Nearly 70 German subjects were removed from the register of honorary members by Moscow University alone and the scientific societies connected with it.[30] Only the A. I. Chuprov Society for the Development of Social Sciences flatly refused to revise its membership on the alleged grounds that it did not have information on the citizenship of its members since its charter did not provide for the collection of this type of data.[31]

ରଃ ଞ

Association with the government's military defense program effected cardinal changes in the paradigm of scientific research and teaching in the physics and mathematics departments of universities and noticeably weakened any of their primary goals that were not directly related to "safeguarding technical work

---

[29] *Protokoly zasedaniia Soveta imp. Petrogradskogo universiteta za 1914 g.,* 79–80.

[30] TsIAM f. 418, op. 92, d. 735 (Ob iskliuchenii iz chisla pochetnykh chlenov universiteta i sostoiashchikh pri nem uchenykh obshchestv vsekh poddannykh voiuiushchikh s Rossiiei derzhav), ll. 12–29.

[31] TsIAM f. 418, op. 92, d. 735.

from the destructive forces of war."[32] In the field of chemistry, for example, priority was given to applied research on pharmaceuticals in order to relieve the acute drug shortage experienced by the active army and the whole population. In 1915 Ignat'ev stated: "The shortage of chemical and pharmaceutical products experienced since the outbreak of war has demonstrated completely clearly our empire's close dependence on the foreign, and chiefly the German, market."[33] In September 1914 the minister of education convened a "Special Session" of professors of chemistry, medicine, and pharmacology to draw up a list of medicines needed by the army which the higher education institutes would be able to prepare using students and lab workers. The first All-Russian Congress to work out a plan to combat "drug starvation" took place in Kazan' from 10–16 August 1917 under the auspices of the regional War Industries Committee. Professors of Kazan' and Saratov universities presented scientific reports.[34] The Physics and Chemistry Society of Kiev University undertook production of medicines in a chloroform factory they had organized. This project was directed by Professor S. N. Reformatskii.[35] Scientists in the chemistry department of the Natural Sciences College of Moscow University undertook pharmacological work after building a chemical-pharmaceutical factory.[36] Non-governmental ("private") higher education establishments were also involved in the struggle to alleviate the shortages of medicine. Odessa University (from 1916), Moscow Advanced Women's Courses (from 1917), and Petrograd Private University (until 1916 the Psycho-Neurological Institute) all operated chemical pharmaceutical departments.[37] They prepared specialists for the pharmaceutical industry, which had been completely absent in prewar Russia and was only now emerging.

The leading centers for the preparation of drugs that were vital for military field medicine were the universities of Kazan' (the laboratories of professors A. Ia. Bogoroditskii and A. E. Arbuzov), Kiev (Reformatskii), and Moscow. Manufacture of morphine, iodine, and salicylic pharmaceuticals was organized in the laboratory of Professor A. E. Chichibabin at Moscow Technical Institute. These medicines were provided primarily "for the needs of military medical units." In March 1916 the Council of Ministers assigned

---

[32] Vernadskii, *Voina i progress nauki*, 234.

[33] RGIA f. 733, op. 156, d. 631 (Ob uchrezhdenii farmatsevticheskikh shkol i o sokrashchenii aptek: Dlia lits, derzhashchikh ispytanie na zvanie aptekar'skikh pomoshchnikov. 1916 g.), l. 3.

[34] TsIAM f. 418, op. 95, d. 924, l. 16.

[35] RGIA f. 733, op. 226, d. 170 (Vsepoddanneishaia zapiska ministra narodnogo prosveshcheniia, o deiatel'nosti vysshikh uchebnykh zavedenii v 1914 g.), l. 5.

[36] M. N. Tikhomirov, *Istoriia Moskovskogo universiteta*, 1: *1755–1917* (Moscow: Izd-vo Moskovskogo universiteta, 1955), 425.

[37] Ivanov, "Rossiiskoe 'uchenoe soslovie,'" 116.

300,000 rubles for the organization of "a model factory for the manufacture of medicine" at Chichibanin's institute.[38] Radiographic research by professors and teachers also acquired a medical orientation. At the Moscow Technical Institute mobile and stationary x-ray machines were developed for use in military field medicine.[39] Professor G. K. Suslov of Kiev University carried out applied medical radiology research in ten military hospitals.[40]

The medical departments of universities applied themselves completely to military-specific applications. Firstly, in teaching, their primary task was to speed up the preparation of "ordinary doctors" for the military in an abbreviated program. These doctors would receive a full-fledged medical diploma after the war when they finished the complete university program and passed the state exams. Secondly, in their scientific research professors concentrated mainly on the problems of military field medicine. For example, in Tomsk University in 1915 professors worked on such topics as "The Structure and Activities of Bacteriological Laboratories at the Front" (Professor A. P. Avrorov); "War-Related Courses for Doctors" (Professor S. V. Lobanov); "Poisoning by Asphyxiating Gases" (Professor N. V. Vershinin); and "Individual Isolation of Infectious Diseases" (Professor P. N. Lashchenkov).[41]

Medical departments of universities were transformed into centers of hospital care for severely wounded frontline soldiers. V. D. Zernov, a professor of physics at Saratov University (where there was a department of medicine), recalled that "[i]n Saratov the war had little impact at first, but soon new university buildings were transformed into hospitals. The wives of professors and teachers undertook the duties of nurses. In my [Physics] institute a hospital for surgery was organized and an operating theater was located in the large auditorium. I also organized an x-ray room."[42] This was one of three infirmaries located in university buildings that were under the patronage of the Saratov provincial zemstvo, with an overall capacity of 500 beds.[43]

The Council of Moscow University opened a clinic for wounded and sick soldiers on 25 July 1914. In view of the fact that several of the assistants and orderlies had been drafted for military service, and considering the great influx of wounded, the council requested that adjunct senior lecturers of the

---

[38] *Osobye zhurnaly Soveta ministrov Rossiiskoi imperii: 1916 god* (Moscow: ROSSPEN, 2008), 89–90.

[39] V. I. Prokof'ev, *Moskovskoe vysshee tekhnicheskoe uchilishche: 125 let* (Moscow: MASHGIZ, 1955), 149–51.

[40] RGIA f. 733, op. 226, d. 170, l. 5.

[41] P. A. Zaichenko, *Tomskii gosudarstvennyi universitet im. V. V.Kuibysheva: Ocherki po istorii pervogo Sibirskogo universiteta za 75 let (1880–1955)* (Tomsk: Izd-vo Tomskogo universiteta, 1960), 125

[42] Zernov, *Zapiski russkogo intelligenta*, 205.

[43] Solomonov, *Imperatorskii Nikolaevskii Saratovskii universitet*, 180.

Faculty of Medicine "take upon themselves responsibility for the treatment of patients."[44] Wives of professors and university employees suggested creating "their own" university infirmary on 14 October of the same year. The university set aside space and allocations for this. A resolution was also adopted on monthly voluntary personal contributions by professors (no less than 5 rubles per person) for treatment of the wounded.[45]

On 29 June 1915 the Council of Petrograd University resolved to assign funds from its own budget for the organization of a field infirmary in the name of Petrograd higher education institutions, for a permanent infirmary under the Ministry of Education to be located at the Women's Medical Institute, and also an infirmary for the treatment of nervous and mental illnesses to be located at the university.[46] Military infirmaries also operated in non-medical higher education establishments, for example at the Kazan' Institute for Women's Courses, the Divinity Academy, and the Veterinary Institute.

Visits to the theater of war became part of the academic routine for teachers of medicine. S. I. Spasokukotskii and V. I. Razumovskii, professors at Saratov University, were assigned to the Southwestern Front as consultant surgeons in 1915. Several infirmaries were created in the frontline area on the initiative of Razumovskii.[47] In the same year Professor A. S. Ikonnikov of Kazan' University was assigned "by petition" to the front as a "practicing surgeon,"[48] and his colleague Professor V. N. Tonkov was assigned to make improvements in the Military Medical Academy.[49] The university professoriate also took part in organizing the medical operations of the Red Cross and other military health institutions. In 1915 three Saratov professors were seconded as consultants to the Red Cross.[50]

Finally, the war made it necessary for professors and teachers to organize the manufacture of home-produced surgical instruments and medical laboratory equipment. At Kazan' University a special commission headed by Professor N. F. Vysotskii was set up to work out measures for coping with this shortage. It stated: "Until the present war, research and teaching activity in our universities, at least in the medical, physical science, and mathematics faculties, was completely dependent on foreign companies, chiefly German

---

[44] TsIAM f. 418, op. 92, d. 747 (Postanovleniia Soveta Moskovskogo universiteta), l. 9.

[45] TsIAM f. 418, d. 585 (Postanovleniia Soveta Moskovskogo universiteta), l. 25.

[46] *Protokoly zasedaniia Soveta imp. Petrogradskogo universiteta za 1914 g.*, 83.

[47] Solomonov, *Imperatorskii Nikolaevskii Saratovskii universitet*, 181–82.

[48] Natsional'nyi arkhiv Respubliki Tatarstan (NART) f. 977 (Sovet Kazanskogo universiteta), d. 1277 (Protokoly zasedanii), l. 173.

[49] NART f. 977, d. 12907 (Protokoly zasedanii), l. 125.

[50] *Otchet o sostoianii i deiatel'nosti imp. Nikolaevskogo universiteta za 1915 g.* (Saratov, 1915), 5.

ones, from whom we had to order our scientific supplies—instruments, equipment, vessels, chemical and medical supplies, and so on, since Russia did not possess them."[51] The chair of the commission issued information about this matter to all medical universities and invited their cooperation. Such a notification was also sent to Moscow University.[52]

For professors and teachers in higher education institutes the most urgent task in practical scientific research for the military was the development of means of chemical defense against the asphyxiating gases used by German troops.[53] In a very short time three types of gas mask, invented by chemists of the Petersburg Mining Institute—and ordered by the Anti-gas section of the Chemical Committee of the Main Artillery Directorate of the universities—were put into rapid production. At the same time large-scale work was taking place on facilitating the manufacture of new types of gas warfare and explosive material for the military.[54] The developments worked out by the physics and mathematics departments of Moscow University became the technological base for a factory producing chemical weapons.[55] The laboratories of professors Bogoroditskii and Arbuzov conducted a series of studies to find the simplest methods of protection against poisonous substances. The director of the pharmacology laboratory, V. N. Boldyrev, developed a method for protecting against chemical attacks which the armies of Russia's allies adopted. Professor N. A. Shilov of the Moscow Technical Institute constructed a standard model chemical laboratory for work in the war zone. His colleague F. K. Gerke composed methodical guidelines on "Poison Gas in Warfare" and "Brief Information on Gases Used by the Germans and Methods of Combating Them" for distribution to the troops as brochures.[56]

It was primarily the Main Artillery Administration (Glavnoe artilleriiskoe upravlenie) that guided defense-related research activity at the Petrograd Technical Institute. Faculty involved with the defense program at the Petrograd Polytechnical Institute—a different organization from the Technical In-

---

[51] NART f. 977, d. 13128 (Protokoly zasedanii), l. 8.

[52] TsIAM f. 418, op. 421, d. 112, l. 11ob.

[53] A. N. De-Lazari, *Khimicheskoe oruzhie na frontakh mirovoi voiny, 1914–1918 gg.* (Moscow: Gosudarstvennoe voennoe izdatel'stvo, 1935), 29, 45. The first German gas attack on the Russian front took place on 3 June 1915 on the outskirts of Warsaw at Vola Shildlovska. 9,146 persons were gassed, of whom 1,183 died. In 1916 the Germans undertook ten such attacks against Russian forces. The greatest damage was suffered that year on 2 July near Smorgan' in Molodechno region: 3,864 gassed with 286 fatalities.

[54] E. V. Trofimova, *Sozdanie i deiatel'nost' Khimicheskogo komiteta pri Glavnom artilleriiskom upravlenii v gody Pervoi mirovoi voiny* (Moscow: Kompaniia Sputnik, 2002), 135–47.

[55] *Istoriia Moskovskogo universiteta*, 1: 425.

[56] Prokof'ev, *Moskovskoe vysshee tekhnicheskoe uchilishche*, 192.

stitute—undertook a wide array of research on radio-telegraphic appliances, electric fences, aircraft, x-ray equipment, and medicine production.[57] During the war years the experimental-production base of the industrial engineering institutes greatly expanded; in wartime conditions they oriented themselves toward defense-related research and manufacturing. In practical terms these evolved into a number of small faculty-led projects for the production of shells (Petrograd Technological Institute), magnetos, detonators, and micro-telephonic instruments (Polytechnic and Electro-Technical institutes in Petrograd), etc. Similarly, workshops to manufacture components for artillery shells and grenades were organized in the Physics Department at Saratov University; they operated under the auspices of the War Industries Committee.[58]

In addition to their scientific and practical work, the patriotic activity of professors and teachers extended to the sphere of defense management. As expert consultants, they took part in the activity of such governmental bodies as the Special Commissions on defense, transport, and manufacturing; the Central War Industries Committee and its local branches; the Chemical Committee with its chief concentration on artillery; and also the self-governing Union of Cities and the Zemstvo Union for Aid to the Sick and Wounded.

∞ ∞

The war had an impact on the ideology of patriotic militarism in the works of scholars dedicated to military themes in Russian and general history, political economy, political science, as well as in public lectures, museum work, and journalism. They expressed their patriotic fervor by claiming to demonstrate the historically predetermined aggressiveness of Germans, the roots of which were to be sought in the wars they started in the 18th and 19th centuries. "In German culture both past and present," affirmed E. N. Trubetskoi, "there are no small number of examples of arrogant and generally improper relations with other peoples and cultures."[59] V. P. Buzeskul discovered revanchist ideas embedded in German historiography. He entitled an article he published in *Russkaia mysl'* (no. 9, 1915) "Contemporary Germany and German Historical Science: The Ideology of Revanchism." M. P. Antsiferov heard the lectures on classical history by Professor M. I. Rostovtsev of Petrograd University in which he developed the theory that the historical bellicosity of the German nation was caused by its break with the ancient civilization that had fed the

---

[57] *Trudy Leningradskogo politekhnicheskogo instituta im. M. I. Kalinina*, no. 190, *Istoriia instituta* (Leningrad, 1927), 78–81.

[58] Solomonov, *Imperatorskii Nikolaevskii Saratovskii universitet*, 182.

[59] E. N. Trubetskoi, "Voina i mirovaia zadacha Rossii," *Russkaia mysl'*, no. 12 (1914): 94.

culture of all European peoples.[60] Professor of Russian history at Moscow University, M. M. Bogoslovskii, recorded the following maxim in his diary on 20 March 1915: "A moral code obviously does not exist for the modern German. His is the principle of evil armed with all the complex devices of science. After such evil deeds [the sinking of a hospital ship in the Black Sea] the war must naturally take on a merciless character and its end, obviously, will be marked by even more cruelties than its beginning."[61] His colleague D. N. Anuchin, a geography professor, wrote about the expansionist designs of German geographers during the ongoing war.[62] And so on and so forth. A compendium of articles published in Petrograd by M. M. Kovalevskii in three issues, "Russia and Her Allies in the Fight for Civilization" (1916–17), became a platform for the expression of professorial patriotism. The authors included E. V. Tarle, N. I. Kareev, E. D. Grimm, A. N. Veselovskii, and others.

Implying that the imperial ideology of the German burghers and Junkers was characteristic of the nation, the Russian professoriate purposefully created a literary stereotype of the average German as an "arrogantly self-satisfied chauvinist," obsessed with the cult of the "mailed fist," and despising the national interests of other peoples. The German Kaiser Wilhelm II was the epitome of such revanchist views. A belief in his supposed clinical insanity was widespread in Russian society. The eminent psychiatrist V. M. Bekhterev rejected this judgment, yet thought that "the rays of German militarism" emanated from the kaiser's actions. Not finding any obvious psychic impairments in the personality of his hypothetical patient, the doctor still discovered in his behavior signs of clinical ill-health as exhibited by "periods of excitement and the delusional nature of his statements," inherent not only in the mentally sick but in the so-called "degenerate neuro-nervous type."[63]

Student Ensigns, Non-Commissioned Officers, Privates

The Russian Empire went to war without having officers in reserve. Consequently on 30 September 1914 the government issued a "resolution" to cancel the postponement of military service for students until they had completed their higher education coursework. This "extraordinary measure" was motivated by

---

[60] N. P. Antsiferov, *Iz dum o proshlom* (Moscow: Feniks. Kul'turnaia initsiativa, 1992), 162. In this connection the memoirist recalled: "The impassioned Rostovtsev was not able to retreat into academic life during the war. When it became clear that there was a lack of ammunition, Mikhail Ivanovich stood at a lathe and set himself to making shells. He subsequently suffered because of his militant anti-German position" (ibid.).

[61] M. M. Bogoslovskii, *Dnevniki 1913–1919* (Moscow: Vremia, 2011), 165.

[62] D. N. Anuchin, "Predpolozhenie i deistvitel'nost'," *Russkie vedomosti*, 25 August 1914.

[63] V. M. Bekhterev, *Vil'gel'm—degenerat neronovskogo tipa* (Moscow, 1916), 7.

the "significant shortfall in the officer corps, as high as 75% in some places."[64] The student body became virtually the only source for replenishing the young officers lost in battle. From now on undergraduate students were drafted into the "lower ranks" of reserve regiments with subsequent deployment based on speciality and requirements. But in these circumstances, so critical for the army, the government resorted to the usual method of protective selection of intelligent recruits. "The worthy and capable" were sent for short-term study (4–8 months) in military schools to obtain the initial officer's rank of "ensign." The less "worthy" draftees among the students were made non-commissioned officers and the completely "unworthy" were made privates.

Into the category of the "unworthy" fell young people with a reputation for being "politically unreliable," as did all "persons of the Jewish confession" without exception. The issue of limiting the service rank of Jewish students sent into the army caused a difference of opinion within ruling circles. An interdepartmental communication of October 1915 found it generally preferable to refrain from drafting Jews, even as privates, and would not accept them in officer schools. This measure was greeted with outrage by the whole student body. In the "appeal" by representatives of Moscow University student organizations in March 1916, the drafting of Jews into the lowest army ranks was characterized as "a new outrageous act ... stemming from the government's [Russian] nationalist policy." The authors of the "appeal" termed the possible non-drafting of Jewish students as "provocative invective of the authorities aimed at inflaming nationalistic instincts" in society. The students demanded the drafting of Jewish students "on equal terms with all."[65]

Such a reaction by the students troubled the head of the government, Goremykin. In a letter written in October 1916 to the minister of war, A. A. Polivanov, he rejected even the hypothetical non-drafting of Jewish students into the army because of the possibility that it could provoke disorders within higher educational institutes. Moreover, the premier was sure that the implementation of such a plan would lead to a predominance of the Jewish element in universities and special institutes. Goremykin did not see alternatives to the military mobilization of Jews in "lower ranks" and did not see any serious impediments to this.[66]

In accordance with the new law, the draft campaign encompassed all students. Its scale can be judged by the following data: Petrograd Polytechnic sent 1,615 students into the army in 1915–16; the small Petrograd Railway Engineering Institute sent 400 in 1915 alone; Moscow Business Institute sent

---

[64] *Osobye zhurnaly Soveta ministrov Rossiiskoi imperii: 1914 god* (Moscow: RossPEN, 2006), 395.

[65] GARF f. 102.00 (1916), d. 59, ch. 46, Litera "B" (O studencheskikh besporiadkakh v Moskve), l. 9.

[66] RGIA f. 1276, op. 11, d. 1369, ll. 8ob.–9ob.

1,800 in 1916;[67] by this point approximately 50 percent of Petrograd students were under arms.[68] Awaiting them was the front, whose fire incinerated the lives of new student recruits each day and every hour. Within the government only the minister of education, Ignat'ev, expressed alarm at this wasteful squandering of young intellectual talent. He wrote to the Council of Ministers on 3 September 1915 that students should be taken into the armed forces "only as a last resort" to make up numbers in the officer corps; "it is essential to bear in mind that with the end of military action a very significant number of educated workers will be required to ensure the reestablishment of the normal pace of governmental service."[69] However, Ignat'ev's warning had no effect. Student mobilizations continued every two or three months. They literally bled the lower courses of higher education institutes, restricting the intake of upper classmen and consequently the number of graduates. Those students who were not drafted were required to work in the defense industries as substitute engineers, designers, design-technicians, lathe instructors, lathe operators, and so on. From January through August 1917 alone 200 students from the Moscow Technical Institute worked at military enterprises in Moscow city and province.[70] Students were taken for civic work more frequently and in greater numbers, for example loading firewood, and as low- and intermediate-level personnel in field hospitals and on hospital trains. Such distractions were not conducive to the rhythm and productivity of academic life.

The widely practiced intensive, or, more precisely, shortened courses did not provide quality preparation of graduates in higher education. In order to satisfy the ever growing need for doctors at the front and in hospitals at the rear, university medical departments adopted a shortened four-year (instead of five-year) program. The fuel and transport crisis affecting the Russian economy was the reason for the accelerated graduation of specialists from such places of higher learning as the Forestry Institute in Petrograd; the Agriculture and Forestry Institute in Novaia Aleksandriia; the Moscow and Petrograd railway engineering institutes; and civil engineering departments of the Petrograd, Warsaw, and Kiev polytechnics. They then invariably worked for the ministries occupied with government defense—Military, Communication, Trade and Industry, and Agriculture. This type of service was considered as active military duty, and in cases of infringement of discipline these employees fell under the jurisdiction of military justice.

---

[67] A. E. Ivanov, *Vysshaia shkola Rossii v kontse XIX–nachale XX veka* (Moscow: Institut istorii SSSR, 1991), 256.

[68] Rostovtsev, *Universitet stolichnogo goroda*, 324.

[69] RGIA f. 1276, op. 11, d. 1369, l. 4.

[70] TsIAM f. 372 (Moskovskoe tekhnicheskoe uchilishche), op. 6, d. 211 (O komandirovke studentov Moskovskogo tekhnicheskogo uchilishcha Voenno-tekhnicheskoi komissiei na zavody), l. 11.

In Anticipation of Peace

The main burden of military mobilization in higher education was felt in the period when Ignat'ev headed the Ministry of Education (January 1915–December 1916). In order to meet the challenges caused by the war, the minister drafted a strategic plan of postwar reform for the restructuring of higher education up to 1925.[71] Determining the university's place in the plan was the responsibility of the Council for the Affairs of Institutions of Higher Learning, an ad hoc umbrella organization within the Ministry of Education. The Council gave priority to the drafting of a new university charter that would meet European standards of academic autonomy. The Council also proposed a plan for opening new universities in Rostov-on-Don, Perm', Samara, Iaroslavl (based on the Demidov Juridical Lyceum), Voronezh (or Tambov), Ekaterinoslav (or Simferopol' or Kerch'), Vil'na (or Smolensk or Minsk), and Vladivostok (based on the Vostochnyi Institute).

Responsibility for another part of the plan concerning professional-technical education lay with the Council for Professional Education in the empire, which presented a report "On Establishing a Network of Technological Institutes." Its blunt premise was that the war laid bare the inadequacies of "our professional education," which "up to the present has developed weakly and unsystematically; so many technical tasks are beyond Russia's capability due to the lack of a sufficient number of workers." The developers of that part of Ignat'ev's reform program therefore suggested expanding the network of industrial-engineering institutes "twice over," proposing to open 11 new technological colleges, first in Viatka, Samara, Irkutsk, Kishinev, Vil'na, Vladivostok, and Blagoveshchensk; and in a second phase in Ekaterinoslav, Simferopol', and Voronezh. [72]

Post-February Freedoms

Professors, teachers, and students greeted the February Revolution with political and patriotic enthusiasm. Their firm support of the Provisional Government was based not only on expectations of a revolutionary transformation of the state, but on immediate compliance with the obligations to their allies in the war with Germany. The attitude of the professoriate on this fateful issue was expressed succinctly by its Kazan' colleagues: "We are convinced that the freedom we have won can only be preserved by the complete unity of all classes of society standing behind the Provisional Government, which is

---

[71] On Ignat'ev's plans for reform, see Ivanov, *Vysshaia shkola Rossii*, 184–87.

[72] RGIA f. 741, op. 7, d. 485, l. 26ob.

leading the fight against an enemy that is at one and the same time formidable, an age-old ally, and the stronghold of Russian reaction."[73]

The democratic mood of the student body, which was inspired by the idea of protecting the new Russia, was at odds with the antiwar mood of 1915–16 caused by the Russian army's terrible losses. But students returned to the positions they had taken at the beginning of the war, and now replaced the slogan "Down with the War!" with "War to its Victorious End!" At the March assembly of students at the Moscow Business Institute, the only one to vote for the Bolshevik antiwar resolution was the Bolshevik orator himself. The students of Petrograd University booed a Bolshevik among their peers who called for an immediate end to the war.[74] Medical students, who had only recently been preparing a protest against the war, now expressed their readiness to postpone their final exams until a more propitious time, in order not to delay their departure to the front "for clinical duties."[75] In April 1917 students of the Mining Institute in Ekaterinburg passed a resolution to cut short their studies and voluntarily leave for the front.[76]

In short, both ideologically and emotionally, the higher education "population," with the exception of a small number of Bolshevik and Socialist Revolutionary student groups, demonstrated their patriotic attitude to the war. "Now there are slogans around which we can unite with students; for example on pursuing the war to a victorious conclusion," the Council of Moscow University stated with satisfaction in March 1917.[77] Higher education institutions continued to maintain military barracks and military medical agencies. The Provisional Government continued the practice of drafting students into the army and commissioning them for work in war industries. Student volunteers worked at "feeding stations" for soldiers and needy civilians, created civilian militias (*politseiskie druzhiny*) to preserve order in the cities, and carried out patriotic propaganda campaigns among the populace.

However, these activities were unusual for higher education and became more and more unsustainable, due to the deficiencies in supplies for the students' own daily requirements. A crisis of physical survival arose before them in full magnitude. Professor Bogoslovskii wrote in his diary on 5 October 1917: "We have completely lost the habit of eating. We are simply beginning to

---

[73] *Golos Kazani*, 18 March 1917. Cited in A. Iu. Sizova, "Rossiiskaia vysshaia shkola v revoliutsionnykh sobytiiakh 1917 g." (Dissertatsiia kandidata istoricheskikh nauk, Rossiiskii gosudarstvennyi gumanitarnyi universitet, 2007), 57.

[74] Ibid., 180.

[75] Ibid.

[76] Ibid., 220.

[77] *Istoriia Moskovskogo universiteta*, 1: 556.

starve."[78] And on 22 October: "hunger is advancing on Moscow; we will [only] be getting half a pound of bread per person."[79]

Students who did not have family in the towns where they attended school went from house to house in search of food and warmth. Moscow University students issued an appeal for help to the Council of Professors:

> There are no rooms in Moscow. No bread. A huge proportion of the students arriving in Moscow are obliged to roam around looking for shelter, and anyone who finds some considers themselves fortunate. As many as 5 or 6 students can be sharing one room. The crisis in food supply makes itself felt even more sharply since almost every student is starving and spends a significant part of their time standing in line on the streets ..., and the pitiful vegetation they find costs an enormous sum of money.[80]

Confirming the authenticity of this complaint, Bogoslovskii noted in his diary that "[l]ife in Moscow for very many of our students has become barely possible because of the expense of apartments and food."[81] The situation of young students in other Russian centers of higher education was just as hopeless. "The war has caused colossal devastation in higher education. No more than a third of the student body remains in many institutions," stated the author of an article on "The Collapse of Higher Education" that appeared in *Novaia zhizn'* on 29 October 1917.

The everyday crisis of living was exacerbated by discord between professors and the students who demanded their own representation with voting rights on the councils of higher education establishments. The professors considered such claims to be excessive and academically unsound, and in turn offered their opponents collaboration in conciliation organizations. An example of such a committee of professors, junior faculty, and students was one set up at Moscow University for developing "forms of student participation in affairs concerning their interests and mode of life." Similar organizations arose in Petrograd and Kiev universities.[82] In the locations where professors succumbed to student pressure (Kazan' and Perm' universities, the Petrograd Mining Institute, the Warsaw Polytechnic Institute, the latter evacuated at that

---

[78] Bogoslovskii, *Dnevniki*, 436.

[79] Ibid., 445.

[80] Sizova, "Rossiiskaia vysshaia shkola," 241, citing TsIAM f. 418 (Moskovskii universitet), op. 249, d. 112, l. 315.

[81] Bogoslovskii, *Dnevniki*, 168.

[82] O. N. Znamenskii, *Intelligentsiia nakanune Velikogo oktiabria* (Leningrad: Nauka, 1988), 158.

time to Nizhnii Novgorod), conflict immediately arose when the professors' councils disavowed the concessions that had been made.[83]

The students took the refusal to accept their representatives onto governing councils as unwillingness on the professors' part to democratize higher education in accordance with the demands of the new Russia. Extreme alienation of students from teachers followed. The students resorted to their tried-and-tested method of pressuring the academic administration through strikes, which took place across Russia in March and April 1917.[84] The revolutionary chaos in the country was also not conducive to academic studies. As in 1905, the students opened up campus buildings to the public for multiparty protests and meetings. Higher education was paralyzed until the fall of 1917, if one does not include sparsely attended lectures, seminars, and laboratory work at some universities and institutes. Professor Zernov recalled this uncertain time:

> Classes were not officially canceled in the university, but instead of lectures, political meetings were often held in the auditoriums. Indeed, once I came to give a lecture at the Physics Institute and found the auditorium taken over by a thousand-strong crowd of protestors. There were students there, but mainly it was people off the streets. Quite a large group of my own students surrounded me and said they wanted to listen to my lecture. Remembering that during the great French Revolution not a single lecture was canceled in the Sorbonne, I suggested that they come to my library in the Physics Institute.[85]

When, as in 1905, students, exhausted by the strain of political life, decided to return to class, they encountered an unforeseen situation. The Provisional Government lacked the material resources necessary to support the effective work of higher education and resolved to postpone the beginning of the academic year until 2 October. Petrograd was singled out. Classes there were closed until 1918 on the pretext of the threat of a German attack on the capital. In order to unburden the city of "extra mouths to feed" at a time of severe food shortages, out-of-town students were required to continue their studies in the provinces. Yet there was nothing for the "refugee-students" there, due to the same breakdown in the economy.

These actions, which circumstances forced the authorities to take, called forth an explosion of student dissatisfaction since they suspected the Provisional Government of politically motivated anti-student intrigue. Wanting to control the whole educational process at universities, students

---

[83] Sizova, "Rossiiskaia vysshaia shkola," 228–29.

[84] For details, see ibid., 222–33, and A. Ia. Leikin, *Protiv lozhnykh druzei molodezhi* (Moscow: Molodaia gvardiia, 1980), 46–47.

[85] Zernov, *Zapiski russkogo intelligenta*, 212.

challenged the authority of professors. Reinforced by the Russia-wide strikes in the spring and summer of 1917 and the anti-government disorders in September, this became one of the leading causes of the systemic inaction in higher education and one of the factors in the weakening of the political position of the Provisional Government.[86]

Professors conducted themselves more cautiously in the conflict with the students, as they were always prepared to respond positively to outbursts that were aimed at renewing studies. In a session in September 1917 the Council of Moscow University supported an emotional declaration by Professor V. M. Khvostov that blamed the authorities for closing higher education institutions in Petrograd:

> When sites were needed for clinics it was schools that were the first to be allocated for this purpose (not cinemas, cabarets, and other places of entertainment). Now it seems it is necessary to help the capital ..., and once again, it's the schools they close first of all.... We are not so rich in education as to be able to do away with schools. Let the disarray in the country affect something else, but not the schools.[87]

Regarding higher education, the professoriate also reacted more carefully than the student body. They had used the post-February freedoms for the benefit of academic independence and had been able to restore the university positions of colleagues who had been obliged to leave them during the oppressive administration of Minister Kasso. Taking advantage of the prolonged postponement of academic classes because of student disorders, academics made preparations for reforms in higher education. M. M. Novikov, professor of zoology at Moscow University and its elected rector, recalled: "All summer long in 1917, with the thunder of revolution roaring around Russia, I was living in Petrograd working zealously for the most part on peaceful reconstruction in higher education."[88] He was referring to his chairmanship of the Commission for the Reform of Higher Education under the Provisional Government's Ministry of Education. The commission was made up of the minister himself, his vice-ministers, department heads, and, as invited members, the representative of the academic section of the Ministry of Trade and Industry, the Academic Council, and junior faculty from Petrograd institutes of higher learning. The Commission was empowered to initiate legislation. The statutes it prepared

---

[86] O. N. Znamenskii, *Intelligentsiia nakanune Velikogo oktiabria (fevral'–oktiabr' 1917)* (Leningrad: Nauka, 1988), 274–75, 318–21.

[87] Sizova, "Rossiiskaia vysshaia shkola," 228–29, citing TsIAM f. 418, op. 249, d. 112a, ll. 315–315ob.

[88] M. M. Novikov, *Ot Moskvy do N'iu-Iorka: Moia zhizn' v nauke i politike* (New York: Izd-vo imeni Chekhova, 1952), 268.

for signature by the minister and his deputies were immediately forwarded for confirmation to the Provisional Government.

The Commission suggested radically changing the method of paying teaching personnel in higher education by canceling the honorarium collected from students for listening to lectures, which served as a supplement to the relatively modest teaching salary, and replacing it with higher salaries. A resolution was also accepted on replacing non-permanent lecturers with permanent ones, with a precedent in the university charter of 1863.[89]

Professor Novikov considered reform of the university charter to be one of the most substantive achievements of the commission. He recalled that, because of the matter's urgency, the commission decided that, rather than creating a new charter, they would change the current charter of 1884 by issuing legislation that eliminated norms "contrary to the principle of university autonomy."[90] To achieve this it was necessary to do the following: remove universities from the bureaucratic guardianship of academic trustees; provide elective university bodies with independence from the Ministry of Education (with the exception of the minister's right to intervene to avoid cases of "nepotism" in the confirmation of professorial candidates elected by the council); allow representation of "junior faculty" in collegiate bodies of departments and university councils; and permit the unhindered activity of scholarly organizations. In June 1917 the All-Russian Conference of Academics approved these innovations, which were also extended to the economics institutes administered by the Ministry of Education. They were confirmed into law by the Provisional Government.[91]

Under Soviet Rule

The October Revolution resulted in the instantaneous annulment of the Commission for the Reform of Higher Education and its efforts toward democratic reorganization. Students and professors reacted to the new government in different ways. In the capital students had already exhausted their zeal for protest in conflicts with the professoriate and the Provisional Government, and they gave a lukewarm welcome to the Revolution; they did not feel any great sympathy for the Bolsheviks. In the regions caught up in the conflagration of the Civil War, students generally supported the Soviets' enemies.[92] Recognizing the political unreliability of the "old" student body,

---

[89] Ibid., 276.

[90] Ibid.

[91] Ibid.

[92] For example, at the end of 1918 the students of the Novocherkassk Polytechnic Institute organized a student fighting squad for the battle with "anarchic Bolshevism." Thirteen locomotive brigades were formed from among these students which played

the Soviets conceived a quick way of proletarianizing higher education. On 2 August 1918 the government of the RFSFR issued the decree "On Rules for Admission into Institutions of Higher Learning," which stated that any person who was 16 years of age, irrespective of their level of education, may become a student at any university or institute.[93] By a resolution of the Soviet government on 6 August 1918, the Commissar of Enlightenment was ordered to guarantee that members of the proletariat and poor peasantry had priority admission to higher education.[94]

As a result of these decisions universities were flooded with entrants without a high school education. But this influx receded just as quickly. Professor Novikov recalled the conflict that resulted:

Initially the auditoriums were filled with half-literate workers who soon, however, realized that it wasn't as simple to "gnaw the granite of science" as the political leaders had thought. The unprepared public was not capable of doing all the different types of practical assignments in the seminars and laboratories that often played a major role in modern higher education. As a result student numbers decreased to their initial levels.[95]

This obliged the Commissariat of Enlightenment to seek out other means of Sovietizing students in higher education. It attempted to do so through the so-called "workers' faculties" (rabfaki) within universities and institutes which were supposed to accelerate the training of young workers and peasants and prepare them for an advanced curriculum.[96] The Soviet government understood that the formation of a contingent of "red students" required time, and it was obliged to accept vitally needed and highly educated personnel from the "bourgeois" student body. According to the calculations of E. E. Platova, 30 decrees were issued during the Civil War years on the urgent drafting of upperclassmen in engineering and medical schools into the Red Army, and the same number on the resumption of classes for students in

---

a major role in putting down the Bolshevik uprising in Rostov-on-Don. Attached to the Volunteer Army of General Kornilov, the brigades took part in the legendary Ice March. N. A. Reshetova, *Intelligentsiia Dona i revoliutsiia: 1917–pervaia polovina 1920-kh godov* (Moscow: Moskovskii obshchestvennyi nauchnyi fond, 1997), 24, 62.

[93] *Dekrety Sovetskoi vlasti*, no. 3 (Moscow: Akademiia nauk SSSR, 1964), 138, 141.

[94] V. I. Lenin, *Polnoe sobranie sochinenii*, 5th ed. (Moscow: Gosudarstvennoe izd-vo politicheskoi literatury, 1963), 37: 34.

[95] Novikov, *Ot Moskvy do N´iu-Iorka*, 108.

[96] See Sh. Kh. Chanborisov, *Formirovanie sovetskoi universitetskoi sistemy* (Moscow: Vysshaia shkola, 1988), 82–94; A. P. Kupaigorodskaia, *Vysshaia shkola Leningrada v pervye gody Sovetskoi vlasti (1917–1925)* (Leningrad: Nauka, 1984), 85–95.

other fields.[97] All medical colleges were militarized by bringing them under the command of the commander in chief of the Armed Forces. Moreover, the government compelled medical students of both sexes to continue their studies as a form of emergency national service. Students were placed under complete state control and were subject to the same rules governing cadets at military schools.[98]

A resolution of the Soviet government of 24 March 1920 (subsequently renewed), "On the Urgent Graduation of Specialist Engineers," addressed the task of accelerating the preparation of students in industrial institutes, including those who had been drafted into the army, to become engineers in industrial enterprises and various other agencies. They were decommissioned from their student work at the front and ordered to return to their places of study. All of these so-called "accelerators" were transferred to state control and on completion of their courses of study were given compulsory assignments at the discretion of the national economic bodies.[99]

The professoriate regarded the Bolshevik Revolution as a usurpation of the authority of the Provisional Government and reacted indignantly to the Bolshevik rejection of Russia's obligations to its allies in the war with Germany. On 20 November 1917 the Council of Khar'kov University passed a resolution stating: "It is unbearable to us that the birth throes of Russian freedom should be linked in the consciousness of our descendants with memories of a repulsive betrayal."[100] The resolution was passed to the consuls of the Allied powers. Professors at Kazan' University supported their Khar'kov colleagues, asserting that a separate peace "would exclude Russia from the family of nations, which by common toil create science, art, and industry, i.e., create those intellectual and material valuables [tsennosti] without which this life does not exist."[101] This kind of resolution was the last widely publicized declaration by faculty organizations on the question of defense of the fatherland.

Relying on the frailty of Soviet power, the corporate bodies of professors continued to operate under the academic laws of the Provisional Government. According to Professor Novikov, "harmonious agreement within university life ... without any particular disturbances reigned through the first years of the Bolshevik regime up until the time when the Communist government

---

[97] E. E. Platova, *Zhizn' studenchestva Rossii v perekhodnuiu epokhu* (St. Petersburg: Sankt-Peterburgskii gosdarstvennyi universitet aerokosmicheskogo priborostroeniia, 2001), 23.

[98] Ibid.

[99] Ibid., 23–26.

[100] See Sizova, "Rossiiskaia vysshaia shkola," 57.

[101] See A. L. Litvin, "Uchenye kazanskogo universiteta vo vremia smeny politicheskikh rezhimov," in *Vlast' i nauka*, 125.

applied pressure ... to the principle of academic autonomy."[102] Professors in Petrograd acted in the same way as their colleagues in Moscow.[103] The historian M. K. Korbut described the situation during this period at Kazan´ University as follows: "Right up until 1918 the university felt itself to be autonomous in every sense of the word! It was given no commissions from, and took no interest at all in undertaking any kind of obligations to, the new order, all the time waiting impatiently for the restoration of the status quo and stubbornly addressing official documents to the no-longer-existent Ministry of Education."[104]

The Soviet government temporized in reacting to the wilfulness (*svoevolie*) of the professoriate, although they did not refrain from applying selective measures of a repressive nature, most often short-term arrests. A different turn of events took place in the higher education establishments caught up in the crucible of the Civil War (the Volga and Don regions, and the Crimea). There local professors collaborated with anti-Bolshevik forces in the hope of reviving the Constituent Assembly and replacing the Communist government. For example, the Council of Professors at one local university reacted to the capture of Kazan´ in August 1918 by the Samara-based Komuch—Committee of Members of the Constituent Assembly—with a resolution expressing readiness "to exert all our strength, our means, and even the life of our members on behalf of our Motherland" and expressed the intention to open a subscription "for a voluntary one-off financial donation to the people's army."[105] When the Red Army returned to Kazan´ half of the professors left the city together with the retreating Komuch members. It is true that the Bolsheviks acted with a certain degree of caution in this case. Only one professor, the acting rector of the university, D. A. Gol´dgammer, was among the citizens arrested for collaboration with Komuch, and only for a short time. The other professors, under threat of arrest, were ordered to collect a sum for the Red Army ten times greater than that donated to the People's Army of Komuch.[106]

In Rostov-on-Don there was only one professor among the 168 shot for collaboration with the White Guard—A. R. Kolli, who had been evacuated there from Warsaw University.[107] After the expulsion of Kolchak's supporters, the

---

[102] Novikov, *Ot Moskvy do N´iu-Iorka*, 103.

[103] O. M. Beliaeva, "Ervin Davidovich Grimm v Peterburgskom universitete" (Dissertatsiia kandidata istoricheskikh nauk, Sankt-Peterburgskii institut istorii, Rossiiskii akademii nauk, 265–69).

[104] M. K. Korbut, *Kazanskii gosudarstvennyi universitet im. V. I. Ul´ianova (Lenina) za 125 let* (Kazan´: Izdanie Kazanskogo universiteta, 1930), 301.

[105] Ibid., 303.

[106] Litvin, "Uchenye kazanskogo universiteta," 125.

[107] Platova, *Zhizn´ studenchestva v perekhodnuiu epokhu*, 21.

faculty of Tomsk and Irkutsk universities and the Omsk Agricultural Institute were mobilized to carry out "scholarly-work duties" (*uchebno-trudovye povin-nosti*). For the time being the Soviet authorities used similar tactics with the "White Guard" Tavricheskii University in Crimea (founded in 1918 during a period of White rule).

Thus a stalemate arose from 1917 to 1920 in the confrontation between the "men of science" and the Soviet government, in which the two sides, as if feeling each other out, restrained themselves from decisive action. Professors worked to preserve the prerogatives of unlimited academic autonomy, which they had acquired during the brief period of the Provisional Government, while at the same time trying to fight off or neutralize the encroachments of Soviet power for absolute governmental control in the management of higher education. They initially regarded Soviet power as one based purely on force and did not want to collaborate with it. But then, under the pressure of irresolvable circumstances—the financial crisis in higher education and the total impoverishment of teachers and students[108]—they were obliged to turn to the new regime for help and demonstrate their loyalty or at least neutrality ("Neither for you, nor against you").[109] The Soviet authorities, in turn, initially refrained from attempts at splitting the corporate unity of faculty bodies through revolutionary purges, but set the "junior" faculty, traditionally dissatisfied with their academic inequality, against the professors.[110] It was understood that the state would not be able to manage without the senior

---

[108] Those who died of hunger or illness included the historians A. S. Lappo-Danilevskii, M. A. D'iakonov, and B. A. Turaev; the economist M. I. Tugan-Baranovskii; Byzantine scholar P. B. Bezobrazov; law professor V. M. Khvostov; natural scientists A. S. Famitsyn, E. S. Fedorov, and others (Kupaigorodskaia, *Vysshaia shkola Leningrada*, 65). "Faculty meetings now differ little from memorial services for our colleagues," bitterly remarked Associate Professor (*privat-dotsent*) P. A. Sorokin of St. Petersburg University (P. A. Sorokin, *Dal'niaia doroga* [Moscow: TERRA, 1992], 131).

[109] Litvin, "Uchenye kazanskogo universiteta," 127.

[110] By the decree of 1 October 1918 "On Certain Changes in the Make-Up and Management of Government Scholars and Institutions of Higher Learning in the RSFSR," all scholarly degrees and titles were abolished; those who had conducted lectures for no less than three years were granted the title "professor"; those who had worked more than fifteen years could undertake teaching duties only by passing national examinations and with positive character recommendations from well-known scholars (*Dekrety Sovetskoi vlasti*, 3: 381–83). However, the Commissariat of Enlightenment's insistence that newly qualified "professors" promoted from among the junior faculty ranks vindictively blackball their old colleagues was successfully resisted: "The collegiality of the teaching personnel," testified M. M. Novikov, professor of zoology of Moscow University, "fortunately begun in the period of the Provisional Government, now showed itself in full strength. Almost all the old professors were voted in again. In our department [physics and mathematics] as if by an irony of fate, only the professor of astronomy, Shternberg, failed"; he was a Bolshevik (Novikov, *Ot Moskvy do N'iu-Iorka*, 111).

"bourgeois" specialists (*spetsy*) until they could replace them with a "red" Communist professoriate. The long siege of this corporate fortress began with "the strange policy," in the words of American scholar Stuart Finkel, whereby the Soviet government applied a mix of concessions as it attempted to "establish control over higher education and to eliminate the worst of what it considered alien, at the same time aiming to make use of the non-Bolshevik professoriate and do minimal damage to these valuable institutions."[111] The climax of the confrontation was a sharp conflict over the adoption of the higher education charter, codified in a government decree signed by Lenin in September 1921. This finally crushed the autonomy of higher education granted by the Provisional Government. A protest by professors and the initiation of a strike forced the authorities to make a concession in the form of a "Statute on Institutions of Higher Learning" (July 1922), which somewhat expanded the rights of faculty members. But soon many of the active protestors were subjected to arrest, exile, and confiscation of property as counter-revolutionaries. The most "active counterrevolutionary element" was forced to leave the country on pain of being shot (the "Philosophy Steamer"). On behalf of Soviet power, *Pravda* declared that this was a first warning to the "bourgeois intelligentsia." Resistance by higher education activists was finally broken.

However, many Soviet leaders had been students under the old regime, and to them it was clear that the complete removal of the "old" professoriate would be catastrophic to the overall system of higher education and would deplete the scientific and technical potential of the country. In order to avoid this civilizational disaster the government adopted the tactic of creating numerous applied scientific research institutes that were independent of the pre-existing higher education establishment. The idea for these institutes excited prominent scientists such as V. I. Vernadskii, K. A. Timiriazev, and others, and attracted many "men of science" to the comfort of scientific research, which was essentially apolitical as compared to scientific teaching, which was constantly stressful due to the need to protect academic autonomy from the encroachments of the authorities. An original suggestion by A. Kozhevnikov is of interest in this connection: "The gradual departure of scholars from teaching activity into research work eased for the Bolsheviks the replacement of the senior bourgeois professoriate with more politically and ideologically loyal teachers."[112]

Translated by Joan Bridgwood

---

[111] Styuart Finkel′ [Stuart Finkel], "Organizovannaia professura i universitetskaia reforma v Sovetskoi Rossii," in *Vlast′ i nauka*, 173–74.

[112] Kozhevnikov, "Pervaia mirovaia voina," 98–99.

The Russian School System and School Students during the Wars and Revolutions of 1914–22

Evgenii M. Balashov

When the First World War began, the Russian school system still exhibited many of the shortcomings that had emerged over the course of its development. The most pressing of these shortcomings were stubborn remnants of the class system, detachment of the majority of secondary schools from the demands of life, separate education for boys and girls, institutional fragmentation, and a huge number of different kinds and types of schools with no links or coordination between them. There was no direct connection or continuity between the courses and programmes offered by primary and higher primary schools (a four-year superstructure building on the primary school and leading to an incomplete secondary education) and secondary schools. During the entire interval between the revolution of 1905–07 and the beginning of the First World War, Russian society lived in the expectation that the education system would be reformed. The print media repeatedly took up the issue of school reform, as did the State Duma and even the government. However, not one of the projects proposing a far-reaching reorganization of the school system was put into practice.

It was during the First World War that a decisive attempt was undertaken to reform the school system in a liberal democratic manner. At the end of 1914, Count P. N. Ignat'ev, a man with close ties to liberal circles, was appointed minister of education. In February 1915, soon after he came into office, he convened a conference of school district administrators, at which he outlined the general direction of the new educational policy. His words were: "It is necessary for school education to foster the development of our country's productive forces. School education must serve the lives and needs of the population, and in order to do so, those who work and lead in our schools must penetrate into the psychology of the average citizen, approach his needs in a sympathetic and friendly manner, and look for ways and means of satisfying them. The issue of school education needs to be considered from the viewpoint of the demands of life."[1]

---

[1] Cited in N. A. Konstantinov, *Ocherki po istorii srednei shkoly: Gimnazii i real'nye uchilishcha c kontsa XIX v. do Fevral'skoi revoliutsii 1917 g.* (Moscow: Uchpedgiz, 1956), 166.

Russian Culture in War and Revolution, 1914–22, Book 1: Popular Culture, the Arts, and Institutions. Murray Frame, Boris Kolonitskii, Steven G. Marks, and Melissa K. Stockdale, eds. Bloomington, IN: Slavica Publishers, 2014, 315–48.

In spring 1915, a special conference under the leadership of the minister himself began drafting the school reform project. Some of these documents were published shortly afterwards.[2] They stipulated that secondary school education ought to: 1) become national; 2) become "self-sufficient," i.e., providing a general education without the main goal being the preparation for higher education; 3) be seven years in duration; 4) consist of two levels of three and four years of classes respectively. The first level ought to correspond to three years of the higher primary school course; this would guarantee the unity of the levels. It was true that the first class of the first level was intended for children with a slightly better preparation than the one provided by primary school. The curriculum for the second level was based on a tripartite division, i.e., it was divided into three main currents, namely modern humanities, classical humanities, and non-classical (real'noe).[3] In May 1915 a project was drafted on the status of parents' organizations. Their purpose was defined as assisting in teaching and pedagogical work and attending to the needs of the students. The quorum for general parents' assemblies was laid down as one-fifth of the overall number of parents and lowered to one-tenth if the assembly failed to convene.[4] Ignat'ev implemented this project through personal orders, alongside a number of other elements of the school reform, ignoring harsh criticism from the right. Naturally he could not really put the reform into practice under these conditions. The minister submitted a petition to the emperor in which he asked for the "backbreaking burden of service against the call of my conscience" to be removed from him, and on 28 December 1916 he was allowed to stand down.[5] Exactly two months later the February Revolution began.

Once the February Revolution was over, the question of reform was on the agenda once again; moreover, people started defining the new school system in terms such as "free" and "democratic." The first step of the Provisional Government was to remove individual reactionary functionaries and administrative structures. In March 1917 the replacement of school district administrators and other functionaries began. In May the government abolished city, provincial, and district school councils that had had protective functions. In June it disbanded the conservative academic committee and the minister's council of the Ministry of Popular Education (Ministerstvo

---

[2] See *Materialy po reforme srednei shkoly: Primernye programmy i ob˝iasnitel′nye zapiski* (Petrograd: Senatskaia tipografiia, 1915).

[3] N. A. Konstantinov, "Iz istorii proekta reform srednei shkoly v Rossii pri ministre narodnogo prosveshcheniia grafe Ignat′eve (1915–1916 gg.)," *Sovetskaia pedagogika*, no. 8–9 (1943): 29, 30.

[4] Ibid., 35.

[5] S. S. Ol′denburg, *Tsarstvovanie imperatora Nikolaia II* (1981; repr., St. Petersburg: Petropol′, 1992), 615.

Narodnogo Prosveshcheniia, or MNP).[6] The preconditions were created for unifying the educational organizations of the different departments under the jurisdiction of the MNP. On 8 May the government passed a resolution that ordered the synod to hand over all parochial schools to the ministry, and on 20 June another resolution was passed ordering the transfer of all schools that were part of the network of general education or received budgetary funds. These measures were not implemented completely; the parochial schools remained under the synod's authority. Also, the MNP could not take over the educational institutions belonging to the Mariinskii Institute, which were subject to transfer according to a resolution of 4 March, together with the institutions run by the Philanthropic Society. Special government commissars were appointed to lead these institutions.[7]

During spring and summer a few preliminary steps were undertaken to close the gap between the individual levels of education. A resolution of the Provisional Government that was published on 18 May 1917, gave power to the minister of education to establish four-year grammar schools (*gimnazii*) and non-classical secondary schools (*real'nye uchilishcha*) which were open to children who had completed higher primary school (*vysshee nachal'noe uchilishche*).[8] The conference of school district administrators on 12 August 1917 outlined the rules for admission to higher primary school and to classical and non-classical secondary school. They foresaw admission without examination for adolescents who had completed at least three years of primary school. The conference expressed a "general desire" for "classical grammar schools to constitute a complete cycle of secondary education."[9] The implementation of these measures meant that for wide sections of society, secondary school became significantly more accessible. Moreover, a government decision from 24 April gave the minister of education the right to establish classical grammar schools, pre-grammar schools, and non-classical secondary schools for pupils of both sexes, funded by the government, or to allow the establishment of such schools on funds provided by local governments.[10]

Most fruitful, however, were the efforts toward draft legislation on educational reform. In May 1917 an advisory commission, formed on the initiative of the pedagogical community for the purpose of debating the reform, began its work. Later it was given official status and named the State Committee for Popular Education. Its members included representatives of the All-Russian

[6] *Vestnik Vremennogo pravitel'stva*, 7 July 1917; *Sbornik ukazov i postanovlenii Vremennogo pravitel'stva*, vyp. 2, chast' 1 (Petrograd: Gostipografiia, 1918), 49–51.

[7] F. F. Korolev, *Ocherki po istorii sovetskoi shkoly i pedagogiki, 1917-1920* (Moscow: Izd-vo APN RSFSR, 1958), 58–59; *Vestnik Vremennogo pravitel'stva*, 18 August 1917.

[8] *Vestnik Vremennogo pravitel'stva*, 18 May 1917.

[9] Ibid., 13 August 1917.

[10] Ibid., 5 May.

Teacher's Union, the Academic Union, the Petrograd Soviet of Workers' and Soldiers' Deputies, the Executive Committee of the State Duma, and other organizations. The committee drafted a large number of bills that could have significantly altered the old system of education, steering it in the direction of democratic, evolutionary development. But none of the bills drafted in May and June were passed by the government. The passivity of the MNP under the direction of A. A. Manuilov led to a conflict between the committee and the ministry. In early June the work of the committee was interrupted for almost a month; it resumed only under the new minister, S. F. Ol'denburg.[11]

The content of the bill "On the Management of Popular Education in the Regions" was based on the concept of wide-ranging decentralization of the local education management. In order to adapt new structures to the ones already existing within the system of local government, the project envisaged the organization of district and municipal committees on popular education, which had the right to manage schools directly. The same principle of self-government on a collective basis, while the individual institution remained relatively autonomous, was to define the internal organization of each school. The bodies of school self-government were envisaged to comprise pedagogical councils consisting of teachers, representatives of the local government, and parents' organizations.[12] A number of bills drafted by the State Committee for Popular Education put forward the idea of a united school. This meant preserving the main types of existing schools while establishing unity and continuity between their syllabuses. In accordance with this idea there were plans for the creation of a single united, comprehensive school comprising three levels. The duration of each level was to be regulated by law. The course of the first level (primary school) would last four years, that of the second level (higher primary school) four years, and that of the final level (the senior years of the classical grammar schools, non-classical secondary, and other secondary schools) would last three years. Any digressions from this norm must not conflict with the basic aims of the integrated school.[13]

The curriculum reform consisted in identifying a so-called "minimum curriculum" among the material in the present curriculum. The authors of the bill considered it necessary to highlight among the entire content of the school curriculum "the basic nuclear curriculum, which must consist only of subjects the educational value of which is beyond any doubt"; the remainder of school hours "will be left at the discretion of the local leaders of the school

---

[11] Ia. G. Kordo, *Reforma narodnogo obrazovaniia v svobodnoi Rossii* (Moscow: Russkoe t-vo izdat. dela, 1917), 5–7; N. N. Smirnov, "Gosudarstvennyi komitet po narodnomy obrazovaniiu (istoriia sozdaniia i deiatel'nosti)," in *Petrogradskaia intelligentsia v 1917 g.: Sbornik statei i materialov* (Moscow–Leningrad: Institut istorii SSSR, 1990), 4–19.

[12] Gosudarstvennyi arkhiv Rossiiskoi Federatsii (GARF) f. 1803, op. 1, d. 4, l. 10–11, 15–17.

[13] Ibid., ll. 29–33ob., 40–51.

and can be used in different ways." Thus dividing all subjects into two categories, the bill established that both categories could be compulsory or not compulsory for the pupils of a given school. "The result is four subject groups: 1) compulsory for all schools of a given level and for all pupils at these schools; 2) compulsory in that they must be available at a certain level, but optional for the pupils; 3) additional compulsory subjects; and 4) additional optional subjects." The bill identified three subject groups that were to form the basis of the minimal comprehensive curriculum. They were: a) natural sciences (physics, chemistry, botany, etc.), b) humanities (native language and literature, history, and social science); and c) mathematics.[14] Moreover, the committee planned regulations for the introduction of compulsory schooling and access to primary education, drew up proposals regarding changes to school syllabi, the abolition of compulsory Holy Scripture lessons, and changes to the conditions for acceptance into educational institutions in order to facilitate students' transition from the lower to the higher level, etc.[15] The school system's educational work had to be based on concern for the all-round development of the child and his or her preparation for practical and social activity within the democratic order. Pedagogues were faced with the task of stimulating in children and young people "love for their neighbor and their Fatherland, understanding of human dignity and of the rights and obligations of each citizen in the future democratic society."[16]

Overall the bills did not pursue the goal of breaking apart the education system or creating a new system. Their aim was to remove obstacles to the further development of progressive elements within the existing school system and to cleanse it of remnants of class-consciousness and other limits. Also, the bills were concerned with restructuring school education so as to make it more democratic and universally accessible. The main direction of the envisaged reorganization of educational management presupposed replacing rigid governmental structures with public structures based on the model of town and district government. The liberation of school collectives from the obtrusive patronage of the state could offer opportunities for developing self-governing structures and exploring pedagogical models.

The bills drafted by the State Committee for Popular Education were not passed under either Manuilov, whose passivity was perhaps a result of his desire to avoid "rash measures,"[17] nor under his successors Ol'denburg or S. S. Salazkin, although all bills were fully drafted and in the hands of the ministry

---

[14] I. Lapshov, "Gosudarstvo i organy mestnogo samoupravleniia v pervyi period revoliutsii," *Pedagogicheskaia mysl'*, no. 1–2 (1918): 147–48.

[15] Kordo, *Reforma narodnogo obrazovaniia*, 7–25; GARF f. 180, op. 1, d. 4, ll. 22–22ob., 71–76, 96.

[16] *Narodnyi uchitel'*, no. 29–30 (1917): 12.

[17] Korolev, *Ocherki po istorii sovetskoi shkoly*, 63.

by October 1917.[18] One of the reasons for the delay in passing these bills might have been the high turnover of ministers. Yet in Russian schools the new academic year 1917–18 began in conditions that had hardly changed since the fall of tsarism. A large proportion of teachers continued to desire the long-awaited reforms. However, in opposition to the pedagogical communities, the majority of the population was strongly against decisive reforms. It is likely that this mood, most clearly expressed by the parents, was one of the main reasons for the sluggishness of the MNP.

The activity of parents' organizations increased greatly from the very first days of the revolution. The parents' committees of individual schools began to unite and form regional unions and committees, loudly announcing the role they played in school and society. The council of the Petrograd Union of Parents' Committees proclaimed: "We are fulfilling our obligations, explaining to Russian society and the government the role an organized parent force plays in the fate and life of the renewed school system. We must exercise our inalienable right, a right that is ours more than anyone else's—that is, the right to voice the demands that life is placing on school education."[19] In summer 1917 the unification process reached a national scale. The first All-Russian Congress of Parents' Organizations took place on 7–10 August in Moscow, presided over by N. S. Kartsov, the head of the Petrograd union. It was attended by 250 delegates, who represented a large number of regional committees that had already formed unions in provincial areas, such as Vladivostok, Irbit, Eisk, Shadrinsk, and Kamenets-Podol'skii. The congress was also attended by representatives of the Moscow pedagogical community and by delegates of the All-Russian Student Union. The congress discussed several principles related to the organization of the new school system. At the same time, the majority of delegates expressed a very conservative stance. A major bone of contention was the teaching of Scripture. Two conflicting viewpoints were at loggerheads. The first, that of the clergy (i.e., those who taught Scripture), was that the subject ought to be compulsory for all students. The second, expressed by pedagogues and students, was that religious education should be left to the family, and later, for older students, be given to the school and the students themselves. In the end the majority voted in favor of compulsory Scripture lessons. Moreover, the delegates resolved to approach the government with the urgent request to quickly raise the age at which students could freely decide for or against the subject from 14 to 17 years.[20]

The activity of the State Committee for Popular Education was rated very negatively by the congress of parents' organizations. The delegates thought that the "decisive breakup of the entire structure of school education" that was

---

[18] Smirnov, "Gosudarstvennyi komitet po narodnomy obrazovaniiu," 19.

[19] "Pervyi Vserossiiskii s"ezd roditel'skikh organizatsii," *Psikhologiia i deti*, no. 5 (1917): 50.

[20] Ibid., 51.

underway—and without the necessary sanction of the All-Russian Congress for Popular Education—was "risky and dangerous." One of the resolutions called for the congress to convene and for parents' committee representatives to be included in its activities. Moreover, the congress considered it necessary to hold preliminary comprehensive discussions of any future major legislation that would affect popular legislation in the regions. The congress passed a bill on the new status of parents' organizations and proclaimed the creation of the All-Russian Parents' Union, the permanent office of which was established in Moscow.[21] The leadership of the union defined one goal to be "the attainment of the greatest possible influence of parents on school life, school management and *the complete reorganization* of school education."[22] The contradictory character of the statements made by representatives of parents' organizations was a reflection of their heterogeneous membership. After all, members hailed from the provinces and the capital, were of diverse political, religious, and social circumstances and different social status and educational background. Naturally, the leadership of the Parents' Union in Moscow had a different attitude than those who had voted for the resolutions at the congress of parents' organizations. On the whole, however, the attitude of parents was significantly more conservative than that of the majority of teachers, let alone the pedagogical elite. Because of this it is not surprising that the MNP, when it lingered over the reforms, kept an eye on the reaction of broader social circles, parents in particular. Considering further political developments, it is highly probable that even if the bills of the State Committee for Popular Education had been passed, they would hardly have changed the path that Russian school education took after October 1917. No "bourgeois" reforms could have satisfied the radical demands of the Bolsheviks.

Soviet state policy in the field of education, as in other spheres, was defined by the aims formulated in the programmatic documents of the Communist Party. Over the course of time, however, these documents underwent certain changes. The sections concerning school education in the first programme of the Russian Social Democratic Workers' Party, adopted by the Second Party Congress in 1903, were characteristic of a social democratic party. They contained a number of social democratic demands: separation of school and church, introduction of free compulsory general education, and prohibition of child labor.[23] Between 1903 and February 1917 these general positions were developed in party documents, in the press, in the speeches of Bolshevik delegates in the State Duma, and in the addresses of Bolshevik pedagogues at congresses on popular education. Criticizing the management of popular education in Russia and the government's educational policy,

---

[21] Ibid., 51–52.

[22] Lapshov, "Gosudarstvo i organy mestnogo samoupravleniia," 149–50. The italics in this and further citations are the author's, unless stated otherwise.

[23] *Vtoroi s˝ezd RSDRP: Protokoly* (Moscow: Godlitizdat, 1959), 421–22.

the Bolshevik press supported the democratic idea that the immediate management of schools should lie in the hands of local government and that the population should be involved. Particular attention was paid to the establishment of a united school as an issue that had not only pedagogical, but also social implications. The question of the democratization of school life was also raised.[24] In her 1915 book *Popular Education and Democracy*, Nadezhda K. Krupskaia gave the first overview of the historical development of labor schools and of Marxist criticism of all "bourgeois" theories of labor education. And although the book did not contain a constructive Bolshevik programme on this issue, the author reached the following general conclusion: "As long as the organization of school education remains in the hands of the bourgeoisie, school will be a tool directed against the interests of the working class. Only the working class can turn labor school into a 'tool for the transformation of society.'"[25]

After the February Revolution this idea acquired special significance. The rejection of the existing Russian school system as a tool of "bourgeois class domination" and the demand to replace it with "proletarian" labor schools would become the basis of the Bolsheviks' view on the reorganization of education. "For the bourgeoisie, school, like the press, is a tool in the struggle against the working class, a tool of domination," the party publicist K. S. Eremeev wrote, "school curricula and the organization of the whole matter are directed towards a single aim: to build and strengthen bourgeois viewpoints and thoughts."[26] More concrete measures were outlined in Krupskaia's article "The Municipal School Syllabus," published in May 1917 as a pre-election programme for the elections to the regional dumas of Petrograd. The first point of the programme concerned the improvement of pupils' material situation and the provision of free meals for children. It proposed establishing "children's houses" with dormitories, playgrounds, and workshops so that extracurricular activities could be organized. The article underlined the significance of a single school form for all classes of society and its connection to "productive labor."[27] In June 1917 the "Materials on the Revision of the Party Programme" were published, edited by Lenin. The section dedicated to education was compiled by Krupskaia. Compared to the first programme, the new one included a slightly expanded body of democratic demands: the abolition of compulsory state language in schools, free compulsory education until the age of 16, free school meals, clothing and learning materials, responsibility for education to be transferred to local government, election of teachers by the populace, a

---

[24] Korolev, *Ocherki po istorii sovetskoi shkoly*, 76–77; *Bol'shevistskaia pechat' v bor'be za demokratizatsiiu obrazovaniia: Nachalo XX veka* (Moscow: Pedagogika, 1990), 63–212.

[25] N. K. Krupskaia, *Narodnoe obrazovanie i demokratiia* (Moscow–Leningrad, 1930), 131.

[26] *Pravda*, 16 April 1917.

[27] *Pravda*, 18 May 1917.

completely secular school, polytechnization of education, and a link between teaching and "social-productive child labor."[28]

For another few months after they came to power in October 1917, the Bolsheviks' declarations concerning the overall direction of their educational programme continued to stress the position of a democratic school system, although they highlighted its class-based "proletarian" character. In his address "On Popular Education" of 29 October 1917, A. V. Lunacharskii, head of the People's Commissariat of Enlightenment (Narkompros), put forward the aims of universal literacy, universal compulsory free education, creation of a unified school, decentralization of education management, and so forth.[29] What remained unchanged was the Bolsheviks' demand for a "totally secular school."

The situation changed in summer 1918. Having rid themselves of the Left Socialist-Revolutionaries in July, the Bolsheviks monopolized power. Their policies toward "class enemies" became harsher, and soon they would initiate the Red Terror. Around this time Lunacharskii managed to block the influence of those teachers who were opposed to the Bolsheviks, both politically and organizationally, and to make the loyal teachers cooperate. It was precisely in the second half of 1918 that official documents started to demand a radical restructuring of the school system, alongside statements stressing the political significance of school education. The "Statutes of the Unified Labor School of the RSFSR," approved on 30 September, were published in October. This document constituted the most radical, maximally "revolutionary" approach to the reorganization of the school system, even among the Bolsheviks themselves. It was adopted only after prolonged discussion.

The "Statutes" abolished all existing types of educational institution and made legal provisions for a two-level, nine-year unified labor school. The first level was for children between 8 and 13 years of age (five-year course) and the second for children between 13 and 17 years of age (four-year course). The "Statutes" confirmed the previously adopted decrees on coeducation in a free secular school and declared the universality and compulsory nature of education.[30] However, the aims pursued with the reorganization of the education system were not limited to the articles of the "Statutes" that detailed the universal accessibility and democratization of school education. The "Declaration of the Basic Principles of the Unified Labor School," published at the same time as the "Statutes" and written by Lunacharskii, highlighted the radical difference between the old and new school systems. It stipulated:

---

[28] V. I. Lenin, *Polnoe sobranie sochinenii*, 5th ed. (Moscow: Institut marksizma-leninizma pri TsK KPSS, 1969), 32: 47–56.

[29] *Sbornik dekretov i postanovlenii Rabochego i krest'ianskogo pravitel'stva po narodnomu obrazovaniiu*, vyp. 1 (Moscow: Gos. izd-vo, 1919), 156–59.

[30] A. A. Abakumov et al., comps., *Narodnoe obrazovanie v SSSR: Obshcheobrazovatel'naia shkola. Sbornik dokumentov 1917–1973 gg.* (Moscow: Pedagogika, 1974), 133–37.

"The matter does not consist in making school education as it is, that is, school education in the form devised by the previous regime, universally accessible. This school education is not suitable for the laboring masses. The task consists in a radical reformation of school education in the spirit of a school that is truly intended to benefit the people."[31] Slightly earlier, in a speech given at the First All-Russian Congress on Education in August 1918, Lunacharskii had phrased this intention more clearly: "It is not a matter of taking control of the school system: the school system is just as decrepit and useless as the bureaucratic apparatus. We could not consider instructing regional inspectors to make a few changes, as the Provisional Government had done; we had to destroy everything; it was totally clear that the school system was subject to revolutionary demolition."[32]

The section on "popular education" in the new party programme, which was adopted by the Eighth Party Congress in March 1919, contained not only the provisions of the "Materials on the Revision of the Party Programme" from 1917, but also advanced purely political directives as part of the main objectives of school education. The preamble to the section stressed: "In the area of popular education the Russian Communist Party pursues the aim of bringing to completion the transformation of the school system from a tool of the bourgeois class reign into a tool for breaking down the division of society into classes, into a tool of the communist rebirth of society." Among other things the programme announced that education workers would be prepared so that they would be "steeped in the ideas of communism" and that "the apparatus and the means of state power" would be used for this end.[33] Thus the programme considered school education to be not only a means of political education, but also a means of forming a new type of human being, a "new man." This was to become the main objective of schooling, and it was to encompass all aspects of education and teaching.

In order to form this "new man" it was necessary to cleanse human consciousness of all old spiritual values and to completely destroy the existing way of life and the related psychological structures. Breaking down these structures in order to implement a new social model was the explicit goal of Bolshevism. In the words of the British philosopher Bertrand Russell, the new model represented "an alien philosophy of life that cannot be imposed on the people without changing their instincts, habits and traditions, in such a way as not to dry out the most important sources of their vitality and not to engender apathy and despair amidst the ignorant victims of belligerent education."[34] As the part of society least attached to the old ways, children were most receptive

---

[31] Ibid., 137.

[32] A. V. Lunacharskii, *O narodnom obrazovanii* (Moscow: Izd-vo APN RSFSR, 1958), 33.

[33] *Kommunisticheskaia Partiia Sovetskogo Soiuza v rezoliutsiiakh i resheniiakh s'ezdov, konferentsii i plenumov TsK*, 2: 1924–1930, 9th ed. (Moscow: Politizdat, 1983), 76–83.

[34] Bertrand Russell, *Praktika i teoriia bol'shevizma* (Moscow: Nauka, 1991), 97.

to political and psychological influence. Not in vain did Lenin remark at the First All-Russian Congress of Education Workers that "the victories of the revolution can be cemented only by the school system."[35] At the same time the new educational system was based on the assumption that the youngest children were the most open to new ideas. Lunacharskii said that "pre-school education is a matter of greatest importance for socialism. During those years a socialist foundation of such strength is built in a child that a stronger one you will never build."[36] The basics of "communist feelings," he maintained, must be instilled in a child beginning at five years of age. Wresting children from the spheres of the peasantry and petty bourgeoisie and subjecting them to communist influence was "easier to do with young people, even easier with teenagers, very easy with school children and easiest of all with children of preschool age."[37] In accordance with these guidelines, preschool education was included in the general education system as early as December 1917, in order to "initiate a child's social education at the first developmental stages."[38]

Political and ideological instruction became a paramount goal in Soviet schools, and not just in extracurricular work. It spread to all forms of teaching. Schools were to be transformed into "a tool of communist regeneration." Lunacharskii continued to stress that Soviet school policy must be based on political ideology. "School is a political institution, established by the state in order to serve the aims of the state. Our school must be communist."[39] Absolutizing his own thesis, he proclaimed: "We do not imagine and must not imagine any form of education that does not have a direct connection to the tasks of building communism and because of this is not steeped in the spirit of communism."[40] Communist education had to be based strictly on the principle of collectivism. Krupskaia singled out three main objectives of collectivist education: the formation in the children of "a social instinct, social consciousness, and social habits."[41] These objectives became the foundation of the so-called "social education."

In order to correspond to the main principles of the new system of general education as laid down in the documents of the State Commission on

---

[35] Lunacharskii, *O narodnom obrazovanii*, 463.

[36] A. V. Lunacharskii, *Prosveshchenie i revoliutsiia: Sbornik statei* (Moscow: Rabotnik prosveshcheniia, 1926), 199.

[37] Lunacharskii, *O narodnom obrazovanii*, 464.

[38] *Sbornik dekretov*, 119.

[39] Lunacharskii, *Prosveshchenie i revoliutsiia*, 170, 180.

[40] Quoted in *V. I. Lenin i A. V. Lunacharskii: Perepiska, doklady, dokumenty*, comp. V. D. Zel'dovich and R. A. Lavrov, Literaturnoe nasledstvo 80 (Moscow: Nauka, 1971), 98.

[41] N. K. Krupskaia, "Obshchestvennoe vospitanie," *Na putiakh k novoi shkole* 1 (1923): 14.

Education in 1918, the school system had to become unconditionally secular, unified, labor-based, and accessible to both sexes. The first of these statutes was a consequence of the party's policy towards religion and the church. The intolerance towards religion, founded on the party ideologues' and leaders' extreme rationalism and belligerent materialism, aimed to cleanse human psychology of the "remnants of religion" in order to affirm the ideas preached by the adepts of the new faith. N. A. Berdiaev wrote in 1917 that,

> Bolshevism wants to be not just something, not just a part or separate field of life, and not a social policy, but everything in its entirety. As a fanatical faith doctrine it does not tolerate anything else nearby. It does not want to share anything with anything else in order to be everything and in everything. Bolshevism is socialism that has reached religious dimensions and the exclusivity of religion.... Like all religious fanatics, the Bolsheviks divide the world and all humankind into two kingdoms—the kingdom of God, i.e., the kingdom of the socialist proletariat, and the kingdom of the devil, i.e., the kingdom of the bourgeoisie. [42]

The Sovnarkom decree that separated the church from both state and schools (20 January 1918), as well as the State Commission on Education's resolution on a secular school system dated 18 February 1918, proclaimed complete freedom of religion and the possibility of receiving a private religious education.[43] However, one year later, in March 1919, the new programme of the Bolshevik Party declared the positions expressed in the decree insufficient.[44] N. I. Bukharin and E. A. Preobrazhenskii's *ABC of Communism*, a popular explanation of the party programme, categorically declared: "The liberation of children from the reactionary influence of their parents is an important objective of the proletarian state.... [W]e must not limit ourselves to driving religion out of our schools. School must take the offensive against religious propaganda in the family."[45] This turned the corresponding article in the decree into a straightforward declaration.

The second principle, the creation of a unified school, appeared mostly in its historical meaning, in which it had been considered before 1917 and to which a significant number of Russian pedagogues had aspired for a long time. It had been a reaction to the disunity and lack of continuity between different school types. The unity would be manifest in the creation of a single comprehensive educational chain from kindergarten to university, with

---

[42] N. A. Berdiaev, *Sobranie sochinenii* (Paris: YMCA-Press, 1990), 4: 29–30.

[43] *Sbornik dekretov*, 17; *Dekrety sovetskoi vlasti* (Moscow: Politizdat, 1957), 1: 373–74.

[44] *Kommunisticheskaia Partiia Sovetskogo Soiuza v rezoliutsiiakh i resheniiakh*, 2: 83.

[45] N. Bukharin and E. Preobrazhenskii, *Azbuka kommunizma* (Moscow: Gos. izd-vo, 1919), 214.

each link constituting a higher level. However, in connection with the task of creating the "new man" it assumed yet another meaning: the unity of the content of teaching and policy. The consistent implementation of this objective led to a unification of syllabuses, textbooks and teaching methods, in particular in the humanities. When the New Economic Policy (NEP) was adopted in spring 1921 and private publishing houses increased their activity, Sovnarkom hastily issued a special resolution called "On the Procedure for Publishing Textbooks." This resolution awarded the exclusive right to publish textbooks, and to republish them for all kinds of educational institutions, to the State Publishing House (Gosizdat).[46]

In addition, the unity of the school system became manifest in its nationalization, as the state took upon itself all education management, thus taking it out of the hands of private individuals, as well as local government. This policy contradicted the statement on the necessity of decentralizing school management and keeping it on a lay basis, which the Bolsheviks had repeatedly put forward before October 1917 and during their first months in power. In August 1918 Lunacharskii gave the following reasons for the new position: "We desire a genuine people's sovereignty, that is, the transfer of all power to the masses ... but the mass of the petty bourgeoisie and the mass of the unenlightened part of the peasantry ... does not welcome our reform, and therefore it is necessary to leave to the government the final jurisdiction in many questions concerning the school system."[47] As a result the Soviet education system was much closer to the state than the prerevolutionary system had been. All its parts, without exception, had to be managed by the state and correspond to the state's ideology, interests, and needs.

The labor principle of education was one of the most critical and controversial moments in the genesis of the new school system. The concept of a "labor school" was considered the cornerstone of the new education system. In the programmatic documents it appeared both as a teaching method (the perception of subjects through labor) and as an educational principle (the introduction of children to labor). Lunacharskii said that

> [t]he first interpretation of the labor principle is that the child must perceive school subjects through labor.... The essence of the new teaching method is not study, not setting homework and asking the children to repeat it, but excursions, walks, sketches, modeling, and all kinds of labor processes, through which the child can himself enrich

---

[46] *Narodnoe obrazovanie v SSSR*, 145–46. However, when it considered the conditions of NEP, Sovnarkom issued a new directive in March 1922 that allowed private publishing houses to print textbooks, albeit under the very strict control of Narkompros. I. F. Zakolodkin and A. Ia. Podzemskii, comps., *Osnovnye uzakoneniia i rasporiazheniia po narodnomu prosveshcheniiu*, ed. V. N. Kasatkina (Moscow–Leningrad: Gos. izd-vo, 1929), 663.

[47] Lunacharskii, *O narodnom obrazovanii*, 35–36.

his own experience.... Moreover, the labor school has yet another sense. We cannot produce a literary intelligentsia as the previous secondary school did. The labor school must teach everyone to labor. That means we must not only take care to ensure that subjects are perceived through labor, but we must also teach the children to labor.[48]

This dual understanding of the labor principle was confirmed on 30 September 1918 in the "Statutes of the Unified Labor School of the RSFSR," which proclaimed productive labor as the basis of school life "not merely as a teaching method, but as productive, socially necessary labor."[49] Teaching must be general, comprehensive, and polytechnical. Alongside the exaggeration of the role of productive labor in teaching, to the detriment of the teaching of the basics of scientific knowledge, it contained a number of other radical positions: the abolition of homework, exams, marks, the year group system, etc. It suggested replacing division into groups according to age by division into groups according to the students' degree of qualification.

The radical reform faced major difficulties that were insurmountable in some respects. The banishment of Scripture from the school syllabus was greeted with resentment everywhere, and in some places triggered resistance in the population. Krupskaia recalled that "this decree was difficult to implement."[50] The resistance was especially large and persistent in the countryside and in the provinces. Upon hearing the mere rumor that Scripture might be excluded from the school syllabus, the local population declared that they had no need for such a school.[51] According to the pedagogue V. A. Desnitskii,

local Soviet power placed the entire burden of formally implementing the decree effectuating the exclusion of Scripture from the syllabus on the teachers. They were threatened with repressions should the school continue to teach Scripture, they were ... obliged to see to the removal of all accessories of worship ... and at the same time they were under strict instruction to replace the icons that had been removed with portraits of Marx and Russian revolutionary activists, representatives of the state authorities in the respective Soviet republic, then there was the prohibition banning clergy from teaching Scripture to children, even outside school hours, and even in church itself. It is easy to

---

[48] Ibid., 108–10.

[49] *Narodnoe obrazovanie v SSSR*, 135.

[50] N. K. Krupskaia, *Pedagogicheskie sochineniia v 10 tomakh* (Moscow: Izd-vo APN, 1958), 2: 95.

[51] N. V. Chekhov, "Zakon Bozhii v shkole," *Uchitel'*, no. 7–8 (1918): 8.

imagine what kind of psychological atmosphere was created in order to implement the reform.[52]

In the large cities the majority of parents also expressed support for the continuation of teaching religious subjects. However, when it came to religion the policies of the authorities were particularly harsh. The resistance mounted by parents' committees against the implementation of the decree separating church and school (as well as other reforms) was one of the main reasons that these committees were dissolved. According to the statute on unified labor schools, parents' committees on school councils were to be replaced by "representatives of the working population" who were to make up one-fourth of the number of teachers. They were elected mostly via the party collectives and women's sections and were intended to establish "proletarian" control over schools and teachers. The very first elections showed that these representatives, who were not parents themselves, had absolutely no interest in visiting schools, and so the utopian idea of "class control" in schools suffered a crushing defeat.[53] As a result of the difficult material situation of popular education at the beginning of NEP there appeared, spontaneously and semi-legally, so-called aid committees or aid councils (*sovsod*) in the schools. In contravention of the "Statute" these councils consisted of parents who were interested in the success of the school. Their main task became finding means that would enable the school to work normally. The educational leaders were forced to accept the councils, and they took over, in effect, the roles of the former parents' committees.

Many problems beset the introduction of the unified school. The "Statute" outlined the following plan for the reformation of the old educational institutions. Three-year and four-year primary schools were due to be turned into five-year first-level schools. To achieve this aim, each primary school added a further year, beginning in the academic year 1918–19. Four-year higher primary schools were transformed into second-level schools. To achieve this, the first year of teaching was scrapped and a senior year was added for those who had graduated from one of these institutions in the current year. The first three years of the eight-year secondary school, together with the two preparatory years, were restructured to form the first level. Years 4 to 7 were due to become the second level, while year 8 was scrapped.[54]

---

[52] A. V. Desnitskii [Stroev], "Tserkov' i shkola," *Vestnik prosveshcheniia*, no. 1–3 (1919): 23–24; Desnitskii, *Tserkov' i shkola* (Berlin: Gos. izd-vo RSFSR, 1923), 43.

[53] See further E. M. Balashov, "Uchastie rabochikh v zhizni petrogradskikh shkol v pervye poslerevoliutsionnye gody," in *Rabochie i rossiiskoe obshchestvo: Vtoraia polovina XIX–nachalo XX v. Sbornik statei i materialov, posviashchennyi pamiati O. N. Znamenskogo*, ed. S. I. Potolov (St. Petersburg: Glagol, 1994), 208–23.

[54] *Narodnoe obrazovanie v SSSR*, 136–37.

The practical implementation of this plan was marred by great difficulties. In the vast majority of rural primary schools it proved impossible to offer an additional fifth year due to the absence of premises and teachers. And in places where a fifth year was established, it was impossible to find a sufficient number of students who wanted to continue their education in the five-year school. The result was a gap between rural first- and second-level schools. It was just as impossible to reach full unity in the towns, where many primary schools also continued to comprise four years. There were not enough second-level schools, and in the places that had enough schools for those wishing to enter, it turned out that the students, who came from many different former school types (with different curricula), were so heterogeneous in their prior knowledge that it was very difficult to teach them. This led to the establishment of unofficial tests (violating the "Statute") for those wishing to enter a second-level school, which in some places turned into proper selective exams. With the abolition of year 8 of the classical grammar school and other secondary schools, the curriculum covered by the second-level school in practice no longer corresponded to the demands set by higher schools. The result was that higher schools also introduced exams based on the curriculum of the previous eight-year classical grammar school.[55] As we can see, full unity was not achieved.

Implementing the labor principle proved even more difficult. The attack on the "school of study" was painfully under-resourced in terms of material, staff, and methodology; this was only natural given the circumstances of war and devastation. The devastation of schools during the Civil War rendered nearly impossible not only polytechnical teaching, but also teaching in general. Teachers were wholly unprepared for teaching "labor processes." Drawing conclusions from the attempts of teachers to comprehend the labor principle, Krupskaia wrote: "It was understood to mean that the children should not only learn, but also work. Study remained the same, but alongside it the children were made to sweep floors, wash dishes, collect firewood, unload carriages, and run errands."[56] Lunacharskii noted the same thing: "Many pedagogues understood it to mean that if they made a former workshy grammar school student carry firewood they would by that very act transform the previous school into a new labor school."[57] The "labor principle" was introduced into schools on a formal level, with no impact on the teaching process. This was to be expected, as proper implementation required time, significant resources, and a proven practical programme. In 1920 the leadership of Narkompros became firmly convinced that it was impossible in the near future to turn mass schools into labor schools. Work on labor processes turned into a laboratory

---

[55] N. V. Chekhov, *Tipy russkoi trudovoi shkoly v ikh istoricheskom razvitii* (Moscow: T-vo "Mir," 1923), 63–65.

[56] Krupskaia, *Pedagogicheskie sochineniia*, 4: 23.

[57] Lunacharskii, *O narodnom obrazovanii*, 125.

project and was concentrated in a small number of exemplary educational institutes. Narkompros created its own section of experimental model institutions.[58]

The Civil War led to a sharp decline in the standards of teaching, in particular in secondary schools. The decline had three main causes: firstly, economic devastation and the absence of the basic necessities for supporting the teaching process (heating, light, textbooks, learning aids, and so forth); secondly, the disastrous material situation of teachers, many of whom were forced to abandon pedagogical work, while the young people who took their place as a rule lacked the necessary knowledge and experience; thirdly, irreparable damage was inflicted by the implementation of the radical task of "revolutionary demolition" of the school system. The old school system was to a large extent destroyed, yet attempts to build a new one, let alone an "ideal" one, all failed. Lunacharskii admitted as much when he reflected on the path that had been traveled:

> During the first period of maximal revolutionary enthusiasm, having outlined the ultimate ideal of a school system for our time with a high degree of accuracy, we set out to realize it without looking back, but we had none of the necessary resources and therefore frequently inflicted unnecessary destruction (although there was much that needed to be destroyed) and often ended up suspended in mid-air.[59]

At the same time, he continued,

> [I]ndividual ONOs [local departments of popular education] took one of two paths: some did not drive out the old school and just paid lip service, others did destroy the old school but failed to build the new one. This could be done on the cheap: fire the teachers who were saboteurs, unite boys' and girls' schools, etc. Tell the teachers "hush!" and convene a large meeting of student mischief-makers. All this was even more harmful than the preservation of the old school... But we could not provide anything new, except for a few experimental model units.[60]

The destruction of the school system in conditions of sharp material decline led to a deterioration in the quality of teaching, while the number of students rose. The quantitative side became the main indicator for the development of the education system. Lunacharskii noted:

---

[58] N. V. Chekhov, "Opyt trudovoi shkoly v Rossii," in *Trudovaia shkola v svete istorii i sovremennosti* (Leningrad: "Seiatel'" E. V. Vysotskogo, 1924), 82–84.

[59] Lunacharskii, *O narodnom obrazovanii*, 225–26.

[60] Ibid., 236–37.

We began to set quantitative tasks. This was a transition from the acutely revolutionary period, during which we were busy drawing up a new idea. We started relegating the methodological goals of school to the background. This conviction was held very strongly among our responsible education-alists: we must teach them something, and anything we teach them will be good; but we, who faithfully held on to the "unified labor school" did not have the heart to speak of it.... We all were preoccupied by one thing: how to maintain student numbers, how to make sure teachers did not leave.[61]

The first three years of school reform dispelled all illusions regarding the possibility of achieving fast radical transformations. The unsuccessful attempt to rapidly implement the principles of the polytechnical labor school to a certain extent discredited these principles in the eyes of some Soviet edu-cation leaders, a trend reinforced by the following circumstances. The creation of the unified labor school in 1918 was accompanied by a mass liquidation of trade, technical, economic, and other related educational institutions, with-out the real conditions and demands for additional labor being taken into account. In order to rectify this mistake Narkompros founded the State Committee for Professional Education in late 1918, but this was not enough to satisfy the demands of industry even under the conditions of civil war and economic devastation.[62] The situation changed for the worse with the tran-sition to economic growth in the second half of the 1920s, when the demand for skilled workers rose sharply. Around this time some Soviet leaders began to voice opposition to the unified labor school of polytechnic orientation, instead favoring the liquidation of the second level of the comprehensive secondary school and an early start to vocational training. The first to express this view was F. Grin'ko, the people's commissar for enlightenment of the Ukrainian Soviet Republic, with the support of several Narkompros leaders, headed by the chairman of the Main Administration of Vocational Training (Glavproforb), O. Iu. Shmidt. Lunacharskii, Krupskaia, L. R. Menzhinskaia, and others opposed early and narrow specialization. The discussion about the alternative of polytechnical or monotechnical education came to an end at the party meeting on public education, held by the Central Committee of the Bolshevik Party from 31 December 1920 to 4 January 1921. The result of the five-day discussion was a compromise. The main Soviet school was declared to be the seven-year labor and comprehensive school for children aged 8–15. The seven-year school comprised two levels: level 1 lasted four years (the

---

[61] Ibid., 237. The italics are the author's.

[62] Iu. S. Borisov, "Shkol'nye reformy i podgotovka kadrov (1917–1941 gg.)", in *Dukhovnyi potentsial SSSR nakanune Velikoi Otechestvennoi voiny: Iz istorii sovetskoi kul'tury 1917–1941 g. Sbornik statei*, ed. Borisov (Moscow: Institut istorii SSSR, 1985), 96–100.

fifth year of teaching was added to level 2) and level 2 lasted three years. The meeting proposed to transform the two senior years of level 2 into vocational schools (*tekhnikumy*).[63] Thus what happened was a sharp turn away from the goal of rapidly establishing a comprehensive polytechnic labor school towards the opposite idea, namely to make secondary education vocational. Lunacharskii was forced to admit: "We got carried away by illusions with regard to the speed with which we could introduce if not the ideal unified labor school, then something close in spirit.... We must become realistic, we must distinguish between the aim of a school for the masses, which we must maintain, so to speak, and the demands of Russia, so that they don't become separate."[64] Lenin took care to stress that this was a temporary measure, writing: "We are destitute. We need carpenters, metal workers, *now. Without any doubt.* All must become carpenters, metal workers and so on, *but* with the addition of a minimum of general education and polytechnical knowledge."[65] However, this temporary measure dragged on for ten years (into the academic year 1931–32); moreover, vocational training started ever earlier, spreading to the seven-year school as well.

Even the new reform could not be implemented completely. The plan outlined for the gradual abolition of second-level schools with the simultaneous establishment of vocational schools in their place was shelved as a result of the lack of means for organizing and equipping vocational technical schools. Second-level schools continued to exist, while only a very small number of seven-year schools were established. As a result this reform was discontinued at the end of 1922.[66] A year later Narkompros conceived the idea of making the two senior years of the second-level school vocational instead of replacing them with technical schools.

The reform of school education that had begun in the first years of Soviet rule, mainly as a search for new forms and methods of teaching, continued throughout the next decade and was stopped in the early 1930s.

 C8   80

The First World War had been the first link in the successive chain of social upheavals that would have a tremendous psychological and psycho-physical impact on the rising generation of Russians. It triggered the Revolution, and

---

[63] Iu. S. Borisov, "Razvitie gosudarstvennoi sistemy narodnogo obrazovaniia v SSSR: Sovershenstvovanie soderzhaniia obucheniia," in *Iz istorii partiino-gosudarstvennogo rukovodstva kul'turnym stroitel'stvom v SSSR: Sbornik statei*, ed. L. V. Ivanova (Moscow: Institut istorii SSSR, 1983), 155–56.

[64] Lunacharskii, *O narodnom obrazovanii*, 190–91.

[65] Lenin, *Polnoe sobranie sochinenii*, 42: 230. The italics are Lenin's own.

[66] Chekhov, "Tipy russkoi shkoly," 76.

the Revolution was followed by the Civil War. The subsequent stages of deepening social crisis determined the consciousness of the new generation to a certain degree. The pedagogue S. A. Zolotarev wrote in 1925:

> The most characteristic patterns in the combination of emotional experience and acts of will must be placed in the context of such psychophysical factors as war, revolution, famine, epidemics, unprecedented mortality, and economic devastation; and in the context of such intellectual and emotional factors as the ideology of external and civil war, the general intensity of perception, sharp transitions from an overabundance of impressions to their scarcity, and similar transitions in the sphere of volitional activity.[67]

War, revolution, and the subsequent civil war and famine marked the stages of a deepening transformation in the consciousness of children and young people.

When fighting began in 1914 the conditions in which lessons were held in city schools changed. Parts of school buildings were turned into military infirmaries. Moreover, cities had a large contingent of students from refugee families from the western provinces. A directive from the Ministry of Popular Education dated 10 August 1914 stipulated that such students be admitted outside the specified quota. In bigger cities, large numbers of students were admitted above quota—up to 100 students per school.[68] The result was an acute shortage of school buildings. For the first time in the history of the Russian school, two shifts of lessons were introduced, one in the morning and the other after lunch. Children attending the second shift spent the entire morning in the streets, idling, playing games and fighting, and the lessons that followed after lunch made them tired and irritated. Consequently, the after-lunch groups consisted of a crowd of children who were nervous, restless, and fatigued from the impressions of a morning spent running around in the streets. Now they were sitting down, tired, in the heavy atmosphere of premises that had been poorly aired after the morning lessons.[69]

The war agitated the country's youth and triggered a wave of patriotism. Pupils participated in patriotic demonstrations. The exalted nature of these demonstrations, characterized by extreme manifestations of mob psychology and even appeals for anti-German pogroms, naturally had a very negative effect on the spirits of young people. There were instances of pupils taking part in anti-German pogroms. One crowded student demonstration in Moscow

---

[67] S. A. Zolotarev, *Chetyre smeny molodezhi (1905–1925): Iz nabliudenii pedagoga* (Leningrad: Sovremennik, 1926), 67.

[68] *Vestnik vospitaniia*, no. 8 (1914): 80.

[69] S. Bakhrushin, "Bor'ba s detskoi prestupnost'iu v sviazi s voinoi," *Prizrenie i blagotvoritel'nost' v Rossii*, no. 5 (1916): 386–88.

culminated in the destruction of shops owned by the German merchants Mandel and Einem. In order to prevent similar excesses, the administrators of the Petrograd school district even issued an order banning pupils from staging demonstrations during "school hours."[70]

A mass exodus began when students joined the army. This was considered a manifestation of patriotic feelings, but the boys were drawn to the front mainly by the usual need of young men to experience change and romantic adventures. It is impossible to give precise numbers of how many adolescents left school to join the army. The papers wrote that in September 1914 alone, in Petrograd twelve pupils from non-classical secondary schools, one from a classical grammar school, and one cadet disappeared to the front. All of them were between 13 and 17 years of age. In Moscow, eleven cases of disappearance were recorded, including that of a female grammar school pupil who changed into the uniform of an army volunteer. The papers recorded cases where children (some of them only 10 to 12 years old) ran off to the front in Kaluga, Yaroslavl, Kostroma, Serpukhov, Rybinsk, and many other towns and cities.[71] They usually fled without money, warm clothing, or a change of clothes, and often ate nothing for two or three days. In October 1914 they swamped the Western and Southwestern districts. During the first three months of the war, more than 400 young volunteers, whose parents in their panic sent telegrams to the local authorities, imploring them to arrest their children, passed through Vil'no (Vilnius) in the direction of the front.[72] The number of children who were not officially sought is nowhere recorded. A similarly large number of runaways tried to reach the Galician Front. On some days, the police caught and sent to Kiev between 30 and 40 young people.[73] It is significant that out of the 120 children under 14 who were questioned in early 1915, 37 percent (40.5 percent of the boys and 33 percent of the girls) expressed a desire to go to war, while 64 percent said they wanted to see fighting (among those over 9 years of age this number was 76 percent).[74]

Those young runaways who did reach the front and managed to join an army unit entered a blood-soaked atmosphere of killing and violence that invariably affected the psychological balance of adults, let alone children. In 1917 (with a significant delay due to censorship) the journal *Russkaia shkola* (The Russian School) published an article written by a frontline officer about

---

[70] *Vestnik vospitaniia*, no. 9 (1914): 110; N. P. Malinovskii, "Voina i deti," *Russkaia shkola*, no. 11 (1914): 68.

[71] R.G., "Iz srednei shkoly (Khronika)," *Vestnik vospitaniia*, no. 9 (1914): 109.

[72] Malinovskii, "Voina i deti," 69.

[73] V. M. Levitskii, "Bezprizornye deti i voina," in *Deti i voina: Sbornik statei* (Kiev: Kievskoe frebelevskoe obshchestvo, 1915), 14.

[74] V. V. Zen'kovskii, "O vlianii voiny na detskuiu psikhiku (po dannym ankety)," in *Deti i voina*, 62.

two 12-year-old boys, Mishka and Vas'ka, who had joined his regiment. The soldiers call them "imps." The officer wrote: "The war did their heads in. They fantasized aloud and told the soldiers how they would kill the Germans, distinguish themselves, and return home bedecked with the Cross of St. George." However, they volunteered to go on reconnaissance and disappeared for around four days. The officer remembered:

> They returned caked in mud and exhausted, but on horseback; they had stolen the horses from the Austrians.... "We crept into the village of S," Mishka told, "where we ran into a sentry.... He was leaning against a haystack, smoking and mumbling some kind of song; he didn't see us.... And I, I snuck up to him, grabbed his throat from behind and, whack, I strangled him." "He stuck his tongue out and went all blue," Vas'ka added, "but nothing, he didn't scream. He kicked his legs a couple of times and snuffed it." In the same village they had to kill yet another sentry, whom they skewered on a bayonet, and "all this blood came out and he wheezed like a slaughtered pig." They talked so naturally and with such abandon about how they had killed two people; they painted such a colorful picture of how the soldier they slaughtered "floundered" and "sniveled" and how they pulled the satchel off the corpse, in which they found dry biscuits and wine, how they ate them on the spot, next to the dying man, that one is terrified for these children without knowing them.... "This is awful," said our company commander, Lieutenant N. "Because after the war they will be criminals, downright cutthroats, God knows what that is."[75]

Teenage runaways all shared one desperate wish, and that was to achieve a feat, to become famous and to receive an award. The example of a 15-year-old boy is characteristic. Having endured privations in a camp at the Southwestern Front for two months, he did not hold out until he got an award. Instead, he went to Kiev, bought himself a Cross of St. George in a shop and proudly walked around with it on the Kreshchatik, Kiev's main street, until he was arrested by the police.[76]

Different kinds of patriotic propaganda had a great influence on children's consciousness. The war brought forth a torrent of boulevard, folk, and "public-patriotic" literature. Newspapers, journals, brochures, leaflets, and colorful lithographs inundated the market of cheap publications. They described with relish and a clownish humor the glorious victories of Russian soldiers and Cossacks who killed pathetic and cowardly "prussaks" by the dozen, depicted the horrific "atrocities" committed by the Germans and the Turks and played

---

[75] Iak. Okunev, "Deti na voine (Iz boevykh vpechatlenii)," *Russkaia shkola*, no. 5–8 (1917): 3.

[76] Levitskii, "Bezprizornye deti i voina," 14.

up the image of the mustachioed Kaiser Wilhelm in his pointy helmet in every possible way. Publications aimed at children also actively exploited the war as a topic. All the patriotic propaganda, irrespective of whether it featured in official or other publications, created an atmosphere dominated by a cult of brutality and a glorification of murder and violence, which had a pernicious effect on the young generation. This did not fail to horrify some contemporaries. In January 1915 the papers told the story of a commander in chief who had personally awarded the Cross of St. George to a 12-year-old hero for chopping down 13 Austrians with his own hands. After reading this notice, one intellectual from Petrograd wrote in his journal: "The last words are a nightmare. In normal times this would be a world event due to its sheer horror—a crime totally out of line ... a 12-year-old boy chopped down 13 people!... Now it's the other way round. The boy is a hero. The boy received a St. George from the commander in chief himself. The boy is surrounded by a halo of glory. Hundreds of thousands of boys envy him. Millions are enraptured by him..."[77] This spirit of merciless brutality, which at any time and during any war hovers over the image of the warrior hero being extolled as an example of highest moral valor, was the moral substance in which the world view of young Russians was formed from August 1914 onwards.

After the February Revolution the spiritual atmosphere within the school system started to change. The sociological polls carried out during the 1910s in various Russian cities show that a large proportion of young people attending a prerevolutionary state secondary school in a city in the years after the revolution of 1905–07 were not content with the atmosphere and the prevalent customs in school. The list of reasons for this discontent included the formalistic way of teaching and assessment, the pointless harshness of discipline and the lack of pupils' rights, surveillance of pupils and school inspectors who were informers, pedantry of teachers, etc.

Since the very beginning of the Revolution all efforts of the re-established student unions were aimed at "independent student activities and the creation of a free school." "School used to be separated from the family and from life," proclaimed the students at a meeting of the representatives of Petrograd schools in March 1917 in the hall of the Tenishev Institute. "We left school unprepared not only for practical life, but also for continuing education. We must make efforts for secondary school, to which we give eight years of our lives, to be for us a second family and to make citizens out of us."[78] Regardless of the fact that the Revolution changed the general situation in school and rendered the relationship between pupils and their tutors closer and less forced, no real transformations took place in the school system during 1917.

---

[77] G. A. Kniazev, "Iz zapisnoi knizhki russkogo intelligenta," *Russkoe proshloe*, no. 2 (1991): 102.

[78] *Vestnik vospitaniia*, no. 3 (1917): 56.

The Soviet school reform that began in the academic year 1918–19 introduced significant changes. The social composition of the student body began to change, coeducation became the norm, the grading system, exams, Scripture lessons, Latin, school uniforms, and strict discipline became a thing of the past. Students began to behave very freely, and by the measure of the past their behavior sometimes bordered on anarchy. The decline in student discipline happened very fast and was noted everywhere as early as 1918–19. One female teacher working in a town school wrote: "During my 35 years as a teacher I have never seen pupils on whom school has as little influence as the present cohort."[79] This phenomenon was a consequence of the abolition of rigid demands on the behavior and appearance of pupils who, suddenly freed from harsh discipline, gave in to a wild outburst of mischief, wilfulness, and disorderly conduct. The confusion of the teachers, the school administration's loss of authority, and the devastation of the schools all played their role in the disintegration of discipline, but the main reasons were found in the chaotic conditions of the Civil War and the fall of all previous authority figures and moral principles. The behavior of the pupils fully corresponded to the moods and mores reigning in society as a whole.

Under the new social conditions the psychological atmosphere within the school walls started to change. During the implementation of the decree on coeducation the management of popular education, in particular in the capitals and other large cities, tried to "democratize" the student contingent of the secondary schools. A widespread practice for achieving this end was to mix students from different types of educational institutions (for example, students from the gymnasium and students from the higher primary school, i.e., the incomplete secondary school, which was attended mostly by the children of the lower strata of the urban population). This mixing immediately created an imbalance in the established life of a given school. O. D. Dediulin, chairman of the pedagogical council of a former private girls' gymnasium of Petrograd, remembered that in autumn 1918 the school faced huge difficulties,

> having accepted some of the children who had attended the now-closed private educational institutions, as well as all students of the Voznesenskii higher primary school for boys. The new children, wholly unaccustomed to the traditions ... of our school ... were unable to merge immediately with our indigenous student body. There was feuding, distrust appeared between students and teachers, something hidden and hostile was in the air.[80]

---

[79] Zolotarev, *Chetyre smeny molodezhi*, 89.

[80] *Nasha shkola. 1912. X. 1922. Istoriia vozniknoveniia i razvitiia 25-i trudovoi shkoly* (Petrograd: 25-ia trud. shkola, 1922), 6–7.

The structure of school life, which had been upheld over decades not only by the pedagogues, but also by the students themselves, as well as the traditions that had been passed from generation to generation, gradually receded into the past, alongside the corresponding social order and way of life. Academician D. S. Likhachev, who attended the K. May Gymnasium, remembered:

> The schools of Petrograd, as well as the city's people, had their individuality, their traditions, their customs. We were "May Bugs," and to this day I enjoy it when I can recognize in an acquaintance that they also studied at May's. For a long time still it seemed to me that in a crowd I could recognize people who had studied at May's—by the way they held themselves, even by their gait.... [In 1918–19] May's school gradually began to fall into decay. The students scattered, some went with their parents to places where there was more food.... You could watch the class empty. The teachers left, too.... And I already started feeling pity for the school.[81]

But the traditions that had formed over decades proved remarkably stable. Another memoirist, who entered the May Gymnasium in 1918, wrote that "although it was already a Soviet school, it still maintained the old traditions, which were carefully preserved by the old teachers, and also by the children themselves, especially the senior years."[82]

The preservation of old traditions was fostered by the fact that the principles of the new Soviet school were introduced for the most part merely on a formal level in the academic year 1918–19. In April 1919 Lunacharskii admitted: "In practice we have not managed to create a unified school in Russia which even remotely corresponds to our declaration."[83] And it hardly would have been possible in a single year to change, or even to change the face of, the structure of a school system that had formed over many decades. It was insufficient to remove the old icons from the school premises and replace them with portraits of the new leaders. "The label 'unified labor school' now graces all educational institutions of St. Petersburg," wrote A. E. Kudriavtsev, an expert at the Petrograd branch of Narkompros, in spring 1919,

> but everywhere the recent old times are hiding behind that label, totally untouched. In some places the portraits of Marx, Lenin, Trotskii, and Lunacharskii hang in close and touching proximity to the honorary diplomas of the Empress Mariia or Aleksandra, sealed in their gilded

---

[81] D. S. Likhachev, N. V. Blagovo, and E. B. Belodubrovskii, *Shkola na Vasil'evskom* (Moscow: Prosveshchenie, 1990), 139.

[82] Ibid., 140.

[83] *Severnaia kommuna*, 27 April 1919.

frames.... On a visit to one of the schools I had to attend the school breakfast. I take my place at table next to the students. Above us hangs a large portrait of Karl Marx in all its splendor, while from the opposite wall the face of A. V. Lunacharskii, so well known to all Petrograders, is looking at us. I point at him and ask the girl sitting next to me who he is. "Uritskii, I think." And above us, who is that? "That's Karl Marx." And who was that? No answer. None of the other student girls could solve the riddle either...[84]

Secondary schools preserved their originality, which they merely camouflaged with outward correspondence to the new demands. Because of that the psychological atmosphere in Soviet schools during the first year of their existence was a rather strange mixture of old and new values. In any case the aggregation of the old with the new in school lasted not very long and took place mostly in people's heads rather than in visible acts, as those attracted the irritation of the party inspectors.

The social composition of senior students at the former classical grammar schools was to a lesser degree subject to change. By the early 1920s the senior year groups, unlike the junior ones, were still dominated by the children of the intelligentsia and of those working in various ranks of the administration, diluted by children of the new (and to some degree the old) bourgeoisie and some children from working families. Profound changes affected only the appearance, behavior, mentality, and attitude to life of the pupils. A teacher with many years of experience in prerevolutionary schools wrote in 1922:

Meeting this new audience, an old teacher might be amazed at the students' appearance, their heterogeneous attire, and their free and unforced behavior. When testing knowledge and "successfulness" according to the old curricula the teacher would have found many defects.... But during a regular conversation with the students he would quickly convince himself that they were the same young people as of old.... There is a simple explanation for this paradox: the social composition of those studying at the second level ... has changed very little. All the hardships of life could not exhaust the stock of education and knowledge that existed in the families of the bourgeoisie and of those working in the administration.[85]

The predominance of children from intellectual families in urban secondary schools was tenacious, regardless of all attempts by the authorities to

---

[84] A. Kudriavtsev, "Petrogradskaia shkola v minuvshem godu (Iz vpechatlenii raionnogo eksperta)," *Vestnik prosveshcheniia*, no. 4–5 (1919): 27.

[85] G. Rogov, "Obliki sovremennoi molodezhi," in *Sovremennyi rebenok* (Moscow: Rabotnik prosveshcheniia, 1923), 5.

"proletarianize" the second-level school. The main reasons were these: the children of office workers were better prepared for attending secondary school, both in terms of their stock of knowledge, which was usually acquired at home as well as at school, and their psychological orientation towards education, which was formed by the sphere in which they grew up. Working-class children, as a rule, chose the path of early vocational training. The biggest dropout of working-class children happened between years 5 and 7. During these years a large proportion of these children changed to primary or secondary vocational schools. The most popular schools for working-class children were factory training schools, where they accounted for up to 79 percent of the student body.[86] However, all the reasons listed for the disproportionate social composition of the student body can be attributed ultimately to one basic fact, namely the life goals of a certain social stratum. Workers usually primed their children to learn a trade as early as possible, i.e., to have a slice of "real bread" in their hands. Intellectual and office-worker families prized knowledge as the highest possession. Correspondingly, their scale of values was different and favored education (including higher education) and the corresponding career path.

In 1918 separate education for male and female adolescents was abolished and replaced by coeducational secondary schools. This had a serious impact on the general atmosphere in schools, and also on the development of young men and women respectively. Separate education was founded on ideas about the social function and also the intellectual and psychological particularities of each sex. Women's role in the family determined the secondary education they received. This was not only true for women's institutes, which prioritized the development of aesthetic sensibilities and the art of housekeeping, but also women's classical grammar schools, the curricula of which were significantly reduced in comparison to those taught at men's grammar schools. Women could only receive a commercially oriented secondary education in private institutions, and most of these could be found only in large towns. A non-classical secondary education for women, with an emphasis on natural science subjects, was virtually non-existent.

The coeducational school system accorded girls the same rights and opportunities as boys. If we can judge by a student poll in the town of Orel from autumn 1918, a certain proportion of girls immediately valued these opportunities. They wrote that the coeducational school brought them more knowledge, as girls were taught the same curriculum as boys, and that besides it was easier to develop as a person among boys. Yet coeducation swiftly triggered a negative response from the majority of male students. Three-quarters were opposed to coeducation and only one-quarter in favor. The supporters of single-sex education wrote that it offered more opportunities for boys to gain knowledge, that there was less gossip and flirting, that boys did not have to

---

[86] *Kul'turnoe stroitel'stvo Soiuza Sovetskikh Sotsialisticheskikh respublik: Sbornik diagramm*, 2nd ed. (Moscow–Leningrad, 1929), 37.

feel embarrassed in front of "repulsive girls," and girls did not have to suffer insults from "disgusting boys."[87] And yet the majority of those opposed to coeducation were girls. One of the students of the former Petersburg Boys' Gymnasium No. 3 remembered that the internal life of his year group became significantly more difficult after the introduction of coeducation. "The group's self-esteem suffered a bit from the fact that suddenly and for no reason they squeezed eight girls from the corresponding year of the Iurgens Classical Grammar School for Girls, which was being fused with our grammar school, into the friendly family that was our year group." On the other hand, he continued: "The old journals and poems from those times tell that during the first half of the year we were much more preoccupied with flirting and other nice things than with science."[88] At the same time, during the first years after the Revolution the effort to reject the other sex was just as evident as in prerevolutionary times. This was particularly visible among the girls. In winter 1918–19, right after the introduction of coeducation, in the town of Vetluga (Nizhegorodskaia province) the female students stubbornly formed clubs that were girls-only and refused to admit boys.[89] It was a form of protest against coeducation and at the same time an attempt to preserve the spirit of the women's grammar school, at least outside the school walls. Thus the process of overcoming the legacy of the old single-sex school was rather painful.

It is crucial to take into account the profound impact of the era's social upheavals, i.e., war, revolution, and famine, on the psycho-physical state of school children. The mass-scale crisis of family life, a consequence of the loss of large parts of the male population during the First World War, reached unprecedented numbers during the Civil War. War, famine, epidemics, and other misfortunes cost the lives of many. Everywhere families were destroyed very quickly, causing massive psychological trauma in children. One of the polls among Petrograd school children in late 1919 yielded several hundred stories about death in the immediate family. In every questionnaire filled in by the children there was a list of dead relatives: "my dear grandmother died of hunger," "Dad was killed in the war," "my uncle died of food poisoning after eating horse meat," "my grandfather was executed, my uncle went mad and died," "two brothers were killed in the war," "my brother and sister are missing," "my uncle died of hunger, my aunt of the Spanish flu," "my brother was killed in the war, my father during the revolution," "my uncle went missing during the October Revolution," "two of my cousins shot themselves,"

---

[87] D. Azbukin, "Psikhologiia shkol'nikov v nachale Oktiabr'skoi revoliutsii," *Pedologicheskii zhurnal*, no. 3 (1923): 70.

[88] 13-ia Sovetskaia trudovaia shkola, Peterburgskaia Tret'ia gimnaziia, *Za sto let: Vospominaniia, stat´i, materialy* (Petrograd: Izd-vo 13-oi sovetskoi trudovoi shkoly, 1923), 154–55.

[89] G. A. Fortunatov, "Svobodno voznikaiushchie soobshchestva podrostkov," *Pedologiia*, no. 4 (1929): 530.

etc.[90] The worries tied to these tragedies left a special "grown-up" mark on the children, as their world view lost its childlike immediacy and carefreeness. One teacher who was involved in the research noted that

> pupils who have been asked to write something "funny" or something "sad" tend to choose the "sad" assignment and what they write is not sad in a childish sense, is not about a lost doll or theater ticket that failed to materialize, but it reveals the genuine sorrow of people who have been affected by a terrible life. Few have something "funny" to tell, and even then we find not laughter, but grimacing and sarcasm.[91]

Another, significantly more widespread reason for the depression, apathy and loss of vitality in children that was noted by many pedagogues and doctors was the protracted state of starvation. Starvation (or insufficient nutrition) had in practice begun during the First World War, but the most acute starvation happened between 1919–22, and the last two years, 1921 and 1922, were the harshest. "Although I am only 16 years old," a schoolboy from Smolensk wrote in early 1923, "I've seen many bad things in my life ... and I've become apathetic. The famine had a big impact on me, when I had to work with my hands for a piece of bread."[92] The protracted starvation caused major physical changes in an enormous number of schoolchildren. The visible results were noticeably stunted growth, significant weight loss (up to 40 percent), smaller chest circumference, and reduced muscle strength. Moreover, researchers observed atrophy of the thymus gland, which plays a major role in growth, thyroid glands that reached only 45–70 percent of their normal weight, and major changes in the pituitary glands and the gonads.[93] Emaciation had many highly disadvantageous consequences, including anaemia and a general lack of psychological and physical energy. A new syndrome appeared, called "emaciation neurosis."[94] Schoolchildren suffered from fatigue, attention deficit, irritability with simultaneous apathy and limited liveliness. Depression was manifest alongside extreme touchiness. Doctors noted that children increasingly exhibited base, animal interests and desires.

---

[90] Zolotarev, *Chetyre smeny molodezhi*, 81.

[91] Ibid., 81–82.

[92] A. P. Serebrennikov and A. V. Serebrennikova, "K voprosu o professional'noi orientatsii smolenskikh shkol'nikov," *Nauchnye izvestiia Smolenskogo universiteta*, no. 2 (1924): 207.

[93] V. G. Shtefko, *Vliianie golodaniia na podrastaiushchee pokolenie Rossii* (Simferopol': Krymizdat, 1923), 42, 105, 107–10; L. P. Nikolaev, "Vlianie sotsial'nykh faktorov na fizicheskoe razvitie detei," *Put' prosveshcheniia*, no. 9 (1924): 25; I. A. Ariamov, *Osnovy pedologii* (Moscow: Moskovskii rabochii, 1927), 33–34, 36.

[94] G. D. Aronovich, "Nevrozy istoshcheniia u detei," *Voprosy izucheniia i vospitaniia lichnosti*, no. 4–5 (1922): 557–73.

This included a pathological greed for food and endless dwelling on variations of the "hunger theme," which in some cases became obsessive.[95]

Hunger dominated the responses to a poll in 1919 in which children were asked what they would like to do. Reading and going to the cinema were replaced by the desire to "eat and drink tea with sugar," "fill my belly," "have a substantial meal," receive "two French buns with butter" and "galoshes without holes," while instead of playing games they wanted to "lie in the sun," "stand in a queue while peasant women swear at each other," "trade," and "speculate."[96] Persistent hunger made children steal, take food from the weak, lie, and cheat their elders. Physical emaciation led to complications of the usual children's diseases, with the result that child mortality reached unprecedented heights. There was also an unusual prevalence of disease, including nervous and psychological disease. According to data collated by the academician V. M. Bekhterev, of more than 1,500 children examined in one of the prophylactic school dispensaries in Petrograd, 18 percent had a nervous illness, while the overall number of those suffering from disease was 61 percent.[97] The conclusions reached by doctors at the First All-Russian Congress on Child Defectiveness, Delinquency, and Abandonment in summer 1920 read: "The deviations in the nervous and psychological health of these children are a sad portent of the future potential for an increase in nervous and psychological disease in the entire country.[98]

As a consequence of general mobilization after the start of the First World War, the majority of families where a member had been conscripted were in a difficult material situation. The following numbers speak for themselves: in Petrograd, 35,983 families were registered with the municipal trusts for the poor in August 1914, while by November 1915 their number had reached 83,848. That means that during the first 14 months of war the number of poor families increased by a factor of 2.3.[99] "Poverty, high prices, and the large number of families who have lost their breadwinner are the factors that spawn penury," wrote one author researching the problem in 1916.[100] During the Civil War families found themselves in significantly more calamitous situations when rationing was introduced as a result of severe food shortages. Material hardship forced children to undertake adult labor early in life. The peak of early labor activity among school children was in 1919–20 and early

---

[95] *Detskaiia defektivnost', prestupnost' i besprizornost': Po materialam I vserossiiskogo s"ezda 24/VI–2/VII 1920 g.* (Moscow: Gos. izd-vo, 1922), 21.

[96] Zolotarev, *Chetyre smeny molodezhi*, 82.

[97] *Detskaiia defektivnost', prestupnost' i besprizornost'*, 22.

[98] Ibid.

[99] V. N. Ogronovich, "Polozhenie besprizornykh detei v Petrograde v sviazi s voinoi," *Prizrenie i blagotvoritel'nost' v Rossii*, no. 1–2 (1916): 73.

[100] A. Gudvan, "Deti i voina," *Gorodskoe delo*, no. 5 (1916): 217.

1921. During this period not only the majority of senior year students worked, but also a significant proportion of younger children. Work took up a large amount of the children's time. School attendance plummeted. According to data from an inspection of Moscow schools in 1920, even out of those 40 percent of pupils who remained registered with the schools, only 20–25 percent really attended lessons.[101]

One consequence of the changes in both school, family, and everyday life was a shift in pupils' attitude towards school. In 1918, 40 percent of schoolchildren questioned in the town of Orel said that they preferred being at school to being at home, with 38 percent claiming the opposite.[102] The shortcomings of school listed by the children included lack of discipline and poorly prepared teachers, while the main virtues included the closeness between teachers and children, the fact that education was free and accessible to all, and the free school breakfast. In 1919–20, when the devastation of schools reached its peak, the spectrum of attitudes pupils displayed towards school became very varied. They gave replies such as: "Now it is better only because the teachers are more relaxed in their behavior towards us ... but overall school has become worse, because it is in ruins"; "Previously school was like the barracks, we blindly obeyed the directors, but now it is the other way round"; "In the old school we were scared of bad marks and studied hard, but now no one cares"; "Now you manage both to go to school and stand in a queue"; "Previously it was better because there was discipline, while ... now there are commotions"; "In the past we had enough to eat and so we learned, but now we are hungry and so we don't learn"; "The school we have now is better than the old one.... [P]reviously I couldn't go, because my father is a peasant"; "In the past they paid for us and valued us, and now they don't"; "Now our teacher is a friend, and before it was almost the other way round."[103] Overall one can say that, during this period, those who had the highest opinion of the new school system were the younger pupils, who had no memory of the old system, while those in the senior years were for the most part critical.

According to the plan of the Soviet school reform's authors, the basis of school life now was student self-government. This had to build on "the development of activity, creativity, self-discipline, and initiative in the children," and its aim was to "impart social habits to the students, awaken their consciousness of public obligations, responsibilities, and rights, prepare them for conscious participation in the civic life of the country and draw them into this life."[104] The basics of self-government were outlined for the first time in October 1918 in the "Basic Principles of the Unified Labor School

---

[101] *Detskaiia defektivnost', prestupnost' i besprizornost'*, 33.

[102] Azbukin, "Psikhologiia shkol'nikov," 71.

[103] Zolotarev, *Chetyre smeny molodezhi*, 86–87.

[104] A. M. Lebedev, *Samodeiatel'nost' i samoupravlenie uchashchikhsia: Sbornik pedagogicheskikh statei* (Leningrad-Moscow: Gosudarstvennoe izd-vo, 1925), 12.

of the RSFSR." This document set three goals for student self-government: 1) participation in the work of the pedagogical councils of the school, 2) self-administration of student groups and the creation of an electoral apparatus, 3) political and educational work.[105] The apparatus of electoral self-government consisted of senior students' councils (*starostaty*) or students' committees (*uchkomy*), which were accountable to the general school assembly. At city or town level the self-government of individual schools was coordinated by students' unions. Sometimes the school organs of self-government were even considered local cells of the union. Each year group elected its own organ of self-government, a so-called *gruppkom*, the functions of which included monitoring the discipline, order, and cleanliness of the classroom. In addition, the school self-government was entitled to organize different kinds of circles, clubs, and organizations to do with science, education, art, and sport, as well as the editing of school journals, and so forth.

Once the first cells of the Communist Youth League (Komsomol) had been established in school, the Komsomol became responsible for organizing school self-government. When general student unions were disbanded,[106] Komsomol cells tried to take over all work inside the student body, substituting for the structures of self-government and sometimes even disbanding the students' councils. Moreover, Komsomol cells exhibited a desire to supervise all aspects of school life, right down to teaching and administration. Such pretensions forced the delegates to a conference of local school leaders in August 1920 to note that the role of Komsomol cells "consists in working with the students and in actively participating in the life of the school, without interfering in the administrative functions of the school."[107] The intrusion of the Komsomol in all school matters, including questions of administration, pedagogy, and teaching, which pedagogues had considered their exclusive prerogative, created significant tensions in schools, in particular between Komsomol members and teaching staff.

The work of student committees and executive committees was limited to, firstly, the assignment of duties, which often went in alphabetic order and, secondly, the use of disciplinary penalties for various order violations.[108] The second area found wide application in all schools. Student "courts" developed frantic activity in order to weed out lateness and other violations of order. Towards the beginning of the 1920s they sometimes took the form of

---

[105] *Narodnoe obrazovanie v SSSR*, 143.

[106] The last of the local student unions—the Student Union of the Petrograd Unified Labor Schools (previous named the Student Union of Proletarian Labor Schools)—stubbornly refused to discontinue its activities and was ultimately disbanded in early February 1920. *Krasnaia gazeta*, 1 February 1920 and 5 February 1920; *Iunyi kommunist*, no. 4 (1920): 15.

[107] *Narodnoe prosveshchenie*, no. 67–70 (1920): 8–11.

[108] Krupenina, "Detskoe kommunisticheskoe dvizhenie i shkola," 34–35.

extraordinary revolutionary trials. Thus in one of the second-level schools the "komobs" convened—the abbreviation stands for "Committee for Public Salvation." In another school in which an increase in lateness was observed the decision was taken to organize an "Extraordinary Commission for the Struggle against Lateness," which adopted the decision not to admit latecomers to the classroom until the end of the lesson.[109] Later, when the revolutionary spirit of the period of war communism had become a thing of the past, such merciless names became rare and were swapped for more peaceful ones, such as "disciplinary commission" or "commission for order," etc. However, the nature of the imposed "sentences" remained the same. The teachers complained about the harshness of the commissions' members towards their own peers and were often forced to defend the delinquents. The students applied the measures they witnessed in the world in which they lived. They included a rather broad spectrum of punishments: public admonition, revocation of the right to receive theater tickets and attend school performances, revocation of the vote in elections to the school's self-government, recording of the delinquent's name on the "black board," a minor fine, or forced labor, etc. Ultimately, the most severe punishment was exclusion from school, although this required the sanction of the school council.[110] The existence of peer trials in schools caused division among teachers, some of whom were categorically against them.

The organization of revolutionary festivities played a special role in the life of any school. They were considered very important for the political education of the students. They were organized by young pioneers and Komsomol members, as well as members of all "representative" organs of self-government. They usually took the form of meetings with concerts or "evenings," during which the students gave speeches and declamations, read poetry, sang revolutionary songs, and so forth.

Yet another completely new phenomenon in schools was the appearance of the so-called "wall newspapers." This was a new phenomenon in Russia as a whole. It was initiated by the papers *Izvestiia* and *Pravda*, which were glued to walls. The bulletins of the Russian Telegraph Agency (ROSTA) followed suit, and finally there were handwritten newspapers in factories, etc. The first wall newspapers in schools appeared only in 1922. They were preceded by newspapers in leaflet form—one or two pages of standard format, with both sides used for text. They had appeared in individual schools as early as 1917, but had mostly fallen into disuse by the early 1920s.[111] When school wall newspapers became popular, political topics were clearly predominant. The most widespread type of wall newspaper was the festive (anniversary) paper.

---

[109] N. Kavyrshin, "O distsiplinarnom uklone v rabote organov uchenicheskogo samo-upravleniia (Obzor literatury)," *Na putiakh k novoi shkole*, no. 1 (1928): 118.

[110] Ibid., 118–19.

[111] I. I. Rufin, *Shkol'noe literaturnoe tvorchestvo* (Moscow, 1929), 33.

Another variation of the agitational wall "press" were papers dedicated to different political campaigns. Just like festive papers (*prazdnichnye gazety*), they did not stand out for particular originality of content, and they appeared much less frequently. There were papers intended for the entire school, as well as those concerning a particular year group, which mostly reflected the current life of the school or year group. Usually the papers for individual years were produced more quickly and had more issues than those affecting the entire school. Their content was rather heterogeneous. In addition, second-level schools began to produce literary papers, a new form of paper that originated in Soviet times. In the first years after the Revolution literary journals were widespread in secondary schools. Subsequently they became less frequent, and by the early 1920s they had become a rare phenomenon. They were replaced by literary wall newspapers, smaller in volume but accessible to anyone who wanted to read them.[112]

By the early 1920s the "civic" creativity and activity that had been awakened in the consciousness of children had reached a significant stage of development within the school. In this the pupils differed radically from the pupils of prerevolutionary times. Another important peculiarity of the postwar generation of schoolchildren was their practical orientation, which noticeably distinguished them from the previous generation. As a result of the impact of social cataclysms, starvation, and privations, they grew up very early. A utilitarian outlook became a mass phenomenon among adolescents.

Translated by Josephine von Zitzewitz

---

[112] V. Chistiakov, "Stennaia shkol′naia gazeta i rol′ slovesnika," *Rodnoi iazyk v shkole*, no. 6 (1927): 232–33.

The Russian Orthodox Church during the First World War and Revolutionary Turmoil, 1914–21

Pavel G. Rogoznyi

From the very beginning of the First World War, the Russian Orthodox Church was actively involved in the patriotic movement that drew in a significant proportion of the Russian population. From the pulpits came sermons on the "Teutonic threat" and "German dominance." Churches held prayers for "the gift of victory" and the healing of the wounded, and those fallen in battle were remembered. On the orders of the Holy Synod, field hospitals were opened in many monasteries.[1] The title of a sermon by Bishop Nikodim (Krotkov)—the suffragan (*vikarii*) of the diocese (*eparkhiia*) of Kiev—"Go to war as if called by God," which was published as a leaflet and distributed in hundreds of thousands of copies, was characteristic.[2] Germanophobia also affected the functionaries of the spiritual office, to the point that V. K. Sabler, the chief procurator of the Holy Synod, changed his "German" surname and took that of his wife, henceforth calling himself Desiatovskii.[3]

Priests actively called on their parishioners to go to war and fulfil their duty.[4] Sometimes the bishops themselves—for example Nikon (Bezsonov), the bishop of Enisei diocese—joined the army in the field.[5] Moreover, representatives of the Institute of Military Clergy fulfilled their pastoral duties among the troops. The head of military and naval clergy was the archpresbyter

---

[1] For more detail, see S. G. Runkevich, *Velikaia otechestvennaia voina i tserkovnaia zhizn´* (St. Petersburg, 1916).

[2] D. N. Shilov, *Gosudarstvennye deiateli Rossiiskoi imperii 1802–1917: Biobibliograficheskii spravochnik* (Moscow: Dmitrii Bulanin, 2001), 577.

[3] Rossiiskii gosudarstvennyi istoricheskii arkhiv (RGIA) f. 796, op. 204, ot. 1, st. 1, d. 176, l. 16ob.

[4] Priests and deacons were exempt from military service. Men without a theological education could be ordained as deacons, a practice widely abused by those keen to evade conscription.

[5] See P. G. Rogoznyi, "Votchina episkopa Nikona (Eniseiskaia eparkhiia v 1913–1917 gg.)," in *Istoriia povsednevnosti: Istochnik. Istorik. Istoriia*, vyp. 3 (St. Petersburg: Evropeiskii universitet, 2003).

Russian Culture in War and Revolution, 1914–22, Book 1: Popular Culture, the Arts, and Institutions. Murray Frame, Boris Kolonitskii, Steven G. Marks, and Melissa K. Stockdale, eds. Bloomington, IN: Slavica Publishers, 2014, 349–75.

(*protopresviter*), a position held during the war by Georgii Shavel'skii; overall there were more than 2,000 priests in the army and navy by 1915.[6] The conflict was called a "Great Patriotic War" and members of the clergy were actively involved in propagating its "holiness." Did the clergy's activity encourage the patriotic mobilization of the population? The historian D. Beyrau writes: "Considering what we know about the revolutionary events that followed in 1917, the activity of the church can be called ineffective."[7] Beyrau also notes that it is hard to identify the reason for this. At the same time it is presumed that there is an answer: the problem was the general political crisis that the Russian Empire experienced at the time and that affected all parts of society. The crisis could not possibly pass by the Orthodox faith as an institution. And while at the beginning of the war patriotism seemed to consolidate Russian society, the first defeats at the front exposed the empire's weak spots.

The church's weaknesses came to the fore with particular force in 1915, when its internal problems were superimposed on the general political contradictions that had caught up with the empire's government and led to the replacement of the supreme commander in chief and the dismissal of several ministers. Among those dismissed was Sabler-Desiatovskii, accused of having links to Rasputin. His dismissal, however, did not help overcome the church's weaknesses, since his replacement, A. D. Samarin, a leader of the Moscow nobility who was popular in church circles, positioned himself as a categorical opponent of so-called "dark forces" in the church right from the beginning. Unfortunately, historiography has so far failed to produce studies specifically dedicated to the ecclesiastical crisis of 1915 (although there are many works on the general political crisis in Russia during that period).[8]

The ecclesiastical crisis of 1915 was linked to the resignation of Samarin. The reason for his resignation was that the chief procurator contravened Varnava (Nakropin), the bishop of Tobolsk, who had become a bishop despite lacking the most basic ecclesiastical education, and who had tried to "glorify" the Orthodox hermit Ioann (Maksimovich), who was revered in Siberia, against the resistance of the synod, that is, unlawfully. The one who resigned as a result of the conflict was not the bishop, but the chief procurator of the

---

[6] Archpresbyter Shavel'skii wrote that overall more than 5,000 priests "spent some time" at the front. More than 30 died from injuries. G. I. Shavel'skii, *Vospominaniia poslednego protopresvitera russkoi armii i flota* (Moscow: Krutitskoe podvor'e, 1996), 2: 93, 106.

[7] D. Beyrau, "Fantazii i videniia v gody Pervoi mirovoi voiny: Pravoslavnoe voennoe dukhovenstvo na sluzhbe Vere, Tsariu i Otechestvu," in *Petr Andreevich Zaionchkovskii: Sbornik statei i vospominanii k stoletiiu istorika*, ed. L. G. Zakharova, S. V. Mironenko, and T. Emmons (Moscow: ROSSPEN, 2008), 767–68.

[8] On the political crisis of 1915, see M. F. Florinskii, *Krizis gosudarstvennogo upravleniia v gody Pervoi mirovoi voiny* (Leningrad: Izd-vo Leningradskogo universiteta, 1988); and B. I. Kolonitskii, *"Tragicheskaia erotika": Obrazy imperatorskoi sem'i v gody pervoi mirovoi voiny* (Moscow: Novoe literaturnoe obozrenie, 2010).

Holy Synod. People in the church and in secular circles alike linked all these events to the hated name of the "elder" (*starets*) Grigorii Rasputin.[9] Recent research has denied the role of Rasputin in the appointment of his protégés to high government office.[10] And indeed it is difficult to prove Rasputin's influence on politics with official documents. Public opinion, however, was convinced that his influence was real, and this conviction was even more important than Rasputin's activities themselves.

People holding the most diverse political opinions were united in the belief that "the sectarian [*khlyst*] manages everything." After the February Revolution P. V. Gur'ev, the director of the synod's office, compiled a list of so-called "Rasputin appointments" among the leading clergy. According to this document, the ruling bishop (*arkhierei*) in both capitals had been personally appointed by the emperor without prior consultation with the synod, as foreseen in the "Spiritual Regulations" adopted under Peter the Great. Thus the synod's members found out about the appointment of Metropolitan Pitirim (Oknov) in Petrograd and Metropolitan Makarii (Nevskii) in Moscow only after the event.[11] Public opinion could not forgive such rude interference in church matters. Both hierarchs were dubbed "Rasputin's men" for life, and the church community did not accept their appointments as legitimate.

While Metropolitan Makarii of Moscow was merely considered "a decrepit old man" who "remembers nothing and knows nothing," Metropolitan Pitirim became the most hated figure in the church. Among the many "sins" ascribed to him was homosexuality.[12] The hierarch of Petrograd was a rather colorful figure whose portraits frequently featured in the press, while he himself tried to play the role of a liberal. According to Professor Titlinov, Pitirim displayed "progressive tendencies and freely proclaimed liberal thoughts" which he would later quickly change to mean the opposite.[13]

The question of the parishes, which also included the search for resources for the clergy to live on, especially in the countryside, was a big problem,

---

[9] For more detail, see S. L. Firsov, *Russkaia tserkov' nakanune peremen (konets 1890-kh–1918 gg.* (Moscow: Kruglyi stol po religioznomu obrazovaniiu i diakonii, 2002), 445–84.

[10] See, for example, S. V. Kulikov, "Kamaril'ia i 'ministerskaia chekharda': Sootnoshenie verbal'nykh i biurokraticheskikh praktik v pozdneimperskoi Rossii," in *Novaia politicheskaia istoriia: Sbornik nauchnykh rabot*, ed. M. M. Krom (St. Petersburg: Izd-vo Evropeiskogo universiteta v Sankt-Peterburge; Aleteiia, 2004), 77–97.

[11] RGIA f. 796, op. 445, d. 745, ll. 1–2.

[12] For detailed information on Metropolitan Pitirim, see S. L. Firsov, *Iskusivshiisia vlast'iu: Istoriia zhizni Petrogradskogo Pitirima (Oknova)* (Moscow: Pravoslavnyi Sviato-Tikhonovskii gumanitarnyi universitet, 2011).

[13] B. V. Titlinov, *Tserkov' vo vremia revoliutsii* (Petrograd: Byloe, 1924), 54.

which the authorities had been unable to solve for many years.[14] During the First World War the problem became more acute, and according to the data provided by the commission, there were cases in some dioceses where lower-ranking clergy had starved to death. Distrust in the authorities increased, and military defeat only strengthened the rumors about betrayal at the very top. The process of the de-sacralization of the monarchy directly affected what seemed to be the autocracy's greatest ideological buttress—the Orthodox Church. For that reason, it is not surprising that the majority of Orthodox clergy genuinely welcomed the February Revolution.[15]

In contrast to the October Revolution, which divided the country, the February Revolution provided a short interlude that united the overwhelming majority of the empire's population. Public consciousness perceived it as "Russia's Spring" and "Red Easter."[16] Nicholas II abdicated and Grand Prince Mikhail Aleksandrovich refused to accept supreme authority. As a result even the monarchists, following the entire Romanov house, had no choice but to accept the new regime.[17] The church also accepted the new authorities. The Holy Synod designed a new form of intercessory prayer for the authorities, if somewhat belatedly. Many priests genuinely welcomed the change and saw it as the beginning of a new epoch in the life of the church. The "Ecclesiastical Revolution" was the name given to this short-lived period in the history of the Russian Orthodox Church, first by contemporaries and then by historians.

An important trait of postrevolutionary Russia was that the authorities, including the ecclesiastical ones, ceased to be the only source of law-making, i.e., the Provisional Government did not monopolize that process. The arch-presbyter N. Liubimov, a member of the synod, said at the All-Russian Council of the Orthodox Church (Pomestnyi sobor): "Life has outpaced us. We don't manage to issue orders, and then we receive news such as: the bishop of this place has been dismissed, in that place the holy fathers have taken power into their own hands. What should the synod have done?"[18] In other words, public

---

[14] For more detail, see Vera Shevzov, *Russian Orthodoxy on the Eve of Revolution* (Oxford: Oxford University Press, 2004), published in Russian as V. F. Shevtsova, *Pravoslavie v Rossii nakanune 1917 goda* (St. Petersburg: Dmitrii Bulanin, 2010).

[15] See M. A. Babkin, *Rossiiskoe dukhovenstvo i sverzhenie monarkhii v 1917 godu: Materialy i arkhivnye dokumenty po istorii Russkoi pravoslavnoi tserkvi* (Moscow: Indrik, 2006).

[16] See B. I. Kolonitskii, *Simvoly vlasti i bor'ba za vlast': K izucheniiu politicheskoi kul'tury Rossiiskoi revoliutsii 1917 goda* (St. Petersburg: Dmitrii Bulanin, 2001).

[17] The assertion of M. A. Babkin that the synod allegedly had an alternative and could have refused to accept the new authorities is wholly inconclusive. M. A. Babkin, *Dukhovenstvo Russkoi Pravoslavnoi Tserkvi i sverzhenie monarkhii* (Moscow: RPIBR, 2007); and Babkin, *Sviashchenstvo i Tsarstvo: Rossiia, nachala 20 veka–1918 god* (Moscow: Indrik, 2011).

[18] *Deianiia Sviashchennogo Sobora Pravoslavnoi Rossiiskoi Tserkvi 1917–1918 gg.* (Moscow: Izd-vo Novospasskogo monastyria, 1994), 2: 192.

initiatives outpaced any decisions made by the highest church authorities. One example is the position of commissar for spiritual matters, which appeared in a number of dioceses. Sometimes it was held by a priest, other times by a person unfamiliar with the church and its problems. These commissars came into conflict with the old ecclesiastical structures because they demanded extraordinary competencies. Revolutionary tendencies affected almost all dioceses of the Russian Church. After April 1917 a new collocation appeared in the lexicon of the church: "Ecclesiastical Bolshevism." During the year, the concept changed dramatically: initially it meant simply disobedience towards the church authorities, but later, after the Bolshevik coup, it came to mean cooperation between priests and "Lenin's men."[19]

A mutiny of the Danilov Monastery's monks caused a big stir in society. The cenobites not only chased away the superior, but also turned the monastery into a den, with a home distillery and women of easy virtue. A correspondent of the Moscow paper *Utro Rossii* spent some time in the mutinous monastery. In his words "everywhere the cells are littered with cigarette butts and on the tables there are bottles of wine and *khanzha* [bread vodka]." He was unable to interview the main mutineer and ideologue of the uprising—Archdeacon Sofronii was drunk during the correspondent's visit.[20] Archpresbyter Nikolai Liubimov, the synod member sent to the monastery, confirmed that the newspaper notice "fully corresponds to reality." The diocesan inspection, whose report reached the synod only towards the end of 1917, identified the former superior of the monastery as the main culprit of the monks' mutiny, because "his goodness, according to the inspectors, was worse than theft."[21]

And yet, regardless of all the excesses that were characteristic of the revolutionary period, the main church reforms were implemented from below, for example during meetings between clergy and laity in the spring of 1917, and only later written into law by the Holy Synod. The most important of such reforms was the creation of institutes like the ecclesiastical-diocesan commissions and the ubiquitous introduction of elective elements into the church hierarchy. In certain dioceses congresses of clergy and the newly formed church commissions spoke out against their bishops and appealed to the synod for the removal of hierarchs they disliked. However, with the exception of Pitirim (Oknov), the metropolitan of Petrograd, and Varnava

---

[19] For more detail on this expression, see P. G. Rogoznyi, "'Tserkovnyi Bolshevizm': K izucheniiu iazyka bor'by za vlast' v Rossiiskoi Pravoslavnoi Tserkvi (aprel' 1917–mart 1918 g.)," in *Politicheskaia istoriia Rossii pervoi chetverti XX veka: Pamiati professora V. I. Startseva* (St. Petersburg: D.A.R.K, 2006), 329–40.

[20] *Utro Rossii*, 6 May 1917.

[21] RGIA f. 796, op. 204, ot. 1, st. 5, d. 222, l. 1ob. For more detail, see P. G. Rogoznyi, "Vzbuntovavshiisia monastyr' v buntuiushchei Rossii," in *Politicheskaia istoriia Rossii XX veka: K 80-letiiu professora V. I. Startseva*, ed. B. D. Gal'perina (St. Petersburg: D.A.R.K., 2011).

(Nakropin), the archbishop of Tobolsk, who were swiftly removed from the pulpit, the process of dismissing a bishop usually lasted several months. Many contemporaries gained the impression—and this impression has been reflected in the historiography—that the main initiator of the "purges" of the episcopate was V. N. L'vov, the new chief procurator of the synod. In reality, the initiative for dismissing a bishop almost always came from below, and the dismissals themselves were carried out not by the chief procurator, who did not have the legal right to dismiss anybody, but by the synod itself.

The role of L'vov, who is sometimes portrayed as a persecutor of the church, has been heavily exaggerated. He had an unbalanced character and frequently imagined himself in the role of an ecclesiastical dictator. However, when his initiatives conflicted with any strong public movement within the church, he was powerless to do anything. For example, regardless of his personal support, his protégé, Bishop Andrei (Ukhtomskii) was defeated in the elections for the post of Metropolitan of Petrograd. Regardless of the seemingly "counterrevolutionary" position taken by Andronik (Nikol'skii), the Bishop of Perm', who had publicly confessed his monarchist sympathies, the chief procurator was powerless to do anything, due to the archpastor's (*arkhipastyr´*) immense popularity among both clergy and laity. It is possible that the negative evaluation of L'vov has been influenced retrospectively by his role in the Kornilov affair, as well as his subsequent adventures in Soviet Russia following his return from emigration, when he proclaimed himself an "Ecclesiastical Bolshevik." The malicious legend that the former chief procurator was a member of the League of Militant Atheists probably originated in the emigration.[22]

The main source of trouble for hierarchs, therefore, was not the "revolutionary" chief procurator but conflicts with their own clergy or the new authorities. For example, it was the lay authorities who initiated the arrest of Tikhon (Nikanorov), the archbishop of Voronezh, who was handed over to the Petrograd Soviet in July 1917. This episode, which did not have any serious repercussions for Tikhon himself, caused a big uproar and was falsely interpreted by the Holy Synod as an act of "Ecclesiastical Bolshevism." At the same time, both the clergy of Voronezh and the chief procurator of the synod defended the bishop, who was released without charge soon afterwards and allowed to return to his diocese.[23]

In some of the dioceses where a strong opposition formed against the ruling archbishop, the struggle for power lasted throughout 1917. This was the case in Riazan', Tver', Orel, Enisei, Ekaterinburg, Ekaterinoslav, Vladimir, Tomsk, and a few other dioceses. The biggest scandal was caused by an incident in the

---

[22] This version circulated among émigrés. It was also adopted by George Katkov, the well-known historian of the 1917 Revolution. However, its sources are unclear and it has proved impossible to find any reliable evidence on this question.

[23] RGIA f. 796, op. 2004, ot. 1, st. 5, d. 223, l. 6.

diocese of Orel, which became the subject of a special inquiry by the synod's court commission. First, all diocesan power had been seized by a committee headed by a local priest, Sergei Arakin. Not only did the "Arakinists" strip Bishop Makarii (Gnevushev) of his power, they also "stormed" the building of the local consistory. In response, the moderate "Society for Ecclesiastical Renovation" (Obshchestvo tserkovnogo obnovleniia) was founded, chaired by the archpriest (*protoierei*) Aleksandr Obolenskii (in the diocese its members were known as "Renovationists" [*obnovlentsy*]). Bishop Serafim (Ostroumov), who came to Orel after the dismissal of Bishop Makarii, took the side of Arakin's committee, with the result that Archpriest Obolenskii nearly ended up before an ecclesiastical court. What saved him was the mediation of the new chief procurator of the synod, A. V. Kartashev.[24]

In Tver', the ecclesiastical congress opposed archbishop (*arkhiepiskop*) Serafim (Chichagov), who had convened the congress in the first place. The bishop's main opponents were the deacons and sextons. Shortly before the Revolution, Serafim had introduced a special examination for them, testing their basic knowledge of Scripture, liturgy, and church history. He was right to worry that the people applying for those jobs were often completely illiterate and motivated not by a yearning to serve the church but by a desire to avoid military service. The church in Tver' was split into supporters and opponents of Serafim. A synodal inspection was sent to the diocese and found the arguments of his opponents largely unfounded. The Holy Synod did not dismiss Serafim, but the secular powers, i.e., the local soviet, became involved, with the result that the archbishop was forced to leave the diocese of Tver' for good.[25]

One archbishop who managed to keep his diocese was also one of the most hated: Agapit Vishnevskii, the archbishop of Ekaterinoslav. He was saved by his connections to the top, in particular his friendship with Archbishop Platon (Rozhdestvenskii), the chair of the Holy Synod. However, the ecclesiastical authorities soon came to regret their decision, as the political "flights" of this hierarch only brought discord to the church. Previously an active member of the Black Hundreds, after the February Revolution Agapit took the side of "civil society" (*obshchestvennost'*) and blessed the "most useful activity" of the soviet. After Simeon Petliura seized power in Ukraine, he spoke out as an open Ukrainophile.[26] It proved impossible to bring the "schismatic archbishop" to trial, despite the wishes of L'vov.[27] We must also note that the majority of accusations against the episcopate were based on rumors and anonymous

---

[24] P. G. Rogoznyi, *"Tserkovnaia revoliutsiia" 1917 goda* (St. Petersburg: Liki Rossii, 2008), 165.

[25] Ibid., 98–110.

[26] See Evlogii (Georgievskii), *Put' moei zhizni* (Moscow: Krutitskoe podvor'e, 1994), 360–61.

[27] "Sud nad episkopami," *Svobodnaia tserkov'* (Petrograd), 28 July 1917.

denunciations that were unsubstantiated. The only bishop whose links to Rasputin could be documented was Aleksei (Dorodnitsyn), the archbishop of Vladimir.[28]

Historiography often attributes the revolutionary mood of rank-and-file clergy to the "antiecclesiastical" activity of the main church newspaper, *Vserossiiskii tserkovno-obshchestvennyi vestnik* (All-Russian Messenger of Church and Society), which was credited with provoking the clergy to stage revolutionary acts.[29] It was sometimes asserted that the paper was a Renovationist organ, or even, as the archimandrite Tikhon (Shevkunov) believed, a "Bolshevik mouthpiece."[30] The *Messenger* was a publication of the professoriate of the Petrograd Ecclesiastical Seminary. The editor, B. V. Titlinov,[31] and his colleagues, all of them well-known scholars and metropolitan priests, had managed to create the most readable and interesting church newspaper of their time. It was a relatively moderate paper, as indicated for example by its electoral support for the Kadets, the most "ecclesiastical" of Russia's political parties at that time.

One of the main results of the "ecclesiastical revolution" was the widespread introduction of elective elements. Elections were a crucial symbol of the revolutionary process that occurred in the church. In 1917 the male and female superiors of the monasteries, parish priests, deacons, and psalmists were elected. However, the central element of this process was the election of the highest hierarchs. Elections of bishops were held between spring and autumn of 1917 in 11 dioceses: Petrograd, Moscow, Chernigov, Tula, Kursk, Vladimir, Riazan′, Khar′kov, Orel, Saratov, and Ekaterinburg. Two elections were held in Riazan′, three in Ekaterinburg; their results, however, were not confirmed by the Holy Synod, and the dioceses' bishops were appointed by administrative means. It is worth noting that elections were held only in those places where the diocesan bishop had been dismissed for some reason or other.

---

[28] Archbishop Aleksei himself did not agree with this version and regarded himself as a victim of "Ecclesiastical Bolshevism." When he arrived in Ukraine in autumn 1917, he became a fierce champion of "ecclesiastical Ukrainianism." At the All-Russian Council of the Orthodox Church of 1917–18, his activity was regarded already as schismatic.

[29] This assertion is incorrect because the first issue of the newspaper appeared on 7 April, yet the strongest wave of "revolutionary activity" among the clergy occurred in March 1917.

[30] Archimandrite Tikhon (Shevkunov), "Sobor ili revoliutsiia?" www.patriotica.ru/religion/shevk_sobor.html (accessed 19 September 2009).

[31] It is interesting to note that, during the period of repression, Titlinov was accused, among many other things, of having given "counterrevolutionary" speeches at the All-Russian Council of the Orthodox Church. At the Council, he had spoken out decisively against the "lawless" reprisals against the emperor's family.

The attitude that contemporaries adopted towards the elections is also important: while at first they were regarded as a long-awaited return to Christian foundations, subsequently some regarded them merely as a "reshuffle" during which "everyone is trying to secure for himself a larger, sweeter slice of the cake."[32] Yet, at the time, it was difficult to argue against the use of the elective principle. Those who drafted the synodal rules for elections referred to the authoritative opinion of the late Professor V. V. Bolotov about the "undisputable" presence of the elective principle in the ancient church.

There were different mechanisms for nominating a candidate to the pulpit. Some people actively advanced their own candidature, whereas others discovered they had been nominated only when they received a telegram. The nomination of lay candidates for the position of diocesan bishop was an exclusive phenomenon in the history of Russian Orthodoxy. At the same time not a single candidate not already a bishop (*episkop*) was ever made diocesan bishop, even if he won the elections.[33] It is possible that this was due to the absence of a precedent, but also the distinct fear triggered in some of the electorate by the prospect of having a diocesan bishop (*arkhierei*) who was a layman or a representative of the "white clergy" (i.e., the married rather than the monastic clergy, who were known as the "black clergy").

The confirmation of election results in 1917 took place in two steps. First the Holy Synod announced its decision, followed by the Provisional Government. The approval of an elected bishop by the secular authorities was a mere formality, as they confirmed all the decisions of the synod. It is difficult to imagine which form elections within the church would have taken had they become established. In 1917 they were a consolidating element for the church and legitimized the power of the diocesan bishops. An elected bishop could no longer be regarded as a protégé of "dark powers."

We must bear in mind one important factor about 1917. The power of the Provisional Government was often imaginary, especially in the provinces, where power was usually exercised by various committees and soviets. Subsequently many of them "became bolshevized," which helped "Lenin's men" quickly to seize power in the provinces. These new organs of power constantly interfered with church business, regardless of resistance on the part of the Holy Synod, the chief procurator, or the Provisional Government. The myth that the Provisional Government pursued anti-ecclesiastical policies formed during this period. The myth's source was not just the activity of the "revolutionary" chief procurator, but also the authorities' attempt to secularize elementary schools: the Provisional Government issued a decree ordering all

---

[32] This is how the elections were seen by Nikon (Bezsonov), the former bishop of Enisei diocese (RGIA f. 796, op. 204, d. 94, l. 186).

[33] For example, in the first round of elections in Moscow, Archbishop Tikhon (Bellavin) and A. D. Samarin received an equal number of votes, while in Vladimir the majority of votes in the first round of elections went to Archpriest Timofei Nalimov, a former professor of the Ecclesiastical Academy in St. Petersburg.

parish schools managed by the synod to be transferred to the Ministry of Education.[34] Some "hotheads" already had labeled the government a "Mongol Horde." Subsequently, certain émigré authors described its policies in a similar way, as did a number of church historians.[35] This does not correspond to reality—on the contrary, the new authorities did everything in their power to enable the church to function independently of the state.

With regard to institutional relations, the separation of church and state would have occurred anyway, although it would not have had the grievous consequences of the well-known Bolshevik decree. The Provisional Government's resolution "On the Freedom of Conscience," adopted on 14 July, provided a legal basis for freedom of religion for the adult population and for the first time allowed people to profess no religious adherence at all.[36] Many people, however, could not imagine a church that would function freely within a secular state. In autumn 1917 several public church figures failed to spot the difference between the Provisional Government and the Bolsheviks. Bishop Aleksei (Simanskii) remarked in a private letter that he could not see any difference between Kerenskii and Lenin. Professor N. D. Kuznetsov, who represented the Holy Synod in negotiations with both the Provisional Government and the Bolsheviks, even thought initially that it would be easier to reach agreement with the latter as opposed to the "sad memory" of the Provisional Government.[37]

The election of the patriarch took place against the backdrop of the events of October–November 1917. During the summer it had still seemed impossible to elect a patriarch: at the pre-Council meeting, a majority was in favor of a collective administrative body for the church. Towards the end of the summer, however, the church community started shifting to the right, prompted by ever more frequent anti-clerical acts directed against church property and the clergy themselves, which were sometimes nothing but thuggery and which had begun long before the Bolsheviks came to power. There is a well-known description in the memoirs of A. I. Denikin of soldiers who, after the

---

[34] See A. V. Sokolov, "Gosurdarstvo i Pravoslavnaia Tserkov' v fevrale 1917–ianvare 1918 g.: Vopros o sud'be tserkovno-prikhodskikh shkol i Zakone Bozh'em," in *Politicheskaia istoriia Rossii 20 veka*, 249–68.

[35] For example, according to the author of a biography of Metropolitan Antonii (Khrapovitskii), the authorities "were not trying to identify the will of the people, but to find support, first and foremost among the country's criminal elements ... and they took strong measures in order to demoralize the Russian Orthodox Church from within." See Nikon (Rklitskii), *Mitropolit Antonii (Khrapovitskii) i ego vremia, 1863–1936* (Nizhnii Novgorod: Bratstvo Aleksandra Nevskogo, 2004), 2: 509–11; and V. Tsypin, *Istoriia Russkoi Tserkvi 1917–1997* (Moscow: Pravoslavnaia entsiklopediia, 1997), 12.

[36] *Tserkovnye vedomosti*, 29 July 1917.

[37] "Aleksei (Simanskii)—Arseniiu (Stadnitskomu) 28 oktiabria 1917 goda," in *Pis'ma patriarkha Aleksiia svoemu dukhovniku* (Moscow: Izd. Sretenskogo monastyria, 2000), 81.

Revolution, built a latrine in the altar room of the regimental church, which they had previously refurbished with their own hands.[38] Archival materials and periodicals published in 1917 show that the scope of various anticlerical and antiecclesiastical acts committed by peasants and soldiers foreshadowed the carnival mockery of the 1930s. For example, the soldiers of the Guard Regiment billeted in Nova-Pochaev not only staged a pogrom there, but also destroyed the town's monastery and, as the head of the regiment recounted, "dressed in clerical robes and held a sacrilegious service."[39] At the same time the church authorities also changed. Kartashev, the new chief procurator and soon the first minister of religion, was more compliant and gentle than his predecessor with regard to church figures.

The All-Russian Council of the Orthodox Church in August 1917 was a major ecclesiastical event. Heated debates on the patriarchal elections coincided with the October coup in Petrograd. The vote at the Council was divided: 146 members voted for the reinstatement of the patriarchy, 12 voted against, and 12 abstained. And, as one researcher justly remarked, those opposed to the election of the patriarch cannot be regarded as forerunners of Renovationism in any form.[40] On 5 November 1918, Tikhon, the metropolitan of Moscow, was elected patriarch by lot, a practice fully compliant with the Gospel tradition. His election to the patriarchal throne coincided with the first battles of the Civil War in Moscow. The church's attempt to broker a peaceful solution to the conflict remained fruitless. In Petrograd, the Bolsheviks came to power without much bloodletting, while in Moscow hundreds died. At first, the Bolsheviks, having seized power in both capitals, did not have time to deal with church matters. However, the ecclesiastical question quickly made it onto Sovnarkom's agenda.

The "Decree on Freedom of Conscience and on Ecclesiastical and Religious Communities"—better known as the "Decree on Separation of Church and State"—was published in January 1918.[41] It resulted from a collaboration between the Orthodox priest Mikhail Galkin[42] and Lenin, who composed its

---

[38] A. I. Denikin, *Ocherki russkoi smuty: Krusheniia vlasti i armii* (Moscow: Nauka, 1991), 79–80.

[39] Tsentral'nyi gosudarstvennyi istoricheskii arkhiv Ukrainy (TsGIA) f. 315, op. 2, d. 736, l. 9.

[40] I. Solov'ev, *Vosstanovlenie patriarshestva v Russkoi Pravoslavnoi Tserkvi, 1917 god: Tserkov' i sud'ba Rossii* (Moscow: Sviato-Tikhonovskii universitet, 2008), 117.

[41] *Dekrety Sovetskoi vlasti* (Moscow: Gosudarstvennoe izd-vo politicheskoi literatury, 1957), 1: 373–74.

[42] Mikhail Galkin was a priest at the Spaso-Koltovskaia church and published the newspaper *Svobodnaia tserkov'* (The Free Church) in the capital. In late 1917 he offered his services to the new authorities in the matter of separating church and state. In the summer of 1918, he renounced his priesthood and began to work officially at the Ministry of Justice. Subsequently he became an active member of the "League

opening point: "The church will be separate from the state." Neither Galkin nor the Bolsheviks had developed anything new. The decree was reminiscent of the French law on the separation of church and state, adopted in 1905.[43] The Bolshevik decree was shorter and more declarative, but the main difference from the French case was that it did not stipulate a mechanism for implementation.[44] Even before the publication of the document the Bolsheviks had tried to requisition the premises of the Aleksandr Nevskii Monastery. However, after the superior of the monastery was arrested, the monks raised the alarm and a crowd assembled, which was dispersed by Red Guards. There were victims, too: the first to die was the archpriest (*protoierei*) Skipetrov, who had tried to enter negotiations with the invaders.[45] After these events, a procession was joined by up to 300,000 people on Nevskii Prospekt alone.[46] The Bolsheviks retreated, having understood that a sudden revolutionary onslaught would not be enough to eradicate religion.

On 19 January the patriarch published his famous epistle with the anathema against "those who commit outrage." Although the term "Bolshevik" did not

of Militant Atheists." His articles were published under the pseudonym "Mikhail Gorev." See Daniel Peris, "*Commissars in Red Cassocks*: Former Priests in the League of the Militant Godless," *Slavic Review* 54, 2 (1995): 340–64.

[43] The decree has always been interpreted in a tendentious way, depending on whether the writer was a member of the Party or the church. Cf. Titlinov, *Tserkov´ vo vremia revoliutsii*; M. M. Persits, *Otdelenie tserkvi ot gosudarstva i shkoly ot tserkvi v SSSR* (Moscow: Izd-vo Akademii nauk SSSR, 1958); R. Iu. Plaksin, *Krakh tserkovnoi kontrrevoliutsii 1917–1923 gg.* (Moscow: Nauka, 1968); A. N. Kashevarov, *Tserkov´ i Vlast´: Russkaia Pravoslavnaia Tserkov´ v pervye gody sovetskoi vlasti* (St. Petersburg: Izd-vo Sankt-Peterburgskogo gosudarstvennogo tekhnicheskogo universiteta, 1999). The Moscow philologist A. K. Kravetskii has published several instructive articles that detail the prehistory of the decree: A. K. Kravetskii, "K istorii poiavleniia 'Dekreta ob otdelenii tserkvi ot gosudarstva i shkoly ot tserkvi,'" in *Sviashchennyi Sobor Pravoslavnoi Rossiiskoi Tserkvi: Obzor deianii. Pervaia sessiia* (Moscow: Krutitskoe podvor´e, 2002); A. K. Kravetskii, "K istorii Dekreta ob otdelenii tserkvi ot gosudarstva," in *1917 god: Tserkov´ i sud´ba Rossii. K 90-letiiu Pomestnogo Sobora i izbraniia patriarkha Tikhona* (Moscow: Sviato-Tikhonovskii universitet, 2008).

[44] See *Zakon ot 9 dekabria 1905 goda: Obshchie soobrazheniia po povodu dekreta ob otdelenii tserkvi ot gosudarstva* (Moscow, 2006), 277–381.

[45] For more detail, see M. V. Shkarovskii, *Aleksandro-Nevskaia Lavra v gody revoliutsionnykh potriasenii (1917–1918): Gorod na vse vremena* (St. Petersburg: Dmitrii Bulanin, 2011).

[46] According to church data, up to half a million people took part in the demonstration; in any case, the turnout was significantly higher than for the defense of the Constituent Assembly. It is worth noting that the author of a recent high quality monograph on 1918 in Petrograd seems not to have noticed this event: Alexander Rabinowitch, *The Bolsheviks in Power: The First Year of Soviet Rule in Petrograd* (Bloomington: Indiana University Press, 2007), published in Russian as A. Rabinovich, *Bol´sheviki u vlasti: Pervyi god Sovetskoi vlasti v Petrograde* (Moscow: Novyi khronograf, 2007).

appear in the text, everybody understood that it was directed against those in power.[47] Subsequently, historians' opinions diverged as to whether this really was an anathema against the Bolsheviks, or whether it was directed against all "those who commit outrage." But this debate began significantly later, and contemporaries understood clearly whom Tikhon's epistle addressed.[48] Moreover, the patriarch himself called his epistle an anathema against the Soviet authorities, and the document itself contained unambiguous references to the existing authorities.[49]

The government's reply was not long in coming. On 23 January the abovementioned "Decree on Freedom of Conscience" appeared in the press. It contained a number of democratic clauses, one of which deprived the church of its rights as a legal actor. Iurii Got'e wrote in his diary, "The force of the decree on the separation of church and state wholly depends on how it is implemented,"[50] and he was right: in a genuinely democratic state, such a decree—despite a few dubious clauses—would not indicate any threat of repression; furthermore, the persecution later suffered by the Orthodox Church happened in spite of the decree.

And of course we must refrain from identifying this decree as an act of "malicious persecution of the church," as some contemporary historians like to call it. Such a claim can be made only by someone who has not read the text of the decree itself. Just like the other early decrees of the new authorities, the decree is too diffuse and "declarative." Nobody, including the authorities, knew how to put it into practice. A commission was established "to put into

---

[47] *Akty Sviateishego Patriarkha Tikhona i pozdneishie dokumenty o preemstve vysshei tserkovnoi vlasti 1917–1943* (Moscow: Sviato-Tikhonovskii universitet, 1994), 82–85.

[48] Soviet historians dubbed Tikhon's edict an anathema against the Soviet authorities. Conversely, most post-Soviet researchers have considered it an anathema not against the Bolsheviks, but against "all those who commit outrage." However, as T. G. Leont'eva rightly remarks, at the time "no one was in any doubt as to whom he had in mind." T. G. Leont'eva, *Vera i progress: Pravoslavnoe sel'skoe dukhovenstvo v Rossii vo vtoroi polovine 19–nachale 20 veka* (Moscow: Novyi khronograf, 2002), 208.

[49] *Sledstvennoe delo patriarkha Tikhona* (Moscow: Sviato-Tikhonovskii universitet, 2000), 202. Compare the following: "The conjugal union of a Christian family is openly declared unnecessary" (a reference to the recently adopted decree on civil marriage—see n. 52); "The sacred cathedrals are destroyed by shots from deadly weapons (the sacred cathedrals of the Moscow Kremlin) ... the monasteries considered sacred by the faithful people (such as the Aleksandr Nevskii Monastery and the Pochaev Monastery) are seized by the godless lords of this century and declared apparently property of the people ... and finally the authorities, who promised to bring order to Russia, truth and justice, to ensure freedom and order, display nothing but the most unbridled wilfulness wherever they go and exert nothing but violence against anyone." These examples make it abundantly clear against whom Tikhon's edict was directed. *Akty Sviateishego Patriarkha Tikhona*, 83

[50] Iu. V. Got'e, *Moi zametki* (Moscow: Terra, 1997), 109.

practice the separation of church and state." Its meetings were chaired in May 1918 by Bonch-Bruevich, and among its several tasks it was required to "investigate the many instances of precedent that have arisen due to the direct application of individual clauses of the decree to the tangled legal relationships of today."[51] Despite the cumbersome phrasing, it was hardly possible to provide a more precise formulation.

Many of the decree's clauses remained unimplemented for a long time, such as the introduction of civil marriage (in the original sense of the term, not the one used today).[52] Marriages were usually registered in church, just as before, and the church conducted divorces according to well established principles. The "marriage codex" of imperial Russia was substantial and complicated, and much literature on family law was produced, in particular before the Revolution. Already then people had commented on its shortcomings and archaic nature.[53] Infidelity was the fastest way to a divorce, but in order to file for divorce on these grounds it was necessary to bring witnesses who could testify to the adultery of the "guilty" party. Naturally it was problematic to attest the fact of "coupling," although money and connections would always procure the necessary witnesses. The synodal functionaries in charge of divorce proceedings quickly amassed large fortunes. Gregory Freeze has written ironically about the ease with which witnesses were found in cases of adultery: the doors in Russian houses "were never closed, it seems."[54] Soviet decrees did little to change the situation.

After the Revolution, not everybody wanted to make use of such a complicated procedure. In 1918, the commissar of Samara province ordered the clergy "immediately to start fulfilling the will of the people, that is, to carry out wedding ceremonies in church for citizens who have been divorced before a lay court according to the decree of the People's Commissars. Those who refuse to do so will be dismissed from their position and face court proceedings." Did that mean that a priest who refused to bless a "dubious"

---

[51] Gosudarstvennyi arkhiv rossiiskoi federatsii (GARF) f. 353, d, 688, l. 11.

[52] In contemporary Russia, a "civil marriage" (*grazhdanskii brak*) means that a couple cohabits without a marriage license (which in English would be called common-law marriage), while the Bolshevik decrees implied the issuing of marriage licenses by civil authorities.

[53] Compare the following recent studies: E. V. Beliakova, *Tserkovnyi sud i problemy tserkovnoi zhizni* (Moscow: Kul'turnyi tsentr "Dukhovnaia biblioteka," 2004); V. A. Veremenko, *Dvorianskaia sem'ia i gosudarstvennaia politika Rossii* (St. Petersburg: Evropeiskii dom, 2004); and V. Iu. Leshchenko, *Sem'ia i russkoe pravoslavie 11–19 vv.* (St. Petersburg: Izd-vo Frolovoi, 1999).

[54] Gregory Freeze, "Mirskie narrativy o sviashchennom tainstve: Brak i razvod v pozdneimperskoi Rossii," in *Pravoslavie: Konfessii, instituty, religioznost'*, ed. M. D. Dolbilov and P. G. Rogoznyi (St. Petersburg: Izd-vo Evropeiskogo universiteta, 2009), 142.

marriage could be dismissed like a state functionary? The Commissariat of Justice received a multitude of complaints, from officials and ordinary citizens, asking for an explanation of this clause. The main question concerned the relationship between the decree and an ecclesiastical marriage. To make matters worse, it was explained differently in different places. And the clause was highly topical and problematic—the definition of a civil marriage and how to conclude it remained unclear, especially in the countryside. Although the decree on civil marriage was issued as early as December 1917, it was hardly noticed at the time: nobody took the Bolsheviks seriously at that point, and during the height of the Civil War, with "Lenin's men" controlling central Russia, the issue of so-called "civil marriage" concerned only a small part of the population.

The question of marriage and divorce was certainly the most widely discussed element of the decree. In the countryside the question was often decided amicably. There are only a few documented cases, and so each one is important, for example that of A. N. Okninskii, a former functionary of the department of the Ministry of Justice who, as luck would have it, spent the two years from 1918–20 in a village in Tambov province and recorded "civil acts." As the Bolsheviks soon confiscated the parish registers, Okninskii himself had to register all deaths, births, and marriages. He described the operation of the unwritten "marriage codex" as follows. He would issue "certificates," evidently after checking the parish registers to determine if a couple could get married, because "without such a certificate the priests would not baptize, marry, or bury anyone."[55] Once a peasant had received a certificate, he could have the marriage solemnized in church. Divorce was more difficult. Okninskii recalled divorcing two couples where the spouses both wanted to end the marriage, "but as far as I remember, the church authorities did not recognize this kind of divorce."

This was understandable. It was easier to obtain a civil divorce: divorce was not a sacrament, but, by contrast, marriage was supposed to happen in church, and the Bolsheviks' decrees were unable to change the opinion of the populace. Okninskii also recalled that he had to write down his entries on non-working days, "on Sundays and feast days... they were still holidays in Soviet Russia" (this really was the case—when Okninskii writes of feast days he means ecclesiastical feasts) and that once a local Bolshevik rudely demanded a certificate that his daughter could get married in church.[56]

With the parish registers confiscated, a priest was unable to verify whether he was administering the sacrament lawfully, but the civil certificate would provide some information—at least confirmation that bride and groom were not already married to other people. We can imagine that this practice was

---

[55] A. L. Okninskii, *Dva goda sredi krest'ian: Vidimoe, slyshimoe, perezhitoe v Tambovskoi gubernii s noiabria 1918 goda do noiabria 1920 goda* (Moscow: Russkii put', 1998), 44.

[56] Ibid., 45.

ubiquitous in the countryside, at least in the areas under Soviet authority.[57] It is interesting that the decree on marriage and divorce issued by the All-Russian Council of the Orthodox Church was less radical. Written documentation was not compulsory under the new conditions; only the signatures of bride, groom, and four witnesses were required.[58] It was clearly possible to dupe a priest, which is why many of them started to demand a written certificate.

Sometimes curious things occurred. A. I. Tikhomirov, a priest in Olonets province, wrote to Lenin seeking permission to marry for the second time. Both Patriarch Tikhon and Metropolitan Veniamin, the ruling bishop, opposed this. The priest expressed his genuine support for the "dictatorship of the proletariat" and asked for his province to be liberated from the "black usurpers," meaning monastic clergy. Tikhomirov described the patriarch as a protégé of "a small group of landowners, counts, monks, and other reactionaries."[59] The priest justified his request to remarry in a manner that was both practical and cynical: he needed "a cheap pair of hands ... in order to improve his personal wellbeing," and to hire a maidservant would be too expensive. He also asked for the sincerity of his wishes to be taken into account, and passed on his good wishes for "many years of proletarian dictatorship."[60] It is unlikely that Lenin read the letter himself—it was sent to the eighth "ecclesiastical" department of the Commissariat of Justice for "clarification," where it triggered astonishment and genuine interest. Tikhomirov was regarded as a real "ecclesiastical Bolshevik" and received a more than gracious answer, personally signed by Krasikov, the head of the department, which stated that according to the decree "the state of so-called Holy Orders is no obstacle to first and subsequent marriages ... while Tikhomirov's fear of oppressive monks and certain reactionary priests had no basis in Soviet legislation."[61]

According to conventional wisdom, the Bolsheviks disseminated atheist propaganda as soon as they came to power, organizing a kind of "storming of the heavens."[62] Reality, however, brought them back down to earth very quickly. In a country where 90 percent of the population were believers,

---

[57] The testimony of Okninskii's memoirs is trustworthy, and in this case it seems unbiased. It is not important in the overall canvas of the memoirs themselves, where it takes up only two pages, and it is evident the episode had no political conclusions for the author. It is also important that the memoirs were written two years later and had absolutely no ideological subtext.

[58] *Akty Sviateishego Patriarkha Tikhona*, 99.

[59] GARF f. 353, op. 3, d. 761, l. 93.

[60] Ibid.

[61] Ibid., l. 95.

[62] See, for example, V. A. Alekseev, "*Shturm nebes*" *otmeniaetsia: Kriticheskie ocherki po istorii bor'by s religiei v SSSR* (Moscow: Mysl', 1992).

such propaganda was doomed to failure. The Bolsheviks had to act much more subtly. They endeavored to explain the new decree to the people. Why should religious education be private? A leaflet of the Petrograd Bolshevik Party answered as follows: "In public schools children of Orthodox, Catholic, Muslim, and Jewish families are learning together and these schools are funded by the state, therefore religion cannot be taught there. But if parents so wish they can see to it that their children are instructed in whatever religion they want, at their own expense."[63] The peasant masses were unimpressed by this kind of agitation. The demand to retain Scripture lessons was voiced even at soviet peasant meetings during the Civil War, and even among workers.

In its reaction to demands by workers to hold public prayers in factories, the Petrograd committee of the Bolsheviks, in another leaflet, recommended to those "whom the priests are still leading on a leash, firstly, not to confuse the priests' faith with Christianity and, secondly, not to forget the role of the state church in the history of the fight of the oppressed against their oppressors … and not to follow the priests who sell the name of Christ." The leaflet also stipulated that "the powerful of this world have perverted this teaching with the help of the priest and turned it into a teaching that safeguards the rights of the oppressors. Those preachers who fought for genuine Christianity in its original form were burnt at the stake by the priests, drawn and quartered and annihilated by all means possible. Thus Christianity was annihilated."[64]

The main ecclesiastical feasts continued, in practice, to be state holidays and non-working days. Sometimes ecclesiastical and state feasts were celebrated together, especially in the provinces. For example, at a meeting of the Executive Committee of Ustiug the delegates who planned the May Day and Easter celebrations declared a week-long school holiday for Easter and resolved "to buy for the Red Army comrades who will organize the festivities three eggs per person, one pound of sausage for each group of four people, and a bucket of vodka for each group of forty."[65] A touching form of class unity, without any discrediting of religious matters. Another sore issue was the instruction of the new authorities to remove all icons from "state and juridical public buildings." The decree itself did not mention this, but it appeared in the instructions on "how to implement the decree" published by the Commissariat of Justice in August 1918.[66] Icons were also to be removed from educational institutions

---

[63] *Listovki petrogradskikh bol'shevikov* (Leningrad: Lenizdat, 1957), 3: 161.

[64] Ibid., 222.

[65] Cited in N. Kedrov, "Gosudarstvo i tserkovnaia obshchina v 1920-e i 1930-e gody: Evoliutsiia vzaimootnoshenii v Ustiuzhenskom raione," in *Ustiuzhna: Kraevedcheskii al'manakh*, vyp. 6 (Vologda: Vologodskii gosudarstvennyi pedagogicheskii universitet, 2008), 178.

[66] Resolution of the Commissariat of Justice: "O poriadke provedeniia v zhizn' dekreta ob otdelenii tserkvi ot gosudarstva i shkoly ot tserkvi (Instruktsiia)," 24 August 1918.

and factories. This endeavor frequently triggered strong resentment and was evidently not pursued very eagerly, especially in the early days.

For example, the removal in 1919 of icons from the shop floor of the Shuia factory on the initiative of local Bolsheviks caused genuine unrest among the workers, who stopped working and demanded "that the icons be returned to their previous place." The Communist Iazykov, who was responsible for the deed, had to confess that he began his task "clumsily and without sanction from the Executive Committee and the party, and acted only for myself, which is why I alone am guilty of everything and ask for punishment if I deserve it."[67] When even the workers—supposedly the most "revolutionary" class—reacted to antireligious action in this way, we can only imagine the peasantry's response.

The removal of icons from factory buildings, public offices, schools and so forth was a very painful issue. As in the example of the Shuia factory, such actions often caused a storm of protest and forced the Bolsheviks to explain their objectives publicly. Rumors about icons spread quickly and acquired surprising forms. There was even a rumor that all icons would be confiscated. "There is no lie more foul and vile than this one," a leaflet of the Petrograd Bolsheviks proclaimed. "Who would have an idea as stupid as the confiscation of icons? Who needs icons apart from believers? Can we use them to feed the hungry or melt them to make cannons?"[68] However, such explanations were of no avail.

Iaroslavskii, the Moscow District commissar, told Sovnarkom in December 1918 that implementation of the decree was meeting stubborn resistance in the countryside: "a whole range of sometimes violent clashes occur because the population opposes the removal of icons and religious objects from schools." Local soviets, wrote the commissar, "often do not reckon with the will of the overwhelming majority, which is often unanimous." As a result, there was agitation against the Soviet authorities, and the slogan was "they agree with the Bolsheviks in everything."[69] With regard to the confiscation of icons, the commissar—according to Lev Tolstoi's former secretary Chertkov—remarked that a special kind of bribe had become widespread: "a bribe so that they wouldn't touch the icons ... for an icon of Jesus Christ they take five rubles, less for the Mother of God."[70] In conclusion, the commissar remarked that he had several letters from Communists, all asking the same question: "Does it

---

[67] Gosudarstvennyi arkhiv Ivanovskoi oblasti f. r-708, op. 1, d. 35a, ll. 7–7ob. I am grateful to N. V. Mikhailova for this reference.

[68] Listovki petrogradskikh bol'shevikov, 160.

[69] GARF f. 353, op. 3, d. 696, l. 216.

[70] Ibid.

make sense to damage relations with the peasant masses further over this issue?"[71]

How did the central authorities react? The Commissariat of Justice published a special circular, in which it specified that

> when confiscating icons from public premises it is strongly advised not to turn the event into an antireligious demonstration ... it is not at all necessary for the confiscation to take place during the business hours of the given institute and in the presence of the public, since such a demonstrative confiscation of icons ... in particular if it is accompanied by completely unnecessary attacks against one or another religious cult, as has happened in some places, only creates a false impression in the eyes of the populace about the way in which the Soviet authorities struggle against popular prejudices.[72]

The answer that Iaroslavskii received was that "resentment against the act is caused not so much by the confiscation of icons as such, but by the way in which this is done, which often takes an uncouth or even brutal form."[73] The complete removal of icons from all public premises was apparently completed only in the mid-1920s. Naturally, the implementation of the decree led to fundamental changes not just in relations between church and state; it also affected the entire population that found itself under Bolshevik rule.

The church did what it could to oppose the efforts of the new authorities, which it had not even considered legitimate at first. The All-Russian Council of the Orthodox Church, which continued to meet in Moscow until autumn 1918, introduced significant changes to the way the Russian Church was administered. The council was the highest organ of church authority, and it possessed legislative, administrative, judicial and controlling powers; the head of the church was the patriarch. The Holy Synod and the Supreme Church Council were designated its administrative bodies for the period between the convocations of the All-Russian Council.[74] The council's definition of the church's legal position "within a changed government order" was already obsolete at the time of its adoption: according to the definition of the head of the Russian state, the minister of religion and the minister of education had to be Orthodox.[75] When this regulation was adopted, there were no longer any ministers, and the Russian state itself had ceased to exist.

---

[71] Ibid., l. 216ob.

[72] GARF f. 353, op. 2, d. 690, l. 80.

[73] Ibid., l. 217.

[74] *Sobranie opredelenii i postanovlenii Sviashchennogo Sobora Pravoslavnoi Rossiiskoi Tserkvi 1917–1918*, vyp. 1 (orig. 1918) (Moscow: Novospasskii monastyr', 1994): 3, 7.

[75] Ibid., vyp. 2: 7.

In March 1918 the All-Russian Council tried to establish at least some kind of relationship with the new authorities. An ecclesiastical delegation headed by Samarin, the former chief procurator, expected to meet Lenin, but the meeting did not happen, and the church figures had to be content negotiating with second-order Bolsheviks, such as Bonch-Bruevich and Lunacharskii.

In Petrograd, attempts were undertaken to preserve the Ecclesiastical Academy by incorporating it into a university. But the permission of Petrograd University notwithstanding, this project remained confined to paper, and the academy was closed down.[76] By autumn 1918 the confrontation between authorities and church had come to a head. During the "Red Terror," thousands of priests were shot, but the lawless reprisals against the clergy had begun significantly earlier, and not always at the initiative of the Bolsheviks. For example, in January 1918 in Kiev unknown persons killed Metropolitan Vladimir (Bogoiavlenskii). One of the church's most popular leading clergy, Andronik (Nikol'skii), was killed in Perm' during the summer; a commission of the All-Russian Council of the Orthodox Church headed by Archbishop Vasilii (Bogoiavlenskii), sent to Perm' to investigate the murder, disappeared without trace. According to some sources the members had fallen victim to robbers on the way back to Moscow. "The oprichniks [a reference to Ivan the Terrible's henchmen] will shoot you like a partridge," Patriarch Tikhon wrote to Metropolitan Antonii (Khrapovitskii).[77]

On the first anniversary of the October Revolution the patriarch published an address to Sovnarkom. "You have divided the people into warring camps and plunged them into a fratricide that is unprecedented in its brutality. You have openly replaced love towards Christ with hatred, and instead of spreading peace you have artificially unleashed class hatred."[78] This was the patriarch's last "counterrevolutionary" appeal; a year later he would talk of loyalty and non-interference in the political struggle.

The main antiecclesiastical and anticlerical action of the Bolsheviks during the Civil War was the desecration campaign of the holy relics, which began officially in 1919.[79] The occasion for this campaign was an incident in the Aleksandr Svirskii Monastery in the autumn of 1918. During an inventory of the monastery's property, the shrine of Aleksandr Svirskii was found to contain a doll instead of his relics (according to the church, it was bones).

---

[76] For more detail, see T. A. Bogdanova and N. N. Glubokovskii, *Sud'ba khristianskogo uchenogo* (Moscow-St. Petersburg Al'ians-Arkheo, 2010).

[77] *Sledstvennoe delo*, 662.

[78] *Akty Sviateishego Patriarkha Tikhona*, 149.

[79] Quite a lot has been written about the desecration of relics. While the campaign used to be regarded, almost exclusively, as an exposure of clerical fraud, it is now considered a sacrilegious profanation of sacred objects. Serious studies also exist: S. A. Smith, "Bones of Contention: Bolsheviks and Struggle against Relics 1918–1930," *Past and Present*, no. 2004 (2009): 155–94.

The Soviet leadership evidently appreciated the potential to exploit such an advantageous moment for the government's cause.

It seems that the central authorities first learned of the incident from the report of an expert, the now-former priest Galkin, who was in Petrozavodsk and Olonets province in autumn 1918. In his report he wrote that in September 1918 a commission of 15 people from the provincial executive committee arrived at the Aleksandr Svirskii Monastery, the monks raised the alarm, and the crowd that assembled forced the unwelcome guests to retreat. Later, the Red Army came to their assistance, and the superior of the monastery and the most active monks were arrested and shot. On 22 October, members of the district soviet of Lodeinoe Pole visited the monastery and requisitioned all valuables, including three relic shrines. According to Galkin, when the relics were opened in the presence of "numerous representatives, a very ordinary doll was found to be lying in the shrine in place of the incorruptible remains of four saints." A few days later, on 30 October, evidently when the rumors about the wax doll and the "astonishing relics" had reached the "masses of the people," a town meeting declared: "We hold up to shame the monks and priests as those who cause darkness by perverting the holy ideas of Christ, our teacher."[80]

Almost simultaneously the commissar of justice received a complaint by the surviving monks of the ill-fated monastery, which stated that they had inspected the relics shortly before they were confiscated. They claimed to have found ascetic clothing that had decayed in parts and "when we raised the *nalobnik* [an embroidered ribbon] we saw the face of the saint, his lower jaw fell onto his chest, the teeth in his mouth were all in order, only two lower ones had fallen out, on his head there was a bit of hair, and part of his beard was preserved ... some ribs had dropped from his chest and part of the backbone was visible." Further the letter detailed, in high rhetoric, how a group of Red Army soldiers consisting of "up to 30 people" had come to the monastery and looted it. They had taken whatever they fancied and, after discovering the monastery's wine stock, "some of them got blind drunk." The monks pointed out that among the looters were some who previously lived in the monastery as lay brothers or workers and who knew where the valuables were hidden.[81] At first sight one version of events contradicts the other, yet in any event there were no incorruptible relics.

No other antiecclesiastical measure received so much press coverage. It seems curious that the Bolsheviks, at the height of the Civil War, created such problems for themselves and made enemies among hundreds of thousands, even millions, of simple people who were loyal to the new authorities but continued going to church. Some have argued that the desecration of relics was

---

[80] GARF f. 353, op. 3, d. 691, ll. 16–16ob. Galkin's report, sent to the Commissariat of Justice, was dated 24 November 1918.

[81] GARF f. 353, op. 3, d. 731, l. 62.

a crude, sacrilegious act like the carnivalesque mockery of Emel'ian Iaroslav-skii's time during the 1930s. In reality the situation was much more complex. Moreover, the desecration of the relics was the most successful anticlerical and antiecclesiastical campaign during the entire Soviet period. Its results were used for atheist propaganda right up to the beginning of perestroika in the 1980s.

Many thought that relics were the incorruptible bodies of holy hermits. Moreover, it was the incorruptibility of the body that determined the holiness or sinfulness of someone connected to the church. Suffice it to recall the famous episode of Elder Zosima's death in Dostoevskii's novel *The Brothers Karamazov*. The fact that the elder's body began to decompose and "smell" was perceived as an indicator that Zosima's life had been sinful. The body's incorruptibility was regarded, even by educated congregations, as a symbol of holiness. In the late 19th century, however, the renowned church historian E. E. Golubinskii demonstrated that this idea was incorrect and that in antiquity people had venerated corruptible as well as incorruptible relics; he also wrote about many cases of fake Orthodox relics in Greece.[82] Ecclesiastical censorship meant it was impossible to write the same about Russia. Church figures remembered Golubinskii's book at the height of the desecration campaign; however, by then it was too late, and besides the views of a single academic counted for little in comparison to popular beliefs about holiness that had been held for centuries. [83]

Even before the Revolution the Russian church authorities understood only too well the "temptation" into which "wrong" relics could lead. This was the reason why the synod had forbidden the transfer of the relics of Stefan Permskii from Moscow to Perm', disregarding the numerous requests of the local population (the synod's archive holds an impressive folio of signatures with the request to transfer the relics). But it turned out there were no relics; instead there were a few jumbled bones that could not possibly be identified, and for this reason the ecclesiastical and lay authorities were keen to put the brakes on the process.[84] But the objectives of the Bolsheviks, once they seized power, were different altogether.

As a rule, relics would be opened by the clergy themselves, in the presence of representatives of the authorities, medical workers who had been invited to examine the state of the remains, and representatives of the press, etc. Facts were documented and the results photographed, and often filmed. The first openings yielded shocking results that even church figures had not expected, and for which the convinced atheists had waited so badly. All kinds

---

[82] E. E. Golubinskii, *Istoriia kanonizatsii sviatykh v russkoi tserkvi* (Moscow: Krutitskoe patriarshee podvor'e. Obshchestvo liubitelei tserkovnoi istorii, 1998), 34–35.

[83] Patriarch Tikhon mentioned Golubinskii's book during his interrogation.

[84] RGIA f. 797, op. 79, ot. 2, st. 3, d. 173, ll. 46–49 (Vypiska iz opredeleniia Sv. Sinoda ot 3–16 dekabria 1909 g.).

of things were found in the saints' sepulchres: jumbled bones in the best case, sometimes half-rotten skeletons, in the worst case wax dolls, rags, cotton wool, nails, boots, even women's stockings. The one thing they did not contain was incorruptible relics.

When he discovered the first results of the openings, Patriarch Tikhon circulated a confidential edict "on the removal of causes for mockery and temptation regarding holy relics," in which he demanded the removal from sepulchres of all objects unrelated to the remains of saints.[85] Yet this did not change the essence of the situation: there were few incorruptible relics, and where they were found, they could be explained by the influence of the environment in which the body originally was buried. As a rule, once they had been opened, the remains would be exhibited in the same church, in order to show people the "fraud" the church had perpetrated "for centuries." The flurry caused by these exhibitions was enormous, and people from all social strata wishing to look at the real "relics" formed long queues.

Got'e, who visited the Troitskii Monastery and after the service kissed the "naked skeleton" of Sergei Radonezhskii, thought that the initiative not to conceal the remains under shrouds belonged to the church. He wrote:

Even the doctors admitted that the skeleton was at least 500 years old and that the hairs discovered were grey, although time had yellowed them. Thus our priests came to their senses and left the remains uncovered, because they rightly want to show 'here, look, we don't hide what was and what is,' and thereby they naturally strengthen religious sentiment.[86]

For Got'e, a pious historian, the most important thing was the bones' authenticity—they really were old and dated from the time of Sergei Radonezhskii. For the majority of simple believers all this was a fraud. The refined intellectual Got'e, who had dedicated his life to the study of the past, had a worse grasp of popular psychology than the less well educated organizers of the desecration campaign. Unlike him, many clergymen had a good understanding of what future researchers would call "popular Orthodoxy." They understood the "temptation" caused by the exposure of saints' remains and therefore protested against it as best they could. Lenin also understood this when he gave the order to show the film made at the opening of Sergei Radonezhskii's relics: "we must see to it and check that this film is shown across the whole of Moscow as quickly as possible."[87]

---

[85] *Sledstvennoe delo*, 497.

[86] Got'e, *Moi zametki*, 277.

[87] V. I. Lenin, *Polnoe sobranie sochinenii* (Moscow: Gosudarstvennoe izd-vo politicheskoi literatury, 1970), 50: 279.

Of course the "fake relics" on their own could not fundamentally under-mine popular faith in God, but they were capable of seriously discrediting the church and the clergy, and the authorities knew how to use this, sometimes even referring to the Gospel. For example, M. Vetoshkin, chairman of the Vologda provincial soviet, wrote as follows to Bishop Aleksandr (Trapitsyn) on the subject of the opening of relics belonging to Feodosii Totemskii, condemn-ing the clergy for conscious forgery and lies:

> Is this what the great revolutionary preached to the world, the son of the carpenter from Nazareth? What would he have said, the ardent defender of the poor and the humiliated and insulted, who gave his life for his friends, if he had found out the great fraud committed on earth in his name. What has the church made of his teachings? It turned the revolutionary teachings of the naive and wise carpenter to the service of the rich and sated of this world, it turned his teaching into the object of shameless exploitation of the masses and a tool for deceiving them.[88]

Vetoshkin's letter displayed pure anticlericalism without a hint of antire-ligious sentiment. On the contrary, he cleverly used popular religiosity for propaganda purposes.

After the Bolshevik victory in the Civil War, the situation with regard to "freedom of conscience" began to change. Lenin and Trotskii knew very well that the church would now be the Soviet system's main ideological opponent. To get rid of the church once and for all through a "cavalry raid" was clearly impossible. Their dogmatism notwithstanding, the Bolshevik leaders were also pragmatists. The majority of those who supported the Soviet authorities remained believers. Trotskii wrote in a note to the Politburo: "There is a church outside my window. Out of ten passers-by (counting everyone, including children) at least seven, if not eight, cross themselves when they walk past. And many of those who walk past are Red Army soldiers, many are young."[89]

Resolution of the church question required measures more subtle than simple repression. Soon enough a pretext presented itself in the form of a severe famine in the Volga region. In order to help the starving it was decided to use valuables belonging to the church. The Bolsheviks interpreted attempts at resistance by believers in their own favor.[90] Lenin decided to exploit the

---

[88] *Sledstvennoe delo*, 519–21.

[89] O. Iu. Vasil'eva, comp., *Russkaia pravoslavnaia tserkov' i kommunisticheskoe gosudarstvo 1917–1941: Dokumenty i fotomaterialy*, ed. Ia. N. Shchapov (Moscow: Bibleisko-bogoslovskii institut Sv. Apostola Andreia, 1996), 1005.

[90] A number of studies have appeared recently that consider the blow the Bolsheviks dealt to the church after the Civil War: N. A. Krivova, *Vlast' i Tserkov' v 1922–1925 gg.* (Moscow: AIRO-XX, 1997); M. Iu. Krapivin, *Nepridumannaia tserkovnaia istoriia: Vlast' i Tserkov' v Sovetskoi Rossii (oktiabr' 1917–konets 1930-kh gg.)* (Volgograd: Peremena, 1997);

events in the town of Shuia, where the confiscation of church valuables had caused an uprising against the authorities. It was after these events that he wrote his famous "secret" letter to the Politburo, published in the USSR for the first time only in 1990. Lenin stated unambiguously that the events in Shuia "are not just a rare propitious instance, but the only event where we have a 99 in 100 chance of successfully hitting our enemy on the head and establishing the position that we need for many decades ahead." Lenin argued that the confiscation of church valuables should be carried out "as decisively and fast as possible … the more representatives of the reactionary clergy and the reactionary bourgeoisie we manage to execute for this reason, the better. Now is the moment to teach this audience a lesson so that they won't dare to even think about resistance for the next few decades."[91]

Lenin had become pragmatic. Five years in power had taught him many a lesson. He had ideological enemies—the church and religion—and they would not die away of their own accord, but continue to live for many years. This meant it was necessary to deal this enemy a decisive blow when a favorable moment presented itself. Lenin had no illusions with regard to the atheism of the population of the former Russian Empire and wrote, paraphrasing Machiavelli: "One clever commentator of government issues was right when he wrote that if the implementation of a given political idea requires a number of brutal measures, these measures must be carried out in the most energetic way possible and in the shortest possible time-span, because the popular masses will not bear cruelty over a long period of time."[92]

The term "popular masses" deserves our attention: Lenin was not talking about a handful of "clergy from the Black Hundreds" or "landowners the Bolsheviks haven't managed to kill off." He was referring to the same peasants and workers for whose sake the Bolsheviks had fought the Civil War. As mentioned above, Trotskii, who was considered the main "expert" on Orthodoxy in the Politburo, also understood this.

This was precisely the moment when he wrote his note on how to demoralize the Orthodox Church from within. The method, he thought, was to set the pro-Soviet part of the clergy, i.e., those who adhered to the Change of

---

Kashevarov, *Tserkov' i Vlast'*; V. M. Lavrov, V. V. Lobanov, I. V. Lobanova, and A. V. Mazyrin, *Ierarkhiia Russkoi Pravoslavnoi Tserkvi, patriarshestvo i gosudarstvo v revoliutsionnuiu epokhu* (Moscow: Russkaia panorama, 2008); M. V. Shkarovskii, *Russkaia Tserkov' v 20 veke* (Moscow: Veche, 2010); I. A. Kurliandskii, *Stalin, vlast', religiia (religioznyi i tserkovnyi faktory vo vnutrennei politike sovetskogo gosudarstva v 1922–1953 gg.)* (Moscow: Kuchkovo pole, 2011). The exploration of sources by S. G. Petrov deserves special mention: S. G. Petrov, *Dokumenty deloproizvodstva Politbiuro TsK RKP(b) kak istochnik po istorii Russkoi Tserkvi (1921–1925)* (Moscow: RossPEN, 2004).

[91] "Pis'mo V. I. Lenina chlenam Politbiuro o sobytiiakh v g. Shue i politike v otnoshenii tserkvi," in *Tserkov' i Politbiuro 1922–1926: Arkhivy Kremlia* (Moscow: Sibirskii khronograf-RossPEN, 1997), 140–44.

[92] Ibid., 142

Landmarks (Smena vekh) school of thought, against the conservative adherents of the Black Hundreds and to wait for the result—since "there is no more frenzied accuser than a priest from the opposite camp"—and afterwards to get rid of the Smena vekh clergy as well, "who ought to be considered the most dangerous enemy of tomorrow."[93]

This was how the "renovation schism" in the church began—with a political decision, taken by the secular authorities. With the active help of the authorities the Renovationists quickly usurped the key positions in the church. However, their initial success soon met a degree of passive resistance from the believers that neither the Bolsheviks nor the Renovationists themselves had expected. The believers' cultural conservatism turned out to be stronger than all the political vacillation of the entire ecclesiastical elite taken together. The masses of ordinary people accepted neither the new calendar, attempts to hold church services in Russian instead of Church Slavonic, nor married bishops.

cs so

One can say that the Russian Orthodox Church was already in a profound state of crisis when the First World War began. The origins of that crisis lay in the synodal structure itself. The church was subordinate to the state authorities, and its highest-ranking clergy often had to submit to state interference in church affairs. The nascent war brought the contradiction in the ecclesiastical sphere to a head, and the "class" hatred between higher- and lower-ranking clergy intensified with the burdens of the war period.

The story about how Rasputin was interfering with church business triggered protest from even those churchmen who were most loyal to the autocracy. The Orthodox Church was forced to welcome the February Revolution, albeit belatedly. The lowest-ranking clergy were the most radically inclined, which created a "revolutionary situation" within the church. Despite the general paralysis of the authorities, the synod more or less mastered this situation, although it was forced to carry out far-reaching reforms, which completely changed the legal framework of the church. The All-Russian Council legally strengthened the basic outcomes of the "church revolution."

The Bolsheviks' ascent to power initially had no consequences for the church. However, it became clear very quickly, in particular once the "Decree on Separation of Church and State" was published, that difficult times lay ahead, and persecution of the church during Soviet times constituted a serious violation of this decree. The patriarch's anathema on the Bolsheviks was of little help to the White opposition and overall had no influence on the general political situation. The decree was implemented only on paper

---

[93] "Zapiska L. D. Trotskogo v Politbiuro TsK RKP(b) o politike po otnosheniiu k tserkvi," in ibid., 162.

and often depended on the goodwill or, conversely, the ill intent of the local authorities.

In their struggle against the church during the Civil War, the Bolsheviks employed an almost exclusively anticlerical rhetoric that won sympathies even among the religious peasants and workers. On the other hand, the attempts at antireligious propaganda failed almost everywhere and finally triggered a negative reaction from the central authorities. Even the Bolsheviks' main antiecclesiastical action of the Civil War years—the desecration of relics—was accompanied by anticlerical propaganda which portrayed the clergy as "deceitful" people who had forgotten the teachings of Christ.

Many clergymen fell victim to repression during the Civil War years, especially once the "Red Terror" was proclaimed. However, not all clergy who died a martyr's death during the Civil War were victims of Bolshevik terror. Robbery and murder were committed by the Reds as well as by the Whites and Greens, and sometimes simply by bandits and criminals.

Only after the Civil War did the Bolsheviks deal a painful blow to the Orthodox Church under the pretext of confiscating its valuables, allegedly in order to alleviate starvation. Simultaneously, the "Trotskii-Lenin plan" to demoralize the church was drawn up, when the Bolsheviks exploited the administrative resources and existing contradictions within the church and organized the so-called "Renovationist schism." And yet the Bolsheviks' plan to demoralize the church with the help of pro-Soviet Smena vekh priests failed, and this forced the authorities to concentrate on the repressive element of their "church policy." The consequences of this course became apparent a few years later, when NEP was canceled and the authorities set out to completely eradicate any form of dissenting thought.

Translated by Josephine Von Zitzewitz

The Church's Revolutionary Moment:
Diocesan Congresses and Grassroots Politics in 1917

Catherine Evtuhov

The role of religious institutions and movements in revolutions is one of the most fraught issues in modern history. The assault on the church was conducted with exceptional violence and fury in 18th-century France and 20th-century Russia and Spain; while faith has also, notably in our own times, served as a clarion call to arms.[1] The history of the Orthodox Church in Russia, speaking generally, suffered from 70 years of neglect and distortion, followed now by two decades of innovative exploration by young scholars in Russia, Ukraine, the United States, and elsewhere.[2] It is an interesting moment to pause and take stock of the slowly emerging synthetic picture of the church and its place in the larger historical narrative of war and revolution. I wish, in this chapter, to take a brief look at the immensely creative and tumultuous era in the church as a community that preceded the outbreak of the First World War, and then to focus in on a yet-unwritten but fascinating episode of revolutionary politics—the empire-wide calling of local diocesan congresses in the spring of 1917. While a good deal of research on the history of the church itself has been accomplished in recent years, I would like to suggest that a consciously place-specific approach, focusing not on national issues but on local politics, can begin to integrate events within the church with the history of the Revolution itself. The history of the church is not a separate sphere for specialists in religion, but the locus of key events that can help us reach a better understanding of revolutionary politics on the ground. Paradoxically, this very local focus forces us to broaden our vision: the events of spring and summer 1917 in various locales throughout the empire had their continuation not only in the Soviet Union, but in the very rich life of the Orthodox Church in emigration. Therefore, I suggest that a new and intrinsically fragmented, yet globally present, Orthodox Church had emerged by the end of 1922.

---

[1] An interesting link between religion and violence is explored by Arno Mayer in *The Furies: Violence and Terror in the French and Russian Revolutions* (Princeton, NJ: Princeton University Press, 2000).

[2] As is well known, the beacon of outstanding scholarship on the social history of the Russian Orthodox Church for decades has been the work of Gregory Freeze.

Russian Culture in War and Revolution, 1914–22, Book 1: Popular Culture, the Arts, and Institutions. Murray Frame, Boris Kolonitskii, Steven G. Marks, and Melissa K. Stockdale, eds. Bloomington, IN: Slavica Publishers, 2014, 377–402.

A Russian Reformation?

Already in 1937, Georges Florovsky wrote of the Russian Silver Age as an era of intensive theological innovation and creativity, in which, perhaps unexpectedly, lay thinkers took the lead in questioning and reevaluating religious doctrine.[3] Like philosophers and poets throughout Europe in the fin de siècle, Russian thinkers challenged the prevailing positivism in philosophy and realism in literature; the Russian search led to a creative exploration of metaphysics and ultimately religion.[4] Over the past two decades, literary scholars and historians of ideas have pointed, in particular, to the Christological dimensions of fin-de-siècle literary polemics about the nature of the Word or Logos. Arguments between literary schools, in other words, were about theology as much as aesthetics. Indeed, early 20th-century thinkers seriously debated, in the guise of literary discussion, the key theological difficulties of the divine and human natures of Christ that had once formed the crux of the concerns of the patristic tradition and the Ecumenical Councils of the Christian Church.

Irina Paperno proposed in a 1993 article that the disagreement between Acmeists and Symbolists revolved significantly around theological issues, and indeed that Osip Mandel'shtam increasingly construed the Symbolist theory of the Word as symbol as heretical. Mandel'shtam, she suggests, eventually came to his understanding of the Word (*slovo, kak takovoe*) through a reading of the Church Fathers at the Council of Chalcedon. In her words,

> The Chalcedonian creed maintains the oneness of Christ's two natures, the human and the divine. This oneness in no way diminishes the distinction between the two natures united within the one figure of Christ. In the person of Christ (the Word made flesh) human nature, in no way lessened, is united with the divine. In a similar manner,

---

[3] G. V. Florovskii [Georges Florovsky], *Puti russkogo bogosloviia* (Paris: YMCA Press, 1937), chap. 8.

[4] Several synthetic sketches of the Silver Age as a historical epoch and as theological exploration exist, in addition to Florovsky. See especially Catherine Evtuhov, "The Silver Age as History," introduction to *The Cross & the Sickle: Sergei Bulgakov and the Fate of Russian Religious Philosophy* (Ithaca, NY: Cornell University Press, 1997); Marc Raeff, "Enticements and Rifts: Georges Florovsky as Russian Intellectual Historian," in *Georges Florovsky: Russian Intellectual and Orthodox Churchman*, ed. Andrew Blane (Crestwood, NY: St. Vladimir's Seminary Press, 1993); and the older Nicholas Zernov, *The Russian Religious Renaissance of the Twentieth Century* (New York: Harper & Row, 1963).

Mandelshtam's "word as such" represents a unity of the word's denotative ("common") and symbolic meanings.[5]

The discussion in literary and aesthetic circles coincided, further, with a contemporaneous controversy within the Orthodox Church: the *imiaslavie* movement among monks on Mount Athos who, in an adaptation of medieval hesychasm, developed a theory of prayer that culminated in the claim, by some adherents, that the Name of God was itself God.[6] The questioning and elaboration of dogma took a variety of forms in lay and clerical circles, ranging from carefully planned and frequently frustrating meetings between the lay intelligentsia and reform-minded clerics in the Moscow, St. Petersburg, and Kiev Religious-Philosophical Societies,[7] to concerted plans for church reform in the revolutionary years of 1904–07,[8] to the emergence of a rich and original tradition of religious philosophy that included such famous names as Vladimir Solov'ev, Sergei Bulgakov, Pavel Florenskii, Nikolai Berdiaev, Aleksei Losev, and others.[9]

---

[5] Irina Paperno, "On the Nature of the Word: Theological Sources of Mandelshtam's Dialogue with the Symbolists," in *Christianity and the Eastern Slavs, 2: Russian Culture in Modern Times*, ed. Robert P. Hughes and Paperno (Berkeley: University of California Press, 1994), 301.

[6] This controversy, too, has attracted an immense amount of attention in contemporary scholarship. See, first, the above-mentioned article by Paperno; but also Thomas Seifrid, *The Word Made Self: Russian Writings on Language, 1860–1930* (Ithaca, NY: Cornell University Press, 2005); Catherine Evtuhov, *The Cross & the Sickle: Sergei Bulgakov and the Fate of Russian Religious Philosophy, 1890–1920* (Ithaca, NY: Cornell University Press, 1997); and others. The most extensive claims for the importance of the Name of God movement are made by Loren Graham and Jean-Michel Kantor, who trace the origins of descriptive set theory, as well as its home, the Moscow School of Mathematics, to the Mount Athos polemic. Loren Graham and Jean-Michel Kantor, *Naming Infinity: A True Story of Religious Mysticism and Mathematical Creativity* (Cambridge, MA: Harvard University Press, 2009).

[7] Jutta Scherrer, *Die Petersburger religiös-philosophischen Vereinigungen: Die Entwicklung des religiösen Sebstverständnisses ihren Intelligencija-Mitglieder* (Wiesbaden: Otto Harrassowitz, 1973); Temira Pachmuss, *Zinaïda Hippius: An Intellectual Profile* (Carbondale: Southern Illinois University Press, 1971). See also in Randall Poole, "The Moscow Psychological Society, 1885–1922: Neo-Idealism and the Search for Philosophic Consciousness in Russia's Silver Age" (Ph.D. diss., University of Notre Dame, 1995).

[8] See especially James Cunningham, *A Vanquished Hope: The Movement for Church Renewal in Russia, 1905–1906* (Crestwood, NY: St. Vladimir's Seminary Press, 1981); but also an important more recent article by Freeze, "All Power to the Parish? The Problems and Politics of Church Reform in Late Imperial Russia," in *Social Identities in Revolutionary Russia*, ed. Madhavan K. Palat (Harlow, UK: Palgrave, 2001), 174–208.

[9] These figures, too, have experienced an unprecedented outpouring of translations and new research.

Parallel to such developments in lay theology (and here, naturally, I have sketched only the bare bones of a multifaceted discourse), the outlines of a reform movement within the institutional Orthodox Church are by now well established. The impulse for reform can be traced at least as far back as the 1860s. The era of the Great Reforms witnessed not only concrete measures affecting the life of the church, but also an explosion of spiritual journals, and the seminal and controversial endeavor by Aleksandr Bukharev (Archimandrite Fedor) to relate Orthodox theology to the exigencies of modern life.[10] The parish clergy in the half-century that followed played a dynamic role in education, charity, scientific investigation, and politics. Not the least of the stimuli to this effusive religious self-examination was the 25-year domination of the church by its remarkably activist secular overseer, Konstantin Pobedonostsev—whose dramatically conservative theories and policies prompted an equally dramatic response on the part of the religious left.[11]

The vibrancy of popular piety,[12] social activism and charitable efforts on the part of the clergy,[13] constructive engagement in the imperial capital,[14] pastoral

---

[10] Paul Valliere, *Modern Russian Theology: Bukharev, Soloviev, Bulgakov. Orthodox Theology in a New Key* (Grand Rapids, MI: Eerdmans, 2000); and B. F. Egorov, ed., *Arkhimandrit Feodor (A. M. Bukharev): Pro et contra* (Moscow: Izd-vo Russkogo Khristianskogo gumanitarnogo instituta, 1997). See also P. Znamenskii, *Bogoslovskaia polemika 1860-kh gg. ob otnoshenii pravoslaviia k sovremennoi zhizni* (Kazan´: Tip. Imperskogo universiteta, 1902).

[11] Gregory Freeze, *The Parish Clergy in Nineteenth-Century Russia: Crisis, Reform, and Counter-Reform* (Princeton, NJ: Princeton University Press, 1983); Jennifer Hedda, *His Kingdom Come: Orthodox Pastorship and Social Activism in Revolutionary Russia* (DeKalb: Northern Illinois University Press, 2008); Argyrios Pisiotis, "Orthodoxy versus Autocracy: The Orthodox Church and Clerical Political Dissent in Late Imperial Russia, 1905–1914" (Ph.D. diss., Georgetown University, 2000). On Pobedonostsev, see A. Iu. Polunov, *Pod vlast´iu Oberprokurora: Gosudarstvo i Tserkov´ v epokhu Aleksandra III* (Moscow: AIRO-XX, 1996); and the older biography by Robert Byrnes: *Pobedonostsev, His Life and Thought* (Bloomington: Indiana University Press, 1968).

[12] Vera Shevzov, *Russian Orthodoxy on the Eve of Revolution* (New York: Oxford University Press, 2004); Chris J. Chulos, *Converging Worlds: Religion and Community in Peasant Russia, 1861–1917* (DeKalb: Northern Illinois University Press, 2003).

[13] G. N. Ul´ianova, "Tserkovno-prikhodskie popechitel´stva kak strukturnaia edinitsa blagotvoritel´nosti vnutri mestnogo soobshchestva v pozdneimperskoi Rossii," in *Blagotvoritel´nost´ v Rossii: Istoricheskie i sotsial´no-ekonomicheskie issledovaniia* (St. Petersburg: Izd-vo imeni N. I. Novikova, 2004), 166–76; Daniel Scarborough, "The White Priest at Work: Orthodox Pastoral Activism and Social Reconstruction in Late Imperial Russia" (Ph.D. diss., Georgetown University, 2012).

[14] Hedda, *His Kingdom Come.*

creativity,[15] workers' mutual aid,[16] a wide spectrum of political positions among the clergy,[17] and absolute absence of evidence of secularization[18] have all been convincingly established. Particularly significant are local studies, in which historians have managed to recreate the practice of piety in Russia's parishes.[19] The monastic world has been brought to life in studies by Scott Kenworthy and William Wagner.[20] Together, these works definitively overturn a tired and dismal older vision of a corrupt, drunken, clerical caste functioning as informers and slaves to the state, with little to offer to Vissarion Belinskii's iconic peasant "scratching his backside" while speaking of God; a monastic hierarchy motivated by sheer self-interest; and a Holy Synod that was never anything more than a subservient ministry of the autocracy. Thus, the larger framework and vision of the Russian Orthodox Church in society have shifted decisively.

Decades of religious discussion culminated in the calling of the All-Russian Council of the Orthodox Church (Vserossiiskii Pomestnyi Sobor Pravoslavnoi Tserkvi), whose sessions opened on the festival day of the Dormition of the Virgin (15 August) in 1917 and petered out during 1918 as the Bolshevik Revolution gathered strength.[21]

---

[15] Nadieszda Kizenko, *A Prodigal Saint: Father John of Kronstadt and the Russian People* (University Park: Pennsylvania State University Press, 2000).

[16] Page Herrlinger, *Working Souls: Russian Orthodox and Factory Labor in St. Petersburg, 1881–1917* (Bloomington, IN: Slavica, 2007).

[17] Pisiotis, "Orthodoxy versus Autocracy."

[18] Gregory Freeze, "Subversive Piety: Religion and the Political Crisis in Late Imperial Russia," *Journal of Modern History* 68, 2 (June 1996): 308–50, here 308–09; Catherine Evtuhov, *Portrait of a Russian Province: Economy, Society, and Civilization in Nineteenth-Century Nizhnii Novgorod* (Pittsburgh: Pittsburgh University Press, 2011), chap. 9; Scarborough, "White Priest."

[19] See, for example, Gregory Freeze, "A Pious Folk? Religious Observance in Vladimir Diocese, 1900–1914," *Jahrbücher für Geschichte Osteuropas* 52, 3 (2004): 323–40; Chulos, *Converging Worlds*, which focuses on Voronezh province; and Shevzov, *Russian Orthodoxy*, whose larger study is firmly anchored in the detailed investigation of Vologda diocese.

[20] Scott Kenworthy, *The Heart of Russia: Trinity-Sergius, Monasticism, and Society after 1825* (New York: Oxford University Press, 2010); William Wagner, "The Transformation of Female Orthodox Monasticism in Nizhnii Novgorod Diocese, 1764–1929, in Comparative Perspective," *Journal of Modern History* 78, 4 (December 2006): 793–845.

[21] *Pomestnyi* (local) is here used in opposition to "ecumenical," and signifies the national character of the council, hereafter All-Russian Council. The documents of the council were published as *Sviashchennyi Sobor Pravoslavnoi Rossiiskoi Tserkvi: Deianiia* (Moscow, 1918), while further archival materials are located in the Russian State Historical Archive: Rossiiskii gosudarstvennyi istoricheskii arkhiv (RGIA) f. 833, "Sviashchennyi Sobor Pravoslavnoi Rossiiskoi Tserkvi." On the council, see Catherine

On the Ground: The Diocesan Congresses of Spring 1917[22]

Some of the most remarkable developments in Orthodoxy during the years of war and revolution occurred on the local level. Church policy unquestionably played a certain role in regional military strategy. For example, as the General Staff prepared to launch the Brusilov offensive, army chaplains—in the expectation of military success—developed a plan for the assimilation of Uniate parishes into the Orthodox fold.[23] In Galicia and Ukraine, confessional politics formed a key part of occupation policy, as a sharp conflict—in Mark von Hagen's words, a "war of faiths"—developed between Archbishop Evlogii, the synod's plenipotentiary to the region, and Metropolitan Andrei Sheptyts´kyi, defender of the Uniate Church's independence. The 16th-century effort to achieve union between Orthodoxy and Catholicism played out once again on the battleground of Ukraine.[24] National politics resonated on a local level in other ways as well: controversy raged over "Rasputin appointees" in certain dioceses, and the bishop of Tobol´sk, for example, was nearly removed until the emperor intervened in his defense.

Historians of the Orthodox Church in Russia have only just begun to turn their attention to the local diocesan congresses that took place throughout the empire in the spring of 1917. Most notably, M. A. Babkin has mined their materials in a worthwhile effort to reconstruct the church's position on key issues such as attitudes towards the monarchy, the legitimacy of the Provisional Government, and the war effort, while P. G. Rogoznyi uses them as part of his fascinating study of why and where parishioners sought to replace, or keep, their bishops.[25]

Evtuhov, "The Church in the Russian Revolution: Arguments For and Against Restoring the Patriarchate at the 1917–1918 Church Council," *Slavic Review* 50, 3 (1991): 497–511; and a good deal of newer literature such as K. V. Kovyrzin, "Pomestnyi Sobor 1917–1918 godov i poiski printsipov tserkovno-gosudarstvennykh otnoshenii posle fevral´skoi revoliutsii," *Rossiiskaia istoriia*, no. 4 (2008): 88–97.

[22] The Russian term is *eparkhial´nyi s˝ezd*. I have chosen to translate *s˝ezd* literally, as "congress," although the term "assembly" is also sometimes used in the historical literature.

[23] O. Georgii Shavel´skii, *Vospominaniia poslednego protopresvitera russkoi armii i flota*, 2 vols. (New York: Izd-vo imeni Chekhova, 1954), 1: chap. 9.

[24] See Mark von Hagen, *War in a European Borderland: Occupations and Occupation Plans in Galicia and Ukraine, 1914–1918* (Seattle: University of Washington Press, 2007), 37–42; and A. Iu. Bakhturina, *Politika Rossiiskoi Imperii v vostochnoi Galitsii v gody Pervoi mirovoi voiny* (Moscow: AIRO-XX), 2000.

[25] M. A. Babkin, "Prikhodskoe dukhovenstvo Rossiiskoi pravoslavnoi tserkvi i sverzhenie monarkhii v 1917 godu," *Voprosy istorii*, no. 6 (2003): 59–71; P. G. Rogoznyi, *Tserkovnaia revoliutsiia: 1917 god* (St. Petersburg: Liki Rossii, 2008).

Still, the congresses themselves are in desperate need of systematic examination, precisely because they became a crucial arena for the expression of religious and also political ideas at the grassroots level. Here I would like to look in some detail at the meetings of two such congresses—in the distant Siberian diocese of Tobol´sk, which was at the same time a key playing field for ecclesiastical politics, and the dynamic, politically charged central Russian diocese of Nizhnii Novgorod, with a brief glance at some other regions as well.

The creation of "diocesan congresses" belongs to the reform era of the 1860s, and forms part of the comprehensive package of diocesan reform. The congresses were meant to provide a local participatory organ for decision-making at the parish and then diocesan level. So far, they have been seen largely as a rubber-stamp mechanism, although this is likely an inaccurate assessment.[26] The "diocesan congresses" themselves were a sort of figment of reformers' imagination: a legalistically-minded 1908 document construed informal consulting committees of three diocesan clergy recommended by an 1864 seminary rule as the original congresses, which subsequently acquired increasing local power and ultimately official status in 1903–07.[27]

Their true role surfaced in an astounding fashion in the months that followed the February Revolution. The congresses were meant, at that moment, to be convened for the relatively straightforward task of electing delegates to the All-Russian Council of the Orthodox Church. Yet even a cursory glance at their operations shows that these local bodies, called at the height of war, became a vehicle for the expression of religious and political currents far beyond mere selection of candidates. They serve, on the one hand, as a sort of prism for understanding the political passions of this critical phase of revolutionary development; on the other, they point to the church as a genuine locus of revolutionary activity and an integral part of the larger revolutionary process.[28]

The All-Russian Council of the Russian Orthodox Church, when it convened on 15 August 1917, marked the culmination of an extensive network of local congresses and a reform movement with deep roots back to the 1860s and especially to the post-1905 period. Two key innovations of the council— the first since the 17th century—were the all-important elective principle (*vybornoe nachalo*) and lay participation.[29] Although the council has received

---

[26] See Scarborough, "White Priest."

[27] V. Beliaev, A. Viktorov, and M. Mansurov, *Eparkhial´nye s˝ezdy: Sbornik deistvuiushchikh zakonopolozhenii ob eparkhial´nykh s˝ezdax. Ikh praktika za 1903–1907 gg. Predstoiashchaia reforma s˝ezdov. Prilozheniia.* (St. Petersburg: Bereg, 1908).

[28] The complicated term *tserkovnaia revoliutsiia* was used by some contemporaries and is picked up and developed by Rogoznyi.

[29] Earlier congresses had brought together bishops and some lower clergy but not lay people, and the composition of the congress was one of the most controversial issues.

a good deal of attention, we still know very little of the on-the-ground local mechanisms by which it was convened. How significant were the diocesan congresses, specially called between March and August to elect delegates to the national council? What follows is a highly preliminary examination of two case studies, with a more cursory comparative glance across the empire. I would like to suggest that we need to see these councils *in their local context* if we are to understand the on-the-ground workings of revolutionary politics, rather than merely using them as a means to address empire-wide questions.

Tobol'sk. The diocesan congress to elect delegates to the All-Russian Council did not meet until 4 August, much later than in many other dioceses in response to a synod decree of early May mandating diocesan councils in the interests of greater participation; not only local but also general and national issues were to be discussed to this end. Distances assured a staggered pattern for the local meetings. The Extraordinary Congress therefore had multiple examples to follow, including that of Tiumen', which met on 20–27 May. "At that congress, extraordinary and specially convened, primarily church issues of general interest were discussed, with little attention to questions of local ecclesiastical-social life; therefore, an ordinary diocesan congress of the clergy was scheduled for Tobol'sk for 20 August."[30] The date, however, was moved up because of one crucial agenda item: the election of delegates to the All-Russian Council which would take place earlier. According to the Pre-Council Commission (*sovet*), parishes would choose lay members, superintendent districts would choose two clergy and three laity, and the diocesan congresses themselves would select two clerics and three lay members.[31]

On 4 August 1917, the Tobol'sk Diocesan Congress convened from all districts, with electors chosen from the parishes, superintendencies, and parish schools. The delegates numbered 114 total, because representatives of three superintendencies could not make it in time. The *Tobol'sk Diocesan News* reported, "This local ecclesiastical diocesan celebration was conducted with all possible majesty. All the participants of the congress well understood and appreciated, with their entire soul, the importance of this day which marked the renewed sobornost' of the Russian Orthodox Church; everyone experienced a special and rarely-repeated spiritual mood through the course of the entire day."[32] The day began with an 8 a.m. liturgy, at which Father Kronid Olerskii was promoted to archpriest. Many parishioners having no role in the Congress attended although it was a weekday—a circumstance the *Diocesan News* chronicler interpreted as marking a religious renaissance. The congress itself opened at 2 p.m., with the reading of Article 58, the decree on the convocation of an all-Russian council. The congress proceeded with

---

[30] *Tobol'skie eparkhial'nye vedomosti* (hereafter *TEV*), no. 26 (8 July 1917): 356.

[31] Ibid.

[32] *TEV*, no. 30 (8 August 1917), 427.

admirable efficiency (no minutes are available in the *vedomosti*), and concluded its deliberations at midnight, having chosen four priests, one psalmist, and six laity as delegates to Moscow.[33] The journalist rhapsodized over the beauty of the ceremony, "just like at Easter," while the Cossack F. G. Zibarev, elected from the laity, gave an acceptance speech: "I thank you, fathers and brothers, for electing me; my conscience bears witness that I will stand firm in favor of God's Church and Holy Orthodoxy; I ask you to pray for God's servant Fedor both in church and in your home prayers; while I, so long as God gives me strength, will be stalwart in my faith, firm in holy Orthodoxy, and courageous in the defense of Christ's Church, and will perform my duty in all humility until the end."[34]

However, far from remaining content with this satisfying ceremony and the stipulated election of delegates, congress members immediately took matters into their own hands, creating a parallel institution to the diocesan consistory (the primary ecclesiastical administrative institution at the diocesan level in the imperial period), namely the Ecclesiastical Diocesan Commission of Tobol'sk Diocese (Tserkovno-eparkhial'nyi Sovet Tobol'skoi Eparkhii), which would *coexist* with the consistory. The consistory itself also was made elective, and Tobol'sk was one of 15 dioceses to throw out their bishop.[35] An article of 8 August commented that he had siphoned off money designated for poor clergy to the cathedral for decorations, and this gossip spread through the dioceses.[36] The new organization insisted on financial independence and created its own administrative structures. In other words, we see in Tobol'sk not just a struggle for power but a successful example of restructuring. The newly elected Bishop Germogen agreed with everything the commission proposed.

The commission itself seems markedly modeled on the zemstvo. The Temporary Decree on the Ecclesiastical Diocesan Commission of Tobol'sk Diocese contained the following provisions: 1. The commission included two priests,

---

[33] The delegates actually listed from Tobol'sk, of 564 total, in the All-Russian Council roster, are: P. I. Aleksandrov, priests, and superintendent, Ishimskii district; I. A. Andronikov, lay juror, Tiumen'; Germogen, bishop; A. A. Vasil'ev, lay teacher, Tobol'sk; Voronin, lay delegate from Omsk; N. Ia. Zaborovskii, psalmist, Kurgan district; F. G. Zibarev, lay peasant, Akmolinsk.

[34] *TEV*, no. 30, 430.

[35] Rogoznyi, *Tserkovnaia revoliutsiia*, 213; see also Dimitry Pospielovsky, *The Russian Church under the Soviet Regime, 1917–1982*, 2 vols. (Crestwood, NY: St. Vladimir's Seminary Press, 1984). According to Rogoznyi, the provincial meetings tended to be more radical and revolutionary because they were subject to less scrutiny and supervision.

[36] According to Shavel'skii, Bishop Varnava was a Rasputin appointee; he was saved from dismissal by the synod already in 1915 by an appeal to Nicholas II (Shavel'skii, *Vospominaniia*, 1: 369–73).

one deacon or psalmist, and three laity elected to a three-year term; 2. it was the executive organ of the Diocesan Congress and the highest point of appeal of diocesan governance; 3. all affairs of the diocese were subject to the review of the commission; and 4. decisions were to be made by majority rule, with a possible appeal to the synod by the bishop (much like the governor's appeal to the Senate in zemstvo matters) if things could not be worked out. Last but not least, the commission was to receive 21,000 rubles per year for support, and each member would have a salary of 3000 rubles.

In Tobol'sk, as in a number of other dioceses, an important role was played by the newly-formed Union of Laity and Clergy (Pravoslavno–tserkovnoe obshchestvo edineniia klira i mirian), which pronounced its goal to be

> the complete spiritual unification of clergy and laity of the Orthodox Church according to the principle of sobornost for the defense and strengthening of the holy Orthodox faith, for the preservation of Divine ecclesiastical decisions, rules and laws of the Orthodox Church and its established rituals and customs, for the study of requirements and needs of local church civic life and the provision of means and resources to satisfy them according to the principles of the holy New Testament and holy church canons, and for the cultivation and affirmation of Orthodox Christian principles in all aspects and manifestations of social life (state, public, family, and private).[37]

All this would depend not on the imminent council but on "the living members of the Orthodox Russian Church themselves in their various locales and dioceses."[38] The Union's aims were more abstract and utopian than those of the official Diocesan Congress and Commission, and envisioned an ideal structure beginning at the parish level and proceeding upwards to the diocesan and finally the national level with a central organ in Moscow.

> This brotherly unification of members of the Orthodox Church must take shape freely, in accordance with the wish of parishioners themselves, as a result of their own realization of the necessity and utility of such an organization—which understanding will in turn assure the viability of the Union as a whole, independent of arbitrary influences. And if such a union has members across the entire Orthodox Russian land, and if local subdivisions are united in their activities and have a national All-Russian central organ, then the voice of such a society will have significant strength in shaping Russian Orthodox Church life.[39]

---

[37] *TEV*, no. 32 (22 August 1917), 1.

[38] Ibid.

[39] Ibid., 3.

The board of the union would consist of three clergy and ten laity, each elected for a single-year term. This vision, replicated in Tiumen', was given full support by the newly elected Bishop Germogen, himself a delegate to the All-Russian Council, with the words "a lovely idea" and "I deeply sympathize."

Late summer and early fall witnessed the formation of a Union of Orthodox Clergy of Tobol'sk diocese, with the avowed purpose of uniting the clergy and its religious-civic activity in contemporary conditions, namely: a free church life, reforms of clerical conditions, material and legal improvements, and mutual aid for moral perfection.[40]

Events in Tobol'sk in the spring of 1917 convey an impression that matters in Siberia proceeded more or less as they were supposed to.[41] Following a classic pattern of Russian governance,[42] the synodal decree of early May 1917 (see above, page 384), was met by an active local response including an efficient diocesan congress and the formation of new religious-civic groups, to the point that the unpopular bishop was removed and replaced with the more congenial Germogen. The *Tobol'sk Diocesan News*, at a significant physical remove from the tumult of the capitals, continued publication until quite late, in contrast to the "metropolitan" norm. Nonetheless, conversations already in August 1917 convey a sense of emergency, and local clergy discussed the need to hire a lawyer to defend their interests.[43] A closing speech at the lay and clerical congress noted that, in the three weeks it had been meeting, attrition had been significant. Kronid Olerskii asked, "Don't you feel, dear brothers, a certain fatigue, a cooling of thought and feeling, a certain hesitation in the movement forward." He evoked imagery he had used at the founding Tiumen' district congress months earlier, where he feared that the swollen spring waters might not find their appropriate riverbed and overflow into chaos; but now, stagnation could be equally dangerous.[44]

Nizhnii Novgorod. The situation was far more dramatic in Nizhnii Novgorod, where revolutionary passions, most notably in the longtime workers' settlement of Sormovo (the site of several of Maksim Gor'kii's novels), infused developments in the local life of the church. We catch a glimpse of the atmosphere in the city center: on the day that Nizhnii Novgorod province

---

[40] *TEV,* no. 28 (18 August 1917), 108; no. 39 (15 October 1917).

[41] It is possible that political passions formed an underwater current in Tobol'sk; at present I can only base my impressions on the discussions as they are reflected in the *vedomosti.* Some dioceses changed the title, and with it the political orientation, of their *vedomosti* in the course of the 1905 Revolution. The Nizhnii Novgorod organ, for example, became *Tserkovno-obshchestvennyi vestnik.*

[42] See Evtuhov, *Portrait of a Russian Province,* chap. 7.

[43] *TEV,* no. 23 (15 August 1917).

[44] *TEV,* no. 28 (18 August 1917), 107.

voted to join the new Provisional Government, thousands of people flocked to the Duma, including 5,000 Sormovo workers brandishing red flags.[45] Two diocesan congresses were held in Nizhnii Novgorod, the first on 15–18 May and then, after major controversy erupted, on 8–9 August. The latter congress was attended by 198 persons.

Almost immediately, parties emerged. The primary groupings were the Committee of the United Clergy (Komitet ob˝edinennogo dukhovenstva i mirian, hereafter KODM), and the Holy Transfiguration Brotherhood (Spaso-Preobrazhenskoe Bratstvo, SPB). What were the main points of conflict? In the early days, they focused primarily on electoral procedures, although these ostensibly anodyne discussions concealed deep class divisions. Essentially, the KODM demanded the famous Kadet four-tail formula—universal, secret, direct, and equal elections. The clerical congress, while accepting this basic principle, wanted in addition to introduce a curial system, in which clergy would elect clergy, lower clergy would elect lower clergy, and laity would elect laity. The fear was that, without this stratification, the lower clergy would take over by virtue of their greater numbers; the presence of laity complicated matters still further, and the priests, as essential members, needed to have their voice. Seeking a compromise, Father Spasskii suggested that the local superintendents' councils should be permitted to choose between these two possible procedures.[46]

The KODM, further, called for urgent meetings at the parish level, which would include women; they rejected any automatic status for the superintendents; and, echoing the projects of the religious-philosophical societies in the capitals 15 years earlier, advocated links with the lay intelligentsia.[47] "Everything points to the immediate emergence, without waiting for directives from on high, of the clergy from that passive state in which it has found itself due to the infelicitous circumstances of the old order."[48] The clergy's job in the new situation was to *care for its flock*, not to pursue estate interests or political slogans. What should be the content of sermons? "To appeal to the population to follow calmly the directives of the Provisional Government, along with a call to bear the burdens of the war until its victorious conclusion," not to get

---

[45] *Nizhegorodskii tserkovno-obshchestvennyi vestnik* (hereafter NTsOV), no. 7 (8 March 1917). Sormovo was one of the first working-class communities in Russia, dating back to the 1840s. The primary industry was the huge shipbuilding plant (Red Sormovo in Soviet times). Part of Balakhna district in the 19th century, Sormovo has now been absorbed into the city of Nizhnii Novgorod and forms one of its suburbs. An interesting landmark is the impressive Sormovo cathedral, erected in 1905 and funded by a collection among the workers.

[46] NTsOV, no. 13 (30 April 1917), 25.

[47] NTsOV, no. 11 (16 April 1917), 178–80.

[48] Ibid., 178.

distracted by rumors, and not to identify freedom with lawlessness.[49] "All truly faithful people in the parishes, particularly those acting as luminaries in the village—teachers, physicians, agronomists—must be won over by the pastors to join them in working together, and should become the pastor's retinue. The clergy themselves, further, should function as an "enlightened force" (intelligentnaia sila), with a duty to go to the people and explain the situation to them, including the urgent need for an All-Russian Council.[50]

The KODM published a complete list of agenda items for reform, many of them harking back to projects from the abortive church councils of 1905 and 1911–12; they included an agenda for the church as a whole, but also items addressing particular local diocesan concerns. They are fascinating enough to quote in full, as I do in the appendix. A few key highlights concerned electoral procedures, including urgent parish-level meetings to elect laity to the superintendents' council, the inclusion of women at all levels, and the omnipresent four-tail formula. Particularly significant agenda items included, for the church as a whole, the implementation of a conciliar (sobornaia) form of governance, building up from diocesan to regional and finally all-Russian councils; equal civic rights for the clergy; "the restoration of relations among bishops, hierarchs, and priests to the way they were in the ancient apostolic church, and destruction of the spirit of despotism and secular domination prevalent beginning in the fourth century [!]"; bishops to be appointed from the white clergy and elected by a regional council; discussion of lay participation. On the local level, the KODM, borrowing the language of the Social Democrats, requested the creation of a diocesan executive committee (ispolkom), the re-election of consistory members and an increase in their numbers, the implementation of the elective principle at all levels, the abolition of marks for behavior, and the cessation of censorship of sermons.

The apparent impartiality with which the Vestnik initially reported the events of 15–18 May in fact concealed a deepening and dramatic rift. The opening ceremony of the congress was scheduled for 1 p.m. in the building of the diocesan women's college in the provincial capital, with more than 300 delegates in attendance.[51] However, the radical left, goaded by a certain V. Rakitin, a Sormovo worker, showed up early in the morning. By 11 a.m. stormy meetings were going on in various rooms of the college, with the radicals explaining matters to the rural delegates; the left in this manner managed to get itself elected to a plethora of responsible posts. Among the radicals was I. Liubimskii—the very priest who got the cross from his parish and who made

---

[49] The insistence with which all intrachurch groups spoke of continuing and winning the war, and the pervasiveness of the church's support of the war, raise interesting questions about the possible degree to which the church hierarchy might have influenced the Provisional Government's famously unbending stance.

[50] NTsOV, no. 11 (16 April 1917), 179.

[51] NTsOV, no. 15 (21 May 1917), 161.

an "extremely agitated, destructive [*pogromnaia*]" speech against the urban clergy.[52] The composition of the congress bore witness to a particular electoral process, and was questioned by more conservative delegates. "The dominant element was representatives of the clergy—deacons and psalmists—and laity. Among the latter category there are members of the bureaucratic rank and file [*chinovnyi klass*], the intelligentsia, the upper bourgeoisie, but still primarily peasants—workers of the land, for the first time summoned to discuss church and parish issues."[53] This predominance of lower clergy and peasants in part reflected a decision, by open vote, to admit members of the KODM *in corpore* (a decision later condemned as imposed by the left) as well as representatives of the established church brotherhoods and parish schools. In the meantime, membership was denied to the new SPB on the grounds that they already had ten representatives from the parishes.[54] The first task was the election of officials. The KODM's V. S. Gaginskii won the presidency with 254 secret votes (out of twelve candidates), while the runner-up had only 34; Gaginskii was confirmed 245–75. Nine vice-presidents—four clergy (two of them priests) and two laity, and ten secretaries—five clerical, five lay—were also confirmed.

Gaginskii followed up with an inspirational speech—he was later accused of preparing it in advance, thus bearing witness to manipulated elections—in which he spoke of the free conciliar (*sobornaia*) church as having been within us, and only now open to realization in real life. "To embody the principle of freedom, sobornost', and the elective principle in the entire structure of church life—this is our first task."[55] The new council would build on the achievements of the previous, abortive but important meeting in 1905, and in this sense was "second in its nature, first by its circumstance."[56] The congress, on the next day, broke up into sections, and reconvened in the evening to hear reports from each. The sections were dedicated to issues of parish organization and reform; diocesan governance reform; the legal status of clergy; facilities management; education; canons and mission; and verification of delegates (i.e., proper election procedures). In the evening, delegates heard a paper by D. Dneprovskii on the conciliar form of governance of the church in the first century; discussed problems with an accountant at the candle factory; set up a special commission to resolve misunderstandings between clergy and parishioners; took up a collection for Russian POWs (231 rubles); and prepared

---

[52] "Zhaloba Sviateishemu Pravitel'stvennomu Sinodu," *NTsOV*, no. 20 (12 July 1917), addendum.

[53] *NTsOV*, no. 15, 161.

[54] Ibid., 162.

[55] Ibid., 164.

[56] Ibid., 163.

a sermon to the flock to "explain" principles of freedom. Last but not least, the congress passed a vote of no confidence to Archbishop Joachim.[57]

All of these proceedings took place in a somewhat tense and occasionally sentimental atmosphere. The success of the collection was due to an inspiring speech about the POWs, delivered just previously. The first female participant in a church congress—a rural teacher—quietly took the podium and "spoke of spiritual concerns." Outside, the delegates heard the noise of a funeral procession of a technician named Andreev who had been killed by the mob; some congress members went outside to pay tribute to his family. Yet, the rejection of the bishop, at least according to this account which belongs to P. A. Almazov (an interesting character who belonged to both groups), proceeded with due decorum.[58] As we learn from a later complaint filed by the urban clergy and center right, however, this harmony was achieved by the KODM's cooptation of the congress: they had begun their campaign early, promulgating a program of immediate parish reform already on 12 March, and printing a telegram criticizing Bishop Joachim. Three "local *intelligenty* [members of the intelligentsia]" showed up at the Council and were listened to patiently. Deacons and psalmists (the "lower clergy") formed their own meetings and tried to subvert the group project; they resolved, among other things, "not to accept blessings from the priests, not to kiss their hands, to stop preparing Sunday and holiday services." Yells and stomping accompanied the discussion.[59] Delegates voted with their feet, so that by the time the actual poll to confirm the congress's legitimacy (*doverie*) was held, the vote was indeed 44 to 8—but 48 delegates of the original 100 had already drifted away and did not participate. It was in response to all of this that the urban clergy formed a six-person Pastoral Soviet—in turn accused by the KODM of "Presbyterianism." All of this caused much worry, including "in the district towns and villages of the diocese" (this is reflected in the discussion of districts, below).[60] Then, the SPB was formed; only Almazov was able to straddle both groups. The KODM pushed for an early convocation, but the bishop insisted on 15 May, with adequate time for preparation. Faith in the KODM was undermined among the urban clergy and parishioners, and they did not elect them. This is why they plotted to get in by other means. In short, what was going on was quite clear: it was a largely successful effort by "proto-renovationists" in the shape of the KODM to seize control of the diocesan congress.

The congress concluded by sending telegrams to everybody under the sun. They sent a missive to the synod in support of the Provisional Government and Constituent Assembly in the faith that "the Orthodox Church will always

---

[57] Ibid., 165.

[58] *NTsOV,* no. 16 (28 May 1917), 178–79.

[59] *NTsOV,* no. 19 (28 June 1917), addendum, 3.

[60] Ibid., 4.

benefit from the rights of freedom and self-determination in its inner life, while the Orthodox faith remains *first among equals.*[61] More telegrams went to the Petrograd Soldiers' Soviet, the Workers' Soviet, the Peasants' Soviet ("a fraternal greeting"), and to the aging archpriest F. Vladimirskii of Arzamas: "The free congress sends a greeting to the venerable representative of the semi-free congress of 1905."[62] The SPB, in the meantime, convened its own congress and ceremonial liturgy at 1:30 p.m. on 16 May, with speeches about parish life and choral singing. A "spontaneous pre-congress meeting" convened at 8:30 p.m. with discussion of issues and answers to "perplexed" questions of other persons in attendance.[63]

The whole story was ultimately resolved by an appeal to the synod, which took these circumstances very seriously. The May congress was not annulled, but was "discontinued"; in other words, a next meeting of the congress, scheduled for 8–9 August, would proceed as an independent event rather than a continuation of May's achievements.[64]

One of the most fascinating aspects of church politics in Nizhnii Novgorod diocese in spring 1917 was the abundant manifestation of civic activity at the most grassroots level—that of the provincial districts. In Ardatov, parishioners convened a congress on 12 April, attended by 78 people—40 priests, 15 deacons, 12 psalmists, and 11 laity. The congress decided: 1) to support the Provisional Government and popularize its recently issued Liberty Bonds (*zaem svobody*); 2) to be at one with the people and support them and participate without proposing any political platforms; 3) to forget narrow professional interests, given the current crisis; 4) to facilitate lay participation, given the conciliar structure (*sobornoe ustroistvo*) of the church; 5) to consider the elective principle (*vybornoe nachalo*) appropriate to the times; 6) to divide up the district into units of 10–12 parishes so that the clergy could work most usefully together. In Balakhna, in a classic move by the "proto-renovationists," the radical clergy of the First Superintendency (*blagochinnyi okrug*) on 20 April demanded the transfer of the *Tserkovno-obshchestvennyi vestnik* to the KODM. The Sormovo meetings were the most sophisticated and detailed. Here, on 23 April, a parish meeting worked out a specific agenda for the imminent diocesan congress, addressing, first, the organization of the Orthodox parish in accordance with principles of extensive self-government; and, second, the structure and governance of the Orthodox Church as a whole. On the first point they proposed that the parish commune control all incoming and outgoing expenses and elect a committee to this end; that the membership of

---

[61] *NTsOV*, no. 15 (21 May 1917), 165. The age was rife with catch-phrases and "first among equals" was certainly one of them. This principle was much discussed at the All-Russian Council with respect to the patriarch's status vis-à-vis the bishops.

[62] *NTsOV*, no. 15, 166.

[63] Ibid.

[64] *NTsOV*, no. 26 (8 September 1917), 348–49.

the parish be regulated through a registration process; and that the question of an elected clergy and their material support be raised, along with guidelines for election. On the national issue, they urged the speedy convocation of a council to decide all questions; a decision on the crucial question of who was the head of the Russian Orthodox Church;[65] and the implementation of the elective principle at all levels of the church administration. In Gorbatov district, the local clergy held a meeting in the town of Vorsma on 24 April, attended by the activist KODM priest P. A. Almazov. The Gorbatov clerics, like those of Balakhna, went over to the KODM side, endorsing the activities of that group and also demanding the transfer of the *Vestnik*; they demanded the ouster of diocesan missionaries as "useless to the cause."[66]

More evidence of the penetration of politics to the absolute grassroots level, on both sides, also emerged. A piece from 10 May cites examples of the aggression of peasants against clergy, where parishioners took away church land without compensation or chased away priests. In a particularly challenging case, peasants in a Balakhna parish petitioned for the award of a cross for their beloved priest but the award was not granted. The peasants proceeded to take matters into their own hands and gave him a cross themselves, causing considerable consternation among the hierarchy: if parishioners could reward, they could also potentially punish, and had thus created a dangerous precedent.[67] A group of church watchmen, in June, demanded higher pay (100 rubles per month), vacation, and release from janitorial chores.[68] On the opposite side of the spectrum, there was also on-the-ground support for the complaint. Rural clergy wrote in to protest against the KODM, including the priest of the Second Superintendency of Ardatov district and priests from Balakhna, Kniaginin, Vasil', Nizhnii Novgorod, and Arzamas; these petitions were sometimes signed by deacons as well.[69]

Even in these circumstances, not everything was about politics—religious matters were also central. On 21 May, Almazov reported an incident which made him nearly faint with joy (my evaluation based on his tone). A priest wrote in to the *Vestnik* to report that several Old Believers had showed up, uninvited, at their local electoral meeting on 30 April, inspired by the coming diocesan congress and wanting to participate: "The Old Believers announced that, because the program contained points about the restoration to the Orthodox Church of ancient church canons, they would be delighted to

---

[65] This did, indeed, become the most important decision by the All-Russian Council, which restored the patriarchate and elected Tikhon within days of the October Revolution. See Evtuhov, "Church in Revolution," and others.

[66] All of these district happenings are reported in *NTsOV*, no. 14 (10 May 1917), 141–42.

[67] Ibid., 135. The priest in question was I. Liubimskii (see above).

[68] *NTsOV*, no. 18 (14 June 1917), 210.

[69] *NTsOV*, no. 25 (25 August 1917), 339–41.

participate in the discussion of these points in cooperation with the Orthodox clergy. At the same time the leader announced that, if the future All-Russian Council restored all ritual and hierarchical matters appropriate in the liturgy in accordance with ancient practice, they, the Old Believers, would immediately join the fold of the Orthodox Church."[70] The reticent parish priest agreed, accepting the prior's membership as one of the elected delegates—but sought the approval of higher authorities. Almazov emotionally responded "with a shout of his joyous heart!": "Your report is enough to rouse the dead. Because what you are telling me is what the Church has been waiting for for more than two hundred years."[71] This was the whole point—to restore the church and connect back up with the ancient, canonical church! Gaginskii also expressed a desire "to break down barriers among Christians," and, further, "to rip out by the roots the weeds of Pharisean disdain for those of other faiths, sown by the old regime, and to show them the richness of the Christian soul"; while Almazov, once again, saw one of the main achievements of the Council as the joint discussion between Orthodox and Old Believers.

It is significant that actual representation at the All-Russian Council, when delegates finally made their choice at the new 8–9 August gathering,[72] seemed to tilt rather in favor of the establishment; and there was one representative of the united faith and no Old Believers.[73] The temporary triumph of the conservative forces, however, was undone by 1918, when the SPB was liquidated and some of its key members shot.[74]

Other Regions. Religious politics in the spring of 1917 were as varied as Russia's dozens of dioceses, and research on this fascinating panorama is still

---

[70] *NTsOV,* no. 15 (21 May 1917), 155.

[71] Ibid.

[72] *NTsOV,* no. 24 (15 August 1917), 319–20.

[73] Members from Nizhnii Novgorod diocese were A. G. Al'bitskii, a priest from Semenov; A. M. Chernoutsan, a lay instructor at the Nizhnii Novgorod parish school; V. A. Demidov, a Nizhnii Novgorod landowner; Archbishop Joachim, dismissed on 22 March 1918; M. R. Kudriavtsev, archpriest from the Nizhnii Novgorod Theological Academy; I. E. Lavrent'ev, a merchant of the united faith from Gorbatov; and a Lebedev, lay seminary administrator and candidate in theology from Pochinki.

[74] P. G. Protsenko, *Biografiia episkopa Varnavy (Beliaeva): V nebesnyi Ierusalim. Istoriia odnogo pobega* (Nizhnii Novgorod: Izd-vo Bratstva vo imia Sv. Kniazia Aleksandra Nevskogo, 1999), 188. The SPB did not go down without a fight. They were responsible for setting up a kindergarten, publishing house, free religious instruction, various charitable activities, and more throughout the winter of 1917–18, and organized the Nizhnii Novgorod religious procession (*krestnyi khod*), held throughout the empire in February 1918, in protest against persecution of the church (ibid., 175–76).

embryonic. *Vedomosti* tended to mention briefly events in other dioceses.[75] The diocesan congress in Kiev numbered 800 delegates divided into a conservative minority and a progressive majority; projected reforms included parish councils chosen by direct, equal, universal, and secret ballot, to be reproduced as well on the district and okrug level. In Saratov, 145 delegates, in a "passionate" meeting, asked to remove the bishop, abolish (or at least profoundly reform) the diocesan consistory, and shut down church schools.[76] In Orenburg the bishop was well loved, worked *with* the clergy, and had a record of defending clergy who were accused of political unreliability.[77] The congress, when it met in May, proposed a series of reforms ranging far beyond the strictly ecclesiastical sphere: these included labor legislation—an eight-hour day justified by the spiritual needs of workers; democratization of education and the retention of religious instruction on a voluntary basis; and, once the war was over, the abolition of armies, navies, arsenals, and munitions factories, and the creation of an international court.[78] In Khar'kov parishioners wanted to petition to retain Bishop Antonii, and a business school student who opposed this petition was beaten up, resulting in scandal and a meeting on the Sobornaia Square following the Sunday liturgy.[79] On Monday evil rumors resumed, and the laity met in the Church of the Annunciation to try to keep Antonii, who in turn asked them to let him resign and enter a monastery.[80]

In Tver', the congress was opened by its president, F. V. Tikhvinskii, a former priest but now army veterinarian in Rzhev. They voted in unison for a democratic republic, for giving church lands to the people, and a majority

---

[75] On occasion, these brief notes provide the most valuable insight into events in different dioceses, particularly where the *Eparkhial'nye vedomosti* had already ceased publication (e.g., Volhynia on 1 April 1917), or where the reporting function had been displaced by a thick-journal type edition (e.g., Khar'kov's *Vera i razum* and Kazan"s *Pravoslavnyi sobesednik*). Where possible, I have corroborated the notes with a local edition.

[76] *NTsOV*, no. 13 (30 April 1917), 203–04. The precise wording of this last radical measure was: "to acknowledge the existence of parish schools as a disseminator of religious-moral instruction [*vospitanie*] of the people as quite desirable, but in different and better conditions than has been the case up to this point." These conditions were defined as subjecting the schools to the parish councils; the parish councils and parish assemblies would then decide their fate. "Eparkhial'nyi S"ezd dukhovenstva i mirian aprel'skoi sessii 1917 g. Protokoly," *Saratovskie eparkhial'nye vedomosti*, no. 13 (1 May 1917), 436–60; no. 15 (21 May 1917), 530–36; 536.

[77] *NTsOV*, no. 13 (30 April 1917), 203–04.

[78] *Orenburgskii tserkovno-obshchestvennyi vestnik*, no. 13 (21 May 1917): 1–4; no. 14 (25 May 1917): 1–2; no. 18 (8 June 1917): 1.

[79] According to the *Vedomosti*, the student turned out to be a Jew named Kaufman.

[80] *NTsOV*, no. 13 (30 April 1917), 203–04.

voted for the separation of church and state. They did not endorse Bishop Serafim and asked him to leave the diocese. The council thought it necessary to invite the professors of state law Iu. V. Sergeevskii and of economic law I. M. Gromoglasov (former professor of the Moscow Theological Academy).[81] Events in Krasnoiarsk unfolded in a "strained atmosphere." The priest A. Muranov called Bishop Nikon a despot, tyrant, and careerist. "Nikon's autocracy has no bounds. He made it his goal to wreck and paint red the clergy of Enisei diocese. He did this in order to further his career. Bishop Nikon did not disdain to bow before Rasputin, plead before Varnava and the salon of Baroness Ignatieva." Nikon traveled through the Turukhan region and forced the *inorodtsy* to drop their subsistence fishing to accompany him. Muranov comments: "The church is an organization. We, the pastors, are its body and our head is the bishop. But who will object if we say that our organization has an unhealthy head? Such a sick head needs to be removed from a still healthy organism." This pronouncement was met by cries of "Bravo," "Right on," and "Away with Nikon."[82] In Zhitomir, the congress came out against the Black Hundreds and for a democratic way of life, including autonomy for Ukraine, separation of church and state, the elective principle in the life of the clergy, reform of schools, the immediate calling of a church council based on democratic principles, and the distribution of church lands to the peasants. The Ispolkom wanted to get rid of Archbishop Evlogii, but the congress disagreed, and wanted to appeal to General Brusilov and Prince L'vov (at this time head of the Provisional Government) to leave him in Volhynia. They also wanted to appeal to the synod to revise the composition of the consistory because they were too preoccupied with politics.[83]

In Kazan', the congress essentially decided to support the Provisional Government; that the task of the clergy was to be in the church and with parishioners, as close as possible to the people ("The spirit should be popular and democratic"); and that the church must have inner freedom regardless of the form church–state relations would take. Finally, Kazan' members suggested that the pastor must engage in politics!—but, should instruct rather

---

[81] *Protokoly Chrezvychainogo Eparkhial'nogo s"ezda dukhovenstva i mirian Tverskoi eparkhii. 20–25 aprelia 1917 g.* (Tver', 1917). See also Rogoznyi, *Tserkovnaia revoliutsiia*, 99–100.

[82] *NTsOV*, no. 13 (30 April 1917), 220. Interestingly, the final instruction (*nakaz*) to the delegates to the church council, worked out at the subsequent local congress (*s"ezd*) on 8–10 August, bore no trace of this conflictual stance. This latter document proposed: 1) the realization of the conciliar principle on all levels of church organization; 2) the impossibility of the separation of church and state; 3) the necessity of religious instruction in all schools; 4) the right of the Orthodox parish to open whichever schools it may wish; 5) intensification of religious discipline; 6) dissemination of the work of the All-Russian Church Council as broadly as possible. *Nakaz deputatam na vserossiiskii pomestnyi sobor v gorode Moskve, vyrabotannyi na obshcheeparkhial'nom s"ezde dukhovenstva i mirian 8, 9 i 10 avgusta 1917 g.* (Krasnoiarsk, 1917).

[83] *NTsOV*, no. 13 (30 April 1917), 220.

rather than guide, so that parishioners would choose the party that was best for church and moral life. If a concrete party was recommended, the pastor should do this only as a citizen, not by authority of the church.[84] Gregory Freeze adds, focusing on the specific issue of parish reform, that the Vladimir congress insisted on the recognition of the parish as a juridical entity, the inclusion of all laity over age 18 in the parish assembly, clerical appointment through parish recommendation and consent, and local management of diocesan funds; and that the same body in Kherson and in Perm' came out in favor of elections for all positions in the church and, in the latter case, satisfactory explanation by the bishop if a candidate were found "unworthy."[85]

Mikhail Babkin has compiled an extremely interesting statistical summary, indicating percentages of parishes supporting various positions.[86] Yet, the actual local detail gives us a better sense of what was going on on the ground, even if until this point the picture is rather impressionistic. So far I have come across two specifically local studies—one of Khar'kov diocese and another of Smolensk. A. D. Kaplin and M. V. Matveenko describe the successful election, in Khar'kov, of delegates followed by the resignation of a group of laity; a resolution to melt down the church bell to spend on a children's colony; and the election of a new bishop.[87] An interesting article by M. V. Kail' places the Smolensk diocesan congress in the context of earlier efforts at church reform, while pointing out the importance of specifically local circumstances. According to Kail''s study, the Smolensk congress, which numbered close to 300 lay and clerical participants, addressed the pressing issue of parish reform, implementation of the electoral principle, support for parish schools, and the appropriate role for priests in politics, while in the end focusing above all on diocesan administration. Like many other congresses, the Smolensk group deferred to the future All-Russian Council on this essentially canonical question of who, indeed, was legitimately responsible for the election and appointment of bishops. In confirmation of the Nizhnii Novgorod congress's clearly radical nature, it is interesting to note that the Smolensk congress, while sending the standard telegram of support to the Provisional Government, discussed sending one to the Petrograd workers' and soldiers' soviets but decided against it.[88]

---

[84] *NTsOV,* no. 18 (14 June 1917).

[85] Freeze, "All Power to the Parish," 194.

[86] Babkin, "Prikhodskoe dukhovenstvo."

[87] A. D. Kaplin and M. P. Matveenko, "Khar'kovskaia eparkhiia v usloviiakh revoliutsionnykh sobytii 1917 g.," *Sumskii istoriko-arkhivnyi zhurnal,* no. 8–9 (2010): 165–67.

[88] M. V. Kail', "'Revoliutsiia v tserkvi': Diskussii o tserkovnoi reforme i Smolenskii eparkhial'nyi s"ezd dukhovenstva i mirian 1917 g.," www.moscowia.su/images/konkurs_raboti/2008/2.22.doc (accessed 6 June 2012). Thanks to Scott Kenworthy for bringing this article to my attention.

It is too early to draw up a general profile of the diocesan congresses as a whole. Still, it is clear that, first of all, the individual congresses strongly reflected their particular local context. The Tobol'sk congress, physically located far from the center, followed a pattern recognizable from the zemstvo politics of the preceding half-century: central initiatives met an active local response, and the reorganization of local structures and even the removal of the bishop (impossible under Nicholas II's regime) proceeded in orderly fashion. The Nizhnii Novgorod congress, in contrast, became a lively arena for the expression of political conflict in which radical currents collided with conservative forces at the most grassroots-possible level; even here, however, the synod still had a strong voice and intervened to mitigate the confrontation. We can propose, however, that the diocesan congresses taken as a whole shared some common features as well: even though they met for a matter of days, they usually not only elected delegates to the All-Russian Council as officially charged but also promoted considered agendas for diocesan and national reform, and in some cases were able to raise dogmatic issues for ultimate discussion in Moscow. One element remains constant: the level of engagement and participation of clerical and lay members alike was extremely high. The issues of parish and diocesan reform, elections, control over finances, and juridical status—among the most central of the questions dominating discussions since at least 1905[89]—had deep roots throughout the provinces. The eventual delegates to the All-Russian Council brought with them concerns that had taken shape in daily dialogue and struggle in Russia's regions.

A "Global" Orthodox Church for the 20th Century

The story of the church in revolution is one of fragmentation. The remarkable unity achieved in Moscow in 1917–18 proved a mere flash, and episodes more typical of the ensuing years include the bizarre spectacle of the main army chaplain scurrying around southern Russia, trying to gather support for a miniature All-Russian Council that would provide leadership for the Denikin government.[90] In purely institutional terms, the patriarchate, restored by the council, was annulled by the Bolshevik regime in 1925, until its reemergence as an arm of the Soviet state during and after the Second World War. The church to some degree went underground, with parishioners using local organs of secular organization to come to the defense of their priests.[91] Sect-like groups met in private apartments in the late 1920s to perpetuate worship

---

[89] See Freeze, "All Power to the Parish," for one angle on these issues.

[90] Shavel'skii, *Vospominaniia*, 2: 329–55. This was the Temporary Ecclesiastical Administration that later formed the kernel of the Synod in Exile.

[91] Glennys Young, *Power and the Sacred in Revolutionary Russia: Religious Activists in the Village* (University Park: Pennsylvania State University Press, 1997).

under the radar.[92] The most brutal and violent part of the story—executions, exiles, and camps—is by now fairly well known; but this quieter tale of the parishes in retreat still contains many unwritten chapters. This is one of the reasons why a specifically local approach to church history is so important.

The outlines of the new dis-organization of the church had emerged with some clarity by the end of 1922. The key elements of this dispersal were the remarkable forced emigration—Lenin's original solution—of intellectuals who had played a part in the lay theological elaboration of doctrine in the years of the Silver Age.[93] The ironic effect of the deportation was the flowering of theology in "Russia Abroad": Sergei Bulgakov wrote far more in terms of sheer volume in his "second life" as a theologian in Paris (he was 50 when he was deported);[94] Georges Florovsky wrote his brilliant history of Russian culture through a theological prism; and an ecumenical movement flourished in the 1930s in Europe and the United States, particularly engaging the Catholic and Anglican churches.

A new chapter in the institutional history of the Orthodox Church opened with the establishment of a Synod in Exile at Sremski Karlovci in the Kingdom of Serbs, Croats, and Slovenes—a relic of the Temporary Ecclesiastical Administration in Southern Russia, and headed by Metropolitan Antonii (Khrapovitskii), formerly of Kiev.[95] National Orthodox churches such as the Orthodox Church of America followed various thorny paths in establishing their independence. Within the Soviet Union the renovationist wing of collaborationist clergy took control of the hierarchy and administration; the Living Church was officially established in May 1922.[96] Patriarch Tikhon was briefly imprisoned before being coopted back into the church administration

---

[92] One such group is described by Carol Dockham, "War with the Red Dragon: The Case of a Counter-Revolutionary Monarchist Church Group in Kiev and Neighboring Regions, 1932–1933," unpublished seminar paper, Georgetown University, May 2011.

[93] See Stuart Finkel, *On the Ideological Front: The Russian Intelligentsia and the Making of the Soviet Public Sphere* (New Haven: Yale University Press, 2007); and Lesley Chamberlain, *Lenin's Private War: The Voyage of the Philosophy Steamer and the Exile of the Intelligentsia* (New York: St. Martin's Press, 2007).

[94] See, for example, Antoine Arjakovsky, *Le père Serge Boulgakov, un philosophe et un théologien chrétien* (Paris: Parole et Silence, 2007); Valliere, *Modern Russian Theology*; and a number of important articles by theologian Barbara Hallensleben.

[95] Marc Raeff, *Russia Abroad: A Cultural History of the Russian Emigration, 1919–1939* (New York: Oxford University Press, 1990), 122. This was on 13 September 1922.

[96] "Russian Orthodox Church Outside Russia," Wikipedia, http://en.wikipedia.org/wiki/Russian_Orthodox_Church_Outside_Russia. On Renovationism, see Edward Roslof, *Red Priests: Renovationism, Russian Orthodoxy, and Revolution, 1905–1946* (Bloomington: Indiana University Press, 2002); and an interesting reinterpretation: Scott Kenworthy, "Russian Reformation? The Program for Religious Renovation in the Orthodox Church, 1922–1925," *Modern Greek Studies Yearbook* 16/17 (2000/2001), 89–130.

not long before his death. The crucial turning point, as Jonathan Daly and others have argued, was the confiscation of church possessions by the Bolsheviks, ostensibly in order to facilitate famine relief.[97] By the autumn of 1922 the fragmented and dispersed elements of 20th-century Orthodoxy were in place; together they comprise the many faces of the Russian Orthodoxy we have inherited from that difficult era.

ↂ ↄ

It is perhaps easiest to see the history of Russian Orthodoxy in the 20th century as one of martyrdom and suffering juxtaposed with moral failing. Yet as this brief and preliminary foray into the history of the critical months of revolution indicates, the role of the church and its members was far from passive: the spring of 1917 was a moment of new beginnings and new struggles, whose history forms an essential and inalienable chapter of the Revolution itself. Inevitably, the conciliar movement of the early 20th century was inscribed in the political struggle; at the same time, the congresses, large and small, sought to resolve genuine issues of dogma as well as of local and national administration, and evidenced an extraordinary degree of popular involvement and participation, as well as a diversity of perspectives. From the vantage point of the 21st century, when the Russian Orthodox Church in Exile and the Moscow Patriarchate have forged an uneasy reunion, it is clear that the theological debates and political conflicts engaged at the empire-wide diocesan congresses and culminating in the All-Russian Council of the Orthodox Church in 1917–18 provided an impetus for spiritual development over the intervening century. The theological debates in lay circles that began in the fin de siècle, the intensive work of on-the-ground reform of the months between February and October, and the experience of fragmentation and dissemination in "Orthodoxy Abroad" are all part of one story. This story holds a key to the difficult relation between politics and religion whose complexities we have only begun to explore.

---

[97] Jonathan Daly, "'Storming the Last Citadel': The Bolshevik Assault on the Church, 1922," in *The Bolsheviks in Russian Society: The Revolution and the Civil Wars,* ed. Vladimir Brovkin (New Haven: Yale University Press, 1997), 235–66.

Appendix

The Nizhnii Novgorod KODM's proposed electoral procedures and agenda items:[98]

Electoral Rules:

1. Urgent meetings [s˝ezdy] of parishioners to elect laity to the superintendents' assemblies.
2. Everyone is desired to participate, including women.
3. Delegates (or female delegates [delegatki]) are chosen in equal numbers as clergy, with a minimum age of 21.
4. A general superintendents' assembly is to be called at once.
5. The president of the assembly will not be the superintendent [blagochinnyi], but instead will be chosen by universal, secret, direct, and equal elections.
6. Presided over by the above, the assembly will choose 2 priests, 2 deacons or psalmists, and 2 laity.
7. Those who receive an absolute majority are considered elected.

Agenda:

A. For the church as a whole:
   1. Review canon law where it may not apply, e.g., with respect to the age of the deacon.
   2. Establish a conciliar [sobornaia] form of governance, i.e., diocesan, regional, and all-Russian councils.
   3. Church and State. Because the Provisional Government is well-behaved, there is no need to separate from it; "but the church must be free in its inner life and restore the ancient right of petitioning to the secular powers in matters of governance and society."
   4. Representatives of the church must participate in all government and social institutions.
   5. The clergy has equal civic rights with everyone else.
   6. The parish clergy and the parish have the right of a juridical entity [iuridicheskoe litso].
   7. Decentralization of clerical institutions regulating economic and educational life.
   8. Instructions for bishops and clergy must accord with canon law.
   9. "The restoration of relations among bishops, hierarchs, and priests to the way they were in the ancient apostolic church, and destruction of the spirit of despotism and secular domination prevalent beginning in the fourth century."

---

[98] Source: *NTsOV*, no. 11 (16 April 1917), 217–19.

10. Review of the liturgy and especially the role of the "archpriest bureaucrat" [*chinovnik*].

11. Reform of the ecclesiastical courts, with "the restoration of canonical judgment over bishops and clergy; the introduction of transparency [*glasnost'*] and principle of individual participation in a trial between two parties."

12. Bishops are to come from the white clergy.

13. Bishops are to be elected at the Regional Council.

14. Elected clerical officers cannot be removed except by court trial.

15. Proper compensation for clergy.

16. Bishops should be paid by the state treasury [*kazna*] or diocese, and should not use income from monasteries, archpriests' houses, or "the usual extraction of money on the side."

17. Discuss lay participation and an autonomous church commune.

18. The clergy is not responsible for illegal marriages.

19. Discuss divison of income among the parish's clergy.

20. Parish schools are the responsibility of the parish. The status of church schools is to be equalized with those of the state and others.

B. Local diocesan concerns:

21. Create a diocesan executive committee [*ispolkom*].

22. Re-elect consistory members and increase their numbers.

23. Resolve the question of a chancellery and secretariat at various levels.

24. Implement the principle of elections [*vybornoe nachalo*], and hold elections at the diocesan level.

25. Institute superindendents' committees instead of superintendents.

26. Create a court based on natural law [*sovestnyi sud*] for the clergy.

27. Set up investigative commissions and put them to work.

28. No marks for behavior.

29. Get rid of censorship of sermons.

30. Establish inter-parish communications.

31. Lay participation in congresses involving diocesan issues.

32. Create a superintendency for schools.

33. Various material (household) issues.

Cultural Heritage and "the People's Property": Museums in Russia, 1914–21

Susan Smith

During the early years of World War I, the artist and preservationist Nikolai Rerikh published several articles in Petrograd addressing different war-related threats faced by Russian antiquities and historic sites. He noted the German destruction and theft of artifacts from Belgium; reported rumors that Germans deported into Russia's central provinces were buying up Russian art and antiques at precisely the moment when many of those protecting the monuments were fighting the war; bemoaned the idea of building a railroad for military purposes that would mar views of Novgorod; and reminded his countrymen to look after the graves and memorials for earlier Russian heroes.[1] Rerikh was right to be worried; as scholars have long noted, the destruction and loss of Russian artifacts and art were extensive over the course of World War I and the subsequent civil war.

That these very threats and losses promoted a dramatic shift in the conceptualization of "cultural heritage" and the development of a massive museum network, however, has rarely been discussed. The upheaval of war made more urgent a growing European-wide sense that historic and artistic monuments, witnesses to the past worthy of study and appreciation—in Russian, *pamiatniki*—needed to be protected. The term *pamiatniki* corresponds to a narrow definition of "cultural heritage," the inherited material objects and the intangible ideas related to these objects that have been deemed to have collective value and that are, therefore, to be protected for future generations.[2] In Russia the threats, both foreign and domestic, to monuments interacted with war-related changes in class dynamics and politics to shift notions of

---

[1] These articles include N. K. Rerikh, "Beregite starinu," "Divinets," "Luven sozhzhen," and "Novgorodskim stroiteliam," in *Beregite starinu*, ed. E. B. Dement'eva (Moscow: Mezhdunarodnyi tsentr rerikhov, 1993), 47–50.

[2] The definition used here is based on the works of others, including UNESCO, ed., *The Protection of Movable Cultural Property I. Compendium of Legislative Texts* (Paris: UNESCO, 1984); David J. Murphy, *Plunder and Preservation: Cultural Property Law and Practice in the People's Republic of China* (Hong Kong: Oxford University Press, 1995); and Wayne Sandholtz, *Prohibiting Plunder: How Norms Change* (New York: Oxford University Press, 2007).

Russian Culture in War and Revolution, 1914–22, Book 1: Popular Culture, the Arts, and Institutions. Murray Frame, Boris Kolonitskii, Steven G. Marks, and Melissa K. Stockdale, eds. Bloomington, IN: Slavica Publishers, 2014, 403–23.

who was responsible for the country's cultural heritage. While these wartime developments were presumably not necessary for the dramatic growth in museums and their holdings of the Civil War years, they probably made Bolshevik policies of expropriation more palatable to the prerevolutionary museum organizers and amateur historians who helped carry out these policies, and who organized the new museums and reorganized the old to contend with the influx of objects deemed monuments. From 1914–21, Russian museums, as the public depositories and interpreters of such objects, promoted and benefited from the developing idea of cultural heritage and the corresponding notion that preservation is a duty of the modern state.

Indeed, in the years immediately after the October Revolution, Russia experienced a museum explosion—until the current museum explosion in China, likely the greatest the world had ever known.[3] According to one list based on materials from 1920, the number of museums still operating on Russian territory by the October Revolution was 213.[4] Forty-six of the museums were in Petrograd and 32 in Moscow. The provinces that were more economically advanced, defined as more industrialized and with more developed capitalism, were more likely than others to be home to several of the 135 local museums.[5] Of the 213, roughly 20 percent were historical and 12 percent artistic, while more than 16 percent addressed natural sciences and more than 25 percent were multidepartmental or "complex" museums of regional studies (kraevedcheskie muzei).[6] Although not all of them would survive for long, according to a similarly framed 1920 count, 246 museums were

---

[3] Holland Cotter, "A Building Boom as Chinese Art Rises in Stature," New York Times, 21 March 2013, http://www.nytimes.com/2013/03/21/arts/artsspecial/a-prosperous-china-goes-on-a-museum-building-spree.html?emc=eta1&_r=0.

[4] D. A. Ravikovich, Formirovanie gosudarstvennoi muzeinoi seti (1917–polovina 60-xx gg.). Nauchno-metodicheskie rekomendatsii (Moscow: Ministerstvo kul'tury RSFSR, Akademiia nauk SSSR, Nauchno-issledovatel'skii institut, 1988), 13. Ravikovich used the Russian borders of 1987 when he was writing.

[5] Ibid., 16. My own research focuses on one such region, Vladimir province, to the east of Moscow. Among other things, Vladimir's proximity to Moscow meant that the region's monuments were well known and of great importance to preservationists in the capitals, and that the impact of policy changes was felt relatively quickly.

[6] Those unaccounted for in these categories were mostly local museums apparently so unsystematically created as to be very difficult to classify. The list of 213 museums did not include the following: those museums whose existence could be "doubted due to a lack of hard evidence"; the regimental museums; a significant number of the handicraft and agricultural museums organized by zemstva; or the nearly 100 museums of visual aids designed for school teachers and students (Ravikovich, Formirovanie gosudarstvennoi muzeinoi seti, 14). Tamara P. Spiridonova found nearly 220 regimental museums. See her "Muzei voiskovykh chastei v dorevoliutsionnoi Rossii (Stanovlenie i istoriko-kul'turnoe znachenie)" (Candidate diss., Rossiiskii institut kul'turologii, 2005), 15–17.

founded in Russia between 1918 and 1920.[7] Overall, then, by the end of 1920, after a few closures, there were 457 museums in Russia of which 67 were in the Petrograd area, 83 in Moscow and the surrounding areas, 113 in the provincial capitals and 194 in the district cities.[8] Even the leading alternative count of museums, which identified significantly fewer than 213 museums operating by October 1917 and roughly 200 museums created between 1918 and 1920, found that the number of museums more than doubled in those three years.[9]

Due to Bolshevik expropriation policies designed to secure the material wealth of institutions, the upper classes, and the church, it is very likely that the vast majority of these new museums collected and displayed the materials—historical, archaeological, ethnographic, and artistic—that, at that time, in part because of the war, came to be considered part of the Russian cultural inheritance. The increased number of *pamiatniki* available in a greater number of locations made possible the expansion of the museum-going public and, for most viewers, presumably made more likely the acceptance of such an inheritance.

The Impact of World War I

Two discussions engaged the museum world in the years before the start of the war. The first, regarding the creation of a legal framework for the protection of antiquities, took place in the Duma and elite journals and built on long-running conversations.[10] The second was a growing professional discussion of museum practices, roles, and networks—the concerns of a nascent profession—that took place in sessions at national and regional archival, archaeological, and historical congresses and meetings, and at the 1912 Preparatory Congress for the Organizing of the First All-Russian Congress of Museum Workers. To the last, the Chairman of the Imperial Russian Historical Museum invited all historical, archaeological, church, and military museums in the Russian Empire to discuss problems such as insufficient funding, the lack of training for museum workers, the loss to museums in the capitals of items found in the provinces, and the absence of agreed upon means for the

---

[7] Ravikovich, *Formirovanie gosudarstvennoi muzeinoi seti*, 26.

[8] Ibid., 37. Despite these numbers, materials on Russian museums from 1914–16 are difficult to come by. Even Geraldine Norman's "biography" of the Hermitage mentions the war before 1917 only in passing. Geraldine Norman, *The Hermitage: The Biography of a Great Museum* (New York: Fromm International Publishing, 1997).

[9] V. K. Gardanov, "Muzeinoe stroitel'stvo i okhrana pamiatnikov kul'tury v pervye gody Sovetskoi vlasti," in *Istoriia muzeinogo dela v SSSR: Sbornik statei. Trudy NII muzeevedeniia*, vyp. 1 (Moscow: Gos. izd-vo kul'turno-prosvetitel'noi literatury 1957), 29–30.

[10] For example, see the coverage dating from 1909 in the journal *Starye gody: Ezhemesiachnik dlia liubitelei iskusstva i stariny.*

categorization, restoration, and conservation of objects.[11] The participants also discussed means for promoting a shared consciousness, including the creation of a museum bureau, the publication of a journal specifically for museums, and conferences, such as the First All-Russian Congress scheduled for Christmas break in early 1915.[12] Unfortunately, the war intervened and the Congress never met. For the participants in this conversation, World War I, and particularly German destruction of the historical centers of Louvain and Rheims—despite Article 56 of the Hague Convention protecting historic monuments and works of art —made the risks to cultural heritage much more immediate, and the broader importance of museums and preservation much clearer.[13]

Unsurprisingly, during the war, the experiences and responses of Russian museums varied according to their circumstances—location in relation to the front; the space demands of their particular towns for war-related purposes; and the draft eligibility, professions, and, occasionally, the political beliefs of their organizers. All museums would suffer some shortages and logistical difficulties and even those museums far from the frontlines experienced up-heaval. In the Far East, for example, Chita's museum was closed in order to house in its buildings 500 men wounded at the front.[14] Regardless of whether their museums were closed to the public, organizers and activists attempted to continue their preservation and cultural activities, sometimes even protecting others' objects. The Kremlin Armory, for example, housed objects evacuated from Poland, as well as objects from Romania, western and southern Russian provinces, and Petrograd's palaces.[15] Finally, some museums raised funds for suffering soldiers, as did the Museum of Baron Stieglitz when it hosted a

---

[11] Representatives from some art institutions, including the Academy of Art, attended the congress, but natural science, technical, craft (*kustar*), and pedagogical museums were not represented.

[12] "Protokol pervago zasedaniia Predvaritel'nogo s"ezda deiatelei muzeev," in *Predvaritel'nyi s"ezd po ustroistvu pervogo vserossiiskogo s"edza deiatelei muzeev* (Moscow: Postavshchik dvora Ego Velichestva tovarishchesto skoropechatii A. A. Levenson, 1913), 17 and 24; Khristina Tur'inskaia and K. P. Kalinovskaia, *Muzeinoe delo v Rossii v 1907–1936 gody* (Moscow: Institut etnologii i antropologii RAN, 2001), 36.

[13] "Laws of War: Laws and Customs of War on Land (Hague II): July 29, 1899," in *Treaties and Other International Agreements of the United States of America, 1776–1949* (Washington, DC: Government Printing Office, 1968), available at http://avalon.law.yale.edu/19th_century/hague02.asp.

[14] L. V. Korneva, *U istokov muzeinogo dela na Dal'nem Vostoke Rossii* (Khabarovsk: Ministerstvo kul'tury Khabarovskogo kraia, Khabarovskii kraevoi kraevedcheskoi muzei im. N. I. Grodekova, 2002), 143.

[15] E. I. Smirnova, "Moskovskii kreml'," in *Bol'shaia Rossiiskaia entsiklopediia muzeev, chastnykh sobranii i kollektsii*, ed. V. L. Ianin et al. (Moscow: Ripol klassik, 2009), 382.

benefit exhibit of church antiquities for which tickets were sold to thousands of visitors.[16]

Although some museums collected materials relating to the war and there were temporary exhibits of war trophies, at a time when museums could have helped more explicitly to mobilize popular patriotism, there is little evidence that many non-military museums propagandized the history of Russian military heroes or the victories of Russian armed forces.[17] A museum dedicated to Russian military glory—organized in 1913 in Tsarskoe Selo with materials and funds given by Elena Tret'iakova to Nicholas II in 1911—was transformed into a museum about World War I when both Tret'iakova and the Artillery Museum supplemented the collection with war trophies displayed in a 1915 trophy exhibit at the Admiralty. The museum opened in February 1917 but closed in 1918.[18] At least one group outside of the capitals, the Society for Archaeology, History, and Ethnography at Kazan' University, attempted to create a museum on World War I, albeit unsuccessfully.[19] The seemingly general absence in non-military museums of exhibits that unambiguously promoted the war effort may have been a result of the brief duration of what Aaron Cohen refers to as "public patriotism." Cohen found that during the first months of the war, "a complex visual culture of war diffused throughout the public and society" but that when it had become clear that the war would not be short, this "public patriotism" declined and life returned to "normal" with the war becoming a subject to avoid.[20]

---

[16] "Otrazheniia voiny," *Starye gody: Ezhemesiachnik dlia liubitelei iskusstva i stariny*, June 1915, 49.

[17] Melissa Kirschke Stockdale, "United in Gratitude: Honoring Soldiers and Defining the Nation in Russia's Great War," *Kritika: Explorations in Russian and Eurasian History* 7, 3 (2006): 470.

[18] S. Ia. Lastochkin and Iu. F. Rubezhanskii, *Tsarskoe selo—rezidentsiia rossiiskikh monarkhov: Arkhitekturnyi i voenno-istoricheskii ocherk* (St. Petersburg: Voennyi inzhenerno-tekhnicheskii universitet, 1998), 198. There is some confusion regarding the dates when this museum operated although it appears that it closed no later than 1919. Interestingly, this project has been revived and what will be Russia's only museum dedicated to World War I is to be opened in Tsarskoe Selo in 2014. "Rekonstruktsiia, restavratsiia, tekhnicheskoe pereosnashchenie i prisposoblenie Ratnoi palaty dlia muzeinogo ispol'zovania" and "Ratnaia palata," Gosudsarstvennyi muzei-zapovednik Tsarskoe Selo, http://tzar.ru/science/restoration/upcoming/martial_chamber and http://www.tzar.ru/museums/palaces/alexander_park/landscape_park/martial_chamber (accessed 2 October 2012).

[19] M. I. Burlykina, *Universitetskie muzei dorevoliutsionnoi Rossii (XVIII–pervaia chetvert' XX vv.)* (Syktyvkar: Syktyvkarskii gosudarstvennyi universitet, Rossiiskii institut kul'turologii, 1996), 158.

[20] Aaron J. Cohen, *Imagining the Unimaginable: World War, Modern Art, and the Politics of Public Culture in Russia, 1914–1917* (Lincoln: University of Nebraska Press, 2008),

The most common direct contribution to the war made by museums that remained open seems to have been offering themselves as places of respite. Indeed, the war appears to have accelerated the democratization of the museum experience of the late 19th and early 20th centuries, a phenomenon experienced elsewhere as well.[21] As *Apollon,* a leading art journal, commented in 1915, "Never has such a democratic public visited museums, it seems, as now." The following year the journal reported that nearly 20 percent of the visitors to the Hermitage were convalescing soldiers, presumably including many from the hospital in the Winter Palace next door.[22] The February Revolution continued and apparently deepened this trend, bringing even more members of the lower classes into the museums. That they were often first-time museum visitors was clear from their behavior.

> The Petrograd soldiers, anxious to instruct themselves and occupy the leisure that the revolution has given them, are great visitors to the museums. Their anxiety to investigate everything leads them to pass their hands over the pictures and caress the statuary (often marking it with their nails). Notices have been put [up] begging comrades to touch nothing.[23]

A few new museums even managed to open during the war—among them the Azov City Museum and that of Perm' University—offering new cultural destinations to all classes.[24]

The February Revolution

If the start of the war witnessed the closure of some museums and slackened the pace of work in others, the fall of the monarchy in February 1917 and

---

87–88, 93.

[21] As Frederic Lucas, the director of the Brooklyn Museum, suggested in 1907, "this museum of today is a great deal more than a place where objects are merely preserved, it is an educational institution on a large scale, whose language may be understood by all, an ever open book whose pages appeal not only to the scholar but even to the man who cannot read." Frederic A. Lucas, "Purposes and Aims of Modern Museums," in *Museum Origins: Readings in Early Museum History and Philosophy,* ed. Hugh H. Genoways and Mary Anne Andrei (Walnut Creek, CA: Left Coast Press, 2008), 58.

[22] Cohen, *Imagining the Unimaginable,* 93.

[23] Correspondents of the Associated Press, "Queer Stories of New Russia: Elementary Mentality of the Masses Demonstrated by Amusing Examples," *New York Times,* 30 September 1917.

[24] E. A. Shulepova, *Regional'noe nasledie: Opyt izucheniia i muzeefikatsii pamiatnikov Dona* (Moscow: Ministerstvo kul'tury Rossiiskoi Federatsii, Rossiiskaia Akademiia nauk, Rossiiskii institut kul'turologii, 1998), 89; Burlykina, *Universitetskie muzei,* 126.

the increasing radicalization of much of the population meant that political questions sometimes overshadowed scholarly and preservationist concerns. Although political differences among the organizers apparently led to the closure in February 1917 of the Blagoveshchensk Museum in Amur province in the Far East, for example, problems resulting from the revolution unsurprisingly had the greatest impact on collections tied to the royal family.[25] For the Russian Museum, created as a state institution to serve as a "living remembrance" of Alexander III, the start of the war had made little difference, but the fall of the monarchy led to major changes, particularly the closure of art exhibit halls for reorganization.[26] The museum's ethnographic division remained open, but it too had new problems beyond the general disruption caused by the war of networks abroad and at home for the exchange and acquisition of ethnographic objects.[27] According to correspondents from the Associated Press reporting from Petrograd at the end of September,

> The founder and curator of the "Ethnographic" Museum recounts that his staff (caretakers, cleaners, & c.) has petitioned the Government for the suppression of his office, on the ground that a curator is useless in a museum, that he does nothing, costs money, and is of no service, as they who carry the keys, wield the feather brooms, and clean the floors are the real curators.[28]

While this curator struggled with his newly empowered staff, his counterparts in the Hermitage—closed due to unrest after the February events—were clearly worried about their own staff; they began speaking to one another in French and German in order to discuss sensitive topics around the gallery attendants.[29] Like those working with the Russian Museum's art collection and at the Marble Palace, these curators prepared for the first evacuation of valuable works on the night of 29–30 September. Riga, less than 500 kilometers from Petrograd, had fallen to the Germans in early September, intensi-

---

[25] Korneva, U istokov muzeinogo dela, 143.

[26] E. V. Basner, "Nachalo," in Iz istorii muzeia: Sbornik statei i publikatsii, ed. N. N. Dubovitskaia and A. L. Saminskii (St. Petersburg: Gosudarstvennyi Russkii muzei, 1995), 24; V. A. Aseev, "Russkii muzei, 1908–1922," in Iz istorii muzeia, 38.

[27] I. I. Shangina, Russkii fond etnograficheskikh muzeev Moskvy i Sankt-Peterburga: Istoriia i problemy komplektovaniia, 1867–1930 gg. (St. Petersburg: Ministerstvo kul'tury Rossiiskoi Federatsii, Rossiiskii etnograficheskii muzei, 1994), 71.

[28] Correspondents of the Associated Press, "Queer Stories."

[29] S. Varshavskii and B. Rest, Riadom s zimnim (Leningrad: Sovetskii khudozhnik, 1969), 78.

fying concerns about the imminent German threat to the capital's cultural treasures.[30]

Unfortunately, the German menace had domestic counterparts with regards to cultural heritage: benign neglect, concealment, sales, export, theft, vandalism, and destruction. As Douglas Smith makes clear, the fall of the monarchy led to extensive destruction of noble property in the countryside, which, for many terrified nobles, brought back memories of the violence after the 1905 Revolution. During the brief tenure of the Provisional Government, large numbers of significant objects left the country or simply disappeared, accelerating a process that dated from the beginning of the war.[31] Preservationists throughout the country, including leading cultural figures in the capitals, drew the new government's attention to this issue although the authorities generally did little.

The archival materials for the Provisional Government in Vladimir province suggest that, despite the creation of cultural-enlightenment committees, the provincial representatives of the Provisional Government did not prioritize such concerns—a situation most likely found everywhere. Rather, they dealt with strikes, struggled to find sufficient supplies of basic items, and focused on arresting high-ranking imperial officials and revolutionaries.[32] Like their counterparts in other regions, the museum activists, in this case the Vladimir Archival Commission organizers, did what they could. In their July appeal to the residents of the region, they offered those unable or unwilling to care for their objects space in which to keep them.

> People of Vladimir! In the difficult year through which our Fatherland is living today, the Vladimir Learned Archival Commission turns to you with a fervent plea: care for our artistic and historic monuments! Danger threatens them on all sides, from our external enemies and from our own carelessness and from ignorance, and from maliciously self-interested people. Damage or destruction of each such object causes irreparable harm not only to its actual owner, but to all of us, the entire Russian people, all of our Fatherland, for a work of art or historical monument is the property of the whole country, [it] has state

---

[30] See, for example, Rerikh's call to action from 1915 ("Beregite starinu"). For more on the evacuations from the Hermitage, see Norman, *The Hermitage*, 142.

[31] Douglas Smith, *Former People: The Final Days of the Russian Aristocracy* (New York: Farrar, Straus and Giroux, 2012), chap. 6; I. E. Grabar', *Moia zhizn': Avtomonografiia. Etiudy o khudozhnikakh* (Moscow: Izd-vo "Respublika," 2001), 262.

[32] Gosudarstvennyi arkhiv Vladimirskoi oblasti (GAVO) f. 1186 (Vladimir Provincial Committee of the Provisional Government), op. 2.

value. [Monuments] should be preserved as sacred objects—no matter whether they will remind us of light or dark pages of our history.[33]

The objects listed were diverse, but they were all rhetorically transformed from private property into public or national property. While Krista Sigler has argued that the Provisional Government failed, in part, due to its inconsistent record in defending private property rights, in the case of monuments, the transformation of privately-held items and structures into the people's property had already begun. This trend was not unique to Russia, as indicated by the 1913 French law requiring the registration of private objects designated of national value.[34]

In a 1915 review of the aforementioned Stieglitz Museum exhibit, the archaeologist Nikolai E. Makarenko raised other reasons for treating cultural artifacts as public property. He argued that objects in church and monastery vestries and depositories, such as those then on exhibit, should be available for everyone to view precisely because "over many years and centuries many [such] artworks were created from metal, minted, written and embroidered at the expense of the people." Although the objects had been made by master craftsmen and used by people who deeply believed in their meanings and appreciated their craftsmanship, attitudes had changed, leaving these artworks

> like old invalids, to spend their days in dark, musty vestries, that are, in the majority of cases, poorly maintained.... The objects of the vestries are state property, not private property, therefore the place of their depositing [is] the museum. There they will be available for the use of the country and science, a benefit not material ... but spiritual, [a benefit] immeasurably greater.

Such objects had been insufficiently studied by art historians and, therefore, could be of use to both science and to the country; accordingly, they should be placed in public museums, whether civic or clerical.[35] Clearly, with so many objects held by churches, monasteries, and lay religious organizations, such arguments had ramifications beyond this one exhibit.

The rhetorical transformation of private property into public accelerated at least partially as a result of the climate created by the war and the resulting blows

---

[33] Vladimirskaia uchenaia arkhivnaia komissiia, "Vozzvanie," *Staryi Vladimirets* (1917): 3–4.

[34] Krista Sigler, "The Kshesinskaia Mansion: Elite Culture and the Politics of Modernity in Revolutionary Russia" (Ph.D. diss., University of Cincinnati, 2009); UNESCO, *The Protection of Movable Cultural Property I. Compendium of Legislative Texts*, 121–34.

[35] N. E. Makarenko, "Vystavka tserkovnoi stariny v muzee barona Shtiglitsa," *Starye gody: Ezhemesiachnik dlia liubitelei iskusstva i stariny*, July–August 1915, 73.

to the monarchy and then the Provisional Government. The war mobilized adults of all classes, and many people believed these contributions deserved a return. Some scholars believe the war heightened individuals' identification to the community, rather than the state, developing what Hubertus Jahn has termed a patriotism "of social consciousness and philanthropy" that increasingly emphasized ethnic identity.[36] At the same time, the war's negative impact on everyday life on the domestic front promoted what Boris Kolonitskii has referred to as "anti-'burzhui' consciousness"—a distrust of those actually or potentially better-off, who appeared to have put their own interests above those of others.[37] This was a volatile and confusing mixture, as suggested by the above appeal to residents of Vladimir; if an owner was capable and willing to protect his property (the monument in question) he would be thanked for fulfilling his duty, but, if he was not, the property belonged with the community. The Bolsheviks would take the argument further: no individual or institution had the right to hold onto such property because the simple fact of ownership of the monument suggested that the individual could not be trusted.

Why Did the Bolsheviks Preserve Monuments?

As Aleksandr Mosiakin and Sean McMeekin have shown, claiming but not destroying property meant that the state was grabbing assets that were potentially liquid on international markets. Indeed, Mosiakin has made a largely convincing argument that critical decrees limiting exportation and later calling for expropriation resulted from the new authorities' fiscal needs. As he has shown, financial crises in 1918, including the need to pay reparations to the Germans after the Russians pulled out of the war at Brest-Litovsk, and the famine of the early 1920s led to the sale of tens of thousands of expropriated objects.[38] Given the Bolsheviks' then tenuous grip on power and the general economic and social problems in the country, it is all the more surprising that the regime turned its attention not just to expropriation, the *taking* of private property, but also to appropriation, the process of *making this property its own*. After October, responsibility for cultural heritage came to reside with the state, the professed defender of the interests of the masses. Accordingly, appropriation took place in new frameworks of meaning, most

---

[36] Hubertus F. Jahn, *Patriotic Culture in Russia during World War I* (Ithaca, NY: Cornell University Press, 1995), 148–49 and 74–75.

[37] Boris Kolonitskii, "Antibourgeois Propaganda and Anti-'Burzhui' Consciousness in 1917," *Russian Review* 53, 2 (April 1994): 183–96.

[38] Aleksandr Mosiakin, "Antikvarnyi eksportnyi fond," *Nashe nasledie*, no. 3 (1991): 35–47; Sean McMeekin, *History's Greatest Heist: The Looting of Russia by the Bolsheviks* (New Haven: Yale University Press, 2009).

clearly articulated through rhetoric that reflected the Marxist war against the upper classes and the church.[39]

Through their early administrative steps, the Bolsheviks who made policy and who were concerned with preservation—and this was by no means all of them—demonstrated that they knew whom to approach from among the educated classes of the prerevolutionary period and that they shared with those individuals an appreciation for material culture, and a belief in its power to elicit emotional connections and to make history tangible. The Bolsheviks also developed the mechanisms—albeit more frequently on paper than in reality—to preserve cultural monuments. Moreover, they appeared to be doing so in ways that the prerevolutionary activists themselves desired, most immediately by issuing preservation laws and creating a museum and preservation infrastructure. When possible the new authorities made available scarce manpower, funds, and vehicles to the newly appointed preservation and museum workers. In 1919 Lunacharskii referred to prerevolutionary activists among these preservation authorities as "angels, who, with the help of intelligent peasants and workers" kept an eye on the treasures that were public property even in the farthest reaches of the country.[40] Of course, not all of the prerevolutionary museum and cultural figures were willing, or hungry enough, to label such treasures as the people's property and work with the new authorities, as recalcitrant organizers in Novgorod and other cities made clear.[41]

Most prerevolutionary museum activists were concerned with particular forms of identity—whether regional, ethnic or civic. The Bolsheviks, however, were primarily concerned with class identity and believed that the assets seized (expropriated) and protected, put to proper use and correctly interpreted (appropriated), could and should be used to raise class "consciousness" among the masses. The utility in such a scheme of making public such conspicuous examples of wealth and power as the Hermitage and Winter Palace was immediately apparent. Although it did not prevent the Hermitage staff from joining the boycott of the new regime by civil servants, the Bolsheviks declared both buildings state museums on 30 October 1917.[42]

---

[39] For a fuller examination of expropriation and appropriation, see Susan N. Smith, "The Accidental Museum: Expropriating and Appropriating the Past," *Russian Review* 67, 3 (July 2008): 438–53.

[40] Ravikovich, *Formirovanie gosudarstvennoi muzeinoi seti*, 29.

[41] N. G. Porfiridov, *Novgorod, 1917–1941. Vospominaniia* (Leningrad: Lenizdat, 1987), 60–61. Nikolai Porfiridov recalled how the old leadership of the museum, regional officials that had made up the core of the Society of Lovers of Antiquity, responded to the official act of transfer of the museum to the Division of Public Education by reading a prepared statement about the act's illegality before leaving the April 1918 meeting en masse. The collection's keeper also left.

[42] Norman, *The Hermitage*, 156.

While examining the luxurious property of the royal family or the wealthy, the lower classes would viscerally understand that the wealth they had generated could have been better distributed. In other words, collecting and displaying objects allowed the Bolsheviks to wage class warfare financially by denying owners the ability to dispose of their objects, and psychologically by utilizing the items to propagandize their own cause. The use of museums as instruments for the collection, preservation, and use of these objects was good Marxist practice for another reason as well: it served as a base on which proletarian culture could be built.

Indeed, in Soviet historiography, the most frequently mentioned reason for preservation of cultural heritage was the Leninist notion that the proletariat must build on the best of the past, a position laid out by Lenin in October 1920 in "On Proletarian Culture."[43] This position spoke against the spontaneous acts of destruction taking place around the country and was directed against the Proletkul't and others who called for the cultural slate to be wiped clean.[44] In determining the fate of buildings and physical objects they themselves designated as significant, the Bolsheviks demonstrated who was in control to those both inside and outside the country. Yet, as Nikolai I. Ruban reminds us, in the more contested areas during the Civil War, such as the Russian Far East, where museums struggled through various regimes simply to preserve the network created before the revolution, gaining control could take the Bolsheviks several years.[45]

Organizing the Museum Network

On 25 October 1917 the Petrograd Military-Revolutionary Committee appointed commissars for the protection of art collections and museums.[46] In the immediate aftermath of that day's events, the new cultural authorities formed preservation collegia in Petrograd and then in Moscow, and eventually created parallel organizations throughout the country. When the capital was moved in March 1918, the Moscow collegium—renamed in late May the Central Division for Museum Affairs and the Protection of Monuments of Art

---

[43] V. I. Lenin, "On Proletarian Culture," in *V. I. Lenin: Selected Works*, ed. Institut Marksizma-Leninizma pri TsK KPSS (Moscow: Progress Publishers, 1971), 484–85.

[44] For a brief summary of this debate, see Richard Stites, *Revolutionary Dreams: Utopian Vision and Experimental Life in the Russian Revolution* (New York: Oxford University Press, 1989), chap. 3, particularly 68–72.

[45] N. I. Ruban, *Sovetskaia vlast' i muzeinoe stroitel'stvo na dal'nem vostoke Rossii (1920–1930-e gg.)* (Khabarovsk: Ministerstvo kul'tury pravitel'stva Khabarovskogo kraia, Khabarovskii kraevoi kraevedcheskii muzei im. N. I. Grodekova, 2002), 42–43.

[46] L. N. Godunova, "Organy upravleniia muzeinym delom v SSSR, 1917–1941 gg.," in *Muzeinoe delo v SSSR: Muzeinoe stroitel'stvo v SSSR. Sbornik nauchnykh trudov* (Moscow: Ministerstvo kul'tury SSSR, Tsentral'nyi muzei revoliutsii SSSR, 1989), 13.

and Antiquity—became responsible for the country's artistic and historical monuments, whether structures or objects. Throughout the country, in the areas under Bolshevik control, bureaucratic changes in Moscow were replicated in the provinces. As already suggested, these regional collegia, later subdivisions, were too understaffed, underfunded, and educationally and experientially underprepared to deal effectively with the expropriation process and the resulting influx of objects. Expedient and partial solutions to these shortcomings included the creation of the National Museum Fund, for which the authorities in Moscow were ultimately responsible and to which all museum collections technically belonged; the convocation in February 1919 of the First All-Russian Conference on Museum Affairs to continue prewar conversations; and the increasing circulation of works such as Igor' E. Grabar"s *For What Purpose Do We Need to Protect and Collect Treasures of Art and Antiquity*, designed to bridge the enormous gap between ideal and actual museum practices.[47] All of these mechanisms addressed, if not necessarily in ways that the prerevolutionary activists would have preferred, the concerns of preservationists and, by increasing the standardization of museum practices, made the work of these and other untrained and ideologically unsound museum employees easier for a nervous state to guide and monitor.[48]

Such steps towards professionalization were particularly important given the museum explosion of the immediate postwar years. Two Soviet museum researchers, D. A. Ravikovich and V. K. Gardanov, published tallies, noted earlier, of the number of museums in Russia before the October Revolution and by the end of 1920. Although their numbers vary widely, both found that the number of museums within Russia more than doubled between 1918 and 1920. As Gardanov noted, the "organization of museums in such remote corners [of Soviet Russia] is the most striking fact in the development of museum affairs in these years."[49] Indeed, Ravikovich found that 186 of the 246 new museums created from 1918–20 were located outside of the capitals, so that by the end of

---

[47] Division of Written Sources of the State Historical Museum (GIM) f. 54 (Museum Division of Glavnauka of People's Commissariat of Enlightenment), op. 1, d. 17, l. 55; I. E. Grabar', *Dlia chego nado okhraniat' i sobirat' sokrovishcha iskusstva i stariny* (Moscow: Komitet po okhrane khudozhestvennykh sokrovishch pri Sovete vserossiiskikh kooperativnykh s"ezdov, Tipo-litografiia T-va I. N. Kushnerev, 1919), 28. Grabar' was a leading prerevolutionary preservationist and cultural figure who worked extensively with the Bolsheviks.

[48] The frequency of state questionnaires makes this nervousness clear. See, for example, the answers from 14 different expropriation commissions in Gosudarstvennyi arkhiv Rossiiskoi Federatsii (GARF) f. a. 353 (Commissariat of Justice), op. 4, d. 417. For more on issues of professionalization, see Susan N. Smith, "Museum Practices and Notions of the Local in a Provincial Russian Museum, 1898–1935" (Ph.D. diss., University of Washington, 2005), chaps. 4–6.

[49] Ravikovich, *Formirovanie gosudarstvennoi muzeinoi seti*, 13–14, 26 and 37; Gardanov, "Muzeinoe stroitel'stvo," 29–30. Gardanov, whose criteria were unstated, found 151

1920, 307 of the 457 museums he counted were in the provinces. Of these, 113 museums were located in provincial capitals and 194 in the district capitals; in other words, they were all in administrative seats. Due to the preponderance of noble estates and monasteries in European Russia, most of these new museums would have been in European Russia and would have included at least some man-made objects that were considered *pamiatniki*.[50]

As the number of museums, objects in state hands, and museum employees grew, bureaucratic ties and oversight became more extensive. In 1921, perhaps because Bolshevik victory in the Civil War was assured and "the period of collecting" was winding down, there occurred the last bureaucratic adjustment of significance until the end of the 1920s. All non-pedagogical museums within the purview of the Commissariat of Enlightenment were concentrated into one agency, Glavmuzei. Each provincial subdivision was replaced with a *gubmuzei*, or a "Provincial Committee for Museum Affairs and the Protection of Monuments of Art, Antiquity, People's Everyday Life, and Nature." Among other tasks, each *gubmuzei* was to determine and coordinate the activities of each institution under its authority; oversee the work of district museum authorities; protect works of art and monuments of everyday life, history, and nature; undertake archaeological digs; organize enlightenment work such as exhibits, lectures, congresses, and excursions; and produce scholarly and popular literature.[51]

Expropriating and Collecting

Following the October Revolution, "class warfare" had a direct impact on museum affairs through the nationalization of land and structures and the logistical challenges resulting from the expropriation of objects. The concept of class warfare, however, also mirrored and could serve to justify destructive and brutal behavior by the masses, useful to the new regime in its destruction of the upper classes, but difficult to rein in when so desired. It comes as no surprise that the notion that "significant" objects had become public property and were worthy of protection was frequently unrealized despite having been promoted from the very first moments of the revolution. In some cases, such as that of Dmitrii P. Riabushinskii's Moscow home, destruction and theft by soldiers during the "Red Terror" led to the flight of the owners and to the

---

museums in existence at the end of 1917 and over 200 new museums founded between 1918 and 1920.

[50] Ravikovich, *Formirovanie gosudarstvennoi muzeinoi seti*, 38–39.

[51] GAVO f. r-1826 (Vladimir-Suzdal' History, Art, and Architecture Museum Reserve), op. 1, d. 8, ll. 1–3ob.

loss of their collections.[52] Although Aleksei V. Morozov's home was officially under the protection of the Moscow preservation authorities, anarchists destroyed or damaged many of its contents and hung their black flags on its exterior walls.[53] Clearly the new authorities were not always able or willing to control their ostensible followers; nor could they be everywhere at once.

Accepting the impossibility of physically removing monuments from their settings, placing them elsewhere and caring for them, in autumn 1918 the new regime issued decrees preventing the moving or disposal of monuments and then requiring that monuments be registered.[54] Just as the activists of the Vladimir Learned Archival Commission effectively acknowledged the nationalization of the museum they had built, individual owners were to become complicit in the loss of their property. The important 5 October 1918 decree "On the Registration, Cataloging, and Protection of Monuments of Art and Antiquity in the Possession of Individuals, Societies, and Establishments" gave owners one month from its publication to notify the appropriate local authorities that they possessed monuments and to provide a list of objects to either the appropriate provincial or central authorities. If registered objects were threatened with poor care or other hazards, the decree mandated their transfer for safekeeping to state preservation organs. Anyone who did not comply with the decree would be "held responsible to the full extent of revolutionary law up to the confiscation of all of their property and the deprivation of freedom."[55]

In this and related decrees, and in those targeting the church, the terms "monument" and "all-state significance" were vaguely defined; whether this was unintentional or deliberate is unknown.[56] Nevertheless, the flexibility of the terms best served the state's financial and ideological goals, since the

---

[52] Iu. A. Petrov, *Dinastiia Riabushinskikh* (Moscow: Russkaia kniga, 1997), 173–74. McMeekin provides a good overview of the looting of private property not held in banks (*History's Greatest Heist*, 35–53).

[53] "Anarkhisty," *Apollon*, no. 8–10 (1917): 113–14.

[54] See, for example, "Dekret Soveta narodnykh komissarov o zapreshchenii vyvoza za granitsu predmetov iskusstva," 19 September 1918.

[55] GAVO f. r-1048 (Division of Public Education of the Executive Committee of the Vladimir Uezd Soviet of Workers, Peasants, and Soldiers Deputies), op. 1, d. 12, ll. 84–84ob. ("O registratsii, prieme ne uchet i okhranenii pamiatnikov iskusstva i stariny, nakhodiashchikhsia vo vladenii chastnykh lits, obshchestv i uchrezhdenii," 5 October 1918); G. A. Kuzina, "Gosudarstvannaia politika v oblasti muzeinogo dela v 1917–1941 gg," in *Muzei i vlast': Gosudarstvennaia politika v olbasti muzeinogo dela (XVIII–XX vv.)*, ed. S. A. Kasparinskaia (Moscow: Nauchno-issledovatel'skii institut kul'tury, 1991), 114.

[56] GARF f. a-2307 (Main Administration of Scientific, Scientific-Artistic, and Museum Institutions and Institutions for the Protection of Nature of the People's Commissariat of Public Enlightenment/Glavnauka RSFSR), op. 3, d. 2, l. 5ob.

government could alter the relative status and significance of objects when the need arose. Provincial authorities issued parallel decrees, examined and sometimes took collections in their provinces, and passed information (or did not) up the chain. Most of the new items that these authorities dealt with came from four types of expropriation—those from institutions or organizations, such as archival commissions and other learned bodies; from the church; from noble estates; and from private individuals, the type of expropriation least likely to present the state with rivals for the objects.[57]

The results of expropriation in Vladimir province provide a sense of the scale of change in museum holdings in a region with a large number of wealthy noble estates and monasteries. At the time of the revolution, the collection of the Vladimir Historical Museum contained roughly 5,200 objects. The collections in the town of Vladimir with which the prerevolutionary organizers and new authorities were most familiar entered the collection first, a presumably typical start to the expropriation process. By the beginning of summer 1918, this had resulted in the confiscation of a sizeable percentage of the nearly 3,500 items and object sets in Vladimir. Nearly a quarter of those items came from the collection of church artifacts belonging to the lay Brotherhood of Aleksandr Nevskii, since the January decree separating church from state had transformed the property of the church and religious organizations into that of the people.[58] In 1919 and 1920, over 1,700 objects entered the Historical Museum's collection, including the collection confiscated earlier by the Cheka from the former Provincial Noble Assembly and the most important objects from the 12th-century Dmitrievskii and Uspenskii Cathedrals.[59] Moreover, even though decrees of November 1917 and January 1918 stipulated that historic relics located in Russia were to be returned to Poland and Ukraine, the Vladimir museum acquired objects that had been evacuated in 1914 from the western provinces and stored in the Rozhdestvenskii Monastery down the

---

[57] As Daniel Sherman points out, French revolutionary decrees ranging from the nationalization of church property in November 1789 to the official confiscation of the property of émigrés in November 1791 forced the new authorities to protect "a cultural patrimony gravely threatened by vandalism." Daniel J. Sherman, *Worthy Monuments: Art Museums and the Politics of Culture in Nineteenth-Century France* (Cambridge, MA: Harvard University Press, 1989), 99, 101, and 103.

[58] GIM f. 54, op. 1, d. 681 (Documents of the Vladimir Historical Museum, 1918–23), ll. 60–65ob., 28 April 1920. Arkhiv Vladimiro-Suzdal'skogo muzeia-zapovednika (VSMZ) f. 420 (Materials on the history of the museum reserve), n.p. VSMZ f. 2096 (Museum affairs in Vladimir province in the first years of Soviet power), l. 4.

[59] GIM f. 54, op. 1, d. 681, ll. 60–65ob.; GAVO f. r-1826, op. 1, d. 4, ll. 13–13ob. In fact, the Dmitrievskii Cathedral itself came under the Vladimir subdivision's purview at this time. Alisa Aksenova, "Khronika zhizni 'Muzeia-skital'tsa'," in *Zhivaia istoriia: Pamiatniki i muzei Vladimiro-Suzdal'skogo istoriko-arkhitekturnogo i khudozhestvennogo muzeia-zapovednika*, ed. T. A. Kniazeva (Moscow: Pamiatniki otechestva, 2000), 49–50.

street.[60] It is thus unsurprising that the first item on the museum's working plan for 1920 was locating more space for storage and display, a problem that became significantly worse in 1921 when another 3,851 objects entered the collection.

The Vladimir museum authorities did not have much time to process, organize, or utilize these materials, nor did they always succeed in getting to the objects first. Some expropriations, such as those at the province's wealthiest monastery, Spaso-Evfimiev, had been spurred on by theft by unknown parties. In cases where museum personnel were particularly concerned about objects disappearing or being threatened with damage, they occasionally searched for objects in markets or purchased objects directly from their owners. In other words, sometimes the authorities treated objects like private property in order to guarantee that they became public property.[61]

The distinction between private property and public good could be muddied in other ways as well. The authorities occasionally allowed former owners, such as Dmitrii G. Burylin in Ivanovo, to continue working with their expropriated collections. Predictably, such arrangements could prove problematic; the Ivanovo authorities eventually released Burylin from his obligations because he had continued to use museum items for his own purposes.[62] In other cases as well, prerevolutionary museum organizers tried to continue treating their collections as private property while ostensibly recognizing the state's right to them. For example, Julia Fein found that members of the Irkutsk Section of the Geographic Society appeared to be working with the regional authorities, who claimed ownership of the museum they had created, while simultaneously and successfully asking the central authorities to allow them to keep the museum. When the regional authorities ignored the central authorities, society members took museum objects home for safekeeping and were denounced and sued accordingly.[63]

Central, regional, and local authorities wrangled for the spoils not just amongst themselves but also with local populations who were not the prerevolutionary owners of objects. This happened in Vladimir province at the Vorontsov-Dashkov estate, Andreevskoe, home to a famous collection of portraits of political and military figures. Surprisingly—given the fact that the estate peasants had, for reasons we can only guess at, thwarted its attempt to sneak items out of the region in April 1919—the Central Division for Museum Affairs and the Protection of Monuments of Art and Antiquity suggested (unsuccessfully) 13 months later that the estate should be considered

---

[60] GAVO f. r-1826, op. 1, d. 4, ll. 13–13ob.

[61] GIM f. 54, op. 1, d. 681, ll. 60–65ob. and 141–141ob.; Aksenova, "Khronika," 49; GAVO f. r-1826, op. 1, d. 5, ll. 32–33ob.

[62] A. Dodonova, *Dmitrii Gennad'evich Burylin* (Ivanovo: Izd-vo "Ivanovo," 1997), 81, 85.

[63] Julia Fein, "Cultural Curators and Provincial Publics: Local Museums and Social Change in Siberia, 1887–1941" (Ph.D. diss., University of Chicago, 2012), 320–21.

"inviolable" and transformed into a museum "in view of [its] exceptional artistic-historic significance."[64] When it proved possible, central authorities claimed that they wanted valuables to remain in the areas, and sometimes the very buildings, where they were located, and, therefore, somewhat in context. This preference appears to have been stated particularly when a high level of wealth was concentrated in one place, resulting in the possibility of having an "instant" *in situ* museum, or when the place itself could serve to memorialize an important cultural figure, such as Lev Tolstoi's Iasnaia Poliana, decreed to be under state protection in June 1919.[65] Although such a museum was not created at Andreevskoe and over 500 of the estate's objects entered the regional museum in Vladimir, such museums were created from 1918–23 at 19 estates and 12 monasteries, particularly in the area around Moscow.[66]

Museums mushroomed nearly everywhere, if not necessarily on the scale found in Vladimir province. By the beginning of January 1920, the Vladimir Subdivision of Museum Affairs and the Protection of Monuments of Art and Antiquity claimed to be responsible for 18 museums, at least 2 of which existed only on paper, and 14 of which were historical-archaeological or artistic-historical museums.[67] In addition to overseeing these museums, in 1920–21 alone, the subdivision's employees inspected 7 estates, 15 monasteries, 52 churches, and 1 private individual's collection, registering 8,000 items of "an art-historic character," many of which were transferred to these new local museums.[68] Given that the logistical challenges of expropriation—a shortage of funds, space, packing supplies, vehicles, and manpower—existed everywhere, it is no wonder that museum authorities continued to make direct appeals to the population for its assistance.

The following appeal is from the Central Division and likely dates from spring or summer 1920. It is a good example of the rhetorical framework

---

[64] D. I. Kopylov, ed., *Istoriia Vladimirskogo kraia* (Vladimir: OOO "Diuna," 2001), 291–92. The peasants might have asked, if, after all, the property of the wealthy had been acquired on the backs of the working classes and had thus become public property, were the local peasants not the most suitable public? GAVO f. r-1826, op. 1, d. 1, 497. For more on this story, see Smith, "The Accidental Museum," 445–46.

[65] The State Memorial and Natural Preserve "Museum-Estate of Leo Tolstoy "Yasnaya Polyana," "Yasnaya Polyana after Leo Tolstoy's Death. Foundation and Development of the Museum," http://ypmuseum.ru/en/2011–04-13-17-30-44/mhistory/44-2011-08-16-21-22-37. html (27 November 2012).

[66] Aksenova, "Khronika," 49. Evgraf Konchin, *Revoliutsiei prizvannye. Rasskazy o moskovskikh emissarakh* (Moscow: Moskovskii rabochii, 1988), 44. For more on the case of Andreevskoe, see Smith, "Museum Practices," chap. 5.

[67] GAVO f. r-1826, op. 1, d. 1, l. 351.

[68] A. I. Ivanov, "Muzeinoe delo vo Vladimirskoi gubernii za vremia revoliutsii i ego blizhaishie zadachi," *Trudy 2-i konferentsii po izucheniiu prizvoditel'nykh sil Vladimirskoi gubernii* (1926): 3.

that justified expropriation while laying the groundwork for appropriation through the presentation and interpretation of objects in a museum.

> Comrades and Citizens, the life of the landowners and capitalists was beautiful not only in its full material satisfaction, but because in their hands were found spiritual valuables, uncountable treasures of antiquity and art. All [of these] the working class made with its callused hands....
>
> The October Revolution, having given the people all of the property of the country—the fields and forests, the mines and factories—turned the objects of art and antiquity also into a public good.... Museums have been founded in big and little cities and small towns, where all of these valuables reside; museums are the people's houses of rest and of great pleasure, which any work of art gives an individual....
>
> *The Red Army in its victorious procession, having liberated the people from the oppression of the landowners and bourgeoisie, returns to [the people] all these innumerable works of art, makes them public property and makes [the people] responsible for their preservation.*[69]

The rhetorical transformation of private property into cultural heritage was complete. The truth of at least part of the public appeal could not be denied; beautiful objects had been collected and museums had been founded in cities and towns.

The Rise of the Revolutionary History Museum

A new type of museum not based on expropriated antiquities and artifacts did appear in this period: the revolutionary museum, grounded in and providing a justification for class warfare. In October 1919, the Petrograd Soviet decided to create a museum to glorify the names of revolutionary fighters and to propagandize the correct understanding of revolutionary history. It made the creation of the collection a national undertaking, calling on the "working masses and the soviet establishments of the RSFSR" for assistance. When the museum opened in January 1920 in the former nursery in the Winter Palace, its display began with the history of the Pugachev and Razin rebellions.[70]

---

[69] GARF f. a-2307, op. 3, d. 2, l. 20. Emphasis in the original.

[70] L. N. Godunova, "Istoriko-revoliutsionnye muzei: Voprosy formirovaniia i razvitiia muzeinoi seti 1917–1941 gg.," in *Muzeinoe delo v SSSR: Muzeinaia set' i problemy ee sovershenstvovaniia na sovremennom etape. Sbornik nauchnykh trudov*, ed. I. A. Antonova et al. (Moscow: Tsentral'nyi muzei revoliutsii SSSR, 1985), 182; Svetlana Ivanovna Kytmanova, "Istpart i stanovlenie istoriko-revoliutsionnykh muzeev (1920–1928 gg.)" (Candidate diss., Moskovskii gosudarstvennyi universitet imeni M. V. Lomonosova, 1983), 50–51.

That spring, the American anarchist Emma Goldman joined the staff and found her new coworkers "shivering with cold" and with frostbitten hands, a very common situation due to the shortage of basic supplies during the Civil War.[71]

Returning from a collecting expedition in the fall, Goldman was appalled to learn that a newly created body in Moscow, Istpart (the Commission on the History of the October Revolution and the Russian Communist Party [Bolsheviks]), had been made responsible by Sovnarkom for shaping the revolutionary narrative and, therefore, the museum exhibits.[72] As Frederick Corney has written, October would come to be presented "as the culmination of an organic revolutionary movement within the Russian Empire, directed by a conscious revolutionary agent—the coherent and inspired Bolshevik Party."[73] Much smaller museums of revolutionary history were also created in several provinces, although their proponents had even greater difficulty in finding ideologically reliable organizers and objects for display, as well as sometimes struggling to link their locales to the greater revolutionary narrative.[74]

Conclusion

World War I served as the framework for both the overthrow of the imperial regime and the failure of the Provisional Government. Nevertheless, the war and the resulting logistical problems, worries about cultural heritage, and the related shifting understandings of private property were probably not necessary for the museum boom of the immediate postwar years; the Bolshevik ideology of class warfare and the necessity of building proletarian culture on the accomplishments of the past made expropriation and the public presentation of its results all but certain once the Bolsheviks had secured power, just as they would the extensive sale of cultural objects in the 1920s and 1930s to fund Soviet modernization and, ostensibly (and ironically), the

---

[71] Emma Goldman, *My Two Years in Russia: An American Anarchist's Disillusionment, and the Betrayal of the Russian Revolution by Lenin's Soviet Union* (St. Petersburg, FL: Red and Black Publishers, 2008), 87–88.

[72] Ibid.

[73] Frederick C. Corney, *Telling October: Memory and the Making of the Bolshevik Revolution* (Ithaca, NY: Cornell University Press, 2004), 2.

[74] Indeed, a similar process took place in Vladimir, although the revolutionary history museum would eventually be grafted onto the regional museum and provide the exhibits' historical framework. See Susan N. Smith, "A Weapon in the Battle for Socialism? The Rise of the Vladimir Kraevedcheskii Museum," *Museum History Journal* 3, 2 (2010): 189–208.

museums themselves.[75] That said, expropriation may have been more palatable to prerevolutionary museum organizers because of the anxieties of the war and, therefore, easier to carry out.

Grabar' was undoubtedly writing for many museum organizers when he argued that the protection of such monuments in a period in which the state and the way of life was being completely re-created was an urgent state task. Moreover, he maintained that cultural activists should "cover all of Russia with a dense network of museums, these preservers of living creativity and breeding grounds of culture."[76] As we have seen, this "dense network of museums" did, in fact, quickly come into being. In the absence of studies of popular reception or even the most basic information on many museums, it is not possible to demonstrate that the museums became "breeding grounds of culture." Nonetheless, many of these museums continue to preserve examples of Russian cultural heritage and serve their local communities today.

---

[75] For an important collection of recent work on the sales of artistically and historically significant objects, particularly in the post-Civil War period, see the articles in *Treasures Into Tractors: The Selling of Russia's Cultural Heritage, 1918–1938*, ed. Anne Odom and Wendy R. Salmond (Washington, DC: Hillwood Estate, Museum & Gardens, 2009). See also Smith, "Museum Practices," 233–37.

[76] Grabar', *Dlia chego*, 5.

Notes on Contributors

Evgenii M. Balashov is a Senior Research Fellow at the St. Petersburg Institute of History, Russian Academy of Sciences, St. Petersburg.

William C. Brumfield is a Professor of Slavic Studies at Tulane University, New Orleans.

Vladimir P. Buldakov is a Senior Research Fellow at the Institute of Russian History, Russian Academy of Sciences, Moscow.

Aaron J. Cohen is a Professor of History at California State University Sacramento.

Catherine Evtuhov is a Professor of History at Georgetown University, Washington, DC.

Murray Frame is a Senior Lecturer in History at the University of Dundee.

Ben Hellman is a Senior Lecturer in Russian Literature at the University of Helsinki.

Page Herrlinger is an Associate Professor of History at Bowdoin College, Maine.

Anthony Heywood is a Professor of History at the University of Aberdeen.

Anke Hilbrenner is an Associate Professor in East European History at the University of Bonn.

Anatolii E. Ivanov is a Senior Research Fellow at the Institute of Russian History, Russian Academy of Sciences, Moscow.

Russian Culture in War and Revolution, 1914–22, Book 1: Popular Culture, the Arts, and Institutions. Murray Frame, Boris Kolonitskii, Steven G. Marks, and Melissa K. Stockdale, eds. Bloomington, IN: Slavica Publishers, 2014, 425–26.

Boris Kolonitskii is a Professor at the European University at St. Petersburg and a Senior Research Fellow at the St. Petersburg Institute of History, Russian Academy of Sciences, St. Petersburg.

Julia Mannherz is an Associate Professor of History at the University of Oxford.

Steven G. Marks is a Professor of History at Clemson University, South Carolina.

David MacLaren McDonald is the Alice D. Mortenson/Petrovich Professor of Russian History at the University of Wisconsin-Madison.

Christopher Stolarski is a Social Sciences and Humanities Research Council Post-Doctoral Fellow at the Department of History, University of Toronto.

J. Alexander Ogden is an Associate Professor of Russian and Comparative Literature at the University of South Carolina, Columbia.

Christopher Read is a Professor of History at the University of Warwick.

Pavel G. Rogoznyi is a Research Fellow at the St. Petersburg Institute of History, Russian Academy of Sciences, St. Petersburg.

Susan Smith is an independent scholar, Washington, DC.

John W. Steinberg is a Professor of History at Austin Peay State University, Tennessee.

Melissa K. Stockdale is an Associate Professor of History at the University of Oklahoma.

Denise J. Youngblood is a Professor of History at the University of Vermont.